CATHOLIC REFORMATION IN IRELAND

Catholic Reformation in Ireland

The Mission of Rinuccini, 1645–1649

TADHG Ó hANNRACHÁIN

OXFORD

UNIVERSITY PRESS

OXFORD

UNIVERSITY PRESS

Great Clarendon Street, Oxford OX2 6DP

Oxford University Press is a department of the University of Oxford.
It furthers the University's objective of excellence in research, scholarship,
and education by publishing worldwide in

Oxford New York

Auckland Bangkok Buenos Aires Cape Town Chennai
Dar es Salaam Delhi Hong Kong Istanbul Karachi Kolkata
Kuala Lumpur Madrid Melbourne Mexico City Mumbai Nairobi
São Paulo Shanghai Singapore Taipei Tokyo Toronto
with associated companies in Berlin Ibadan

Oxford is a registered trade mark of Oxford University Press
in the UK and in certain other countries

Published in the United States
by Oxford University Press Inc., New York

British Library Cataloguing in Publication Data

Data available

Library of Congress Cataloging in Publication Data

Ó hAnnracháin, Tadhg.
Catholic reformation in Ireland: the mission of Rinuccini, 1645–1649/Tadhg Ó hAnnracháin.
p. cm
Includes bibliographical references (p.) and index.
1. Counter Reformation—Ireland. 2. Rinuccini, Giovanni Battista, 1592–1653.
3. Ireland—Church history—17th century. I. Title.
BX1504.O43 2001   282′.415′09032—dc21   2001036409
ISBN 0-19-820891-X

1 3 5 7 9 10 8 6 4 2

Typeset in Sabon
by Hope Services (Abingdon) Ltd
Printed in Great Britain
on acid-free paper by
Biddles Ltd.,
Guildford and King's Lynn

To BORCSA

Preface

AN ENORMOUS number of people have helped, encouraged, and supported me in the course of writing this book. While living in Florence I incurred huge debts of gratitude to Pinella di Gregorio, Marisa Meli, Marie-Claire Ponthoreau, and Elke Atzler. Much of the Roman research was made possible by the generosity of Paolo Taviani, Maria-Linda Odorisio, Antonio, Lorenzo, Andrea, and Jeanne Marchesi in offering me lodging and friendship. Professor Daniel Roche was also an inspiring presence and guide during this time.

My colleagues past and present in the Combined Departments of History in University College Dublin, in particular Mary Daly, Margaret MacCurtain, Judith Devlin, and Eddie Coleman have been unstinting with assistance and encouragement since I first returned to Ireland. Sincere thanks as well to my Head of Department, Tom Bartlett, for his genial support and sound advice. I owe more than I can say to Nicholas Canny of the National University of Ireland, Galway whose perceptive criticism did so much to shape whatever is positive in this book. Thanks also to Bríd MaGrath, Pádraig Lenihan, Jane Ohlmeyer, Robert Armstrong, and Micheál Ó Siochrú and to the cordial staff of all the libraries and archives who have offered me such patient assistance.

As always my family has been a constant source of love and affirmation. I could never have asked for more from Mairéad, Donncha, Máire, and Gar while my parents, Eamonn and Deirdre, constantly surpassed even their unsurpassable selves. In Budapest I have been fortunate to acquire another family of equal wonder. Many, many thanks to Gergő, Klára, and Ferenc from the Irish interloper who robbed your city of its most luminous presence. I have no words to convey the joy which my children Lóránt and Liadh have brought into my life. Equally my gratitude and love for my wife Borcsa is beyond my compass to express. This book is far too little to offer her in return for all that she has given me but with passionate thanks I dedicate it to her.

TÓhA

Acknowledgements

THE AUTHOR would like to thank Oxford University Press for permission to reproduce published material in Map 1.

Contents

List of Maps   xi

List of Abbreviations   xii

Note on Dates   xiii

I.   THE GENESIS OF THE NUNCIATURE

Introduction   3

1. The Rebellion of 1641 and the Evolution of the Confederate Catholics of Ireland   16

2. Development and Reform in the Irish Church, 1618–1645   39

3. The Background and Formation of the Nuncio   82

II.   RINUCCINI IN IRELAND

4. Resistance to the Ormond Peace   123

5. The Attrition of Influence, December 1646–February 1648   166

6. The End of the Nunciature   198

7. The Nuncio, Religious Reform and the Irish Clergy   232

8. Conclusion   253

Appendix A. The Irish Episcopacy during the Nunciature   268

Appendix B. Supplementary Biographical Details   270

Appendix C. Chronology   279

Bibliographical Note   284

Bibliography   287

Glossary   309

Index   311

List of Maps

1. Catholic Dioceses of Ireland, *c.*1630   38
2. Rinuccini's Journey to Ireland, 1645   114
3. Rinuccini's Major Journeys in Ireland   122

List of Abbreviations

AAF	Archivio Arcivescovile di Fermo
ACCS	Archivio della congregazione per le cause dei Santi
AGS	Archivio General, Simancas
AG(V)	Archives de la Guerre (Vincennes)
Aiazzi, *Nunziatura*	G. Aiazzi, *Nunziatura in Irlanda di Monsignor Gio. Baptista Rinuccini Arcivescovo di Fermo negli anni 1645 à 1649* (Florence, 1844)
AMAE	Archives du Ministère des Affaires Étrangères, Paris
APF	Archivio della Sacra Congregazione di Propaganda Fide
ASCM	Archivio Storico Comunale di Milano
ASF	Archivio di Stato di Firenze
ASV	Archivio Segreto Vaticano
BAV	Biblioteca Apostolica Vaticana
BNP	Bibliothèque Nationale, Paris
Bodl., Carte MSS	Bodleian Library, Oxford, Carte Manuscripts
Comment. Rinucc.	Stanislaus Kavanagh (ed.), *Commentarius Rinuccianus, de sedis apostolicae legatione ad foederatos Hiberniae catholicos per annos 1645–9* (6 vols., Dublin, 1932–49)
CSPI	*Calendar of State Papers Relating to Ireland*
FAK	Franciscan Archive, Killiney
Gilbert, *Irish Confederation*	J. T. Gilbert (ed.), *History of the Irish Confederation and War* (7 vols., Dublin, 1882–91)
NA	National Archives, Dublin
NLI	National Library of Ireland
SOCG	Scritture Originali riferite nelle Congregazioni Generali

Note on Dates

TWO DIFFERENT calendars existed in Europe during the period of this book: on the continent the Gregorian reform had been generally adopted while in Ireland and in England the Julian style was still normally in use, resulting in a ten-day differential in dates. A further complication in these islands was the general reckoning of Lady Day, or 25 March, as the first day of a new year. Dates in this book are generally given according to the Julian calendar. When dating is according to the Gregorian style this is signified by the use of (ns). The first day of the year, however, is always taken as 1 January rather than Lady Day.

I. The Genesis of the Nunciature

Introduction

The critical importance of the catholic church in Irish history since the early modern period is indisputable. That the majority of Ireland's inhabitants adopted a confessional identity centred on Rome was critical to the post sixteenth-century evolution of the various communities which inhabited the island. It was also profoundly important in terms of the Irish relationship with Britain. Indeed, to the present century no one factor was more influential in distinguishing and dividing the histories of the two islands than the (in archipelago terms) localized success of the post-tridentine Irish catholic church.

This book is a case study of a particular, important, and relatively neglected episode in the penetration of Ireland by the catholic reformation. Its chronological scope is the second quarter of the seventeenth century, a period which in European terms is generally conceived as lying towards the end of what might be termed the 'high counter-reformation', that rough century between the first convocation of the Council of Trent in 1545 to the treaty of Westphalia in 1648 which represented a critical epoch in the remodelling of post-reformation catholicism. From an Irish perspective, however, rather than representing the tail-end of a period of reform, this was an era of dynamic religious innovation which telescoped together a number of developments that occurred more gradually in less peripheral parts of the catholic world. It was during these decades that the distinctive Irish pattern of an illegal episcopally directed catholic church functioning within a protestant state was first established. This unlikely and in European terms highly anomalous development was ironically the template to which the Irish catholic church, having failed to establish a legal right to jurisdiction and property in the 1640s, and having escaped annihilation in the 1650s, basically conformed for most of the rest of the early modern period.

The long-term political implications of the extension of the catholic reformation to Ireland during this period were enormous. In the shorter term, this development also had a critical bearing on the Irish theatres of the Wars of the Three Kingdoms in the 1640s. The reinterpretation of that decade has been central to the New British history which has rightly stressed the interconnectedness of the crisis which engulfed the triple Stuart monarchy in the latter stages of Charles I's reign. Yet, as a number of scholars have recently emphasized, it was in Ireland that the Wars of the Three Kingdoms took on their most European aspect[1] because nowhere else in the archipelago had the

---

[1] Nicholas Canny, 'Religion, Politics and the Irish Rising of 1641', in Judith Devlin and Ronan Fanning (eds.), *Historical Studies*, 20 *Religion and Rebellion* (Dublin, 1997), 40–70; Jane Ohlmeyer,

forces of the counter-reformation established such a decisive presence. Throughout the three Stuart monarchies issues of religion were central to conflict, but in Ireland this reached a pitch closer to the continental experience because the distance between the competing religious positions was greater than in Britain. Thus, while the personality as well as the government of Charles I is integral to an understanding of the crisis in England and Scotland, this is less obviously true of Ireland. As in the contemporary crisis in Germany, there were deep structural reasons why a conflict centred on religion was likely to ignite and why a negotiated settlement to restore equilibrium would prove hugely difficult.[2]

The central protagonist and the focusing lens of this book is GianBattista Rinuccini, who served as nuncio to the confederate catholics of Ireland between 1645 and 1649. During this period he was a figure of pivotal importance who aroused intense and diverse emotions. Towards the end of his nunciature, for instance, his confederate enemies asserted that he:

by himself, and by his continual practices, ministers, and accomplices, hath endeavoured to withdraw this nation from their allegeance to his majestie, to subvert the fundamentall lawes and gouernement of the land; and instead thereof, to introduce a forraigne, arbitrary, and tyrannicall gouernement, as by the course of his lordship's proceedings is to be undenyably evidenced. By means of all which, and other his lordship's proceedings and actions in this kingdome, many hundreds of churches and chappells, wherein catholique service was publiquely said, are fallen into the enemies hands. Great numbers of religious convents dispersed, whole and great countryes inhabited by confedrats left wast and unpeopled, and a generall famine, unparaleld in this kingdome by any age before, occasioned, and universall desolation like suddenly to ensue, if not speedily preuented.[3]

With similar bitterness another commentator described him as 'fitted up for grand station with an exterior grandeur and seemly deportment which served for a cloak and varnish to his ambition, falsehood and folly'.[4] For his part, the confederate secretary, Richard Bellings, argued that what he saw as Rinuccini's disastrous interference in Ireland was motivated by the nuncio's ambition to be elevated to the sacred college of cardinals.[5] In contrast with this, however, Nicholas French, the bishop of Ferns, declared to the pope in 1648:

'Ireland Independent: Confederate Foreign Policy and International Relations during the Mid-seventeenth Century', in ead. (ed.), *Ireland from Independence to Occupation, 1641–60* (Cambridge, 1995), 89–111.

  [2] See Robert Bireley, 'The Thirty Years' War as Germany's Religious War', in K. Repgen (ed.), *Krieg und Politik, 1618–1648* (Munich, 1988), 85–106.

  [3] Abstract of charges against the nuncio, 19 Oct. 1648 (Thomas Carte, *The Life of James, Duke of Ormond* (6 vols., Oxford, 1851), vi. 577).

  [4] The war and rebellion in Ireland begun in 1641 (NLI MS 345, p. 1221).

  [5] Bellings's narrative (J. T. Gilbert (ed.) *History of the Irish Confederation and the War in Ireland* (7 vols., Dublin, 1882–91), v. 5).

in what concerns Rinuccini's character, and good example to all, even his enemies honour his piety. All acknowledge his good and irreproachable life. And in merit he could be judged the light and exemplar of bishops, a man most apt to his great duty, in which by the pope's wise choice and to the great edification of the church of God he has shown himself extremely worthy. He encourages the splendour of religion, honour to bishops and esteem to the clergy against the hate of certain nobles. They begrudge this virtue in him . . .[6]

Ferns's perception was certainly closer to the general Italian opinion of Rinuccini. To one observer, the Irish nuncio was simply 'a wise and much admired prelate',[7] while the secretary of the congregation of Irish affairs lauded his 'blameless life . . . virtue . . . ardent charity . . . Apostolic zeal' and his 'not ordinary prudence'.[8]

It was my original intention in opening this field of research to concentrate quite narrowly on the years of Rinuccini's nunciature and in particular on his profound political influence within the confederate association which was responsible for the intensity of the reactions which he provoked. This rapidly proved impractical. Not only was it necessary to link the nunciature much more firmly to the previous political evolution of the confederate catholics, the subject of Chapter 1 of the present study, but it also became clear that the natural context in which to situate Rinuccini's career in Ireland was the European counter-reformation and its extension to Ireland. In particular there were three crucial and wider processes to be taken into account and it was from that realization that the structure of the present book developed.

The most important of these processes was the manner in which Rinuccini's mission connected to the previous development of the Irish church, in particular to the evolution of a resident and pastorally active hierarchy in the period between 1618 and 1641. That is the subject of Chapter 2 of the present study. The general tendency in the Irish historiography has been to view the Rinuccini mission as a rather exotic interlude. It is a central contention of this book, however, that his nunciature can only be understood as an aspect of a broader Roman strategy which for several decades had aspired to integrate Ireland as fully as was possible into the wider continental pattern of episcopally directed

---

[6] Si de Rinuccini moribus agatur, et bono versus omnes exemplo, vel hostes ipsius colunt in eo pietatem. Omnes enim vitam bonam et irreprehensibilem in eo fatentur. Et merito censeri potest lumen et exemplar Episcoporum, vir sane ad tantam legationem aptissimus, in qua ad magnam Ecclesiae Dei aedificationem Vestrae Sanctitatis electione prudentissima se perquam dignum praebuit. Fovet continuo splendorem religionis, honorem episcoporum, et existimationem Cleri, contra odium quorundam nobilium. Huic in ipso virtuti invident . . . Ferns's memorial to Pope Innocent, May 1648 (Stanislaus Kavanagh (ed.), *Commentarius Rinuccianus, de sedis apostolicae legatione ad foederatos Hiberniae catholicos per annos 1645–9* (6 vols., Dublin, 1932–49) iii. 43).

[7] 'Prelato di molta stima e sapere'. Anonymous, undated Informazione à S.R. dello stato d'Hibernia in tempi della Nunziatura de Mons. Rinuccini (BAV Barberini Latini 4994, fo. 86ʳ).

[8] 'Vita innocente . . . virtù . . . prudenza non ordinarie . . . ardente sua carità . . . apostolico suo zelo'. Instruzione al nuncio (G. Aiazzi, *Nunziatura in Irlanda di Monsignor Gio. Baptista Rinucccini Arcivescovo di Fermo negli anni 1645 à 1649* (Florence, 1844), p. xxxv).

catholic reform. Rather than a break with previous policy, the mission was intended as its culmination.

Not only should the Rinuccini nunciature be viewed in the context of previous Irish policy, but it should be noted also that Vatican perceptions of Ireland were integrated into a wider matrix of concerns. This phenomenon was particularly evident in the 1640s but it was not restricted to that decade. Since its foundation in 1622, the *Congregatio de Propaganda Fide* had included Ireland within its jurisdiction. *Propaganda Fide* was itself an expression of a buoyant sense of confidence within the Roman church: a major rationale behind its creation was the papal commitment to support a strategy of recatholicization in the territories which the early victories of the Thirty Years War had delivered into the Emperor's hands, most notably in Bohemia.[9] Contemporaneously with this development, *Propaganda* pushed forward expansively in Ireland: the bold and influential policy of appointing an Irish hierarchy which included even Gaelic bishops, despite the potential problems deriving from the protestant nature of the state, can be rightly seen as a particular expression of a more general confident mood inspired by the belief that the confessional frontiers of the continent had not yet been stabilized. In the 1640s the profound influence which Rinuccini was able to wield in Ireland stemmed in large part from the similarity between his objectives and those of the Irish hierarchy which *Propaganda* had created since 1618. It derived also from the manner in which their acquisition of moral authority in the preceding decades furnished him with enormous political leverage. The coincidence of interest between nuncio and native episcopate was the result partly of the European education and formation of the Irish bishops, which conditioned them to aspire towards similar conditions to those enjoyed by catholic clergy on the continent, and partly of their discontent with the conditions which they had endured prior to the collapse of the English state in Ireland following the rebellion of 1641.

The second major process which urgently demanded analysis was the personal experience and formation of the nuncio himself, in particular during his term as Archbishop of Fermo in the Marche of Italy from 1625 to 1653. This topic is the principal material of Chapter 3 of the present study. Carlo Borromeo has tended to throw a gigantic shadow over the subject of episcopal reform in Italy, and indeed elsewhere in Europe.[10] Yet, although on research it became increasingly clear that Rinuccini was an ardent apostle of episcopally directed reform, neither Borromeo nor any other post-tridentine Italian figure acted as one of his primary models or sources of inspiration. It

---

[9] Geoffrey Parker, *The Thirty Years' War* (London, 1984), 6–7, 39, 92–3; Thomas Munck, *Seventeenth Century Europe: State, Conflict and the Social Order in Europe, 1598–1700* (London, 1990), 3–11; see also Bireley, 'The Thirty Years' War as Germany's Religious War'.

[10] A. Degert, 'S. Charles Borromée et le clergé français', *Bulletin de littérature ecclésiastique*, 4 (1912), 145–59, 193–213.

was striking to note merely a tiny handful of references to the cardinal-archbishop of Milan in Rinuccini's extensive writings on the subject of a bishop's position and duties. Rather, a strong sense of Rinuccini's own originality on the subject of church reform, together with a covert desire for a new general council of the church to complement the legacy of Trent, was clearly present. In this way, the archbishop of Fermo emerged not as a passive clone of sixteenth-century predecessors but as a more autonomous thinker adapting actively through personal experience to the demands of his own time and in particular to what he saw as the sapped elasticity of catholic vitality in the early modern period. Transferred to an Irish stage, these pastoral and personal preoccupations threw his behaviour as nuncio in Ireland into much sharper relief, particularly with regard to his determination to achieve the public exercise of catholicism in Ireland which was the central feature of his mission and around which most political tension accumulated.

Yet if Rinuccini's personal formation was a critical determinant of his actions in Ireland and only explicable in terms of his personal convictions concerning religious reform, it was in his institutional capacity as papal nuncio that he wielded political influence. The wider forces which shaped his mission were thus the third process which needed to be addressed. In the past the tendency has been to consider the Rinuccini nunciature in terms only of its impact on Ireland. To do so, however, is to ignore that the Vatican's Irish policy was merely one aspect of a greater and interlocking matrix of international concerns. From the perspective of Rome, Ireland was a distant and not particularly important location, not only in comparison with more important continental theatres of influence, but also in comparison with protestant England. It is striking that the Irish nuncio himself after several years in the island felt it necessary to appeal to his superiors to look beyond Ireland's obvious insignificance: 'Miserable Ireland, always obscured by English greatness, has remained separated from the earth as [somewhere] distant from knowledge, and lost in the rays of the overshadowing monarchy, it shows no lights which do not appear to be feeble sparks.'[11] Although the avowed purpose of the nunciature was the complete restoration of the damaged structures of the Irish church, beyond that again existed the glittering lure that a regenerated Ireland might serve as a springboard for an even greater confessional advance, namely the recapture of England for the catholic fold. In dreaming dreams of this nature concerning England, the papal secretariat was trespassing on the realm of fantasy but the existence of such a dimension to Rome's Irish policy was significant. The Rinuccini mission was never intended to act within a purely Irish framework or according to purely Irish imperatives. Rather it was part of a wider web of European

---

[11] 'Misera Irlanda oscurata sempre dalle grandezze inglesi, è rimasta tanto staccata dalla terra, come lontano dalle cognizioni, e abbagliata dai raggi di questa Monarchia soprastante non porta lumi che non appariscono fiaccole'. Rinuccini's relation to the pope (Aiazzi, *Nunziatura*, 402).

policy, a fact which increased its vulnerability to external influences. At various times the political tension generated by the papal election of 1644, the diplomatic roller coaster between Paris and Rome during the pontificate of Innocent X, the behaviour of the envoys of Henrietta Maria in Italy, and Turkish activity in the Mediterranean all intruded on the handling of the Irish nunciature. In broader terms, the war in Germany acted as a critical background to all aspects of papal activity in Ireland during the period of this book. Events in Ireland could never be permitted to compromise the activity of the Vatican's representatives in the peace negotiations in Münster. In addition the German war was certainly psychologically significant with regard to the framing of Irish policy, both in terms of generating confessional optimism during the 1620s and in terms of the frustrations of the 1640s when Ireland became an alternative theatre for international catholic action which carried lighter risks of antagonizing the French government.

The dominant theme of Part I of this current study, therefore, is that the dynamic evolution of the catholic church in Ireland during the period under discussion cannot be understood within a purely Irish context. The natural corollary to this point, of course, is that neither should this process be regarded as of merely Irish relevance: it is also an episode in the wider history of the catholic reformation. The situation in which Rinuccini found himself as papal delegate to the confederate catholics was rich with many contemporary resonances. During the middle decades of the seventeenth century, in central Europe, in America, in India, and in Asia a whole generation of catholic activists, like Rinuccini formed in the crucible of tridentine reform, and imbued with a sense of mission and confidence by the success of confessional renewal in the territory of the catholic states of Europe, struggled to adapt that heritage to profoundly different environments. To a considerable extent, it was Rinuccini's era, the last period of fluidity in the religious borders of Europe, which tested and defined the limits of the tridentine impulse then successfully consolidating itself in the catholic confessional states of its European heartland.[12]

In certain areas such as Bohemia, with firm support from the Habsburg dynasty, tridentine catholicism was implanted with relative success into an area previously largely lost to the reformation. On the contrary, in Asia (and in North America), the threat to orthodoxy from the pursuit of acculturation served to limit the missionary effectiveness of the catholic reformation.[13] One of the purposes of this present book is thus to examine the

[12] A. D. Wright, *The Counter-Reformation: Catholic Europe and the Non-Christian World* (London, 1982); Natalie Zemon Davis, *Women on the Margins: Three Seventeenth Century Lives* (Cambridge and London, 1995), esp. pp. 63–139; R. Po-Chia Hsia, *The World of Catholic Renewal, 1540–1770* (Cambridge, 1998).

[13] Po-Chia Hsia, *Catholic Renewal*, 73–9, 165–93; Zemon Davis, *Women on the Margins*, 63–139.

collision of that confident and global tridentine impulse, spearheaded initially by continentally trained Irish clergy and later by papal delegates, of whom Rinuccini was the most important (and concerning whom most documents have survived), with the catholic periphery of seventeenth-century Ireland.

One of the central conclusions of the book, presented particularly in Chapters 2 and 7, is of the decisive impact which catholic reforming activity made on Ireland in the second quarter of the seventeenth century. Such a conclusion may appear surprising. Recently Raymond Gillespie has argued with great force that popular religion in seventeenth-century Ireland was stubbornly resistant to the imposition of official theologies and that it retained a great deal of its traditional character throughout this period.[14] Gillespie's conclusion dovetails neatly with those of scholars of early modern France which have also emphasized the resiliency of popular religious mentalities in the face of learned elites' attempts to inculcate change.[15] The incomparably greater evidence available to French historians in making evaluations in this regard is also indicative of a need for caution by their Irish counterparts in exaggerating the impact of catholic reform.

Yet the gap between conclusions of this nature and my own is probably more apparent than real. It is certainly likely that there has been an underestimation of the impact of the catholic clergy on the belief systems of the general population in Ireland during this period. In that regard the tone of the testimony of the bishops and of the Italian mission presented in Chapter 2 is of great interest. It is undoubtedly suggestive when a body of administrators report to their central superiors in an atmosphere of general satisfaction, deploring not so much the obstinacy of the people but exterior impediments to reform.[16]

Nevertheless, the most important factor in reconciling my conclusions with those of others is the probability that different categories are being utilized to evaluate the impact of catholic reform. That the seminary-trained clerical elite failed completely to replace popular theologies and other manifestations of folk religion with the official doctrines of the church is fairly obvious: the resources for such a vast programme of cultural indoctrination among a largely illiterate population were simply not available. Yet it is

---

[14] Raymond Gillespie, *Devoted People: Belief and Religion in Early Modern Ireland* (Manchester, 1997); Alison Forrestal's analysis, based almost exclusively it is true on synodal decrees, also points out the limitations of what was achieved by catholic reform outside of ritual forms: see *Catholic Synods in Ireland, 1600–1690* (Dublin, 1998), esp. pp. 49–50, 190–2; the thrust of Patrick Corish's work in *The Catholic Community in the Seventeenth and Eighteenth Centuries* (Dublin 1981) and in *The Irish Catholic Experience* (Dublin, 1985) would also tend to support this viewpoint.

[15] See for example Robin Briggs, *Communities of Belief: Cultural and Social Tensions in Early Modern France* (Oxford, 1989); Jean Delumeau, *Catholicism between Luther and Voltaire* (Paris, 1977).

[16] I am grateful to Dr John Morrill for bringing this point to my attention.

eminently arguable that neither Rinuccini nor his Irish episcopal colleagues considered this a failure. In that regard Italian and Irish clerical expectations may have been somewhat lower than those of their French contemporaries, or of modern historians. The central concerns of the Irish hierarchy were to transmit to the generality of the laity a very basic catechesis, almost certainly learnt by rote, to ensure that the rites of passage of birth, marriage, and death were accompanied by the sacraments of the church, and that at least annually penance and the Eucharist were received. What was required of the clergy was of course a good deal more and my conclusion is that considerable advances were achieved in this direction, advances which have perhaps been underestimated in the past because of the institutional damage sustained by the catholic church during the 1650s which was not overcome again until at least the 1690s.[17]

That these modest ambitions came fairly close to fulfilment was a major achievement on the part of an illegal body of pastors. Despite the direct competition from the church by law established, they had managed to confirm their position as the body of religious professionals in whom the mass of the laity reposed their confidence. Certainly relatively few of the general population could aspire to any profound level of understanding of Christian doctrine but most in any case considered this to constitute the proper domain of the clergy. In that regard it was greatly significant that the clerics of the catholic church became widely trusted as adequate in a professional capacity to meet the doctrinal needs of the lay populace and that they were viewed as worthy and impressive intermediaries between the people and God. Moreover, although it was certainly beyond the resources of the catholic clergy to eliminate completely what they perceived as the superstitious abuses of popular religion, they were effective in maintaining a widespread respect for the official sacraments of the church and for the clergy's role as the vehicles by which those sacraments were offered to the people, something which was indicated very powerfully by the effectiveness of the threat and actuality of excommunication throughout the turbulence of the 1640s.

Therefore, I would argue that the impact of catholic reformers in Ireland is to be measured less by the extent to which they managed to substitute popular religious practices with the devotions of the educated elite than in the manner in which they acquired popular legitimacy as a professional clerical body mediating between the people and God. Ironically their illegal status may have acted as an advantage in this regard. During this period the coercive apparatus of the state was generally not applied in a consistent fashion to disrupt their activities. There were occasional outbursts of overt repression but in the main the catholic clergy were exposed more to the fear than the actuality of danger and persecution. Thus, in terms of confirming their

---

[17] In this regard my conclusions are similar to those of Forrestal, *Catholic Synods*, 190–3.

moral authority with the population at large, they were exposed to sufficient difficulties to boost their credibility but not so many as to undermine their pastoral activities. The legacy of this experience was subsequently critical in allowing the clergy to emerge as a formidable and distinctive interest during the 1640s, when the question of their corporate right to jurisdiction and property became the burning political issue within the confederate association.[18]

This, of course, is not to deny the existence of a lay catholic elite capable of internalizing a far more sophisticated religious awareness than that of the populace in general. Ironically, it was from their ranks that the chief internal opposition to the clergy within the confederate association emerged and it was these under the umbrella term of 'Old English' who became the chief targets of Rinuccini's ire in the latter years of the decade. This topic is probed more extensively in Chapter 6. None the less, at this juncture it is germane to note that the convulsions which struck the confederate catholics during the 1640s mirrored similar conflicts on the continent. It is not an exaggeration to suggest that two of the major currents which divided catholicism during the Thirty Years War, namely the confessional impulse to define conflicts on religious lines and the more political perspective which ultimately triumphed at Westphalia are evident also in the political debates of the confederates. The turbulence created by the intersection of these currents was the principal factor in the political instability which engulfed the confederate association in the latter part of the decade.

As Chapter 1 of this study demonstrates, already by 1644 many confederates believed that they had attained the necessary conditions to allow for a reconciliation and coalition with the royalist party in Ireland. Their aspiration, however, of achieving this transition ran counter to the wishes of the more militantly catholic party who continued to nourish hopes and expectations that more radical advances for their religion might be achieved with large-scale assistance from the continent. Such hopes were indicative of a belief that the catholic powers of Europe could be mobilized to protect the interests of Irish co-religionists. Nor was this attitude entirely naïve: both French and Spanish perceptions of the war in Ireland were at times influenced by confessional sympathy, and more substantial aid did arrive from the papacy in the hands of genuinely religiously motivated papal ministers. Nevertheless, the inadequacy of the assistance which the catholic militants received, even from Rome, meant that as elsewhere in Europe the war in Ireland ultimately testified more to the limitations of confessional solidarity than to its strength.

---

[18] There are evident similarities between what developed in Ireland and what Po-Chia Hsia has referred to as the emergence of 'a politico-confessional consciousness' in central Europe: see *Catholic Renewal*, 74–6.

Indeed, direct continental interference in the affairs of the confederates during this period was not limited to support of the clerical party among the confederates. The covert opposition between papal and Bourbon diplomacy in Germany also eventually replicated itself in Ireland. In the contemporary continental struggle, the cardinal ministers of France and the monarchs they served, despite certain personal susceptibilities to aspects of tridentine piety and despite internal dévot opposition, consistently placed urgent dynastic and national interests before the pursuit of strictly confessional objectives.[19] Similar French attitudes also became apparent in Ireland.

Ironically, in 1645 it initially appeared possible that the principal French influence in Ireland would represent dévot interests. In that year the *Compagnie du Très-Saint Sacrement* contemplated making use of the Irish war as a new and relatively uncontroversial field for confessional action. The duc de Ventadour held negotiations with Rinuccini in Paris concerning a possible donation of 100,000 scudi to the confederate war,[20] in the hope that advances for the catholic religion in Ireland and thereafter, and, more importantly, in Britain would help compensate for the losses being endured, largely as a result of Bourbon diplomacy, in Germany. But the rising threat of the English parliament eventually focused the French government's attention on Ireland in a manner similar to its preoccupations in central Europe. Particularly in 1646 Mazarin's agents attempted to mediate a settlement in the Irish war which involved the surrendering of gains previously made on behalf of the catholic church in order to create an archipelago wide coalition of support against parliament. The internal confederate opposition to this plan was focused by Rinuccini, with assistance from the Spanish agent in Ireland, and it was eventually defeated although at tremendous cost to the internal unity of the association. The following year French concern at a time of crisis to recruit soldiers for the European war contributed materially to confederate disunity and helped to thwart the papal nuncio's attempts to steer the association in a more militant direction.[21]

Not only, therefore, did the polarization of catholic politics in Ireland during the latter half of the 1640s occur in a fashion reminiscent of the contemporary European struggle, but the representatives of a variety of catholic powers also exerted a direct influence on the passage of events in the island and the policies which they adopted in Ireland mirrored those of their counterparts on the continent. Yet although the fractures within the unity of Irish catholicism during this period are eminently comprehensible within a wider continental framework, the logic of events in the island was also dictated by

[19] J. H. Elliott, *Richelieu and Olivares* (Cambridge, 1984); Richard M. Golden, *The Godly Rebellion: Parisian Curés and the Religious Fronde, 1652–62* (Chapel Hill, NC, 1981).

[20] For the details of this scheme see Rinuccini to Pamfili, 14 July (ns) 1645 (Aiazzi, *Nunziatura*, 28).

[21] See Ch. 5.

developments intrinsic to Ireland and to its relationship with England and Scotland. In this regard, the linguistic and cultural heterogeneity of the catholic population of the island is of importance. It is certainly apparent that a rigid dichotomy between Old English and Old Irish is hugely inadequate to explain the evolution of the various factions within the confederate association. It is equally obvious that issues of property, localism, and religious conviction were of critical significance in this regard. Yet there is a danger of dismissing too completely ethnic intolerances or of substituting them with notions of merely provincial antipathies.[22]

The identity which the confederates attempted to construct tried consciously to subsume differences between Old English and Gaelic Irish under a confessional banner. The overt nature of this endeavour was itself a testimony to the need to do so. This represents one of the most interesting aspects of catholic confessionalism in an Irish context. Confessionalization along national lines resulting in the creation of religiously intolerant nation states was a typical feature of early modern Europe. In Ireland, however, the politicization of catholic identity required the creation of a bridge between previously existing and potent identities of *Gall* and *Gael*, Old English and 'meere Irish'. In the estimation of the papal nuncio, that bridge was only imperfectly constructed during the 1640s. Indeed the realization of the inadequacy of a flatly confessional analysis of the political landscape of Ireland was one of the more bitter pieces of wisdom which he acquired during his nunciature.

Throughout this period events in England and Scotland exercised a gravitational pull over the catholic confederates which Rinuccini was powerless to dissipate. Ultimately, it was the catholic opposition which forced his departure through their insistence that religion should accommodate itself to the English constitution of the island and loyalty to the protestant Stuart dynasty. Significantly, the final push towards the second Ormond peace, which sealed Rinuccini's departure, was provided by a deeply felt sense of horror at the remonstrance of the army which compelled both Ormond and the confederates to shape an arch across the confessional divide.

This was a bridge which Rinuccini could never cross. At no time during his sojourn in Ireland did he demonstrate any sympathy with the dilemma which the conflicting demands of catholicism and English allegiance created for many confederates. Ultimately it was this failure to engage with the wider British dimension of the Irish problem which ruined his mission: by the end of the nunciature it was evident that his most unambiguous supporters were Owen Roe O'Neill and the Ulster army, returned exiles and men with little material and psychological stake in the pre-1641 constitution of the island. Yet the nuncio's intransigence in this regard did not derive merely

---

[22] The best discussion of these issues is Micheál Ó Siochrú, *Confederate Ireland, 1642–1649: A Constitutional and Political Analysis* (Dublin, 1999), 16–22 but my own analysis does not entirely concur with his.

from personal intolerance. He was a faithful exponent of Roman policy towards Ireland and the actions which he took were broadly consistent with the responsibilities with which he had been entrusted.

The actual conduct of his nunciature is the principal material of Part II of this book. Chapters 4, 5, and 6 concentrate primarily on the nuncio as a political actor, while Chapter 7 analyses his mission in terms of its avowed primary objective of religious reform. A reinterpretation of the nuncio's role in the 1640s is long overdue.[23] There can be no doubt that he was a figure of real significance in terms of the Wars of the Three Kingdoms. It seems certain that without his presence the confederate catholics would have amalgamated with the royalist forces in the island at a far earlier date and that the intention of this union would have been intervention in England. That this would have had important implications for British politics in the years between the battle of Naseby and the outbreak of the second civil war seems certain. The nuncio's importance within a specifically Irish context is naturally correspondingly greater. Only the marquis of Ormond could be considered a figure of comparable influence within the island during the 1640s.

Despite his evident centrality, the nuncio has been a curiously neglected figure. Partly this can be ascribed to the formidably difficult context in which he operated. As a decade the 1640s in Ireland have been regarded by Irish and non-Irish historians alike as one of the most complex in the island's history.[24] Written over three hundred years ago, the words of Richard Bellings, one of the first chroniclers of the period, still stand as a fit motto for the daring individual attempting to present that complexity to a wider audience: 'a war of many parts, carried on under the notion of so many interests, perplexed with such diversity of rents and divisions, among those who seemed to be of a side.'[25]

None the less the last ten years have witnessed a notable expansion of research concerning the rebellion of 1641 and the confederate association to which it gave rise. Michael Perceval-Maxwell and Jane Ohlmeyer have added considerably to the existing knowledge concerning the constitutional and conspiratorial background to the outbreak of rebellion.[26] The work of Nicholas Canny has presented a fundamental reappraisal of the social and

[23] The only existing major study of the nuncio is that of Michael Hynes, *The Mission of Rinuccini, Nuncio Extraordinary to Ireland, 1645–49* (Louvain, 1932).

[24] 'The bewildering number of hands . . . in the game' is Roy Foster's descriptive phrase: see *Modern Ireland, 1600–1972* (London, 1988), 99; one can note also John Morrill's description of 1640s Ireland as 'a seventeenth-century Lebanon' in *The Nature of the English Revolution* (London, 1993), 36. For his part, John Kenyon, *The Civil Wars of England* (London, 1989), 203–5 is lured into a number of factual errors in his attempt to summarize Irish affairs.

[25] Bellings's narrative (Gilbert, *Irish Confederation*, i. 1).

[26] Michael Perceval-Maxwell, *The Outbreak of the Irish Rebellion of 1641* (Dublin, 1994); Ohlmeyer, *Civil War and Restoration in the Three Stuart Kingdoms: The Career of Randall MacDonnell, Marquis of Antrim, 1609–1683* (Cambridge, 1993).

sectarian unrest to which that rebellion gave rise.[27] After a long period in the historiographical wilderness the confederate catholics have also been the subject of renewed attention. Pádraig Lenihan's excellent study on the confederate military has been supplemented by Micheál Ó Siochrú's fine political and constitutional analysis of the association.[28] At the same time, the politics of Irish protestants during the 1640s have been lucidly investigated by Robert Armstrong.[29] This research has been extremely illuminating in many respects. The dominant theme of the current study, however, is that what happened in Ireland in the reign of Charles I both can and should be situated within a wider context, not only that of the archipelago but of the continent as a whole. As a religious war, it is arguable that in some respects Ireland is closer to Germany than to England or Scotland during the 1640s.[30] Certainly the closest parallel to Rinuccini is the papal nuncio at the negotiations at Münster, Fabio Chigi. This is not to belittle the enterprise of the new British history but merely to note that just as Scotland connected naturally to the world of the North Sea and the Baltic as well as to England and Ireland, so through religion Ireland was linked also to the catholic world of the continent and that these connections must be acknowledged in a more holistic history of the archipelago. It is in that spirit that the current study has been constructed.

[27] See in particular Canny, 'In Defence of the Constitution? The Nature of Irish Revolt in the Seventeenth Century', in Louis Bergeron and Louis Cullen (eds.), *Cultures et pratiques politiques en France et en Irelande XVIe–XVIIIe siècles* (Paris, 1991), 23–40; id., 'What Really Happened in 1641', in Ohlmeyer, *From Independence to Occupation*; and id., 'Religion, Politics and the Irish Rising' in Devlin and Fanning, *Historical Studies*, 40–70.

[28] Pádraig Lenihan, *Confederate Catholics at War, 1641–49* (Cork, 2001); Ó Siochrá, *Confederate Ireland*.

[29] Robert Armstrong, 'Protestant Ireland and the English Parliament, 1641–1647' (unpub. Ph.D. thesis, Trinity College Dublin, 1995).

[30] See Bireley, 'The Thirty Years' War as Germany's Religious War', 85–106.

CHAPTER ONE

The Rebellion of 1641 and the Evolution of the Confederate Catholics of Ireland

I

Henry VIII's breach with Rome, culminating in his assumption of the Supreme Headship of the Church of first England and then in 1536 of Ireland, inaugurated the Irish reformation. In 1541 Henry became the first English monarch to style himself King rather than Lord of Ireland and it was intended that all the inhabitants of the island, whatever their ethnic origin, would now be regarded as his subjects and would form part of the church of which he was head. For the rest of the century, with the exception of a brief interlude under Mary in the 1550s, the official religion of the Irish kingdom was a form of protestantism. The executive, however, was notably ineffective in spreading the new religion. Few of the indigenous population became convinced protestants. In contrast, the direct political authority of the state, which prior to 1534 had largely been confined to certain areas on the island, the dwindling remnants of twelfth- and thirteenth-century Anglo-Norman colonization, increased steadily during this period as a series of Gaelic and Gaelicized lordships were absorbed into its jurisdiction. The accession of James I in 1603, following the defeat of a massive rebellion by a confederation of Gaelic lordships, which had made a degree of use of counter-reformation rhetoric, marked the end of the process of assimilation and conquest and ushered in a period of peace and rapid economic change.

Despite the now unchallenged supremacy of the Stuart state in Ireland, the official church nevertheless continued to make little headway in terms of converting the native population. Catholicism, increasingly influenced by post-tridentine reform, established itself securely as the religion of the majority of the population, although the catholic community was itself divided by a number of factors. The most politically influential and economically prosperous catholic group were of Old English origin, essentially the product of that pre-reformation Anglo-Norman colonization.[1] The other and, in terms of numbers, major component of the catholic population were the Old or Gaelic Irish, the descendants of the pre-Norman indigenous population of the island and those Gaelic Scots and English which had assimilated to that

---

[1] Aidan Clarke, *The Old English in Ireland, 1625–42* (London, 1966), 9–27.

culture over the course of several centuries. The protestant population of the island was largely of recent English or Scots provenance of whom roughly 100,0000 had arrived in the island in the decades between 1580 and 1641, partly through state-sponsored plantation of the confiscated lands of elements of the Gaelic and Gaelicized population. This community had generally enjoyed the favour of the Dublin administration and had shown great energy and success in the pursuit of profit in Ireland.[2]

The political position of all catholics, including the traditionally loyal Old English community, was weakened by the crown's perception that their temporal loyalty was compromised by their religious allegiance to Rome. The single most important political issue in Ireland, therefore, during the period 1603–1641 revolved around the question of the legal toleration of the catholic religion.[3] In the late 1620s, taking advantage of Charles I's anxiety about a continental invasion of Ireland following the outbreak of the Anglo-Spanish war, catholic representatives bartered financial contributions to the upkeep of an army for a variety of concessions, termed the Graces, concerning the security of their lands and the limited recognition of their religion.[4] These concessions were not, however, confirmed by statute and only some came to be applied, leaving catholics disgruntled and the Graces as a potential focal point for catholic political pressure.

The appointment of Thomas Wentworth as Lord Deputy in 1632 initially raised hopes for the attainment of the Graces but in the event his governorship significantly increased the alienation of the catholic population and also heightened tensions in the New English and Scottish communities. Wentworth, later made lord lieutenant and earl of Strafford, enjoyed an unusual level of support from London which rendered his administration largely independent of the existing political interests in Ireland. His administrative zeal and ability meant that he used this freedom of action to put the finances of his government on a firm footing, to launch attacks on the weakness of land title in both the protestant and catholic communities, and to institute a religious policy which alienated the protestant interest without soothing the fears of catholics.[5] This created enormous resentment and insecurity: catholic landowners had hoped and believed that Wentworth would

[2] Nicholas Canny, 'Migration and Opportunity: Britain, Ireland and the New World', *Irish Economic and Social History*, 12 (1985), 7–32; id., *Kingdom and Colony: Ireland in the Atlantic World, 1560–1800* (Baltimore, 1988), 69–102; id., 'In Defence of the Constitution? The Nature of Irish Revolt in the Seventeenth Century', in *Cultures et pratiques politiques en France et en Irelande XVIe–XVIIIe siècles* (Paris, 1991), 25–6; Michael MacCarthy-Morrogh, *The Munster Plantation* (Oxford, 1986); Victor Treadwell, *Buckingham and Ireland, 1616–1628: A Study in Anglo-Irish Politics* (Dublin, 1998).

[3] Clarke, *Old English*, 25–7 and id., 'The Army and Politics in Ireland, 1625–30' *Studia Hibernica*, 4 (1964), 32–3; Canny, 'In Defence of the Constitution?', 25–6.

[4] See Clarke, *The Graces, 1625–41*, Irish Historical Series, 8 (Dundalk, 1968).

[5] Hugh F. Kearney, *Strafford in Ireland, 1633–1641: A Study in Absolutism*, 2nd edn. (Cambridge, 1989), 216–19; Clarke, *Old English*, 117–18.

implement the Graces: the New English objected to being forced to disgorge the profits from decades of administrative corruption and to Wentworth's religious policy.[6] Representatives of both religious interests, therefore, but particularly the protestant, co-operated with the English parliament's impeachment and judicial murder of Strafford in May 1641.[7]

Nevertheless, even before the fall of the lord lieutenant the interests of the two groups had been diverging once more and his death accelerated this process. Following Strafford's imprisonment at the end of 1640, the government in Dublin had devolved into the hands of two Lord Justices, Sir William Parsons, a representative of the New English interest, and the English master of the ordnance, Sir John Borlase.[8] This development caused great unease among the catholic population who feared above all an administration dominated by Irish protestants.[9] Moreover, the developing assault on the king's power and prerogatives by the English parliament, availing of the military pressure of a hotly protestant Scottish army which had already defeated the king in the Bishops' wars, was acutely threatening to Irish catholics.[10] Consequently, as early as February 1641, a group of Old Irish conspirators were already vaguely planning a rising.[11] In the course of the summer of 1641 a separate plot to capture Dublin castle, involving disgruntled Irish military entrepreneurs, in which members of the Old English community also participated and which may have enjoyed at least a tacit element of approval from the embattled monarch himself, was also developed.[12] Old English interest in this scheme, however, subsequently waned as increasingly it appeared that

[6] Kearney, Strafford in Ireland, 104–29; Canny, From Reformation to Restoration: Ireland, 1534–1660 (Dublin, 1987), 188–204; R. Buick Knox, James Ussher, Archbishop of Armagh (Cardiff, 1967), 44–53.

[7] Robert Ashton, The English Civil War: Conservatism and Revolution, 1603–1649, 2nd edn. (London, 1991), 136–7; Kearney, Strafford in Ireland, 199–208; Michael Perceval-Maxwell, 'Ulster 1641 in the Context of Political Developments in the Three Kingdoms', in Brian Mac Cuarta (ed.), Ulster 1641: Aspects of the Rising (Belfast, 1993), 98–102.

[8] Clarke, Old English, 136–7.

[9] Raymond Gillespie, 'The End of an Era: Ulster and the Outbreak of the 1641 Rising', in Ciarán Brady and Raymond Gillespie (eds.), Natives and Newcomers: Essays on the Making of Irish Colonial Society, 1534–1641 (Dublin, 1986) 199–200.

[10] The appointment in May of a representative of the English puritan faction, Robert Sidney, earl of Leicester as lord lieutenant of Ireland initially heightened tension still further: see Perceval-Maxwell, 'Ulster 1641 in the Context of the Political Developments in the Three Kingdoms', 102–5; Conrad Russell, The Causes of the English Civil War (Oxford, 1990), 14–15; Ashton, English Civil War, 134–40.

[11] Gillespie, 'End of an Era', 193–201.

[12] Ibid., 201–3; Clarke, 'The Genesis of the Ulster Rising of 1641', in Peter Roebuck (ed.), Plantation to Partition. Essays in Ulster History in Honour of J. L. McCracken (Belfast, 1981), 29–45 and id., Old English, 158–60; Perceval-Maxwell, 'Ulster 1641 in the Context of Political Developments in the Three Kingdoms', 96–104; Gillespie, 'End of an Era', 201–3; Russell, 'The British Background to the Irish Rebellion of 1641', Historical Research, 61 (1988), 177–81; for the details of Charles's previous plans to use Irish forces as a response to his British problems see Jane Ohlmeyer, Civil War and Restoration in the Three Stuart Kingdoms: The Career of Randal MacDonnell, Marquis of Antrim, 1609–1683 (Cambridge, 1993), 77–101.

such a plot was necessary neither to put pressure on the king nor to assist him.[13] In addition, during the summer the new lord lieutenant, the earl of Leicester, seems to have convinced the Old English representatives in England that he was not to be feared. Moreover, Charles' negotiations with his Scottish subjects during this period worked to diminish both catholic fears of a Scottish assault on their liberties and the king's own need of a counterweight to the Scottish army.[14]

The Ulster Irish, however, seem to have been isolated from the negotiations which cooled the anxieties of the Old English community and had in any case problems and grievances distinct from those of their co-religionists.[15] A group of largely Gaelic Irish conspirators, therefore, continued with a plot for a rising in Ulster which they planned to coincide with the capture of Dublin castle, the seat of Irish government. The attempt on the castle was frustrated but the rising in Ulster did take place, beginning in the evening of 22 October 1641.[16]

II

More than anything else, the confederate catholic association to which Rinuccini was subsequently accredited was the heir to this rising. On the one hand the rebellion established the context within which Irish and British affairs interacted for the rest of the decade. The rebellion itself was a major cause of the English Civil War.[17] The preoccupation of England and Scotland with the military and constitutional resolution of this crisis over the next seven years, which meant that sufficient resources could not be spared for the effective repression of the Irish rebellion, was an essential condition in allowing the development of the confederate association.[18] Nevertheless,

[13] By early April 1641 the king had already agreed to enact legislation which would secure the principal Old English objective, namely the security of their estates. See Perceval-Maxwell, 'Ulster 1641 in the Context of Political Developments in the Three Kingdoms', 101; Russell, 'British Background', 173.

[14] Perceval-Maxwell, 'Ulster 1641 in the Context of Political Developments in the Three Kingdoms', 104–5; see also id., *The Outbreak of the Irish Rebellion of 1641* (Belfast, 1994), 105–66.

[15] Id., 'Ulster 1641 in the Context of Political Developments in the Three Kingdoms', 105–6; see also id., *The Outbreak of the Irish Rebellion of 1641*, 110–51.

[16] Brendan FitzPatrick, *Seventeenth-Century Ireland: The War of Religions* (Dublin, 1988), 133–67 has deconstructed some of the evidence to argue that the plot to take Dublin castle never existed. Ohlmeyer, *Civil War and Restoration*, 101 n. 8 notes the force of his argument but Perceval-Maxwell, 'Ulster 1641 in the Context of Political Developments in the Three Kingdoms', 208 n. 44 points out the existence of other evidence which Fitzpatrick has ignored. See also Clarke, *Old English*, 161 n. 1.

[17] The refusal of parliament to allow the king control of an army to repress the rebellion in Ireland, or of the local militia forces which were considered necessary to oppose any invasion of England by Irish rebels, enormously escalated the constitutional crisis in England, which eventually collapsed into civil war in 1642. Russell, *Causes of the Civil War*; Ashton, *English Civil War*, 140.

[18] A Scots army was sent to Ireland but it was slow to arrive and rarely penetrated outside Ulster. The central text on the Scots in Ireland is David Stevenson, *Scottish Covenanters and Irish*

the confederates were in no doubt that the eventual victors in the English Civil War would turn their attention once again to Ireland.[19] Confederate interest in the outcome of events in England was further sharpened by the fact that Irish catholics had far greater reason to fear a Parliamentary victory in England.[20] The Adventurers' Act of March 1642, supplemented by the doubling ordinance of July, which proposed to pay for the repression of the Irish rebellion through wide-ranging confiscations of Irish land, naturally intensified these anxieties.[21] The king had actually assented to the Adventurers' Act but during the 1640s the confederates could hope realistically that a settlement with Charles would protect the lands of the catholic proprietors in the island.[22] Consequently, throughout the 1640s the confederates' pursuit of their goals, and in particular their religious objectives, was to be compromised by the desire to bolster the royalist position in England, whether by moderating the demands which they made in negotiations with royalist commissioners so as not to alienate moderate protestant opinion from the king, or by the dispatch of actual military assistance to the royalist war effort.

The rising spread first through Ulster and then the rest of the country in a manner which the original leadership had clearly not intended.[23] From the beginning, the rebel leaders insisted that they were in arms to protect the

Confederates (Belfast, 1981). See especially 43–65 with regard to the manner in which even prior to the outbreak of the first civil war the crisis in England militated against any response to the Irish rebellion.

[19] The horror felt in England at the rebellion, intensified by the belief that an impossible number of protestants had been murdered in an organized conspiracy involving practically all the catholics of Ireland, defies exaggeration. This testified to the skill with which the Irish protestant community publicized this particular version of the rising: in this regard see Toby Barnard, '1641: A Bibliographical Essay', in Mac Cuarta, *Ulster 1641*, 173–7; Aidan Clarke, 'The 1641 Rebellion and Anti-popery in Ireland', ibid., 149–57; Gillespie, 'End of an Era', 191–3.

[20] Even in 1641 Irish catholics had feared that parliament's assault on the king's prerogatives would lead to parliamentary persecution of their religion. See Canny, 'In Defence of the Constitution?', 28.

[21] Robert Armstrong, 'Protestant Ireland and the English Parliament, 1641–1647' (unpub. Ph.D. thesis, Trinity College Dublin, 1995), 39–45; K. S. Bottigheimer, *English Money and Irish Land* (Oxford, 1971), 39–42.

[22] In this regard see Clarke, *Old English*, 208–9; Patrick Corish, 'The Rising of 1641 and the Catholic Confederacy, 1641–45', in T. W. Moody, F. X. Martin, and F. J. Byrne (eds.), *A New History of Ireland*, iii, *Early Modern Ireland, 1534–1691* (Oxford, 1976), 295–6.

[23] As a group this leadership represented those 'deserving Irish' who had been accommodated in the settlement of Ulster after the Nine Years' War and the Flight of the Earls, who occupied positions of some importance within the new order and who had come to share some of the characteristics and preoccupations of the Old English. Their economic difficulties in adapting to the new order, however, had been accentuated by the recession of the 1630s, and they seem to have been particularly resentful of insulting behaviour in their regard by a new breed of men who had entered the localities on the tails of the recession. See Clarke, 'Genesis of the Ulster Rising', 34–7; Gillespie, 'End of an Era', 193–9; id., 'Destabilising Ulster, 1641–2', in Mac Cuarta, *Ulster 1641*, 107–10; id., 'Harvest Crises in Early Seventeenth-century Ireland', *Irish Economic and Social History*, 2 (1984), 5–18; id., *Colonial Ulster: The Settlement of East Ulster 1600–41* (Cork, 1985), 202–3; Canny, 'In Defence of the Constitution?', 35–7.

king's prerogatives and to safeguard their religion from protestant forces which intended to destroy both it and them. The character of the rebellion, however, was decided as much by their inability to control its development as by their original objectives. Throughout the country attacks were launched on the local protestant population. In contrast to the turbulence of the sixteenth century, by 1641 Ireland had enjoyed over thirty years without the outbreak of a major rebellion, which meant that in the face of these attacks both the government and the protestant population of the country were psychologically and materially ill-equipped to cope.[24] This pattern of aggressive behaviour reflected considerable economic motivation: recession and poor harvests accentuated the condition of those who had difficulty in adapting to the developing market economy in Ireland, and who had watched protestant settlers occupy and develop better agricultural holdings and acquire numerous bonds and mortgages on native property.[25] Those who had little or no place within the developing economic structures took the opportunity to engage in pillage and violence and they seem to have been chiefly responsible for the actual massacres of protestants which occurred.[26] Nevertheless, religion provided the normative structure which justified the onslaught. The steady consolidation of an explicitly catholic identity throughout Ireland in the previous decades evidently helped create popular hostility towards those not members of the Roman church.[27] Wentworth's religious policy and the increasing radicalism of Ulster presbyterianism in

[24] Gillespie, 'Destabilising Ulster, 1641–2', 110–11; for contemporary but opposing views of the quiet before the storm see Sir John Temple, *The Irish Rebellion or an history* (London, 1646) and Bellings narrative (J. T. Gilbert (ed.), *History of the Irish Confederation and the War in Ireland* (7 vols., Dublin, 1882–91), i. 2).

[25] Gillespie, 'Destabilising Ulster, 1641–2', 111–13; Canny, *Kingdom and Colony*, 61 and id., 'In Defence of the Constitution?', 30–3; the type of economic pressure exerted on landlords and tenants is outlined in Mary O'Dowd, *Power, Politics and Land: Early Modern Sligo, 1568–1688* (Belfast, 1991), 63–86; see also ead., 'Land Inheritance in Early Modern County Sligo', *Irish Economic and Social History*, (1983), 5–18; Brendan Ó Bric, 'Galway Townsmen as Owners of Land in Connacht, 1585–1641' (unpub. MA thesis, University College, Galway, 1974), 357–97; Ciarán Ó Murchadha, 'Land and Society in Seventeenth Century Clare' (unpub. Ph.D. thesis, University College, Galway, 1982), 16–21 notes the manner in which protestant settlers were able to take advantage of the economic difficulties of natives to establish themselves in Clare; see also Gillespie, *Colonial Ulster*, 125–6, 140–2, 200–1 which points out the greater difficulties confronting Gaelic landholders in a period of general economic difficulty although members of the Old English community also suffered in this process of economic decline.

[26] Canny, 'In Defence of the Constitution?', 37–9.

[27] Michelle O'Riordan in 'The Native Ulster *Mentalité* as Revealed in Gaelic Sources, 1600–50', in Mac Cuarta, *Ulster 1641*, 83, 90–1 emphasizes that the learned Gaelic literature of the pre–1641 period did not advocate such sectarian hostility: but extreme sectarian antagonism, which the catholic clergy evidently strove to control rather than promote, did emerge during the rising. See Canny, 'In Defence of the Constitution?', 33, 38; Mary Catherine Kennedy, 'Eagla an Ghallsmacht: The Religion and Politics of Irish Catholics, 1620s–1670s' (unpub. MA thesis, University College, Galway), 7–8; in view of the depth of hostility which did emerge in the 1640s, the psychological unpreparedness of the protestant population was even more remarkable: see Ó Murchadha, 'Land and Society', 37–8.

the 1630s had served to sharpen distinctions still further.[28] Resentment of tithes and other exactions by the protestant clergy also played their part.[29]

Thus it is necessary to distinguish between the original and limited objectives of the Ulster leadership and the sectarian and economically motivated hostility and disorder which erupted in the wake of the rebellion, which the leadership had not planned but which in a sense engulfed them.[30] The combination of these different impulses was also important in the spread of the rebellion. The manner in which the rebel leaders articulated their aims was to be a vital factor in attracting the support of the Old English landowners of the Pale, the rich hinterland of Dublin.[31] This group's natural distrust of the Lord Justices had been heightened by the government's behaviour, in particular by its refusal to distribute arms to the Old English population to protect themselves and their property from the southern advance of Ulster rebel forces. At the end of November the rebels' victory at Julianstown over a force of government troops was a further indication of their strength and the vulnerability of the lands of the Old English Pale. Distrust of the government was intensified by the manner in which parliament was not allowed to debate a response to the rebellion at any length, and by the extreme severity towards the catholic population with which detachments of government troops behaved at Santry and, under the command of the much feared Sir Charles Coote, in Wicklow. Rumours abounded that a Scots army was to be introduced to extirpate catholicism within the kingdom. Although no hard evidence could be adduced to link the Lord Justices to such a plan, few believed that the government would regret such a development if it occurred.[32] The Old English members of parliament in November 1641 in fact addressed a petition to their monarch pleading that the government of the country and the suppression of the rebellion be entrusted to the earl of Ormond.[33] This was of considerable significance. There is every reason to believe that if Ormond had dominated the Irish government at this point then the Old English leadership would not have become involved in the rebellion. Thus when Ormond became lord lieutenant in 1643, a post which he held also during Rinuccini's nunciature, he found himself negotiating with a confederate leadership dominated by individuals who might conceivably have never entered rebellion if he had supplanted the Lord Justices, Parsons and

[28] Gillespie, 'End of an Era', 197–8.   [29] Ó Murchadha 'Land and Society', 40–1.
[30] Canny, 'In Defence of the Constitution?', 36–7; Hilary Simms, 'Violence in County Armagh, 1641', in Mac Cuarta, Ulster 1641, 123–38.
[31] In this regard see Gormanston to Clanricard, 21 Jan. 1642 (Gilbert, Irish Confederation, i. 255); Clarke, Old English, 219.
[32] Bellings's narrative (Gilbert, Irish Confederation, i. 35–41); Bodl. Carte MS 64, fo. 464[r–v]; 'The war and rebellion in Ireland begun in 1641' (NLI MS 345 (Plunkett-Dunne MS), p. 1216); Clarke, 'A Discourse between Two Councillors of State, the One of England, the Other of Ireland', Analecta Hibernica, 26 (1970), 171–4 and id., Old English, 174–86.
[33] Clarke, Old English, 173–4.

Borlase, two years earlier.[34] The attachment to Ormond is thus fundamental to an understanding of the extremely conciliatory stance later adopted by the confederates in subsequent negotiations with the lord lieutenant and, during the nunciature, their determination to persist with those negotiations in the face of Rinuccini's opposition.

Distrust of the government, vulnerability to the Ulster rebels' forces, and an identification with the objectives of the rebel leadership all encouraged the Old English landowners of the Pale to join forces with the insurgents. Local popular pressure also played its part. From an extremely early date, the Old English leadership had been worried about the opportunistic pillaging which the rebellion encouraged in their own localities.[35] Fear of the consequences of standing aloof from the rebellion also operated in forcing involvement elsewhere in the country. Although a catholic, the earl of Castlehaven had cattle stolen in 1642, apparently because of his refusal to join the rebellion.[36] Richard Bellings later explained the decision of his father-in-law, Viscount Mountgarrett, to throw in his lot with the insurgents as heavily influenced by: 'the apprehensions he had of the height to which the meaner sort of people might grow up against the nobility and gentry.'[37] It has been suggested also that the involvement of the lords of the Pale in the rebellion operated to confer respectability on participation.[38] Moreover, the involvement of the greater gentry and catholic nobility also evidently had a momentum of its own. As more of the catholic community implicated itself in rebellion, it became increasingly obvious to those such as Viscount Muskery in Munster, who initially stood aloof, that the failure of the rebellion would lead to the eradication of the landed catholic community which had existed prior to 1641. In such a case, even if the catholic gentry who had refused to join the rebellion were exempted from a general protestant retribution, they would be left as a small and vulnerable minority in the new Ireland.[39]

Another vital ingredient in the spread of the rebellion was the involvement of the catholic towns whose citizens later played an important role during Rinuccini's nunciature, particularly in 1646. The reactions to the rebellion of the various towns with predominantly catholic populations varied from

[34] In this regard see 'The war and rebellion in Ireland begun in 1641', p. 1216.

[35] Indeed, in December the Dublin government was convinced that the Lords of the Pale were following rather than leading their tenants and adherents into rebellion. See Clarke, Old English, 164, 185; Bodl. Carte MS 64, fo. 460ʳ; Historical Manuscripts Commission, Calendar of the Manuscripts of the Marquess of Ormonde KP, NS (8 vols., London, 1902–20), ii, 42–3.

[36] J. C. Beckett The Making of Modern Ireland, 1603–1923 (New York, 1977), 85–6; Corish, 'The Rising of 1641', 292–4; James Touchet, The earl of Castlehaven's review: or his memoirs (London, 1684), 25.

[37] Bellings's narrative (Gilbert, Irish Confederation, i. 65).   [38] Clarke, Old English, 193.

[39] See for example Bellings's discussion of the reasons which persuaded Viscount Muskery to join the insurgents (Gilbert, Irish Confederation, i. 70); Micheál Ó Siochrú, Confederate Ireland, 1642–1649: A Constitutional and Political Analysis (Dublin, 1999), 65 points out in addition that Muskery, like Mountgarrett, was influenced by a fear of social unrest and actual personal danger.

place to place and over time.[40] Divisions within the urban communities between pro- and anti-rebel factions certainly occurred in Galway, Cork, and Waterford but were probably also present in other cities. In general, the opponents of the rebellion seem to have been among the more prosperous citizens. Genuine religious enthusiasm was possibly a more important factor in the towns than anywhere else. Independent behind their walls, the major ports were in no real danger from anything other than the most concerted siege by any of the armies in Ireland. But it was in the towns that the impact of catholic reform on the daily practice of people's lives had been greatest.[41] Forty years earlier the southern corporations had already given evidence of their commitment to catholicism by the repossession of churches after the death of Elizabeth and in the interim this commitment had strengthened.[42] The towns were generally well-supplied with well-trained secular clergy, a greater than average proportion of regular clergy, and were often also the seat of a bishop, or subject to particular episcopal attention. Throughout this period in fact the urban populations were often to show greater susceptibility to clerical influence than to any of the decrees of the confederate Supreme Council.

The institutionalized involvement of the catholic church crucially strengthened the movement towards greater organization in 1642. Some such development was increasingly necessary because of events in England[43] and

---

[40] Some pillaging of protestants evidently occurred in the towns of Kilkenny and Wexford which probably helped their citizens to decide they had little to lose in throwing in their lot with the rebellion: see Bellings's narrative (Gilbert, *Irish Confederation*. i. 56, 65), but this was evidently uncommon: see Ohlmeyer, *Civil War and Restoration*, 110. The influence of local magnates was evidently of some importance. In Kilkenny's case, as an inland town surrounded by territory in open revolt, there was less possibility of staying aloof, while Galway and Limerick's slow involvement in the rebellion was influenced by the local opposition of the earls of Thomond and Clanricard. With regard to the stance of the 'English' catholic Clanricard see John Lowe (ed.), *Letter Book of the Earl of Clanricarde, 1643-7* (Dublin, 1983), pp. xvii-xxvi; see also Clarke, *Old English*, 193-5; Ó Murchadha, 'Land and Society', 45-50. Cork never came into the hands of the confederates. Although the population was probably over 85 per cent catholic, the mayor opened the gates to the troops of St Leger in 1642 and from then on the city remained securely in protestant hands. See MacCarthy-Morrogh, *The Munster Plantation*, 265; Stanislaus Kavanagh (ed.), *Commentarius Rinuccianus, de Sedis apostolicae legatione ad foederatos Hiberniae catholicos per annas 1645-9* (6 vols., Dublin, 1932-49) (*Comment. Rinucc.*), i. 307-8. In Waterford too it is evident that the mayor was more inclined to surrender the city to government troops than to insurgent forces. He was, however, opposed by the majority of the townspeople marshalled by the recorder: see the Briver correspondence (Gilbert, *Irish Confederation*, ii. 12, 22-3).

[41] Corish, *The Catholic Community in the Seventeenth and Eighteenth Centuries* (Dublin, 1981), 31-2; the great influence of the local clergy on the passions of the townsfolk can be seen for instance in the riots of 1648 in Galway (*Comment. Rinucc.*, iii. 493-5) and in Limerick in 1646 (Gilbert, *Irish Confederation*, vi. 119-23).

[42] See A. J. Sheehan, 'The Recusancy Revolt of 1603: A Reinterpretation', *Archivium Hibernicum*, 38 (1983), 3-13 and id., 'Irish Towns in a Period of Change, 1558-1625', in Brady and Gillespie, *Natives and Newcomers*, 110-11.

[43] On 8 Dec. 1641 the English House of Commons passed a resolution demanding an end to the toleration of catholicism in any of the Stuart dominions. By the end of Mar. 1642 the king had accepted the Adventurers' Act and had agreed not to pardon the Irish rebels without parliamentary

because of the need to improve the military capacity of those in rebellion,[44] particularly after the landing of considerable troops from England and the first detachments of a strong covenanter force in Ulster in April.[45] The arrival in Ireland of returning military exiles, in particular Owen Roe O'Neill in July and Thomas Preston in September 1642, provided the rebels with a limited store of munitions and a pool of several hundred experienced officers around which to build armies.[46] The outbreak of the English Civil War in August which severely limited supplies to the English forces operating in Ireland and the reluctance of the covenanter army to risk its forces outside east Ulster also gave the rebels respite to organize, recruit, and train.[47]

A vital stage in this process was the establishment, at the initiative of the catholic hierarchy, of a provisional executive council of clerical and lay leaders in June 1642. It was this body which organized the election of the first quasi-parliamentary but unicameral confederate General Assembly at the end of October 1642.[48] The general assemblies were essentially gatherings of the major catholic property owners in the island,[49] with a common interest in defending both property rights and their shared religion, as was reflected by the decisions of the first assembly.[50] The representative nature of the assemblies conferred legitimacy on the Supreme Councils which they elected to conduct affairs between meetings of the quasi-parliamentary body. The

consent and it was becoming known in Ireland that he had categorically condemned the rebellion. By this time also reinforcements from England had led to a government offensive which had driven the Ulster rebels from the Pale. These factors meant that the Old English of the Pale were willing to negotiate an end to their participation in the rebellion but the behaviour of the government in Dublin, still under the control of elements hostile to catholicism, acted to discourage them from doing so. See Armstrong, 'Protestant Ireland and the English Parliament', 9–63; Clarke, Old English, 190–208; Corish, 'The Rising of 1641', 295–6.

[44] This point was brought home by the battle of Kilrush in Kildare in April 1642 which demonstrated the inability of the irregular rebel army to confront even small forces of trained soldiers. See Bellings's narrative (Gilbert, Irish Confederation, i. 80).

[45] For the background to the dispatch of this force and for its initial deployment see Stevenson, Covenanters and Confederates, 43–83, 103–21.

[46] See Jerrold Casway, 'Owen Roe O'Neill's Return to Ireland in 1642: The Diplomatic Background', Studia Hibernica, 9 (1969), 60 and id. Owen Roe O'Neill and the Struggle for Catholic Ireland (Philadelphia, 1984), 60–4.

[47] Stevenson, Covenanters and Confederates, 120–3.

[48] Ó Siochrú, Confederate Ireland, esp. pp. 205–36 is now the definitive text on the workings of the confederate governmental institutions; see also D. F. Cregan, 'The Confederation of Kilkenny', in Brian Farrell (ed.), The Irish Parliamentary Tradition (Dublin, 1973), 103–5: confederate assemblies of course never pretended to constitute a parliament since the convocation of parliament was one of the prerogatives of their monarch which they had sworn to uphold.

[49] Having taken possession of most of the property pertaining to the Church of Ireland, the catholic clergy were once again formidable landowners although the fact that prior to Rinuccini's arrival two-thirds of their revenues were under lay management for use in the war probably diminished their influence. See Comment. Rinucc., ii. 92, 149: with regard to the secular delegates it has been estimated that the average holdings of those who were not peers amounted to about 7,000 acres. See Cregan, 'The Confederation of Kilkenny: Its Organization, Personnel and History' (unpub. Ph.D. thesis, National University of Ireland, 1947), 106.

[50] See Gilbert, Irish Confederation, ii. 72–85.

second buttress of confederate legitimacy was the oath of association, the Irish equivalent to the Scottish covenant.[51] This oath commenced with a pledge of allegiance to the king and to the upholding of his prerogatives. It then obliged the taker to defend the lives, just freedoms, possessions, patrimonies, and rights of every person who had sworn or who would swear the oath in future. It forbade any attempt by any confederate to seek a separate peace or pardon without permission from the Supreme Council and it enjoined obedience to the council in every matter concerning the common cause.[52] It was thus both an oath of obedience and association which established a brotherhood or society of 'confederate catholics' committed to the achievement of certain goals. What emerged from the first General Assembly, therefore, was a potentially formidable union. Arguably the single most important ingredient in the stabilization of the new association among the general population, which was to have enormous implications in the years of Rinuccini's nunciature, was the support of the church.[53]

III

It has been argued that the initial objectives of the confederate catholics, demonstrated in the decrees of the first confederate assembly, were defensive and that this reflected the fundamental conservatism, not only of the Old English interest, but of the original leaders of the rebellion. In religious terms, their goal has been portrayed as the preservation of the existing toleration of catholic worship rather than the improvement of the conditions under which catholicism had previously been practised.[54] Such an analysis traces the intrusion of an extremist religious outlook to the influence of the continent during the 1640s.[55] While acknowledging the force of this argument, it can be qualified to some degree. Recently it has been argued convincingly that too great a focus on constitutional matters blurs the picture of what occurred in the original rebellion and that even those catholic landowners who appeared to participate in the rebellion 'in defence of a vaguely defined constitution were really seeking after a new political order'.[56] With regard to specifically religious extremism, it must be stressed that pressure

---

[51] The most detailed analysis of the confederate oath is Fitzpatrick, *War of Religions*, 188–91 but this analysis is questionable on a number of grounds; see also Beckett, 'The Confederation of Kilkenny Reviewed', *Historical Studies*, 2 (1959), 29–41 and Corish, 'The Rising of 1641', 299; with regard to the Scottish covenant see Stevenson, *Covenanters and Confederates*, 122–3, 130; in this regard note the interesting reference to the 'confederate calvinists in Scotland' in 'The war and rebellion in Ireland begun in 1641' (NLI MS 345 (Plunkett-Dunne MS), p. 946.

[52] *The memoirs and letters of Ulick, marquiss of Clanricarde* (London, 1757), 325.

[53] This was something of which Rome was aware, as is apparent in Rinuccini's instructions (G. Aiazzi, *Nunziatura in Irlanda di Monsignor Gio. Baptista Rinuccini Arcivescovo di Fermo negli anni 1645 à 1649* (Florence, 1844) (Aiazzi, *Nunziatura*), p. xli).

[54] Clarke, *Old English*, 216–19.   [55] Ibid., 216.

[56] Canny, 'In Defence of the Constitution?', 40.

towards a more extreme 'continental' position in this regard was not exerted by Rinuccini alone. A considerable element of sectarian radicalism had surfaced in the course of the rebellion. Long before the nuncio's arrival, the native Irish hierarchy were demanding a radical alteration of the constitutional status of the catholic church, demands which cannot be solely or even primarily attributed to the efforts of Rinuccini's predecessor as papal agent, PierFrancesco Scarampi, who arrived in the island in 1643. Moreover, it is clear that a majority of the confederate laity accepted the justice of a number of the clergy's demands as was to be shown by the events of 1646–7. It is true, however, that the nuncio's arrival brought the more radical confederate positions increasingly to the forefront.

That these positions were not articulated with the same force in the earlier years of the association owed much to the influence of the earl and later marquis of Ormond. Over the course of the winter of 1642–3, as the English war showed signs of developing into a protracted struggle, the king became interested in securing the return of the army which had been sent to Ireland in the wake of the rebellion and, ultimately, in acquiring Irish troops for use in England.[57] To this end, in January 1643 he authorized Ormond and six other commissioners to hear the grievances of the Irish rebels which opened the possibility of a negotiated peace in Ireland. Over the course of the next ten months, Ormond gradually emerged as the dominant force in the Dublin government and was finally appointed lord lieutenant in November 1643. By that time a year long cessation of hostilities, commencing in September 1643, had already been arranged between royalist and confederate forces.[58] During the truce, confederate commissioners were to have the opportunity to present their demands to the king himself in England. In the event, this cessation was to be steadily extended and actually ended only when Rinuccini overthrew the government established by the first Ormond peace in 1646. The 1643 truce thus marked the end of conflict between forces loyal to Charles and the confederates for three years and inaugurated a period in which the confederates were chiefly concerned with achieving their objectives through negotiations with Ormond. So exactly was this development in tune with the wishes of many prominent confederates that the association's commissioners were prepared to accept remarkably poor financial terms for the original truce[59] and they were also willing to continue negotiations even in the face of the king's evident reluctance to grant their demands, and

---

[57] Joyce Lee Malcolm, 'All the King's Men: The Impact of the Crown's Irish Forces on the English Civil War', *Irish Historical Society*, 22 (1979), 239–64.

[58] Corish, 'The Rising of 1641', 304–9.

[59] Despite holding considerable military advantages the confederates agreed to pay £30,000 for the truce, the equivalent of a normal year's revenue to the king from the area under their control: see Gilbert, *Irish Confederation*, ii. 360–8; iv. 244–8. The collection of this sum placed a huge strain on the confederate economy.

despite the hostility towards the policy of truce and negotiation of Rinuccini's predecessor, Scarampi.[60]

The negotiations with Ormond, however, did not mean a complete end to confederate military activity during this period. The Scots in Ulster opposed the cessation and in July 1644 the protestant enclave in Munster under the command of Murrough O' Brien, Baron Inchiquin, also declared for parliament and against the cessation. In 1644 the confederates mounted an offensive against the Scots in Ulster, and the following year they attacked the protestant forces in the south. Neither campaign, however, effected a major change in the military balance in the island. Militarily, the cessation of 1643 thus inaugurated something of a stalemate. The truce with Ormond precluded any change of positions in Leinster while in Munster and Ulster neither the confederates nor their foes were able to make significant headway.

A number of reasons can be identified why the confederates rejected the advice of the papal agent in 1643 and elected to make a truce with the king. Eagerness to demonstrate their genuine loyalty to the king and by doing so to obtain his goodwill were important factors.[61] In addition, by securing the removal of the English army many confederates probably believed that, at a stroke, they could strengthen both the king in England against parliament and their own position in Ireland. And many evidently hoped also that the truce would give them time to organize their own government properly and receive aid from abroad.[62] In the event, the sum paid for the truce, the drain of soldiers from Ireland to the king's armies, and the doubts raised in the Vatican about confederate commitment to war in the catholic interest possibly outweighed any advantages which did accrue.[63] Nor did the king demonstrate any great willingness to accept confederate professions of loyalty: contrary to their expectations the royalist forces in Ireland never joined with the confederates against the covenanter Scots in the north,[64] and the confederates' costly outfitting of the earl of Antrim's expedition to Scotland on behalf of the king failed to excite any major demonstration of royal favour.[65] In 1643, however, the leaders of the association clearly did not

---

[60] For details of the negotiations see Ó Siochrú, *Confederate Ireland*, 68–86.

[61] Corish, 'The Rising of 1641', 307.

[62] See the arguments concerning the truce put forward by Richard Bellings in *Comment. Rinucc.*, i. 413–21.

[63] The details of Antrim's activities in Scotland and on the continent are covered in Ohlmeyer, *Civil War and Restoration*, 127–73; see also Stevenson, *Covenanters and Confederates*, 165–89. It has also been suggested that far larger forces arrived more unobtrusively to bolster the main royalist armies in England: see Lee Malcolm, 'All the King's Men', 239–64. This argument is strengthened by Ronald Hutton, 'The Royalist War Effort', in John Morrill (ed.), *Reactions to the English Civil War, 1642–9* (London, 1982), 57 which agrees that no more than 7,000 of the troops transported could have come from the original English army sent to Ireland.

[64] Even as late as May 1644 the confederates were contemplating conferring the command of their own army against the Scots on Ormond. See Gilbert, *Irish Confederation*, iii. 170–1.

[65] Ohlmeyer, *Civil War and Restoration*, 147; Stevenson, *Covenanters and Confederates*, 180–1.

anticipate such an attitude from the king. Moreover, Ormond's emergence as the dominant figure in Dublin and the trust which he inspired in the catholic community offered further encouragement to the confederates to adopt conciliatory positions.[66]

Perhaps most importantly of all, the secular confederates clearly believed that a negotiated settlement with the king which would satisfy their principal grievances was *possible*. This is of great importance. Modern historical research has focused attention on the constitutional difficulties involved in any attempt to negotiate a settlement between a protestant monarch and catholic subjects, particularly with regard to the exercise of jurisdiction by catholic prelates appointed by the pope.[67] The far greater difficulties which confronted Charles in negotiating with Irish catholics than with Scots presbyterians have been emphasized.[68] Yet in the early stages of negotiations with royalist commissioners even relatively moderate lay confederates evidently believed that, in addition to their secular grievances,[69] it was necessary to insist on the formal abrogation of the reformation legislation and even several fourteenth-century statutes which ordained the prosecution of any beneficed cleric appointed without royal consent.[70]

[66] See Cregan, 'The Confederation of Kilkenny' (thesis), 104–5 concerning Ormond's personal connections with prominent confederates; id., 'The Confederation of Kilkenny' (article), 112 offers a superb succinct analysis of Ormond's relationship with the association: with regard to Ormond's own determination not to be suspected of favouring the confederates because of personal and familial ties see Ormond to Charles I, 14 Nov. 1645 (Gilbert, *Irish Confederation*, i. 197).

[67] See esp. Corish, 'The Rising of 1641', 311–12; the deposing power of the pope had been an issue of prime importance in the last decades of the sixteenth century and the first decades of the seventeenth, brought into prominence by the papal excommunication of Elizabeth and James's own love of theological debate. See J. J. Silke, 'Primate Lombard and James I', *Irish Theological Quarterly*, 22 (1955), 124–50; see also Kenneth Fincham and Peter Lake, 'The Ecclesiastical Policies of James I and Charles I', in Kenneth Fincham (ed.), *The Early Stuart Church, 1603–1642* (London, 1993), 28–48; however, Charles's marriage to a catholic princess pointed up the decline in importance of this issue: indeed the confederates made much play of the natural harmony between catholicism and monarchy in memorials to Ormond. See for example Gilbert, *Irish Confederation*, iii. 298.

[68] Corish, 'The Rising of 1641', 311–12; Canny, *From Reformation to Restoration*, 208; the confederates, however, consistently underestimated these difficulties: they seem to have believed their religion to be closer to that of the king than the king's was to that of English puritans. In this regard see the memorials distinguishing between the king's religion and puritanism in APF, Scritture Referite nei Congressi, Irlanda, vol. i, fo. 137r and in APF, SOCG 295, fo. 6. The king himself may have been in a tiny minority within the Church of England who agreed with them: see Russell, *Causes of the English Civil War*, 197–8.

[69] Their demands in this regard included a review of all confiscations since the time of Elizabeth; the abandonment of all claims concerning land title made by the crown since 1634; the end of the Court of Wards; the opening of all offices to catholics; and the establishment of an Irish Inn of Court and a university.

[70] See Muskery to Ormond, March ?1644 (Gilbert, *Irish Confederation*, iii. 128–30); Confederate commissioners to Ormond, 17 July 1645 (ibid., iv. 332); John Lowe, 'Charles I and the Confederation of Kilkenny 1643–9', *Irish Historical Society*, 14 (1965), 5; Cregan, 'Confederation of Kilkenny' (thesis), 147–8; some indication of the confederate belief in the reasonableness of their position can be gained from Bellings's description of Ireland prior to 1641 (Gilbert, *Irish Confederation*, i. 2–3).

If Charles consented to a settlement with the authors of the 'massacres' of 1641 on these terms he would have alienated protestant opinion throughout his domains.[71] The confederates can hardly have been unaware of this but it should be noted in this regard that none of the protagonists during this period, not the king, nor the confederates, nor the English parliament, nor indeed the pope's representatives, believed that a settlement in Ireland would not lead to an intervention in the English Civil War. It was evidently a long-term component of confederate strategy that the settlement in Ireland could be secured principally by assisting the king to victory against his English and Scottish rebels.[72]

The disappointing response to their demands first from the king and then from Ormond (to whom conduct of the negotiations had devolved in the course of 1644)[73] might have been expected to dampen confederate enthusiasm for the attempt to achieve their objectives through negotiation. That the negotiations continued after the end of the first truce in September 1644 was the result of a combination of factors. In particular, an influential group of Old English confederates was frankly desperate to continue them. Alarmed about events in England, and having tasted the atmosphere at Oxford in the spring of 1644, it seems clear that this group was already prepared to settle for the removal of their principal secular grievances and immunity from the penalties of the penal laws, with the hope of further concessions at a more auspicious time. This was the group which, despite Rinuccini's opposition, was to be at the forefront in the conclusion of the first Ormond peace in 1646.[74]

Their eagerness for a treaty was increased by the growing militancy of the clerical party within the association which they found deeply alarming because it acted as an additional barrier to any negotiated settlement. This second faction was not only determined to secure the immediate and public abrogation of the penal legislation against catholicism but also to retain control of all church property which had been transferred from the Church of

---

[71] In this context see Robin Clifton, 'The Popular Fear of Catholics During the English Revolution', *Past and Present*, 52 (1971); Keith Lindley, 'The Impact of the 1641 Rebellion upon England and Wales', *Irish Historical Society*, 18 (1972); and John Wilson (ed.), Buckingham Contributions for Ireland 1642 (*Buckingham Record Society*, 21 (1983); Thomas Carte, *An history of the life of James, first duke of Ormond* (6 vols., Oxford, 1851), vi. 119, 146.

[72] In this regard see the Supreme Council's instructions to Hugh Bourke (Gilbert, *Irish Confederation*, iv. 93); see also the Supreme Council's instructions to Wadding (ibid., ii. 119); for Charles' view and use of Irish resources see Fitzpatrick, *War of Religions*, 77–108; Aidan Clarke, 'The Earl of Antrim and the First Bishops' War', *Irish Sword*, 6 (1963–4), 108–15; Stevenson, *Covenanters and Confederates*, 166–74; Lee Malcolm, 'All the King's Men', 251; and Ohlmeyer, *Civil War and Restoration*, 77–173; Parliament's very real worries about Irish intervention were reported by the Venetian secretary in England, Gerolamo Agostini, to the Doge and Senate of Venice, 22 Apr. 1644 (*Calendar of State Papers and Manuscripts Relating to English Affairs, Existing in the Archives and Collections of Venice, 1947–52* (London, 1927) 91–2; moreover if the European war had ended sooner than it did then the entire religious dynamic of the English war might have changed: in this context see Russell, *Causes of the English Civil War*, 193.

[73] Corish, 'The Rising of 1641', 311–12.   [74] Lowe, 'Charles I and the Confederation', 6.

Ireland in the course of the rebellion and war.[75] This party clearly had far less to hope for in negotiations since the king was unlikely to consent to this last proposition.[76] Rank and file members of the association had considerable sympathy with the demands of the clergy on this issue, who could thus muster considerable support in any confederate assembly. The clergy, however, were poorly represented in the confederate delegations which actually conducted the negotiations with Ormond.[77] As a result, there was always danger of a disjunction between the main body of the association and its official representatives. Throughout this period the assembly was in fact inclined to act as a check upon the process of negotiation. This not only created delays but ultimately it produced a situation in which the confederate assembly of 1647 repudiated the peace made by the confederate negotiators in 1646.[78]

Following that repudiation, many of the principally but not exclusively Old English members of the 'peace party' became totally alienated from the rest of their colleagues and from Rinuccini to whom they ascribed most of the blame for this development. None the less, the seeds of this alienation had been laid in the era prior to the nuncio's arrival. The increasing frustration of a group of influential Old English confederates at the failure to make peace with the king during this period was linked to the knowledge that they themselves, in the words of their arch apologist, 'could claim no other pretence of title to their estates than graunts from the crowne of England'.[79] From their perspective therefore, the continued security of their landownership depended on the maintenance within the constitution of the authority which had originally conferred it upon their families. Of crucial importance in this regard was the suspicion which Old English landowners came to entertain that the title to these estates might be challenged both by elements

[75] This issue of the churches was explicitly confronted in the assembly of May 1645: see *Comment. Rinucc.*, i. 527–9. Already in August of the previous year, however, the clergy had given notice of this demand: see the Duchess of Buckingham to Ormond, 20 Aug. 1644 (Gilbert, *Irish Confederation*, iii. 258).

[76] Even in the wake of the second civil war in England the king could not be brought to countenance the permanent alienation of the lands of the Church of England bishops: see Ashton, *English Civil War*, 337–8.

[77] Two factors were principally responsible for this: in the interests of harmony the confederates deliberately chose commissioners who they believed would be acceptable to Ormond and these tended to be religiously moderate Old English. Most importantly in this regard, the confederates unofficially accepted Ormond's refusal to deal with any member of the catholic clergy: see Cregan, 'Confederation of Kilkenny' (thesis), 153–4; Lowe, 'Charles I and the Confederation', 16–18. Second, the constitutional matters under discussion meant that a high proportion of the confederate delegates were lawyers and these tended to be less interested in the attainment of clerical demands. At least three and possibly five of the eight confederate commissioners who conducted the first negotiations with Ormond were lawyers: see Gilbert, *Irish Confederation*, iii. 252.

[78] See Lowe, 'Charles I and the Confederation', 16–19; Corish, 'Ormond, Rinuccini, and the Confederates, 1645–9' 319.

[79] Bellings's narrative (*Irish Confederation*, i. 19).

within the Gaelic Irish community and by the religious orders of the catholic church.

Suspicions of the objectives of the Gaelic rebels in Ulster, in many ways their hereditary foes, had evidently been nourished within the Old English community of the Pale from the beginning of the rebellion. As Viscount Gormanston informed the earl of Clanricard in 1642:

When first this action was discovered, most of the lords towards Dublin, to whom the design was not communicated, resorted to the Justices for armes, thinking at that time that the Irish had revived the old quarrel, and thought to expel us, who this four hundred years have been possessed of the most considerable parts of this king-dome . . . it was a blessing from God that the Irish had proposed to themselves fair ends, for otherwise, by the distrust of the State, we might have been compelled to seek new dwellings.[80]

As events were to demonstrate, Old English confidence in the 'fair ends' of the Old Irish, or in the degree to which they had indeed laid aside the 'old quarrel', was never absolute. In particular, after the summer of 1642 when Owen Roe O'Neill displaced Sir Phelim O'Neill and Roger Moore as the most important figure among the northern confederates, Old English anxieties about O'Neill's ultimate ambitions became acute. This was to prove one of the most destabilizing features of Rinuccini's nunciature.[81] Old English landowners also felt vulnerable to the claims of the religious orders whose property had been confiscated by the crown in the previous century,[82] and their anxieties in this regard increased steadily as the decade wore on.[83]

Fears that clerical pressure might eventually be put upon them to restore such property to its original owners was thus an incentive for some impor-tant confederates to seek peace with the king. From their perspective the sep-arate but not entirely dissimilar claim of the secular clergy of the catholic church to the property of the Church of Ireland, while not without justice, was dangerous in two ways. In the first place it would set a precedent in terms of the restoration of church property.[84] Second, and far more importantly, by obstructing a settlement with the king it raised the spectre that the confed-erates would be forced to vindicate their demands in arms. If this failed,

---

[80] Gormanston to Clanricard, 21 Jan. 1642 (Gilbert, *Irish Confederation*, 255).

[81] See for instance how Robert Talbot attempted to play on Preston's fears of the Old Irish in the crisis of 1646: Talbot to Preston (Latin trans.), 3 Sept. 1646 (*Comment. Rinucc.*, ii. 361); in this regard, it is evident that in 1641 the knowledge that Roger Moore (who by his marriage to Sir Patrick Barnewall's daughter was linked to most of the major families of the Pale) was prominent in the councils of the Ulster rebels proved a major factor in earning the trust of the lords of the Pale: see Bellings narrative (Gilbert, *Irish Confederation*, i. 35–6).

[82] In this regard see Brendan Bradshaw, *The Dissolution of the Religious Orders under Henry VIII* (Cambridge, 1974).

[83] This issue is discussed in greater detail in Ch. 2.

[84] In this regard one can note that Wentworth's recent recuperation of many revenues for the established church helped bring this issue even more sharply into focus.

savage reprisals from England could be expected. If it succeeded, however, the entire constitutional status of the monarchy from whom the Old English landowners held their land would be thrown into discussion. In 1647 the nuncio believed that this was the reason for the outrage aroused by the attack on the legitimacy of the Stuart monarchy by a radical Jesuit text, Conor O'Mahoney's *Disputatio Apologetica*. As the nuncio noted, the ideas contained in the *Disputatio* were seen as 'the final fatal ruin for all those who hold ecclesiastical property from the king'.[85] The determination of landowners to maintain the negotiations because of the potentially appalling consequences of not reaching a settlement was thus a major reason why talks continued. Moreover, while the other foes of the confederates in the island remained unsubdued, there was a certain logic in maintaining a truce in Leinster and in continuing to negotiate with Ormond. In a sense by doing this it was open to the confederates to pursue both a military and a conciliatory policy, namely negotiating with the king while strengthening their own military position by attacking their own and the king's enemies in Ulster and Munster. At face value, this twin policy is indeed what occurred. As noted above, while negotiating with Ormond, the confederates did mount (largely ineffective) offensives against the Scots in 1644 and against Inchiquin in 1645. Of critical importance, however, for the later conduct of Rinuccini's mission were the differing conclusions which the developing 'peace' party and the clerically dominated 'war' party drew from the failure of these campaigns. For the 'peace' party, the revelation of confederate military weakness increased the urgency of concluding a treaty with the king and of obtaining security for Irish catholicism by contributing to a royalist victory in England or, at the very least, of strengthening the anti-parliamentarian position in Ireland by joining their forces and garrisons to those of Ormond. If the retention of the churches continued to obstruct a settlement then this group were increasingly inclined to waive the attainment of this article, at least until the king had recovered his position in England.

The hardline clerical position was very different. This ascribed the military failures to the government of the Supreme Council. A reluctance to trust O'Neill with the command of the 1644 expedition was seen to have been compounded by massive administrative inefficiency and corruption.[86] Far more ominously, the suspicion developed that the peace party had actually conspired to bring about the failure of the 1645 campaigns and possibly of the 1644 campaign as well. This suspicion was fuelled by the conviction that

[85] 'Come l'ultima fatale rovina di tutti quelli che tengano beni Ecclesiastici dal Re' (as the final fatal ruin of all those who hold ecclesiastical goods from the king): Rinuccini to Pancirolo, 1 Oct. 1647 (Aiazzi, *Nunziatura*, 257).

[86] In this context see 'An Aphorismical discovery of treasonable faction' in J. T. Gilbert (ed.), *A Contemporary History of Affairs in Ireland (1641–1652)* (3 vols., Dublin, 1879), i. 82–8; see also the anonymous memorial 'Multae sunt' presented to Rinuccini on his arrival in Ireland (*Comment. Rinucc.*, ii. 44–5).

some of the most important councillors, military figures, and negotiators such as Viscounts Muskery and Mountgarrett, the earl of Castlehaven, Richard Bellings, Gerrott Fennell, Sir Robert Talbot, Geoffrey Browne, Richard Martin, and Patrick Darcy had a personal interest in reaching peace with Ormond because they expected to benefit from his patronage and that of the catholic marquis of Clanricard after the peace was finalized.[87] The logic of these suspicions was that military success for the confederates would strengthen the case for no compromise on the issue of the churches.[88] Since the dominant party in the Supreme Council and among the negotiators[89] favoured such a compromise it was arguably in their interests therefore to prevent major confederate military victories.

Little attention and less credence have been attached to these suspicions in the past. The blanket accusations in this vein of the text known as the *Aphorismical Discovery* are so manifestly false that they have perhaps helped cloud consideration of the topic.[90] Yet the fact that Rinuccini himself rapidly accepted the plausibility of these theories means that they require attention, if for no other reason than the degree to which his own behaviour in Ireland became predicated on a basic distrust of the advocates of peace.

If the 'peace' or 'Ormondite' party did fear that military victories might damage their position within the association then it seems unlikely that this development could have occurred before the autumn of 1644. It was only at this point that the negotiations with Ormond had clearly revealed the futility of hoping to retain the churches in negotiations with the king.[91] The first major military operation which the confederates undertook after this point had been made clear was the siege of Duncannon. Commenced in January 1645, the siege of what Rinuccini later saw as the most important fortress in

[87] Rinuccini certainly developed this conviction from an early stage in his *nunciature*: see Relazione del Regno d'Irlanda, 1 Mar. 1646 (Aiazzi, *Nunziatura*, 108); prior to the nuncio's arrival the confederates' Jesuit agent in Paris voiced similar suspicions: see Matthew O' Hartigan to Supreme Council, 16 Nov. (ns) 1644 (Gilbert, *Irish Confederation*, iv. 62); the same point was voiced in the memorial 'Multae sunt' presented to Rinuccini on his arrival (*Comment. Rinucc.*, ii. 43–5): Ormond for his part was convinced that slaking confederate ambition for places was one of the keys to securing a peace: see his letter to Digby, 13 Jan. 1644 (Carte, *Ormond*, vi. 6); Ormond was of course the kinsman and patron of many of the confederate leadership while Clanricard had close personal contacts with important Galway lawyers, particularly Patrick Darcy: see 'Patrick Darcy, Galway Lawyer and Politician', in Diarmaid Ó Cearbhaill (ed.), *Galway Town and Gown* (Dublin, 1984), 90–101.

[88] In 1646 the intransigence of the clerical party, now led by Rinuccini, was greatly enhanced by the military victories of that summer.

[89] The dominance of this group is discussed briefly in Lowe, 'Charles I and the Confederation', 16–18.

[90] 'An Aphorismical discovery of treasonable faction', in Gilbert, *Contemporary History*: this is one of the most important surviving narratives from immediately after the confederate period, containing a considerable amount of material unavailable elsewhere but written from a hotly partisan point of view.

[91] Supreme Council to Luke Wadding, 26 Nov. 1644 (Gilbert, *Irish Confederation*, iv. 35–6).

Ireland[92] was finally successfully completed in March. Very interestingly in the context of the present discussion, the siege was successful only because Rinuccini's predecessor as papal agent, Scarampi, personally supplied the requisite funds:[93] for their part the Supreme Council were set to abandon the siege in March, insisting that they lacked the resources to continue to supply the besieging army. Yet just before the fall of Duncannon, the council offered to equip one thousand men to aid the royalist cause in Scotland in return for the loan of Carlingford fortress.[94] Possession of Carlingford would certainly have strengthened the confederate position,[95] but that it was of the same strategic importance as Duncannon is doubtful. Significantly, the council seemed to hope that the temporary transfer of the fortress would demonstrate to the world, and in particular to the disgruntled clerical extremists, the king's genuine willingness to reach an equitable settlement with the confederates. On the other hand, the fall of Duncannon might well strengthen the radical position. Overall, therefore, the council's stance with regard to Duncannon is of interest in what it reveals about their priorities although there is no evidence that they sabotaged the siege.

Accusations of sabotage were, however, to be levelled at the council and the earl of Castlehaven concerning the major confederate offensive against the protestant enclave in Munster in the summer of 1645.[96] This offensive followed in the wake of a number of furious debates in the confederate assembly during May and June 1645 concerning the status of the churches and the church livings. In these debates, the 'peace' party essentially tried to convince the clergy that the issue of the churches should not be allowed to undermine the negotiations with Ormond.[97] Though divided on this subject and reluctant to adopt a confrontational position,[98] the clergy basically insisted on the retention of the churches as a *sine qua non* of peace. Interestingly, they justified their position partly on the grounds that 'at this time, we are in numbers, forces, arms and money far stronger than the

---

[92] A view which Ormond shared: see his letter to Digby, 8 Mar. 1644 (Carte, *Ormond*, vi. 52).

[93] Paolo Aringhi, *Memorie istoriche della vita del venerabile servo di Dio Pier Francesco Scarampi* (Rome, 1744), 40–1.

[94] Supreme Council to Ormond, 14 Mar. 1645 (Gilbert, *Irish Confederation*, iv. 173–4); Ohlmeyer, *Civil War and Restoration*, 153.

[95] See Stevenson, *Covenanters and Confederates*, 169–71.

[96] These accusations of course came to Rinuccini's ears as soon as he landed in Ireland: see the Relazione del Regno d'Irlanda, 1 Mar. 1646 (Aiazzi, *Nunziatura*, 109).

[97] *Comment. Rinucc.*, i. 524–33; this is discussed in greater detail in Ch. 2.

[98] Three Old English bishops (probably Dease, Rothe, and Tirry) seem to have argued that the king should not be forced to concede the churches: see *Comment. Rinucc.*, i. 527–9); these three bishops had been appointed at the heyday of the influence of the Old English 'politiques' in Rome: see F. X. Martin, *Friar Nugent: A Study of Francis Lavalin Nugent, 1569–1635, Agent of the Counter-Reformation* (Rome and London, 1962), 249–50; Silke, 'Later Relations between Primate Peter Lombard and Hugh O Neill', *Irish Theological Quarterly*, 22 (1955), 15–30 and id., 'Primate Lombard and James I', 124–50).

Protestant party in this kingdom',[99] and they insisted on the capacity of the association to continue to wage war to obtain its just demands.[100]

In the face of this clerical attitude, there were logical reasons why members of the peace party might have preferred to see the offensive of 1645 fail rather than succeed. Whether they went so far as to sabotage the expedition is, however, more difficult to establish. Castlehaven was of course a prominent member of the peace faction and the following year Rinuccini had certainly heard rumours that he had deliberately allowed the campaign to peter out.[101] A chronological point glossed over by Bellings,[102] the apologist of the peace party, but noted in passing by the *Aphorismical Discovery*,[103] provides some corroborative evidence. This point also dovetails with the most explicit accusation of sabotage, that of Walter Enos, a Wexford cleric. Enos claimed that in a confession prior to his death the lieutenant-general of Castlehaven's army in 1645 admitted that the council and the general deliberately halted the campaign of that year, because of fears of what such a military success would do to the internal equilibrium of the association.[104] Exactly what status should be accorded this confession is open to question.[105] Nevertheless, it is evident that, first, persistent doubts about the commitment of the 'peace' party to the war had begun to circulate in Ireland before Rinuccini's arrival in October 1645, and, second, that the credence which Rinuccini gave to these suspicions was to exert a profound influence on his own stance in Ireland.

By the time the nuncio had embarked upon his journey to Ireland in March 1645, internal tensions between an influential group of secular confederates and the clerical interest had begun to polarize the association. A major reason for this development was the accelerating decline of the royalist party in England which focused Irish attention on the probability that the island's recent relative immunity from British intervention was not likely to continue indefinitely. Yet on whom should this place the onus of compromise in the confederate/royalist negotiations? Certainly the catholic property holders of Ireland had everything to fear from a parliamentary triumph but the royalist need for assistance was, in the short term, of greater urgency. The problem was made still more knotty by the fact that there was

[99] 'Hac tempestate cum sumus numero, viribus, armis, et numis hoc regno parte Protestantica longe superiores', Rationes Congregationis (*Comment. Rinucc.*, i. 528).

[100] See the clerical response to the lay inquiry ibid., 536.

[101] Relazione del Regno d'Irlanda, 1 Mar. 1646 (Aiazzi, *Nunziatura*, 109).

[102] This relates to Castlehaven's return to Kilkenny during the summer: Bellings's discussion of the campaign does not mention this detail: see Bellings's narrative (Gilbert, *Irish Confederation*, iv. 13).

[103] Gilbert, *Contemporary History*, i. 96; as Donal Cregan notes in 'The Confederation of Kilkenny' (thesis), 2, the anonymous author of this text is generally reliable on matter of fact.

[104] See *Comment. Rinucc.*, i. 570.

[105] At least one anonymous royalist observer ascribed the fiasco simply to the rivalry between Preston and Castlehaven: see Bodl. Carte MS 16, fos. 292^v–293^r.

as yet no indication that the catholic clergy, as a corporate body, would receive any satisfaction in the peace negotiations. It was around these issues that the core of the confederate crisis during the Rinuccini nunciature came to revolve.

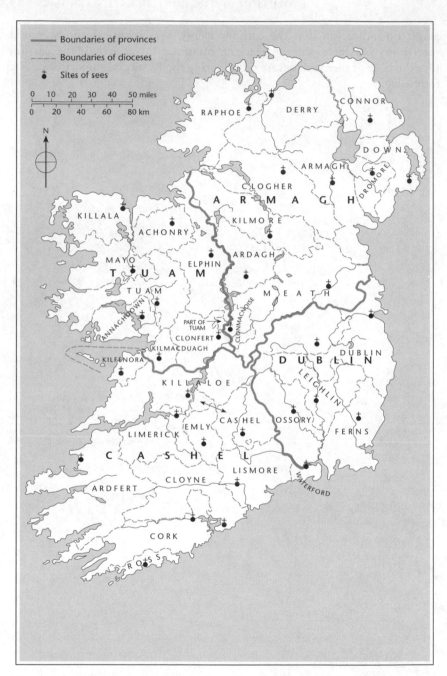

MAP 1. Catholic Dioceses of Ireland, *c.* 1630 (fo. 78A)

Reproduced with permission from T. W. Moody, F. X. Martin, and F. J. Byrne (eds.), *A New History of Ireland*, ix, *Maps, Geneologies, Lists* (Oxford, 1984), Map 27.

CHAPTER TWO

Development and Reform in the Irish Church, 1618–1645

I

An understanding of the development of the Irish catholic church in the decades prior to Rinuccini's arrival is integral to an understanding of his mission. Despite the revolutionary changes of the 1640s which made it possible, the creation of the Irish nunciature was firmly rooted in previous Roman policy. In certain ways indeed, the provision of a nuncio to Ireland in 1645 was merely the elaboration of the consciously tridentine policy of strengthening the Irish hierarchy which had been applied to the island over the previous thirty years.

The aftermath of Trent saw the pastoral bishop emerge as the key figure in the implementation of religious reform in most of catholic Europe. The major exception to this rule were catholic communities like those of England, Holland, or Transylvania which were subject to the jurisdiction of a protestant state. In such areas, catholicism tended to be organized along the lines of a mission.[1] Transylvania, for instance, under the protestant prince, Bethlen Gábor, was not the seat of its designated bishop who instead resided hundreds of miles away in Pozsony, the capital of Imperial Hungary. As a result, the focus of catholic reform in the principality was not the episcopacy but the small Jesuit mission.[2] Ireland also was ruled by a protestant monarch but there—for a variety of reasons, of which the most important was the sheer weight of numbers of the catholic population—the catholic church was organized from Rome in a manner closer to the orthodox structures of the continental mainland than to those of a mission.[3] Nineteen

---

[1] Robert Sauzet, *Contre réforme et réforme catholique en Bas-Languedoc* (Paris, Brussels, and Louvain, 1979), *passim*; James D. Tracy, 'With and Without the Counter-Reformation: The Catholic Church in the Spanish Netherlands and the Dutch Republic, 1580–1650', *Catholic Historical Review*, 71 (1985); Wolfgang Reinhard 'Reformation, Counter-Reformation and the Early Modern State: A Reassessment', *Catholic Historical Review*, 75 (1989), 383–404; the use of the word reform to describe the activity of the tridenine clergy throughout the course of this book is naturally not intended as a positive value judgement. What they considered reform was in many cases dogmaticaly repressive.

[2] See Mihály Balázs, Ádám Fricsy, László Lukács, and István Monok (eds.), *Erdélyi és Hódoltsági Jezsuita Missziók*, I/2, *1617–1625* (Szeged, 1990), esp. 279, 292, 345, 355, 439.

[3] See P. Corish, *The Catholic Community in the Seventeenth and Eighteenth Centuries* (Dublin, 1981), 17–21.

episcopal provisions were made to Irish sees between 1618 and 1630. By the early 1630s archbishops, supported by one to five suffragans, were resident in each of the four metropolitan provinces of the Irish church and the extensive missionary faculties which the regular clergy had previously enjoyed in Ireland had been largely revoked.[4]

From a Roman perspective the collapse of the protestant government in Ireland in 1641–2 offered the opportunity to take this process further and to transform the approximate structure of the Irish episcopacy into a fully articulated, post-tridentine, national church. It was to this end that Rinuccini was sent to Ireland with instructions to secure the full acceptance of the Council of Trent and the political and economic status of the diocesan clergy.[5] In addition, by establishing a tribunal he was to provide a disciplinary forum to settle ecclesiastical disputes within the Irish church, the lack of which had been the occasion of considerable inconvenience to the Irish clergy in the previous decades with all such disputes either transmitted to Rome or else settled by sometimes partisan bishops.[6] It is important to establish these connections because the nuncio was not merely an Italian exotic who came to Ireland, saw the problems that confronted him, and failed to overcome them. Rather his mission was a logical development of previous Roman policy.

Moreover, the conduct of Rinuccini's mission was crucially affected by the catholic culture which had developed prior to his arrival and by his relationship with the native clergy of Ireland, above all with the bishops. The Irish hierarchy, as Donal Cregan has argued, in certain respects resembled the blueprint of a counter-reformation episcopate because it was the first in Europe to be wholly seminary-trained; because its members were appointed to their sees with an unprecedented lack of interference from the temporal ruler of the country in which they were to function; and because, in contemporary European terms, they were quite exceptionally resident in their dioceses.[7]

Rinuccini was himself a prelate of great pastoral experience and a theorist on the importance of the episcopacy in church government. To a considerable extent, his mission in Ireland was aided by the fact that the previous twenty years had witnessed a definite growth of episcopal authority within the Irish church. Consequently, the most powerful ecclesiastics with whom

---

[4] D. F. Cregan, 'The Social and Cultural Background of a Counter-Reformation Episcopate, 1618–60', in A. Cosgrove and D. MacCartney (eds.), *Studies in Irish History Presented to R. Dudley Edwards* (Dublin, 1979), 85–117; Brendan Jennings (ed.), *Wadding Papers* (Dublin, 1953), 581.

[5] See the Nuncio's instructions (Aiazzi, *Nunziatura*, pp. xxxv, xlv–xlviii).

[6] In this regard see Jennings, *Wadding Papers*, *passim* and in particular 204, 240–3, 594–5, 633; from a Roman perspective the tribunal would also put an end to the scandalous situation which had developed among the confederates of dealing with ecclesiastical and secular cases in the same court: see 'Miscellanea Vaticano-Hibernica' in *Archivium Hibernicum*, 6 (1917), 119.

[7] See Cregan, 'Social and Cultural Background', 117.

Rinuccini had to deal were themselves bishops made sympathetic by training and difficult pastoral experience to the settlement of the church which the nuncio hoped to obtain in Ireland, although at times their ties of blood and friendship with the native secular communities could create cross currents of interest. To a very real extent, these Irish bishops were in a position to confirm or limit the nuncio's authority. Probably the key factor in Rinuccini's coup against the executive established by the Ormond peace in 1646 was the support of the Irish bishops and other major members of the Irish clergy expressed in a national convocation.[8] Correspondingly, the nuncio's failure to unify the Irish hierarchy over the issue of the Inchiquin truce was one of the most influential factors in his defeat in 1648.[9] The key to understanding the stance of the Irish bishops in the 1640s and their relationship with the nuncio thus lies in an appreciation of how their attitudes were shaped by the triple interaction of their continental training, their loyalty to their native communities, and their experiences as pastors in the period prior to 1641. This last point in particular has been neglected in the past and is the subject of section two of this chapter. Section three examines the penetration of counter-reformation influence in Ireland in the decades prior to Rinuccini's arrival, focusing on particular on Gaelic Ireland, and examining how the origins of the influence which he was to wield can be located in this period; while section four examines the role of the catholic clergy within the confederate catholic association prior to the nuncio's arrival.

II

Prior to 1641 the Irish catholic hierarchy operated in conditions which were utterly outside the norm of their European contemporaries. All the catholic clergy of Ireland were affected by the illegal status of their church. The most obvious danger which this presented was that the clergy might become the subject of a sustained governmental persecution involving death, banishment, or imprisonment, as was to happen in the Cromwellian era when the Irish episcopate was destroyed and the numbers of clergy hugely reduced.[10] But even in the 1620s and 1630s clergy, and bishops in particular, encountered less dramatic forms of persecution which severely hampered their endeavours and which were to influence the stance they adopted within the confederate catholic association.

---

[8] For the bishops present see Cregan, 'The Confederation of Kilkenny: Its Organisation, Personnel and History' (unpub. Ph.D. thesis, National University of Ireland, 1947)', 231; see also *Comment. Rinucc.*, ii. 324–46.

[9] For details of episcopal opposition to Rinuccini in 1648 see *Comment. Rinucc.*, iii. 284–8, 327, 335, 342, 491, 500.

[10] See Toby Barnard, *Cromwellian Ireland, English Government and Reform in Ireland* (Oxford, 1975); Corish, *Catholic Community*, 47–51.

One point that has been largely ignored in the past relates to the question of whether it was possible for an illegal body of pastors to preside successfully over a tridentine-type movement of reform and discipline.[11] In less anomalous parts of catholic Europe bishops were in a position to coerce conformity with what was in many ways a highly authoritarian conception of reform, either by virtue of their own authority, or by recourse to the secular arm.[12] In Ireland this situation was reversed. Not only were the bishops destitute of any support from the state but secular authority could be (and frequently was) invoked against them by the very individuals whom they were attempting to discipline. This was particularly the case because (as was to be emphasized again during the negotiations for peace between Ormond and the confederates in the 1640s)[13] the royal government in Ireland tended to differentiate between, on the one hand, the exercise of the catholic religion, including the celebration of mass which arguably was not subject to the penalties of the Act of Supremacy,[14] and, on the other, the exercise of a jurisdiction derived from Rome. One result of this was that a bishop was particularly vulnerable to accusations in the secular courts from his own clergy. This created significant problems for the Irish hierarchy who were committed to a programme of activity predicated on the exercise of authority derived from Rome.

In the metropolitan province of Armagh, for instance, the catholic primate of all Ireland, Hugh O'Reilly, was imprisoned for six months in 1637. It was an experience which he shared with his suffragans John O'Cullenan, the bishop of Raphoe, and Edmund Dungan of Down and Connor. Another bishop of the province, Eugene MacSweeny, may or may not have been imprisoned but was certainly arraigned before a royal tribunal. In each case their offence was apparently that of having exercised papal jurisdiction in Ireland and their principal accusers were their own priests. The basic root of the problem appears to have been that the bishops' attempts at reform were resented by the local catholics of the diocese.[15]

[11] P. Hoffmann, *Church and Community in the Diocese of Lyons, 1500–1789* (New Haven, Conn. and London, 1984), 6, for example, contrasts the hierarchical episcopal model of tridentine reform with less conservative models of missionary work.

[12] G. Alberigo, 'Studi e problemi relativi all'applicazione del Concilio di Trento', *Rivista Storica Italiana*, 70 (1958), 239–98; J. A. Bergin, 'The Crown, the Papacy and the Reform of the Old Orders in Early Seventeenth Century France', *Journal of Ecclesiastical History*, 33 (1982), 234–55; Sauzet, *Contre Reforme*, *passim*; Henry Kamen, *The Phoenix and the Flame: Catalonia and the Counter-reformation* (London, 1993), 54.

[13] Concerning this point see the documentation in J. T. Gilbert (ed.), *History of the Irish Confederation and the War in Ireland* (7 vols., Dublin, 1882–91), iv. 326–35.

[14] In the course of negotiations during the 1640s Ormond obtained a judicial opinion confirming immunity from penalties under this act for both the hearing and saying of mass: see Robert Armstrong, 'Protestant Ireland and the English Parliament, 1641–1647' (unpub. Ph.D. thesis, Trinity College Dublin, 1995), 187, n. 74.

[15] In this context, it is interesting to note the parallel behaviour of the apparently unreformed Bosnian franciscans in Pécs and Belgrade who bitterly resented either episcopal or Jesuitical interference and were prepared to stir up the Turkish authorities against their opponents in order to protect their local positions: see Balázs *et al.*, *Erdélyi*, 343, 356–7. Balázs *et al.*, *Erdélyi* 343, 356–7.

This can be demonstrated very clearly in the see of Raphoe. Maurice Ward, a priest of the diocese, objected to Bishop O'Cullenan's punishment of his clergy for their lapses. O'Cullenan appears to have used an array of sanctions, up to and including suspension to repress his clergy's tendency to error, excess, and scandalous behaviour. Ward, therefore, accused his bishop of *lèse-majesté* in the royal courts. The case was heard before the viceroy and O'Cullenan was imprisoned for three months, and even after his release his freedom was curtailed by a number of legal restrictions.[16] The bishop of Raphoe was at least luckier than Edmund Dungan who was also imprisoned on a charge of *lèse-majesté* but who died in prison before his case was decided.[17]

MacSweeny was the victim of something similar. In his case, the local laity co-operated with the clergy of Kilmore, disgruntled with episcopal interference, to accuse the bishop before the secular courts.[18] Significantly both O'Cullenan and MacSweeny were subsequently eager to be transferred to another diocese. O'Reilly accredited his imprisonment to the malice of one Donal Casey and it is reasonable to suppose that resentment of the archbishop's reforming activities was once again at the centre of the problem. The timing suggests that Casey betrayed the archbishop of Armagh with regard to the convening of a synod, for the archbishop was apparently arrested within days of the synod's conclusion.[19] In each case it is clear that it was the bishops' attempts to fulfil the role of post-tridentine pastors which were responsible for the antagonism they created.

This development was not confined to Gaelic Ulster but was common to all four provinces of the Irish church. The origins of this danger to the bishops from their own clergy was traced by some to Dublin and the example of an English priest, Paul Harris.[20] Harris became embroiled in a pamphlet war with members of the regular clergy in the early 1630s and by taking action for libel caused two of his opponents to be bound to the peace by the Lord Chief Justice.[21] He also supported two members of the diocesan clergy of Dublin, Luke Rochford and Patrick Cahill, against the attempts of Thomas Fleming, the Franciscan archbishop of Dublin, to impose his authority in the diocese. As a result of their efforts, one of the archbishop's nominees to a parish in Dublin was imprisoned and the archbishop was forced to tread very carefully in case they invoked the state against him in turn.[22] In 1635 the

[16] APF, SOCG 140, fos. 169ʳ–171ᵛ; P. F. Moran (ed.), *Spicilegium Ossoriense: Being a Collection of Original Letters and Papers Illustrative of the History of the Irish Church* (3 vols., Dublin, 1874–84), i. 180–4.

[17] See Thomas Strange to Luke Wadding, 5 Aug. 1628 (Jennings, *Wadding Papers*, 268).

[18] APF, 'Lettere Latine', 9 fo. 69ʳ⁻ᵛ; *Spicilegium Ossoriense*, i. 209; see also 'Miscellanea Vatico-Hibernica', *Archivium Hibernicum*, 3 (1914), 82–3.

[19] *Spicilegium Ossoriense*, i. 228–31.

[20] APF, SOCG 140, fos. 333ʳ–335ᵛ; *Spicilegium Ossoriense*, i. 198.   [21] *CSPI*, 1633–47, p.14.

[22] See Jennings, *Wadding Papers*, 326, 456, 469, 507, 558, 565, 570, 577, 604–5.

bishop of Meath, apparently because of fear of the priest's contact with the Irish government, refused to act on instructions from Rome to help the archbishop discipline Harris.[23] In a related incident, Fleming was also worried that the replacement by papal bull of one of Cahill's supporters, Terence Coghlan, as vicar apostolic of Clonmacnoise would incite Coghlan to 'run *ad brachium seculare*' to protect his position.[24]

One of Fleming's suffragans, Ross MacGeoghegan, the bishop of Kildare, was embroiled in a similar situation in 1638. Having deprived a certain Bartholomew Moore of his parish for what seems to have been fairly flagrant misconduct, the bishop discovered that Moore had accused him before the viceroy of having exercised papal jurisdiction. As a result, the bishop found himself so harassed that he was unable to discharge his functions.[25] Also in the metropolitan province of Dublin, it can be noted that two vicars apostolic of the see of Leighlin, Matthew Roche and Moriarty Dowling, were imprisoned during the 1630s, Dowling for an entire year.[26]

The archbishop of Cashel, Thomas Walsh, was also gaoled for a short period in 1633.[27] His suffragan in Waterford, Patrick Comerford, apparently escaped this fate but wrote worriedly to Rome of the hatred for his person which his efforts at promoting reform had caused.[28] In another letter to Luke Wadding, Comerford bitterly bemoaned the state of ecclesiastical discipline in the country, complaining that members of the regular clergy not only resisted episcopal authority but that the prelates of the regular orders themselves were often afraid to try and discipline their members 'such is their liberty, and the advantage they take of these turbulent times'.[29]

Matters were no easier in Connacht. In 1632 the practice of taking ecclesiastical cases to the secular courts was forbidden in the provincial synod of Tuam.[30] In 1634, nevertheless, it was reported in Rome that the archbishop, Malachy O'Queely, suspected by the state of having consecrated priests, found it necessary to go into hiding for several months.[31] In the same province, the vicar apostolic of Clonfert, John Bourke, was forced out of Connacht for a period to escape punishment for having exercised papal jurisdiction.[32] In 1637 the issue flared up again when O'Queely's attempts to

[23] See *Spicilegium Ossoriense*, i. 204–5.
[24] Fleming to Wadding, 20 July 1631 (Jennings, *Wadding Papers*, 557).
[25] APF, SOCG 140, fos. 308ʳ–309ʳ; see also MacGeoghegan to Colgan, 4 Oct. 1638 (*Analecta Hibernica*, 6 (1934), 229–30).
[26] APF SOCG 140, fo. 229ʳ⁻ᵛ; Jennings, *Wadding Papers*, 610.
[27] See C. P. Meehan, *The Rise and Fall of the Irish Franciscan Monasteries and Memoirs of the Irish Hierarchy in the Seventeenth Century* (Dublin, 1877), 113.
[28] APF, SOCG 140, fos. 335ʳ–336ᵛ.
[29] See Comerford to Wadding, Nov. 1631 (Jennings, *Wadding Papers*, 616).
[30] APF, 'Scritture riferite nei Congressi' 1, Irlanda, fos. 171ʳ–180ᵛ.
[31] See *Spicilegium Ossoriense*, i. 194.
[32] See Cathaldus Giblin, 'The Processus Datariae and the Appointment of Irish Bishops in the Seventeenth Century', in Franciscan Fathers, *Father Luke Wadding: Commemorative Volume*

assert his authority over the collegiate church of St Nicholas in Galway were resisted with the threat of reporting him to the state for the exercise of powers derived from Rome.[33]

Given the difficulties which bishops and other prelates encountered if catholic clergy chose to resist their authority by appealing to the state, and in view of the fact that the problem showed more signs of intensifying than of disappearing as the 1630s wore on, it is hardly surprising that this point was to emerge as a major issue among the catholic confederates in the following decade. In the negotiations with the king during the 1640s, the catholic clergy were determined to secure immunity for the exercise of a jurisdiction derived from Rome, despite the difficulties which this point created.[34] Indeed, as an obstacle to a settlement, this issue was to rank alongside the other great and problematic demand of the catholic clergy, namely the right to the churches and the church livings which they had acquired in the aftermath of the rebellion. Once again, the context of the previous decades helps explain the fervour with which the catholic bishops pushed for this latter point also to be included in the treaty of peace during the 1640s.[35]

That the ambitious Roman policy of attempting to institute a continental model of bishop-directed reform would encounter financial difficulties was close to inevitable. As illegal competitors with the established church, the catholic clergy lacked access to existing churches or to revenues from church lands. Such lack of institutional support was a particularly acute problem for bishops. Their duties of visitation required that bishops maintain a certain number of horses and servants.[36] In addition, the contemporary notion of episcopal dignity demanded that its spiritual dimensions be affirmed by outward manifestations of eminence.[37] Their inability to maintain themselves according to their dignity was a constant complaint from Irish bishops to Rome during the period under review.[38] Thomas Walsh, the archbishop of Cashel, was particularly bitter that a bishop should be forced to prepare his own food and to dress without assistance,[39] and echoes of his resentment can be found in the letters of other prelates.[40]

To a very large extent, the episcopate were dependent on the local laity, particularly their own kinsfolk, for the ordinary means of subsistence. For this reason, it was an enormous benefit to a bishop to be appointed to his

(Dublin, 1957) 578; Thomas Gilroy Connors, 'The Impact of English Colonial Expansion on Irish Culture' (unpub. Ph.D. thesis, Urbana, Ill., 1997), 237.

[33] See letters of O'Queely to an unnamed correspondent (*Analecta Hibernica*, 14 (1944), 21–7).
[34] In this regard see Bodl. Carte MS 15, fos. 287^{r-v}, 750^{r}–754^{v}; see also the documentation in Gilbert, *Irish Confederation*, iv. 325–41.
[35] See *Comment. Rinucc.*, i. 524–9.   [36] APF, SOCG 140, fos. 34^{r}–35^{v}.
[37] One can note that even in Ireland Rome insisted that the first goal of ecclesiastical revenue was to support archiepiscopal ceremonies: APF, SOCG 295, fo. 40.
[38] See for example ibid. 140, fos. 21^{r-v}, 169^{r-v}, 351^{r}, 342^{r-v}; *Spicilegium Ossoriense*, i. 221.
[39] APF, SOCG 140, fo. 79^{r-v}.   [40] See Jennings, *Wadding Papers*, *passim*.

native diocese as this vastly increased the likelihood that he could find accommodation in a secure network of friends and relations. The bishop of Waterford, for instance, habitually lived with his brother; the bishop of Ossory alternated between his brother's house and that of his cousin Viscount Mountgarrett; and the archbishop of Dublin, son of the baron of Slane, resided with kin and friends on the edge of his diocese.[41] A bishop who was not native to his see, however, and dependent on the kindness of strangers could encounter very severe financial problems. Moreover, the lack of a local network rendered a prelate far more vulnerable to other difficulties. Opposition was frequently expressed at the intrusion of outsiders into ecclesiastical positions.[42] When this was added to the common resentment of a bishop's reforming activities, the result could be a backlash of antipathy which rendered it impossible for a bishop to function effectively. It was this lethal cocktail of financial insecurity and fear of the priests whom they had been sent to govern which led both the bishop of Raphoe, John O'Cullenan, and the bishop of Kilmore, Eugene MacSweeny to petition Rome to be transferred to the vacant diocese of Derry.[43] It is not unlikely that Thomas Walsh's financial difficulties in Cashel were related to the fact that he himself was a native of Waterford and not of his diocese.[44] The archbishop of Tuam, Malachy O'Queely, also apparently encountered problems in Galway partly because he was a native of Killaloe and not of the archdiocese.[45]

Local provenance, of course, meant far less if the bishop lacked eminent relations. Edmund Dungan, the bishop of Down and Connor, for instance, was a native of his see[46] but his miserable death in prison may well have been related to the fact that he was of an obscure family.[47] It was thus very useful if, as well as native to their dioceses, bishops were of wealthy or aristocratic stock, as in fact was the case with many of the members of the Irish hierarchy.[48] One of the reasons why the bishops of the province of Armagh were eager in 1632 to have the earl of Antrim's illegitimate son, Francis MacDonnell, elevated to the hierarchy was their realization that his father's wealth and support would make it easier for him to function in the uncertain climate of Ulster.[49] In 1637 the bishop of Elphin insisted to Rome that in order to protect the dignity of the episcopal state only those with secular kin able to provide for them should be promoted to bishoprics.[50]

[41] See Jennings, *Wadding Papers*, 345, 516; Meehan, *Franciscan Monasteries*, 183; Cregan, 'Social and Cultural Background', 91.

[42] See for instance Jennings, *Wadding Papers*, 315, 136–7, 165, 351, 362, 435, 452.

[43] APF, SOCG 140, fos. 159ʳ–162ᵛ.   [44] Jennings, *Wadding Papers*, 612.

[45] In this regard see Aiazzi, *Nunziatura*, 102; Giblin, 'Processus Datariae', 557–8; Connors, 'The Impact of English Colonial Expansion', 231.

[46] Jennings, *Wadding Papers*, 75.   [47] Ibid., 216, 268, 349.

[48] See Cregan, 'Social and Cultural Background', 85–117.

[49] See letter of bishops of province of Armagh to Urban VIII, 12 July 1632 (Jennings, *Wadding papers*, 623–4).

[50] APF, SOCG 140., fos. 351ʳ.

Rome seems to have been relatively slow to appreciate the great importance of means and local family connections. Wealth was not apparently the
decisive factor in the nineteen provisions which were made to Irish sees
between 1618 and 1630.[51] But the freeze on appointments between 1630 and
1641, despite the fact that many sees remained empty, can probably be traced
to the gradual realization in Rome of the precarious economic position of
the Irish episcopacy. The last three provisions to the hierarchy, immediately
before the rebellion of 1641 transformed the Irish situation, were all from
wealthy families and Rome had been supplied with detailed information
about their families' willingness and capacity to support them in a manner
suitable to the episcopal dignity.[52] In 1642, also, the extremely wealthy
Edward O'Dempsey was appointed: a provision not unrelated to the
munificent offers of support made by his father, Viscount Clanmalier, on his
behalf.[53]

Rome was fortunate that candidates from the higher echelons of catholic
society were available in such numbers and eager for presentation to sees.
But, although by the early 1640s the appointment of wealthy aristocrats to
their native dioceses was emerging as the preferred solution to the lack of
ecclesiastical revenues, it was by no means an infallible remedy for the problems of the Irish hierarchy. In the first place, the bulk of the episcopate had
already been appointed by 1630 and many of its members were in very severe
difficulties. Second, in some parts of Ireland, particularly in Ulster, wealthy
catholic aristocrats were in short supply because of the impoverishment of
the local community. Two of the most important prelates of the province
of Armagh for instance, Heber MacMahon, vicar apostolic and then bishop
of Clogher, and Hugh O'Reilly, bishop of Kilmore and then primate, were of
eminent local stock but their families had fallen on hard times.[54] Nor was the
wealthiest candidate for a see necessarily the best: Rome refused in fact to
appoint the earl of Antrim's son to a see, and was slow to elevate the well-
connected John Bourke who, in Rinuccini's estimation, was a somewhat
mediocre prelate. Fourth, even the support of local and powerful kin was not
a certain guarantee of stability. Ross MacGeoghegan was from a wealthy
family; his sister was married to the Viscount Clanmalier and his links to
that family were further strengthened when he selected one of her sons,
Fiacra, as his vicar general in Kildare.[55] Nevertheless, the accusation of one
of his priests almost completely curtailed his activity. Perhaps most importantly of all, the dependence of bishops on wealthy secular kin represented a
potential threat to their independence of action. In 1641, when the bishop
of Meath, Thomas Dease, found himself at odds with his kinsman and

[51] Jennings, Wadding Papers, passim.
[52] Giblin, 'Processus Datariae', 563–6; Cregan, 'Social and Cultural Background', 90–1.
[53] APF, SOCG 140, fo. 127[r].   [54] Cregan, 'Social and Cultural Background', 91–4.
[55] APF, SOCG 140, fo. 96[r–v]; Cregan, 'Social and Cultural Background', 94–5.

longtime patron, the baron of Delvin, he deprived himself of his home for the previous twenty years.[56] Even when dramatic clashes of this kind did not occur, it seems clear that debts of gratitude and familial links with wealthy catholics helped sway the stance of certain bishops in the 1630s and 1640s. In the earlier decade, this probably contributed to the willingness of some bishops to accept, contrary to official Roman policy, that secular catholics could with a clear conscience retain former monastic property confiscated at the reformation.[57] In the 1640s bishops like Tirry of Cork, Rothe of Ossory, Dease of Meath, and Bourke of Tuam seem to have been influenced towards a less militant stance at moments of crisis by their close connections to Old English aristocrats.[58]

Yet, however unsatisfactory, the reliance on wealthy secular kin was fundamental to the maintenance of the episcopal system prior to 1641 because, until the uprising transferred the property of the protestant hierarchy to the catholic bishops, no other source of finance could be found to replace it. The most important supplement to familial largesse up to 1641 was the bishops' taxation of their diocesan clergy. This, however, was not a lucrative source of funds. The catholic parish clergy were themselves of course dependent on the voluntary contributions of the population and often had little to pass on to their superiors. John Roche of Ferns wrote to Luke Wadding in Rome in 1630 that he had drawn less than five pounds from his diocese in the previous year, (although he was fortunate enough to be able to spend more than a hundred pounds of his own money in the same period).[59] In the late 1630s the metropolitans of Ireland indicated to Rome that hardly eight of the sixteen resident bishops had more than 100 scudi (20–5 pounds sterling) a year and they believed that none could have more than 200 scudi per annum. The archbishops pointed out that these were grossly inadequate sums given a bishop's duty of visitation which necessitated the maintenance of several horses and servants.[60]

Nowhere were bishops in worse straits than in Ulster. John O'Cullenan of Raphoe, for instance, evidently lived in very great difficulty. As he reported to *Propaganda Fide*, there were only nineteen (in another place sixteen) beggarly priests in his diocese to contribute to his upkeep and hardly seventy secular catholics of any substance to offer him hospitality. Indeed, Raphoe claimed in 1636 that there was hardly a house in the whole see which could afford to take him in except at his own expense. Constant protestant immigration into the diocese was evidently making matters consistently worse.

[56] Meehan, *Franciscan Monasteries*, 167.
[57] Memorial of 23 Dec. 1630, APF, SOCG 295, fo. 27^{r-v}; James Barron to the cardinal protector, 21 Aug. 1631 (Jennings, *Wadding Papers*, 564).
[58] *Comment. Rinucc.*, i. 524–9, iii. 284–8, 327, 335, 342, 491, 500.
[59] See Ferns to Wadding, 26 May 1630 (Jennings, *Wadding Papers*, 370).
[60] APF, SOCG 140, fos. 34^r–35^v; see also Tadhg Ó hAnnracháin, 'Rebels and Confederates: The Stance of the Irish Clergy in the 1640s', in John Young (ed.), *Celtic Dimensions of the British Civil Wars* (Edinburgh, 1997).

He reported to Rome of 'the new colony of heretics that every day come to live here', to such an extent that the bishop's poverty was forcing him to reside for periods outside his diocese.[61]

The same processes were clearly at work in other parts of Ulster. In 1637, two days after a provincial synod, the bishops of Armagh wrote to the cardinals of *Propaganda Fide*. They informed the congregation that their revenues did not allow them to maintain even the most modest conception of a bishop's dignity. Not a single diocese was worth more to its bishop than 600 Belgian florins (about 60 pounds sterling) per annum.[62] But what was worse was the effect of protestant immigration into the province and the simultaneous impoverishment of the native population. Consequently, a diocese which had been worth 600 florins to its bishop in 1635 was at that time worth only 400, and the bishops prognosticated gloomily that in a further two years the value would have declined to 200 florins.[63]

In November of the same year the bishop of Down and Connor, Hugh Magennis, echoed the same pessimistic message. Although he admitted that the king's clemency meant that outright persecution was at a low level,[64] the economic situation was nevertheless disastrous. Magennis pointed out that many of his priests were operating in parishes where only a minority of the population was catholic. Magennis's purpose in writing this letter was to convince the congregation that the various religious orders who had once maintained establishments in the province should not be given permission to seek to revive them. As a Franciscan himself, the bishop may have been tempted to help secure the position of his order who had numerous 'convents' throughout Ulster.[65] Magennis, however, specifically denied this motivation. His concern was that the area simply could not feed additional clergy and if the bishops attempted to organize something on behalf of new regular clergy he was worried that the overburdened common people would have recourse to the state courts.[66]

This evidence corroborates the theory that economic conditions were vital factors in the rebellion of 1641.[67] It also indicates how vitally the interests,

---

[61] 'La nuova colonia di heretici che ogni di vengono ad habitarvi' (APF, SOCG 140, fo. 162ʳ); see also ibid., fos. 169ʳ⁻ᵛ, 170ʳ⁻ᵛ, 173ʳ⁻ᵛ, 185ʳ⁻ᵛ.

[62] One can compare this with the diocese of Solsona in Catalonia during the early seventeenth century: this was considered one of the poorest in the region but still provided its bishop with roughly £4,000 per annum: see Kamen, *Phoenix and the Flame*, 46.

[63] *Spicilegium Ossoriense*, i. 220–1; see also Ó hAnnracháin, 'Rebels and Confederates', 107.

[64] His family had reason to appreciate this as his own father, John Magennis, had been imprisoned on religious grounds some time prior to 1630: see Giblin, 'Processus Datariae', 555.

[65] Jennings, 'Brussels MS 3947: Donatus Moneyus Provincia Hiberniae S. Francisci', *Analecta Hibernica*, 6 (1934), *passim*.

[66] APF, SOCG 140, fo. 342ʳ⁻ᵛ.

[67] In this context see Raymond Gillespie, 'The End of an Era: Ulster and the Outbreak of the 1641 Rising', in Ciarán Brady and id. (eds.), *Natives and Newcomers: Essays on the Making of Irish Colonial Society, 1534–1641* (Dublin, 1986), 193–9; id., 'Destabilising Ulster, 1641–2', in Brian Mac Cuarta (ed.), *Ulster 1641: Aspects of the Rising* (Belfast, 1993), 107–10.

and indeed the ministry, of the catholic clergy were being compromised by the economic hardships of their congregations. This may go some way towards explaining why priests were, in many cases, to the forefront of the disturbances in 1641 and why the Ulster bishops were so eager to legitimize the war in their provincial synod in 1642.[68] It is also a factor to be borne in mind when assessing the militant stance of the Ulster clergy during the confederate wars.[69] To those who had experienced how severely their attempts at reform had been compromised by the political and economic conditions of Ulster in the 1630s, there were sound ecclesiastical reasons for insisting on a peace which would prevent the re-emergence of the same problems. Reversal of the plantations was thus on both the political and ecclesiastical agendas of the Ulster Irish in the 1640s. Without a dependable source of finance, an episcopally directed movement of reform close to what Rome (and the bishops themselves) hoped for was subject to enormous difficulty.

But Ulster militancy, it is important to stress, was merely a more intense manifestation of a common clerical attitude during the 1640s. Among the confederates it was the clergy as a whole who represented the chief obstacle to compromise with the king's viceroy. This was very obviously the case even before the nuncio's arrival. It was particularly evident in May 1645, when the congregation of the clergy decided to insist on the retention of the churches and church livings which they had gained since 1641 as a necessary condition of peace. Of the fourteen bishops present only three refused to give assent to this position.[70] With the exception of Edward O'Dempsey (who had served as provincial of the Dominicans), these bishops had vast pastoral experience in Ireland for many years before the 1641 rebellion. Even Heber MacMahon, the least experienced after O' Dempsey, had been vicar apostolic in Clogher for at least four years before his promotion to the episcopate in 1642.[71] Most of the others had been bishops for fifteen years or more.[72]

One reason why the Irish clergy united on such a stance was the fact that many aspects of the Ulster experience detailed above were familiar also to prelates in the other provinces. The fear of further plantation, for instance, haunted the bishop of Elphin, Boethius MacEgan, in 1637. Like other members of the hierarchy such as Ross MacGeoghegan of Kildare, MacEgan

---

[68] Nicholas Canny, *From Reformation to Restoration: Ireland, 1534–1660* (Dublin, 1987), 209–10; *Comment. Rinucc.*, i. 314–19.

[69] The bishop of Clogher, Heber MacMahon, actually succeeded Owen Roe O'Neill as commander of the Ulster army: see Jerrold Casway, *Owen Roe O'Neill and the Struggle for Catholic Ireland* (Philadelphia, 1984), 264–6, 34, 48, 51, 122, 140, 192; The primate, Hugh O'Reilly, played a less prominent role but Massari has left a record of O'Reilly's militant perspective and desire to crush Ormond after Benburb: see APF, Miscellaneae Varie 9, 137; all the Ulster bishops supported Rinuccini in the excommunications of 1646 and 1648: see below Chs. 4, 6, and 7.

[70] *Comment. Rinucc.*, i. 524–9: the identity of these three is uncertain; all were Old English, of whom one was certainly Thomas Dease, another David Rothe of Ossory, while the third was probably Tirry of Cork.

[71] Giblin, 'Processus Datariae', 568.   [72] Cregan, 'Social and Cultural Background', 87.

considered his person to be anything but safe, reporting that he spent his time fleeing from place to place in the country. And like bishops from every province of Ireland, MacEgan constantly had to struggle with the difficulties created by his own poverty and that of his clergy.[73]

Such poverty represented a particularly acute problem for bishops because of the tridentine role which they were expected to play, involving not only the expense of visitation but also the maintenance of episcopal dignity. The fact that the hierarchy was largely drawn from an Irish social elite with wide experience of the continent[74] probably accentuated both their sense of grievance at the discrepancy between their status and their penury, and their determination to make use of the upheavals of the 1640s to effect change. Nevertheless, it is clear that some of the bishops' problems were replicated at a lower level by the parish clergy. And, as with the bishops, the tridentine notion of pastoral care to which they were expected to conform put particular stress on the poverty of the diocesan priests.

The creation of an efficient parochial system was a major priority for the Irish bishops.[75] Patrick Comerford of Waterford and Lismore, for instance, arriving in the late 1620s into a diocese deprived of a resident bishop for five decades, took immediate steps to establish parish priests with responsibilities for specific areas. In doing so he was clearly following the example of other bishops and his (classically tridentine) motivation was to ensure a more regular and orderly administration of pastoral sacraments. In particular, he wanted to address the problem that the towns of his diocese had an over-abundance of clergy while the countryside suffered from a severe deficiency.[76] To protect the jurisdiction of the priests within their newly allocated parishes he also followed the common pattern of abolishing the missionary faculties of the religious orders within his diocese.[77] Episcopal behaviour of this kind, particularly in southern dioceses such as Cork, Cashel, Ossory, Ferns, and Waterford led to great antagonism between the hierarchy and the regular clergy.[78] But it also served to alter the relationship between the clergy and laity in a fashion which, from the bishops' own perspective, was not always entirely positive.

The new parochial system was more orderly and tidy. It provided for greater hierarchical control because a bishop (provided that Rome did not

[73] APF, SOCG 140, fos., 34ʳ–35ᵛ, 351ʳ–352ᵛ; 'Scritture riferite nei Congressi' 1, Irlanda, fo. 172ʳ.

[74] Cregan, 'Social and Cultural Background', 85–117.

[75] In this regard see for example the petition and reply concerning parochial divisions in Connacht (Jennings, *Wadding Papers*, 445, 454–5); the diocesan statutes of the bishop of Cork (ibid., 451); Comerford to Wadding, 8 Jan. 1629 (ibid., 334); see also the report from Elphin in 1631 in *Archivium Hibernicum*, 3 (1914), 361–5.

[76] A not uncommon problem in other parts of Europe as well: see Kamen, *Phoenix and the Flame*, 88–9.

[77] Comerford to Wadding, 8 Jan. 1629 (Jennings, *Wadding Papers*, 334); same to cardinals of *Propaganda Fide*, 6 July 1630 (*Spicilegium Ossoriense*, i. 165–9).

[78] Jennings, *Wadding Papers*, 366, 381–3, 393–404, 409.

undercut him by giving papal bulls of appointment to particular parishes)[79] could move or threaten to move parish priests who were not performing adequately. And it meant that the laity did not have to depend for sacraments on the potentially haphazard efforts of missionary regulars who had been, in Comerford's words, 'at liberty to administer the sacraments to whom and when they pleased.'[80] But the new system rephrased with greater urgency than ever the perennial question of the payment of the clergy. Prior to the restriction of the missionary faculties of the religious orders in the 1620s, the regulars apparently bestowed sacraments free of charge and relied on the more or less voluntary generosity of the people for their subsistence.[81] The diocesan priests, appointed to particular parishes and expected by their bishops to act as intrusive and not necessarily popular agents of reform in the localities, were naturally concerned to achieve some independence from the sporadic goodwill of their parishioners. The role which they were expected to perform had of course been designed with the beneficed clergy of continental Europe in mind.[82] This is the context in which the practice of demanding direct payment for sacraments became the subject of many complaints.[83]

In 1632 a decree in the provincial synod of Tuam forbade clergy, with what success cannot be known, to withhold sacraments until payment had been received.[84] In any case the practice clearly was not confined to Connacht.[85] Such behaviour could lead to the deaths of babies without baptism and adults without extreme unction.[86] The habit of refusing confession at Eastertide unless the priest received a sizeable donation[87] also threatened to erode respect for the sacrament of penance and ran directly counter to the tridentine spirit of reform and sacramental regularity which the Irish bishops were attempting to inculcate. None the less, in the absence of benefices in Ireland, it was in one sense logical that the diocesan clergy would look to bolster their financial position by bartering sacraments for payment.

This was yet another reflection of the difficulty of applying continental patterns of tridentine reform to Ireland's anomalous conditions. This period has been rightly identified as one of growth and vigour in Irish catholicism but this does not necessarily imply that the Irish clergy were content with the situation in which they found themselves. In particular, without a secure eco-

[79] APF, SOCG 140, fos., 327–32; Jennings, *Wadding Papers*, 309, 315, 389, 552, 633.
[80] Comerford to Wadding, 8 Jan. 1629 (Jennings, *Wadding Papers*, 334); see also same to same, Nov. 1631 (ibid., 617); see also Questions for solution at Rome (ibid., 631).
[81] See the report to the nuncio at Brussels, 22 Aug. 1630 (ibid., 393–5).
[82] Although it is true that even on the continent, clergy were not always successful at extracting tithes: see Kamen, *Phoenix and the Flame*, 157.
[83] See Jennings, *Wadding Papers*, 355, 393–5.
[84] APF, 'Scritture riferite nei Congressi', 1, Irlanda, fos. 171r–180v.
[85] Questions for solution at Rome (Jennings, *Wadding Papers,* 631).
[86] See the letter of Owen Field, 10 Apr. 1630 (ibid., 353–7).
[87] Report to the nuncio at Brussels, 22 Aug. 1630 (ibid., 394–8).

nomic position for the parish clergy and the episcopacy then the more authoritarian dimensions of religious reform were difficult to institute. Such a conclusion had already been reached on the other side of the confessional divide during the 1630s, and a parallel can be detected between Wentworth's concentration on improving the revenues of the established church as a prelude to sustained ecclesiastical reform[88] and the concerns of the Vatican secretariat which dispatched Rinuccini to Ireland in 1645 with instructions to secure the economic position of the pastoral clergy.[89] A further ironic parallel with catholic behaviour is the manner in which protestant bishops attempted to compensate for the dissipation of their sees' revenues by exploiting the pecuniary possibilities of their ecclesiastical jurisdiction:[90] from a lay perspective there was a certain symmetry between payment for catholic sacraments and fines for not receiving those of the established church. And there is a further parallel in the manner in which the catholic bishops mirrored their protestant counterparts' response to inadequate livings by conferring a plurality of parishes on a priest. As in the case of the established church, this increased the net from which an individual priest could draw revenue and, as in the case of the established church, it decreased the amount of pastoral care and attention which he could supply to any one parish.[91] This structural convergence between the churches in the 1630s laid the groundwork for the conflict of the 1640s when the catholic clergy occupied the lands of their protestant counterparts and refused to countenance their return during the peace negotiations: the clerics of both confessions were animated by the belief that the competition for resources represented a vital element in the competition for souls.

As noted above, the new emphasis on parishes was also a recipe for conflict between the catholic regular and secular clergy. To the bishops, aware of the financial difficulties which afflicted their priests, the regular clergy represented competition for the generosity of the catholic population. In addition, the religious orders were often unwilling to accept the primacy of the ordinary jurisdiction within a diocese.[92] Several bishops, therefore, particularly those of Ossory, Meath, Cork, Waterford, Cashel, and Ferns, together with the vicar apostolic of Leighlin, launched a more or less open and co-ordinated

---

[88] Canny, 'The Attempted Anglicisation of Ireland in the Seventeenth Century: An Exemplar of "British History"' in J. F. Merritt (ed.), *The Political World of Thomas Wentworth, Earl of Strafford, 1621–1641* (Cambridge, 1995), 171–3, 181; Hugh F. Kearney, *Strafford in Ireland, 1633–41: A Study in Absolutism*, 2nd edn. (Cambridge, 1989), 70–82; *CSPI*, 1633–47, pp. 131, 167, 189, 208.

[89] See the nuncio's instructions (Aiazzi, *Nunziatura*, pp. xxxv, xlv–xlviii).

[90] In this regard see John Roche to Wadding, 26 May 1630 (Jennings, *Wadding Papers*, 370).

[91] See letter of Owen Field, 10 Apr. 1630 (Jennings, *Wadding Papers*, 354); S. G. Ellis, 'Economic Problems of the Church: Why the Reformation Failed in Ireland', *Journal of Ecclesiastical History*, 41 (1990), 239–65; Alan Ford, 'The Reformation in Kilmore before 1641', in Gillespie (ed.), *Cavan: Essays on the History of an Irish County* (Dublin, 1995), 82.

[92] Corish, *Catholic Community*, 27–8; APF, SOCG 140, fo. 341ʳ.

campaign to restrict the operations of the regular clergy within their dioceses, and in particular to limit the amount of money which they garnered from the population.[93] The regular clergy's resistance to this process was sustained and even in the 1640s they were capable of convincing many in *Propaganda Fide* that more freedom should be restored to them but on the whole the bishops experienced a considerable measure of success.[94]

As certain observers noted, none the less, success in this regard was not an unmixed blessing. The antagonism and bitterness which were aroused led to a great deal of polemic and controversy which did little to increase respect for catholic ecclesiastics and in fact seems to have acted as a source of consolation for the clergy of the established church. Moreover, since priests might have several parishes, the exclusion of the regular orders from a pastoral role could lead to a diminution in the availability of the sacraments to the laity: in particular there were accusations that the poorer laity who lacked the funds to pay their parish priests for the administration of sacraments and who previously had availed of regular generosity were being neglected. In addition, it was the regular orders who provided most of the catholic preachers in Ireland because on the whole they were better educated and freer of pastoral duties.[95] By curtailing their ability to canvass for money to support themselves, there was an obvious risk that the number of regular preachers would decline.[96] Judging by their behaviour, many of the bishops in the south of Ireland seem to have been prepared to run this risk in the interests of maintaining hierarchical discipline,[97] but once again it was clear that there were hidden costs in the policy of centring the restructuring of the Irish church around episcopal authority.

This problem with the regular clergy, although much commented on in the existing secondary literature, was, however, less intractable than others faced by the Irish hierarchy.[98] There seems, in any case, to have been less friction between the bishops and the religious orders in Ulster and Connacht.[99] Moreover, even the southern bishops appear to have been prepared to accept regulars as parish priests if they in turn were prepared to give up their mis-

[93] Corish, *Catholic Community*, 26–9; id., *Irish Catholic Experience* (Dublin, 1985), 101–5; Jennings, *Wadding Papers*, 320, 341, 355, 357–8, 366, 397, 398, 400, 409, 438, 495, 525, 549–50, 579.

[94] Scarampi to Barberini, Aug. 1644 (APF, SOCG 89, fos. 390–4).

[95] See the report to the nuncio at Brussels, 22 Aug. 1630 (Jennings, *Wadding Papers*, 393–5, 396–7, 402); Thomas Bray to Wadding, 15 Nov. 1630 (ibid., 438–9) and ibid., 240, 342, 373, 438; see also *Spicilegium Ossoriense*, i. 177.

[96] See Thomas Strange to Francis Matthews (ibid., 440–1).

[97] One can note a parallel in this regard with the bishops of the Caroline church of England: see Kenneth Fincham, 'Episcopal Government, 1603–1640' in id. (ed.), *The Early Stuart Church, 1603–42* (London, 1993), 71–92.

[98] Corish, *Catholic Community*, 26–9 and G. Rice, 'Thomas Dease, Bishop of Meath, and Some Questions Concerned with the Rights to Ecclesiastical Property Alienated at the Reformation', in *Riocht na Midhe*, 6/1 (1975), 69–89.

[99] Wadding to the cardinal protector, 1634(?) (Jennings, *Wadding Papers*, 624–8); Comerford to cardinals of *Propaganda Fide*, 6 July 1630 (*Spicilegium Ossoriense*, i. 165–9).

sionary privileges and take responsibility for particular parishes.[100] Indeed, one of the hidden sources of the conflict may have been the fact that the bishops of Munster wished to make use of the, on the whole, better educated cadres of regular clergy[101] in a pastoral context under their own supervision, not as independent agents. One reason why this would have been attractive to the bishops was the fact that they had relatively little control over the supply of educated priests.

Trent ordained that bishops should establish seminaries in their dioceses but this was impossible in an Irish context. The Irish church was dependent for seminary trained personnel on the continental colleges. The work of these institutions was hugely appreciated by the Irish hierarchy, who themselves were all products of continental education, but the colleges operated more or less outside the possibility of control, influence, or succour by the Irish bishops. The archbishop of Cashel, for example, expressed great resentment in 1627 that the Jesuits in charge of various Irish seminaries in Spanish possessions were not sufficiently interested in the recommendations of the Irish hierarchy.[102] The fact that the colleges were often run by religious orders also increased the possibility that the best students would be canvassed by their teachers to become regulars.[103] Even worse was when the religious governors of an institution had little interest in its mission: within the college of Seville, Irish students believed that the Spanish Jesuits who governed the college were negligent in the recruitment of students and in sending graduates back to Ireland. Significantly, their complaint in this regard was not directed to the powerless Irish bishops but to Rome.[104] The Irish bishops also lacked the financial resources to help fund any of the often desperately needy colleges abroad. The impoverishment and decline of the college at Douai in the late 1620s was lamented by a variety of Irish bishops but there was little they could do beside the writing of ineffectual letters to the cardinal protector.[105]

Even this recourse was not open to the bishops in certain other situations. The religious orders were of course not the only clerical rivals of the catholic diocesan clergy: they also faced competition from the church by law established. Despite the fears expressed by some, catholic clerical controversies did not apparently result in a discernible alienation of the secular population. In fact, that the two branches of the catholic clergy felt free to engage in at times vicious controversy is perhaps an indication of how unattractive they believed the established church to be to the general population. But if

---

[100] See Thomas Strange to Francis Matthews, 24 Nov. 1630 (Jennings, *Wadding Papers*, 440–1).
[101] Jennings, *Wadding Papers*, 32, 103–4, 373, 438.
[102] Walsh to Roche, 14 Mar. 1627 (ibid., 245–6).
[103] Thomas Messingham to Ingoli, 1 Aug. (ns) 1634 (APF, 'Lettere Antiche' 134, fo. 57).
[104] Irish students at Seville to Ludovisi, 9 Apr. (ns) 1630 (Jennings, *Wadding Papers*, 352–3).
[105] Jennings, 'Documents of the Irish Colleges at Douai', *Archivium Hibernicum*, 10, 179–92; Jennings, *Wadding Papers*, 246–7, 302–3.

the evangelical mission of the established church inspired relatively little fear in their catholic counterparts, the ability of the protestant clergy to extract finance from the catholic laity was an entirely different matter. The evidence suggests that the powers of the established church in this regard were an increasing source of worry to the catholic clergy in the twenty years prior to 1641.[106] In the often difficult economic climate of Caroline Ireland[107] the population could struggle to support one church establishment, let alone two. And during the 1630s the efforts of the resident Irish hierarchy to restructure the catholic church in Ireland coincided rather unhappily with Wentworth's determination to improve the financial basis of its protestant rival. The Court of High Commission was viewed as a deadly threat by the catholic clergy[108] and the capacity of protestant bishops to levy fines on the catholic population was hardly less resented.[109] It was not surprising, therefore, that during the 1640s the confederate catholics, spurred on by the clergy, were determined to secure an end to High Commission and to exempt themselves from the jurisdiction of the protestant hierachy.[110]

It is clear, therefore, that the clerical position of the 1640s had its roots in the development of the church over the previous decades. A Roman-appointed hierarchy, trained on the continent of Europe, had evolved and had committed itself to the restructuring of Irish catholicism. The relative success of this process provided the bishops and later the nuncio with a platform to become significant actors within the politics of the confederates during the 1640s. This was used to press for the removal of what had been perceived by the catholic hierarchy as the key obstacles to the smooth functioning of the alternative church, in particular the illegality of the bishops' authority, and the lack of clerical revenue. The Irish episcopate's concern over these matters reflected the fact that they were the products of the same culture of tridentine reform as Rinuccini himself. Consequently, Rinuccini's position during his nunciature was to find strong support among the Irish hierarchy and in many ways, indeed, was merely a strong restatement of views they had already expressed on these issues.

[106] APF, SOCG 140, fo. 327^{r-v}; ibid., fo. 342^{r-v}; John Roche to Wadding, 26 May 1630 (Jennings, *Wadding Papers*, 370); Hugh Bourke to cardinal protector, 17 Nov. 1624 (ibid., 90); Ciaran Ó Murchadha, 'Land and Society in Seventeenth Century Clare' (unpub. Ph.D. thesis, University College, Galway, 1982); *CSPI*, 1633–47, pp. 131, 167, 189, 208.

[107] Gillespie, 'The End of an Era', 204–8 and id., 'Harvest Crises in Early Seventeenth-century Ireland', *Irish Economic and Social History*, 2 (1984), 5–18.

[108] George Conn to Barberini, 23 Oct. 1636 (ASV, Inghilterra 6, fos. 68–70^{v}); APF, SOCG 140, fo. 327^{r-v}.

[109] John Roche to Wadding, 26 May 1630 (Jennings, *Wadding Papers*, 370).

[110] Gilbert, *Irish Confederation*, iii. 298–300, iv. 290–1, 319, 338.

III

If Rinuccini benefited from the support of an episcopate with demonstrably similar attitudes to his own, he also benefited from the changes in Irish catholicism which these bishops had helped to bring about in the previous decades and which rendered much of the general population susceptible to clerical influence and leadership. Despite the difficulties which the catholic clergy encountered, it is clear that prior to the rebellion of 1641 the religious culture of the counter-reformation had bitten deeply into all levels of Irish society. Indeed, it is possible that the realization of the strength of their position in Ireland and of the potential which existed to bring Irish catholicism into the European mainstream helped fuel the determination of the catholic clergy to wring major concessions from the king during the 1640s.

One index of the progress of the Irish counter-reformation was the steady increase in the numbers and quality of the Irish clergy.[111] In 1618 Donncha Mooney counted, probably reliably, no more than 160 Irish Franciscans in Ireland and abroad: by 1623 sources within the order estimated that the Irish province had swelled to 300 members, while Carlo Invernizzi in 1644 believed that there were a thousand Franciscans in Ireland alone.[112] This last figure may not be wholly accurate but it seems clear that there had been a dramatic increase in the order's membership over a period of twenty-five years. Not all of these friars were of the highest quality but the expulsion of six members of the order for incorrigible behaviour in 1615 and the passing of stern ordinances in the provincial chapter of the same year bear testimony to a determination to promote reform.[113] Moreover, like their Dominican counterparts and rivals, the provincial of the Franciscans visited all the convents of his order more or less annually in an attempt to maintain standards.[114] That this had real effect is indicated by the testimony of James Plunkett, vicar general of Meath, who insisted in 1624 that the efforts towards reform on the part of the Irish Franciscans compared favourably with what he had experienced of the order in Spain.[115]

Changes were also to be seen among the parish clergy. Between 1630 and 1637 the number of priests with care of souls in the diocese of Tuam jumped

---

[111] As early as 1624 the prelates of Cashel were adverting to a marked increase in learned and disciplined secular clergy: see Jennings, *Wadding Papers*, 87–8.

[112] See id., 'Brussels MS. 3947', 18; Answer of the Franciscans at Drogheda to the charges of the Vicar-General, 1623 (id., *Wadding Papers*, 45); Patrick Conlan, *Franciscan Ireland* (Mullingar, 1988), 37; 'Miscellanea Vaticano-Hibernica', *Archivium Hibernicum*, 6 (1917), 123; the contrast between these numbers and the paucity of catholic missionaries in Transylvania or Turkish Hungary is hugely interesting: the Jesuit mission in Transylvania hovered between one and four operatives in the 1620s while the mission in Pécs generally had two members of the society: see Balázs, *et al.*, *Erdélyi*, *passim*.

[113] Jennings, 'Brussels MS. 3947', 124–5.   [114] Id., *Wadding Papers*, 545, 592, 599–600.

[115] Testimony of James Plunkett, 4 Apr. 1624 (ibid., 65–6).

from 34 to 57;[116] between 1625 and 1637 the increase in Elphin was from 13 to 42.[117] In 1634 Rome decided to stand by its decision not to allow any further missionary faculties to Ireland because the island was plentifully supplied with clergy.[118] The following year the bishop of Ossory, David Rothe, expressed his belief that, when the absence of ecclesiastical revenues and the laity's poverty were taken into account, his diocese was actually overstaffed. In the town of Kilkenny eight secular priests other than the bishop exercised pastoral duties and they were supported by roughly double that number of regular clergy. More than thirty pastoral clergy, exclusive of personal chaplains, resided in the rural parts of the diocese.[119]

Certainly, not all these priests were seminary trained on the continent[120] but even those who had not been abroad for education were evidently subject to close monitoring. The bishop claimed to hold a synod every year and conducted annual visitation for confirmation and the correction of morals. In addition, Rothe had appointed eight vicars forane from the most qualified clergy in his diocese whose monthly task was to assemble the priests of their deaneries to discuss difficult cases they might have encountered in confession, to study together, and to prescribe reading for the next meeting. (This appears to have been a common tactic among the Irish bishops who in this way were able to maximize the talents of their continentally trained clergy.[121]) The vicars forane of Ossory in turn were convoked four times a year together with the urban clergy to discuss matters of general pastoral importance. Rothe's clergy were also expected to spend one week a year in retreat with one of the diocese's three resident Jesuits.[122]

As Rinuccini would certainly have agreed, the provision and organization of clergy on this model, even if the model functioned more imperfectly than episcopal reports suggest, was the essential first step to influencing the

[116] See Malachy O'Queely's 'Relatio Status' in 'Miscellanea Vatico-Hibernica', *Archivium Hibernicum*, 3 (1914), 84–9.

[117] APF, SOCG 140, fos. 351ʳ–352ᵛ; again the contrast with Transylvania is very great: there in the 1620s the Jesuits, other than unorthodox and often married Székely clergy, could count on the support of only four or five other priests: see Balázs *et al.*, *Erdélyi*, 428, 442.

[118] See 'Miscellaneous Documents I, 1588–1634', *Archivium Hibernicum*, 12 (1946), 198.

[119] See Rothe's 'Relatio Status' in 'Miscellanea Vatico-Hibernica', *Archivium Hibernicum*, 3 (1914), 84–9.

[120] An analysis of the clergy who received bulls of appointment from Rome during the 1640s indicates that 36 of 195 appointments are mentioned as having acquired seminary qualifications. The true number was almost certainly greater and this list may in fact give more indication of those who held higher degrees in theology than anything else: see Jennings, 'Ecclesiastical Appointments in Ireland, Aug. 1643-Dec. 1649', *Collectanea Hibernica* 2 (1959), 18–64.

[121] See for instance the Relationes Status of Tuam and Down in 'Miscellanea Vatico-Hibernica', *Archivium Hibernicum*, 3 (1914), 98, 106; see also the report from Elphin in 1631, ibid., 364; Connors, 'The Impact of English Colonial Expansion', 244 notes that Francis Kirwan of Killala apparently insisted that inadequately educated priests reside with him in Galway until retraining had been completed.

[122] Rothe's 'Relatio Status' in 'Miscellanea Vatico-Hibernica', *Archivium Hibernicum*, 3 (1914), 88.

religious culture of the people. An indication of the impact on the general population was the presence of no fewer than four sodalities in the diocese, one of which was clearly an exclusive group to which only the social elite were allowed entrance.[123] In terms of the bishop's social authority, one can note also the almost casual manner in which Rothe seems to have been able to summon a local aristocrat to enquire concerning his relatíons with a certain catholic gentlewoman.[124]

Bishops themselves were in little doubt that clerical activities, and in particular their own, had a notable impact on the population at large. Hugh O'Reilly in his short spell as bishop of Kilmore claimed to have restored respect for marriage and put an end to divorce in his diocese. He also believed that he had practically extinguished the previously common occurrences of theft, robbery, and open drunkenness.[125] Such large claims indicate that wariness is necessary when dealing with the reports of bishops to their own superiors. Yet it does seem evident that a reforming prelate could have a dramatic influence on a diocese.[126] Malachy O'Queely, for instance, evidently brought enormous dynamism to his role first as vicar apostolic of Killaloe and then as archbishop of Tuam. The attestations given in his favour during the 1620s were designed to win him a bishopric but, even when this is taken into account, it is evident that various bishops, regular clergy, including the provincials of various orders, and the inhabitants of his own diocese accepted that he had made a dramatic impact on the behaviour and morals of the population of Killaloe.[127]

As archbishop of Tuam, O'Queely demonstrated the same restless energy. Shortly after his consecration he convoked a provincial synod with the principal objective of securing the acceptance of the council of Trent in the province. The synod's decrees, approved by Rome in 1634,[128] followed a classical post-tridentine pattern in their articles about clerical dress, parish records, restriction of penances, the Eucharist, admission to clerical orders, marriage, and catechism. Some of the measures, such as those stressing the non-repeatability of confirmation and the extent of the obligations of god-parentship, indicated a pressing need to disseminate simple doctrinal information among the people of the province. The decrees also had to take into consideration very considerable levels of ignorance among some of the clergy, such as a belief that extreme unction was to be given to the dead. Yet the overall impression is of an essentially orthodox programme tailored to

---

[123] Ibid.   [124] See Rothe to Wadding, 13 July 1630 (Jennings, *Wadding Papers*, 430).
[125] See O'Reilly's 'Relatio Status' in 'Miscellanea Vatico-Hibernica', *Archivium Hibernicum*, 3 (1914), 81.
[126] In this context, it is interesting to note that the Jesuit missionaries in Transylvania believed that the application of episcopal authority was of fundamental importance in the consolidation of reform: see for example István Szini to Muzio Vitelleschi, 21 Nov. 1617 (Balázs *et al.*, *Erdélyi*, 278–90); same to same, 3 Jan. 1625 (ibid., 439–40).
[127] In this regard see Jennings, *Wadding Papers*, 77–83.   [128] APF, 'Lettere Latine' 9, fo. 58.

the fact that Tuam had been without a resident bishop for decades.[129] Naturally to make a synodal decree was one thing and to have it observed was quite another but it would be unwise to dismiss the impact which a determined bishop could have in a diocese.

O'Queely evidently backed up the synod with dedicated visitation. He appears to have been the first bishop in several centuries to reach the Aran islands. In 1632 he was already claiming to have confirmed 100,000 people, both within and outside his diocese.[130] By 1637 he had consecrated forty-five priests and at that time he claimed that a comprehensively remodelled system of pastoral care was functioning in his diocese. Like the bishop of Ossory he had created vicars forane to supervise individual deaneries in terms of catechesis (which he claimed was given by parish priests every Sunday and feast day), administration of sacraments, and confession. They were also entitled to fine clerics absent without leave from their parishes. At least twice a year the practice was for the priests of an individual deanery to go on retreat together. O'Queely himself, as befitted a doctor of theology, preached frequently and he had licensed various other qualified clergy to perform the same function.[131] His chapter consisted of a dean, precentor, archdeacon, provost, twelve canons, and five vicars choral while in the individual dioceses of his metropolitan province a penitentiary, sub-penitentiary, and synodal examiners had been appointed.[132] O'Queely's role in the disturbances following the rebellion of 1641 was also in the mould of a classic counter-reformation prelate. By that stage he had apparently acquired the social authority to act as a major bulwark against the looting and destruction of the general population.[133]

O'Queely's career in Killaloe and Tuam is of particular interest because there is a tendency in much of the historiographical literature on this subject to underplay the impact of the counter-reformation on Gaelic Ireland, particularly in comparison with its progress in areas of the country with a higher Old English population.[134] Such an approach contrasts strongly with the work

[129] APF, 'Scritture riferite nei Congressi' 1, Irlanda, fos. 171ʳ–180ᵛ.

[130] Ibid., fos. 168ʳ–171ʳ; Connors, 'The Impact of English Colonial Expansion', 247.

[131] See O'Queely's 'Relatio Status' in 'Miscellanea Vatico-Hibernica', *Archivium Hibernicum*, 3 (1914), 97–100; Jennings, *Wadding Papers*, 80–1; Connors, 'The Impact of English Colonial Expansion', 243–6.

[132] Connors, 'The Impact of English Colonial Expansion', 246.

[133] Gillespie, 'Mayo and the 1641 Rising', *Cathair na Mart*, 5 (1985), 40–1; although Connors, 'The Impact of English Colonial Expansion', 237–8 notes that English sources considered him a prime mover in attacks on protestants.

[134] In this regard see Rice 'Thomas Dease, Bishop of Meath', 66; Aidan Clarke, 'Pacification, Plantation and the Catholic Question', in T. W. Moody, F. X. Martin, and F. J. Byrne (eds.), *A New History of Ireland*, iii, *Early Modern Ireland, 1534–1691* (Oxford, 1976), 226–7 and id., 'Colonial Identity in Early Seventeenth-century Ireland', in T. W. Moody (ed.), *Historical Studies*, 11, *Nationality and the Pursuit of National Independence* (Dublin, 1978), 69; and Brenden FitzPatrick, *Seventeenth-Century Ireland: The War of Religions* (Dublin, 1988), 177–8; Corish, *Catholic Community*, 40; and id., *Catholic Experience*, 102.

of those scholars who have detected significant influences from the European counter-reformation in the religious sensibility of the literature produced in Irish during the first part of the seventeenth century.[135] It also contrasts with Rinuccini's analysis of Irish catholicism: by the end of his mission the nuncio was very sharply critical of the Old English as catholics and eager to see all future aid from Rome directed to the Gaelic Irish community.[136] Why such an ardent exponent of tridentine reform as Rinuccini should have evolved opinions of this kind is obviously a question of considerable importance and one which had considerable implications for his behaviour in Ireland.

A significant factor in influencing Rinuccini's opinions was clearly that, as is evident in the Gaelic literature of the period, the European counter-reformation had sunk deeper roots into Gaelic Ireland than has often been accepted. In this regard, it is important to note that the chief agents of religious reform in Gaelic Ireland were not Old English missionaries but continentally educated Gaelic clergy. And, as in the more anglicized parts of the country, the chief directors of catholic reform in Gaelic areas were bishops. In the earlier part of the seventeenth century there was considerable opposition within the Old English wing of the Irish church to the appointment of bishops of Gaelic origin, on the grounds that they, especially if they were identified as partisans of the exiled earls of Tyrone and Tyrconnel, might incite a general persecution of catholics in Ireland.[137] Supplementing this fear was probably a certain degree of cultural condescension.[138] But during the 1620s such opposition was largely defeated by the sustained campaign of Gaelic petitioners to Rome who emphasized the pastoral failure of those Old English bishops previously appointed to predominantly Gaelic areas.[139]

---

[135] In this regard see Tadhg Ó Dúshláine, An Eoraip agus Litríocht na Gaeilge, 1600–1650, Gnéithe den Bharócachas Eorpach i Litríocht na Gaeilge (Dublin, 1987); Breandán Ó Buachalla, 'Annála Ríoghachta Éireann is Foras Feasa ar Éirinn: An Comhthéacs Comhaimseartha', Studia Hibernica, 22–3 (1982–3), 59–105, his introduction to Foras Feasa ar Éirinn (Irish Texts Society Reprint, 1987), 1–8 and Aisling Ghéar: Na Stíobhartaigh agus an t-aos léinn (Dublin, 1997); Canny, 'The Formation of the Irish Mind: Religion, Politics and the Gaelic Irish Literature', Past and Present, 95 (1982), 91–116; Marc Caball, 'Faith, Culture and Sovereignty: Irish Nationality and its Development, 1558–1625', in Brendan Bradshaw and P. Roberts (eds.), British Consciousness and Identity (Cambridge, 1998); Bernadette Cunningham, The World of Geoffrey Keating: History, Myth and Religion in Seventeenth-Century Ireland (Dublin, 2000); Michelle O'Riordan, The Gaelic Mind and the Collapse of the Gaelic World (Cork, 1990) is significantly more cautious in assessing the impact of the counter-reformation on Gaelic poetry but she indicates that by the mid-seventeenth century evidence of at least a limited influence is visible: see for example pp. 254–5.

[136] In this regard see also Ch. 6.

[137] In this regard see John Roche to the cardinals of the Holy Office, 1626 (Jennings, Wadding Papers, 141–2); see also ibid., 123–5; J. J. Silke, 'Primate Peter Lombard and Hugh O Neill', Irish Theological Quarterly, 26 (1959), 15–30 and id., 'Primate Lombard and James I', ibid., 22 (1955), 124–50.

[138] In this regard see John Roche's comments on his Gaelic colleagues in Patrick Corish (ed.), 'Two Reports on the Catholic Church in Ireland in the Early Seventeenth Century', Archivium Hibernicum, 22 (1959), 146.

[139] See Jennings, Wadding Papers, 125–78.

There was clearly also bitter resentment among many Gaelic Irish clerics at the imputation that they and the culture from which they sprang were less civilized than their Old English counterparts, and a keen desire to assert the compatibility of Gaelic culture and post-tridentine catholicism.[140] The result of successfully convincing Rome of the practicality of appointing bishops to Gaelic Irish areas was the rapid development of a Gaelic wing of the hierarchy. Indeed, the majority of bishops at work in Ireland during this period were of Gaelic origin.[141]

That fact generally has been accorded little significance.[142] Yet there are at least two points of importance in this regard. First, it is surely indicative that candidates suitable for elevation to the episcopate were freely available in Gaelic Ireland. The fact that members of the Gaelic social elite had in such numbers over the previous decades sought education in continental seminaries,[143] despite their occasional complaints that they were the subject of discrimination by their Old English colleagues, must be taken as a symptom of a religious shift within Gaelic Ireland.

Second, that bishops of the stamp of Malachy O'Queely were being produced helps illuminate the preference which Rinuccini was to show for the Gaelic Irish. As the product of post-tridentine Italy, Rinuccini was keenly aware of the centrality of the bishop's role in the programme of religious change. Although the extent to which reform was solicited from below during the reformation and the counter-reformation cannot be ignored, the programme of the post-tridentine church was essentially linked to the imposition of new doctrinal formulae and information by an educated elite.[144] Rinuccini certainly conceived of catholic reform as something to be imposed on the general population from above by a revitalized series of church institutions, in particular the pastoral episcopate.[145] To a considerable extent he believed that the successful implementation of the tridentine programme depended on two conditions: the availability of suitable bishops to implement reform, and their endowment with the necessary power to enforce their authority, first on the clergy, and then, in combination with the newly disciplined clergy, on the laity. If Gaelic Ireland had not produced clergy who were capable of discharging the responsibilities of a post-tridentine bishop then

[140] APF, SOCG 140, fo. 5ʳ⁻ᵛ; in this regard see also Comment. Rinucc., ii. 187.

[141] And the majority of the Gaelic bishops were drawn from the secular clergy not, as has sometimes been asserted, from the regular orders: see Corish, Catholic Community, 21.

[142] Cregan, 'Social and Cultural Background', 102; Hugh Kearney, 'Ecclesiastical Politics and the Counter-Reformation in Ireland, 1618–48', Journal of Ecclesiastical History, 11 (1960), 202–12.

[143] Cregan, 'Social and Cultural Background', 88–103.

[144] Denis Richet, 'Sociocultural Aspects of Religious Conflict in Paris during the Second Half of the Sixteenth Century', in Robert Forster (ed.), Ritual, Religion and the Sacred (London, 1982), 183.

[145] In this he was in line with the dominant current of the Italian counter-reformation since at least the last two decades of the sixteenth century: see Giovanni Romeo, Inquisitori, esorcisti e streghe nell'Italia della Controriforma (Florence, 1990), esp. pp. 201–74; with regard to France see Hoffmann, Church and Community, 70–87.

an individual such as the nuncio would surely have formed a different opinion of the Gaelic Irish.

That Gaelic bishops were capable of fulfilling the role of tridentine pastor is indicated by the career of Malachy O'Queely. It is clear, moreover, that O'Queely was not an isolated figure in the Gaelic wing of the hierarchy. There were, for example, considerable similarities between the archbishop of Tuam and his senior suffragan, the bishop of Elphin, Boethius MacEgan. MacEgan was one of the first of the resident bishops of Gaelic Irish stock to be appointed.[146] In 1637, some twelve years after his provision, he dispatched a memorial about the state of his diocese to *Propaganda Fide* which clearly indicates that he was committed to a recognizably tridentine form of episcopal activity, although he admitted to Rome that the political climate necessitated certain modifications in his behaviour. An annual diocesan synod was considered too hazardous so the bishop met secretly once a year with the priests of the seven individual deaneries within the see. Parish priests, he reported, were catechizing the population regularly and celebrating mass in secluded rural areas. The bishop reported further that he was enforcing the decrees of O'Queely's provincial synod on his clergy.[147]

The bishop of Ardfert, Richard O'Connell, represents another example of a Gaelic prelate with a very tridentine appetite for pastoral activity. This diocese is of particular interest as it was here that Rinuccini landed in Ireland. In 1645 the future secretary of *Propaganda Fide*, Dionysio Massari, recorded the expedition's impressions of the catholicism of the remote district of Kenmare at a time when the Italians had freshly arrived from the continental mainland. The diocese of Ardfert was one of the least anglicized areas of the country but Massari was impressed by the state of religious instruction among the people. As he reported to Rinuccini's brother in Florence:

It is certainly an astonishing thing. Among mountains and barren places, with the inhabitants so reduced to poverty by the depopulation of their heretical enemies, I saw the knowledge of the holy catholic faith flourish so much that there was not a man or woman or any little boy who could not recite the lord's prayer, the Hail Mary and the precepts of the holy church.[148]

Elsewhere, in slightly different terms, he recorded that even the smallest child was capable of reciting the creed, the Our Father and the Hail Mary in Latin, and to his amazement many also knew the ten commandments.[149] Massari was equally impressed by the tremendous reverence which the people

---

[146] Giblin, 'Processus Datariae', 533.   [147] APF, SOCG 140., fos. 351ʳ–352ᵛ.

[148] 'Res sane est miranda. Inter montes et loca aspera, et incolas hostium haereticorum depopulatione ad inopiam redactos adeo vidi sanctae fidei Catholicae florere notitiam, ut non occurreret vir, mulier, nec puer quantuluscunque, qui Orationem Dominicam, salutationem Angelicam, et Sanctae Ecclesiae praecepta non recitaret.' (*Comment. Rinucc.*, ii. 13).

[149] APF, Miscellaneae Varie, 9, p. 56.

demonstrated towards the foreign ecclesiastics.[150] His evidence would appear to indicate a very successful diffusion of a tridentine notion of cate-chesis in an exclusively Irish-speaking area of very difficult terrain.[151] In this regard, it is interesting to note that an Italian cleric considered such a trans-mission of basic prayers to be a very considerable achievement.[152] The fact that these dimensions of catechesis have been considered 'rudimentary' in the Irish historiography carries the risk of ignoring the slow rate at which many areas of the European mainland were brought to a similar level of knowledge.[153] The problem of teaching prayers in a foreign language to an illiterate population was by no means confined to Ireland.

Like O'Queely, O'Connell had a formidable appetite for pastoral work. Indeed, when Rinuccini landed O'Connell was away on visitation in one of the remote peninsulae of the Kerry coast.[154] Quite clearly too, O'Connell benefited in his pastoral work from the support of highly educated local clergy. A memorial to *Propaganda Fide* in the 1630s, at a time when O'Connell was still vicar apostolic, declared that the diocese had 52 secular priests, including 6 doctors of theology, 3 doctors of canon law, 4 bachelors of theology, and another 6 who had studied theology but had no degree. Another 23 or 24 of these priests were defined as having mediocre learning. In addition there were 12 Dominicans, 7 Franciscans, and 12 Augustinians who were all either theologians, or authorized to preach, or both. There were naturally many other less qualified regular clergy as well.[155] Thus for the 80 parishes in his diocese O'Connell appeared to have a core of perhaps 50 con-tinentally educated clergy with another 22 or 23 of reasonable education. In terms of numbers and quality of clergy, therefore, the little anglicized diocese of Ardfert compared favourably with any other area in the country, and the high opinion which Massari formed of the state of religious instruction among its population is to a considerable extent explained.

---

[150] Rinuccini and Scarampi were also struck by this point: see *Comment. Rinucc.*, ii. 8, 14; see also the account of Scarampi's mission (BAV, Barberini Latini 4729, fo. 463ʳ) and the following chapter.

[151] Massari's noting of the harsh landscape is of interest. That he was impressed to see the mark of catholic reform in such conditions is not surprising: mountainous areas of difficult access on the continent were often entirely neglected by reforming clergy into the eighteenth century: see Kamen, *Phoenix and the Flame*, 84–7, 105–7.

[152] In this Massari was in line with many continental missionary groups: see E. William Monter, *Ritual, Myth and Magic in Early Modern Europe* (Brighton, 1983), 89–90.

[153] Corish, *Catholic Experience*, 105; Delumeau, *Catholicism between Luther and Voltaire* (London, 1977) 175; one can note that on a number of levels Ireland enjoyed a substantial advantage over other areas of Europe; in Ireland bishops were appointed on pastoral grounds, not merely as a means of obtaining the revenues of a see; the self-elected oligarchies in the cathedral chapters who slowed the impulse of reform elsewhere had been largely swept away by the reformation in Ireland, and Irish sees were quite small in European terms and so more amenable to episcopal visitation: see Kamen, *Phoenix and the Flame*, 84, 104–8, 115–16, 123.

[154] *Comment. Rinucc.*, ii. 15.

[155] APF, SOCG 140, fos. 69ʳ–77ʳ; Jennings, 'Miscellaneous Documents II, 1625–40', *Archivium Hibernicum*, 14 (1949), no. 9.

Massari was also favourably impressed by the Gaelic population of Ulster and reported the uplift in his spirits when his journey took him into a province which he regarded as more tenacious in its faith than the others and the home of a people 'so catholic' (si cattolico) and reverential to the Holy See. Here again he found the people well instructed in catholic faith and dogma.[156] Rinuccini, for his part, considered Ulster to be the most catholic of the four provinces and believed it to be the 'seat' of the Gaelic Irish whom he praised as catholics at the expense of the Old English.[157] To some extent these later judgements may have been influenced by political sympathies but, given the nature of the observers involved, it seems probable that the Italian evidence is a further indication of the roots which counter-reformation ideology and practice had already sunk in Gaelic Ireland. Once again the record of the pastoral activity of Ulster bishops such as Hugh O'Reilly, Eugene MacSweeny, John O'Cullenan, and Bonaventure Magennis provide corroboration of this theory.[158] In this context it is interesting to note that the clergy of the largely Gaelic province of Armagh (minus the Old English bishop of Meath) responded to the northern crisis in 1641–2 by resorting to one of the essential instruments of counter-reformation practice, namely a provincial synod. Nor is the synod's programme without interest in its highly tridentine concern for legitimacy and discipline, its regulation of the sacraments of penance and communion in the new situation, its edicts concerning the repossession of churches, the provision of clerical services in the army and the excommunication of offenders, together with its expressed desire for a union of ecclesiastical and secular authority to combat disorder.[159]

Of course, post-tridentine catholicism involved more than the implementation of the pastoral reforms of Trent. The 'rallying of the less articulate to the slogans of denominational division'[160] cannot be excluded any more than it can be suggested that the counter-reformation consisted of no more than this. The inculcation of denominational affiliation was a feature of the counter-reformation all over Europe because the goal of post-tridentine catholicism was not just to produce a more practising and more knowledgeable catholic community, but also to disseminate orthodoxy and to repress heterodoxy, whether superstitious or heretical.[161] In contemporary catholic terms, Christianization came second to orthodoxy: the peasant who could just about mumble his *Credo*, *Ave Maria*, and *Paternoster* and who made his Easter confession and communion was still safer from hellfire than

[156] APF, Miscellaneae Varie, 9, pp. 127, 139.

[157] *Comment. Rinucc.*, ii. 185; (sede): Aiazzi, *Nunziatura*, 391.

[158] See the various 'Relationes Status' in 'Miscellanea Vatico-Hibernica', *Archivium Hibernicum*, 3 (1914), 80–107; see also APF, SOCG 140, fos. 169ʳ–171ᵛ.

[159] *Comment. Rinucc.*, ii. 314–19.

[160] A. D. Wright, *The Counter-Reformation: Catholic Europe and the Non-Christian World* (London, 1982), 36.

[161] Romeo, *Inquisitori*, 201–74.

a bishop of the Church of England. An awareness that they were catholics as opposed to heretics,[162] even if they were unencumbered by any great awareness of the theological niceties involved, was an important aspect of the religious affiliation of the catholic population throughout Europe during this period. Nor is this surprising when one considers how much of the population was illiterate. Religious identity was probably determined, to a large extent, by the strength of the bonds of fear or trust which linked the less educated to a particular body of clergy.

By 1641 Ireland certainly corresponded to this pattern of denominational affiliation, a pattern which had been cultivated by the catholic clergy of both Gaelic and Old English Ireland. One of the major objectives, indeed, of catholic religious literature in Irish was to heighten sectarian differences and create an abhorrence of protestantism.[163] The success which this and other measures had had was to be seen with the explosion of sectarian violence against protestants in the aftermath of the 1641 rebellion. This is not to suggest that the catholic clergy were content with the pattern of violence which swept the country in the winter of 1641–2. On the contrary, many individual clerics exerted themselves to channel and control the violence which occurred. But the very success which many of them enjoyed in their endeavours was an indication that the sectarian hostility was a foster child of their own missionary activity.

A widespread diffusion of counter-reformation influence can thus be glimpsed throughout Ireland prior to 1641. The fact that Gaelic Ireland shared in this pattern in a manner not generally accepted certainly had implications for the Rinuccini nunciature, because it allowed the nuncio to believe that by choosing to oppose the policies of the confederate peace party he was aligning himself with an alternative party of good catholics, rather than with semi-christian barbarians. If Rinuccini had not come to this conclusion then it is difficult to believe that he would have involved himself so vehemently in confederate politics, particularly in 1648 when he had come to believe that ethnic differences were an important element in confederate divisions.

Of even greater significance, of course, was the fact that even in 1648 Rinuccini's influence was not *confined* to the Gaelic community. Throughout the island, and especially in the towns, there were those who were made profoundly uncomfortable by the thought that they were in opposition to the pope's nuncio. Such opposition ran directly counter to the reverence for the

---

[162] John O'Malley stresses how widely operative anti-protestant impulses were within the catholic reformation: see his introduction to John O'Malley (ed.), *Catholicism in Early Modern Europe: A Guide to Research* (Ann Arbor, Mich., 1988).

[163] Ó Buachalla, '*Annála Ríoghachta Éireann*', 65; Canny, 'Formation', 91–116; although Michelle O'Riordan in 'The Native Ulster *Mentalité* as Revealed in Gaelic Sources, 1600–50', in Mac Cuarta, *Ulster 1641*, 83, 90–1 argues that the learned Gaelic literature of the pre-1641 period did not advocate sectarian hostility.

catholic clergy which seems to have been strengthened and consolidated by the post-tridentine programme of reform. According to Donncha Mooney, even in the Nine Years' War Irish soldiers fighting for Elizabeth were prepared to take arms against their English colleagues for the protection of catholic clergy.[164] The intervening decades served to heighten the status of catholic religious. In 1611 the reaction of the population of Dublin to the execution of Conor O'Devaney was indicative of extreme fervour and the manner of his death further intensified emotions.[165] Certainly in the following decades it seems to have been commonplace that catholic women and youths in Dublin and elsewhere would riot with stones to rescue clergy captured by state officials or soldiers.[166]

The confederate period was to furnish further examples of widespread respect for the clergy. The citizens of Waterford gave public evidence of their determination to see the church's demands fulfilled in 1644.[167] Two years later respect for the clergy carried Waterford and other corporations even further into overt opposition to the Ormond peace. An analysis of the towns' behaviour in rejecting that peace suggests that the actual details at issue between the nuncio and the Supreme Council were largely irrelevant to the urban populations. What was important was the belief that the ecclesiastical demands must be satisfied, even before the clergy supplemented the reverence which normally accrued to them with the excommunication of the supporters of the peace.[168] This type of affiliation proved extremely stubborn. Even in 1648, with the nuncio's influence in decline and despite the local prestige of the marquis of Clanricard, the town of Galway continued to demonstrate enormous respect and loyalty to the nuncio and the clergy of his party.

In his retrospective history of the confederates, Richard Bellings rather maliciously suggested that the unusual respect which the Irish showed the nuncio was a factor in puffing up his arrogance and inclining him to interfere in matters beyond his competence.[169] There may have been an element of truth in this but the key point about the nuncio's interference in confederate politics was not so much his personal motivation as the degree of influence which he was able to exert. And the basis of that influence, other than of course the money he brought from Rome, was first the strength of the institution which he had been sent to lead and second the strength of the hold which that institution had acquired over the loyalty of the general population, including the

---

[164] Jennings, 'Brussels MS. 3947', 97.

[165] Richard Conway's narrative, 1612 (*Spicilegium Ossoriense*, i. 123–6).

[166] Ibid.; Jennings, 'Brussels MS. 3947', 33; id., *Wadding Papers*, 330, 333; adult men may have been absent from such demonstrations because of their greater vulnerability to prosecution.

[167] See 'Miscellanea Vaticano-Hibernica', *Archivium Hibernicum*, 6 (1917), 108.

[168] In this regard see Bodl. Carte MS 18, fos. 204ʳ–206ᵛ, 287ʳ–289ʳ, 383ʳ⁻ᵛ; Gilbert, *Irish Confederation*, vi. 94–5, 110–30.

[169] Gilbert, *Irish Confederation*, i. 154.

soldiers of the armies, in the previous decades. To a very considerable degree, Rinuccini inherited the power of the Irish counter-reformation and it was that which made him such a formidable figure.

IV

Rinuccini did not of course arrive in Ireland until 1645, four years after the outbreak of the 1641 rebellion. The evolution of the confederate association in the intervening period helped determine the parameters of his influence. In particular, the role which had been allotted to the clergy within the association and the development of clerical attitudes towards the peace negotiation were to be factors of critical importance.

From the outset the 1641 rebellion presented the catholic church with an important challenge. Although the rebel leadership claimed to be in arms to protect the king's prerogatives, at a lower social level the uprising signalled the beginning of widespread attacks on protestants, first in Ulster and then, as the rebellion spread, throughout the country. As noted previously, these attacks owed much to economic factors but the normative structure which justified the onslaught on protestants was provided by religion. Throughout the country protestants were a uniquely vulnerable, foreign, threatening, visible, and resented presence who could be represented as a 'pollution' of the religious community and dehumanized by rites of violence which allowed for their murder, expropriation, and banishment.[170] Moreover, the providential context in which events in seventeenth-century Ireland were seen by members of all religious groups meant that catholics could see the collapse of state authority as a divine intervention on their behalf and as a punishment of heresy.[171]

This popular sectarian unrest demanded a response from the church. Priests and bishops of a tridentine stamp could not stand idly by in the midst of such turbulent events. The basic thrust of the initial clerical reaction seems to have been to try and channel the violence with individual clerics attempting to ensure that only those protestants who refused to convert became targets for expropriation and expulsion.[172] It was not until March 1642, however, and the synod of the province of Armagh, that the ecclesiastical response transcended the local efforts of individual priests and bishops.[173] In

---

[170] Ó Murchadha, 'Land and Society', 42, 52–6; see also Yves-Marie Bercé (trans. J. Bergin), *Revolt and Revolution in Early Modern Europe: An Essay on the History of Political Violence* (Manchester, 1987), 15–19; Canny, 'Religion, Politics and the Irish Rising of 1641', in Judith Devlin and Ronan Fanning (eds.), *Historical Studies*, 20, *Religion and Rebellion* (Dublin, 1997), 40–70.

[171] Mary Catherine Kennedy, 'Eagla an Ghallsmacht: The Religion and Politics of Irish Catholics, 1620s–1670s' (unpub. MA thesis, University College, Galway), 21–2.

[172] Canny, *From Reformation to Restoration*, 209 and id., 'Religion, Politics and the Irish Rising of 1641', 40–70.

[173] 'Ó hAnnracháin, 'Rebels and Confederates', 98–9; Gillespie, 'Mayo and the 1641 Rising', 38–44.

May of the same year the first post-tridentine synod of the entire island came together at Kilkenny to enunciate an official church position, to which practically all the catholic clergy of the island quickly conformed.[174] By legitimizing the idea of a war in the interests of the catholic religion, by articulating uncompromising support for the rights of catholic property owners, and by appealing to influential lay catholics to join them in creating a political structure to replace that shattered by the rebellion, the church provided an essential foundation for the development of the confederate catholic association during the summer and autumn of 1642. The backing of such a respected institution was also crucial in legitimizing the authority of confederate institutions. It was the clergy who administered the confederate oath of association, the Irish equivalent of the Scottish covenant, which bound the general population to obedience to the Supreme Council. Not only was the threat of excommunication levelled at those who perjured this oath but all catholics who refused to subscribe were warned that they too would be cut off from the body of the church.[175]

Events in Ireland also demanded a response from the Vatican. The pope's nephews, Francesco and Antonio Barberini, were the cardinal protectors of Britain and Ireland respectively, and they showed themselves cautiously disposed to patronize the rebellion as a war for the catholic religion.[176] Rome, however, was reluctant to antagonize the French crown which was linked by marriage to the Stuarts. Instructions were therefore sent to the nuncio in France that he should persuade Richelieu that the Irish rebellion was a religiously meritorious undertaking which deserved the support of all catholic powers.[177] At the same time steps were taken to remedy the chronic lack of information concerning the true nature of the Irish rebellion. In February 1642 the future bishop of Limerick, Edmund O'Dwyer, was sent to Ireland as a secret papal agent to survey the situation in the island, to encourage the rebels with hope of aid from abroad, and to exhort them to fight for the freedom of the catholic religion.[178] By the beginning of April O'Dwyer was in Brittany preparing to ship to Ireland,[179] which indicates that he was probably present at the national synod convoked in May and that the stance articulated by the clergy on this occasion was influenced by consultation with the pope's agent. This may well have been a factor in ensuring such a high degree of clerical unanimity.

Roman influence was mobilized on behalf of the rebellion not only in France but in Spain and its dependencies as well. It was partially as a result

---

[174] The clergy who stood out from this overwhelming consensus are discussed in Ó hAnnracháin, 'Rebels and Confederates', 99.
[175] Ibid.   [176] Barberini to Grimaldi, Feb. 1642 (BAV, Barberini Latini 8247, fos. 1–18).
[177] Ibid.
[178] Instructions to Edmund O'Dwyer, 3 Feb. (ns) 1642 (BAV, Barberini Latini 8626, fos. 29ʳ–33ᵛ).
[179] O'Dwyer to Barberini, 1 Apr. (ns) 1642 (ibid., fo. 37).

of this that Irish officers serving in Spanish forces were released to return to Ireland in the course of 1642.[180] Rome also gave some financial support. In March 1642 Antonio Barberini sent 10,000 scudi (circa £2,500) via Avignon and Paris and other small grants followed. The subsequent eruption of the War of Castro severely limited the amount of finance which the papacy had available for Ireland and total Vatican aid to Ireland prior to Rinuccini's arrival probably did not exceed £8,000: a sum, however, which still made Rome the biggest single source of foreign support.[181] The papacy also led the way in diplomatic recognition of the confederate regime, less hampered than other European states by its rebellious status *vis-à-vis* the Stuarts.[182] The confederates were undoubtedly helped by the existence of several non-monarchical states, most notably Genoa and Venice, in the Italian peninsula, which provided a ready-made paradigm for the accommodation of the new confederate government within the framework of papal diplomacy.[183] The arrival of the papal envoy PierFrancesco Scarampi in late June or early July of 1643 was a notable boost to the authority of the Supreme Council, serving to consolidate its appearance of legitimacy.[184]

Church support was thus of vital importance in ensuring the stability of confederate government during its early years. Members of the clergy were also prominent in confederate institutions. Several bishops and, at various times, all four archbishops sat on the confederate Supreme Council and every bishop had a seat by right in the General Assembly, the unicameral quasi-parliamentary body of the confederates.[185] Members of the clergy were used as diplomats to continental powers, providing a service which was cheap and linguistically competent,[186] and the bishop of Clonfert, John Bourke, held the office of confederate Lord Chancellor.[187]

Nevertheless, as a corporate body the clergy do not appear to have been particularly assertive in the early years of the confederate association. Whether the unicameral structure of the confederate assembly operated to

---

[180] Jerrold Casway, 'Owen Roe O'Neill's Return to Ireland in 1642: The Diplomatic Background', *Studia Hibernica*, 9 (1969), 48–64; Barberini to Grimaldi, 6 Sept. (ns) 1642, (BAV, Barberini Latini 8249).

[181] *Comment. Rinucc.*, i. 422; Wadding to Bourke, 22 Mar. (ns) 1642 (HMC, *Report on Franciscan Manuscript* (Dublin, 1906)), 127; Gilbert, *Irish Confederation*, ii. 68.

[182] Jane Ohlmeyer, 'Ireland Independent: Confederate Foreign Policy and International Relations during the Mid-seventeenth Century' in ead. (ed.), *Ireland from Independence to Occupation 1641–60* (Cambridge, 1995), 90–5.

[183] See Pamfili to Rinuccini, 25 Mar. (ns) 1646 (*Comment. Rinucc.*, ii. 27–8); Herbert Rowen, 'Kingship and Republicanism in the Seventeenth Century: Some Reconsiderations', in C. H. Carter (ed.), *From the Renaissance to the Counter-Reformation: Essays in Honour of Garrett Mattingly* (London, 1966), 428.

[184] Ó hAnnracháin, 'Rebels and Confederates', 100.   [185] Ibid., 101.

[186] Ohlmeyer, 'Ireland Independent', 90–2.

[187] 'Miscellanea Vaticano-Hibernica', *Archivium Hibernicum*, 6 (1917), 115.

decrease or preserve the bishops' influence is open to question.[188] The fact remains, however, that the clergy represented a minority bound to accept majority decisions within the Supreme Council and a tiny and apparently timid minority within the assembly.[189] This institutional imbalance was somewhat redressed by the clerical habit of sitting in convocation at the same time as the assembly was in progress. But prior to Rinuccini's arrival the determination to use this forum to lock horns with the confederate executive over issues of importance to the clergy was not particularly apparent. The advanced age of many of the bishops, most of whom had been appointed before 1631, militated against their enjoying a high political profile. In addition, certain of the bishops, in what was an exceptionally pastorally orientated hierarchy, seem to have been uninterested in political activity, particularly if it might bring them into conflict with their secular colleagues. Rome's representatives in Ireland were dismayed, for instance, that the Irish clergy were prepared to allow ecclesiastical cases come before the Supreme Council for decision.[190] The ostensible justification for this erosion of ecclesiastical immunity was that the council was not a purely secular body but one on which clergy were also represented. More important was probably the determination of certain secular confederates, especially lawyers, to prevent the establishment of a separate ecclesiastical tribunal. Once again, there was to be a notable difference between the determination of Rinuccini, who faced down fierce opposition in order to establish such a tribunal, and the more acquiescent demeanour of the Irish clergy.[191]

Although the catholic clergy inherited the churches and livings of the Church of Ireland in all areas controlled by the confederates, the importance of their financial contribution to the association was somewhat disguised. Two-thirds of all clerical revenues were devoted to the war but the property from which this revenue was drawn was administered by lay farmers and assessors, not by the clergy themselves. It was not until Rinuccini exerted his influence against what he saw as an unacceptable lay intrusion into ecclesiastical affairs that the clergy regained control of their own contribution to confederate finances.[192]

The clergy were also largely marginalized from one of the main preoccupations of confederate government, namely the conduct of peace negotiations with the king and his representatives. One major reason for this was the reluctance of the royalist party to have any immediate contact with catholic clergy. Some attempt was made to compensate for this difficulty: the confederates

---

[188] Kearney, 'Ecclesiastical Politics', 209 suggests the former while Micheál Ó Siochrú, *Confederate Ireland*, 207 argues the contrary.

[189] See Ó hAnnracháin, 'Rebels and Confederates', 101–4 for a more detailed discussion of this point.

[190] 'Miscellanea Vaticano-Hibernica', *Archivium Hibernicum*, 6 (1917), 119.

[191] See Ch. 6.   [192] Ó hAnnracháin, 'Rebels and Confederates', 102–3.

insisted on their right to have a bishop on the negotiating team with Ormond in 1644 (although in practice he may not have been present at any of the meetings)[193] and the exclusively secular party of negotiators who went earlier that year to Oxford was accompanied by a clerical watchdog, Robert Barry, charged to ensure that they protected the church's interests.[194] None the less, inevitably this situation operated to diminish the clergy's influence, in particular because the confederate negotiators came to operate as something close to auxiliary Supreme Councillors.[195]

Another reason why the clergy had relatively little input into the negotiations with the king may have been the belief that their own particular demands, above all the right to exercise a jurisdiction derived from Rome and the retention of the churches and church livings taken from their protestant counterparts, were unlikely to be achieved at the negotiating table. To some extent, the confederates seem to have pursued a dual strategy in 1643 and 1644: while the negotiations with the king basically addressed the matters of especial interest to lay catholic property owners, on the continent confederate diplomats lobbied catholic powers for the substantial assistance required to obtain the key clerical demands by force of arms. The nuncio of France reported to Rome in April 1643, for instance, after consultation with an envoy from Ireland, Geoffrey Baron, that the confederates' intention was to drive all heretics out of the island.[196] The same militant note was sounded in other correspondence in the following year.[197] Carlo Invernizzi, sent by Scarampi to Rome in 1644, reported that the Supreme Council had promised never to make peace if they received even a modicum of assistance.[198] Meanwhile, Scarampi evidently did his best to convince the confederates that such assistance might be forthcoming from the Vatican.[199]

From the moment of his arrival Scarampi had disagreed with the confederate policy of truce and negotiation. Like Rinuccini after him, he favoured a much harder negotiating stance with the royalist camp and was bitterly opposed to the idea of paying for a cessation, particularly the first year-long agreement from September 1643, for which the confederates had paid £30,000. The papal envoy believed that the real bargaining leverage which the confederates possessed lay in their military strength. The logic of his position was identical to that of Rinuccini later, namely that the confeder-

[193] Ó hAnnracháin, 'Rebels and Confederates', 102–3.
[194] 'Miscellanea Vaticano-Hibernica', *Archivium Hibernicum*, 6 (1917), 106.
[195] Ó hAnnracháin, 'Rebels and Confederates', 103.
[196] Grimaldi to Barberini, 24 Apr. (ns) 1643 (BAV, Barberini Latini 8238, fo. 63).
[197] Ó hAnnracháin, 'Rebels and Confederates', 104.
[198] 'Miscellanea Vaticano-Hibernica', *Archivium Hibernicum*, 6 (1917), 107–8.
[199] See Duchess of Buckingham to Ormond, 20 Aug. 1644 (Gilbert, *Irish Confederation*, iii. 258).

ates' best security was to conquer the entire island and to hold it by force until their demands had been granted.[200]

The rejection of the papal agent's advice may have reflected the fact that Scarampi himself had arrived in Ireland with relatively little money and what he had may have been donated directly to O'Neill. Nor, although he convinced many in Ireland that he was a genuinely holy man, does Scarampi appear to have been a particularly adept diplomat. As well as lacking the title of nuncio and the financial resources which favoured Rinuccini in his dealings with the confederates, he seems also to have lacked the verbal and written eloquence and the hard-nosed negotiating skills of his successor.[201] He detested pomp, was genuinely humble, moved secretly whenever he could to avoid displays in his honour[202] and in general seems to have been a figure which the confederate government found relatively easy both to admire and ignore for the first year of his sojourn in Ireland.

By the autumn of 1644, however, tensions were beginning to rise between secular and lay interests within the confederate camp. No large-scale assistance had arrived from the continent thus, in the short term at least, making it unlikely that the clergy's goals could be attained by military force. As a result these points came more into focus in the negotiations with Ormond. The lord lieutenant was shocked to discover that the confederates wanted the repeal, not just of the Acts of Supremacy, Uniformity, and Faculties, but also the Act of Appeals, parts of the Act of Marriages, and several fourteenth-century statutes which ordained the impeachment of clergy appointed without royal consent[203] and was deeply unwilling to entertain these demands.[204] For his part, Ormond made it clear that he would not countenance the retention of the churches by the catholic clergy.[205]

During the winter of 1644–5 this last issue began to develop explosive potential. Ormond was to the fore in heightening tension over this point with his insistence that any peace treaty should explicitly return ecclesiastical property to the established church,[206] despite warnings that the catholic clergy would by no means consent to the loss of the churches.[207] There is

---

[200] See the exchange of views between Scarampi and Richard Bellings in *Comment. Rinucc.*, i. 413–21; see also John Lowe, 'Charles I and the Confederation of Kilkenny', *Irish Historical Society*, 14 (1964), 8–9; Cregan, 'Confederation of Kilkenny', 138.

[201] Paolo Aringhi, *Memorie istoriche della vita del venerabile servo di Dio Pier Francesco Scarampi* (Rome, 1744), 17, 23–5, 28, 18; Viaggio in Irlanda di Dionysio Massari (APF, Miscellaneae Varie 9, 11).

[202] Account of the life of Scarampi (BAV, Barberini Latini 4886, fo. 6ᵛ); see also Aringhi, *Scarampi*, 47.

[203] Confederate commissioners to Ormond, 17 July 1645 (Gilbert, *Irish Confederation*, iv. 332).

[204] Ó hAnnracháin, 'Rebels and Confederates', 105.

[205] Gilbert, *Irish Confederation*, iv. 319, 35–6.

[206] I am indebted to Micheál Ó Siochrú for pointing out to me Ormond's role in forcing this issue.

[207] There had been warnings of this since the middle of the previous year. On 20 Aug. 1644, for instance, the Duchess of Buckingham wrote to Ormond that she found 'it impossible to make the

evidence that many among the clergy were beginning to distrust the Supreme Council's conduct of both the war and the negotiations with Ormond. Concern was growing that the dominant clique on the council were not sufficiently interested in obtaining the clergy's particular demands, provided that the needs of secular property holders could be met. As noted previously, distrust was growing that many prominent confederates with personal links to Ormond were eager for a peace treaty because they expected to benefit from his patronage following its completion. The level of inefficiency and corruption in confederate government was also the target of criticism.[208] The developing peace party for their part was increasingly worried about the parlous position of the royalist party in England[209] and saw the necessity of a speedy conclusion of their dealings with the king. In addition the issue of former monastic lands now in lay catholic possession lurked like a dangerous reef beneath the surface of all debates on ecclesiastical property.

The potential divisiveness of this issue had been gaining momentum for several years. A large amount of land, originally the property of the religious orders of the catholic church, was owned by catholic laymen who joined the confederate association during the 1640s.[210] The nuncio, who was forced to consider the problem in detail, believed that little of this property was in Old Irish hands, something which was to facilitate the development of his relationship with prominent figures within that community.[211] Catholic occupiers of monastic land were naturally eager to retain their possessions, preferably with clerical approval.[212] A case could be made by a well-disposed judge that Cardinal Pole's dispensation of 1554, obtained from Rome for English catholics during the Marian catholic restoration, legitimized lay possession of monastic lands in Ireland also, but Rome had shown little sign

---

clergie or those that run that way to be satisfyed without their churches': see Gilbert, *Irish Confederation*, iii. 258.

[208] Ó hAnnracháin, 'Rebels and Confederates', 108.

[209] Martyn Bennett, *The Civil Wars in Britain and Ireland, 1638–1651* (Oxford, 1997), 210–13.

[210] *Comment. Rinucc.*, i. 424–5; in Meath, monastic possessions had been so extensive that various religious orders had been entitled to present priests to over half the parishes in the diocese: in Cloyne the proportion was even higher: see Rice, 'Thomas Dease, Bishop of Meath', 70; Corish, *Catholic Community*, 22; the Earl of Westmeath received an income of £1,000 per annum from former ecclesiastical property which may help explain his wariness of the confederate cause: see *Comment. Rinucc.*, i. 402; the confederate secretary Richard Bellings held former monastic land at Killashee; the confederate president Viscount Mountgarrett held the lands of the former abbey of Kells; another Supreme Councillor, Geoffrey Browne, was heir to the abbey and lands of Mayo; the chairman of the confederate assembly in 1648, Sir Richard Blake, was also the possessor of former church property and there were other confederates such as Viscount Galmoy and the Allens of St Wolstans whose patrimony was centred to an even greater degree on the possession of what had once been the property of the regular orders: see Cregan 'The Confederation of Kilkenny' (thesis), 107–8.

[211] See Rinuccini's report to the pope (Aiazzi, *Nunziatura*, 391.)

[212] Little monastic land was in the hands of Gaelic landowners in Ulster because the government had seized control of all church lands in the plantation of Ulster.

of making such a judgement in the years prior to 1641.[213] The earl of Westmeath, for instance, had applied to Rome in 1635 concerning the legitimacy of his holdings. He and his heirs had been confirmed in safe and total enjoyment of the property in question but only while Ireland was ruled by a protestant government. Indeed, by the same dispensation, they were warned that the property must be returned to church ownership if it became possible once again for catholic religious to possess it legally.[214] Whether in this matter the policy of the Barberini papacy was influenced by the contemporaneous crisis concerning secularized church lands in the German war remains uncertain, but a definite similarity can be detected in the papal determination not to abandon church claims lightly in either area.[215]

In 1642 the provincial synod of Armagh declared that no catholic in possession of former church property was to be disturbed in any manner if they were engaged in promoting the common cause.[216] This declaration was not, however, repeated by the national synod in May, possibly because the clergy were warned by O'Dwyer that, without definite instructions from Rome, they were not in a position to make a definitive declaration. In October of that year, the first confederate assembly was convened in Kilkenny and came immediately under pressure from the regular clergy to restore monastic land recovered from protestant ownership, a point with obvious implications for the position of such holdings in secular catholic possession.[217] In the end, after stormy discussions, the issue was effectively deferred by the decision that lay catholics should be permitted to retain ecclesiastical goods until the matter was conclusively settled in Parliament.[218]

In December 1642 the Supreme Council wrote to Luke Wadding in Rome in a tone of some confidence asking him to seek a bull like that of Cardinal Pole 'for ensuring the tranquillity of the kingdome and restraining the undue ambition of some ecclesiastics'.[219] Seven months later, following the arrival of the papal envoy, Scarampi, in the island without the requisite bull, the council wrote again more urgently to Wadding to 'procure such a bull as Cardinal Poole had in Queene Marye's dayes for settlinge the estates devolved to the Croune by the suppression', explaining that there was great need for such a bull to: 'quiet the minds of many who, without assurance in this kinde, will, of all likelyhood, be wonn to adheare to them with whom

[213] APF, SOCG 140, fo. 311ʳ.   [214] Comment. Rinucc., i. 402–3.

[215] In this regard see K. Repgen, Die römische Kurie und der westfälische Friede. Papst, Kaiser und Reich 1521–1644 (Tübingen, 1962), 329–88 and Robert Birely, Religion and Politics in the Age of the Counter-Reformation. Emperor Ferdinand II, William Lamormaini, S.J., and the Formation of Imperial Policy (Chapel Hill, NC, 1981), 52–9, 74–94.

[216] Corish, 'The Rising of 1641', 318; Comment. Rinucc., i. 318.

[217] Richard Martin to Clanricard, 2 Dec. 1642 (Bodl. Carte MS 99, fo. 297ʳ⁻ᵛ).

[218] Comment. Rinucc., i. 349.

[219] See the Instructions to Wadding (Gilbert, Irish Confederation, ii. 119.).

theire possessions will be unquestionable'.[220] One reason why this issue had become more immediately important was the fact that, at this juncture, negotiations for a truce with Ormond were well under way and the possibility of some kind of settlement with the Dublin government, which had seemed impossible at the end of 1642, had begun to appear more likely. Any negotiation raised the possibility of some defections from the confederates by those who believed that they could get reasonable terms from the king. In this context, the prospect of continuing in rebellion for a cause whose success might bring heavy financial disadvantages was naturally less appealing. Scarampi also wrote to Rome about the importance of this issue for the confederates and asked for information about the official status of Pole's dispensation. Rome, however, was unwilling to respond definitively on this point. On 11 November 1643 the cardinal-nephew Francesco Barberini wrote to Scarampi that, on receipt of various memorials from Ireland, the congregation of cardinals for Irish affairs had discussed the feasibility of a general faculty of dispensation. Probably aware of the potential ramifications of this decision, in Germany as well as in Ireland, the congregation took the by no means unprecedented decision to defer an answer until the case had been debated further. Scarampi was told, however, to offer the customary faculties to anyone whose conscience was affecting them on this matter.[221]

On 4 April 1644 Barberini wrote to Scarampi that it had been decided that the regular orders were to be forbidden to sue for the restitution of their former properties without a special licence from Rome which Scarampi was to supervise.[222] This seems to have been the last decision prior to the death of Urban VIII. The new pope, Innocent X, who dispatched Rinuccini to Ireland, had the innovative idea of using the land in question, not to restore the former monastic possessors, but to guarantee that the parish clergy of the restored catholic church would be adequately provided for financially.[223] To this end, Rinuccini was given wide powers, either to give a dispensation to the occupying laity, or to insist on restitution as he would think fit.[224]

---

[220] Supreme Council to Wadding (Gilbert, *Irish Confederation*, ii. 277); during the rebellions of the late sixteenth century, James Archer had urged the necessity of providing Old English possessors of monastic property with a dispensation similar to Cardinal Pole's: see Thomas Morrissey, 'Archdevil and Jesuit: The Background, Life and Times of James Archer from 1550 to 1604' (unpub. MA thesis, University College Dublin, 1968).

[221] See Barberini to Scarampi, 11 Nov. (ns) 1643 (*Comment. Rinucc.*, i. 399–400). This decision was probably more likely to provoke than to dispel anxiety in Ireland since, as noted above, the customary dispensation evidently mandated the eventual return of all such property to the church.

[222] Barberini to Scarampi, 4 Apr. (ns) 1644 (*Comment. Rinucc.*, i. 492).

[223] A parallel can be noted here with the establishment in Germany of Jesuit colleges using regained monastic resources, on the grounds that the regular orders lacked the personnel to make effective use of the property: see Ludvig Von Pastor (trans. Ernest Graf), *History of the Popes from the Close of the Middle Ages*, xxviii–xxx (London, 1938–40), 28, 183–4.

[224] See Albizzi's instructions to Rinuccini, Dec.(?) 1644 (Aiazzi, *Nunziatura*, pp. xlv–l).

Yet, to a considerable extent, the damage had already been done before the arrival of the nuncio. The Barberini papacy found itself simply unable to make a firm decision on a matter of great importance to the confederates.[225] The lack of a concrete decision created a climate of distrust and anxiety that Rome's intention was to force the restitution of all former monastic property. Consequently, when Rinuccini arrived, there was a general reluctance to avail of his faculties in case this would be seen as an admission of illegal ownership. How far the nuncio really exerted himself to dispel these suspicions is perhaps open to discussion. His instructions had been stringent that he must provide adequately for the financial support of the parish clergy out of this resource,[226] and it is possible that he erred on the side of caution in attempting to break the impasse.[227] In the long run there was probably real ground for accommodation between the landowners and the nuncio in this regard. In 1643 (probably) the Supreme Council had already decided, in principle, to restore to the Cistercians their monasteries, churches, one-tenth of other properties which had belonged to the order, and one-tenth of the tithes which they had previously enjoyed. This was done on condition that the order make no further claims and similar conditions were offered to the far more numerous members of the mendicant orders.[228] These conditions were concrete evidence of the confederate laity's willingness to provide for impoverished clergy. A settlement with Rinuccini might well have represented no more than a legally binding obligation to endow the parish clergy with what wealthy catholics had been donating voluntarily for decades. Indeed, the areas, such as Ulster and North Connacht, where the clergy had been poorest prior to 1641, were precisely those areas where very little monastic land had been distributed to lay catholics in the wake of confiscation.[229] In the event, no such settlement was to occur and the issue remained as one of the major destabilizing factors within the association throughout the nunciature.

While that rumbled in the background, the future of property confiscated from the church of Ireland post-1641 came sharply into focus during the debates of May and June 1645 in the confederate General Assembly. What these debates revealed was that the clergy were determined to retain the churches but that they wished to be as conciliatory as possible to their secular colleagues. Consequently, they were prepared to countenance a treaty which did not explicitly retain the churches for catholic use provided that this end could be obtained in some other fashion. The debates indicated further

---

[225] Fears that an Irish decision might create a precedent for the more important problem of former ecclesiastical property in Germany may have been one factor promoting caution in Rome.

[226] Albizzi's instructions to Rinuccini Dec.(?) 1644 (Aiazzi, *Nunziatura*, p. xlvi).

[227] In addition, Innocent's plan of using former monastic land to endow the diocesan clergy meant that for the first time the most influential section of the Irish clergy, the bishops, had a real incentive to pursue this topic. This may possibly have heightened tensions still further.

[228] *Comment. Rinucc.*, i. 403–6.

[229] My analysis here differs substantially from FitzPatrick, *War of Religions*, 176.

that a party among the confederates was probably prepared to allow the protestant clergy to regain the churches, provided they were not called upon to do violence to their consciences by relinquishing them explicitly in the peace treaty. The evidence suggests that this peace party was prepared to deceive the clergy about their intentions in order to keep them quiescent and that they hoped to persuade Ormond to forgo any explicit mention of the churches in the treaty in the expectation of effecting a quiet transfer following the conclusion of peace.[230] Ormond, however, was reluctant to accept this compromise and, in any event, there were a number of other clerical demands which the General Assembly agreed to insist upon over the course of the summer which the lord lieutenant refused to countenance and which continued to block the possibility of peace.[231]

The arrival of the earl of Glamorgan in Kilkenny in August 1645, however, at first seemed to offer a way of satisfying both the peace party's eagerness for a settlement and the clergy's determination to retain the churches. Glamorgan, a fervent royalist catholic, landed in Ireland in June 1645,[232] equipped with a wide-ranging private mandate from the king. On his arrival in Kilkenny, Glamorgan negotiated a subsidiary agreement concerning religious matters with the confederates. In this, in return for a promise of 10,000 men for the king's service, he offered extremely wide-ranging concessions.[233] This agreement was probably concluded without Ormond's knowledge,[234] but the terms offered were conditional on the successful outcome of the negotiations with the lord lieutenant. In essence, two linked treaties between the king and the confederates were now being finalized. The public treaty with Ormond dealt principally with the secular grievances of the confederates: the secret articles were separate from but dependent on this public treaty and dealt with religious concessions. The Glamorgan arrangement was opposed by Scarampi who urged the confederates to delay an agreement

---

[230] See Ó hAnnracháin, 'Rebels and Confederates', 108–11; see also Clanricard's correspondence with Ormond in John Lowe (ed.), *The Letter Book of the Earl of Clanricard, 1643–7* (Dublin, 1983), 155–76.

[231] In particular the clergy insisted on their right to spiritual jurisdiction over the catholic population and the complete freedom of the catholic population from the spiritual jurisdiction of the protestant clergy. This position was eventually endorsed by the assembly in August 1645 and presumably at this time the assembly also voted that the Oath of Supremacy should never again be offered to catholics in Ireland: see *Comment. Rinucc.*, i. 536, 567, 730.

[232] This is the date suggested by John Lowe, 'The Glamorgan Mission to Ireland', *Studia Hibernica*, 4 (1964), 161.

[233] In particular he accepted that the churches then in confederate hands were to be retained by the catholic clergy; he also offered complete satisfaction concerning the respective jurisdictions of the protestant and catholic clergy and a commitment that all catholics would be safeguarded against the existing penal legislation: see Lowe, 'The Glamorgan Mission', 166; see ibid., 155–67 for the background and progress of the negotiations.

[234] FitzPatrick, *War of Religions*, 188–93 questions this but Lowe, 'The Glamorgan Mission', 171 is probably correct on this score.

until Rinuccini's arrival.[235] Despite his arguments to the Irish clergy, how-ever,[236] seven of the thirteen bishops consulted on the matter voted in favour of the Glamorgan articles thus confirming the conciliatory stance which they had demonstrated earlier in June.[237] This seemed to clear the way for a quick settlement,[238] but in the event matters had not been finalized by the time Rinuccini arrived in Ireland in October. The basic stumbling block seems to have been Ormond's ignorance, or else his refusal to take any cognizance, of Glamorgan's arrangement.[239] In addition, all sections of the confederate association were eager for the nuncio's arrival: even the peace party coveted the money and supplies which he was bringing with him[240] and they had been made aware by Scarampi that the definitive conclusion of peace would jeopardize his arrival.[241]

In a sense with Rinuccini's arrival the Supreme Council were forced to confront the consequences of previous behaviour. The secular confederates had previously been eager to strengthen their position with the authority of the church. In 1643 they themselves had requested Rome to supply them with

[235] The basis of Scarampi's opposition has been somewhat inaccurately represented in Lowe, 'The Glamorgan Mission', 165; Scarampi's position was in fact almost identical to that of Rinuccini later: he objected to the fact that the agreement did not make provision for the catholic bishops' rep-resentation as lords spiritual in parliament; far more importantly he believed that Glamorgan's mandate, granted only under the king's private seal, was inadequate and not legally binding. He also objected to the secrecy of the mandate because a secret agreement on these matters was not conso-nant with papal dignity; furthermore, he saw the king's conferring of a doubtful as well as a secret mandate on Glamorgan as evidence of the king's dubious good faith and he believed that the laity's eagerness for the treaty was an indication that they themselves would do nothing to force the king to honour the Glamorgan concessions if Charles subsequently repudiated them: in this regard see Pamfili to Rinuccini, 5 Nov. (ns) 1645 (*Comment. Rinucc.*, i. 722); see also Pamfili to Scarampi, 6 Nov. (ns) 1645 (APF, Nunziatura d'Inghilterra 8, fo. 3ᵛ) which confirms that Rome also found the Glamorgan mandate inadequate.

[236] See *Comment. Rinucc.*, i. 556–7.

[237] At least five of these seven bishops, Tirry, Rothe, Dease, Walsh, and Comerford were Old English prelates of exceptionally moderate views. It is eminently possible that no Gaelic Irish bishop voted in favour: see *Comment. Rinucc.*, i. 722–3, ii. 332–3; Gilbert, *Irish Confederation*, v. 70.

[238] Glamorgan certainly believed so: see his letter to Ormond, 30 Aug. 1645 (Gilbert, *Irish Confederation*, v. 78).

[239] There was thus some difficulty in ensuring that the public treaty with Ormond contained no articles which contradicted the secret arrangement with Glamorgan. In this context see the confed-erate memorial to Rinuccini, Nov. 1645 (*Comment. Rinucc.*, ii. 48–9); specifically Ormond held out for the explicit restitution of the churches, his attitude in this regard suggests ignorance of the Glamorgan articles: see Ormond to unnamed correspondent, 17 Oct. 1645 (Bodl. Carte MS 16, fo. 46ʳ): see also ibid., fos. 36ʳ, 38ʳ⁻ᵛ, 48ʳ, 49ʳ⁻50ʳ, 57ʳ, 70ʳ, 149ʳ–151ʳ; Gilbert, *Irish Confederation*, v. 134–5, 163–4; the exact status of the Book of Common Prayer also remained a difficulty: see Confederate commissioners to Ormond, 11 Sept. 1645 (Gilbert, *Irish Confederation*, v. 80–1).

[240] Clanricard to Ormond, 26 May 1645 (Gilbert, *Irish Confederation*, iv. 261–2); Rinuccini left Italy with roughly 50,000 scudi (roughly £12,000) in pontifical subsidies. From Mazarin, from the Spanish agent, and from Antonio Barberini, however, he received an additional £6,000–7,000 which largely covered his expenditure on munitions and transport in France: see *Comment Rinucc.*, ii. 39–40, 161, 186; Aiazzi, *Nunziatura*, xv–xvi.

[241] The undated Latin text of Scarampi's arguments is in *Comment. Rinucc.*, i. 568–9.

a nuncio,[242] and had done so portraying their war as primarily in the interests of religion.[243] They had also been keen to mobilize the force of the church's excommunications to force all catholics to join the rebellion, something which was to turn awkwardly in their hands in 1646.[244] At the same time they applied to Rome for an indulgence for all catholics who joined in the rebellion.[245] The dominant faction in the Supreme Council had been rather blithe about accepting the countenance and patronage of the church. While making use of Scarampi, they had contrived to pay little attention to any unwelcome request which he made. They had also benefited for a substantial period from the rather timorous behaviour of the Irish hierarchy. When they accepted the papal nuncio into their midst, these carefree days, already shadowed by the increasingly assertive stance of the native clergy, were definitively over, something which the council was rather slow to grasp. Rinuccini's personality, background, and the diplomatic context in which he operated are outlined in the following chapter. That his arrival would precipitate changes in Ireland was close to inevitable. The nuncio's personal zeal, the fact that his instructions more or less mandated disapproval of the confederate policy of truce and negotiation,[246] and the fact that he controlled a larger sum of ready cash than was available from any other source in Ireland, all combined to make a clash between the nuncio and the confederate council very probable. Moreover, he arrived in Ireland at a moment when the fragile equilibrium which the confederate association represented was coming under increasing strain.

The original rebellion of 1641 had unleashed a wave of sectarian and social violence which had only been contained by an alliance of catholic clergy and gentry. These popular discontents and prejudices, however, had only been restrained, not eliminated, and an awareness of this may partly explain the stiffening posture of the clericalist party in 1644–5. Certainly the extreme religious preferences of elements of the populace and some of the lower clergy represented a resource which the clerical leaders could tap to bolster their opposition to the movement towards peace. What made this situation doubly destabilizing was that, by the time of Rinuccini's arrival, the Supreme Council and the negotiations with Ormond were both substantially under the direction of a group of Old English confederates who had already decided that religious concessions would have to be made in order to acquire peace. This group centred around Bellings, Muskery, Mountgarrett,

---

[242] See Ch. 3.

[243] Supreme Council to Pope, 23 Nov. 1644 (Bodl. Carte MS 64, fos. 150ʳ–151ʳ).

[244] Wadding to Barberini, Oct.(?) 1642 (Barberini Lat. MS 6483, fo. 36ʳ).

[245] By the time this arrived it may well have caused the council some embarrassment as it alarmed many of the protestants, with whom they were now busy negotiating a peace, who interpreted the indulgence as a mandate for catholics to murder those of a different religion: see the Instructions to Luke Wadding (Gilbert, *Irish Confederation*, ii. 118); and *Comment. Rinucc.*, i. 503–7.

[246] 'Instruzione' (Aiazzi, *Nunziatura*, pp. l–li).

Castlehaven, Fennell, and Browne largely consisted of individuals who had entered into rebellion with reluctance. They would probably have been far slower to have done so if Ormond had been made head of the Dublin government in 1641 rather than in 1643. Deeply alarmed at events in England, their prime objective was to aid the king in upholding his authority in both England and Ireland, thus earning his goodwill and averting the spectre of either parliamentary or radical ecclesiastical and Gaelic Irish control of Ireland. The fact that many of them were nervous about clerical designs on the former monastic property which they possessed provided an additional spur in this direction, but, even if this problem had not existed, their realization that peace with the king could only be attained by watering down their religious demands would have meant little possibility of avoiding a clash with Rinuccini. Rinuccini, for his part, had even less room for manœuvre. His instructions bound him to oppose any peace which did not grant free exercise of catholicism and which did not endow the clergy financially with an adequate and independent income.[247] Translated into the Irish context, this meant that the nuncio would oppose any peace which did not guarantee the catholic clergy the right to exercise freely an ecclesiastical jurisdiction derived from Rome, and which did not ensure the retention by the catholic clergy of property formerly belonging to the Church of Ireland. As a result, that there would be friction between the nuncio and the council concerning the Ormond peace was never really in doubt. What remained to be resolved was the degree to which both parties would be prepared to risk conflict in the pursuit of their objectives.

[247] Ibid., pp. xxxv, xlv–vi, li.

CHAPTER THREE

The Background and Formation
of the Nuncio

I

The archbishop of Fermo, GianBattista Rinuccini, finally made a rather bedraggled landfall at Kenmare in County Kerry in October 1645. To observers from an Irish perspective, the sea-tossed prelate has traditionally appeared as a classic product of the European counter-reformation, the 'tridentine bishop dispatched in mint condition from Italy' in John Bossy's elegant and economical phrase.[1] That Rinuccini carried the stamp of seventeenth-century Italian catholicism is undeniable. But like 'absolutist king', the phrase 'tridentine bishop' is a convenient shorthand to describe a complex reality. There were many many tridentine bishops, far more than absolutist kings indeed, among whom even Carlo Borromeo was only one exceptional individual. A bishop such as Rinuccini, born eight years after the archbishop of Milan's death, did not conceive of himself as a passive elaboration of a Borromeon prototype[2] but rather as another participant and shaper in a tradition of catholic reform. It is as a variation rather than a replication of the counter-reformation theme that the archbishop of Fermo can best be understood.

Rinuccini brought a rich cocktail of experience to bear upon his work as nuncio to the catholic confederates of Ireland. During his previous career, he had been at various times an outstanding student, a curialist, a jurist, an author, and a pastoral archbishop. Born in Rome of Florentine parents in 1592, he was of noble stock.[3] His father's family, although not to compare with the Pazzi or the Medici, was one of the seigniorial houses of Florence: at the time of his appointment as nuncio, his brother Tomasso was the chief gentleman of the bedchamber of the grand-duke of Tuscany.[4] His mother

---

[1] John Bossy, 'The Counter-Reformation and the People of Catholic Ireland', *Historical Studies*, 8 (1971) 170; Patrick Corish, 'Rinuccini, and the Conferates, 1645–9', in T. W. Moody, F. X. Martin, and F. J. Byrne (eds.), *A New History of Ireland*, iii, *Early Modern Ireland, 1534–1691* (Oxford, 1976), 317.

[2] Rinuccini revered Borromeo as a saint, but there is no evidence in Rinuccini's writings on episcopal duties to suggest that he modelled much of his performance as a bishop on Borromeo's specific example: see below.

[3] ASV, Processus Episcoporum Sacrae Congregationis Consistorialis 21, fos. 164, 171.

[4] *Comment. Rinucc.*, i. 590; a chapel in Santa Croce still bears the Rinuccini family name.

was Virginia Bandini, the sister of the important cardinal Ottavio Bandini, who, in addition to many other duties, sat as a member of the Roman congregation on Irish affairs during the 1620s.[5] Rinuccini's career path within the church, therefore, was that of a well-connected aristocrat.

The future nuncio's early education had been in the hands of the Jesuits in Rome. He had then studied law in the famous but declining faculty of law in the university of Bologna which had produced many of the figures who had driven forward the reform of ecclesiastical structures in post-tridentine Italy,[6] and also in Perugia, before receiving a doctorate of *Utrumque Ius* from the university of Pisa.[7] The doctorate in canon law was a classical stepping stone to a variety of important ecclesiastical careers. It is notable also that his studies in civil law were apparently exclusively in a brand of Roman law deeply penetrated and influenced by medieval developments in canon law.[8] He probably shared the common assumption that a grasp of the basis of Roman and canon law equipped a jurist to interpret adequately the legal system particular to an individual kingdom:[9] certainly, he was incensed on at least one occasion by the attempts of confederate lawyers to argue legal principles with him and bemoaned their lack of respect for anything other than common law.[10]

Rinuccini served in the Roman curia for a number of years as secretary to the Congregation of Rites,[11] the body charged with regulating liturgical uniformity in post-tridentine catholicism, where his legal qualifications could be expected to serve in the tribunal which investigated the canonization of saints.[12] He seems, however, to have devoted relatively little attention to this post.[13] Rather, most of his time was occupied as a referendary in both the

---

[5] In the 1623 papal election Bandini actually amassed the highest number of votes in the first ballot: thus Rinuccini could conceivably have become cardinal-nephew in the 1620s: see Ludvig Von Pastor (trans. Ernest Graf), *History of the Popes from the Close of the Middle Ages*, xxvii–xxx (London, 1938–40), xxviii. 11; for Bandini's influence in Rome see ASV, Pontificio. Misc., ii, 150, n. 3.

[6] Antonio García García, 'The Faculties of Law', in Hilda de Ridder-Symoens, *A History of the University in Europe* (Cambridge, 1992), 388; Antonio Ferri e Giancarlo Roversi, *Storia di Bologna* (Bologna, 1978), 228; Paolo Prodi, *Il Cardinale Gabriele Paleotti*, i (Rome, 1959), 80.

[7] See ASV, Processus Episcoporum Sacrae Congregationis Consistorialis 21, fos. 164ᵛ, 165ᵛ.

[8] See Pierre Legendre, 'Le Droit romain, modèle et langage. De la signification de l'*Utrumque Ius*', in Centre National de la Recherche Scientifique, *Études d'histoire du droit canonique dédiées à Gabriel Le Bras* (Paris, 1965), ii. 913–30; Prodi, *Paleotti*, i. 57.

[9] García, 'Faculties of Law', 393, 402.   [10] See Aiazzi, *Nunziatura*, 201–2, 391–2.

[11] ASV, Acta Vicecancellarii SRE 17, fo. 57.

[12] See Niels Krogh Rasmussen, 'Liturgy and Liturgical Arts', in John O'Malley (ed.), *Catholicism in Early Modern Europe: A Guide to Research* (Ann Arbor, Mich., 1988), 273–92; Simon Ditchfield, *Liturgy, Sanctity and History in Tridentine Italy* (Cambridge, 1995), 217–20.

[13] Rinuccini is rarely noted as present in the Decreta Liturgica of the congregation: on 24 Nov. 1625 he certainly expedited a considerable amount of business but by this time he had already been appointed archbishop of Fermo and the session may have been something of a desk-clearing exercise: see ACCS, Decreta Liturgica, 1622–6, fos. 187ʳ–191ʳ: I am grateful to the archivist of the congregation, Mons. Jaroslav Nemec, for drawing my attention to the far greater activity in the post of other secretaries such as Rinuccini's successor, Julius Benignius. It can be noted also that some of

Segnatura di Giudizio and the *Segnatura di Grazie* in Rome.[14] Rinuccini was appointed to both of these bodies in the early 1620s. He was also a *giudice civile* in the special tribunal of the cardinal vicar of Rome[15] and his involvement in these extensive legal duties presumably explains his limited activity in the Congregation of Rites. Although his university education and his administrative experience were thus concentrated in the field of law, it is clear that, as befitted a member of the family which had established the first humanistic academy in Florence,[16] Rinuccini's academic interests were not restricted to jurisprudence. He displayed a breadth of intellectual interests typical of many seventeenth-century figures of the catholic reformation, such as Bérulle, Arnauld, and Bellarmine.[17] Rinuccini combined a reverence for St Augustine with a deep interest in Aristotelian philosophy and elements of the tradition of Christian platonism also appear in his writings.[18]

He was particularly interested in history. One of the now destroyed manuscripts attributed to him in the *Biblioteca Trivulziana* concerned ecclesiastical history and he also produced a book on aspects of Greek and Roman history drawing upon Livy, Polybius, Tacitus, Plutarch, and other authors.[19] A manuscript entitled 'Compendio di Geografia' still survives in the *Trivulziana* collection which was evidently compiled before his journey to Ireland.[20] Another surviving manuscript deals with the theory and practice of logical argument,[21] while a third is a massive exploration of Aristotle's

those who testified on Rinuccini's behalf at the moment of his elevation to Fermo were apparently unaware of his position in the Congregation of Rites although they were fully aware of his legal experience: see ASV, Processus Episcoporum Sacrae Congregationis Consistorialis 21, fos. 164ᵛ–165ᵛ.

[14] See ASV, Processus Episcoporum Sacrae Congregationis Consistorialis 21, fo. 165ᵛ; the *Segnatura di Giudizio* was the highest tribunal in Rome in the normal course of events. Extraordinary cases could, however, be brought before the *Segnatura di Grazie*, which effectively functioned as the Roman Supreme Court. Three years' experience in the *Segnatura di Giudizio* was generally necessary before elevation to the *Segnatura di Grazie* but this requirement was evidently waived in Rinuccini's case: see Niccolò del Re, *La Curia Romana: Lineamenti Storico-Giuridici* (Rome, 1970), 227–34.

[15] ASV, Processus Episcoporum Sacrae Congregationis Consistorialis 21, fo. 165ʳ⁻ᵛ.

[16] Walter Rüegg, 'The Rise of Humanism', in Ridder-Symoens, *History of the University*, 451.

[17] A. D. Wright, *The Counter-Reformation: Catholic Europe and the Non-Christian World* (London, 1982), 26.

[18] Ibid.; see also H. Bremond, *Histoire littéraire du sentiment religieux en France. Depuis la fin des guerres de religion jusqu'à nos jours* (Paris, 1924–33), i. 9–13.

[19] See Varie considerazioni sulla Storia Ecclesiastica (ASCM, Biblioteca Trivulziana Cod. n. 1954); G. B. Rinuccini, *Considerazioni sopra la Storia Romana e Greca di Dionigi d'Alicarnasso, Tito Livio, Polibio, Plutarco, Tacito ecc.* (Rome, 1634?).

[20] Compendio di Geografia (ASCM, Biblioteca Trivulziana Cod. n. 1958): this is a simple, meticulous, and organized text, which deals first with the theory of Geography, then classifies geographical terms, and then briefly summarizes the physical details of various European countries, including Ireland.

[21] Libellus de recta argumentandi ratione ad quaestiones logicas intelligendas (ASCM, Biblioteca Trivulziana Cod. n. 1964); this is an exhaustively taxonomic treatise on how to construct an argument, with detailed information on the nature and application of propositions, syllogisms, etc.

work concerning the classification of the physical universe.[22] In the late 1630s also he produced *Il Cappuccino Scozzese*, a narrative close in form to a novel loosely based on the life of a Scottish friar, George Lesley.[23] Theology does not, however, seem to have figured high among his interests: Rinuccini had apparently no university experience in that subject and he consistently showed himself more interested in the practical performance of ecclesiastical duties than in theological disputation.[24]

In 1625, having been hurriedly ordained, and thus in breach of canonical requirements, Urban VIII promoted Rinuccini to succeed his deceased cousin as archbishop of Fermo in le Marche[25] and it was partly on the basis of his pastoral experience there that he was subsequently appointed as nuncio to the confederates.[26] It was an important see[27] and one where his maternal family enjoyed extensive interests. His mother's brother, Cardinal Bandini, was evidently the chief arbiter of ecclesiastical appointments in the archdiocese. Bandini himself had been archbishop there prior to becoming a cardinal. Three of Bandini's nephews, of whom Rinuccini was the last, in turn followed him as archbishops in Fermo and until his death in 1629 the cardinal continued to draw substantial revenues from the archdiocese.[28] Rinuccini's considerable personal wealth, however, probably shielded him from the worst effects of Bandini's retention of archiepiscopal revenues: certainly by the time of his nunciature in Ireland he was in a

---

[22] Quaestiones in octo libros Aristotelis de phisica (ASCM, Biblioteca Trivulziana Cod. n. 1963); this massive manuscript examines such features of Aristotelian thought as the manner in which matter takes form, the difference between creation and reproduction and the nature and origins of material bodies.

[23] Rinuccini, *Il Cappuccino Scozzese* (repr. Rome, 1863), 119. All page references to this edition. The other version consulted in the course of research, *Il Cappuccino Scozzese* (In Roma per il moneta, 1645), differs only in one section from this edition. Martino Capucci, 'Caratteri e Fortune di un cappuccino scozzese', *Studi Secenteschi*, 20 (1979), 43–4 n. 2 affirms the existence of at least twenty-six seventeenth-century editions of this immensely popular text.

[24] Rinuccini's extant writings on episcopal duties are the subject of a detailed analysis in this chapter: in passing it may be noted that one of his destroyed manuscripts was entitled 'Selva di varii pensieri disposti per materia ed estratti della sacra Scritture e dai Ss. Padri per tesserne sermoni e prediche' (ASCM, Biblioteca Trivulziana Cod. n. 1979).

[25] ASV, Acta Vicecancellari 17, fos. 57–9.

[26] See my article 'Vatican Diplomacy and the Mission of Rinuccini to Ireland', *Archivium Hibernicum*, 48 (1993), 81.

[27] The population of the city was about 10,000, divided into eight urban parishes; the archbishop had four suffragans and there were four collegiate churches. In financial terms the see yielded about 7,000 scudi (about £1,500) per annum. There were 21 clerics with independent income in the cathedral chapter, three convents of nuns, and twelve houses of regular clergy: see ASV, Processus Episcoporum Sacrae Congregationis Consistorialis 21, fos. 166ʳ–171ᵛ; ASV, Lettere di Vescovi e Principi 29, fo. 32ᵛ.

[28] *De Ecclesia Firmana eiusque Episcopis et Archepiscopis Commentarius* (Fermo, 1783), 284–9; of the 7,000 scudi which the see rendered per annum, 4,000 went to Bandini: see ASV, Processus Episcoporum Sacrae Congregationis Consistorialis 21, fo. 171; see also ASV, Acta Miscellanea 97, fo. 677.

position to supplement his salary from the pope with his own personal fortune.[29]

The formidable mass of documentation relating to his visitation in the diocese stands witness to the devotion with which Rinuccini engaged in pastoral work in Fermo, although it would appear that he held only two provincial synods during his time as archbishop.[30] His devotion to his cathedral church was also strong enough to resist the temptation to transfer to the more prestigious archiepiscopal see of Florence in 1631.[31] This was offered to him by the grand duke of Tuscany with the full consent of the pope. Rinuccini was urged to accept the position by the cardinal-nephew, Francesco Barberini, who dwelt on the political advantages to be gained by the installation of a loyal curialist in such an important see. None the less, Rinuccini repeatedly refused to be swayed by the cardinal's representations, asserting in his final answer that the interests of his soul must take precedence over the interests of the world.[32]

The archbishop of Fermo was not just a conscientious pastor: he also wrote at length on the subject of a bishop's duties. His work on this subject is of immense value in clarifying the attitudes, beliefs, and theories which Rinuccini brought to bear on his role as an ecclesiastical administrator and later as nuncio to the catholic confederates. In this respect, the two most useful works are an unpublished treatise extant in the archiepiscopal archive in Fermo entitled 'Instruttione pratica per la cura episcopale' and the large two-volume published work called *Della Dignita et Offitio dei Vescovi*.[33] In the preface to the 'Instruttione pratica' the author disclaimed the intention of discussing any topic other than those which his personal experience had taught him to consider as relevant. Consequently, it provides an insight into how the archbishop integrated his conception of the role and duties of a prelate with a practical programme for their performance. It was probably written around 1632. The much longer *Della Dignita* complements rather

[29] He was to spend approximately £4,000 of his own fortune during the course of his mission in Ireland. This sum was roughly equivalent to the amount paid to him over the four years from the Vatican treasury for his personal maintenance and that of the twenty or so members of his household: see Aiazzi, *Nunziatura*, pp. ix–xvii.

[30] As is evident from the decrees of the synod of 1650: see *Decreta Synodi Secundae Dioec. Firmanae* (Fermo, 1650).

[31] Concern to protect the see from the savage effects of papal justice, in the aftermath of a rebellion in Fermo during 1648, may also have been one of Rinuccini's motives for eventually abandoning the Irish mission in 1649: in this regard see the reports from Imperiale to Pancirolo July–Nov. (ns) 1648 (ASV, Lettere di Vescovi e Prelati 29, fos. 25ᵛ, 32ᵛ, 33ᵛ, 35ʳ⁻ᵛ, 136ʳ⁻ᵛ, 137ʳ⁻ᵛ) and Rinuccini to Pope Innocent, 24 Jan. 1649 (Aiazzi, *Nunziatura*, 358).

[32] Rinuccini to Barberini, Aug. (?)1631 (Archivio Arcivescovile di Fermo, iii C/11).

[33] 'Instruttione pratica per la cura episcopale di Monsignor Gio. Battista Rinuccini, Arcivescovo di Fermo' (AAF, iii C/13): the manuscript is paginated somewhat confusedly, any pagination referred to is my own based on the logical sequence of page to page; *Della Dignita et Offitio dei Vescovi: Discorsi Quaranta di Monsignor Gio. Battista Rinuccini, Arcivescovo e Prencipe di Fermo* (Rome, 1651).

than incorporates the unpublished treatise. It is a more theoretical work, divided into forty 'discorsi' of unequal length and is based to a much lesser extent on the author's personal experience in Fermo. The bulk of the *Della Dignita* was probably written in 1639 but it was published only after Rinuccini's return from Ireland, in 1651.[34] Its object was to attack the common concept of the importance of secular pomp and power which, the author believed, occluded the true character of the church and thus hampered it in disseminating its message in the world. To accomplish this, he chose to concentrate on the nature, importance, and role of what he, in common with most of his contemporaries, considered to be the key figure in the ecclesiastical hierarchy, the pastoral bishop.[35]

The nature of the episcopal institution had been debated in the twenty-third and later sessions of the council of Trent but had proved a thorny problem. A precise formulation of the nature of episcopal authority carried a risk of limiting the rights of the papacy. Eventually, an emphasis on the bishop as pastor was to emerge as one of the pre-eminent features of Trent but curial opposition successfully prevented the formulation of a solid doctrinal foundation for episcopal authority.[36] In the wake of the council, the need for a stronger definition of the episcopal role inspired a series of treatises on the subject. Among the most notable of these was Gabriele Paleotti's *Archiepiscopale Bononiense sive de Bononiensis Ecclesiae administratione*, published in Rome in 1594, which passed over much of the same ground that Rinuccini was to investigate fifty years later.[37] Whether the archbishop of Fermo had read any of these texts, however, is open to question. A strong sense of his own originality informs his writing on this subject which reflects perhaps the shifting focus of the post-tridentine Italian church. It has been argued that by the middle decades of the seventeenth century energetic analysis of the episcopal role was increasingly superseded by a reliance on precepts derived from curial interpretations of tridentine decrees and the careers of figures such as Borromeo.[38] *Della Dignita*, therefore, seems to represent another example of Rinuccini's unease with the fossilization of norms derived from Trent.

The archbishop, however, took pains not to ruffle feathers in the curia. He subscribed wholeheartedly to the pre-eminent authority and personal infallibility of the pope[39] and was extremely careful to voice no open criticism of

---

[34] My surmise here is based on internal evidence.   [35] *Della Dignita*, i, 'Ai lettori'.

[36] G. Alberigo, 'The Council of Trent', in O'Malley, *Catholicism in Early Modern Europe*, 213–21; id., *Lo sviluppo della dottrina sui poteri nella Chiesa universale. Momenti essenziali tra il XVI e il XIX secolo* (Rome, 1964), esp. ch. 1; Wright, *The Counter-Reformation*, 12; Jean Delumeau, *Catholicism between Luther and Voltaire* (London, 1977), 15.

[37] Prodi, *Paleotti*, ii (Rome, 1967), 7–13, 18, 26, 28.   [38] Ibid., ii. 28.

[39] On the important question of the relationship between conciliar and papal authority within the church, he accepted that a council was unable to dictate to the pope, or proclaim any decision without the pope's consent. He also stressed that the pope was the sole authority capable of convening a general council of the church: *Della Dignita*, ii. 247, 254–7.

the papacy, even though one of his basic contentions was that Christianity had suffered a corruption of its earlier purity. In the *Della Dignita,* for instance, while unhappy with the retention of benefices by absentee clergy who enjoyed the revenues while their duties were performed by a proxy, he was keen to emphasize that he questioned neither the pope's rights nor his judgement in relaxing ecclesiastical discipline in such cases.[40] It seems certain that his often expressed reverence for the authority of the Roman pontiff was sincere. For Rinuccini, the truths of catholicism were divinely preserved in Rome and his belief that only proximity to Rome could keep ecclesiastical institutions vigorous was subsequently confirmed by his experiences in Ireland.[41]

Having safely exalted the claims of the papacy, Rinuccini freed himself to pursue his chosen subject, even into those areas where the council of Trent had been unwilling to make definitive statements, such as the status of bishops in the eyes of God.[42] Rinuccini's work is deeply imbued with tridentine influence: indeed the 'Instruttione pratica' is essentially a manual for the implementation of a tridentine pastor's tasks, with regard to visitation, preaching, synodal legislation, etc. Nevertheless, in the *Della Dignita* and the 'Instruttione', his inspiration concerning the episcopacy owed as much to his conception of the bishops of the early Christian church as to Trent. The archbishop was convinced that a 'modern gloom had cheapened the splendour of the primitive light' of the church. There was a great need, he believed, for 'senescent Christianity' to look to its past for inspiration and, in particular, for its bishops to do so.[43] In his work, there are strikingly few references to any of the great episcopal champions of post-conciliar Italian reform such as Carlo Borromeo, Gabriele Paleotti in Bologna, or the bishop of Brescia, Domenico Bollini.[44] Borromeo is mentioned just once in the 'Instruttione pratica' when his system of parish records is warmly approved and he is the protagonist of a single anecdote in the *Della Dignita.*[45] In fact, Rinuccini like the first generation of post-conciliar reformers sought to model his behaviour on the bishops of the ancient church.[46] He displays far more interest in Borromeo's distant predecessor in the see of Milan, St Ambrose, than in Borromeo himself. St Augustine is also mentioned frequently but, above all, it is Pope Gregory the Great (590–604) whom

---

[40] *Della Dignita,* i. 162–5. [41] Ibid., ii. 267, 274, 286; i,'Alla Santita', 3–4.

[42] Alberigo, 'Council of Trent', 213–21; *Della Dignita,* i. 25–30.

[43] 'Il fosco moderno habbia avvilito i splendori della luce primitiva' (*Della Dignita,* ii. 127); 'Cristanesmo invecchiato' (ibid., 137).

[44] See Alberigo 'Studi e problemi relativi all'applicazione del Concilio di Trento', *Rivista Storica Italiana,* 70 (1958), *passim;* Prodi, 'S. Carlo Borromeo e il cardinale Gabriele Paleotti: due vescovi della riforma cattolica', *Critica Storica,* 3 (1964), 135–51.

[45] 'Instruttione pratica', 30; *Della Dignita,* ii. 71; there is also an approving reference in Rinuccini's 'Libellus de recta argumendandi ratione ad quaestiones logicas intelligendas' (ASCM, Biblioteca Trivulziana Cod. n. 1964, p. 19).

[46] Prodi, *Paleotti,* ii. 128–9.

Rinuccini portrays as the 'pastor of pastors without peer in vigilance and solicitude for souls'.[47] In this regard, Rinuccini was as much within the tradition of twelfth-century notions of episcopal duty as that of Trent.[48]

Nor was he reluctant to express definite opinions about certain aspects of tridentine practice. Although Trent ordained, in the interests of saving expense, that a bishop should conduct his diocesan visitations as quickly as possible, Rinuccini argued that it was difficult to visit properly at speed. He suggested that bishops pay for an extra number of days in a parish out of their own revenues. He was also somewhat dubious about the tridentine emphasis on synods, arguing that they should be run off swiftly with no more than thirty decrees.[49] Far from believing that Trent had closed the book on church reorganization, Rinuccini even suggested the need for a new general council to sort out the provision of adequate clergy to poor benefices.[50]

A textured subtlety can thus be detected in Rinuccini's relationship with the tridentine legacy, the fruit of careful thought and experiment. The archbishop was not always so questioning of his intellectual heritage, however. His view of the world was undeniably Italocentric.[51] Like those who gave him his instructions in 1645, it was natural for him to divide the world into Italians and suspicious 'ultramontani'. One of the pre-eminent indices of Italian superiority was, of course, that the peninsula represented the centre of the catholic world: indeed in his writings protestantism seems almost ontologically non-Italian, something which could only threaten by importation from abroad.[52]

By the time Rinuccini came to operate as a pastor in Fermo, this of course was substantially true. The only resident non-catholics in his own archdiocese were probably Jews and gypsies.[53] It is interesting to note the possibility

[47] 'San Gregorio, Pastor de i Pastori, non hebbe mai pari nella vigilanza, e sollecitudine delle anime' (*Della Dignita*, i. 126).

[48] In the twelfth century, as a theology of the episcopate developed, Gregory the Great was taken as the model for constructing the role and requirements of a bishop: see Jean Gaudemet, 'Patristique et Pastorale: La Contribution de Grégorie le Grand au "Miroir de l'Evêque" dans le décret de Gratian', in Centre National de la Recherche Scientifique, *Études d'histoire du droit canonique dédiées à Gabriel Le Bras* (Paris, 1965), i. 129.

[49] 'Instruttione pratica', 20, 36; in this regard Rinuccini's flouting of tridentine orthodoxy concerning the regularity of synods seems to have been common elsewhere in seventeenth-century Italy: see Prodi, *Paleotti*, ii. 153.

[50] 'Instruttione pratica', 18–19.

[51] One can note his exaltation of Italy in his 'Compendio di Geografia' (ASCM, Biblioteca Trivulziana Cod. n. 1958).

[52] 'Tolga da i liti d'Italia la providenza del Cielo, che portata dalle navigationi heretiche una simile perfidia infetti il gregge, & oscuri la luce degl'intelletti Cattolici' (*Della Dignita*, ii. 218. See also ibid., 100).

[53] Restrictions concerning the freedom of movement of Jews and their right to sell goods in towns had been a feature of the synodal legislation of Archbishop Dini, Rinuccini's predecessor and first cousin, in 1623. Rinuccini himself, in a synod in 1650, prohibited any of his priests from saying mass for the benefit of 'Ungarini', by which term he probably meant gypsies: see *De Ecclesia Firmana*, 285–6; *Decreta Synodi Secundae Dioec. Firmanae* (Fermo, 1650), 11.

that Rinuccini had more direct contact with muslims than with protestants during his career there.[54] But what is striking about his writings is the casually dismissive nature of his attitude towards protestantism. It is as if the reformation had *never* threatened Italian catholicism, the implication appearing to be that the catholic centre was not vulnerable to what had been able to corrupt the periphery. It is a pervasive impression of reading his work that Rinuccini found it difficult to conceptualize protestantism as something qualitatively different from the popular superstition or ignorance against which he and his contemporaries struggled to assert themselves in Italy.[55] There is no sense that he saw protestantism as posing an intellectual challenge going beyond the need for merely administrative action, possibly because it is doubtful if he had ever read a single work by a protestant author.[56]

The extent to which Rinuccini simply ignores contemporary protestantism in *Della Dignita* is remarkable. Far more attention is paid to a variety of antique heresies and the schism from Rome of the Greek orthodox church than to the reformation. Rinuccini's personal friendship with the Scottish Capuchin, George Lesley, did inspire a certain interest in the reformation in Britain, or more precisely in the catholic suffering which it had caused. Yet it is interesting that a tendency to confuse the various strands of British protestantism occurs even in the version of *Il Cappuccino Scozzese* which Rinuccini revised following his return from Ireland.[57]

In this regard, the words in that text which Giorgio addresses to his presbyterian mother following his conversion are of interest. They can effectively be read as an accurate reflection of Rinuccini's own religious beliefs and his view of the relationship between catholicism and heresy:

Beloved mother, persuade yourself that it was not juvenile inconsiderateness, nor disorderly affection for friends, nor volubility of thought which led me to abandon your religion. The irresistible force of the reasons which stood in favour of catholicism above all faiths; an absolute conviction, fruit of prolonged study, that the catholic faith is truly divine in its every teaching; that where God is there is truth; that God being one, there should be only one religion or cult of him; that God, most

---

[54] There are references to encounters with Turks and even Persians in the *Della Dignita*, i. 64, 257–8.

[55] Carlo Ginzburg, 'Folklore, Magia e Religione nelle Campagne Italiane', in Carla Russo (ed.), *Società Chiesa e vita religiosa nell'Ancien Regime* (Naples, 1976), 434–8.

[56] Such an attitude was not uncommon in the Italian peninsula where, it has been argued persuasively, pre-reformation attitudes towards religious difference survived into the seventeenth century. As a result Italians were less influenced by the modulation in the idea of heresy towards a *de facto* acceptance of the existence of other confessions and churches which occurred in other parts of Europe. See Gaetano Catalano and Federico Martino (eds.), *Potestà civile e autorità spirituale in Italia nei secoli della riforma e controriforma* (Milan, 1984), 9; A. Dupront, 'Réflexions sur l'hérésie moderne', in *Hérésies et sociétés dans l'Europe préindustrielle* (Paris, 1968), 291; see also Prodi, *Paleotti*, ii. 87.

[57] Rinuccini, *Il Cappuccino Scozzese*, 119.

perfect being, cannot be indifferent that his rational creatures should follow a false rather than a true belief; that he would not have assumed human nature to make himself our lord if he had been content with any cult; here you have, mother, what was my guide in my resolutions.[58]

Conversion is simply an acceptance of the irresistible force of the catholic case. Particularly noteworthy here is the stress on the *rationality* of catholic belief and the argument that human beings are God's *rational* creatures. These are themes which echo throughout Rinuccini's writings. There is a striking identification of the spiritual with the intellectual in *Della Dignita*.[59] At times Rinuccini uses 'soul' and 'intellect' as to all intents and purposes interchangeable terms:

If the human compound has the form of a house, the steward-bishop's objective is to ensure that the servant emotions obey the rule of reason, that the soul holds a non-despotic but conjugal dominion over the body.[60]

He constantly emphasizes that the soul is rational whereas human passions are ignorant and blind and the basis of the almost incurable depravity of humanity. The danger of the passions is that they can enslave and blind the intellect. In this way, it is the passions which divide human beings from God and which can make the soul repugnant to its creator.[61] Not surprisingly, highly metaphysical images of God run through Rinuccini's writings: God is truth, God is eternal, God is non-corporeal. Generally God is the father rather than the son and the question of the passion of Christ and Christ's incarnation is largely pushed to the background.[62]

Rinuccini's attitude to the body was at one with his rather cool notion of the rational. He himself was not a particularly ascetic individual. The archbishop admitted to not wearing a hair shirt; he did not eat only vegetables nor drink only water. (He also brought his own bed with him to Ireland.)

---

[58] 'Diletta Madre, Persuadetevi che non giovanile inconsideratezza, non affetto disordinato agli amici, non volubilità di pensiere m'indussero ad abbandonare la vostra religione. La forza irresistibile delle ragioni che stanno a favore del Cattolicismo sovr'ogni credenza; un assoluto convincimento, frutto di prolungato studio, che la fede cattolica è veramente divina in ogni suo insegnamento; che dove è Dio, ivi è la verità; che uno essendo Iddio, una sola debb'essere la religione, o il culto di Lui; che Dio, Ente perfettissimo, non può essere indifferente che le sue creature ragionevoli seguano una falsa piuttosto che una vera credenza: che non avrebbe assunta l'umana natura per farsi nostro maestro ov'egli fosse pago di un culto qualunque; eccovi o madre mia, ciò che mi fu guida nelle mie risoluzioni.' (ibid., 31–2).

[59] In this he echoes certain positions of Blaise Pascal: see for instance Léon Brunschigg (ed.), *Pensées* (Librairie générale française, 1972), 34; there are echoes also of François de Sales: see Bremond, *Histoire littéraire*, i. 124, vii. 56–7 but Rinuccini's distinctions are cruder than those of either French writer.

[60] 'Se il composto humano hà forma d'una casa il Vescovo Economo hà per fine di fare, che i sentimenti schiavi obbedischino all'impero del ragione, che l'anima tenga dominio sopra il corpo non despotico, ma coniugale' (*Della Dignita*, i. 9): the matrimonial image here is of course also of interest.

[61] Ibid., i. 67, 137, ii. 88, 93.   [62] Although not entirely so: see below.

Unlike Borromeo he does not appear to have flagellated himself although he was not opposed to the practice by others. He enjoyed fishing and hunting birds and was prepared to consider that laughter and singing were acceptable in the recreation of a cleric. He went so far as to quote Plato concerning the relationship between virtue and enjoyment, and agreed that it was impossible for vice to cause pleasure.[63] In *Della Dignita,* he even suggested that angels envied human beings their bodies since exposure to sensual temptation gave mortal creatures the possibility of transcending the limits of their flesh.[64]

Rather than perceiving the human body as inherently and repellently sinful, Rinuccini saw the body as the site and potential instrument in and by which sin could blemish the soul. His concept of the mortification of the flesh was not so much punitive as preventive: it was necessary to discipline the body so that the soul would not be engulfed by its appetites and so that it would accept the dominion of the soul. The mortification of the body in this life was promised its reward after death, and the archbishop indeed referred to this process in explicitly commercial terms. In another striking metaphor, which emphasizes the close patterning between his conceptions of the personal and the social, he suggested that the relationship of the body and the soul is that between a lord and a servant, in which the body should offer deference and service as a client in the expectation of patronage and reward.[65]

Yet while acknowledging the rather pallid rationalism which informed Rinuccini's notion of spiritual discipline, it is important to recognize the existence of a more excitable streak in the archbishop of Fermo's catholicism. *Il Cappuccino Scozzese*, for instance, is a highly romantic book. One particularly interesting passage describes the ecstasy experienced by an evangelist in his conversions. Of this joy the author says:

They know it, they understand it, they taste it only the generous and truly humanitarian souls of those heroes who, holding glory, greatness and renown which proceeds from the world cheap and spurned beneath their feet, tire themselves, wear themselves out, consume themselves, expose themselves to die from sufferings, tortures, rendings, pestilence, martyrdoms, for the flame of the love of God, for their neighbours, to free those unfortunate beings of the human family which the infernal prisons hold enthralled and as slaves.[66]

---

[63] *Della Dignita,* i. 122.   [64] Ibid., 29; see also Alberigo, 'Council of Trent', 213–21.
[65] *Della Dignita,* i. 10.
[66] 'Lo conoscono, l'intendono, lo gustano soltanto le anime generose e veramente umanitarie di quegli eroi che avendo a vile, e posti sotto i piedi gli onori, la gloria, la grandezza, la rinomanza che procedono dal mondo, s'affaticano, si logorano, si consumano, espongonsi a morire di patimenti, di strazii, dilaniati, pesti, martoriati, per fiamma di carità verso Dio, verso il prossimo, per riscattare, quegli infelici dell' umana famiglia, cui le infernali ritorte avvinti si tengono e schiavi' (*Il Cappuccino Scozzese,* 125).

Rinuccini was temperamentally attracted to the notion of a martyr's death. Part of the appeal of the Irish mission in 1645 was probably its sheer exoticism, which stimulated the excitable dimension of a personality that seems to have found little expression in his own idealization of cool rationalism and administrative work The adventure of travelling with great danger and difficulty to what he termed 'the most extreme confines of the Christian world' undoubtedly made a huge impression on the nuncio, who prided himself on having penetrated further west than Julius Caesar and of being, he believed, the first papal delegate since St Patrick to come to the island.[67] In this Rinuccini reflected a not uncommon pattern in counter-reformation spirituality which frequently found greatest scope for the expression of religious ardour in missionary activity outside the heartland of catholic Europe.[68]

Rinuccini's conflation of the rational and the spiritual was also tempered by his stress on the importance of faith. Despite the strong identification of the soul with the intellect noted above, he believed that human rationality was imperfect and that on certain matters, therefore, it should submit itself to faith in divinely revealed truth.[69] The mysteries of providence were, he argued, simply too sublime for human comprehension. He thought rationality at its most dangerous when it disbelieved in its own feebleness because this was the road that led to heresy: to arrive at 'the cognition of heaven' it was necessary to put out 'the torch of natural reason'. Rationality, he emphasized, should stand aside while 'holy faith, the worthy daughter of the omnipotence of God' was exalted.[70]

Faith in an afterlife, in his opinion, was the vital component which set Christianity above and beyond those heathen philosophies which sought to organize existence for the attainment of secular ends such as peace, harmony, and order. Even the highest manifestations of pagan thought, such as the idea of the cultivation of virtue for the sake of its innate beauty, were, he declared, orientated towards the things of this world. Consequently they could never comprehend a notion of Christian perfection based on the promise of a transfigured afterlife.[71]

This hierarchicization of the afterlife above life in the world had important consequences for Rinuccini's vision of the role of the bishop within human society. In simple terms, he believed that no human activity was as important

[67] AAF, iii C/10; 'in extremis orbis christiani finibus' (*Comment. Rinucc.*, ii. 248).

[68] See for example, Natalie Zemon Davis, *Women on the Margins: Three Seventeenth-century Lives* (Cambridge and London, 1995), 63–139.

[69] Again one can note a strong similarity to Pascal and de Sales in this position: see for example Brunschigg, *Pensées*, 131–3; Bremond, *Histoire littéraire*, vii. 56–7.

[70] 'Questa piccola fiàccola della ragion naturale, se vuoi arrivare alle cognitioni del Cielo, sei tu medesimo forzato ad occultarla, & estingerla' and 'Stiansi dunque da banda le ratiocinationi humane, e esaltiamo la fede' (*Della Dignita*, ii. 91); there was arguably a sleeping contradiction here in his insistence both on the inherent rationality of catholic belief and the fear that reason could lead to heresy if not controlled by faith.

[71] Ibid., i. 9–11.

as that of the bishop. It was the bishop, he declared, who was responsible for the 'reform of the souls entrusted to him to send them to paradise'.[72] That the bishop should be free to carry out this activity was therefore of prime importance. Inevitably, this belief had profound implications for his concept of political order.

Rinuccini was very ready to accept that temporal rulers were 'raised by god to lordship' and that the 'dominion of princes was a necessary provision of human kind'.[73] Indeed, his hierarchical visualization of intellect and emotion was evidently patterned on his notion of familial and political authority.[74] The form of temporal authority which Rinuccini most favoured was monarchy, particularly if this involved a religious consecration of the king and in this he was well within the mainstream catholic tradition of his day. It is not difficult to suggest that the archbishop was alert to the mutual compatibility of monarchy and early modern catholicism which was to emerge as the basis of the *ancien régime* in France and southern Europe.[75] He quoted Aristotle approvingly on the notion that some were born to rule and some to be ruled. More importantly, he felt it important that the temporal governments of earth should resemble that of heaven.[76] While in Ireland during the 1640s he was considerably anxious about the threat to both monarchy and catholicism from what he identified as a hydra of protestant democracy in Holland, England, and among the Huguenots in France.[77]

Rinuccini wished that princes, since their authority also originated from God, would see themselves as pastors, and indeed servants, to their people. Nevertheless, he was convinced that secular rulers had no right to dominate the ecclesiastical authority or to threaten the immunities of the church.[78] He interpreted the savageries of the Thirty Years War as a possible punishment for the world's lack of respect for papal dignity and the priesthood. In

---

[72] 'Il fine del vescovo è la riforma dell'anime à lui soggette per inviarle al Paradiso' (ibid., 1).

[73] 'Sollevati da Dio al dominio' (ibid., 39); 'un provedimento necessario del genere humano' (ibid., 190).

[74] In *Della Dignita* Rinuccini paralleled the soul with the father and the political legislator 'who must impose the brake of laws and the fear of abused liberty': 'il legislatore, che hà da imporre il freno delle leggi, & il timore dell'abusata libertà'; the emotions on the other hand were given the role of children and the common people (ibid., i. 9). The manner in which the new absolutisms of the seventeenth century benefited from this particular paradigm of order has been noted in the past. It has been suggested that there was a crucial link between 'the repression of the lower social stratum and that of the lower bodily stratum' and that the domination of ego and superego over id was 'the desired psychological equivalent and support of the domination of the reinforced patriarchal authority' of the seventeenth century: see A. Mitzman 'The Civilizing Offensive: Mentalities, High Culture and Individual Psyches', *Journal of Social History*, 20 (1987), 667, 673; see also G. Snyder, *La Pédagogie en France au xvii et xviii siècles* (Paris, 1965) and Bryan S. Turner, *The Body and Society: Explorations in Social Theory* (Oxford, 1984), 2–3.

[75] With regard to the reinforcement of social hierarchy through attendance at religious ceremonies see Gabriel Le Bras, 'La Pratica Religiosa nelle Campagne Francesi', in Russo, *Società Chiesa e vita religiosa*, 195–6; see also Carlo Ginzburg, 'Folklore, Magia e Religione', ibid., 441–2.

[76] *Della Dignita*, i. 38–9. [77] *Comment. Rinucc.*, i. 658.

[78] *Della Dignita*, i. 42, 50.

circumstances of contumacy by the secular authority, the archbishop endorsed the use of ecclesiastical sanctions, citing among other historical examples that of St Ambrose and the emperor Theodosius I.[79]

Prior to becoming nuncio Rinuccini was evidently reluctant to focus on the possibility that in his own era ecclesiastical authority might be forced to exert itself against catholic temporal powers. He was happy to praise the contemporary catholic rulers of Europe for their unprecedented loyalty to the catholic faith and their respect for supernatural power. As might be expected, he gave pride of place to the Holy Roman Emperor, but Louis XIII of France was referred to approvingly for his reduction of Huguenot fortresses: the kings of Spain, Poland, and the rulers of a long list of Italian states were praised as well.[80] Nevertheless, his belief in a prelate's right and duty to oppose secular authority in God's interests was firm enough to act as the basis for action, as events in Ireland were to demonstrate.

Rinuccini also saw a need for bishops to influence the formulation of laws and the training of lawyers. The archbishop had a wide personal experience of both secular and clerical cases in Roman courts and this had rendered him highly sceptical about both secular law and the probity of lawyers. What evil deeds had once been performed by tyranny were in his own time, he believed, more often accomplished under the mantle of law. He was very conscious that skilled lawyers could manipulate courts to their own advantage, in particular to facilitate the oppression of weaker members of society, such as widows and orphans. 'Glossed texts' and 'interpretations of volumes' could be 'instruments of rapacity', he declared in the *Della Dignita*.[81] He exhorted bishops to oppose what he called 'the hydra of legal monstrosity' in favour of the poor.[82] His theoretical position on the law was clear:

Laws are the same as God because they are not good if not confirmed and animated by right [*ragione*] which eminently one finds in the divinity. And to judge rightly so that nothing human interposes itself is the same as to have recourse to God . . . the law by force of justice can in no way be discordant from God.[83]

---

[79] Ibid., 49–50, 193.

[80] Among these last, Rinuccini inserted a special laudificatory reference to the grand duke of his native Tuscany: ibid., 193–5.

[81] Ibid., ii. 186–7.   [82] 'Idra di monstruosità legali' (ibid., 185).

[83] 'Le leggi sono l'istesso che Dio, perché non son buone, se non confirmate, & animate dalla ragione, la quale eminentemente si trova nella Divinità. Et il giudicar rettamente senza che niente di humano vi frapponga, è l'istesso che ricorrere à Dio . . . la legge . . . per vigore del giusto in nessuna maniera può esser discordante da Dio' (ibid., ii. 185–6); Rinuccini was by no means exceptional in holding this view, the idea that a sin could not be legal had been a basis of north Italian law since the twelfth century: see Pietro Vaccari, 'La storia del diritto nell'Italia settentrionale: Diritto romano e diritto canonio', *Études d'histoire du droit cononique*, ii. 1004; echoes of such a position, particularly concerning distrust of lawyers, were common in other early modern societies: see Herbert Rowen, 'Kingship and Republicanism in the Seventeenth Century: Some Reconsiderations', in C. H. Carter (ed.), *From the Renaissance to the Counter-Reformation: Essays in Honour of Garrett Mattingly* (London, 1966), 424; James Sharpe, 'The People and the Law', in Barry Reay (ed.), *Popular Culture in Seventeenth-century England* (London, 1988), 258–9.

Given the nature of his opinions in this regard it is hardly surprising that Rinuccini would later pay scant attention to the arguments of confederate lawyers concerning constitutional and legal precedents in Ireland when they came into conflict with his belief concerning what was due to God. He also believed it vital that bishops should exercise a legal jurisdiction in matters pertaining to God and his determination to establish an ecclesiastical tribunal in Ireland was a further source of tension with Irish common lawyers. Not only did bishops need to exercise jurisdiction over their clergy but they needed also to hold a 'brake on the inconstant liberty of human discourses' by virtue of a tribunal to investigate heretical opinions.[84] This was the most sublime of pastoral tasks because in all other things the bishop's objective was the salvation of human beings whereas in this his goal was the vindication of the honour and dignity of God. Because God was supreme truth, the archbishop considered it an appalling desecration to believe falsely of him. The liberty to believe, he asserted, was not the liberty to err.[85] Rinuccini, therefore, logically believed that protestants had no right to their sacrilegious beliefs. What was to shock him profoundly in Ireland was the idea that catholics could collaborate in the insult to God by permitting public protestant worship when it was within their compass to prevent it. This attitude was responsible for the efforts he made in Limerick in 1645 and 1646 to suppress public protestant ceremonies.[86]

Personal experience had taught Rinuccini that in times of calamity the people were particularly prone to allow their opinions on religion to mutate. In Della Dignita he cited the example of the proliferation of superstitious, by which he meant non-hierarchically approved, practices in Rome during the plague. Rinuccini's response was to demand unyielding orthodoxy. How, he asked, could one think to oppose heresy if there were wars over concepts and even inflections of words and syllables?[87] Rinuccini's determination never to yield an inch over matters of religious orthodoxy was intimately linked to his conception of the church and its history and mode of growth. It would be a grave mistake to assume that the archbishop was never disposed to negotiate or to accommodate the wishes of others. It was only on certain points that

---

[84] 'Il tener a freno la libertà vagante degli humani discorsi' (Della Dignita, ii. 93); in this regard see the discussion of the Mediterranean tradition of inquisition and censorship in E. William Monter, Ritual, Myth and Magic in Early Modern Europe (Brighton, 1983), 46–72.

[85] Della Dignita, ii. 92–7.

[86] The city of Limerick had been tardy in joining the confederates but finally did so in 1645. None the less, protestant services continued to be held in Limerick in a former Augustinian friary for the quite sizeable protestant community in the city. The nuncio regarded this situation as a scandal and exerted his influence to bring it to an end. Following the fall of Bunratty in 1646, his wish was granted and the friary was reconsecrated for catholic worship. The nuncio turned the occasion into a triumphal display of catholicism by publicly celebrating the first mass there himself, to what he described as a vast congregation: see Comment. Rinucc., ii. 272–3.

[87] Della Dignita, ii. 97–100.

he believed a bishop must never concede anything and demand everything. In the *Della Dignita* he suggested that:

everything which relates to the satisfaction of subjects and to their innocent gratification must find the pastor suavely yielding; but contrarily what regards the honouring of God and is directly related to the jurisdiction of heaven must find him constantly inflexible.[88]

He echoed this in his summary of the principles of ecclesiastical government: 'In indifferent matters or in things relating to the profane (the bishop is) indulgent to the popular imbecility; but in sacred matters and what regards heaven's interest, constant and fixed against whatever resistance.'[89] In another passage, rich with implications for his conduct in Ireland, he declared: 'Secular cunning with frequent modifications of justice seeks to unite the interests of earth to those of Heaven, and not wishing to sustain the loss of either, sees at the end that the world has not been gained and that God has most certainly been lost.'[90] He illustrated this point with reference to a variety of heresies in the early church, such as the heresy of images, acacianism, nestorianism, and eutychianism. In particular he emphasized how the dogma of monothelitism, which at first glance had seemed to offer a *via media* for reconciling differences about the divine and human natures of Christ, opened the way to disaster: 'The compromise, which was believed celestial, became frightening and deadly heresy, and the peace introduced through the temporizing of a most false article was the most pestilent war that the church has ever known.'[91]

Rinuccini's study of the early history of Christianity had also confirmed him in the belief that the growth and health of the church were governed by principles directly contrary to those which held sway in the growth of secular institutions. He believed that God would always provide for the church and argued that peace and the 'enjoyment of apparent tranquillity' was actually an obstacle to its growth and that: 'malevolence, the jeering whistles of the people, stonings, deaths, the perils of flight, ambushes and the threats of princes were the means which spread this celestial empire.'[92] In view of this

---

[88] 'Tutto quello, che spetto alla sodisfattione de i sudditi, e quanto à loro ad una compiacenza innocente, deve trovare il custode soavemente pieghevole; mà per l'opposito quanto risguarda l'honoranza di Dio, e di diretto la giurisdittione del Cielo, hà da trovarlo constantamente inflessibile' (ibid., i. 73).

[89] 'Nelle materie indifferenti, ò profane senso indulgente all'imbecillità popolari, mà nelle sacre, e che risguardano il Cielo constante, e fermo à qualsi sia resistenza' (ibid., 77).

[90] 'L'accortezza del secolo con frequentii moderationi del giusto cerca d'unire al Cielo gl'interressi della Terra, e non sostenendo di perdere alcuna delle parti vede alla fine, che non s'è guadagnato il Mondo, e s'è perduto sicurissimamente Iddio' (ibid., i. 75).

[91] 'Il mezzo termine, che fù creduto celeste diventò spaventosa, & esitiale eresia, e la pace introdotta con la temperie d'un fallacissimo articolo fù la più pestilente guerra, che mai provasse la Chiesa' (ibid., 77).

[92] 'Apparente tranquillità' (ibid., 66); 'Le malevolenze, i sibili de i popoli, le lapidationi, le morti, i pericoli della fuga, l'insidie, e le minacce de i Principi sono stati i mezzi, che hanno dilatato questo Impero celeste' (ibid., ii. 279).

belief, it is paradoxical that the system which Rinuccini outlined for a bishop was predicated on the idea of the church as a centrally institutionalized body within society. The development of this system was one of his principal concerns and an awareness of its main features is an important element in interpreting and understanding his behaviour as nuncio in Ireland.

II

Despite Rinuccini's avowed inspiration from the history of early Christianity, the programme of episcopal activity outlined in both the 'Instruttione pratica' and the *Della Dignita* was very much the product of the tridentine era, and the archbishop can certainly be placed within the context of a reinvigorated post-conciliar catholicism. As noted previously, Rinuccini did not refer to Borromeo with any frequency: rather he drew on his own personal experience. Yet it is very apparent that he was writing in the aftermath of Trent. The features of the council which Borromeo's episcopal career did most to establish as the pillars of reformed practice, such as visitation, diocesan synods, parish records, etc. were treated by Rinuccini as part of the normal fabric of a bishop's activity.[93] His concern, above all in the 'Instruttione pratica', was not to suggest that bishops support seminaries, or hold synods, or visit in their dioceses but to indicate the correct manner of performing these tasks and what errors to avoid. His attitude towards the education of priests and seminarians, in which he emphasized education of a practical pastoral value above theological training, was evidently common elsewhere in contemporary Italy.[94]

One of the most striking points about Rinuccini's writings is the faith which the archbishop's personal experience in Fermo had given him in a particular approach to reform. With regard to his later career as nuncio, it is noteworthy that the archdiocese of Fermo was not free of the 'abuses' commonly associated with seventeenth-century Ireland. Among the problems discussed in the 'Instruttione pratica' are extreme ignorance among the laity (defined as insufficient knowledge of the Christian doctrines essential to salvation); quarrels between regular orders; ignorant clergy; problems with godparents in the sacrament of confirmation; abuses against church immunity; insolent young people; concubinage; and separated married couples. Among the 'abuses' to be subjected to episcopal investigation in parish visits, he listed the usurpation of ecclesiastical goods, public blasphemy, irreverence in church, and cohabitation by unmarried couples. This last point was

---

[93] Concerning the manner in which Borromeo became a trail blazer for tridentine practice see Alberigo, 'Council of Trent', 213–21.

[94] See Thomas Deutscher 'The Growth of the Secular Clergy and the Development of Educational Institutions in the Diocese of Novara (1563–1772)', *Journal of Ecclesiastical History*, 40 (1989) and id., 'Seminaries and the Education of Novarese Priests, 1593–1627', ibid., 32 (1981).

the subject of a synodal decree by two of Rinuccini's immediate predecessors but in the synod of 1650 it was declared that the problem was on the increase. A decree was also issued at Rinuccini's earlier metropolitan synod to prevent unseemly demonstrations at funerals.[95]

Rinuccini believed that it was not enough to have good principles of government without the institutions to implement them. The basic tenet of his own system was the establishment of a wide-ranging and unchallenged episcopal authority which would be then used in an intelligent and unobtrusive manner. He was above all concerned with a bishop's authority over the clergy because he believed that the reform of the laity followed easily, almost inevitably, from the reform of the clergy.[96] The archbishop was thus absolutely committed to the preservation of the legal and fiscal immunities of the church from temporal interference. He believed that a bishop should have the capacity to punish and reward both the clergy and the lesser laity. While accepting that princes and the great of the secular world had a right to deference from bishops, he was convinced of the ecclesiastical authority's right to discipline them also if their behaviour threatened its activity. He believed too in a strong episcopal role in education, regretting the passing of 'the more flowering centuries of ecclesiastical perfection' when all academic activities had been conducted in monasteries or in the houses of bishops.[97] To the greatest extent possible, he believed that bishops should occupy themselves with schools and educational institutions so that the young could be instructed in Christian traditions. In Ireland, he was to treat the lack of provision for catholic control of the proposed university as one of the grave deficiencies of the Ormond peace of 1646.[98]

Rinuccini's key tactic in reform was a careful and elaborate bureaucratization. In fact, the archbishop of Fermo was an almost messianic bureaucrat. In this he can probably be assigned to a particular historical moment during the counter-reformation. To some extent, Rinuccini can be depicted as a quasi Weberian figure whose fervour for organization was stimulated by the sense of possibility of what could be achieved as a result of the application of rational techniques of planning. The terms in which he referred to the practice of episcopal visitation convey this sense of excitement very well: 'If I had not known that the visit was the invention of the Holy Spirit as the Councils teach me then the effect of having seen it would have me believe so.'[99]

[95] 'Instruttione pratica', 5, 7, 10, 15, 16, 24, 34, 43–5; *Decreta Synodi*, 9–10, 16; AAF, 'Decreti Synodali di 1628', 136.

[96] 'Instruttione pratica', 7.

[97] 'I più fioriti secoli delle perfettioni ecclesiastiche' (*Della Dignita*, ii. 156).

[98] See *Comment. Rinucc.*, ii. 76; for further details of the Ormond peace and its negotiations see Chs. 1 and 4.

[99] 'Se io non havessi saputo che la visita è inventione dello Spirito Santo, come m'insegnano i concilii me l'haverebbe fatto credere il vederla' ('Instruttione pratica', 19).

That increased rationalization might have implications for the entire religious world view which he professed never appears to have occurred to the archbishop, nor is this surprising.[100] As was noted by Kierkegaard in the nineteenth century, even Descartes seems to have been insulated by his religious convictions from doubt about the future of catholicism in a new mental universe.[101] In Rinuccini's case his belief that the revealed truth of scripture was not realistically threatened by the workings of the human intellect can be identified as a key element of his stance in this regard. As he put it, a competent knowledge of the ten commandments was enough to confound all earthly knowledge.[102]

The basic outline of the system which Rinuccini envisaged was conventionally tridentine and similar to that employed by his contemporaries in Ireland. He insisted on the necessity for a bishop to keep detailed records about the strengths and weaknesses of every individual cleric in his diocese. This would be possible as a result of examination of each priest by the bishop both before ordination and before they received the right to hear confessions. These investigations would be supplemented by the notes which the bishop took of the priest's performance in the diocesan or more local conferences which, the archbishop advocated, should be held at fortnightly or monthly intervals. These would offer confessors the opportunity to discuss and develop opinions on the correct responses to particular cases in confession. They would also be an incentive and a goad for the priests to study.[103] Priests could also expect to be questioned closely, and their responses noted, in ecclesiastical examinations to select candidates for parishes which became vacant.[104] Finally the system would be rounded off by regular episcopal visitation in the parishes which would check priests in the performance of their daily pastoral duties. These interlocking processes were designed to give the bishop a clear knowledge of any particular priest's weaknesses so that, under the relentless attention of his superior, he would be encouraged or forced to improve.[105] The parish clergy themselves would then be expected to duplicate this systematic referencing of knowledge with regard to their parish-

---

[100] In this context see S. S. Acquaviva, *The Decline of the Sacred in Industrial Society* (Oxford, 1979), 22–35, 96–7, 140.

[101] See Soren Kierkegaard, *Fear and Trembling*, trans. Alastair Hannay (London, 1985), 41–2; see also Daniel G. DiDomizio 'Spirituality and Politics: Seventeenth Century France', in M. Fox (ed.), *Historical Spirituality* (Chicago, 1982), 300.

[102] *Della Dignita*, i. 168; probably consciously echoing a position of one of his favourite saints, St Ambrose: see Edgar Faure, 'Saint Ambroise et l'expulsion des pérégrins de Rome', *Études d'histoire du droit canonique*, i. 523.

[103] There is an evident similarity between Rinuccini's idea here and that of the Irish vicars forane in Tuam and Ossory: see Ch. 2.

[104] By the end of his nunciature in Ireland, Rinuccini had, however, accepted that this aspect of the Italian system was impractical in Ireland: see Rinuccini to Pancirolo, 4 May 1648 (Aiazzi, *Nunziatura*, 310).

[105] 'Instruttione pratica', 11–18.

ioners and would be obliged to send a copy of their information about individual members of their parishes to the bishop at regular intervals. They would also have to provide periodic reports about the financial state of their benefices.[106]

Detailed information and constant surveillance were thus the keynotes of the 'Instruttione pratica'. Above all, what Rinuccini addressed in the treatise, however, was the practical mechanics of implementing this system. He evinced a fairly open contempt for bishops who spotted abuses in visitation and prepared a collection of decrees about their reform, and then left without taking steps to oversee their implementation.[107] They would, he declared, return to find exactly the same abuses and to make exactly the same decrees at the time of the next visit. His belief in his own mode of activity was bolstered by the evident success it had enjoyed in Fermo.[108]

There is a high degree of psychological insight in the archbishop's writings on the subject of reform. Rinuccini believed in the indispensability of a firm episcopal authority capable of punishing those who obstructed its activity; none the less, he believed that coercion was not an efficient mode of reform except in the most recalcitrant cases. Whenever possible he urged the importance of virtuous example and the use of private admonitions and tenderness rather than force, a policy which acquired a twofold efficiency from the culprit's awareness of both the power and mercy of the bishop.[109] He preached also the value of consistency: vice was never to be rewarded nor tolerated. More interestingly, he was aware of the value of approbation from a respected authority and was eager that bishops should always be seen both to praise and to favour the dedicated and the virtuous.[110]

He adopted this attitude with regard to education as well. The archbishop believed that internal socialization was far more effective than exterior coercion and that education should aim at the production of a system of cherished interior values. Whenever it was necessary to discipline a child, he argued that the exact reasons should always be explained and that the child should be made to see the justice of its punishment.[111] Rinuccini was so alert to the danger that the punitive aspects of the bishop would become fixed in the minds of the people that he advocated that a prelate should leave all punishment as far as possible to delegated subordinates. Instead, the bishop was to concentrate on preaching, a practice which Trent had done much to revive as an essential staple of episcopal activity.[112] Laws, he declared, were a remedy against evil but eloquence could make evil abominated. He argued

---

[106] Ibid., 30–3.

[107] As could happen only too easily: exactly this process occurred in Mediona in 1574: see Henry Kamen, *The Phoenix and the Flame: Catalonia and the Counter-reformation* (London, 1993), 17–18.

[108] 'Instruttione pratica', 13–16, 32, 34.

[109] *Della Dignita*, i. 70–1.

[110] 'Instruttione pratica', 15–18, 19–20.

[111] *Della Dignita*, ii. 111, 140.

[112] Prodi, *Paleotti*, ii. 76–7.

further that in preaching a bishop should attempt to involve his listeners creatively. Everything should not be spelled out but the audience should be given the material from which to draw simple conclusions of their own. He reasoned that a natural feeling of ownership and pride attached people to their own ideas more than to those of an exterior authority.[113]

Rinuccini was also keenly aware of the possibilities of heightening the impact of a sermon by the use of a particular theme in a particular setting. He advocated a special sermon at the end of a visitation in a parish on the subject of sin or of death while the population were kneeling after the general communion.[114] Immediately afterwards, with a fine sense of theatre, he suggested that the bishop should mount his horse and ride away, leaving in his wake a suitably chastened and meditative congregation.[115] There is an admirable grasp of psychological detail also in the archbishop's description of how to conduct the personal visitation of priests:

The personal visitation of the priests is more fruitful than all other actions. I think that one should do it if one can by lantern light with a crucifix on a little table and the bishop should be in a habit. Each priest should enter one by one and the bishop, with a paternal heart, should investigate before anything else his temporal state, his needs, worries, revenues, responsibilities for nephews or to marriageable wards; the bishop should offer himself to him with great affection and should note his needs in a book. With the priest having been softened in this manner, he should pass to the soul and should penetrate deeply into his conscience and draw from his mouth the remorse he feels, he should propose to him the remedy of the general confession and of such exercises as he can afford . . . the bishop should console him, correct him, and above all exhort him to mental prayer. I profess to that bishop who will observe this practice that he will find more than one who will confess his entire state to him in tears and others who from tender affection will wish to kiss his feet.[116]

Here, once again, Rinuccini's originality is revealed, less in the actions which he advocated, than in the precise manner in which he advocated their performance. The bishop's duty to reform the parish clergy was a staple of the

---

[113] *Della Dignita*, ii. 66, i. 155.

[114] Sermons of this kind were evidently not uncommon in post-Borromeon Italy: see Peter Burke, 'Popular Piety', in O'Malley, *Catholicism*, 119–21.

[115] 'Instruttione pratica', 25.

[116] 'La visita personale de i preti passa di frutto tutte l'altre attioni. Mi par che si deva fare se si può crocifisso sul tavolino, e sia il vescovo in habito. Entri un prete per volta et il vescovo con viscere paterne l'interrogli prima di tutto il suo stato temporale, necessità, fastidii, entrate, resi di nepoti, o di zitelle nubili, se offerisca per lui con gran'affetto, e noti nel libro il bisogno di esso. Addolcito così il prete passi ad anima, s'interni nella sua coscienza e gli cavi di bocca i rimorsi, che sente, gli proponga i rimedii de i confessori generali e di tanti esercitii a spese di esso vescovo e lo consoli, l'emendi, e sopra tutto l'esorti ad oration mentale. Io proferisco à quel vescovo che vorrà osservar questa pratica che ne trovera più d'uno, che con le lacrime gli confesserà tutto il suo stato, et altri che per tenerezza gli vorranno baciare i piedi' (ibid., 28–9); in this regard see the comments on counter-reformation use of pastoral solicitude as a means of establishing contact with those to be evangelized in Ginzburg, 'Folklore, Magia e Religione', 441–2.

catholic reformation, epitomized by varying figures across the continent.[117] The archbishop of Fermo was thus clearly representative of a wider European tradition of reform, although he saw himself as making a personal contribution to the elaboration of that tradition. This excerpt also suggests how formidable Rinuccini's personality could be at close quarters.

Rinuccini was also interested in how the pressures of group conformity could be utilized at a diocesan synod to impel priests towards personal reform.[118] In fact, he regarded this as the single most useful aspect of a synod, which was an aspect of catholic reform which he viewed with a certain scepticism.[119] This is a particularly interesting attitude because it is directly related to the beliefs which the archbishop cherished with regard to public ecclesiastical ceremonies. The nuncio's determination, which was shared by a majority of the Irish clergy, to secure the full and public exercise of catholicism, was one of the chief factors which prevented an accommodation between the confederates and the royal government. It is, therefore, important to consider how public ceremonies operated as an intrinsic element in his strategy of religious reform.

His thinking in this regard probably reflected the modest educational attainments of much of the population among whom he, like every other seventeenth-century bishop, exercised his pastoral ministry. Ritual forms were arguably more important than the printed or even the spoken word as a medium of communication with a population rooted in a pre-literate and technologically rudimentary culture.[120] Despite the post-reformation emphasis on the word,[121] the inculcation of faith probably had as much, if not more, to do with the ritual transmission of impressions of order, beauty, and authority as with the teaching of doctrine and the promotion of an intellectual grasp of Christian doctrine.[122]

[117] Wright, *Counter-Reformation*, 52, 147, 210–17; Robert Sauzet, *Contre-réforme*, 58–60.

[118] *Della Dignita*, ii. 247–8.

[119] A certain degree of synodal irregularity seems to have been common in the post-tridentine Italian church: in this regard see Christopher Black, 'Perugia and Post-Tridentine Church Reform', *Journal of Ecclesiastical History*, 35 (1984), 436.

[120] In this context see the discussion concerning the impact of technological change on religious belief in Acquaviva, *Decline of the Sacred*, 138–58; the question of historical consciousness and desacralization is discussed by E. De Martino, 'Mito Scienze, religiosità e civiltà moderna', *Nuovi Argomenti*, 37 (1959), 9–11; see also the discussion of civic ritual in Jonathon Barry, 'Popular Culture in Seventeenth Century Bristol', in Barry Reay (ed.), *Popular Culture in Seventeenth-century England* (London, 1988), 69–70.

[121] Monter, *Ritual, Myth and Magic*, 90–1, 24–7; W. Maltby, 'Spain', in O'Malley, *Catholicism*, 41.

[122] Kamen, *Phoenix and the Flame*, 113–14; Victor Tapié, 'Iconografia Barocca e Sensibilità Cattolica' in Russo, *Società, Chiesa e vita religiosa*, 313–14, 326; in this regard one can note Edmund Spenser's comment that 'outward show . . . doth greatly draw the rude people to the reverencing . . . whatever some of our late too nice fools say there is nothing in the seemly form and comely order of the Church' (Henry Morley (ed.), *Ireland under Elizabeth and James I* (London, 1890), 204); see also the discussion of the Puritan fear of idolatry in Russell, *The Causes of the English Civil War* (Oxford, 1990), 77–8.

Rinuccini was certainly alert to the need for an evangelical strategy not restricted to the preaching of words.[123] He believed that the pastoral relationship had been different and finer in the early years of Christianity. In his own time, however, he felt it necessary for the authority of the church to be supported in the eyes of the common people by 'external show'.[124] His emphasis on public ceremony was designed to exploit what he considered to be the innate religiosity of human beings.[125] Reverence towards their priests was, he suggested, the only feature common to all societies.[126] Yet he believed equally firmly in the blindness and inconstancy of the ordinary population. The 'body politic' was: 'infected by the disease of private inclinations, a temperament which wants and does not want, which seeks and refuses, which hates and loves at the same time.'[127] The people, in particular young priests in training, had therefore to be wooed and stimulated by beauty:

with grace of ceremonies they [young clerics] adorn the cloaks of the bride of paradise. The beauty of these rites and the sumptuosity of the chalices and ecclesiastical apparatus has unknowable force with the young people, betrayed by this era, that it suffices to induce towards them (the rites) an indissoluble love. One must procure every grace and splendour in the churches so that the third rank of soldiers cherish the cult greatly and so that they will never think to despise it.[128]

On another occasion he described in loving detail the ceremonial of an episcopal mass which he considered the 'clearest model of celestial greatness': the passage climaxes in an apostrophe:

O uniform majesty of ecclesiastical display, how you are admirable. If I could register here how many alienated hearts you have made return to the light of Christianity, and how many minds impenetrable to the truth of dogma you alone have confounded and indoctrinated with this invariable concord.[129]

---

[123] Wolfgang Reinhard, 'Reformation, Counter-Reformation and the Early Modern State: A Reassessment', *Catholic Historical Review*, 75 (1989), 392 argues that this evangelical strategy represented one of the advantages which the counter-reformation church enjoyed over its protestant rivals: in this regard also see Russell, *Causes*, 77–8.

[124] 'Apparenze esterne' (*Della Dignita*, i. 150–1).

[125] In this context see the discussion of the 'religious perspective' in 'Religion as a Cultural System', in Clifford Geertz, *The Interpretation of Cultures* (London, 1973), 87–125 and Tapié, 'Iconografia Barocca', 326.

[126] *Della Dignita*, i. 52, 174.

[127] 'Corpo politico sì, mà infetto dalle malattie delle private inclinationi, temperamento, che vuole, e disvuole, che cerca, e refiuta, che odia, & ama in un medesimo tempo' (ibid., i. 51).

[128] 'Con vaghezza di cerimonie adornano i manti della sposa del Paradiso. La bellezza di questi riti, e la sontuosità de i Vasi, & apparati Ecclesiastici, hà non sò che di forza con la gioventù traviata del secolo, che basta à conciliarne un'indissolubile amore. Ogni splendore, e vaghezza si hà da procurar nelle Chiese, acciò i tironi manipulari accarrezzino di maniera quel culto, che per qual si sia accidente non pensino di disprezzarlo' (ibid., ii. 125).

[129] 'Modello più chiaro delle celesti grandezze' (ibid., i. 209); 'O Maestà uniforme dell' apparenzze ecclesiastiche, quanto sei ammirabile . . . Potessi io qui registrare quanto cuori alienati hai tù fatto tornare alla luce del Cristianesmo, e quanti ingegni impenetrabili alla verità de i dogmi tu sola hai confusi, & addottrinati con questa invariabile concordia' (ibid.).

In addition to the beauty of the rites, Rinuccini believed in an almost infectious enthusiasm from the participation of a group in a religious experience.[130] As noted above, he thought a synod offered an ideal opportunity to stimulate this process in the priests of a diocese. Elsewhere he praised the effect of group prayer and singing: 'because everyone, as if tempering the edge of interior devotion on the stone of others, renders prayer more acute and vigorous and very well sharpened for the conquest of the senses.'[131] The archbishop's belief in the importance of religious ceremonies was complemented by an intense typically post-tridentine interest in the practical details of their performance. In the 'Instruttione pratica', for instance, he advocated that no child of less than five years of age be admitted to confirmation: the archbishop wanted no crying children spoiling the solemnity of the occasion. He insisted further in the ordination of only a small number of priests at any one time so that the laity did not lose sight of the importance of the ceremony.[132] He emphasized the importance of practice as well.

A good master of ceremonies is the most necessary thing for the sacred functions but I would wish further that in this matter the bishop should be insatiable and that so as not to tolerate any defect, even the most minimal, he should practise his functions several times a year in church behind closed doors and particularly those functions which come rarely . . . and that he should call to be present the canons, the servants of the mitre, of incense, of the pastoral, the deacon and the sub-deacon, the master of ceremonies and above all the master of the chapel because he will find that each one, by not knowing his office perfectly will generate the most enormous confusion . . . All which things if done well he can trust they will be marvelled at with such devotion.[133]

Linked to the devotional stimulation of beautiful rites was the admiration which could be evoked in the common people by the sight of disciplined and reformed clergy. When the people saw the 'splendour of the clergy' he declared in the Della Dignita: 'they desire to be transported by them to the beauty of that heaven whose outline they see in the ecclesiastical orders of the earth.'[134] A concern to distinguish the spiritual from the profane,

[130] In this context see the discussion in Acquaviva, Decline of the Sacred, 42–3.

[131] 'Perche ciascuno quasi temprando sù l'altrui pietre il taglio della devotione interiore, rende più acuta, e per l'espugnatione de i sensi molto ben' affilata, e vigorosa l'oratione' (Della Dignita, ii. 133–4).

[132] 'Instruttione pratica', 9, 13.

[133] 'Un buon mastro di cerimonie è la più necessaria cosa per le funtioni sacre ma io vorai di più che il vescovo in questa materia fosse incontentabile e che per non tolerare alcun difetto benche minimo provasse qualche volta l'anno in Chiesa con le porte chiuse le sue funtioni e particolarmente quelle che vengono di(?) raro . . . e però chiami ad esser presenti i canonici, tutti i serventi di mitra, d'incenso, di pastorale, il diacono e subdiacono, il mastro di cerimonie e sopratutto il mastro di capella perche troverà che ciascheduno per non saper fare perfettamente il suo offitio genera grandissima confusione . . . Cose tutte che fatte bene può credere con quanta divotione siano rimirate' (ibid., 8).

[134] 'Lo splendore del Clericato' (Della Dignita, i. 174); 'desiderano d'esser portati da esso alle bellezze di quel cielo, del quale vedono la figura negli ordini ecclesiastici della Terra' (ibid.).

between the quotidian details of the secular world and the differentiated life of the spirit, was a general feature of the European counter-reformation.[135] This entailed the orientation of religious affairs towards tighter clerical control and the suppression of the intrusion of secular rituals into church ceremonies. At the same time, attempts were made to introduce a distinctive clerical discipline, deportment, and dress.[136] Rinuccini can be situated naturally within this process which ultimately tended to reduce and externalize lay participation in the liturgy.[137] His synodal decrees in 1650 are in the classical tradition with their ordinances on clerical dress and celibacy, proscription of unauthorized holy places, and strict regulations concerning clerical contact with the laity for the purposes of gambling or drinking.[138] In the *Della Dignita* he suggested that: 'no object more worthy of wonder is presented to the eyes of the laity than the beauty of the reformed clergy, and they will not receive a more apt motive to generate the mutation of their own emotions than to see it executed first in the choirs of ecclesiastical persons.'[139] This entire notion of clerical 'beauty' was rooted in the hierarchical duality between body and soul noted above. The essential component was the domination of fleshly appetites.[140] When the archbishop adverted to the need for seminarians to display an 'angelic modesty' or when he spoke of the quiet and sober manner which a cleric should present to the world, he intended that the general population be impressed by the clergy's interior discipline and control of their bodies and emotions.[141] Admiration of the clergy on this score then became a powerful motive towards reform in the people themselves. The archbishop also noted acutely that the personal discipline of the clergy focused their inclination to oversee a similar process in their lay congregations.[142]

Respect for the clergy was also channelled by their position among the elite of society. In the same manner, the public ceremonials of the church both added to and were reinforced by the ritual grammar of authority current in early modern society. In the 'golden age of preoccupation with

[135] P. Hoffmann, *Church and Community in the Diocese of Lyons, 1500–1789* (New Haven, Conn. and London, 1984), 56; Burke, 'Popular Piety', 117–18.

[136] Hoffmann, *Church and Community*, 57–70, 91; see also Wright, *Counter-Reformation*, 71–9; Kamen, *Phoenix and the Flame*, 110–11.

[137] In this regard see Russo, 'Storiografia Socio-Religigiosa e i suoi problemi' in Russo, *Società Chiesa e vita religiosa*, pp. xxiv–xxv.

[138] *Decreta Synodi*, 11.

[139] 'À gli occhi de'laici non si presenta oggetto più degno di stupore, che la bellezza del clero riformato, e non ricevono motivo più atto à generare la mutatione de i proprii affetti, che il vederla prima eseguita ne i chori delle persone ecclesiastiche' (*Della Dignita*, i. 175–6).

[140] In passing, one may note that Rinuccini believed the religious life to be a substitute for martyrdom: see ibid., ii. 159.

[141] 'Instruttione pratica', 8, 25; this was very much within the classical post-tridentine spirit: see Sauzet, *Contre-réforme*, 205; A. Dupront, 'Le Concile de Trente et la réforme tridentin', in Actes du Convegno de Trente, 1963, *Le Concile de Trente et la réforme tridentin* (Rome, 1965), ii. 525–38.

[142] *Della Dignita*, i. 137–8, 146.

precedence'[143] the legitimization of authority by the use of various rituals was so prevalent that a definite correspondence existed between power and the capacity to display it.[144] Since public ceremonial was a property of power, the merely secret exercise of catholicism threatened the recognition of the church's authority upon which Rinuccini's notion of religious orthodoxy largely depended.[145] There was, of course, something of a logical inconsistency between Rinuccini's exaltation of the centuries of persecution as the golden age of catholicism and his determination to maintain the public authority of the church in his own time. The difficulty of reconciling these two notions rumbles as a subterranean tension in his writings but it was not openly confronted.[146]

The honour of God was also involved in the issue of public exercise of religion. Whatever about the individual persons of the clergy, Rinuccini believed that God must be accorded tributes of exterior respect. This was expressed in the construction of beautiful buildings for divine worship and the use of precious metals in the vessels which played a part in catholic rites. In Fermo he took steps to insure that the Eucharist should never be taken into the streets without a canopy and a retinue equipped with a bell to summon the people to homage as it passed.[147] In Ireland he was disgusted with the Irish bishops' unwillingness to spend money on the glorification of church ceremonies and with the Irish predilection for private mass.[148] On this last point, the nuncio's chief distress was at the degradation of the sacrament in a profane environment where the removal of the altar cloth often signalled the return of the table to a variety of secular uses, such as gambling, eating, or drinking beer.[149] The metaphysical and anti-corporeal image of God in his writings was probably not irrelevant to the fervour with which he expressed himself on this point.

Yet, with what might be described as a certain prescience, the archbishop was conscious of dangers deriving from a shared ritual language of ecclesiastical and secular authority. In his view the public display of the church's authority was essential but nowhere did he wish the delineation between spiritual and profane to be clearer than in this domain. He was genuinely horrified that the common people might consider ecclesiastical authority

---

[143] Monter, *Ritual, Myth and Magic*, 50.

[144] Turner, *The Body and Society*, 109–10.

[145] In addition, it was the public performance of sacramental functions by a priest which defined priestly status in counter-reformation Italy: see Angelo Torre, 'Politics Clothed in Worship: State, Church and Local Power in Piedmont, 1570–1770', *Past and Present*, 134 (1992), 55–7.

[146] In this regard one can note the manner in which Cardinal Paleotti's attempts to cultivate an apostolic humility in dining with his household was seen as potentially erosive of his authority and he was advised not to do so regularly: see Prodi, *Paleotti*, ii. 37–8.

[147] 'Instruttione pratica', 8, 27.   [148] In this regard see Ch. 7.

[149] Aiazzi, *Nunziatura*, 111–12.

similar to secular or that they would respect and fear the church only, or even principally, for its temporal power and wealth.

That this was a real danger was something of which he was only too aware.[150] He believed the intrusion of 'pomp' and 'the prouder appearances of the secular satellite' threatened a deadly corruption to the church.[151] The archbishop took the ecclesiastical visit as an example:

visits will find it difficult to defend themselves from an accumulation of pomp and will wither very often in profane ornaments . . . The decorum and respect of the people will send all the military ranks to meet the pastor. The sounding trumpets and the excursion of horses will adorn the spectacle and because the messenger and bringer of peace is not realised or seen, the volleys will resound and the gunpowder and saltpetre will make a cloud. The streets and windows adorned, arches raised and crowned trophies, the happiness of the people explained in a harmony of epigrams, the smokes, the fires of joy will be the worm which goes rotting the shoots underground. Nor does the deception stop here. What will you [the pastors] do at the luxury of the meals where under cover of obsequy the fruits of entire dioceses are displayed. There the adorned beliefs, the variety and multitude of foods, the happiness of those present will occupy your minds and the price of those happy hours, which would buy the safety of a soul, are changed to a coin of miserable somnolence and in the lassitude of languid operations.[152]

Other than the enticements of the senses, Rinuccini was convinced that the two greatest dangers to the catholic clergy were avarice for material goods and ambition for honour. Against these he preached the virtues of prudence, gentleness, patience, and humility. Who, he asked, in one of his relatively rare references to the physical nature of Christ could: 'become intoxicated [with authority] who was endowed with blood and the bloodied power of love?'[153] The wealth of the church was, in his eyes, entirely from the donations of faithful Christians in the past and bishops were therefore morally obliged to

---

[150] There are similarities in this respect not only with a figure such as Paleotti here but even with Giordano Bruno: see Frances A. Yates, *Astraea: The Imperial Theme in the Sixteenth Century* (London, 1993), 213 and ead., *The Rosicrucian Enlightenment* (London, 1972), 134; see also Prodi, *Paleotti*, ii. 65–6.

[151] 'L'apparenze più fiere del satellitio profano' (*Della Dignita*, ii. 212).

[152] 'Le vostre visite dureranno fatica à difendersi da un cumulo di pompe, sfioriranno ben spesso in ornamenti profani . . . Il decoro, e la stima de i popoli manderà incontro al Pastore tutte le schiere militari; Le Trombe sonanti, & il campeggiar de i cavalli adornerà lo spettacolo; e perché non si senta, ò si vede l'annuntio, & il portator della pace, strepiteranno le salve, e farà nube la polvere, e l'opacità del salnitro. Le strade, e le finestre adornate, alzati gli Archi, e coronati i Trofei, l'allegrezze de i popoli spiegate in armonia d'Epigrammi, i fuochi, e le fiamme di giubilo, saranno il verme, che và rodendo sotto terra i germogli. Ne qui finische l'inganno. Che farete alla lautezza delle Mense, dove sotto coperta d'ossequio corrono i frutti delle Diocesi intere? Ivi le credenze adornate, la varietà e moltitudine de i cibi, la letitia degli assistenti v'occuperanno la mente; & il prezzo di quell' hore felici, che comprerebbe la salute d'un anima, si cambierà in moneta di misere sonnolenze, & in stracchezza di languide operationi' (ibid., 214).

[153] 'Chi potrà dunque inebriarsi, che fù dotata col sangue e di Potenza insanguinata d'amore?' (ibid., 294–5, i. 140, 146).

use it in the service of Christian compassion.[154] A bishop, he emphasized, must protect the weak of society, in particular although not exclusively, widows and orphans lest their poverty tempt them into sexual misdemeanours.[155] Rather than operating in the same manner as secular power, Rinuccini saw ecclesiastical authority as something fundamentally different and gentler. Above all he wished that ecclesiastical courts should be seen to operate on principles different from those of the secular jurisdiction. Whereas the objective of temporal justice was to punish wrongdoers, he saw the role of the church courts as medicinal and reformatory based on the principles of 'equity, clemency and compassion'.[156]

In such a way, ecclesiastical justice taught the value and example of mercy to the secular world. This, he believed, was a glorious aspect of the church's role but he had a suspicion that it was something which the catholicism of his own time was relinquishing. To his colleagues, he addressed the question:

What would be your spirit if the court, the ministers and everything which is given to you to insure justice, should become fury and, with pity abandoned, justice went armed in every court and ecclesiastical mildness became smoke and poison? What way would remain to you to show to the common people the differences between the authority of heaven and profane tribunals if the people should see the same effects in both?[157]

And again:

How could you justify, O ambassadors of Christ, to those who expect the rays of a pastoral clemency to send instead severe edicts and fiscal penalties on persons? What have legal judgements and the threat of punishments to do with the party of the angel of peace? Instead of drawing souls from the lethargy of vice will blows come forth . . .? Will, I shall say it freely, the examination of souls become an adjustment of domestic revenues and will the earnings of heaven be exchanged for the goods of the earth?[158]

---

[154] Rinuccini's preoccupations in this regard mirror those of Paleotti at the end of the previous century: see Prodi, *Paleotti*, ii. 18–19.

[155] *Della Dignita*, ii. 170, 180, 187–9.

[156] 'L'equità, la clemenza, la compassione' (ibid., 200); see also ibid., 194–9; nevertheless, he wished them to have extensive powers of punishment for contumacious cases and to point up their normal gentleness.

[157] 'E qual sarebbe il vostro animo, se la corte, i Ministri, e quanto v'è dato per assicurar la giustitia, diventasse furore, e sbandita la pietà per tutto il giusto se ne passeggiasse armato, e la soavità Ecclesiastica spirasse fuoco, e veleni? Qual modo, ò strada vi rimarrebbe giammai per distinguere al volgo da i Tribunali profani l'autorità del Cielo, se la corrente de i popoli in tutte due rimirasse i medesimi effetti?' (ibid., 200–1).

[158] 'E come sosterrete voi, ò Ambasciatori di Cristo, à quei ch'aspettano i raggi d'una clemenza Pastorale, d'inviare inanzi la severità negli editti, & i rigori fiscali nelle persone? In cambio di ritrar l'anime del letargo de i Vitii si scaveranno le colpe? . . . Diventerà, lo dirò pure liberamente, la rivista dell'anime aggiustamento dell'entrate domestiche, & il guadagno del Cielo si cambierà in mercantie della Terra?' (ibid., 212–13).

Thus, while in many ways Rinuccini was an exemplar of the Italian counter-reformation, it is important not to underestimate his sensitivity or intellectual vision. To a large extent, such as in his notions of authority and ecclesiastical discipline, his intense attention to practical details, and his openness to the missionary impulse, he stood squarely in the mainstream of the post-tridentine church. Yet he was also deeply reflective about the whole project of reform and this resulted in an individual and complex conception of the church's activity. In particular, he demonstrated an awareness of the dangers for the church which could arise from the post-tridentine stress on ecclesiastical authority. The close alliance between the church and the secular elites of catholic Europe tied catholicism into an increasingly reactionary position in society and arguably created barriers between the clergy and the general population. In *Della Dignita* Rinuccini attempted to marry what he saw as the great need of the church for influence and jurisdiction within society to a conception of the exercise of authority and the use of wealth which would preserve the ecclesiastical institution from the corruption of power. In this respect, he can be viewed as peering out of the immediate shadow of Trent towards the problems of the years ahead.

Nevertheless, Rinuccini's solutions to the problems he detected remained compromised by his essentially authoritarian vision of personal, social, and celestial order. While acknowledging his insight in realizing that the population would be more willing to accept the dictates of a pastor who himself practised what he preached, the repression of the unorthodox remained fundamental to his system. It is not insignificant that the first line of the *Della Dignita* declared that a bishop's role was not to lead, or guide, or encourage but to 'send' the souls entrusted to him to Paradise. A discrepancy existed too between the archbishop's personal fervour and a certain emotional deficiency within his system. This can be distinguished on a number of levels. The programme of activity which he outlined for a bishop, and indeed for the clergy in general, was administrative to an extent which must have been somewhat consumptive of religious enthusiasm. In this respect, the type of personal study which Rinuccini advocated, orientated away from more emotionally stimulating topics towards questions of pastoral care, probably ran the risk of boring the priests involved.[159] In addition, by virtue of its emphasis on the importance of projecting a certain image to the laity, Rinuccini's programme was a recipe to minimize human contact between clergy and laity. A considerable element of his system was orientated towards the manipulation of exterior impressions to convince onlookers of the difference and the superiority of the clergy. In psychological terms such a project was arguably not only empty but exhausting as well.

---

[159] In this regard see Deutscher 'Seminaries and the Education of Novarese Priests, 1593–1627', *Journal of Ecclesiastical History*, 32 (1981), 308–12.

The system was complemented and enclosed by a rather flat and intellec-
tualized conception of God which hardly offered itself as a basis for a rich and
emotionally sustaining spiritual life. An idea of the spiritual as separate from
and in control of the emotions and the body runs through Rinuccini's writings. The proposition might be advanced that a fierce austerity towards the
flesh was one of the energizing principles in the 'century of saints' which followed Trent.[160] Yet Rinuccini's perception of the body was dominated by a
concern with firm and moderate discipline. The passion for self-mortification
which distinguished Borromeo, St Peter of Alcantara, Ignatius Loyala,
Filippo Neri, and their many followers was not integrated into the archbishop
of Fermo's conception of religious reform.[161] Rather, one can imagine him in
this regard endorsing the position of his contemporary bishop novelist, Jean-
Pierre Camus, who believed 'that excess in all things had to be eliminated'.[162]

III

Rinuccini's appointment as nuncio to the confederate catholics in 1645 represented a radical new step in his varied career. The decision to send him to
Ireland was taken without consultation with the confederate Supreme
Council. In 1643 it is true that Rome had been requested to provide the confederates with a nuncio, the Supreme Council having noticed how useful
Scarampi had been 'in drawing the laity to pay a perfect obedience to their
commands, who were thought worthy of being seconded by so awful and
much reverenced an authority.'[163] By 1645, however, the enthusiasm of the
dominant clique within confederate politics for such an appointment had
waned almost completely because their primary objective was now the negotiation of peace with Ormond and they could cherish few illusions that papal
input would facilitate this process.[164]

Why the pope took the political risk of creating the first major new nunciature in sixty-five years[165] and accrediting it to a rather doubtfully legitimate catholic government, which was not particularly receptive to the
honour entailed, can be traced to a number of factors. The influence in Rome
of the Irish Franciscan, Luke Wadding, who had already been instrumental
in securing Scarampi's appointment, was probably of importance.[166] It is

[160] See Massimo Marocchi, 'Spirituality in the Sixteenth and Seventeenth Centuries', in
O'Malley, *Catholicism*, and in particular the analysis of the failure of Erasmianism (p. 166).

[161] Delumeau, *Catholicism between Luther and Voltaire*, 46.

[162] 'Mais je dis que l'excès en toutes choses doit être retranché': quoted in Bremond, *Histoire littéraire*, i. 155.

[163] Bellings's narrative (Gilbert, *Irish Confederation*, i. 153); Supreme Council to Pope, 1 Oct.
1643 (*Comment. Rinucc.*, i. 429).

[164] See the anonymous letter from Paris, 24 Nov. (ns) 1645 (Bodl. Carte MS 16 fo. 213ʳ);
Ó hAnnracháin, 'Vatican Diplomacy', 78.

[165] Igino Cardinale, *Le Saint-siège et la diplomatie* (Paris, 1962), 32.

[166] See O'Hartigan to Wadding, 23 May 1643 (FAK, D II, fos. 986–7).

likely that Wadding's arguments were strengthened by the return to Italy of one of Scarampi's party, Carlo Invernizzi, who submitted a fervent memorial to the Roman authorities concerning the merits of the Irish confederates and the possibility of major gains for catholicism if they were succoured from Rome.[167] Another factor at work was evidently the heated diplomatic atmosphere in Rome following the election of GianBattista Pamfili as Pope Innocent X in September 1644. Pamfili's elevation had been obtained only after an exceptionally bitter conclave of cardinals, deeply riven by the enmity between the supporters and opponents of the previous pope's nephews, cardinals Francesco and Antonio Barberini. Adding fuel to an already furious fire were the influence of France and Spain. Both these great catholic powers, then engaged in a war for European hegemony, were determined to prevent the election of a hostile pope. French support initially operated in support of the Barberini faction while the partisans of Spain hoped to benefit from the great distaste which Urban VIII's nepotism had created.

The eventual election of Pamfili was the fruit of a rather transparent bargain between the Barberini and their enemies in a conclave whose members were becoming desperate to flee the sicknesses which had begun to afflict their numbers. It represented an enormous rebuff to France and to Mazarin personally and it meant that Innocent X began his reign with a dubious aura of worldly politicking and a diplomatic relationship with Paris which bordered on the poisonous.[168]

To a certain extent, the Rinuccini mission was designed to address both these problems. The bold stroke of dispatching a nuncio and 50,000 scudi to the long-persecuted catholics of Ireland with the declared intention of bringing about the full and public restoration of the exercise of the catholic faith in Ireland[169] displayed to the world that Innocent took seriously his responsibilities as supreme pastor of the catholic church. Moreover, by directing Rinuccini's route through France, without fear of rebuff, the new pope was able to introduce one of his own ministers into the French court, thus restoring a diplomatic interface between Rome and Paris which had been disrupted by Mazarin's extreme hostility to the outcome of the conclave.[170]

The choice of Rinuccini for the post neatly complemented the avowed religious purpose of the nunciature. Rather than a career diplomat, Rinuccini was a pastoral bishop of the type which had been employed as nuncios in the immediate post-tridentine period. He was an author with a high reputation for piety and his appointment created an admiring stir in Rome.[171]

[167] 'Miscellanea Vaticano-Hibernica', *Archivium Hibernicum*, 6 (1920), 107–8.
[168] This is treated in greater detail in Ó hAnnracháin, 'Vatican Diplomacy', 78–88.
[169] See Rinuccini's instructions, Dec. (?)1644 (Aiazzi, *Nunziatura*, pp. xxxv).
[170] Ó hAnnracháin, 'Vatican Diplomacy', 82–3.
[171] Albizzi to Fabio Chigi, 7 Jan. 1645 (V. Kybal and G. Incisa Della Rochetta (eds.), *La Nunziatura di Fabio Chigi, 1640–1651* (Rome, 1946), i. 700–1); see also the letter of Hilario Roncati to Rinuccini (*Comment. Rinucc.*, ii. 746).

Rinuccini's acceptance of the post, involving far greater disruption, danger, and more onerous responsibilities than the see of Florence which he had previously refused in order to stay in Fermo, reflected his own belief in its religious importance.[172]

The decision to send him to Ireland was made towards the end of December 1644, within three months of the confirmation of Fabio Chigi, the future Pope Alexander VII, as the representative of the papacy at the peace conference in Münster.[173] Although there is no evidence of contact between the two papal ministers other than through the secretariat to which both reported and from which they received instructions, the Chigi mission formed an indispensable aspect of the background to Rinuccini's nunciature. Given the critical importance which the papacy attached to the Münster negotiations, it was imperative that Rinuccini's demeanour in Ireland towards the Ormond peace should not prejudice Chigi's resistance to protestant pressure for further concessions in Germany. On at least two occasions, Rinuccini was to be reprimanded when, in his eagerness not to be seen to question confederate loyalty to the Stuarts, he contravened papal guidelines on the non-recognition of the rights and prerogatives of heretics.[174]

The attitudes and sometimes the tactics of both nuncios were to be consistently similar. In December 1645, for instance, Chigi made ready a secret protest against any peace which offered damage to the interests of the church, although he waited for an opportune moment to produce it. On 6 February 1646, and possibly directly inspired by Chigi's action, Rinuccini prepared a similar document denouncing the Ormond peace which he eventually made public in June.[175] Subsequently, none the less, Rinuccini was to take more extreme steps than his Münster equivalent in resisting what he saw as a prejudicial treaty. Chigi's more restrained behaviour almost certainly reflected his dealings with great catholic powers such as the Emperor, Bavaria, and France, towards whom a papal delegate could not afford to adopt such a cavalier attitude as a nuncio accredited to the more marginal catholic confederates. Moreover, Chigi never saw the opportunity of stimulating decisive action such as Rinuccini was able to grasp in 1646 or 1648.[176] Consequently, although the papal nuncio's position was even more unyielding than that of the most intransigent members of the native German

---

[172] See for example *Comment. Rinucc.*, ii. 278; see also ibid., 256–7 and i. 632.

[173] Albizzi to Fabio Chigi, 7 Jan. (ns) 1645 Kybal and Incisa Della Rochetta, *Nunziatura di Fabio Chigi*, 700–1.

[174] See my article '"Though Hereticks and Politicians Should Misinterpret their good zeal"': Political Ideology and Catholicism in Early Modern Ireland', in Jane Ohlmeyer (ed.), *Political Thought in Seventeenth-Century Ireland: Kingdom or Colony* (Cambridge, 2000), 155 concerning the context of these reproofs.

[175] Chigi to Pamfili, 15 Dec. (ns) 1645 in J. Ciampi, *Innocenzo X Pamfili e la sua Corte* (Roma, 1878), 55; *Comment. Rinucc.*, ii. 220–2.

[176] See below, Chs. 4 and 6.

MAP 2. Rinuccini's Journey to Ireland, 1645

catholic party, his role in the slow march to the final treaty was essentially that of a dolorous oracle, bitterly protesting the steady drip feed of concessions to protestant importunity.[177]

Despite differences in the scale of resistance which the two nuncios endorsed, there was no indication of any discrepancy between them in their view of what it was permissible to concede to protestants. In this Rinuccini and Chigi were faithful both to their own interior convictions concerning the damnable nature of heresy and their instructions from Rome. Of considerable importance in this regard, also, was their shared belief that internal dissension rather than protestant strength was the key to the undermining of the catholic position in their respective areas of responsibility. Almost from the beginning of the Swedish intervention in Germany, Rome had identified a reconciliation of the great catholic powers and the combination of their forces against heresy as the key to the safeguarding of confessional advances in central Europe. Fruitless embassies to this end were dispatched to Madrid, Vienna, and Paris in 1632.[178] During the Münster nunciature, Chigi continued to bewail French indifference to the fate of their co-religionists in Germany but even Maximilian of Bavaria and the Emperor became the subject of criticism for their refusal to ignore private commodity in the interests of religion.[179] Rinuccini's position in Ireland was to be effectively identical, for like Chigi he considered that the scale of what the catholic party could achieve if it were united should act as the measure of what concessions might be allowable. Attitudes of this nature were securely anchored in the providentialism of contemporary religious thought which interpreted disasters as the fruit of divine displeasure with human sinfulness.[180]

Despite the decision to appoint him late in 1644, the new nuncio did not leave Rome until March of the following year. Preparations for the mission, in particular the amount of money which he was to receive, were probably disrupted by fresh demands made on the papal purse by both the emperor in Germany and the Venetians whose war with the Turks in Candia was in its initial stages.[181] The delay in Rinuccini's departure, however, also reflected the fact that his safe and timely arrival in Ireland was not the only objective of those who appointed him. Given the danger of the Atlantic sea passage, and the urgent need of the confederates for the subsidies which he brought with him before the onset of the campaigning season, it made compelling sense that Rinuccini should travel north, attracting as little attention as possible, and should embark from France before parliamentary ships emerged from their winter harbours towards the end of March. In the event, not only

---

[177] Pastor, *History of the Popes*, xxx. 94–130.   [178] Ibid., xxviii. 304–7.

[179] Ibid., xxx. 101, 113–14, 119–22.

[180] Ó hAnnracháin, 'Hereticks and Politicians', 170–4 provides a further discussion of such ideas.

[181] See Albizzi to Chigi, 29 Apr. (ns) 1645 (Kybal and Incisa Della Rochetta, *Nunziatura di Fabio Chigi*, 1044–6); Pamfili to Chigi, 4 Feb. (ns) 1645 (ibid., 796–7).

was he delayed in leaving Rome but thereafter his journey was both slow and exceedingly public. He was feted as the new Irish nuncio in Genoa which was of advantage to the new pope diplomatically but not to his own safety.[182] Obedient to the dictates of Roman foreign policy he then proceeded, not to the French coast, but to Paris. His original intention had been to reach Ireland before the end of the General Assembly of the summer of 1645 but his embroilment in papal business in the French capital prevented his departure.[183] For over three months the Irish aspect of his mission was relegated to the background as he engaged in an ultimately futile attempt to thaw relations between Mazarin and the new pope.[184]

Rinuccini personally does not appear to have been unduly unhappy about this delay. Parisian observers were pessimistic about his prospects of evading hostile shipping on the last leg of his journey.[185] The nuncio, therefore, became justifiably nervous about the prospect of the sea voyage. Moreover, he had enormous difficulties in arranging transport,[186] and he was worried that he might arrive in Ireland to find an unfavourable peace already concluded. Consequently he was attracted to the idea of negotiating with the Queen of England in France,[187] which would allow him to concentrate on religious matters when he eventually arrived in Ireland. Eventually, however, direct orders from Rome more or less forced him to set out for Ireland.[188]

The marine voyage came close to fulfilling his worst expectations. He was seven days at sea, during which time he was unable to sleep owing to a combination of seasickness and terror. For two days his small frigate was chased by a much larger protestant privateer and the nuncio was well aware that he faced immediate death or incarceration if the pursuit proved successful.[189] Quite apart from fear and the Atlantic's ungentle embrace, he was in very poor health. On his arrival in the French capital he had been stricken by a bad fever which had confined him for nine days to the bed which he had so prudently carried with him from Italy. He fell ill again in July, was still weak in Paris three months later, and felt unable to contemplate a secret journey

---

[182] See *Comment Rinucc.*, i. 630–3.   ·   [183] Ibid., 636; Aiazzi, *Nunziatura*, 443, 445, 447–9.
[184] Ó hAnnracháin, 'Vatican Diplomacy', 82–3.
[185] For example the Venetian ambassador, Giovanni Nani, wrote to his superiors that it was doubtful if the nuncio would ever arrive safely in Ireland: see Nani to Doge and Senate of Venice, 30 May (ns) 1645 (*Calendar of State Papers and Manuscripts Relating to English Affairs, Existing in the Archives and Collections of Venice, 1643–7* (London, 1926), 192).
[186] Rinuccini to Pamfili, 10 Sept. (ns) 1645 (Aiazzi, *Nunziatura*, 53); see also ibid., 25, 44, 57–8.
[187] Rinuccini to Pamfili, 14 July (ns) 1645 (Aiazzi, *Nunziatura*, 29–30); same to same, 4 Aug. (ns) 1645 (ibid., 38); see also Vittorio Gabrieli, 'La Missione di Sir Kenelm Digby alla Corte de Innocenzo X (1645–1648)', *English Miscellany*, 5 (Rome, 1954), 254–6.
[188] See select documents in Aiazzi, *Nunziatura*, 452–7. Interestingly Rinuccini took ship from the French protestant stronghold of La Rochelle: this seems to have been on the advice of Bellings who evidently expected to find other Irish ships there but the decision was probably a mistake as hostile protestant ships seemed to be well aware of the nuncio's movements: see *Comment. Rinucc.*, i. 732–4; ii. 1–9.
[189] Rinuccini to Pamfili, 15 Oct. 1645 (ibid., ii. 1–4).

to the coast because of his need for attendants.[190] As he entered the ship to Ireland his ailment worsened dramatically. He himself ascribed the problem to a blood disorder but it was possibly dermatological, because the chief symptom was a widespread and desperately sensitive rash on his skin. In addition, he was suffering from the attentions of what was evidently some kind of tapeworm.[191] Having finally landed in Kenmare, the archbishop of Fermo spent his first night in a local cow byre, from which the beasts themselves were not expelled. Although he consoled himself with the reflection that Christ's mission on earth had also begun in a stable,[192] his first night provided little rest after the terrors of the journey.

Matters, none the less, rapidly improved. The Italians took easily to the diet of Gaelic Munster. They particularly relished the shellfish, fish, milk, and beer which the mainly impoverished local inhabitants lavished upon them. They noted also the generosity of their hosts who immediately slaughtered a cow, two sheep, and a pig from their slender herds to supply the exalted guests with lightly cooked red meat. This gesture was somewhat wasted on the nuncio as he did not eat beef and had a marked preference for lighter food.[193] The reverence of the population also made a deep impression on the Italian party. As they moved in slow stages towards Limerick, guards with wooden staves were apparently necessary to keep away the crowds who thronged to touch even the hem of the garment of the pope's nuncio and onlookers constantly sank to their knees to implore his blessing.[194]

This interlude marked the first phase of Rinuccini's warm and approving relationship with Gaelic Ireland. Delivered from the terrors of the sea he encountered a hospitable people who greeted him with digestible food and simple reverence. In November, as he came to Kilkenny (where he was to be surfeited with beef to the exclusion of other meats),[195] the real business of his nunciature began less auspiciously. Significantly, the first diplomatic contact was the subject of the first dissatisfaction. His reception into Kilkenny was elaborately contrived but on his arrival the confederate president, Viscount Mountgarrett, did not come to greet him and did not even rise from

[190] See Rinuccini's letters to Pamfili, 26 May (ns), 2 June (ns), 11 Aug. (ns), 28 Sept. (ns) 1645 (Aiazzi *Nunziatura*, 7, 10, 44, 57).
[191] Rinuccini to Pamfili, 25 Oct. 1645 (ibid., 63); *Comment. Rinucc.*, i. 734; ii. 14, 20.
[192] Rinuccini to Pamfili, 25 Oct. 1645 (Aiazzi, *Nunziatura*, 67).
[193] Rinuccini to Alesio Celli(?), Nov. 1646 (AAF, iii. C/10): du Moulin to Mazarin, 24 Mar. 1646 (Gilbert, *Irish Confederation*, v. 276); when Massari ventured into Gaelic Ulster, he was similarly impressed by the food that he was offered, which he found strange but highly palatable: see Viaggio in Irlanda di Dionysio Massari (APF, Miscellaneae Varie, 9, p. 128).
[194] *Comment. Rinucc.*, ii. 8, 14; Scarampi had encountered identical behaviour upon his arrival in Ireland some years before: see the account of Scarampi's mission (BAV, Barberini Latini 4729, fo. 463ʳ): this passage is almost identical to Paolo Aringhi, *Memorie istoriche della vita del venerabile servo di Dio Pier Francesco Scarampi* (Rome, 1744), 38 and was probably therefore written by Aringhi.
[195] Du Moulin to Mazarin, 24 Mar. 1646 (Gilbert, *Irish Confederation*, v. 276).

his chair as the nuncio left the room in which the audience with the confederate leadership had been held.[196] Rinuccini chose not to complain publicly of this laxity. His superiors subsequently applauded his prudence in not antagonizing the Irish and deputized Luke Wadding to inform the Supreme Council of the ceremonial necessary, which was to be modelled on the etiquette in use between the Vatican and the Republic of Genoa.[197] This incident, however, proved somewhat prophetic of future difficulties.

IV

Rinuccini's arrival in Kilkenny was one of the most significant events of the entire decade. The new nuncio was a highly formidable character. In ways he was authoritarian although in situations where his will was not crossed he was evidently capable of great charm. There was perhaps a certain vanity in his personality but it is impossible to deny his genuine religious commitment. In addition to his acute intelligence, he was both determined and methodical and he was adept at utilizing the respect which accrued to him from his high religious office to exert influence and garner support. Moreover, he carried with him a considerable sum of money which was an important source of leverage within the cash-starved confederate association.

As indicated above, Rinuccini was not just a stereotypical product of the Italian counter-reformation. Nevertheless, it is undeniable that his pastoral and intellectual formation in Italy exerted an influence on his behaviour in Ireland and served to create a distance between him and certain influential confederates. Irrespective of personal beliefs, his instructions made it inevitable that the nuncio would press the confederate catholics to confirm the free and public exercise of the catholic religion as a central and non-negotiable objective of their association. But Rinuccini's behaviour in this regard was not motivated only by obedience to his instructions. His personal experience in the use of elaborate public ceremonies to stimulate the religious ardour of his archdiocese, and his belief in the success that this strategy had reaped, ensured that in Ireland he considered opposition to the acceptance of mere toleration for catholicism a pastoral and evangelical imperative.

Within an Irish context, enormous political problems confronted any attempt to secure the public exercise of catholicism, but in his quest to attain this goal the new nuncio was convinced that divine assistance would be forthcoming in return for a sincere commitment to God's cause, and that faith and a willingness to suffer and to take risks in that cause were neces-

---

[196] Aiazzi, *Nunziatura*, 71–2.
[197] See Rinuccini's relation of his entry into Kilkenny, 20 Nov. 1645 (*Comment. Rinucc.*, ii. 25–7) and Pamfili's response to Rinuccini, 25 Mar. (ns) 1646 (ibid., 27–8).

sary. Consequently, the nuncio was never to tire of enjoining the confederates to trust in divine aid, reassured, perhaps, by his belief that occasional martyrdoms would do no harm to the catholic faith in Ireland. Rinuccini was to attribute the confederate victories of 1646 and the continued turmoil in England which prevented the arrival of a parliamentary army to God's protecting hand. By the same logic, he interpreted the defeats of 1647 and later as a divine castigation for the confederates' lack of faith and disunity.[198] The nuncio believed that attempts to compromise on what was due to God for the sake of temporal gain inevitably led to both the loss of the secular objective and alienation from God. His conviction that a faction of the confederate association was acting in precisely this manner was probably not irrelevant to the distaste for the Old English community which he expressed at the end of his mission. Contrarily, the Gaelic Irish exiles of the Ulster army who had had no stake in the pre-1641 system found it easier to present themselves to the nuncio as selflessly committed to God's cause.

Rinuccini's perception of his nunciature as an exotic, exciting, and historic mission of catholic renewal also probably contributed to the lack of sympathy between himself and much of the native catholic community, particularly the wealthier members of the Old English, whom he found distressingly unwilling to match his own religious ardour. The legal background of so many of the confederate executive and their intellectual training in English common law was arguably another obstacle to the development of a harmonious relationship with the nuncio. Rinuccini had little patience with either lawyers or legalistic formulae. He believed that laws had validity only if they were consonant with God's design. The nuncio was therefore peculiarly ill-equipped to understand the preoccupations of constitutionally conservative confederate lawyers who were eager to preserve as much of the traditional framework of law and authority as was practicable. For their part, secular confederates had little experience of dealing with such an assertive catholic prelate who had never been a fugitive before the law but who rather was accustomed to an institutional position within society with a wide-ranging jurisdiction in both temporal and ecclesiastical affairs. The difficulty of dealing with such a figure was augmented by the combination of intelligence, determination, charisma, and certitude in the nuncio's personality which was to make him a very difficult character to satisfy, divert, or defeat while he was in Ireland.

[198] Ibid., ii. 78, 230–2, 235, 237, 420, 682.

II.   Rinuccini in Ireland

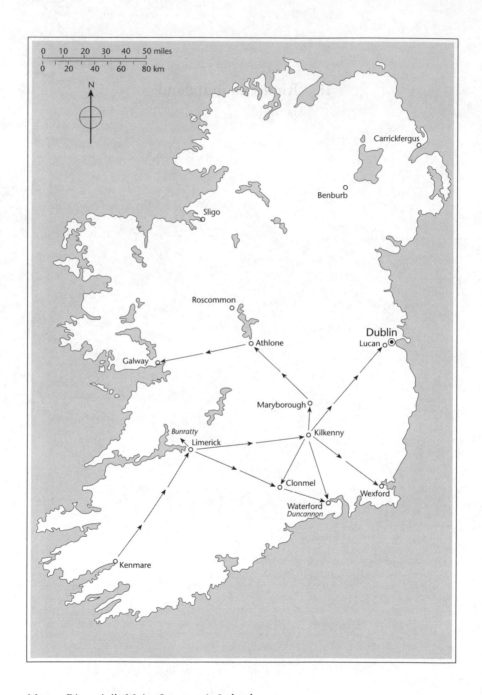

MAP 3. Rinuccini's Major Journeys in Ireland

CHAPTER FOUR

Resistance to the Ormond Peace

I

Rinuccini's first fourteen months in Ireland, from his arrival in October 1645 to his return to Kilkenny after the failure of the campaign against Dublin in December 1646, witnessed some of the most violent transformations of his turbulent nunciature. The backdrop to the unfolding drama both in Britain and on the continent was similarly eventful. In June 1645 the decisive parliamentary victory at the battle of Naseby irrevocably altered the course of the first English Civil War. In Scotland, on 13 September, Montrose was routed at Philiphaugh, which effectively left the royalist cause without a field army in Britain. The king's strongholds fell steadily all over England in the winter of 1645–6 and Charles delivered himself to the Scottish covenanters the following April. On 24 June Oxford surrendered and, by the time the Ormond peace was concluded in Ireland in August 1646, all the major garrisons around the royalist capital had also been taken. Rinuccini's first year in Ireland thus witnessed the effective end of the first civil war in England. On the European mainland the Swedish victory at Jankov in March 1645 and Turenne's destruction of the Bavarian army at Allerheim meant that a Habsburg victory in the German war was effectively impossible and in November 1645 the real negotiations for peace commenced.[1] The dynamic of these events in both Britain and on the continent was to exercise a profound effect on developments in Ireland.

The basic narrative of events in Ireland during this period is sufficiently well known and needs little further elaboration. It has been noted in the past that the months from Rinuccini's arrival in Kilkenny in November 1645 until July 1646 were characterized by intense and ultimately fruitless negotiations between the nuncio and the Supreme Council.[2] During this time, in essence,

---

[1] See John Kenyon, *The Civil Wars of England* (London, 1989), 143–57; David Stevenson, *Scottish Covenanters and Irish Confederates* (Belfast, 1981), 175–82; G. E. Aylmer, *Rebellion or Revolution: England from Civil War to Restoration* (Oxford, 1986), 75–80; Geoffrey Parker, *The Thirty Years' War* (London, 1984), 175–9; Richard Bonney, *The European Dynastic States* (Oxford, 1991), 200; Robert Bireley, 'The Thirty Years' War as Germany's Religious War', in K. Repgen (ed.), *Krieg und Politik, 1618–1648* (Munich, 1988), 104–6.

[2] See in particular D. F. Cregan, 'The Confederation of Kilkenny: Its Organisation, Personnel and History' (unpub. Ph.D. thesis, National University of Ireland, 1947), 188–205; Micheál Ó Siochrú, *Confederate Ireland, 1642–1649: A Constitutional and Political Analysis* (Dublin, 1999), 98–102.

the council was unable to persuade the nuncio to give his consent to a two-pronged peace, in which the chief grievances of the secular confederates would be catered for in a public agreement with Ormond, while the concerns of the clergy would be addressed in an additional and secret arrangement with Glamorgan. That Rinuccini would oppose the suggested compromise of the confederate peace party so stubbornly was highly predictable, first because of his formation and experience in Italy, second because his stance in this regard had already been foreshadowed by that of Scarampi prior to his arrival, and third because in the course of his first year in Ireland the nuncio became aware that the religious sentiments of most of the clergy and of many secular confederates were substantially in line with his own on this issue. Despite this, in the course of the period under review, Rinuccini found himself unable to convince the council to abandon plans for peace until what he saw as essential ecclesiastical concerns had been fully and publicly satisfied.[3]

These tortuous negotiations went through several different phases as various events altered the positions of the different protagonists.[4] The first major turning point was Ormond's imprisonment of Glamorgan in Dublin on 26 December 1645. The lord lieutenant, supported by the king's chief secretary, George Digby, was more or less forced into this action to protect Charles's reputation when news reached Dublin that the English parliament had published details of the Glamorgan articles.[5] This weakened the case for peace by disrupting the two-pronged settlement which had been close to finalization prior to Rinuccini's arrival. In late January 1646 the emergence of the ultimately fruitless papal peace added a new dimension to negotiations,[6] which allowed the nuncio to force the confederates to delay the promulgation of peace until at least the beginning of May. In March the news that Charles had publicly disowned Glamorgan reached Ireland but that did not prevent the council from concluding, although not publishing, their treaty with Ormond on 28 March.[7] In June, following his surrender to the

---

[3] Ó Siochrú, *Confederate Ireland*, 98–102; Patrick Corish, 'Ormond, Rinuccini, and the Confederates, 1645–9', in T. W. Moody, F. X. Martin, and F. J. Byrne (eds.), *A New History of Ireland*, iii, *Early Modern Ireland, 1534–1691*, 318–20; John Lowe, 'The Glamorgan Mission to Ireland', *Studia Hibernica*, 4 (1964), 172–92.

[4] The essential sequence of events is summarized in Corish, 'The Rising of 1641', 317–20; see also Lowe, 'The Glamorgan Mission', 172–92.

[5] Lowe, 'The Glamorgan Mission', 179–86.

[6] This was the product of negotiation between Sir Kenelm Digby, who operated as the agent of Queen Henrietta Maria, and the Vatican secretariat in Rome. The peace was a fairly straight quid pro quo between the Vatican and the Stuart monarchy: in return for religious concessions in the three Stuart kingdoms, but particularly Ireland, the pope promised to provide Charles with up to 400,000 scudi (about £100,000). Ultimately, the peace collapsed because the royalist camp opted to deal with the presbyterian factions in England and Scotland rather than with the pope: see Vittorio Gabrieli 'La Missione di Sir Kenelm Digby alla Corte di Innocenze X (1645–1648)', *English Miscellany*, 5 (Rome, 1954), 247–88; for the actual terms see *Comment. Rinucc.*, ii. 118–20.

[7] Corish, 'Ormond, Rinuccini, and the Confederates, 1645–9', 320; there is an excellent analysis of the articles of peace in Cregan, 'The Confederation of Kilkenny' (thesis), 205–18.

Scots, the king disowned Ormond's right to make peace with the confederates. This put a further obstacle in the way of publication which was not
resolved until the end of July and then only by the application of French
influence. By that time, however, a succession of military victories at
Benburb, Bunratty, and in Connacht had helped create a situation in which
the nuncio was able and determined to oppose the peace.[8]

Rinuccini had previously arranged a legatine national synod in Waterford
which during August first rejected the peace and then excommunicated those
who supported it.[9] Both O'Neill and Preston (eventually), the most important confederate generals, opted to stand by the clergy and in September
Rinuccini returned to Kilkenny and re-established a confederate Supreme
Council under his own presidency. A decision was then made to send the
armies of both Preston and O'Neill against Ormond, who after a brief visit
to Kilkenny had been forced to flee back to Dublin. The lord lieutenant for
his part opened negotiations with parliament to transfer his garrisons to
their control. In the event, the catholic marquis of Clanricard's ability to
influence Preston, added to bad weather and inadequate supplies, undermined the confederate campaign against Dublin. Following the failure of the
attack, Ormond was able to wriggle out of his arrangement with parliament
and maintain his position over the winter. Having returned to Kilkenny,
Rinuccini was persuaded to convene the confederate General Assembly to
discuss the situation and this created a fragile breathing space for all parties
in the weeks prior to its meeting.[10]

II

The general outline of events is thus reasonably clear but, with regard to the
nuncio during this period, what has generally escaped attention is the manner
in which his attitudes towards the peace evolved over time. Prior to 26
December 1645, as has been noted in the secondary literature, Rinuccini
negotiated extensively with Glamorgan, during which time he extracted very
significant concessions from the earl.[11] In the past, possibly because the nuncio
of December 1645 has been obscured by his more belligerent persona of 1646,
Rinuccini's position in these negotiations has been somewhat misunderstood.

[8] Corish, 'Ormond, Rinuccini, and the Confederates, 1645–9', 320; Jerrald Casway, *Owen Roe
O'Neill and the Struggle for Catholic Ireland* (Philadelphia, 1984), 119–40; Stevenson, *Covenanters
and Confederates*, 217–36.
[9] Corish, 'Ormond, Rinuccini, and the Confederates, 1645–9', 320–1.
[10] Ibid., 321–2; Cregan, 'The Confederation of Kilkenny' (thesis), 230–5; Casway, *Owen Roe
O'Neill*, 151–71; J. C. Beckett, *The Cavalier Duke* (Belfast, 1990), 39–41.
[11] Glamorgan committed his king to a catholic viceroy, the seating of catholic bishops in parliament and the right of the catholic clergy to all churches in all places captured by the confederates
before the final confirmation of the treaty: see Cregan, 'The Confederation of Kilkenny' (thesis),
189–91; Corish, 'Ormond, Rinuccini, and the Confederates, 1645–9', 318–19; Lowe, 'The
Glamorgan Mission', 172–3; *Comment. Rinucc.*, ii. 88–9.

The nuncio was neither as satisfied with the worth of Glamorgan's mandate as has been implied,[12] nor in as strong a position to disrupt the peace process as has previously been suggested.[13] Indeed, it must be stressed that throughout his first months in Ireland, the nuncio's posture was basically defensive. He himself declared to his superior, the papal secretary, Cardinal Pamfili, the following summer: 'I confess that for eight months by various stratagems I have restrained the impetus towards peace.'[14]

Rinuccini's negotiations with Glamorgan were critically influenced by his dawning realization of the council's unshakeable desire to conclude peace with Ormond, despite his own best arguments to the contrary.[15] He came to the conclusion that the council did not want to antagonize the pope but believed that no human persuasion could alter their inclinations.[16] In an attempt, therefore, to make the best of a bad bargain, he negotiated with Glamorgan so that the articles concerning religion in the treaty would be the best possible. It is in this light that the nuncio's comment that he had persuaded Glamorgan to promise 'all that which seemed to me to be missing concerning the security of religion' should be interpreted.[17]

Rinuccini's violent opposition to the Ormond peace in August 1646 thus represented a considerable departure from his earlier resigned attitude. Although he realized that the council were prepared to make peace on terms he considered unacceptable, and that a substantial faction of the confederates were eager to reject the peace if he provided leadership,[18] it is clear that Rinuccini had no intention of forcibly opposing the council in December 1645.[19] Rather he

[12] Corish, 'Ormond, Rinuccini, and the Confederates, 1645–9', 318; Rinuccini certainly seems to have accepted that Glamorgan's mandate was not a forgery but, because it was given under the private seal he believed it to be inadequate.

[13] See Lowe, 'The Glamorgan Mission', 173, which suggests that Rinuccini could easily 'wreck' the treaty if he was not 'reassured about the future of the church'; see also Beckett, *Cavalier Duke*, 35.

[14] 'Fateor me cohibuisse variis inventionibus octo mensium curriculo impetum hujus tractatus': Rinuccini to Pamfili, 20 June 1646 (*Comment. Rinucc.*, ii. 234).

[15] Extensive correspondence with the council during these months eventually brought him to this conclusion: see the Latin originals of the documents in *Comment. Rinucc.*, ii. 45–66, 72–84.

[16] Rinuccini to Pamfili, 23 Dec. 1645 (Aiazzi, *Nunziatura*, 79).

[17] '[T]utto quello che mi pareva che mancasse alla sicurezza della Religione': Rinuccini to Pamfili, 23 Dec. 1645 (Aiazzi, *Nunziatura*, 78); as Corish, 'Ormond, Rinuccini, and the Confederates, 1645–9', 318 and Lowe, 'The Glamorgan Mission', 173 have noted this agreement was considerably in advance of anything which had previously been offered to Irish catholics, but this should not be taken to imply that Rinuccini was satisfied with the agreement.

[18] See Rinuccini's description of the mainly clerical, Old Irish and anti-Ormond war-party in his letters to Pamfili of 25 Nov. 1645 (Aiazzi, *Nunziatura*, 74), 23 Dec. 1645 (ibid., 75), 26 Dec. 1645 (ibid., 78–9).

[19] Although it is true that Rinuccini prepared an instrument at this time, which was then signed by two archbishops and six bishops, declaring his inability to approve of any peace which published secular conditions independently of religious ones, or which combined the jurisdiction of the confederates with that of a protestant, his objective was defensive, to protect the pope's dignity. As the authors of the *Commentarius Rinuccinianus* were eager to point out, this declaration did not signify that the clergy would take active measures to undermine a peace which did not meet these conditions (*Comment. Rinucc.*, ii. 88).

informed those who offered to support him in an open resistance to the peace that the pope did not want his minister to be an instrument of division but a mediator.[20] Indeed, he was already making plans concerning his own behaviour when peace was concluded.[21]

Why, apart from distrust of the doubtful value of Glamorgan's commission upon which the religious articles were to depend, was the nuncio so unhappy with the peace?[22] One of his fundamental objections was that the peace would establish the government of a protestant viceroy. The implications which this would have had for Rinuccini's mission were considerable. In effect, its continued existence was under threat. As Scarampi and Spinola, Rinuccini's envoy, had informed the confederates prior to his arrival, it was 'neither seemly nor customary' for a nuncio to reside in an area under the government of a protestant.[23] Consequently, the conclusion of peace meant that the mission which had been announced with such pomp in Rome would be seen to have been publicly rebuffed.[24] The confederates ultimately attempted to smooth over this difficulty by appealing to Ormond to 'countenance' Rinuccini. The lord lieutenant, for whom contact with a papal minister was equally problematic, cautiously responded that he would do so to the extent that it proved conducive to the king's service.[25] None the less, whether any workable arrangement could ever have been implemented remains highly dubious.

Rinuccini contended in addition that the proposed peace would give rise to scandal because the secular articles were to be published while the religious articles were to be kept secret. The confederates were slow to grasp the importance of this matter to the Roman curia. Having sent 'his Apostolic nuncio through so many dangers with arms and money for their use',[26] and having chosen to honour the Irish above the Catalans, or the Portuguese, or the Dutch catholics, the pope's dignity demanded an enthusiastic response from the confederates, not the conclusion of a peace without public guarantees for the catholic religion.

[20] Rinuccini to Pamfili, 23 Dec. 1645 (*Comment. Rinucc.*, ii. 91).

[21] On 26 Dec. he pointed out to Pamfili that the confederates were still committed to war against parliament and the Scots, whether peace was concluded or not. He expressed hopes that the entire island could be liberated with a determined effort and pleaded for more aid from the pope: Rinuccini to Pamfili, 26 Dec. 1645 (Aiazzi, *Nunziatura*, 79).

[22] Cregan, 'The Confederation of Kilkenny' (thesis), 188–91 and Corish 'Ormond, Rinuccini, and the Confederates, 1645–9', 317 largely concentrate on his distrust of the fact that the religious aspects of the treaty would depend on the king's goodwill for implementation.

[23] '[N]eque conveniens nec usitatum sit': see *Comment. Rinucc.*, i. 569; see also Rinuccini to the Supreme Council, 25 June 1646 (ibid., ii. 233).

[24] Moreover, the Rinuccini mission was not intended as a unique interlude but as the beginning of the Vatican's Irish nunciature: Scarampi, for instance, objected to Rinuccini's mode of establishing his tribunal on the grounds that it would prejudice the rights of his successors (ibid., ii. 93).

[25] Instructions to Plunkett, 17 Apr. 1646 (Bodl. Carte MS 17, fo. 171ʳ); and Ormond's response (ibid. fo. 174ʳ)

[26] '[P]er tot pericula Nuncium suum Apostolicum, et ad vestram utilitatem armis etiam et pecunia, atque iis monitis instructum': (*Comment. Rinucc.*, ii. 74).

Rinuccini also objected to the confederates' argument that compromise was necessary in view of the king's weakness and consequent inability to provoke protestant opinion in England by granting concessions to catholics. In Rinuccini's opinion, if Charles was weak then there was actually little to be gained from conciliating him. Indeed, he argued that the crown's weakness meant that the onus of compromise rested on the king's viceroy, not on the confederates.[27] Two radically different perspectives clashed on this point. The peace party among the confederates, centred around Muskery, Bellings, Fennell, Sir Lucas Dillon, Browne, and Mountgarrett, felt it imperative to consider the negotiations in Ireland within the context of the English Civil War, in which they were desperate to prevent a parliamentary victory.[28] If the king lost, then a retributive invasion and the confiscation of their property threatened. Even if the danger could somehow be beaten off successfully, in an Ireland jarred loose from English control their property might still be at risk from claims which could be lodged against it by a combination of Old Irish and clerical interests. Although he had no wish to overthrow the Stuart monarchy in Ireland, Rinuccini's attitude towards the constitutional authority of the king was different. If parliament won the English war, then he believed that the island of Ireland would simply have to stand on its own.[29] If the king emerged triumphant, he was not daunted by the consequences of having alienated him with excessive demands during the crown's weakness, because he believed an acceptable settlement of the church in Ireland was too important to be allowed to depend on a protestant monarch's grace and forbearance. If, as the confederates tried to convince him, the king was favourably disposed towards catholics, then the nuncio would accept any concessions he might make. But he was not prepared to entrust the eventual fulfilment of what he saw as essential religious conditions to the king's good will. If Charles refused to grant certain points then the nuncio's instinct was to attempt to hold the island by force until they were obtained.[30]

Another vital aspect of the nuncio's distrust of the two-pronged treaty was the fear that, having acquired a peace which publicly settled the grievances of secular catholics, the confederate laity would not then be prepared to put this settlement at risk by renewing the rebellion if the secret Glamorgan con-

---

[27] *Comment. Rinucc.*, ii. 75; moreover, Rinuccini was very distrustful of the king: see Cregan, 'The Confederation of Kilkenny' (thesis), 189.

[28] A point which Ormond acknowledged by November 1645, although ironically prior to this he believed that the confederates had been reasonably sanguine about the decline of the royalist cause, precisely because they had hoped it would force further concessions from the king: see Ormond to Dillon, 4 Nov. 1645 (Bodl. Carte MS , 16, fo. 168ʳ)

[29] A point noted previously in Nicholas Canny, *From Reformation to Restoration: Ireland, 1534–1660* (Dublin, 1987), 211–13; Canny's argument is supported by Rinuccini's Relatio Status Rerum, 1 Mar. 1646 (Aiazzi, *Nunziatura*, 115).

[30] *Comment. Rinucc.*, ii. 82.

cessions were subsequently denied by the king.[31] In one memorial to the council, therefore, the nuncio floated the idea that the secular peace be suppressed until the religious articles were confirmed by the king,[32] a suggestion in accordance with the spirit of the original oath of association. The peace party's reluctance to accept this proposition certainly reflected a realization of the impossibility of persuading Ormond to such a course,[33] but it was also an indication that their protestations concerning the worth of the Glamorgan articles were somewhat hollow. Whether Rinuccini adopted a wise policy in the face of constant confederate desire for a settlement is certainly debatable but his analysis in this regard was reasonably shrewd.

For their part, the confederate negotiators had little room for manœuvre in their dealings with the nuncio. Tense debates during the previous months had revealed Ormond's determination to close the door against the saying of mass publicly in churches. In this regard, the confederates had pushed matters as close as they dared, even to the point where the lord lieutenant had begun to believe that they deliberately intended to force a breach on this issue.[34] Aware of his intractability, the Supreme Council enlisted Glamorgan's assistance in convincing the nuncio of the worth of the religious settlement on offer.[35]

It was Glamorgan's imprisonment on 26 December, followed by the arrival in Ireland of a draft in cipher of the papal peace, which first radicalized the nuncio's position. The security of Glamorgan's articles for the catholic church was of course compromised as a result of the disavowal of his authority by both Ormond and the king's secretary, George Digby.[36] Moreover, the proposed terms of the papal peace were substantially better than those offered by Glamorgan.[37] Rinuccini thus became desperate to prevent the

[31] As surely they would have been: it was the king's stubborn attachment to his own religious convictions, which allowed him accept stringent measures against papists but which refused to allow him compromise on what he saw as structures basic to the Church of England, that eventually sealed his fate: see Robert Ashton, *The English Civil War: Conservatism and Revolution, 1603–1649*, 2nd edn. (London, 1991), 335–9; David Underdown, *Pride's Purge: Politics in the Puritan Revolution* (London, 1985), 111–13.

[32] *Comment. Rinucc.*, ii. 75.

[33] The refusal of both Ormond and Clanricard to join openly with the confederates while their status as rebels remained officially unaltered had been a source of considerable frustration to the association's leadership for several years: see for example Muskery to Ormond, 18 Aug. 1645 (Bodl. Carte MS 15 fo. 455) and Ormond's response, 20 Aug. 1645 (ibid., fos. 467–8); see also ibid., 17, fo. 424ʳ).

[34] Ormond to unnamed correspondent, 17 Oct. 1645 (Bodl. Carte MS 16 fo. 45ʳ); see also ibid., fos. 36ʳ, 38ʳ, 48ʳ, 494–50ᵛ.

[35] Ibid., fo. 369ʳ.   [36] Lowe, 'The Glamorgan Mission', 179–86.

[37] In particular, the government of Ireland was to be permanently in the hands of catholics selected by the king; all areas held by royalist garrisons in Ireland were to receive catholic commanders; the royalist forces were to join the confederate armies in attacking the Scots and parliamentarian forces in Ireland; and, in England, anti-catholic legislation was to be rendered harmless so that catholics could enjoy all legal honours, immunities, prerogatives, liberties, and possession of property: see *Comment. Rinucc.*, ii. 118–19.

ratification of the Ormond peace, particularly because he was afraid that the lord lieutenant, once placed in a position of power by the secular peace, would not accept the provisions of the papal treaty when it arrived.[38] In order to secure his point he became ready to threaten civil war,[39] and ultimately forced the postponement of the definitive conclusion of the Ormond peace until May.

In March the arrival in Ireland of news that Charles had publicly disowned Glamorgan's mandate to make peace with the confederates[40] confirmed Rinuccini's belief in the inadequacy of the religious conditions on offer in the Irish negotiations. Yet, at the end of the time allotted for their arrival, not even a public draft of the articles of the papal peace had appeared, and consequently the only alternative to peace with Ormond which the nuncio could offer was the maintenance of an independent confederate government, preferably throughout the whole island.[41] Consequently, towards the end of May the nuncio retreated again from the bellicose position which he had adopted when he had hoped to be able to introduce the papal peace. Once more he had clearly abandoned the intention of promoting rebellion against the council if a treaty was concluded, although he was more convinced than ever that there was no military need for peace.[42] If an unsuitable settlement was signed the nuncio gloomily informed Pamfili on 21 May that he would: 'follow the commandments given to me by Your Eminence . . . to do no act, not to give a positive consent, but to let matters take their course.'[43] In June, still in a defensive posture, he wrote to the council, asking them to summon the General Assembly before any peace was concluded.[44] Rinuccini's coup against the government established by the peace in August–September 1646 was thus the product of a second transformation in his position and was actually at odds with the stance which he had adopted for much of the preceding period. Because these alterations in the nuncio's attitudes have not previously been stressed, the complexity of his reasons for eventually overtly

[38] Rinuccini's arguments against the conclusion of peace before the arrival of the papal peace (*Comment. Rinucc.*, ii. 141–2): from Rinuccini's point of view, one of the great advantages of the papal peace was that it would remove Ormond from his position as lord lieutenant and commander in Dublin. Consequently, he was determined that no peace putting the confederates under Ormond's authority should be signed before the arrival of the papal articles.

[39] He pointed out baldly that the Old Irish confederates would support the clergy's position if his advice was ignored: *Comment. Rinucc.*, ii. 141.

[40] Lowe, 'The Glamorgan Mission', 190–1.

[41] He was prepared to envisage some co-operation with Ormond but only on such stringent conditions that there was no hope that the marquis would accept: Rinuccini to Supreme Council, 5 May 1646 (*Comment. Rinucc.*, ii. 212–15).

[42] Rinuccini to the Supreme Council, 10 June 1646 (ibid., ii. 224).

[43] '[I]l commandamento datomi da V.E. . . . di non far atto, nè dar consenso positivo, ma lasciar fare': Rinuccini to Pamfili, 21 May 1646 (Aiazzi, *Nunziatura*, 131).

[44] *Comment. Rinucc.*, ii. 220; this conformed with an agreement which he had made with confederate negotiators on 19 February, which stated that before the conclusion of the Ormond peace the assembly would be convoked if Rinuccini or Glamorgan felt it necessary.

opposing the published peace have not been thoroughly analysed. In this regard, the hostile and distrustful relationship which developed between the nuncio and the Supreme Council during Rinuccini's first year in Ireland requires consideration.

III

Problems existed in this relationship on a number of levels, one of which was evidently the difficulty of mutual contact and communication. Rinuccini, like Scarampi before him, spoke neither English nor Irish with any fluency. Confederate competency in Latin went some distance towards alleviating this difficulty,[45] but different codes of formal behaviour also posed problems. In his history, Bellings later argued that the nuncio's:

> precise exactness in the least formalities, the great distance between his composed reservefulness and the free-hearted nature of the Irish lessened the esteem which the nation, at first sight, had for him; so that those qualities which gained him the reputation of an excellent courtier at Rome, did in some manner contribute to render him an useless Minister in Ireland.[46]

Sir Richard Blake also found the nuncio's inner thoughts inpenetratable. Even after Rinuccini's humiliation in 1649, following the publication of the second Ormond peace in Galway, he noted that: 'the Italian kept himself close (what his thoughts were I know not nor care not).'[47] The dismissive use of the word Italian in this context is of interest. A stereotypical negativity concerning Italian character may also have helped to create distance between the nuncio and some of the association's leadership, particularly those of Old English extraction. Almost certainly as a result of information from confederate sources, Colonel Barry reported in 1648 that 'the Pope's nuncio is so iniurious, Italian like, he will never forget or forgive an injury'.[48] Sir Kenelm Digby's portrait was perhaps the most unflattering concerning the nuncio's stiff and unyielding character: 'people familiar with the nature and genius of Mons. Rinuccini affirm that through ceremonies, punctilious obstinacies and his own precepts . . . he is more apt to disrupt than to facilitate difficult business.'[49] In this regard, it is relevant to note that it was not only the confederates who failed to measure up to Rinuccini's exacting standards.[50]

---

[45] See Cregan, 'The Confederation of Kilkenny' (thesis), 113–14.

[46] Bellings's narrative, (Gilbert, *Irish Confederation*, v. 10).

[47] Blake to Ormond, 13 Feb. 1649 (Bodl. Carte MS 23, fo. 413ʳ).

[48] Barry to unnamed correspondent, Apr. 1648 (Bodl. Carte MS 22, fo. 67ʳ).

[49] 'Affermano persone pratiche della natura e genio di Mons. Rinuccini che per cerimonie, puntighi e dettami proprii . . . egli sia più atto à sconcertare, che ad accomodare negotii ardue': Sir Kenelm Digby's own summary of his arguments to the pope, undated but clearly either late 1646 or early 1647 (BAV, Barberini Latini 5653, fo. 184ᵛ).

[50] In Paris, in 1645, he complained of the brusque and confused manner in which the French conducted diplomatic encounters: Rinuccini to Pamfili, 2 June 1645 (Aiazzi, *Nunziatura*, 9–10).

Nevertheless, the nuncio's formality and his tendency to measure 'by the standards of Bernini's Rome'[51] should not be exaggerated. In general the confederates evidently were somewhat slipshod in the forms of diplomacy.[52] Moreover, Rinuccini was not so punctilious that he could not react with appreciation to the generosity and reverence which was accorded to him by the impoverished Gaelic community around Kenmare in October 1645. For his part he complained in Kilkenny that Old English confederates showed no desire to develop an easy relationship with him but were careful to maintain all business on a formal level, unlike the Gaelic Irish who visited his house more freely.[53] Rinuccini, indeed, seems to have been relatively understanding of occasional failures in courtesy.[54] As the pope's representative, he frigidly seems to have passed over any perceived slights without drawing undue attention to the incidents in his reports to Rome. Some of the confederates may have found this cold but it could have been a great deal worse. It seems probable, therefore, that the frigid and increasingly hostile relationship between the council and the nuncio was not entirely a product of Italian hypersensitivity concerning formality and order. Whatever the reasons, it was, nevertheless, to be a factor of considerable importance. Poor communications and the council's mistaken reading of the nuncio's determination were to play an important role in the crisis of August 1646.

Formal difficulties were none the less only an aspect of the problem. Of greater long-term significance was the dissatisfaction which the nuncio began to express with the manner and objectives of the council's government. On 1 March 1646 Rinuccini submitted his first major report on the state of affairs in Ireland. He began the second portion of the report with a

---

[51] Corish, 'Ormond, Rinuccini, and the Confederates, 1645–9', 317.

[52] The examples are very numerous: their own agent in Paris, Matthew O' Hartigan, noted the Irish ignorance of diplomatic protocol: see T. Morrissey 'The Strange Letters of Matthew O'Hartigan SJ', *Irish Theological Quarterly*, 37 (1970), 169–70; Mazarin's most trusted emissary in Ireland, Jean Talon, was incensed in 1647 by the 'haute impertinence' of the bishop of Limerick, then a member of the Supreme Council, towards the French resident, du Moulin. When du Moulin presented letters expressing the wishes of his king to the Supreme Council, the bishop declared openly that the king of France was a little boy who signed whatever his advisors put before him: Talon to Mazarin, 21 Dec. 1647 (AMAE, Corr. Pol. (Angleterre) 55, fo. 411ʳ). In the late autumn of 1646 du Moulin had also been deeply offended by the Supreme Council's failure to inform him that they had permitted a levy of troops to Spain, an omission which Rinuccini did his best to smooth over: Rinuccini to Mazarin, 29 Nov. 1646 (AMAE, Corr. Pol. (Angleterre) 52, fo. 666ᵛ); Rinuccini himself had suffered from similar negligence earlier the same year: in June the council sent him a letter informing him of their intentions with regard to peace but gave him no time even to read the letter before implementing their decision: see Rinuccini to Pamfili, 20 June 1646 (Aiazzi, *Nunziatura*, 140–1).

[53] Rinuccini's relation to the Pope (Aiazzi, *Nunziatura*, 395); in this regard one can note that the Old English had frequently been accused of social aloofness by members of the New English community.

[54] In November 1646 he wrote to Mazarin on the confederates' behalf, explaining that their diplomatic clumsiness was not evidence of any malice: see Rinuccini to Mazarin, 29 Nov. 1646 (AMAE, Corr. Pol. (Angleterre) 52, fo. 666ᵛ).

strong condemnation of the confederate policy of truce and negotiation with Ormond, which he believed was inefficient and counterproductive:

It is obvious that if at the beginning of the war they had steadily continued to take control of all the fortresses of the realm, and particularly of Dublin, today the Irish would be certainly the masters of everything; and professing by virtue of their oath to hold all for the king . . . they would have justified their cause much better, than by means of the truces and compromises undertaken afterwards, by which they have not even managed to avoid being called rebels both by His Majesty and all the English.[55]

Yet the nuncio identified something darker than mere inefficiency in this policy. It was the 'Ormond' faction he argued which had introduced the truces, without which 'the war would have been finished absolutely'.[56] This faction, he explained, was motivated by its suspicion of the clergy and of the Gaelic Irish confederates and by a repugnant belief which: 'they are not afraid to profess that if the free exercise of religion was obtained in private houses that it would be superfluous and unjust to seek for more.'[57] He insisted also that, spurred on by the promises which he held out to his partisans, the great aim of Ormond's supporters was to:

place the Marquis in such a state of authority, that he can rule all the provinces according to his will; and to the great infamy of the oath which the realm took from the beginning, to subject to his discretion the exercise and the ceremony of the catholic religion.[58]

Operating in tandem with the schemes of the 'Ormond' faction was, he believed, the general inefficiency of the association.[59] Rinuccini's analysis of the situation in Ireland within this framework provides an essential key to his behaviour in Ireland. In essence, by the spring of 1646 the nuncio had come to believe that most of the confederates' problems could be ascribed to the

---

[55] 'É manifesto, che se al principio della guerra si fosse constantemente continuato ad impadronirsi di tutte le fortezze del Regno, e principalmente di Dublino, oggi gl'Irlandesi sarebbono al sicuro padroni d'ogni cosa; e con professare in virtù del giuramento di tener tutto per il Re . . . assai meglio averebbono giustificato le lor causa, che per mezzo delle tregue e temperamenti presi dopo, con i quali nemmeno hanno potuto fuggire d'esser chiamati rebelli e da S.M. e di tutti gli Inglesi': Relazione del Regno d'Irlanda, 1 Mar. 1646 (Aiazzi, *Nunziatura*, 108).

[56] 'Finita assolutamente la guerra': (ibid.).

[57] 'Non vergognandosi di proferire, che quando s'ottenga l'esercizio libero della Religione per le case, sia superfluo ed ingiusto il ricercar da vantaggio' (ibid., 105).

[58] 'Di collocare il Marchese in tale stato di autorità, che possa reggar a sua voglia tutte le Provincie; e con infamia grandissima del giuramento chi il Regno prestò da principio, soggettare alla discrezione di lui l'esercizio e l'apparenza della Religione Cattolica' (ibid, 108); in this regard, see also Cregan, 'The Confederation of Kilkenny', in Brian Farrell (ed.), *The Irish Parliamentary Tradition* (Dublin, 1973), 111.

[59] He deplored the lack of a council of war, the inflation of the Supreme Council's numbers to the detriment of effective decision-making, the chaotic financial practices, and the lack of forward planning, all of which were particularly distressing to an experienced administrator like the nuncio (ibid., 109); his comments in this regard echoed that of other observers.

ulterior motives and ambitions of the 'Ormondite' leadership and poor organization, a particularly unhappy combination to a meticulous and devout prelate like the archbishop of Fermo.

This report was compiled in the wake of the General Assembly of February 1646 which was convoked to discuss the crisis created by the imprisonment of Glamorgan in Dublin and which evidently hastened the crystallization of Rinuccini's opinions concerning the confederate peace party. From the nuncio's perspective, what he saw as the council's fundamental unwillingness to address the clergy's concerns was thrown into even sharper relief by the enthusiastic reception which was accorded to him by the main body of the association at this time.[60] In the months that followed the nuncio's dissatisfaction with the council was boosted massively by their willingness even to lie to him in an attempt to protect the implementation of the Ormond peace.

The first of the council's deceptions occurred in February 1646. The assembly was then in session and Rinuccini's capacity to sway its members with his orations clearly worried the dominant clique on the confederate executive.[61] The negotiators appointed by the council to deal with Ormond were desperate to conclude peace with the lord lieutenant before his authority expired at the beginning of April, while Rinuccini hoped to postpone any treaty until the arrival of the papal peace.[62] After furious negotiations, a fragile agreement was eventually reached on 19 February.[63] The nuncio, and more particularly the council, both entered into the agreement in something less than total honesty and the failure of both sides to give weight to their

[60] As Patrick Corish has noted, the assembly generally acted as a restraint on the movement towards peace: see Corish, 'Ormond, Rinuccini, and the Confederates, 1645–9', 319. This assembly indeed was only convened because the council had little alternative in the wake of Glamorgan's imprisonment: see Rinuccini to Pamfili, 10 Feb. 1646 (Aiazzi, *Nunziatura*, 88); same to same, 21 Feb. 1646 (ibid., 91). After the earl's release, the council would willingly have postponed the assembly which allowed the nuncio to use the full range of his superb rhetorical skills on the assembled delegates: Cregan, 'The Confederation of Kilkenny' (thesis), 199–200; Glamorgan to Ormond, 28 Jan. 1646 (Gilbert, *Irish Confederation*, v. 253).

[61] In this regard see R.J.'s report to Clanricard, 11 Feb. 1646 (John Lowe (ed.), *The Letter Book of the Earl of Clanricarde, 1643–7* (Dublin, 1983), 209–10).

[62] Confederate arguments in favour of peace before the arrival of the Roman Treaty (*Comment. Rinucc.*, ii. 140–1).

[63] The truce with Ormond was to be prolonged until the beginning of May. If by that time Rinuccini did not produce the articles of the papal peace, signed and sealed by the pope and the Queen of England, then the nuncio would conclude the religious aspects of the peace with Glamorgan. Under this agreement, therefore, if the papal peace failed to arrive, the religious articles of the Ormond peace would be conditional on the king's willingness to honour Glamorgan's authority. Until May, it was agreed, the confederates could continue to negotiate with Ormond, provided they neither concluded nor published anything before the religious articles were also concluded. There was to be no change of government in the intervening period and, if the nuncio and Glamorgan felt it necessary, the General Assembly would be recalled prior to the final conclusion of peace. In the meantime, 3,000 soldiers were to be sent to the relief of Chester: Lowe, 'The Glamorgan Mission', 188–9; Articles agreed between Rinuccini and the confederate commissioners, 19 Feb. 1646 (*Comment. Rinucc.*, ii. 146–7).

opponents' concerns at this point was to be a major factor in the eventual breakdown in August.[64] Rinuccini deliberately suppressed knowledge of some of the details of the papal peace, in particular the provision for a catholic viceroy which the treaty contained, until he had the original documents to hand. Far from believing that the arrival of the papal treaty would finally consummate the settlement of peace, he suspected strongly that it might lead to civil war.[65]

If Rinuccini had been less than forthcoming, then the confederate negotiators were open to the charge of deliberate deceit, in particular Viscounts Muskery and Mountgarrett, and Patrick Darcy. All of these had signed the agreement with the nuncio on 19 February and all were in the party which concluded peace with Ormond, in direct contravention of this agreement, on 28 March.[66] It seems probable that, even in February, and despite their agreement with the nuncio, the peace party were determined to conclude the secular articles before the expiry of Ormond's mandate.[67] Towards the latter end of March, the council repeated their commitment to the nuncio that nothing would be completed until the beginning of May but some days later they secretly concluded the treaty with Ormond although it was not yet to be published.[68] The confederates were keenly aware that this was a breach of their agreement with the nuncio which had been predicated on keeping an avenue open for the more favourable papal peace, and they went to great lengths to conceal it from him.[69] In many ways this was an understandable decision by councillors who saw no reason to jeopardize the secular concessions already granted. While the nuncio's fears that the conclusion of

[64] In this regard see Lowe, 'The Glamorgan Mission', 188 which emphasizes the self-interest of all concerned.

[65] He feared that Ormond would not accept the papal articles and that his supporters among the confederates would prefer to secede from the association than break with the marquis: *Comment. Rinucc.*, ii. 150. This was a risk Rinuccini was prepared to take but he preferred to wait until he had something more substantial than a private cipher copy of the peace in his possession. In the event, the collapse of the papal peace in Rome and Paris meant that this contingency never arose.

[66] That the secret signing of the Ormond peace in March violated the February agreement with the nuncio seems clear but this has previously been passed over: see for instance, Corish, 'Ormond, Rinuccini, and the Confederates, 1645–9', 320; Cregan, 'Confederation of Kilkenny', (thesis) 205.

[67] To this end, the Supreme Council resisted what was evidently severe clerical pressure to renounce one of their most important powers, namely the power to conclude peace independently of the General Assembly: see Rinuccini to Pamfili, 5 Mar. 1646 (*Comment. Rinucc.*, ii. 149); in order to maintain this power, the council seem to have conceded ground to the nuncio elsewhere: see Cregan, 'The Confederation of Kilkenny' (thesis), 202–3 concerning the reform of certain practices to which the nuncio objected.

[68] See Cregan, 'The Confederation of Kilkenny' (thesis), 205–18.

[69] It is interesting that the Bellings's narrative blurs the chronological sequence of these events. Bellings's account clearly implies that the king's disavowal of Glamorgan's mandate (news of which reached Ireland in March) was known to all parties on 19 Feb. when the nuncio concluded his bargain with the confederate representatives about postponing the conclusion of any peace until 1 May. This elision serves to obscure the force of the nuncio's argument that the February agreement had been invalidated by the king's disavowal of Glamorgan: see Bellings's narrative (Gilbert, *Irish Confederation*, v. 8–12).

secular conditions would undermine the council's determination to obtain the clergy's demands were not unjustified, it can be noted that until June the council continued to struggle obstinately on the clergy's behalf.[70] Nevertheless, this deceit was bound to be discovered eventually and was certain to antagonize the nuncio, who would be in a position to assert that the council had done what they had not dared to do while the assembly was in session.

Ormond's co-operation was of course essential to the concealment of the treaty's conclusion from the nuncio. In order to secure his agreement to defer the promulgation of the treaty until June, the confederates agreed to pay the lord lieutenant £3,000.[71] Cheated of their expectation in raising this money and under pressure from Ormond,[72] the council, with some audacity, borrowed the requisite funds from Rinuccini.[73] It was manifestly impossible to tell the nuncio the true reasons for dispatching the money to Dublin, since the nuncio believed that peace had not yet been signed. The council therefore compounded its deceit by fabricating a rather clumsy pretext that the money was to permit Ormond to take the field against the Scots in Ulster.[74] Inevitably the news leaked out that the nuncio's loan was in fact to be used to send some of the most restless protestant officers in the Dublin garrison to England.[75] The nuncio was absolutely outraged. His fury at having been deceived was compounded by the insult offered to the pope by the fact that pontifical funds had been diverted surreptitiously to protestants. Although Rinuccini eventually contrived to regain the money, his correspondence to the whole body of the council about this issue was not given a public reading which further increased his sense of grievance. Following the eventual return of the Italian delegation from Ireland, Rinuccini, Alessandro Neroni, his secretary, and Dionysio Massari, the dean of Fermo, all independently recorded this incident to illustrate the duplicity of the confederates, and, overall, it marked an important stage in the nuncio's growing resentment and distrust of the council.[76]

At this juncture Rinuccini was still unaware of the more important deceit concerning the signing of the peace in March. In the interests of not forfeit-

---

[70] In this regard see the confederate instructions to Plunkett, 17 Apr. 1646 (Bodl. Carte MS 17, fo. 171[r–v]); see also Ormond to Clanricard, 30 May 1646 (*Clanricard Letter Book 1643–7*, 250–4).

[71] Supreme Council to their commissioners, 18 Mar. 1646 (Gilbert, *Irish Confederation*, v. 282).

[72] Ormond to Glamorgan, 14 Mar. 1646 (Bodl. Carte MS 16, fos. 645[r]–646[r])

[73] Ormond to Supreme Council, 11 Apr. 1646 (Gilbert, *Irish Confederation*, v. 327–8; Fennell to Ormond, 14 Apr. 1646 (ibid., 328–9).

[74] See Instructions to Nicholas Plunkett, 17 Apr. 1646 (Gilbert, *Irish Confederation*, v. 331); *Comment. Rinucc.*, ii. 203.

[75] Ormond may well have appreciated the irony of using the pope's money to pay the wages of puritans, and it was reported to the nuncio that he boasted openly of having participated in the papal subsidies: see Rinuccini to Supreme Council, 27 Apr. 1646 (*Comment. Rinucc.*, ii. 204–5).

[76] Viaggio in Irlanda di Dionysio Massari (APF, Miscellaneae Varie, 9, p. 93); Lettera di Alessandro Neroni sul viaggio in Irlanda del Nuncio Apostolico, 1654 (ASF, Miscellanea Medicea 436, ins 19).

ing assistance from the pope, the confederates continued to plead with Ormond to support the way that they had opted to handle the nuncio. On 17 April Nicholas Plunkett, about to set out for Dublin, was instructed: 'to let his Excellency [Ormond] know how much it doth import us to continue the Pope's favour towards us and how great the expectations are which we have of assistance from him.'[77] On 15 May he was instructed to try and convince Ormond:

that the Lord Nuncio should receive no discouragement but rather countenance from his Excellency, having already brought the helps of monies, arms and frigates against the common enemy, and is daily soliciting more from his Holiness, and if encouraged will no doubt prevail therein.[78]

It was thus not until the latter half of June that Rinuccini became certain that the peace had already been concluded. Indeed, unwilling to believe that the confederates would lie to him on this scale, the nuncio seems to have resisted Scarampi's attempts to awaken his suspicions.[79] Because the signing of the peace in March 1646 has not previously been identified as a breach of faith with the nuncio, the degree of his anger when he discovered how his credulity had been abused has been underestimated.[80] The angry and distrustful relationship which existed between the council and the nuncio by the end of June and in particular the nuncio's conviction of the council's deceit, exerted a vital influence on both parties' reactions to a number of important developments during the summer.

In this regard, changes in the military position were of the utmost importance. On 13 June astounding news reached the nuncio that O'Neill had almost completely destroyed the major Scottish army at Benburb. This was highly significant because, by severely weakening the Scottish forces in Ulster, Benburb thus freed both O'Neill and Preston, the major confederate generals, to come to the nuncio's support later that summer.[81] In addition, the

---

[77] Instructions to Nicholas Plunkett, 17 Apr. 1646 (Gilbert, *Irish Confederation*, v. 331).

[78] Additional instructions to Nicholas Plunkett, 15 May 1646 (ibid., 339); on 2 June, in response to the messages which Plunkett had brought, the marquis wrote that he was prepared to 'countenance' the nuncio as the council had asked 'as far as I shall finde necessary for the king's service and the quiet of the kingdom': Ormond to Supreme Council, 2 June 1646 (ibid., 352).

[79] Rinuccini to Pamfili, 21 May 1646 (Aiazzi, *Nunziatura*, 131); Michael Hynes, *The Mission of Rinuccini, Nuncio Extraordinary to Ireland, 1645–49* (Louvain, 1932), 69, 73 in a different interpretation of the evidence implies that Rinuccini was actually aware of the signing of the peace considerably earlier but this appears unconvincing.

[80] One can note the very hot tone of his correspondence with the council after his discovery: see Rinuccini to the Supreme Council, 25 June 1646 (*Comment. Rinucc.*, ii. 228–34); for their part, the council objected to the manner in which Rinuccini presented them on 10 June with a clerical protest, which had been signed on 6 Feb. by a formidable array of Irish clergy, including 13 bishops, and which warned against making peace without the nuncio's approval. The council evidently saw this as a piece of sharp practice against the spirit of their bargain with the nuncio of 19 Feb.: ibid., 221–2, 225.

[81] See Corish, 'Ormond, Rinuccini, and the Confederates, 1645–9', 320–1; Stevenson, *Covenanters and Confederates*, 235–6; J. C. Beckett, *The Making of Modern Ireland, 1603–1923* (New York, 1977), 98.

clergy's resolve to push matters to a crisis was undoubtedly stiffened by the improved military position.[82] The nuncio was also proprietorial about any victory which was achieved with papal assistance. Consequently, the wanton manner in which the Ormond peace seemed to throw away the fruits of this expenditure of papal gold (and his own efforts) irritated him deeply. In addition, his previous attempts to secure additional funding from Rome had been frustrated by the failure of the first subsidies to produce any clear progress and by the confederates' apparent disinclination to prosecute the war.[83] Now, with a major victory to report, the nuncio could entertain justifiable hopes of renewed assistance from Rome if peace was not published.[84] Moreover, the victory at Benburb, followed by the reduction of a strong protestant garrison at Bunratty, in Munster, and of another at Roscommon, in Connacht, caused the nuncio's personal confidence to soar. He interpreted such advances as clear signs of providential favour. Even prior to these successes, Rinuccini had found repugnant the confederates' lack of faith in God's support for the justice and holiness of their cause. In February he had urged the assembly to stiffen their spines and remember that they 'acted and had acted in the cause of God in which it is not sufficient to weigh matters according to human reasons only but something also is to be relinquished to God and to be entrusted to his aid'.[85] After Benburb he roundly upbraided the council, and enjoined them to render thanks to God for their recent miraculous military achievements by showing increased faith in divine protection.[86] It seems probable that the much more aggressive stance which the nuncio was to adopt for the rest of the year can be ascribed partially to a renewed sense of God's guiding hand awakened by the victories of the summer.

The military triumph, added to the revelation of the council's bad faith over the conclusion of the treaty, can be identified as the decisive factors in radicalizing the nuncio's position once again. On 20 June he admitted to Pamfili that he could think of nothing fresh to convince the council against peace, but now optimistically awaited help from God.[87] Effectively, he

[82] Hynes, *Mission of Rinuccini*, 76.

[83] News of the tepid confederate reaction to Glamorgan's imprisonment evidently dampened the Vatican's enthusiasm for investing papal money in Ireland: see Pamfili to Rinuccini, 20 May 1646 (*Comment. Rinucc.*, ii. 95).

[84] See my article 'Vatican Diplomacy and the Mission of Rinuccini to Ireland', *Archivium Hibernicum*, 47 (1993), 83 concerning the transformation in the Roman perspective after news of the victories of 1646.

[85] 'Vos agere, et egisse causam Dei, in qua non sufficit humanis tantummodo rationibus negotia perpendere, sed aliquid etiam Deo relinquendum, atque in ipsius ope reponendum, necesse est': *Comment. Rinucc.*, ii. 78. This attitude on the part of the nuncio should be seen, I think, as a product of his sincere belief, rather than as a display of pious opportunism to cover his dislike of the treaty.

[86] Rinuccini to the Supreme Council, 25 June 1646 (*Comment. Rinucc.*, ii. 228–34). This position is somewhat reminiscent of Lamormaini after the battle of Nördlingen. See Parker, *Thirty Years' War*, 142–3.

[87] Rinuccini to Pamfili, 20 June 1646 (Aiazzi, *Nunziatura*, 142): he also did not neglect to hint to the pope that a sizeable sum of money would help divine intervention along quite appreciably.

appears to have abandoned his earlier intention of standing aside if the peace was published. Personal involvement in the siege of Bunratty further elevated his morale. Since April this siege, which was a response to the sudden opening of a new front in Munster with the arrival of a strong parliamentarian force to occupy the fortress,[88] had proceeded so badly that the nuncio became suspicious that the council was deliberately failing to prosecute it vigorously in order to strengthen the case for peace. Within twelve days of his arrival Rinuccini brought the siege to a successful conclusion.[89] The ease of his victory further increased his suspicions of the council. While the confederates pressed the siege of Bunratty, news of further military success, including the capture of Roscommon by the Leinster army under Preston, was arriving from Connacht.[90] Within the space of a month the confederates had thus recorded significant military advances on three fronts, none of which would have been achieved without Rinuccini's moral or financial input.[91] The nuncio's delight in these victories and his increasing conviction of the untrustworthiness of the council hardened his attitudes to such an extent that not even the sudden application of French influence on behalf of the Ormond peace was enough to return him to his former passivity. This was a vital development which has largely escaped detection and it is necessary at this juncture, therefore, to outline briefly the nature of French involvement in the treaty.

IV

By the summer of 1646 the French government eyed the situation in the three Stuart kingdoms with undisguised alarm. Since the beginning of Charles's crisis, despite the wordy expressions of amity and occasional financial grants, the overriding French interest in Britain and Ireland had remained the

[88] In all probability, one of the principal reasons why the earl of Thomond chose to admit a parliamentary garrison at this juncture was his frustration at the manner in which Rinuccini had obstructed the conclusion of peace: see Thomond to Ormond, 24 Feb. 1646 (Bodl. Carte MS 16 fo. 548ʳ).

[89] Rinuccini to Pamfili, 3 July 1646 (Aiazzi, *Nunziatura*, 144); Viaggio in Irlanda di Dionysio Massari (APF, Miscellaneae Varie 9, p. 147); Gilbert, *Irish Confederation*, vi. 8.

[90] See Mary O'Dowd, *Power, Politics and Land: Early Modern Sligo, 1568–1688* (Belfast, 1991), 126–9 for the background to this campaign; again, the delivery of this important fortress to parliamentary forces probably reflected protestant frustration with Rinuccini's influence over the peace: see Taaffe to Ormond, 4 Mar. 1646 (Bodl. Carte MS 16, fo. 579ʳ).

[91] The importance of these successes in Connacht and the victory at Bunratty has tended to be underestimated. But in Ireland in the 1640s, as elsewhere in early modern Europe, a successful siege was often of greater importance than a victory in the open field, not least because in Ireland, as elsewhere, a high proportion of available troops were stationed on permanent garrison duty. Indeed, until 1649, warfare in Ireland was as siege-orientated as anywhere else in Europe. See Geoffrey Parker, *The Military Revolution: Military Innovation and the Rise of the West* (Cambridge, 1988), 13–16, 40–1; with regard to the significance of the fall of Roscommon see Clanricard to Preston, 14 June 1646 (*Clanricard Letter Book 1643–7*, 265) and concerning the importance of Bunratty see Bodl. Carte MS 17, fo. 600ʳ⁻ᵛ.

recruitment of soldiers. This is very clear from the correspondence between Mazarin's secretariat and his agents in Ireland.[92] The king's military collapse after Naseby in 1645 prompted a considerable reassessment of priorities. French resources were then deeply committed to the European struggle against the Habsburgs. By 1646 this was a struggle in which the French government was reasonably confident of success,[93] but the enormous war effort in Europe meant that no soldiers and little money could be spared for Charles, despite his status as uncle by marriage to Louis XIV. Consequently, any French intervention would, in the short term at least, be primarily diplomatic. The scope of that intervention and the main points of the political analysis on which it was based, are visible in the frank and detailed instructions which on 27 June 1646 were given to Pompone de Bellièvre, the new ambassador to England.[94]

The first part of Bellièvre's instructions expressed disquiet at the rebellions against the Stuarts, particularly in England. Not only was there the prospect of the collapse of a relatively friendly monarchy linked by marriage to the throne of France, but there was the bad example which the rebellion might give to the subjects of other princes. In addition, the instructions expressed concern for the future of catholicism in England and, most interestingly, in Ireland if the parliamentary rebellion was not defeated.[95] Bellièvre's most important instruction was 'to nourish and foment the disunion of the Independents from the Presbyterians and Scots in such a manner that they can never agree and join together to extinguish the monarchy and establish a republic'.[96] Bellièvre was informed that France's interests demanded the restoration of the king. Above all, it was considered necessary to avoid the establishment of a republic, even one prepared to show diplomatic favour to France.[97] The instructions noted the natural hostility between France and

[92] See for instance de la Monerie to Le Tellier, 18 Apr. 1644 (AMAE, Correspondence Politique (Angleterre) 51, fo. 41^{r-v}); Mazarin to de la Monerie, 25 July (ns) 1645 (ibid., fo. 497^{r}): in Scotland also, the cardinal complained that the resident, Jean de Montereul, spent too much time on the affairs of Charles Stuart and not enough on recruitment: see E. de Boccard, *Recueil des instructions donnés aux ambassadeurs et ministres de France depuis les traités de Westphalie jusqu'a la révolution française, xxiv (Angleterre)*, i, 1648–1650 (Paris, 1929), 9.

[93] The battle of Jankov in Mar. 1645 marked a decisive turning point in the war: see Parker, *Thirty Years' War*, 176–7; Bireley, 'Religious War', 104–6; J. H. Elliott, 'Foreign Policy and Domestic Crisis: Spain, 1598–1659', in Repgen, *Krieg*, 198–9; de Boccard, *Recueil des instructions*, 32–3.

[94] He was returning for a second term having previously been appointed there in 1637: see Pierre Gouhier, 'Mercenaires Irlandais au service de la France (1635–1664)', *Irish Sword*, 7 (1965–6), 59.

[95] de Boccard, *Recueil des instructions*, 15–19.

[96] 'De nourrir et fomenter de telle sorte la disunion des Indépendents avec les Presbyterians et Ecossais, qu'ils ne puisent jamais s'accorder et s'unir pour éteindre la royauté et s'ériger en republique': ibid., 35: concerning the divisions which emerged in the victorious coalition in England after the end of the first Civil War see Ashton, *English Civil War*, 290–353.

[97] de Boccard, *Recueil des instructions*, 35–7; this was the view in Paris because the king's revenue had been so limited prior to the great rebellion that his capacity to wage war was dependent on his subjects' consent.

England which made it fundamentally important to prevent the establishment of a strong English state, which was seen as the likely outcome of a
republican settlement. It was also noted that France opposed the destruction
of royal authority in principle and that this would cause inevitable friction
between the French monarchy and any future English republic.[98]

The French government had decided that the best means of restoring the
king would be a coalition of Scots, English Presbyterians, and the Irish confederates. Charles had already been advised from Paris to swallow his pride
and accede to the Scots' demands, as his best hope of salvation seemed to
depend on them.[99] Something remarkably similar to this scenario was actually attempted in 1648, with the Inchiquin truce and second Ormond peace
in Ireland, the second Civil War in England and the engagement in Scotland.
In the event, it failed decisively.[100] The coalition of interests proved too broad
and friable for success. In hindsight, indeed, looking at matters in purely
strategic terms, it might appear that it was something of an error on the part
of Mazarin's government to plan to involve Irish catholics in their plans to
restore the king.

In 1646, however, the French government were apparently motivated by
two factors in their decision to involve the confederates in a new royalist
coalition. In the first place, it obviously counted on its own prestige and
European influence as a sizeable incentive to the warring religious factions in
the Stuart kingdoms to co-operate in the bid to restore their monarch. By the
summer of that year a favourable peace with the emperor seemed inevitable
and Mazarin's government evidently believed that the Spanish would in their
turn be forced to sue for terms.[101] Consequently, the Stuart settlement would
be strengthened by the latent threat of massive intervention from France once
the European war ended. In the event, the second Civil War in England coincided with the bankruptcy and effective collapse of Mazarin's government in
1648, which rendered French influence on English affairs negligible.[102]

The second principal reason why Mazarin's government wished the confederates to participate in the restoration of the king, however, involved a

---

[98] Ibid., 36–7; outside observers were also convinced that France's interest in Scotland and
Ireland was primarily to keep England so preoccupied with internal affairs that it would have no
resources to spare for adventures on the continent: see GianBattista Nani (Venetian ambassador to
France) to the Doge and Senate of Venice, 23 Oct. (ns) 1646 (*Calendar of State Papers and
Manuscripts Relating to English Affairs, Existing in the Archives and Collections of Venice,
1647–52* (London, 1927), 284–5).

[99] Another alternative, which the French government was prepared to consider, was to play
upon the fears of the Independent party. These, it was hoped, might be won by fear of a
Scots/English presbyterian alliance to pledge their forces to the king on acceptable conditions. These
forces might then be supplemented by confederate armies from Ireland: see de Boccard, *Recueil des
instructions*, 20–32.

[100] See Ivan Roots, *The Great Rebellion, 1642–1660* (London, 1983), 126–30; Ashton, *English
Civil War*, 320–39; Kenyon, *Civil Wars of England*, 177–99.

[101] de Boccard, *Recueil des instructions*, 32–3.

[102] François Bluche, *Louis XIV* (Paris, 1986), 52–69; Bonney, *European Dynastic States*, 234.

genuine although hardly indefatigable interest in preserving a catholic population from destruction, particularly one which might turn to Spain if it felt itself abandoned by France. In this regard, Bellièvre was instructed:

As regards Ireland, the Lord Bellièvre will insist principally that it should not be sacrificed in any manner to the rage of the Presbyterians and Scots, nor to some others of the two nations who are in agreement to destroy it. He will not spare any sort of diligence or address to establish this point firmly in which, besides the fact that the reputation and well-being of the King of Great Britain are greatly engaged therein, France has a particular interest as much as not to allow the extermination of the catholic religion in a kingdom where it has been conserved for so long with such care, as that despair will make the inhabitants, seeing themselves abandoned by the king and left as prey to their enemies, have recourse to the Spanish, into whose arms they would throw themselves and to whom they would not make any difficulty about putting into Spanish hands places which they hold and their forces, from which could not but result a very notable prejudice to France.[103]

These two points, first that France could not in conscience stand by while catholicism was wiped out in Ireland, and second that if the Irish were not included in a settlement they would turn to Spain for assistance, were among the keynotes of French policy with regard to Ireland in the summer of 1646.[104] The French government was keenly aware of the historical association between Ireland and Spain. As Bellièvre was informed:

Ireland, being almost entirely catholic and very zealous for religion, there have been up to now many inhabitants of that island who have regarded Spain as that country which has always appeared to protect its interests, and there is even a quantity of officers who have served in Spanish armies and who nourish a secret inclination towards that nation.[105]

---

[103] 'Quant a l'Irlande, le Sr de Bellièvre fera principalement instance qu'elle ne soit point sacrifiée en quelque façon que ce soit à la rage des Presbyterians et Ecossais, ni des uns ou des autres des deux nations qui sont d'accord de la perdre. Il n'epargnera aucune sorte de diligence et d'adresse pour bien établir ce point dans lequel, outre que la réputation et le bien du Roi de la Grande-Bretagne y sont extrêmement engagés, la France a un particulier interêt, tant pour ne pas laisser exterminer la religion catholique en un royaume où elle s'est depuis si longtemps conservée avec tant de soin, que pour ce que les habitants, se voyant abandonnés de leur Roi et laissés en proie à leurs ennemis, le désespoir les ferait recourir aux Espagnols, entre les bras desquels ils se jetteraient, et à qui ils ne feraient point de difficulté de mettre entre les mains leurs forces et les places qu'ils tiennent, d'où il ne pourrait que resulter un très notable prejudice à la France, comme, il est aisé à voir': Instructions to Bellièvre, June 1646 (AMAE, Correspondance Politique (Angleterre) 55, fo. 8ᵛ).
[104] In this regard Jane Ohlmeyer has noted the high degree of interest which both France and Spain demonstrated in the 1640s to become the official 'protector' of Ireland: see *Civil War and Restoration in the Three Stuart Kingdoms: The Career of Randal MacDonnell, Marquis of Antrim, 1609–1683* (Cambridge, 1993), 292–3.
[105] 'L'Irlande étant presque toute catholique et très zelée pour la religion, il y a eu jusque ici plusiers des habitants de cette île qui ont regardé l'Espagne comme celle qui a toujours fait parade d'en proteger les intérêts, et qu'il y a même quantité d'officiers qui ont servi dans les armées espagnoles qui nourissent une secrète inclination pour cette nation': de Boccard, *Recueil des instructions*, 19.

The other vital ingredient in French policy was the determination to secure a settlement in Ireland within the overall context of Charles Stuart's restoration in his three kingdoms, by a coalition of various groups of his subjects. Consequently, the priorities of Mazarin's agents in Ireland were to clash considerably with those of the pope's nuncio. French commitment to protecting Irish catholics from a settlement such as was to occur after the Cromwellian conquest was evidently genuine. Bellièvre pursued this point determinedly in his consultations with the king: on 6 December from Newcastle he wrote to the French Secretary of State, the comte de Brienne, of his belief that he had convinced the king not to abandon the Irish in the negotiations for the royal restoration.[106] Yet the belief that France had a degree of moral obligation to protect a catholic people from dispossession and destruction fell far short of Rinuccini's determination to make the Roman church something close to the established religion in Ireland. In particular, the desire to achieve Charles's restoration without any significant investment of French money or soldiers meant that Mazarin was very willing to accept the necessity of conciliating protestant opinion in England in a fashion which Rinuccini could never condone.

Two important influences on the formulation of French policy were George Digby, who had arrived in France from Ireland in May, and Charles's French wife, Henrietta Maria, who had been installed there the previous year.[107] A memorial from the queen of England was added to Bellièvre's instructions before he left France. The queen admitted that the king had already offered Ireland to parliament but, since it was clear that parliament would extirpate the catholic religion in Ireland, she declared that:

it will be very unworthy of a king to buy peace at such a cruel and unjust price, beyond which the uncertainty of the establishment and continuation of the same would leave him open to the accusation of great imprudence of having thus deprived himself of his strongest resource in the case that it may be necessary to return to arms.[108]

Consequently, she enjoined Bellièvre that: 'in what concerns Ireland one must never fall back nor consent to any accommodation in which it is not included and the peace there ratified.'[109] The peace in question was of course the Ormond peace. Its attractions for the confederates were naturally

---

[106] Bellièvre to de Brienne, 6 Dec. 1646 (AMAE, Correspondence Politique (Angleterre) 54, fos. 776ᵛ–777ʳ.

[107] Hynes, *Mission of Rinuccini*, 80–1; R. Marshall, *Henrietta Maria* (London, 1990), 115–18.

[108] 'Il sera bien indigne d'un roi d'acheter un paix à un prix si cruel et si unjuste, outre que l'incertitude de l'etablissement et de la continuation d'icelle l'accuseroit de beaucoup d'imprudence de s'être ainsi privé de sa plus forte ressource, en cas qu'on eût a revenir aux armes': de Boccard, *Recueil des instructions*, 46.

[109] 'Il ne faut jamais lâcher pied en ce qui est d'Irlande et ne consenter jamais à aucune accomodement qu'elle n'y soit comprise et la paix en icelle ratifiée': ibid., 52.

enhanced to a great degree by the fact that both the French government and the Stuart queen's court in exile were intimating protection for Ireland from the Adventurers' Act if the peace was published. This was an advantage to which not even the most tender consciences on the council could be blind.[110] The person chosen to convey this tempting news to Ireland was none other than George Digby, who had left Ireland some months before. To this end, he received the considerable sum of 10,000 pistols (about £8,000) and the chief French agent in Ireland, Claude du Moulin, was ordered to follow Digby's instructions.[111] So willingly did du Moulin obey this order that his conduct actually became something of an embarrassment to his government.[112]

The nuncio was made quickly aware of the thrust of Digby's policy soon after his return to Ireland. On 7 July he wrote to Pamfili in cipher of the 10,000 pistols which Digby had received in France. He had heard rumours also from the royalist camp in Dublin that the king had secretly given his word that he would honour the Glamorgan concessions.[113] Since the calendar in Ireland was ten days behind that used in France, some three weeks had elapsed since Bellièvre's instructions had been compiled. It seems very clear, therefore, that Digby's mission and Bellièvre's were planned in unison. On 8 July Rinuccini wrote to Pamfili that the new French agent (presumably du Moulin) was urging the confederates that religious splendour along the lines of Rome could not be achieved all at once. The agent was also loud in his praise of Ormond. Rinuccini noted worriedly 'one sees that these are the thoughts of France and those that will now begin to dominate and to overturn everything'.[114] Rinuccini was under the strictest instructions to emphasize his neutrality between the two great catholic powers. Consequently, he was most reluctant to oppose French influence openly. On 17 July he wrote again to Pamfili:

I do not wish to omit to say to Your Eminence that both Lord Eugene O'Neill and Preston, after the victories achieved in their provinces, secretly offered me to go against Dublin if I wished. I felt a great temptation in this affair. But in the end because the most christian king had begun to exert his authority in these matters I

[110] In this regard, few consciences were as tender as those of Nicholas Plunkett and Patrick Darcy who in August insisted to the clergy that French support for the peace was a major reason to accept it: see *Comment. Rinucc.*, ii. 326; moreover, the collapse of the royalist cause in England had brought fears of parliamentary vengeance very much to the fore in the summer of 1646: in this regard see Kenyon, *Civil Wars of England*, 123–57.

[111] Digby to Mazarin, 15 Aug. 1646 (AMAE, Correspondence Politique (Angleterre) 52, fos. 496ʳ–497ᵛ; Convocation of Irish Clergy to Mazarin, 15 Aug. 1646 (ibid., 498ʳ⁻ᵛ).

[112] He was recalled following the nuncio's triumph in 1646, apparently because it was feared in Paris that du Moulin's overt identification with the peace party risked driving the opposing confederate faction into the arms of Spain: see the untitled memorial to the new Irish Agent, July(?) 1647 (AMAE, Correspondence Politique (Angleterre) 55, fo. 301ᵛ).

[113] Rinuccini to Pamfili, 7 July 1646 (Aiazzi, *Nunziatura*, 146–8).

[114] 'Si vede che questi sono i pensieri della Francia, e quelli che adesso cominceranno a dominare ed a rivolgere ogni cosa': Rinuccini to Pamfili, 7 July 1646 (Aiazzi, *Nunziatura*, 148).

did not wish that it be done so that one should not say my authority unseated Ormond without the consent of the council and so as not to cause tensions between our master and that crown.[115]

Since the nuncio seems already to have been contemplating conflict with the council, news of French involvement in the peace evidently came as a most unpleasant shock to him. Fear of confrontation with Bourbon agents was certainly an important factor in restraining him from initiating offensive action. However, not even fear of French reaction could persuade him to stand aside when the council itself took the plunge and published the peace.

While Digby and the French agents disseminated news among the confederates of the stance adopted in France by the queen and Mazarin's government, they also directed their energies and monies to convincing Ormond that it was consonant with the royal will to publish the peace.[116] On 27 July du Moulin wrote to Ormond that his king was ready to support the peace; that he had sent an ambassador to Britain to ensure that the Irish were included in any settlement; that the French king would never abandon his concern for Ireland; and pledged support from France for the unified forces of Ormond and the confederates.[117] The following day Digby made a public declaration that he had firm information that the king positively desired Ormond to conclude peace with the confederates and that the declaration of 11 June had been made unwillingly.[118] On 30 July, therefore, Ormond published the articles which since March had been deposited with Clanricard for

---

[115] 'Non voglio lasciare di dire a V.E. che tanto D. Eugenio O Neil quanto il Preston, dopo le vittorie conseguite nelle loro Provincie, mi hanno segretemente offerto di andar sopra Dublino, se io avessi voluto. Gran tentazione ho sentito in questo negozio: ma alla fine perchè il Re Cristianissimo avevo cominciato a metter la sua autorità in questi trattamenti, non ho voluto che si faccia, acciò non se dicesse che di mia autorità avessi scavalcato Ormonia senza concenso del Consiglio, e per non cagionare nuovi disgusti fra N.S. e quella corona': Rinuccini to Pamfili, 17 July 1646 (Aiazzi, *Nunziatura*, 149): it seems an unlikely coincidence that in the space of three weeks O'Neill and Preston would both independently solicit the nuncio's opinion concerning an attack on Dublin. It seems probable, therefore, that the nuncio used Massari to sound both generals out: see Viaggio in Irlanda di Dionysio Massari (APR, Miscellaneae Varie 9, pp. 127–47); O'Neill to Rinuccini, 29 July 1646 (*Comment. Rinucc.*, ii. 297–8).

[116] On 24 June Ormond had received a letter from the captive king forbidding peace which, to the confederates' horror, he was not prepared to disregard: see Bodl. Carte MS 17, fos. 484ʳ, 608ʳ. One can note that as an (unintentional) tactic to stampede the confederates into peace, Ormond's reluctance was remarkably successful. Once Ormond indicated his willingness to ignore this instruction, the peace party seems to have been understandably determined to seize the opportunity before it disappeared again. In this regard, one can note also that the confederate military victories which helped convince the nuncio to oppose the peace probably inclined Ormond to agree to its conclusion as they indicated that confederate military assistance was worth acquiring: in this regard see Clanricard to Patrick Darcy, 6 June 1646 (*Clanricard Letter Book 1643–7*, 260) and same to Queen of England, 4 Aug. 1646 (ibid., 274).

[117] Du Moulin to Ormond, 27 July 1646 (Gilbert, *Irish Confederation*, vi. 53–5).

[118] Declaration of Lord Digby, 28 July 1646 (ibid., 55–6): this declaration had presumably been requested by Ormond who could hope to use it for his own protection if he ever came into the hands of parliament.

safe-keeping.[119] Six days later Digby wrote with joyful gratitude to Mazarin from Dublin, crediting the 'so effective involvement of France' with the achievement of the treaty.[120] Two days later Ormond also wrote to the cardinal, thanking him for his efforts on behalf of the peace.[121] It seems clear that these expressions of gratitude were not just diplomatic formulae but genuine recognition of the essential role which France had played in the achievement of peace.[122]

On 4 August five of the nine members of the Supreme Council ratified the publication of the treaty in Kilkenny. The council clearly did not expect opposition from the nuncio. In July, prior to leaving Limerick for the legatine synod in Waterford, they had met again with Rinuccini and had presented to him what they apparently assumed were convincing arguments concerning the advisability of making peace. The new information from France was evidently at the core of their position.[123] At the end of the meeting Bellings (writing, it is true, at a much later date) reported that the nuncio declared in Latin: 'I see that much good could result from this peace, but also much harm, God will provide.'[124] Consequently, Bellings and the other members of the council seem to have believed that the nuncio would not oppose the peace. Their conviction in this regard was evidently strengthened by the nuncio's reaction to certain instructions which were then being prepared for confederate agents on their way to France and Rome, and by the behaviour of Rinuccini's subordinate Massari, whose personal attempts to return to Italy seem to have been mistakenly interpreted as evidence of his master's resignation to events.[125]

Probably at least partly by design, the nuncio managed to lull the council into a false sense of security about his likely reactions to the peace. He possibly was not entirely certain of his own future course of action at this junc-

---

[119]   See Gilbert, *Irish Confederation*, 57–8.

[120]   'L'entremise si efficacieuse de la France': Digby to Mazarin, 5/15 Aug. (AMAE, Correspondence Politique (Angleterre) 52, fos. 496–7).

[121]   Ormond to Mazarin, 7/17 Aug. 1646 (ibid., fo. 508[r–v]).

[122]   These words were backed by a more tangible manifestation of gratitude when the council and Ormond agreed to levy 5,000 troops for French service within three months of a French request for such a force: du Moulin to Mazarin, 5/15 Aug. 1646 (Gilbert, *Irish Confederation*, vi. 72, 74).

[123]   Bellings's narrative (ibid., 6–14).

[124]   Ibid., 14: 'Video ex ista pace multum posse provenire boni, multum autem mali, Deus providebit.'

[125]   In these instructions, which were shown to Rinuccini, it was clearly stated that the confederates were eager for peace with Ormond. A private initiative from Massari, unknown to the nuncio, may also have lulled the council's suspicions. Massari apparently approached the council about going back to Rome together with the council's agent, in a similar manner to that in which he later secretly applied to the Irish clergy for the right to represent them in Rome. The council naturally but probably wrongly assumed that he was acting with Rinuccini's full knowledge: ibid., 15–16; Viaggio in Irlanda di Dionysio Massari (APF, Miscellaneae Varie 9, p. 280); during Aug. the council's resentment of what they saw as the nuncio's sharp practice may have created an additional barrier to a negotiated settlement.

ture. But Digby's close involvement in the French patronage of the peace may
have been a factor in inclining him to gamble on opposition to the treaty.
Since his return to Ireland, Digby had consistently insinuated that
Rinuccini's actions had been disowned by the Vatican and that the nuncio
would shortly be recalled from Ireland.[126] Rinuccini was well aware that this
was untrue and his knowledge of Digby's deceitfulness[127] in this instance
seems to have inclined him to doubt his protestations of French support for
the Ormond peace. One can note that during the legatine synod in August
the clergy's spokesmen, probably reflecting Rinuccini's own position, dismissed French involvement in the peace as the product of Digby's machinations in Paris, arguing that he had gained money and credence for the treaty
in France under false pretences.[128] The French factor, therefore, which
weighed so heavily with the council and with Ormond failed to impress the
nuncio to the same degree, particularly when he found the Irish clergy so in
tune with his position during the national synod.

V

The legatine synod in Waterford during August of 1646 has been identified
as an event of very considerable importance. It allowed Rinuccini to oppose
the peace in the name of the entire Irish church and it set in train the creation
of a new Supreme Council and the attack on Ormond in Dublin.[129] But the
complexities of this synod and the evolution of the clerical position in
August and September have not been subject to detailed analysis and a number of important questions remain to be addressed. How strong was the nuncio's influence in Waterford? Did the synod merely endorse the nuncio's
decisions or was there a partnership between Rinuccini and the Irish clergy
in arriving at policy? Was there a genuine attempt to negotiate with the proponents of peace? Why did Ormond and his confederate partisans fail to
take more adequate measures to protect the treaty? And did the clerical decision to reject the peace lead inevitably to the attack on Dublin?

Some of these questions cannot be answered definitively. Rinuccini, for
instance, obviously exerted a considerable influence over the synod. His
position as papal nuncio ensured respect, as did his influence in Rome concerning appointments to Irish benefices. Moreover, his handling of the synod

---

[126] *Comment. Rinucc.*, ii. 280.

[127] Although the secretary clearly exaggerated he may also have been misinformed in Paris; certainly Henrietta Maria appears to have communicated a very sanitized version of her negotiations
with Rome to Digby, which then inclined him to believe that Rinuccini had publicly lied about the
papal peace: see Digby to Ormond, 17 June 1646 (Thomas Carte, *An history of the life of James,
first duke of Ormonde* (6 vols., Oxford, 1851), vi. 397–8).

[128] *Comment. Rinucc.*, ii. 330–7.

[129] Corish, 'Ormond, Rinuccini, and the Confederates, 1645–9', 320–1; Ó Siochrú, *Confederate
Ireland*, 108; for those present see Cregan, 'The Confederation of Kilkenny' (thesis), 231.

was clearly expert.[130] But the nuncio could also count on genuine support for his vision of the church within society. Perhaps the key element in the development of Irish catholicism in the seventeenth century was the decision to create the ecclesiastical structures of a national church and not those of a mission in the island.[131] Throughout the 1640s the basic concern of the clerical party in any peace settlement was to secure and improve the position of a church centred around a national hierarchy. Even before the arrival of Rinuccini, the native episcopate, most of whom had been ardent apostles of the counter-reformation in the previous twenty years, had shown extreme reluctance to compromise on the future shape of the church in Ireland. In this regard it is of interest that Nicholas French's account of the synod, written it is true some thirty years later, attributes little or no significance to the nuncio's role in the rejection of the peace but discusses in detail the manner in which the synod as a whole debated the issue and came to its conclusions.[132] The synod's decree of 12 August also stressed the manner in which all opinions had been heard and unanimous agreement reached.[133] It seems plausible to suggest, therefore, that what Rinuccini supplied in August 1646 was not so much a new direction for the Irish church but strong leadership. Nor should one omit the possibility that Rinuccini's own hesitations and doubts about opposing the peace were eased by the fact that the Irish bishops also found the treaty inadequate.

The question of the peace was considered at the first meeting of the synod on 6 August and, to the nuncio's satisfaction, the clergy found the council guilty of having broken the oath of association and of having disregarded the mandates of the General Assembly. Nevertheless, the assembled clergy were prepared to listen at length to the arguments in favour of the peace which were put forward by the now officially defunct Supreme Council's representatives, Nicholas Plunkett and Patrick Darcy (the same duo who had convinced the clergy to moderate their stance on the retention of the churches during the General Assembly in 1645), and who arrived in Waterford on 8 August.[134] Although the synod was unimpressed by these arguments, there

---

[130] When the assembled clergy first considered the peace on 6 Aug., in a move carefully calculated to stoke their ire (and to emphasize his own essential moderation), the nuncio pointed out that the council had broken their word to him on three occasions. These were, first, a promise made on 3 Oct. 1645 to perform what seemed necessary to the nuncio; second, the agreement of 18 Feb. 1646 to wait until the beginning of May before concluding any peace; and, third, a letter from the council just prior to the conclusion of the peace asserting their willingness to abide by the Feb. bargain: *Comment. Rinucc.*, ii. 324–5.

[131] See Corish, *The Catholic Community in the Seventeenth and Eighteenth Centuries* (Dublin, 1981), 22–40 and id., *Irish Catholic Experience* (Dublin, 1985), 96–122.

[132] S. H. Bindon (ed.), *The historical works of the right reverend Nicholas French, bishop of Ferns* (Dublin, 1846), 44–5.

[133] Bodl. Carte MS 18, fo. 248ʳ.

[134] See the Latin version of the reasons for the conclusion of the peace presented by Plunkett and Darcy (*Comment. Rinucc.*, ii. 325–30).

was little ill will towards the two councillors.[135] It was not until 12 August that the clergy made public their opinion that any confederate who accepted the peace was guilty of perjury of the oath of association. And, more importantly, they temporarily kept the spiritual sword in its scabbard by reserving judgement until a later occasion as to whether perjurers in this regard were to be excommunicated.[136] Instead, representatives were appointed to write to Kilkenny suggesting alternatives to the peace, such as the suspension of the treaty until a General Assembly had debated the matter or, failing that, until an envoy had returned from Rome with the pope's views. The idea was also floated that the Glamorgan articles should be included in the published articles of the peace.[137]

The clergy's position at this juncture thus indicated a willingness to seek a resolution of differences without conflict. Furthermore, the degree and diversity of debate which took place on this issue suggests that the synod did not merely rubber-stamp Rinuccini's decisions. The nuncio may have nurtured and focused his support during the debates but the anti-peace cause was immensely aided by the sheer disarray which their opposition created. The confederates who had concluded the treaty had taken no precautions against the eventuality of clerical resistance. As Richard Bellings later remarked ruefully, if the council had anticipated Rinuccini's later actions:

they would have laboured by preferments and hopes of rewards, to secure for the government the affections of the officers who had greatest power in the Leinster and Connaght army; they would have kept the lord of Muskery in the head of the Munster army, and not sent him to Dublin, to be present at a ceremony which might be performed without him; and they might hinder the congregation at Waterford, as, when experience had made them more wary and circumspect, they interrupted the meeting of the synod to be convened at Galway. But they had not any umbrage of a design in the nuncio to interrupt with so high a hand their proceedings; nor in truth had they any apprehension it could lie in his power to do so.[138]

Having failed to take measures of this nature before the publication of the treaty, the dissolved Supreme Council in addition lacked independent power to react to the burgeoning crisis. Confederate government had officially

---

[135] During these days, despite Plunkett's advocacy of the peace, Rinuccini actually wrote of him approvingly to Rome: Rinuccini to Pamfili, 11 Aug. 1646 (Aiazzi, *Nunziatura*, 152); Cregan, 'Confederation of Kilkenny', (thesis) 231–2.

[136] Significantly, the only decree of excommunication which was issued at this time exclusively concerned any confederate commissioner who actually went to Dublin and assisted in the promulgation of the peace: *Comment. Rinucc.*, ii. 340–1.

[137] This can be deduced from Rinuccini's letter to Bellings, 15(?) Aug. 1646 (*Comment. Rinucc.*, ii. 342) and the memorial from the clergy's spokesmen to the Supreme Council, 22 Aug. 1646 (ibid., 338–9): there was of course no possibility that Ormond would have consented to this last point. He consistently maintained that Glamorgan's articles had nothing to do with him. In his own words 'If they be valid in themselves, they need no corroboration, if invalid, I have noe power to give them strength': Ormond to FitzWilliam, 26 Sept. 1646 (Gilbert, *Irish Confederation*, vi. 143).

[138] Bellings's narrative (Gilbert, *Irish Confederation*, vi. 14).

lapsed with the promulgation of peace which meant that all decisive action was now dependent on Ormond's permission. The patents whereby sheriffs had previously acted on the authority of the Supreme Council were no longer valid, nor was there any promise from the marquis of speedy renewal.[139] Even the peace itself could not be printed in the former confederate capital because the lord lieutenant had ordered that this was to be done only in Dublin.[140] To compound matters, for most of August Ormond remained in his own quarters, creating a semi-vacuum of authority in Kilkenny.[141] Nor were communications between the peace party and their new master always perfect. From the very beginning, the generation of momentum in favour of the treaty was retarded by Ormond's decision that the first city in confederate territory to receive the promulgation of peace should be Waterford. Why the lord lieutenant made this choice remains a mystery,[142] but the peace party who had made extensive preparations for the proclamation in Kilkenny were evidently shocked and dismayed when they discovered where the king-at-arms, William Roberts, had been sent.[143] Waterford was the worst possible choice because the synod was actually in session and the town was full of clergy.[144] It was thus extremely unlikely that the mayor and aldermen of Waterford would take the lead in embracing the peace, particularly because the clergy were apparently threatening to leave the town unless the herald was dismissed.[145]

Plunkett and Darcy finally convinced Roberts to proceed to Kilkenny, where without waiting for Ormond's explicit authorization, he was prevailed upon to proclaim the peace.[146] Despite the loss of momentum at Waterford, the peace party was still reasonably confident about the prospects of overriding clerical resistance, and conferred with Ormond about assembling troops for that purpose.[147] As yet they were not prepared to accept that the synod's decisions had any relevance to the course of action which was to be adopted. The only reply which the clergy in Waterford

---

[139] Ormond to John Walsh and Edward Comerford, 19 Aug. 1646 (Bodl. Carte MS 18, fo. 305r); Mountgarrett to Ormond, 19 Aug. 1646 (ibid., fo. 291r).

[140] Browne to Ormond, 9 Aug. 1646 (Bodl. Carte MS 18, fo. 202r).

[141] Ormond was informed by Castlehaven that 'all face of government [is] amongst us dissolved except that the nuncio and the clergy doe usurpe at Waterford': Castlehaven to Ormond, 28 Aug. 1646 (Bodl. Carte MS 18, fo. 356).

[142] The official reason given, namely that Waterford was the most ancient corporation in the island after Dublin, was evidently merely a pretext: see Roberts to Ormond, 9 Aug. 1646 (Bodl. Carte MS 18, fo. 204v).

[143] Mountgarrett, Bellings, and others to Ormond, 11 Aug. 1646 (ibid., fo. 242r); Muskery and Brown to Roberts, 8 Aug. 1646 (ibid., fo. 201r).

[144] The unfortunate William Kirkby, one of the party sent to proclaim the peace exaggeratedly estimated that 'about a thousand priests and fryars' gazed in a hostile fashion upon the herald and his companions when they entered the city: see the relation of William Kirkby (ibid., fo. 383r).

[145] Roberts to Ormond, 9 Aug. 1646 (ibid., fo. 205r).

[146] Same to same, 12 Aug. 1646 (ibid., fo. 259r).

[147] Mountgarrett, Bellings, and others to Ormond, 11 Aug. 1646 (ibid., fo. 242r).

received to their suggestions for a possible compromise was an independent and dismissive reply from Richard Bellings, under a seal indicating the dissolution of the Supreme Council's government, which denied recognition of any autonomous ecclesiastical authority.[148]

Bellings's letter was received in Waterford on 15 August and it was this which elevated the conflict onto a new plane. The clergy in turn responded with the declaration of an interdict on any town that published the peace. It was declared further that the ex Supreme Council had forfeited its authority and that confederates were no longer oath-bound to obey its orders. The decree also actively prohibited any confederate from paying taxes to the council's treasury or from selling the council arms or powder.[149] This was a bolder assault on the peace than the declaration of perjury five days previously. Perhaps more importantly, it was on this note that the synod itself broke up, delegating authority to act on its behalf to eight men: Rinuccini, Scarampi, the archbishop of Dublin, the bishops of Clogher, Ferns, and Clonfert, the vicar apostolic of Ross (Robert Barry), and Robert Nugent, the prefect of the Jesuit mission in Ireland.[150]

Despite the nuncio's later protestations, it seems likely that he and in particular Scarampi were to the fore in pushing the Irish prelates towards confrontation.[151] It also seems probable that the two Italians were placed in a greater position of influence following the conclusion of the synod. While there is no indication that even later opponents of the nuncio such as Francis Kirwan of Killala or Edmund O'Dwyer of Limerick opposed Rinuccini at the synod, the presence of all shades of opinion in Waterford probably acted as a force for moderation. After 16 August two of the eight clerics with delegated authority were Italians while two others, Clogher and Barry, were

[148] The gist of Bellings's letter was that the prelates in the Supreme Council and the General Assembly had consented to the peace; that no ecclesiastical authority separate from the secular authority could be recognized; and that the council had ratified the peace at the instance of the king of France: see the memorial of the clergy's spokesmen to the council, 22 Aug. 1646 (*Comment. Rinucc.*, ii. 331).

[149] Ibid., 344–6.

[150] The synod actually broke up on 16 Aug., the day before the publication of these decisions. Rinuccini's later testimony suggests, however, that the decision to issue the interdict was authorized by the entire synod: indeed he claimed that what prompted him to sign the interdict was the realization that the entire synod was unanimously in favour and that this 'uniform consensus was the voice of God' (io credendo che questo consenso uniforme della Chiesa fosse voce di Dio): see his relation to the pope (Aiazzi, *Nunziatura*, 401–2). This was probably not merely a case of special pleading advanced by Rinuccini to justify an action which was arguably contrary to his instructions. Rinuccini did sincerely believe that a synod of bishops was a practically infallible interpreter of the will of God.

[151] Indeed Scarampi seems to have put considerable pressure on Rinuccini, insisting to the nuncio that it would be a dereliction of duty if he did not add his authority to that of the Irish bishops: Viaggio in Irlanda di Dionysio Massari (APF, Miscellaneae Varie 9, p. 162): before signing the interdict the nuncio apparently declared, somewhat prophetically, to the gathering that although he acted in unison with them he himself would be especially blamed for this action: Aiazzi, *Nunziatura*, 402.

among the most uncompromising foes of peace with Ormond. Of the remainder, only Clonfert could be expected to show much sympathy for the position of the peace party and his desire to be promoted to the archdiocese of Tuam and to see his brothers Oliver and Hugh elevated to the hierarchy possibly made him wary of antagonizing the nuncio.[152]

The refusal of the confederate peace party to attempt meaningful negotiation in mid-August proved an expensive error. No matter what steps might have been taken it seems clear that the clergy would have condemned the peace. Nevertheless, the manner in which the synod debated the issue, proceeding towards confrontation only by careful stages, indicated a willingness to reach a compromise which the proponents of peace might have been able to exploit to at least reduce the level of confrontation. It was their refusal to make an adequately conciliatory gesture towards the clerical position which ensured that Rinuccini was able to unify the entire Irish church behind his own stance, and in the process confirmed the nuncio's belief in their intransigence and bad faith. With some justification, Rinuccini could argue that his opponents had shown respect neither for the official representatives of the church nor for the position of the main body of the confederate association itself which, during the February assembly, had been far more willing than the council to accommodate the worries of the clergy. With the dissolution of the synod, the peace party thus found themselves in confrontation with a small group of determined clergy who had been authorized to speak on behalf of the whole Irish church and whose leader was clearly the nuncio. This massive endorsement by the Irish clergy obviously increased Rinuccini's freedom of action.

The measures which had been taken in Waterford rapidly began to bite. A more popular injunction than the non-payment of taxes could hardly have been issued and it apparently bore immediate fruit.[153] Ormond's continued absence from the cockpit of the crisis was another significant development. To a large degree the failure of the peace party to make a more constructive response to clerical demands in mid-August probably reflected the fact that they were now tied to Ormond. In that context, as it became evident that the clergy's opposition could not be defused by the intervention of Darcy and Plunkett, they pinned their hopes for the maintenance of the treaty on the marquis's vast personal prestige in confederate quarters. His presence in Kilkenny was put forward as the natural solution to all disturbances.[154] Personal consultation with the lord lieutenant would also clarify whether

---

[152] The family's subsequent attainment of the first of these objectives and their disappointment over the resolution of the latter point possibly help explain their strong opposition to the nuncio in 1648: see *Comment. Rinucc.*, ii. 761–3.

[153] Bellings to Ormond, 21 Aug. 1646 (Bodl. Carte MS 18, fo. 308ʳ); Ormond to the Council in Dublin, 4 Sept. 1646 (ibid., fo. 432ᵛ).

[154] Bellings to Ormond, 21 Aug. 1646 (ibid., fo. 308ʳ); Muskery and others to Ormond, 21 Aug. 1646 (ibid., fo. 306ʳ).

any additional security, outside and above the published treaty which Ormond saw as inviolably concluded,[155] might be offered to the clergy. Yet the marquis's response to the crisis emanating from Waterford was curiously slow. In a letter dated 11 August, Mountgarrett, Bellings, Muskery, Browne, and Lucas Dillon, all key supporters of the peace, had informed him of the difficulties which the clergy were creating.[156] Despite receiving this missive the following day, he waited until the fifteenth of the month before dispatching a reply signifying his intention of shortly leaving for Kilkenny.[157] The days dragged on, however, without news of his departure from Dublin.[158] On 28 August another of his reliable partisans, Castlehaven, directed a frankly desperate letter to the lord lieutenant, signifying the deplorable nature of the situation and how only Ormond's immediate arrival could prevent the inexorable drift of power into the clergy's hands.[159] The lord lieutenant's delay, while understandable in the context of his own position in Dublin and the utterly unexpected nature of the crisis, had serious negative consequences because unrest was spreading like wildfire through confederate territory.

The moral authority of the clergy at a popular level had been critically important in the initial legitimization of confederate institutions. One of the by-products threatened as a result of the deployment of clerical sanctions against the post-peace government appears to have been a recrudescence of the social unrest which had gripped the island in the aftermath of the Ulster rebellion. Looting and ravaging reminiscent of 1641 had broken out in county Laois almost immediately following the announcement of peace.[160] The familiar pattern of attacks on local English inhabitants soon appeared elsewhere.[161] The confederate towns also once again witnessed a frightening cleavage between patrician and plebeian citizens,[162] with many of the former willing to accept the peace while the latter proved more susceptible to clerical injunctions. In Clonmell the local clergy ensured an effective boycott by the lower social orders of the promulgation ceremony, which was attended only by the mayor and a handful of aldermen. In Limerick resistance was far more violent and on 22 August a riot orchestrated by a Dominican friar led to a savage attack on the herald's party and the ultimate deposition of the mayor who had consented to the proclamation of the peace in the city.[163]

---

[155] Robert Armstrong, 'Protestant Ireland and the English Parliament, 1641–1647' (unpub. Ph.D. thesis, Trinity College Dublin, 1995), 241–2.

[156] Bodl. Carte MS 18, fo. 242[r].   [157] Ibid., fo. 279[r].

[158] Although he evidently did authorize his supporters to offer certain guarantees to the clergy: see George Lane to Sir Thomas Nugent, 25 Sept. 1646 (ibid., fo. 570[r–v]).

[159] Ibid., fo. 356[r].

[160] See the letter of an unnamed correspondent to Ormond, 8 Aug. 1646 (Bodl. Carte MS 18, fo. 199[r]).

[161] Ibid., fo. 462[r].

[162] Concerning social urban tension in 1641–2 see Gilbert, *Irish Confederation*, ii. 16–30.

[163] See Bodl. Carte MS 18, fo. 383[r–v].

Even more frightening for gentry already wavering in their consciences concerning the peace was the prospect that clerically stimulated popular fury would be augmented by the military forces of the confederate provincial armies, particularly that of Ulster which had a deserved reputation for rapine and pillage even without the shield of church sanction, and whose intention to plunder those who opposed the peace was soon rumoured.[164] Upon the report of its movement south, therefore, many of the terrified local gentry around Kilkenny and Carlow repaired rapidly to the clergy for protection.[165] The stance which Preston and the Leinster army would adopt, however, was less immediately obvious. From the middle of August the position of the military in fact became the single most important factor in the resolution of the crisis and the positions adopted by the confederate generals largely determined Rinuccini's actions in the following months. It is useful, therefore, at this juncture to examine briefly his relationship with the provincial commanders of confederate forces.

VI

The manner in which O'Neill and Rinuccini co-operated at moments of crisis during the nunciature has been frequently noted in the past,[166] but the vicissitudes of their relationship have only recently received attention,[167] while the nuncio's relations with Preston have been almost totally ignored. Yet, during the period under review in this chapter, the nuncio's interaction with Preston was arguably just as important as that with O'Neill.

From his arrival in 1645 Rinuccini had retained independent control of the subsidies and arms which he had brought from the continent. This provided him, therefore, with a direct input into military matters independent of the decisions of the Supreme Council. In March 1646 the nuncio wished to donate all the papal subsidies to the province of Ulster because it was 'more catholic than the others and professed a singular reverence for the Supreme Pontiff'.[168] In the event, however, Preston's Leinster army received almost twice as much money as O'Neill's (about £7,000).[169] Rinuccini was never again to have such a large sum of money at his disposal and it is arguable that by dividing it in this fashion he had missed the best opportunity he would

---

[164] Lambert to Ormond, 9 Sept. 1646 (Bodl. Carte MS 18, fo. 468ᵛ).

[165] Thomas Harmon to Ormond, 23 Sept. 1646 (ibid., fo. 555ʳ).

[166] See for example Corish, 'Ormond, Rinuccini, and the Confederates, 1645–9', 320–31; Cregan, 'Confederation of Kilkenny' (art.), 111.

[167] See Casway, *Owen Roe O'Neill*, 122–4, 141, 178–81: this account, however, analyses these difficulties almost entirely from O'Neill's perspective and does little justice to the nuncio's criticisms of the general.

[168] 'Più cattolica dell'altre, e professare una singolar reverenza verso il sommo Pontefice': Rinuccini to Pamfili, 21 Mar. 1646 (Aiazzi, *Nunziatura*, 116).

[169] Stevenson ignores this change of heart, *Covenanters and Confederates*, 223; see Casway, *Owen Roe O'Neill*, 122–4 for a discussion of this decision.

have to further his own policies by the use of the Ulster army. When O'Neill and the nuncio finally did become close allies the nuncio lacked substantial resources to support the general's army. On the other hand, by acting in this fashion Rinuccini consolidated his relationship with Preston, who was already grateful to Scarampi for resuscitating his military career at Duncannon in 1645 and this had important consequences in the summer. Scarampi's influence on Preston's behalf was evidently one reason for the nuncio's decision to divide the money in this way. Probably the most influential factor, nevertheless, was the distinctly unfavourable impression of O'Neill which the nuncio had formed during his first months in Ireland, describing the Ulster general on one occasion as a 'very eccentric and self-interested' man.[170]

O'Neill's victory at Benburb,[171] news of which reached the nuncio on 14 June, helped very materially to re-establish the Ulster general in the nuncio's good graces. Nevertheless, although Preston's conduct disappointed him somewhat during the summer, the Leinster army continued to figure very largely in the nuncio's plans for the rest of the year. At the same time as Rinuccini appears to have sounded out O'Neill about an independent attack on Dublin, he also investigated and was satisfied about Preston's willingness to support his plans.[172] When the decision was made to publish the interdict on 17 August, therefore, Rinuccini was quite confident that both O'Neill and Preston would support his own position. Some days later, however, Rinuccini received a very ambiguous letter from Preston which raised doubts about the general's position.[173]

It seems plausible that a sudden doubt about Preston's reliability was the factor in forcing the clergy back to a more moderate position on 24 August when Rinuccini and his associates produced a detailed outline of the conditions which they believed necessary to restore peace among the

---

[170] 'Uomo assai stravagante e interessato': Rinuccini to Pamfili, 24 Apr. 1646 (Aiazzi *Nunziatura*, 124). Another major cause of tension were the ferocious depredations of O'Neill's troops in Leinster which, in the nuncio's view, surpassed the worst excesses of barbarians or Scythians. Rinuccini was particularly upset that the poorly paid Ulster army styled themselves as the army of the pope, thus linking the Holy See to their pillaging. Because of this, prior to Benburb, he would have been perfectly happy to see O'Neill removed from his command or at least punished severely: see *Comment. Rinucc.*, ii. 235–7; the extent of the nuncio's genuine horror at the Ulster army's excesses has been generally ignored even in Casway, *Owen Roe O'Neill*, the most detailed study of the Ulster army.

[171] Which was portrayed as having stopped a Scottish thrust against Kilkenny itself: see Stevenson, *Covenanters and Confederates*, 225–7.

[172] Rinuccini to Pamfili, 17 July 1646 (Aiazzi, *Nunziatura*, 149); Massari seems to have been the emissary chosen to contact the generals on this matter: see Viaggio in Irlanda di Dionysio Massari (APF, Miscellaneae Varie 9, pp. 127–47); O'Neill to Rinuccini, 29 July 1646 (*Comment. Rinucc.*, ii. 297–8).

[173] News also arrived that Preston had greeted news of the peace with jubilant gunfire in his camp and that he had accepted 2,000 pistoles (c.£1,700) from Clanricard to sweeten his army's disposition towards peace: *Comment. Rinucc.*, ii. 299, 358, 360.

confederates.[174] While it was unlikely that Ormond would agree to their conditions,[175] it seems clear that the clergy were serious in their attempt to reach a negotiated settlement at this juncture. Of particular interest is the fact that Rinuccini was prepared to drop the demand for a catholic viceroy, at least temporarily, for what might be termed the 'hard security' of committed catholic military commanders.[176] Yet the most remarkable aspect of the clerical conditions, in the light of Rinuccini's later actions, were the proposals on how to regulate matters in the (probable) event of a failure to agree. The peace party was offered two alternatives in this respect. The first was, in effect, to forget that the peace had ever been published. The confederate association would continue as before in complete control of its own quarters but would ally itself with Ormond's forces against the king's enemies.[177] There was evidently a great deal of merit in this plan and it is arguable that Rinuccini's greatest mistake in Ireland was the decision to shelve this idea when his assumption of government had put him in the best possible position to implement it. The second alternative on offer from the clergy was a General Assembly to debate the merits of the peace.

The clergy demanded a quick reply to their propositions but by 26 August realized that their opponents had no intention of complying.[178] Apparently, the peace party still clung to the hope that the arrival of Ormond could preserve the peace.[179] Information from Kilkenny that no response could be made to their propositions until Ormond's arrival in the capital seems to have inclined the clerical representatives to the conclusion that the supporters of peace lacked the capacity to accommodate their desires but hoped simply to override their opposition. They were strengthened in this conviction by news that, in defiance of the clergy's prohibition, troops had been used to collect overdue taxes.[180] On 26 August, therefore, Rinuccini and his associates authorized the use of violence to resist the collection of these monies. They also decreed the excommunication of any tax collectors who supplied any money to Kilkenny and any soldiers who participated in the collection of taxes, thereby ensuring that the resolution of the crisis would

---

[174] On 25 Aug. the French agent wrote to Mazarin that the clergy had suddenly adopted a more moderate position: du Moulin to Mazarin, 25 Aug./4 Sept. 1646 (Gilbert, *Irish Confederation*, vii. 294); Ó Siochrú, *Confederate Ireland*, 112 notes the return of Plunkett and Darcy to Waterford as another significant factor.

[175] The proposals are outlined in Gilbert, *Irish Confederation*, vi. 99–101.

[176] Ibid.: it was a basic clerical demand that both Preston and O'Neill rather than Clanricard and Castlehaven should receive military commands after the peace. Without such a change, the clergy argued quite reasonably that the clerical party would lack real military security in the event of hostility on the part of Ormond to the implementation of religious conditions.

[177] Ibid.   [178] *Comment. Rinucc.*, ii. 352.

[179] Cregan, 'The Confederation of Kilkenny' (thesis), 232; Bellings to Ormond, 21 Aug. 1646 (Gilbert, *Irish Confederation*, vi. 94–5); Clanricard evidently agreed with this analysis: see his letter to Preston, 24 Aug. 1646 (Lowe, *Clanricard Letter Book 1643–7*, 282–3).

[180] *Comment. Rinucc.*, ii. 354.

almost certainly depend on the respective military strengths of the two camps. In this context, given that O'Neill's religious convictions ensured that he would ignore material blandishments and support the clergy,[181] and that the confederate towns had already shown a clear unwillingness to risk ecclesiastical censures,[182] Preston's stance assumed enormous importance and over the next four months the competition for his loyalty greatly influenced the policy of the respective protagonists.

On 6 September, despite a personal invitation from the recently arrived Ormond to come to Kilkenny, despite attempts to play on ethnic hostility to the Ulster army and despite the promise of rich rewards, Preston opted at least temporarily to support the nuncio's position, thereby ensuring the rejection of the peace.[183] His motives were evidently complex. The peace party was worried that the influence of the Spanish agent in Waterford (Don Diego de la Torre) on behalf of the clergy helped sway Preston's decision.[184] It was the council's misfortune that French patronage of the peace had meant, almost inevitably, that the Spanish agent in Ireland viewed it with disfavour. This was entirely comprehensible since France stood to gain substantial recruitment privileges from the treaty. Unfortunately for the council, Preston continued to have both emotional and financial ties to the Spanish Netherlands.[185] In addition, there was something rather hollow about the council's attempts to sway the Leinster general with hints of lucrative rewards when he had been pointedly omitted from the important military posts in the Ormond peace the previous month.[186] Indeed, Preston had Rinuccini and Scarampi to thank for the funds which had allowed him to achieve his recent successes in Connacht and at Duncannon in 1645. There were sound reasons for Preston to think therefore that the council's sudden interest in his welfare was purely the product of expediency. A ticklish conscience and respect for clerical advice was also clearly a factor in deciding

[181] Ormond was prepared to offer O'Neill a continued military command, custody of all the lands in Oncilland of those not adhering to the peace, and custody of Lord Caulfield's estate, as well as further unspecified advantages: see Ormond to Daniel O'Neill, 28 Aug. 1646 (Bodl. Carte MS 18, fo. 358).

[182] See Hynes, *Mission of Rinuccini*, 91–2; Corish, 'Ormond, Rinuccini, and the Confederates, 1645–9', 321 suggests that the stance of the confederate towns may actually have been the decisive factor in the crisis.

[183] *Comment. Rinucc.*, ii. 364; *CSPI*, 1633–47, p. 503; Sir Robert Talbot to Preston, 3 Sept. 1646 (*Comment. Rinucc.*, ii. 360–2); for their part the clergy attempted to influence him by appealing to traditional anti-Butler prejudice as well as his lack of office under the proposed settlement: see Bodl. Carte MS 118, fo. 29ʳ.

[184] Talbot to Preston, 3 Sept. 1646 (*Comment. Rinucc.*, ii. 360–2).

[185] James Preston to Mazarin, 9 Sept. 1647 (AMAE, Correspondence Politique (Angleterre) 55 fo. 341ʳ⁻ᵛ); in addition to property in Flanders Preston was also in receipt of a Spanish pension: see Ohlmeyer, *Civil War and Restoration*, 180.

[186] The major military positions in the Ormond peace had been conferred on Clanricard and Castlehaven: Gilbert, *Irish Confederation*, vi. 99–101. While Preston's rivalry with O'Neill has been noted many times in the past, his perhaps more serious rivalry with Castlehaven, who competed with him for leadership of the same troops and expeditions, has been largely ignored.

Preston's course of action,[187] as was the question of whether the Leinster army would follow its leader in defiance of a clerical excommunication.[188] Perhaps the factor which weighed greatest with Preston was the fact that O'Neill's forces were apparently stronger than the Leinster army. He evidently wished, therefore, to avoid the possibility of conflict until he had redressed this imbalance and by joining the clergy he acquired time and money to do so.[189]

VII

The creation of a new clerically dominated Supreme Council was possibly inevitable following the rejection of the Ormond peace, but the manner in which this was then followed by an attack on the lord lieutenant in Dublin has been the subject of only limited analysis. Yet this was clearly one of the major turning points of Rinuccini's nunciature, which had a number of important long-term consequences. It has been commonly accepted that after the rejection of the peace there was a logical inevitability about the decision to attempt Dublin.[190] Yet was this the case? Following Preston's adherence to the nuncio, Ormond's position in Kilkenny was untenable and he fled to Dublin on 13 September. Destitute of alternatives, the confederate peace party therefore attempted to negotiate by responding to the earlier proposals of the clergy.[191] When their position is compared with the clergy's moderate attitude on 24 August, it is clear that the distance between the most conciliatory positions of both sides, although not insubstantial, was nevertheless surprisingly small. The degree to which Ormond would have been prepared to endorse the offers which were made to the clergy at this juncture is none the less open to question.[192] A more basic problem was that the two camps were never conciliatory at the same time. By 5 September Rinuccini had heard that Ormond denied having authority to concede anything more than was already contained in the peace. In his opinion, this rendered further negotiation close to meaningless, despite the fact that a secret offer concern-

---

[187] As Clanricard realized after a meeting with him in September: see Clanricard to Ormond, 18 Sept. 1646 (*Clanricard Letter Book 1643–7*, 284).

[188] This had become crucial since 1 Sept. when Rinuccini and his associate delegates, infuriated by the arrival of Ormond in Kilkenny with protestant ministers in his train, published a decree of excommunication against any supporters or favourers of the peace: *Comment. Rinucc.*, ii. 356; Gilbert, *Irish Confederation*, vi. 131–2.

[189] *CSPI*, 1633–47, p. 509.

[190] Corish, 'Ormond, Rinuccini, and the Confederates, 1645–9', 321, for instance, has suggested that 'actions so essentially unconstitutional could only be made acceptable by some striking success and the new council decided on an immediate attack on Dublin'. The decision to attack Dublin, however, actually pre-dated the formation of the new council by a number of weeks.

[191] See Gilbert, *Irish Confederation*, vi. 132–4.

[192] See for instance Ormond to Digby, 24 Sept. 1646 (Carte, *Ormond*, vi. 433); the inability of peace party negotiators to speak for Ormond was also noted distrustfully by the clergy: see the declaration of the nuncio and congregation of clergy, 15 Sept. 1646 (Bodl. Carte MS 18, fo. 513ʳ).

ing the definitive removal of penalties against religious practice and the right to retain ecclesiastical possessions until a parliament was convened in pursuance of the articles of peace, was placed on the table in and around this time.[193]

Clerical militancy was undoubtedly increased by a widespread if mistaken belief that the king himself was prepared to accede to confederate religious demands but that Ormond, or the council in Dublin, or both together, refused to put aside their private prejudices in this matter.[194] In any event, once confident of Preston's support, the nuncio realized that he was in a position to dictate rather than to negotiate terms. On 10 September a new clerical declaration was published in Waterford which, in the attitude expressed towards Ormond, indicated that the decision had already been made to attack Dublin. The lord lieutenant was implicitly accused of having betrayed the king's orders to conclude an Irish peace on any terms. He was also represented as having imprisoned Glamorgan as part of a plot to prevent aid reaching the king from Ireland and of having then published a peace despite the revocation of his mandate.[195] The publication of such fantastic accusations, while undoubtedly opportunistic, may not have been undertaken with complete insincerity. Rinuccini's personal knowledge of the papal peace inclined him to believe that the attitude of the lord lieutenant diverged from that of his monarch on the question of religious concessions. Like the Glamorgan articles, the papal peace had the effect of poisoning the well of negotiations because of the belief it created in certain quarters of the attainability of concessions which neither the king nor Ormond could ever seriously contemplate.[196] This was evidently a point which the marquis subsequently came to appreciate when he re-entered negotiations with the confederates in 1648.

The decision to mount a campaign against Dublin was of great significance. Having left confederate quarters, Ormond opened immediate negotiations with parliament. However, before doing so, he had entirely justifiable suspicions that Rinuccini intended to attack his vulnerable garrisons.[197] Even after his return to Dublin, and despite his disgust with what

[193] See the undated copy of the cipher offer to Rinuccini (Bodl. Carte MS 18, 374ʳ); that this was a genuine offer with Ormond's approval is indicated by Digby's later offer to Preston: see Digby's instructions to Nicholas Walsh, 19 Oct. 1646 (ibid., 19, fo. 221ʳ).

[194] See the letter of Daniel O'Neill to Ormond, 1 Oct. 1646 (ibid., 19, fo. 7).

[195] Comment. Rinucc., ii. 383–6.

[196] In this regard one can note that Geoffrey Baron in early Oct. (ns) 1646 had in his possession a fairly accurate list of the concessions offered in the papal peace and indicated that the confederates were determined to 'stand upon' them: see Bodl. Carte MS 19, fo. 32ʳ.

[197] Sometime before leaving Waterford on 17 Sept., the nuncio urged O'Neill to attack Dublin, hoping to capture either the city or the lord lieutenant. O'Neill, however, refused, preferring to come south and to secure Kilkenny: Rinuccini to Pamfili, 21 Sept. 1646 (Aiazzi, Nunziatura, 160–1). This instruction may even have been sent sometime in Aug. See ibid. 177–8; see also Stevenson, Covenanters and Confederates, 239. Hynes' suggestion therefore that Rinuccini's attack on Dublin was to forestall its transfer to parliament rests on very dubious ground: see Mission of Rinuccini, 107.

he saw as confederate faithlessness, it is clear that Ormond was prepared to negotiate concerning either peace or a new truce.[198] Consequently, the primary responsibility for the fact that the repudiation of the peace led to the resumption of hostilities with Ormond would appear to lie with the nuncio. This is a point of more significance than has perhaps been generally appreciated. Not only was Ormond prepared to negotiate concerning a new cessation, but on 24 August the clerical representatives themselves had been prepared to envisage the renewal of the policy of truce with the lord lieutenant. It was only after the clerical triumph that this idea was shelved. A policy of war with Ormond held many attractions for Rinuccini and it seems clear that his personal input into the arguably imprudent decision to attack Dublin was very considerable.[199] Indeed, the offensive against Dublin really only made sense in terms of the nuncio's own preoccupations. Of greatest importance in this regard was probably his belief that Ormond's pernicious influence among the confederates could only be eradicated by the removal of the lord lieutenant, together with his intuition that the capture of Dublin was the single measure most likely to secure further largesse from Rome. Yet it is arguable that both of these assumptions rested on false premisses. The failure of the peace had already shattered the influence of Ormond's supporters within the association. Those confederates closest to him were in prison accused of perjury. It was actually the unpopular attack on Dublin, massively compounded by the dismal failure of the expedition, which resuscitated the position of the authors of the peace.

Rinuccini was certainly correct when he assumed that the capture of Dublin would be welcomed in Rome. Yet Massari's account of his trip to Rome in the autumn of 1646 suggests that news of Benburb and of the rejection of the peace on their own would have been sufficient to obtain extra papal funds.[200] Rather it was news of the failure of the attack on Dublin which put the new papal subsidies at risk. In addition, Rinuccini's radical behaviour in Ireland, although tolerated as long as it remained successful, was evidently considered somewhat alarming in Rome. This can be sensed in the relief expressed by his superiors when news reached Rome in 1647 that Rinuccini had resigned the presidency of the Supreme Council.[201] In this context, it is probable that a more careful policy of consolidation would not have put additional papal aid at risk.

---

[198] As he made clear to Clanricard who could be expected to act as his intermediary with the confederates: see Ormond to Clanricard, 23 Sept. 1646 (Carte, *Ormond*, vi. 432).

[199] See Rinuccini's relation to the pope (Aiazzi, *Nunziatura*, 407).

[200] Viaggio in Irlanda di Dionysio Massari (APF, Miscellaneae Varie 9, pp. 270–88).

[201] See Pancirolo to Rinuccini, 29 Apr. 1647 (illustrative documents, G. Aiazzi (Annie Hutton, trans.), *The Embassy in Ireland of Monsignor G. B. Rinuccini, archbishop of Fermo, in the years 1645–1649* (Dublin, 1873), 474–5).

The campaign itself was a failure. Although the countryside around Dublin was ravaged, the city itself was never in danger of being taken and the offensive ultimately disintegrated. One of the campaign's great flaws was the necessity which was felt to include the armies of both Preston and O'Neill.[202] This meant that a grossly over-proportioned force of between 15,000 and 20,000 men was involved.[203] The chief reason for the mustering of such an enormous force was the mutual distrust of the two generals, who each saw his own security as dependent on having an army stronger than his rival's. The unnecessarily huge size of the army made it so expensive to maintain in the field that an extended campaign became a virtual impossibility, particularly because the money which Rinuccini had brought from Rome had long since been exhausted.[204]

Apart from shortages of supplies, there were substantial risks that the two confederate armies would fight against each other rather than against Ormond. After prolonged dithering Preston had finally opposed the peace and, in the nuncio's view, partly motivated by hatred of Richard Bellings, had co-operated in the overthrow of the council,[205] but his reliability with regard to the more extreme step of attacking Dublin was clearly open to question. The entire project was clearly against Preston's better military judgement and who, in any case, was still personally attracted to the idea of reaching a peace with Ormond.[206] Moreover, he was understandably nervous about jeopardizing his own supply base in Leinster, and the loyalty of his soldiers,[207] by co-operating with the Ulster army's entry into the province. The decision to include the Leinster army in this campaign has been taken to represent the influence of Old English advisors, in particular Nicholas French, on the nuncio but it is clear that Scarampi's influence on Preston's behalf was also considerable.[208] Nevertheless, the ultimate decision to permit Preston's inclusion was probably Rinuccini's since he had become the president of the new confederate council selected by the clergy which acted as the confederate executive until the

[202] This decision and other complexities of the campaign, including the frantic negotiations to which it gave rise between Digby, Clanricard, Preston, and Rinuccini are traced in detail in Casway, *Owen Roe O'Neill*, 151–71.

[203] Ó Siochrú, *Confederate Ireland*, 120 argues that neither general was strong enough to attack Dublin on their own but the sheer size of the combined army casts doubt on this.

[204] Gilbert, *Irish Confederation*, vi. 22; du Moulin to Digby, 7 Oct./27 Sept. 1646 (ibid., vii. 296; *Comment. Rinucc.*, ii. 391–2; *CSPI*, 1633–47, pp. 536–40.

[205] Rinuccini's relation to the pope (Aiazzi, *Nunziatura*, 406).

[206] Gilbert, *Irish Confederation*, vi. 139: see also Oliver FitzWilliam to Ormond, 24 Sept. 1646 (ibid., 142–3).

[207] The Leinster army were bitterly antagonistic to O'Neill's forces: in this regard see Digby to Ormond, 13 Oct. 1646 (Carte, *Ormond*, vi. 443): the depredations of O'Neill's army in Leinster earlier that year were evidently responsible for much of this animosity.

[208] Casway, *Owen Roe O'Neill*, 151; Ó Siochrú, *Confederate Ireland*, 120; *Viaggio in Irlanda di Dionysio Massari* (APF, Miscellaneae Varie 9, p. 184); Aiazzi, *Nunziatura*, 403, 406–7; and Scarampi also seems to have argued against any attempt to depose Preston in October when it had become clear that his commitment to the campaign was dubious (ibid., 314–15).

General Assembly of 1647.[209] Possibly the key element in the nuncio's decision was the belief that he personally could control Preston through appeals to the Leinster general's conscience. In this he was not wholly incorrect. Although Preston's doubts about the entire enterprise, and his susceptibility to the influence of Clanricard, came close to forcing his defection to Ormond on several occasions in the course of the last three months of 1646, the nuncio was always able to reverse his decision by the application of personal and spiritual pressure.[210] Thus although the campaign against Dublin was a fiasco, it did not result in the complete alienation of the Leinster army from the association.[211]

Yet, however skilfully the nuncio manipulated Preston during these months, it is difficult to see the attack on Dublin as anything other than an act of folly for which Rinuccini himself bore the primary responsibility. Although the offensive revealed Ormond's weakness, the end of the first Civil War in England meant that parliament was in a position to answer any call for assistance from Dublin. However much Rinuccini bemoaned the marquis's pernicious influence on the confederates, it was not in the association's interest to replace him in Dublin with parliamentary forces. In the long term this is exactly what the attack accomplished. It also resulted in the complete abandonment of any attempt to confront more dangerous foes in Munster. After the completion of the Ormond treaty it had been intended to direct an offensive south against Inchiquin, whose strength was causing acute worry in Kilkenny.[212] The clergy's intervention meant that nothing was put in motion in this regard, an omission which was to have extraordinarily expensive consequences in the following year. Of even greater importance was the damage which was done to the internal unity of the association. In many ways the declaration of the Ormond peace and the attack on Dublin were mirror images of each other. Both were attempts by committed factions then in control of the confederate executive to push the association in a direction unacceptable to many of the members. The great majority of the politically important confederates desired a peace with the lord lieutenant which was acceptable to the catholic clergy. It was the incompatibility of these two objectives which defined their unhappy dilemma. The Ormond peace failed

---

[209] Cregan, 'The Confederation of Kilkenny' (thesis), 233: this excited comment from the agents of France, Spain, and the Empire. No one could be unaware of the papal claim to suzerainty over Ireland and speculation abounded that the nuncio was preparing to repudiate the Stuart monarchy in Ireland: see Aiazzi, Nunziatura, 405.

[210] In this regard see Gilbert, Irish Confederation, vi. 150; Aiazzi, Nunziatura, 181–2, 407–9; Digby to Ormond, 13 Nov. 1646 (Carte, Ormond, vi. 455); Casway, Owen Roe O'Neill, 166; Comment. Rinucc., ii. 454–7.

[211] On 22 Dec. Preston made a public declaration in which he humbly admitted that his experiences with Clanricard and Ormond should serve as a warning that no confederate should accept a peace except one approved by the council, congregation, or assembly. The general also signed a public pact to co-operate with O'Neill in future: Comment. Rinucc., ii. 459–60; Aiazzi, Nunziatura, 181–2.

[212] Bellings to Ormond, 18 Aug. 1646 (Carte MS 18, fo. 294[r]).

because the second of these conditions was not met and because the clergy were largely successful in convincing the majority of the association that acceptance of the peace entailed perjury. In September 1646 Rinuccini thus found himself in a position to ensure almost arbitrarily that the key executive posts in the association would pass into the hands of clerical sympathizers. Had he concentrated his energies on purging the association of those most inclined to Ormond and on postponing further radical departures in policy until funds had arrived to finance it, his control over confederate affairs would have been very difficult to shake. The attack on Ormond, on the other hand, effectively helped delegitimize the new executive in a way that the arbitrary selection of the new council had not.

The wisdom of allocating the Dublin campaign to both Preston and O'Neill was also open to question. If the Leinster army was trustworthy then militarily there was no real need for O'Neill. If Preston was not trustworthy, then what could O'Neill really hope to achieve?[213] Had Preston been preferred to O'Neill, then the Ulster general would certainly have been disgruntled, yet he was in no position to break with the clergy. In 1647, in similar circumstances, he was forced to accept his exclusion from Leinster, although with bad grace. In the same vein, if anything was to convince the doubting Old English community that in future policy would not be decided by Ulster Gaelic 'barbarians' then arguably it would have been such a conspicuous gesture of trust in Preston.[214] Ultimately, one can suggest that the two-general approach unhappily succeeded in drastically reducing military efficiency without producing corresponding political gains in terms of conciliating the Old English community.

VIII

The period under review in this chapter witnessed a considerable transformation in the nuncio's position from his reluctant passivity in December 1645 to the highly aggressive stance the following September. That change had been prefigured to some extent by the brief episode of the papal peace, which had indicated that if circumstances allowed the nuncio was prepared to go to very considerable lengths to obtain his way. It would be wrong, therefore, to overestimate the nuncio's reluctance to be drawn into outright opposition to the Ormond peace. None the less, it seems clear that a particular set of circumstances was required before the nuncio could or would have come into conflict with the council. One of those necessary factors was

[213] In this context, Rinuccini's later contention that he believed that O'Neill could be relied on to prevent Preston's waywardness does not really stand up to examination: see Aiazzi, *Nunziatura*, 177–8.

[214] Even Rinuccini himself later admitted that O'Neill's conduct during the campaign had justified some suspicions about his ultimate objectives: see *Comment. Rinucc.*, ii. 461.

certainly the nuncio's conviction that the peace party's commitment to catholicism went no further than the determination to secure toleration for private catholic worship in Ireland and that its desire for peace with the lord lieutenant was influenced by the hope of benefiting from his patronage. The council's actions in signing the Ormond peace despite the collapse of the aspect of the treaty governed by the Glamorgan articles and without waiting for the superior papal peace, their repeated attempts to deceive him, and their inability to prosecute the war with vigour, strengthened the nuncio's conviction of their fundamental untrustworthiness. From his perspective, their final publication of the Ormond peace in August marked a further stage in their lack of concern for the wishes of the clerical party, since the by now patent inadequacy of the Glamorgan articles meant that the treaty was actually the least satisfactory which had been on offer for almost a year.

The council's most significant defence against this last charge was the French involvement in the treaty which promised foreign assistance for the confederates against the increasing threat of the English parliament, something which had become of vital significance in the wake of the collapse of the royalist cause in England. In this context the rather blithe manner in which Rinuccini was prepared to jeopardize French protection for the confederate laity, particularly when one considers the doubts which he seems to have harboured concerning the papal commitment to Ireland, is of interest. The nuncio's awareness, however, that the council had actually signed the peace in March, before any hint of French involvement had emerged, meant that his conviction of their fundamental dereliction of duty to the church was not likely to alter as a result of Bourbon patronage of the peace. The military victories of June/July further strengthened Rinuccini's belief that the peace was unnecessary and organized for the secular commodity of the peace party and that an alternative policy, more militant and more pleasing to God, could be pursued.

Of central importance also was the fact that it was possible for the nuncio to oppose the peace. In this luck played its part, particularly in O'Neill's victory at Benburb which freed the Ulster general to come to Rinuccini's support in September. In addition, the peace party contributed to its own demise. The disjunction between the council's attitudes and those of the General Assembly in February encouraged the nuncio to see the proponents of the treaty as an influential clique within the government rather than as representative of the majority of the association. In introducing the peace, the council gave little thought to the loyalties of either Preston or O'Neill by omitting to provide them with military commands and thus facilitated Rinuccini's task in wooing them to support the clergy. Having lied to and insulted the nuncio and having introduced a peace which failed to satisfy the minimum demands which the clerical party had been making even before Rinuccini's arrival, the council allowed the nuncio to assemble the representatives of the Irish church in a legatine synod and then treated that body's pronouncements with the same cavalier attitude which they had previously shown to Rinuccini. Their over-reliance on Ormond's personal prestige also proved an expensive error, not least because the lord lieutenant found it difficult to react with sufficient speed to the accelerating crisis. Ultimately, and within the context of the negotiating strategy which he had adopted for the previous three years, Ormond did all that could reasonably have been asked of him in his attempt to preserve the peace. But the slow nature of his response meant that he was invariably a step behind the unfolding of events.

Rinuccini's triumph therefore in September 1646 was in some ways attributable to his opponents' mistakes and to luck. Of central importance also was the fact that he had disposed of a considerable sum of money in the preceding months, money which had brought tangible military results. He himself certainly saw the hand of God in the successes of the summer and this was probably partially responsible for the adventurous policy which he pursued after the successful rejection of the peace, despite the fact that he now lacked an independent source of money to support the campaign. His imprudence was punished by the complete failure of the attack on Dublin and the weakening of the authority of the new clerically appointed council. To some extent through a dextrous manipulation of Preston's conscience Rinuccini managed to limit the damage caused by the Dublin campaign but, as the study of the subsequent course of his career in Ireland reveals, his inability to produce finance to support his military policies meant that he was never to recover the dominance which he had enjoyed in September 1646.

CHAPTER FIVE

The Attrition of Influence, December 1646–February 1648

I

The fourteen months from the end of November 1646 to February 1648 marked a particular phase in Rinuccini's Irish career, during which time Nicholas Plunkett and the bishop of Ferns, Nicholas French, exercised a great deal of influence in confederate politics, while the nuncio occupied a less overtly prominent role.[1] This period was inaugurated, and much of its subsequent character determined, by the decision to convene a confederate General Assembly. The writs for this gathering were issued in the wake of the failure of the assault on Dublin and it eventually sat between 10 January and 4 April. The most important problem confronted at this Assembly was the Ormond peace: the lord lieutenant's supporters hoped to have the treaty ratified by the supreme confederate authority,[2] while Rinuccini and his adherents sought the assembly's approval for their overturning of the peace the previous year. The result was a qualified victory for the clerical party because the treaty was indeed rejected. Nevertheless, those who had negotiated it, now bitter personal enemies of the nuncio, were freed from any accusation of having perjured themselves or having been derelict in their responsibilities and were thus free to resume positions of influence within the association.[3] The clergy then secured a second victory when their new formulation of the confederate oath was accepted. This contained four additional articles which committed the taker of the oath to the repeal of all penal laws, the restoration of pre-reformation conditions not only with regard to the free and public exercise of the catholic religion but also with regard to the jurisdiction, privileges and immunities of the catholic clergy, and the retention by the catholic clergy of all churches in the confederates' possession. This seemed to close the door definitively on any revival of the Ormond peace.[4] Again, the clerical achieve-

---

[1] The basic pattern of events during this length of time has already been relatively well established: for a convenient summary see Micheál Ó Siochrú, *Confederate Ireland 1642–1649: A Constitutional and Political Analysis* (Dublin, 1999), 128–70.

[2] Clanricard to Ormond, 8 Jan. 1646 (Bodl. Carte MS 19, fo. 83r).

[3] D. F. Cregan, 'The Confederation of Kilkenny: Its Organisation, Personnel and History' (unpub. Ph.D. thesis, National University of Ireland, 1947) 238–9.

[4] Patrick Corish, 'Ormond, Rinuccini, and the Confederates, 1645–9', in T. W. Moody, F. X. Martin, and F. J. Byrne (eds.), *A New History of Ireland*, iii, *Early Modern Ireland, 1534–1691*, 322.

ment was somewhat qualified by the addition of another clause to the oath which stated that the assembly was to be the only body competent to judge if all sections of the oath were to be insisted on in any future negotiations.[5] The assembly was also given the power, notwithstanding the new oath, to enact any policy which it might judge to be for the good of the kingdom. This decree had the effect of undermining the clergy's position as interpreters of the confederate oath, which they had effectively assumed since August 1646, and allowed Ormond's supporters to hope that a future assembly might reintroduce the peace.[6] The clergy's third victory was in the election of a new council of twenty-four members, of whom only four could be identified with the anti-clerical party.[7] Confederates of whom Rinuccini approved thus controlled the association's executive until the close of the following assembly on 24 December 1647.[8]

The decisions of this first assembly of 1647 had a crucial bearing on Ormond's stance. In the wake of the confederate campaign of the previous year, the area around Dublin was in such a devastated condition that supplies could no longer be found for the lord lieutenant's army. Following the assembly's rejection of the peace, therefore, Ormond reopened communications with parliament which led eventually in July, despite attempts from various quarters to renew his negotiations with the confederates, to the complete transfer of the city and its outlying garrisons to a parliamentary army commanded by Michael Jones.[9] In August 1647 Preston made a determined effort to take Dublin from the newly installed parliamentary forces but his army was virtually annihilated by Jones at the battle of Dungan's Hill. The Supreme Council had previously diverted O'Neill's army to the less important task of retaking Sligo in Connacht. This army was now recalled and managed to hold the line in Leinster against the victorious parliamentary forces.[10] In the south, Inchiquin had taken advantage during 1646 of internal confederate turmoil to win back most of the fortresses he had lost in 1645.

[5] Ibid., 323; Cregan, 'The Confederation of Kilkenny' (thesis), 242.

[6] Comment. Rinucc., ii. 514–15.

[7] Although one of the nuncio's leading opponents, Sir Robert Talbot, believed that in the new council only Muskery, Sir Richard Everard, and John Dillon were not members of the clerical faction: see his letter to Clanricard, 20 Mar. 1647 (John Lowe (ed.), The Letter Book of the Earl of Clanricarde, 1634–7 (Dublin, 1983), 370).

[8] Cregan, 'The Confederation of Kilkenny' (thesis), 246, 256; see also Jane Ohlmeyer, Civil War and Restoration in the Three Stuart Kingdoms: The Career of Randal MacDonnell, Marquis of Antrim, 1609–1683 (Cambridge, 1993), 188–9.

[9] Ó Siochrú, Confederate Ireland, 152–3; Richard Bagwell, Ireland under the Stuarts and during the Interregnum (3 vols., London, 1909–16), ii. 140–1; Thomas Carte, An history of the life of James, first duke of Ormonde (6 vols., Oxford, 1851), vi. 538–9; Comment. Rinucc., ii. 464; J. C. Beckett, The Cavalier Duke (Belfast, 1990), 41.

[10] Ó Siochrú, Confederate Ireland, 155–6; Corish, 'Ormond, Rinuccini, and the Confederates, 1645–9', 324; Bagwell, Ireland under the Stuarts, ii. 146–9; Jerrold Casway, Owen Roe O'Neill and the Struggle for Catholic Ireland (Philadelphia, 1984), 181–200; Pádraig Lenihan, 'The Leinster Army and the Battle of Dungan's Hill, 1647', Irish Sword, 18 (71), 139–53.

By March 1647, with reinforcements from England, he was in possession of a formidable army which may have been as strong as 8,500 foot and 850 horse,[11] and he enjoyed a year of military success. In May 1647 he took Cappoquin, Dromana, and Dungarvan: in mid-summer he ravaged deep into confederate Munster, and, in September, took Cashel by storm with considerable slaughter.[12]

It was against this background of military disaster that the eighth confederate assembly opened on 12 November 1647. Matters quickly became worse as, within days of the opening, news arrived that the Munster confederate army had been routed by Inchiquin at the battle of Knocknanuss. The main decisions and debates of this assembly have previously been the subject of some attention.[13] A factor of considerable importance was the under-representation of the nuncio's supporters among the assembled delegates: as a result of the disruptions of war the province of Ulster, for instance, sent only nine of the seventy-three representatives which it would normally have returned.[14] Deeply alarmed by the succession of military defeats and by developments in England, where on 4 June the army had seized control of the king's person, and on 6 August had occupied London,[15] the assembly debated possible options.[16] It was decided to offer the government of Ireland to the queen of England and the prince of Wales, then resident in France, provided that religious conditions acceptable to the pope could be obtained. If this proved impossible, then a foreign protector, such as the kings of France or of Spain or the pope, would be sought to defend Ireland against parliament.[17] This necessitated the nomination of envoys to the various continental capitals which became the subject of extremely tense debates that brought the association close to rupture. Tensions again rose to a similar height immediately afterwards in the discussions about the creation of a new Supreme Council.[18] Concerning both these issues, the nuncio's party fared

[11] This represented a major increase from his previous strength: in Dec. 1646 William Parsons estimated his forces as 4,000 foot and 300 horse: see his letter to Arthur Annesley, 10 Dec. 1646 (British Library, Egerton MS 917, fo. 26ʳ⁻ᵛ); see also Hugh Hazlett, 'A History of the Military Forces Operating in Ireland' (unpub. Ph.D. thesis, Queen's University, Belfast, 1938), i. 383–7.

[12] Bagwell, *Ireland under the Stuarts*, 150–3; Cregan, 'The Confederation of Kilkenny' (thesis), 254.

[13] In particular by Cregan, 'The Confederation of Kilkenny' (thesis), 256–64 and by Ó Siochrú, *Confederate Ireland*, 159–67.

[14] Casway, *Owen Roe O'Neill*, 200–2; Corish, 'Ormond, Rinuccini, and the Confederates, 1645–9', 324–5.

[15] Robert Ashton, *The English Civil War: Conservatism and Revolution, 1603–1649*, 2nd edn. (London, 1991) 294–309; Ivan Roots *The Great Rebellion, 1642–1660* (London, 1983), 112.

[16] The uncertainty of events in England added very considerably to the tension in Ireland: see for example Clanricard to Daniel O'Neill, 8 July 1647 (*Clanricard Letter Book 1643–7*), 461–2.

[17] Cregan, 'The Confederation of Kilkenny' (thesis), 256–7; Corish, 'Ormond, Rinuccini, and the Confederates, 1645–9', 324–5; Michael Hynes, *Mission of Rinuccini, Nunico Extraordinary to Ireland, 1645–49* (Lovain, 1932), 166–7; French and Spanish views of the protector option are succinctly summarized in the discussion of this assembly in Ohlmeyer, *Civil War and Restoration*, 201–4.

[18] Corish, 'Ormond, Rinuccini, and the Confederates, 1645–9', 325.

badly. In particular, two of the three men entrusted with the embassy to France, Muskery and Geoffrey Browne, were deeply distrusted by the nuncio.[19] As events transpired, the nuncio's unease at their appointment was entirely justified as these envoys plotted with the queen and prince concerning a new settlement in Ireland entirely contrary to his desires. With regard to the council, which was nominated and not elected, itself a sign of almost paralysing tension within the association, the dominance of the faction susceptible to clerical influence which had continued since the change of government in September 1646 was decisively shaken.[20]

II

The basic outline of events is therefore reasonably clear but Rinuccini's own stance during this period between the great excommunication crises of 1646 and 1648 has received relatively little attention from historians and the constraints under which he operated have not been analysed in detail. Perhaps the single most important limitation on his freedom of action was financial. A lack of money had contributed to the nuncio's failure at Dublin and to his consequent loss of momentum and prestige. Something which he had not foreseen, however, was that a similar deficiency would hamper him throughout 1647 as well. Rinuccini had originally left Italy under the impression that, if the situation in Ireland proved favourable, further subsidies would be made available from Rome to supplement those with which he had set out. Upon his arrival the nuncio realized that, from a papal perspective, the situation was anything but favourable but he became convinced the investment of additional pontifical money was actually what was required to transform matters. His correspondence to Rome, therefore, became filled with appeals for more funds.[21] His superiors were unmoved by his arguments and informed him that no fresh monies would be sent until it was known what effect the first subsidies had achieved.[22] The military triumphs of the summer of 1646, followed by the unequivocal opposition of the clerical convocation to the Ormond peace, convinced Rinuccini that further aid would now

[19] Cregan, 'The Confederation of Kilkenny' (thesis), 257–64; Corish, 'Ormond, Rinuccini, and the Confederates, 1645–9', 325–6; Casway, Owen Roe O'Neill, 202.

[20] Hynes, Mission of Rinuccini, 169–70 mentions this nomination process, as does Corish, 'Ormond, Rinuccini, and the Confederates, 1645–9', 325 and Ó Siochrú, Confederate Ireland, 164: see also Comment. Rinucc., iii. 531–14.

[21] See for example Aiazzi, Nunziatura, 101, 125, 142, 150, 158; Rinuccini seems to have been worried that dissatisfaction in Rome with the confederates, added to papal parsimony, would lead to Ireland being written off as a bad investment risk. This possibly explains his rather far-fetched scheme for an independent army in Ireland and his argument that a parliamentary victory might actually benefit Irish catholicism: ibid., 80, 118; Rinuccini's Relatio Status Rerum, Mar. 1646 (ibid., 115).

[22] Pamfili to Rinuccini, 20 May (ns) 1646 (Comment. Rinucc., ii. 94).

be forthcoming from Italy.[23] To this end, his closest friend and advisor, Dionysio Massari, was dispatched to Rome to obtain the additional papal subsidies.

Massari's reports of the victories achieved in Ireland and his general capacity to stir the pope's imagination eventually produced results. Despite incessant pleas from Venice for renewed assistance in the war of Candia against the Turks and the overt protest of the republic's ambassador concerning the diversion of papal funds to Ireland,[24] Innocent made a public commitment in December 1646 to transport an additional sum of 60,000 scudi to Rinuccini via France.[25] News of the failure of the Dublin campaign considerably lessened the pope's enthusiasm for sending this money, however,[26] and a delay of several months ensued while Innocent searched for a face-saving manner of retaining the promised money in Rome. Eventually, a combination of Massari's pleading, the adroit suggestions of the papal advisor, Cardinal Pancirolo, and the public obligation already incurred, persuaded the pope to send the 60,000 scudi. With lesser donations from other cardinals and with 3,500 from Rinuccini's own fortune, the total sum entrusted to Massari actually came close to 70,000 scudi (circa £17,000).[27]

This was quite a considerable amount. Yet it was not until the beginning of May that Massari was able to leave Rome. Nor was any money sent in advance. After news of Benburb in August 1646, the pope had planned to send 15,000 scudi to Ireland immediately, but this money was eventually treated as part of Massari's subsidy and was sent with the dean. Given the minimum two months needed for the journey, Rinuccini could not possibly receive the money until the beginning of July. This was far later than he expected, particularly in view of the fact that the parliamentary fleet was active in the seas around Ireland during high summer and might well intercept the money if it was sent too late in the year. As it transpired, owing to a multiplicity of problems concerning their export from France, these subsi-

[23] Even after the failure of the Dublin campaign, he believed that money was all that was lacking to copper-fasten his own dominance in Ireland, expressing the opinion that even Ormond's supporters could be won over by the promise of finance: see the Report on the Proceedings of the catholic armies against Dublin (Aiazzi, Nunziatura, 183).

[24] See Contarini to Doge and Senate of Venice, 6 Oct. (ns) 1646 (Calendar of State Papers and Manuscripts Relating to English Affaïrs, Existing in the Archives and Collections of Venice, 1647–52 (London, 1927), 282); Ludvig Von Pastor (trans. Ernest Graf), History of the Popes from the Close of the Middle Ages, xxviii–xxx (London, 1938–40), 360–1.

[25] Viaggio in Irlanda di Dionysio Massari (APF, Miscellaneae Varie 9, pp. 268–76); Comment. Rinucc., ii. 380; see also my article 'Vatican Diplomacy and the Mission of Rinuccini to Ireland', Archivium Hibernicum, 47 (1993), 84–5.

[26] The pope had been so confident of success against Dublin that he had already planned the victory procession in Rome to celebrate the city's fall: Viaggio in Irlanda di Dionysio Massari (APF, Miscellaneae Varie 9, pp. 285, 288–90).

[27] Ibid., 290–3, 297; Comment. Rinucc., ii. 717–22; in a further burst of (cost-efficient) generosity Massari was also given permission to take six corpses of presumed martyrs from the catacombs of St Callisto to Ireland.

dies actually failed to arrive until March 1648. Nevertheless, even if the subsidies had not been delayed in transit, the dilatoriness of the Roman curia itself would have been sufficient to deprive the nuncio of money which he needed urgently and which he had anticipated receiving throughout the winter. Rinuccini's plight was accentuated by the fact that uncertain communications left him entirely ignorant of the various shifts in the situation in Rome. From January on, he expected at least the arrival of the first 15,000 scudi with every favourable breeze. The nuncio's lack of money, coupled with his fervent hope that subsidies from Rome would arrive shortly, must constantly be borne in mind, therefore, in analysing his actions throughout this period.

III

At the end of 1646 Rinuccini's short-term objectives remained the same as before, namely the vigorous prosecution of the war in Ireland and in particular the capture of Ormond's garrisons. The failure of the Dublin campaign, however, more or less forced a new departure on the nuncio concerning the manner in which he was to attempt to attain these objectives. It was clear that there were limits to what could be achieved by a *de facto* clerical dictatorship and reliance on the Ulster army. Consequently, in the aftermath of the Dublin campaign, Rinuccini became increasingly amenable to advice from moderate Old English advisors, in particular from Nicholas Plunkett and from the bishop of Ferns, Nicholas French. Although the importance of this duo has been noted in the past,[28] the manner in which they influenced the policies of the nuncio requires further analysis.[29]

Both Plunkett and Ferns had impressed the nuncio with the depth of their religious convictions from an early stage of the nunciature and this was a vital reason for their increasing influence. In March 1646 Rinuccini described Plunkett to Rome as 'absolutely the best councillor which we have at present here for the catholic cause'.[30] Yet Rinuccini was aware that Plunkett was also liked and respected by even the most devoted adherents of Ormond, even if they were somewhat uneasy by the delicacy of his conscience.[31] This increased his political respect for the councillor and thus, despite having

---

[28] Corish, 'Ormond, Rinuccini, and the Confederates, 1645–9', 322; Ó Siochrú, *Confederate Ireland, passim*, emphasizes the critical importance of both men and particularly Plunkett in confederate politics.

[29] This is a point of added importance because Rinuccini subsequently came to regret the degree to which he had followed their advice, which has had a tendency to obscure the co-operation which he afforded them in 1647: see Aiazzi, *Nunziatura*, 409–11.

[30] 'Miglior consigliere che assolutamente abbiamo oggi qui per la causa Cattolica': Rinuccini to Pamfili, 7 Mar. 1646 (Aiazzi, *Nunziatura*, 102); it was also chiefly to honour Plunkett that Rinuccini insisted that his brother, Patrick Plunkett, be elevated to the see of Ardagh.

[31] In this regard see Muskery to Ormond, 18 Apr. 1646 (Bodl. Carte MS 17, fo. 180ʳ⁻ᵛ); Gerrott Fennell to same, 14 Apr. 1646 (Gilbert, *Irish Confederation*, v. 329–30).

originally accepted the Ormond peace, Plunkett was reappointed to the Supreme Council by the nuncio in September 1646. He was joined on this body by Nicholas French, the Old English bishop of Ferns, who was at that time the nuncio's favourite Irish bishop.[32]

These 'good catholics and clever politicians'[33] exerted great influence within the association until their departure from Ireland to Rome in February 1648. Indeed, the fact that the anti-clerical faction, who dominated the second assembly of 1647, were content to see them depart the country on the mission to Rome, is indicative of the influence which they had wielded in the previous Supreme Council.[34] One of the key objectives and, to a certain extent, achievements of Plunkett and the bishop of Ferns during this period was evidently to prevent a total identification of those who had opposed the peace with O'Neill and the Ulster confederates and with extreme constitutional positions.[35] This was attempted in a number of ways, among which the conciliation of Preston, a military figure more likely to inspire trust among the Old English than O'Neill, was of considerable importance. As noted in the previous chapter, French had argued strongly for Preston's inclusion in the campaign against Dublin. He also co-operated with the nuncio in enticing Preston back into the confederate fold after the failure of this campaign, although he subsequently temporarily abandoned the general.[36] The decision to convoke the General Assembly was obviously linked to this broad strategy of moderation.[37]

The importance of this assembly, however, went considerably beyond soothing Preston's anxieties. It seems clear in fact that its convocation set the seal on a definite change of policy in the anti-peace camp, which resulted to some extent in the marginalization of the nuncio himself. By summoning the assembly, Ferns and Plunkett seem to have hoped to relegitimize the authority of confederate institutions through a voluntary renunciation of dictatorship on the part of the clergy. This was the first step in a policy of moderation which, despite his later regrets, Rinuccini clearly tolerated and in ways

---

[32] Aiazzi, *Nunziatura*, 111; as secretary to the congregation of bishops, Ferns had played a vital organizational role in the clerical coup in Aug. and Sept.

[33] This is to paraphrase Rinuccini's own comment: 'buoni cattolici nel resto, ma non senza misura di buona politica' (Aiazzi, *Nunziatura*, 410).

[34] The selection first of the bishop of Clogher and then of the marquis of Antrim for the mission to France was almost certainly made for the same reasons: Jane Ohlmeyer has recently demonstrated that Antrim also played a vital role during 1647, both in orchestrating opposition to the peace in the assembly and then as the president of the clerically dominated Supreme Council: see *Civil War and Restoration*, 183–93.

[35] This analysis differs from both that of Casway, *Owen Roe O'Neill*, 174–5, which argues that the Ormondist party recovered its influence following the first and not the second assembly of 1647, and that of Ohlmeyer, *Civil War and Restoration*, 181–2, who suggests an 'irremediable split' between the Old English and Old Irish confederates from the declaration of the first Ormond peace.

[36] In the assembly Ferns lent support to the attempt to impeach Preston: see Cregan, 'The Confederation of Kilkenny' (thesis), 243; *Comment. Rinucc.*, ii. 554–8.

[37] In this context see Preston to Clanricard, 4 Dec. 1646 (*Clanricard Letter Book 1643–7*), 340–1; see also *CSPI*, 1633–47, 575, 544.

actively encouraged for much of 1647. The most recent analysis of confederate politics underestimates this latter point.[38] It has been suggested that
three identifiable groupings can be identified at this juncture in the association's history: a peace faction, a clerical faction, and the moderates, with
whom 'the clerical faction . . . had to contend' and who 'skilfully manipulated the balance of power between the two main factions'.[39] The painstak-
ing research which has established the names of the various councillors is
impressive but the tripartheid structure advanced can be questioned as too
blunt and absolutist. Under close inspection, the lines between those defined
as 'clerical' and 'moderate' become surprisingly blurred. The majority of the
so-called moderates on the first Supreme Council of 1647 had actually previously sat as members of the clerically appointed executive of the previous
year and thus shared responsibility for the attack on Dublin.[40] Indeed,
Nicholas French, identified as one of the two principal moderates,[41] was a
major influence on that campaign and subsequently participated in the
attempt by the 'clerical faction' to impeach Preston for his unreliability outside Dublin in the first assembly of 1647.[42] For their part, the council members defined almost by default as the 'clerical' faction represent a most
unconvincing ecclesiastical lobby. Only three of the twelve were even members of the clergy: the bishops of Clonfert, Limerick, and Clogher. The last
of these could arguably be represented as an 'extremist', although his true
political orientation lay more towards Owen Roe O'Neill and the Ulster
army than towards ecclesiastical irredentism. Neither Limerick nor Clonfert
was a fire-breathing intransigent. Rather, they were among the bishops most
eager to accommodate the confederate peace party, as was later demonstrated by their position within the episcopal minority which resisted
Rinuccini in the crisis of 1648. Shorn of its clergy, the profile of the lay members of the 'extremist'[43] clerical faction actually resembles very closely that
of their 'moderate' equivalents.[44] Certainly, none of the nine enjoyed the
confidence of the nuncio to the same degree as Nicholas Plunkett, just as
none of the bishops identified with this faction was as close to Rinuccini as
was the supposedly moderate Nicholas French.[45]

Rinuccini himself perceived the new council as highly sympathetic to the
clergy, with the exception of four peace party adherents.[46] His analysis was

---

[38] Ó Siochrú, *Confederate Ireland*, 166.   [39] Ibid., 125–7, 141.

[40] Of the eight 'moderates' named, only Rochford, Blake, and Antrim had not served on the previous council: see ibid., 141, 264–5.

[41] Ibid., 161.   [42] Ibid., 139.   [43] Ibid., 132.

[44] See ibid., 264–5 for a list of the councillors.

[45] Moreover, the political positions identified as classically moderate, namely the search for a settlement with the king which provided religious guarantees, would have been subscribed to by the
most extreme members of the clergy, including Rinuccini: see ibid., 167; see also my article,
'Seventeenth Century Dynamics', *Irish Review*, 24 (1999), 134–7.

[46] Rinuccini to Pamfili, 24 Mar. 1647 (Aiazzi *Nunziatura*, 209).

echoed by the Spanish agent, Diego de la Torre.[47] Perhaps the most telling indication, however, that the 'moderate' leaders, Plunkett and French, were perceived as clericalists emerged in the second assembly of 1647. Given the fraught nature of the debates in progress, it was hardly surprising that a decision was adopted to select rather than elect a new Supreme Council. The four individuals chosen to do so, Muskery, Geoffrey Browne, Plunkett, and French, had all been nominated for foreign service but more pertinently represented different wings of the association. Muskery and Browne carried the banner of the peace party while Plunkett and French were clearly trusted by the clergy to protect their interests. Thus, rather than a tripartheid structure, involving separate and sometimes antagonistic clerical and moderate interests, the political shifts of 1647 are more accurately represented as the pursuit by the clergy and their supporters of more moderate policies, largely orchestrated by one of the most important clerical leaders, Nicholas French, and by Nicholas Plunkett.

The strategy pursued by this duo enjoyed partial success in the first assembly of 1647. The peace was rejected, the clergy remained certain of a sympathetic ear from the Supreme Council,[48] and the prominence of apostles of reconciliation such as Plunkett and Ferns, and of the popular and previously royalist marquis of Antrim within that body's ranks probably did much to reassure many of the Leinster and Munster confederates.[49] Rinuccini was certainly no longer president of the association but the argument that his resignation was part of the decline of clerical ascendancy[50] fails to take into account the nuncio's own reasons for leaving the post. Rinuccini knew that his abandonment of temporal office would be welcomed in Rome and he wished in any case to free his energies for what he considered the more important aspect of his nunciature, namely the supervision of religious reform in Ireland.[51] Moreover, Jane Ohlmeyer has established that Rinuccini was replaced as president by the marquis of Antrim who enjoyed a good relationship with the nuncio and who was dedicated to eradicating Ormond's influence in Kilkenny.[52] Rinuccini was thus well aware that the council remained in the hands of confederates sympathetic to the clergy although it

[47] Diego de la Torre to Spanish Council of State, 30 Apr. (ns?) 1647 (Archivio General, Simancas, Seccion 6, Segretaria de Estado, 94 (Negociaciones de Inglaterra), Legajo 2523).

[48] This was probably partially attributable to the extreme care which the clerical party took in ensuring that their interests would be well represented at the assembly: in this regard see Bellings's narrative (Gilbert, *Irish Confederation*, vi. 47–8); see also Diego de la Torre to Spanish Council of State, 30 Apr. (ns?) 1647 (AGS, Segretaria de Estado, 94 (Negociaciones de Inglaterra), Legajo 2523).

[49] Concerning Antrim, see Ohlmeyer, *Civil War and Restoration*, 188–91; in 1645 he had of course been rewarded with a marquisate for his efforts in the royalist cause (ibid., 152).

[50] This has been suggested by Casway, *Owen Roe O'Neill*, 174.

[51] In this regard see Rinuccini to Pamfili, 14 July 1645 (Aiazzi, *Nunziatura*, 29–30); same to same, 4 Aug. 1645 (ibid., 38); Pancirolo to Rinuccini, Feb.(?) (BAV, Nunziatura d'Inghilterra 8, fo. 41^{r-v}).

[52] Ohlmeyer, *Civil War and Restoration*, 183–91.

was less amenable to his direct control than the nominated council of which he had been president in the last months of 1646.

The key to Rinuccini's subsequent unhappiness with the first assembly of 1647[53] centred around the fact that he personally was committed to positions which only a minority of the confederates at the assembly endorsed. He thus (eventually) came to regret the abandonment of what had been effectively a military and clerical dictatorship because that was the only form of confederate executive which would give an assured commitment to the policy in which he believed. For most of the year, none the less, he was prepared to tolerate and support the conciliatory policy outlined and implemented by Plunkett and Ferns.

IV

A number of areas can be distinguished in which difficulties were created for the nuncio by Plunkett's and Ferns's policy of giving a voice to (largely) Old English opinion, first through the convocation of the assembly, and then through the subsequent election of a new Supreme Council. This development had particularly important implications for the situation in Leinster which the nuncio still saw as the crucial theatre of operations because of Ormond's continued presence in Dublin. Ultimately the convocation of the assembly forced the nuncio to acquiesce in a number of sometimes unpalatable policy decisions such as the renewal of negotiations with Ormond, the confirmation of Preston as the confederate general in Leinster, and the eventual removal of the Ulster army out of the province. Also, the promotion by Plunkett and Ferns of a conciliatory policy towards the authors of the Ormond peace ensured that they reacquired positions of real influence in the association, particularly in Munster.

The resumption of confederate negotiations with Ormond after the convocation of the assembly[54] undoubtedly represented a major rebuff for the nuncio who was in favour of renewing the attack on Dublin at the earliest opportunity. Having agreed to the assembly, however, he was forced to take its wishes into account.[55] In the event, it was not until late July that negotiations

[53] Rinuccini indeed later largely attributed the misfortunes which subsequently afflicted his nunciature to the decision to convene this assembly and to the accompanying liberation of the former Supreme Council from prison: see Aiazzi, *Nunziatura*, 409–11; the nuncio's regrets in this regard smacked of peevishness: the failure at Dublin had already demonstrated that there were clear limits to the capacity of the clergy to force their will on the association, at least as long as the nuncio lacked an independent source of finance.

[54] The terms offered to Ormond in Mar. are summarized in Hynes, *Mission of Rinuccini*, 140–1; see also Ormond to Digby, 20 Mar. 1647 (Carte, *Ormond*, 511); *Comment. Rinucc.*, ii. 529–30, 594.

[55] Although the assembly eventually condemned the Ormond peace, the general inclination was still clearly in favour of some accommodation with the lord lieutenant: see Rinuccini's report of the rejection of the peace, 4 Feb. 1647 (Aiazzi, *Nunziatura*, 193–6); indeed, in as close as the assembly could come to an outright condemnation of the previous attack on Dublin, an additional confederate

with the lord lieutenant were finally abandoned and a genuine campaign launched against the city. This delay was significant because it allowed Jones to establish himself in Dublin, relatively unopposed. What made this doubly frustrating for the nuncio was his appreciation that these renewed negotiations with Ormond enjoyed little hope of success. It seems clear that the only settlement which the lord lieutenant would entertain with the confederates in 1647 was the reintroduction of the original treaty, which by 2 February had definitively been rejected by the confederate assembly.[56] The marquis was understandably jaundiced by confederate behaviour since the initial proclamation of peace. From his perspective, the legitimacy of the authority of those who had concluded the articles of agreement on the association's behalf was incontestable and, therefore, their repudiation lacked any moral foundation.[57] His conviction of confederate criminality was intensified by the subsequent Dublin campaign. As he stingingly observed to lord Taaffe in October 1646:

I find myselfe, after three yeeres treaty of peace, and the solemn conclusion of one at last, now, in less than one moneth, pursued by the united forces of Ireland; whilest Inchiquin and the Scotts, who have been at continuall war with them, are suffered to lye still unmolested. Which shews, that my endeavour to make a peace is in the opinion of some men a greater fault than the declared intention of others to root them out of the kingdom.[58]

The depth of his personal distrust of the 'perfidy of the Irish' reinforced his belief that it was better for 'religion . . . crown and faithful servants here' that his garrisons should 'be given to the parliament, rather than to the Irish rebels'.[59] Consequently, in the main he seems to have used further negotiations after February 1647 merely to forestall any confederate attack on his quarters until he had satisfactorily transferred control to parliamentary forces.[60] While his behaviour in this regard was understandable, and arguably represented another reproach to Rinuccini's imprudent Dublin campaign of the previous year, a sustainable case could be made that Ormond placed his personal concerns and those of Irish protestants above those of the crown at this juncture. Confederate attempts to renew a truce with the marquis were genuine and while the nuncio had managed to ensure

oath binding the taker to try sincerely to bring about an agreement between Ormond and the confederates was instituted at this assembly: see *Comment. Rinucc.*, ii. 523.

[56] Only four days later Ormond dispatched an appeal to London signifying his willingness to negotiate the passage of his garrisons to parliament: Ormond to Charles, 17 Mar. 1647 (Bodl. Carte MS 20, fos. 478ʳ–479ʳ); same to same, Aug. 1647 (Carte, *Ormond*, vi. 541–2).

[57] Ormond to the confederate catholics, 25 Jan. 1646 (Egerton MS 2533, fo. 412ʳ); George Lane to Sir Thomas Nugent, 25 Sept. 1646 (Bodl. Carte MS 18, fo. 570ʳ⁻ᵛ).

[58] Ormond to Taaffe, 26 Oct. 1646 (Bodl. Carte MS 18, fo. 264ʳ⁻ᵛ).

[59] Ormond to the King, 17 Mar. 1647 (ibid., 20, fos. 478ʳ, 479ʳ).

[60] Corish, 'Ormond, Rinuccini, and the Confederates, 1645–9', 323; see also Hynes, *Mission of Rinuccini*, 141–3.

that the proposed religious articles were quite stringent, other aspects were reasonably generous. Indeed, it seems relatively clear that both the Queen and the Prince of Wales, as well as the French government, would have preferred to see Ormond accept such terms rather than turn his garrisons over to parliament.[61]

One of the reasons why Rinuccini proved unable to shape the formulation of confederate policy in Leinster during 1647 was the fact that his influence with the confederate military in the province became increasingly tenuous during the first half of the year. This stemmed partly from his financial difficulties which robbed him of the leverage with the generals which he had enjoyed in 1646, when his subsidies were critical in allowing them take the field, and partly from the changing roles of Preston and O'Neill within Leinster. The first assembly of 1647 in fact saw Preston consolidate his position in the province. This was confirmed in April when the clerical attempt to impeach the general, in which Rinuccini and Ferns both participated, had to be abandoned because of the anxieties which many confederates experienced at the prospect of unchallenged military supremacy by the Ulster army.[62] The clerical party subsequently seems to have decided that it had no option but to support Preston as the confederate general in Leinster. This undoubtedly weakened Rinuccini's chances of reactivating the campaign against Dublin because Preston, now strengthened by the failure of the impeachment, continued to favour doing everything possible to reach an accommodation with Ormond.

Moreover, the activity of French agents during this period also contributed to the reluctance of many officers in the Leinster army, possibly including Preston himself, to adopt an aggressive stance towards Ormond. This was a point of considerable importance. During 1646 French policy in Ireland had been chiefly articulated by the agent, Claude du Moulin, whose enthusiastic support for the Ormond peace was set within a wider French project for the re-establishment of Charles Stuart in his three kingdoms. Despite the clerical coup and the attack on Dublin, du Moulin continued to advocate the Ormond peace in the General Assembly of 1647, which created considerable difficulties for Rinuccini.[63] The French agent undoubtedly believed himself to be acting according to his master's wishes but it appears that at this

---

[61] In this regard see the undated instructions to the new French agent to Ireland (AMAE, Correspondence Politique (Angleterre) 55, fo. 302ᵛ; Scarampi to Rinuccini, 30 Mar. 1647 *(Comment Rinucc.*, ii. 575–6); Charles to Ormond, 13 May 1647 (Carte Transcripts, xxi. 25).

[62] Cregan, 'The Confederation of Kilkenny' (thesis), 243; *Comment. Rinucc.*, ii. 554–8; Diego de la Torre to Spanish Council of State, 30 Apr. (ns) 1647 (AGS, Segretaria de Estado, 94 (Negociaciones de Inglaterra), Legajo 2523); it is impossible to establish who was the prime mover in the case against Preston or with what enthusiasm it was pressed by Rinuccini and Ferns.

[63] Rinuccini to Pamfili, 4 Feb. 1647 (Aiazzi, *Nunziatura*, 196); see also *Comment. Rinucc.*, ii. 504–5; du Moulin was aware that many of those who enjoyed prominent positions after the clerical coup, such as Ferns, Clogher, Antrim, Preston, and O'Neill, were Spanish pensioners: see Ohlmeyer, *Civil War and Restoration*, 180–1.

juncture a fresh policy had already been adopted in Paris.[64] The revitaliza-
tion of the Spanish war effort in Flanders seems to have had the effect of con-
centrating French attention and resources on the continental struggle, to the
exclusion of secondary areas of interest. Consequently French interest in any
type of grand design for the Stuart kingdoms, such as that which had motivated the original involvement in the Ormond peace, diminished rapidly.[65]
Once again the short-term interest of acquiring levies of troops superseded
any other aspect of Mazarin's Irish policy, even if that allowed parliament to
strengthen its position in Ireland.[66] This change of policy on the part of the
French government was to have important effects on Rinuccini's attempts to
revitalize the confederate war effort in 1647.

On 16 March a French fleet of transports under the command of Jean
Talon arrived at Waterford. On the very morning of their arrival they were
met by George Digby who presented them with a proposition from Ormond
concerning the levy of troops.[67] The substance of this proposition was that,
if parliament could be induced to give consent, Ormond would lead 5,500
troops to France, where they would be constituted as a new French army
under Ormond's own command.[68] The point of greatest importance for the
discussion in hand was that the bulk of these soldiers were intended to be
drawn from the *confederate* armies through the suborning and desertion of
key officers and their troops.[69] The Leinster confederate army would certainly have supplied a sizeable proportion of this proposed army: after the
rout of Preston's army at Dungan's Hill, Digby wrote to Ormond of his
'greate greefe' that the battle had taken place since he had had 'soe greate a
part of Preston's army sure for forraigne employment'.[70] The manner in

---

[64] By Feb. 1647 the decision had been made to recall the agent: see Bodl. Carte MS 20, fo. 294^r;
indeed, it seems that, rather than formulating policy on the basis of information received from their
resident in Ireland, Mazarin's government does not appear to have bothered even to decipher many
of du Moulin's dispatches: see Digby to Mazarin, 5 Nov. (ns) 1647 (AMAE, Correspondence
Politique (Angleterre) 55, fo. 379^v).

[65] See the royal memorial to Bellièvre, 30 Mar. (ns) 1647 (AMAE, Correspondence Politique
(Angleterre), fos. 113^r–115^r).

[66] In a royal memorial in Mar. 1647 to the French agent in London, it was noted that the levies
which the French hoped to make in Ireland, comprising one regiment from Ormond's garrisons and
one from the confederates, would have the unfortunate effect of weakening the anti-parliamentary
forces there. This was a price the French government was willing to pay, given its urgent need for
troops in Flanders: see Royal memorial to Bellièvre, 30 Mar. (ns) 1647 (AMAE, Correspondence
Politique (Angleterre) 55, fo. 114^r).

[67] Digby to Ormond, 16 Mar. 1647 (Carte, *Ormond*, vi. 507).

[68] The proposed conditions of service are laid out in Bodl. Carte MS 20, fos. 641^r–642^v.

[69] Digby to Ormond, 27 Feb. 1647 (Carte, *Ormond*, vi. 500); same to same, 6 Mar. 1647 (ibid.,
501–2); Digby to Mazarin, 24 Apr. 1647 (AMAE, Correspondence Politique (Angleterre) 55, fos.
151^r–152^r); see also Ormond to Talon, 23 Apr. 1647 (ibid., fos. 149–50); Ormond to Dudley Loftus,
9 Apr. 1647 (Gilbert, *Irish Confederation*, vii. 325–6).

[70] Digby to Ormond, 19 Sept. 1647 (Carte, *Ormond*, vi. 545); see also *Comment. Rinucc.*, ii.
703–10.

which the confederate armies would be affected was also the point by which Ormond hoped to obtain parliament's sanction for the scheme.[71]

Talon and another experienced French agent, de la Monerie, were certainly interested in Ormond's proposal.[72] Accordingly, Talon went to Dublin to consult with Ormond. On 23 April Ormond guaranteed that, if parliament gave him permission, and if a truce with the confederates could be arranged for several months, he would lead at least 5,500 horse and foot into French service.[73] Talon left for France in the middle of May with details of the scheme which was apparently accepted in principle by the French government, pending parliament's decision to grant permission to transport the troops.[74] The initial response of the Derby House Committee was favourable, but Parliament subsequently decided to reject the scheme, thereby undermining it.[75] This, however, was not made known in Ireland until 26 July.[76] Until that time all parties were rather confident of success. The secret preparations for this scheme thus formed the background to the successful French promotion of renewed truces between Ormond and the confederates between March and July.

In April, as a result of French influence, the confederates were prepared to grant Ormond a six-month truce, provided that the lord lieutenant received no parliamentary troops into his garrisons.[77] Despite Ormond's refusal, subsequent confederate military pressure on his position was half-hearted. The ravages of O'Neill's soldiers, stationed in Leinster but given inadequate

---

[71] Early in April Ormond instructed his emissary to parliament, Dudley Loftus, that if permission was given: 'I am certaine of taking from the Irish a very considerable proportion of their best men, and thereby weakening them exceedingly . . . besides the number of common men which I am confident to draw from them, I shall make no doubt but to bee able to draw also from them (if I have leave) persons and officers of best quality and knowledge in war, which are yet tyed to them for want of meanes otherwise to live or securely to withdraw themselves; and if these be taken from them, they will sudainly be left a very dispicable and inconsiderable number of rebells': Ormond to Loftus, 7 Apr. 1647 (Gilbert, *Irish Confederation*, vii. 326); Ó Siochrú, *Confederate Ireland*, 154 questions whether such a plot existed but advances little evidence to support his doubts: the citation of *Comment. Rinucc.*, iii. 700–16 is a typographical error.

[72] Digby informed the lord lieutenant after the first meeting with Talon: 'the French stand in such need of men for this year's campaign that to purchase a moderate supply of them, they will be content to flatter even those that they contemn most, even the confederate catholicks themselves': Digby to Ormond, 16 Mar. 1647 (Carte, *Ormond*, vi. 508); this was the period in which both France and Spain had identified the struggle for Lerida in Catalonia as of crucial importance. It was thus not only vital for France to acquire recruits but also to deny the Spanish the Irish levies which they coveted so desperately: see R. A. Stradling, *The Spanish Monarchy and Irish Mercenaries: The Wild Geese in Spain, 1618–68* (Dublin, 1994), esp. 52–60.

[73] Ormond to Talon, 23 Apr. 1647 (AMAE, Correspondence Politique (Angleterre) 55, fos. 149ʳ–150ʳ).

[74] See the undated instructions to the new French agent to Ireland, July(?) 1647 (AMAE, Correspondence Politique (Angleterre) 55, fo. 302ᵛ).

[75] Dudley Loftus to Ormond, 15 June 1647 (Bodl. Carte MS 21, fo. 218ʳ); same to same, 21 July 1647 (ibid., fo. 309ʳ).

[76] Ormond to Digby, 26 July 1647 (Carte, *Ormond*, vi. 532).

[77] *Comment. Rinucc.*, ii. 592–3.

supplies, disrupted the activities of Preston's army at this time[78] but the insistence of the French agents, supported by Digby and the emissary sent by the queen of England, George Leyburn, that an accommodation with Ormond was still possible, and the fact that prominent members of the Leinster army were implicated in the plan to desert to French service and consequently reluctant to attack their future commander, also played their part. Towards the end of May the French agents managed to an even greater extent to reopen negotiations between Ormond and the Supreme Council.[79] Since Ormond would not consider any agreement other than the Ormond peace, they supported Leyburn's plan for reconvening the General Assembly to overturn the previous rejection of the peace.[80] Rinuccini was naturally horrified and on 3 June he went to Clonmell and assembled the prelates of the realm to discuss the matter.[81] To the nuncio's disappointment, after a prolonged debate the prelates decided to leave the decision to the discretion of the council. Ultimately it was not Rinuccini's opposition but the arrival of fresh parliamentary forces in Dublin which disrupted the process of negotiation, since this development diminished Ormond's interest in further contact with the confederates. On 20 June he settled definitive articles of transfer with parliamentary commissioners and on 26 July, before departing for England, he resigned all authority to Jones.

There is little evidence that units of O'Neill's command were involved in the French scheme[82] but in 1647, unlike 1646, Rinuccini was unable to make use of the Ulster army to force a breach with Ormond in Dublin. There were several reasons for this, of which the nuncio's financial crisis was the single most important.[83] Since Rinuccini lacked money, the Ulster army could not be outfitted for a campaign without support from the richer confederate provinces, in particular Leinster. These resources were not under Rinuccini's control. Moreover, the first months of 1647 saw a marked cooling in relations between Rinuccini and O'Neill which diminished the nuncio's interest in

---

[78] In this regard see Robert Preston to General Preston, 18 Apr. 1647 (*CSPI*, 1633–47, p. 609); same to same, 21 May 1647 (ibid., 630); see also ibid., 732; as a result of the depredations of O'Neill's troops in Apr., the Leinster army committee began to doubt whether they would be able to supply the Leinster army. On at least one occasion also, units of the Leinster army remained in their quarters to protect the local inhabitants from the Ulster soldiers rather than join the main body of Preston's army, thus weakening Preston's forces and sending internal tensions in the association higher: Edmund Butler to Preston, 24 Apr. 1647 (*CSPI*, 1633–47, p. 614); ibid., 612, 615.

[79] Rinuccini to dei Bagni, 29 May 1647 (Aiazzi, *Nunziatura*, 231); same to Pancirolo, 29 May 1647 (ibid., 232).

[80] Such an assembly would also threaten the dominance of the 'Spanish' party among the confederates: in particular French agents were legitimately worried that Antrim would use his influence as president to ship confederate soldiers to Flanders: in this regard see Ohlmeyer, *Civil War and Restoration*, 180–1, 185–7.

[81] *Comment. Rinucc.*, ii. 606–7.

[82] Although Ó Siochrú, *Confederate Ireland*, 151–2 surmises that this may have been the case.

[83] See Rinuccini to Pancirolo, 12 May 1647 (*Comment. Rinucc.*, ii. 544).

keeping the general in Leinster and indeed actually led to his sponsoring the Ulster army's removal into the less important province of Connacht.

Growing dissatisfaction with O'Neill[84] had been a factor in the nuncio's original decision to accede to the convocation of the assembly and this dissatisfaction steadily increased in the first months of 1647. The general infuriated Rinuccini by his refusal to follow an order from the assembly that the command of the fortress of Athlone be given to Viscount Dillon, who had recently embraced catholicism. O'Neill was reluctant to surrender such a strategic garrison and clearly had not unjustifiable doubts about the worth of Dillon's conversion to the confederate cause: he had previously held the fortress for the king.[85] Rinuccini, however, had personally received the viscount into the catholic church and he hoped Dillon would serve as an inspiration to other protestants to convert.[86] His anger at O'Neill was then increased by the plundering which the Ulster army performed in Leinster during April and May.[87] This devastation was in fact the direct result of the anomalous situation which Rinuccini himself had helped create by introducing the Ulster army into Leinster after the rejection of the peace in 1646. Following the failure of the Dublin campaign those troops had been distributed into winter quarters in Leinster. The question, however, of how they were to be maintained in the future was not addressed. Certainly the Leinster army committee, particularly after Preston had survived the attempt to impeach him in April, seem to have made little or no effort to continue to supply the Ulster army. The response of the Ulster regiments was to forage for themselves which created further antagonism towards O'Neill and his soldiers. Even the bishop of Ferns was deeply shocked by the Ulster troops' conduct. Rinuccini shared this sense of outrage and his sensitivity to the issue was sharpened on 26 April when a large group of women from the vicinity, who claimed to have been victims of O'Neill's soldiers, came to Kilkenny and keened outside his window.[88] The Ulster forces styled themselves as the army of the pope and it was to this that Rinuccini attributed the direction of the women's complaints against his own person.[89]

---

[84] In the aftermath of the Dublin campaign, Rinuccini personally was not happy with either of the principal confederate generals. Although it was clear that Preston had been less reliable than O'Neill, Rinuccini did not wholly absolve the Ulster general from the charge of having provoked Preston's volatility: see Comment. Rinucc., ii. 461.

[85] Even after the Supreme Council allocated command of Athlone to him, he was seeking authorization for his movements from Ormond: see Oliver Jones to Ormond, 6 Jan. 1647 (Bodl. Carte MS 20, fo. 56ʳ).

[86] Comment. Rinucc., ii. 466–9.

[87] See Robert Preston to General Preston, 18 Apr. 1647 (CSPI, 1633–47, p. 609); same to same, 21 May 1647 (ibid., 630); see also ibid., 732.

[88] Comment. Rinucc., ii. 539–40; since the group was exclusively female, their objective may have been to protest against rape as well as pillage.

[89] See the report on the proceedings of O'Neill (Aiazzi, Nunziatura, 224).

The nuncio was incensed. His dignity, and perhaps his vanity, were deeply wounded.[90] The incident contradicted his strongest principles about the manner in which a cleric should be perceived by the people and the fact that the protest was conducted by women probably accentuated his embarrassment. Coming in the wake of the Athlone incident, and of the evident distrust which the General Assembly had shown of O'Neill, the depredations of the Ulster soldiers provoked the nuncio to write to Rome of the general in savagely critical terms.[91] This report was probably a mistake in the context of Rinuccini's own long-term objectives, because it created a great deal of alarm in the curia, which had hitherto perceived O'Neill as the single most reliable confederate, and did nothing to invigorate the pope's rather suspect enthusiasm for the Irish mission.[92] Of even greater significance at this juncture was the nuncio's own acceptance that the Ulster army had become a liability to the clerical cause in Leinster.[93] In a personal meeting with the general at the beginning of May some of the nuncio's anger with O'Neill seems to have been dispelled. Had it been possible to send his forces against Dublin at this juncture, Rinuccini would have done so, despite the danger of antagonizing moderate Old English opinion, but he was unable to supply O'Neill with the requisite money.[94] Because of its potential value, none the less, he was reluctant to see the army disbanded. It seems probable, therefore, that it was actually Rinuccini himself who originally proposed that O'Neill be sent to Connacht, a decision which was to have profound consequences on military matters in 1647 and which was probably almost as significant as the nuncio's decision to attack Dublin in 1646.[95]

There was some superficial merit in the plan. No confederate army existed in Connacht where the Scots still held Sligo owing to the interruption of Preston's 1646 campaign by a combination of the Ormond peace and lack of funds.[96] It was hoped that having taken Sligo, O'Neill would then invade the Scots' quarters in Ulster and in this way provide an Ulster base for his army which would relieve the Leinster population of their intolerable extortions. For the nuncio, the expedition had the added attraction that it would lead to the return into catholic hands of the single most famous religious site in Ireland, the ruined St Patrick's Purgatory in Lough Derg. As he later reported: 'It seemed to me that among the Apostolic expeditions this was

---

[90] Mary O'Dowd, 'Women and War in Ireland in the 1640s', in Margaret MacCurtain and ead. (ed.), *Women in Early Modern Ireland* (Dublin, 1991), 101, has noted that the organization of this demonstration by Viscount Mountgarrett was deliberately to embarrass the nuncio.

[91] See report on the proceedings of O'Neill (Aiazzi, *Nunziatura*, 223–5).

[92] The nuncio's denunciations of O'Neill at this point probably contributed to his later difficulties in receiving additional aid from Rome, which he continued to request throughout 1647 and the first part of 1648: see Pancirolo to Rinuccini, 31 June (ns) 1647 (*Comment. Rinucc.*, ii. 545–6).

[93] Rinuccini to Pancirolo, 28 May 1647 (ibid., 604).

[94] Same to Same, 12 May 1647 (ibid., 544).

[95] See Rinuccini's relation to the pope (Aiazzi, *Nunziatura*, 413–14); *Comment. Rinucc.*, ii. 652.

[96] Preston to Supreme Council, 27 July 1646 (Bodl. Carte MS 18, fo. 111ʳ).

equally glorious as any, and that I would in some ways have fulfilled my duty if in this site covered much more by the hatred of the Puritans than by the soil, it had been conceded to me to replant the cross.'[97]

Yet it is eminently arguable that the diversion of O'Neill's army to Connacht was a grave error and that Rinuccini in particular allowed non-military considerations to cloud his judgement at a particularly inopportune time. St Patrick's Purgatory, however famous as a place of pilgrimage, was of no strategic importance. Moreover, although O'Neill's forces were greatly hated in Leinster, it can be noted that the nuncio and the Supreme Council removed them from Leinster at precisely the moment when they might have compensated for some of their winter excesses by services of military value against the formidable parliamentary army in Dublin.[98]

If the worst effects of O'Neill's absence were felt in Leinster, none the less Rinuccini's plans for the Connacht expedition also turned into disaster, largely because from the beginning O'Neill was very unwilling to go,[99] and because the commissioners charged with supplying the army seem to have been supporters of the Ormond peace.[100] The expedition in fact accomplished little except to heap misery on the civilian population of Connacht, who suffered enormously at the hands of both the Ulster army and the Scots.[101]

Rinuccini's treatment of the Ulster army in the first part of 1647 indicated a genuine willingness to be influenced by moderate Old English advisors. In practice, the nuncio accepted that O'Neill's proven military effectiveness and previous support of the clergy did not entitle him to continue to base his army on the rich and substantially Old English population of Leinster. Given his own lack of money, this decision led essentially to the sidelining of the Ulster army until the end of the campaigning season of 1647 when it was recalled to Leinster in the wake of Preston's defeat. The Ulster army's determination to remain in being, and the nuncio's willingness to provide it with service in Connacht rather than seeking a drastic reduction in its numbers, allowed it to survive this period without disintegration. This was to prove

---

[97] 'Mi pareva che fra le spedizioni Apostliche fosse questa gloriosa al pari delle altre, e che io avrei in qualche parte sodisfatto al mio carico, se in quel sito coperto assai più d'obbrobri che di terreno dei Puritani, mi fosse stato concesso di ripiantare la croce', Rinuccini's relation to the pope (Aiazzi, Nunziatura, 414).

[98] Ó Siochrú, Confederate Ireland, 152 in a different interpretation of evidence argues that the decision to send O'Neill to Connacht was correct but this analysis appears unconvincing.

[99] I differ here from Casway, Owen Roe O'Neill, 181 who suggests otherwise but the nuncio's own analysis in this regard seems plausible: see Rinuccini's relation to the pope (Aiazzi, Nunziatura, 414); Comment. Rinucc., ii. 652.

[100] Rinuccini's relation to the pope (Aiazzi, Nunziatura, 414); personally hostile to O'Neill, there are grounds for suspecting that the commissioners may have planned to force him to disband his army by providing inadequate supplies: in this regard see Casway, Owen Roe O'Neill, 185–9; Comment. Rinucc., ii. 661–3.

[101] Comment. Rinucc., ii. 658, 662–3; Rinuccini's relation to the pope (Aiazzi, Nunziatura, 414).

very significant on two counts: first because by the end of the campaigning season the Ulster army, in contrast to the other two major confederate forces, still survived and remained as ready as ever to support the nuncio and second because it was now even more hated than in previous years.

From the nuncio's perspective the moderate policy advocated by Plunkett and Ferns in Leinster in 1647 ultimately failed. The removal of the Ulster army from the province proved an expensive error, while the continuing negotiations with Ormond not only allowed Jones to establish himself without significant opposition in Dublin, but also opened the way for French agents to suborn many of the Leinster officers. Yet, despite the mistakes which were undoubtedly made, it seems clear that the moderate policy of Plunkett and Ferns in Leinster was dogged by bad luck as much as anything else. The decision to mollify Preston and to trust in his good faith eventually could be said to have justified itself. After Ormond's departure Preston and his officers did turn their backs on the blandishments of the agents of France and committed their forces wholeheartedly to the war. Moreover, they did so with formidable resources[102] which was a tribute to the manner in which the policies of Plunkett and Ferns had united the province of Leinster behind their provincial army. The rout of this army at Dungan's Hill was in many ways simply bad luck for the moderate leadership because that defeat was less the result of military inferiority in numbers, training, or equipment than of an unhappy concatenation of circumstances relating to civilian interference,[103] bad generalship,[104] and the mutual distrust of the Ulster and Leinster armies.[105] If a historical accident had conferred O'Neill's military talents on

---

[102] Rinuccini referred to them as a 'wonderful army' (bellissimo esercito) (Rinuccini's relation to the pope (Aiazzi, *Nunziatura*, 413) while Leyburn described them in these terms: 'the Foot, as lusty appearing men and as well accoutred with Arms and Cloaks, as ever I did see, and the Horse in Appearance equal to our ordinary troops in England' (Clarendon Historical Society, 'The memoirs of George Leyburn', in *Five Scarce Books in English Literature* (London, 1886), 76).

[103] It seems clear that one of the principal reasons that Preston fought at Dungan's Hill was the insistence of the bishop of Ferns that his army could no longer be supplied: since O'Neill maintained a larger force in the same area for four months subsequently, this was evidently not completely true: in this regard see 'The war and rebellion in Ireland begun in 1641' (NLI Plunkett-Dunne MS 345, p. 910); however, O'Neill was almost certainly more ruthless about coercing supply than the bishop of Ferns could countenance. Ferns' religious convictions, the quality which attracted the nuncio to him in the first place, also played their part in the decision to fight. He had come to believe 'this summer is made by God to try the hearts and resolutions of Ireland, and it will be lost or won this very summer': Ferns to Preston, 12 May 1647 (*CSPI*, 1633–47, p. 625); *Comment. Rinucc.*, ii. 296.

[104] 'The war and rebellion in Ireland', p. 910); I am also grateful for a personal explanation of the battle from Pádraig Lenihan.

[105] This distrust contributed both to the shortage of food supplies and to the fact that the Ulster army was not recalled from Connacht to fight in the battle. Both Digby and Leyburn urged the council to recall O'Neill before the battle and Leyburn was convinced that it was not tactical considerations but rather 'their hatred . . . to the Old Irish' which prevented such a summons: see Leyburn 'Memoirs', 70–1; the speed with which O'Neill returned to Leinster after Dungan's Hill indicates how easily he could have reinforced Preston for the actual battle itself.

Preston, and those of Preston on O'Neill, then the policy of Plunkett and Ferns might well have enjoyed considerable success in Leinster during 1647.

V

The disasters which occurred in confederate Munster at this time, on the other hand, do seem to have been directly linked to the policy of conciliation adopted by the confederate moderates towards the authors of the Ormond peace, in particular towards Viscount Muskery. In 1646 Muskery, Ormond's brother-in-law and the most important confederate nobleman in the south,[106] had been made commander of the Munster army.[107] This meant that in the wake of the clerical coup of that year alternative provisions had to be made in the province. Rinuccini was at least partially responsible for the difficulties which later ensued. Obsessed with the need to attack Dublin, he had little attention to spare for the much more dangerous protestant forces in the south. In this way, Inchiquin became one of the beneficiaries of the clerical assumption of control.[108] The clergy eventually decided to replace Muskery with Glamorgan as commander of the confederate forces in Munster, a decision which can possibly be traced to the nuncio.[109] One advantage of this plan from the nuncio's perspective was that the earl's public association with the clerical regime gave a certain colour to the new council's claim that their allegiance to the king was still secure even as they prepared to attack his viceroy.[110]

Despite his political utility, as a general Glamorgan proved a costly failure. Although he commissioned a large number of officers,[111] he seems to have failed to retain many troops in winter quarters to provide a trained nucleus for the following summer's army.[112] His problems became even more pronounced during the assembly. Although the nuncio's supporters dominated proceedings, Muskery's influence among the Munster delegates was particularly pronounced. Once the clerical moderates were persuaded to clear the authors of the Ormond peace of the crime of perjury, Muskery's supporters

---

[106] Ohlmeyer, *Civil War and Restoration*, 190; *Comment. Rinucc.*, ii. 269.

[107] Bellings's narrative (Gilbert, *Irish Confederation*, v. 18).

[108] Had the Ormond peace been established, the intention was apparently to mount an immediate offensive against the Munster ports: see Rinuccini to Pamfili, 12 Mar. 1646 (Aiazzi, *Nunziatura*, 116).

[109] Rinuccini certainly appreciated Glamorgan's religious convictions: on the other hand he had scant respect for his abilities: see Rinuccini to Pamfili, 25 Sept. 1646 (Aiazzi, *Nunziatura*, 162).

[110] Glamorgan was eager to clear himself in this regard but Digby certainly seems to have feared such a development: see Glamorgan to Ormond, 26 Sept. 1646 (Bodl. Carte MS 18, fo. 551ʳ); Digby to Ormond, 18 Oct. 1646 (Carte, *Ormond*, 446).

[111] He did this according to authority which he had from the king: see Gilbert, *Irish Confederation*, vii. 21.

[112] Hazlett, 'A History of the Military Forces', i. 291.

were in a position to clamour for his reinstatement as provincial general. Moreover, Nicholas Plunkett, one of the figures to whom Rinuccini was most prepared to listen, was particularly anxious to conciliate the viscount.[113] In the upshot, an unworkable compromise was devised with regard to the Munster army: Glamorgan remained general but the chief officers and the commissioners entrusted with supplying the army were nearly all adherents of Muskery.[114] Rinuccini certainly does not bear responsibility for this compromise: in fact he advised Glamorgan to abandon the command rather than continue it under those circumstances.[115] But the nuncio was now in no position to insist on his counsel being followed. Glamorgan decided to retain the post, a telling indication of the limits of Rinuccini's influence in Munster. Thus, although confederates on good terms with the nuncio still dominated the Supreme Council, it is obvious that this did not provide him with much leverage in the internal affairs of the southern province, nor, as events were to show, were the council themselves prepared to follow his advice in Munster. His own lack of money increased his helplessness.

As general, Glamorgan tried during the spring to procure supplies for those officers whom he had personally appointed. His commissioners of supply, however, apparently donated all available munitions to those officers who supported Muskery.[116] The result was the complete paralysis of the Munster army which accounts to a considerable degree for the ease with which Inchiquin took Cappoquin and Dungarvan in May[117] and thus undermined the natural defensive line of the Blackwater river and the Knockmealdown and Comeragh mountains which had previously confined him to county Cork.[118] This was to set the stage for his prolonged ravaging of confederate Munster during 1647.[119]

[113] He personally exerted himself to secure Muskery's election to the council and worked with the viscount also to try and persuade the royalist Clanricard to accept office in the association: see Rinuccini's relation to the pope (Aiazzi, *Nunziatura*, 411); Plunkett to Clanricard, 14 Apr. 1647 (*Clanricard Letter Book 1643–7*), 398; Muskery to same, 13 Apr. 1647 (ibid., 399–400); Ferns to same, same date (ibid., 400).

[114] Ó Siochrú, *Confederate Ireland*, 144

[115] Rinuccini to Pancirolo, 22 Aug. 1647 (Aiazzi, *Nunziatura*, 240).

[116] This, at least, is what can be inferred from the accusations which were levelled against the commissioners in June: see Gilbert, *Irish Confederation*, vii. 22–3.

[117] A point acknowledged quite frankly by parliamentary sympathizers: see Bodl. Carte MS 21, fo. 367ᵛ.

[118] See Parsons to Annesley, 10 Dec. 1646 (British Librar Egerton MS 917, fo. 26ʳ⁻ᵛ); Bagwell, *Ireland Under the Stuarts*, ii. 150.

[119] Rinuccini, enormously frustrated by these developments, later believed that if he had had access to as small a sum as 6,000 scudi (about £1,500) he could have saved Dungarvan and Cappoquin and thus have kept Inchiquin pinned to the Cork coast: see Rinuccini to Pancirolo, 22 Aug. 1647 (Aiazzi, *Nunziatura*, 240–1); Inchiquin's ferocity in 1647 was probably influenced by the realization that it would strengthen his position with parliament: see Robert Armstrong, 'Protestant Ireland and the English Parliament 1641–1647' (unpub. Ph.D. thesis, Trinity College Dublin, 1995), 294.

This change in the situation in Munster caused the Supreme Council great alarm and was an additional factor in their willingness to seek an accommodation with Ormond in Leinster during May. On this issue an interesting discrepancy in attitude was revealed between the nuncio and a council which was filled with clerical sympathizers. Because Rinuccini was convinced that the problems in Munster were the product not of weakness but of dissension, he could not contemplate compromising the interests of the catholic religion to the extent of supporting negotiations, simply on the grounds of what he termed 'the unhappy factions of merely one province'.[120] Rinuccini tended to base his estimates of the strength of the confederates on the aggregate wealth, manpower, and military capacity of the entire membership of the association. He was keenly aware that the association was rent with faction and division which, in real terms, weakened it enormously but in conscience he seems to have felt unable to compromise with this sinfulness to the extent of including it as a factor in his political calculations. Thus, somewhat like an exigent confessor, he seems to have believed that he owed it to God to base his estimates of what lay within the compass of the confederates on the potential rather than the actual strength of the association. By May 1647, given that Munster was in a precarious condition, Rinuccini's insistence that the situation be rectified by the composition of the differences which had originally caused the problem was not particularly imaginative. Nevertheless, the alternative and highly conciliatory approach adopted by the council as the situation continued to deteriorate in Munster in May and June was arguably even less constructive than the nuncio's.

During those months the minority party in the army, now led by Richard Butler, son of the viscount of Ikerrin, displayed intense hostility to the army commissioners who were blamed for the military reverses.[121] The Supreme Council, however, evidently believed that the only hope of obtaining service from the Munster army was to allow control to Muskery's faction. In May, therefore, they backed his nominee, Patrick Purcell, as acting commander[122] and in June they were even prepared to tolerate an open mutiny, which resulted in Muskery once again assuming command.[123] This event was to have very significant long-term effects in Munster and it was a telling indication of the decline of the nuncio's influence because the council ignored his advice on the need to deal severely with the mutiny.[124] It is also probable that

---

[120] Rinuccini to Supreme Council, 25 May 1647 (*Comment. Rinucc.*, ii. 600–1: 'nec permitti ut . . . religio privetur suis incrementis ob factiones infaelices unius tantum Provinciae').

[121] *Comment. Rinucc.*, ii. 611–13.   [122] Ibid., 612.

[123] Ibid., 614; Gilbert, *Irish Confederation*, vii. 22–5; in gaining support for his action, Muskery seems to have played on the fears of the Munster confederates that the Ulster army would be introduced into their province: see *Comment. Rinucc.*, ii. 617, 621–2; Rinuccini to Pancirolo, 30 June (Aiazzi, *Nunziatura*, 235–6); see also Muskery to Clanricard, 17 June 1647 (*Clanricard Letter Book 1643–7*), 448–9.

[124] *Comment. Rinucc.*, ii. 615–16; Rinuccini to Pancirolo, 30 June (Aiazzi, *Nunziatura*, 235–6).

in this regard Rinuccini's instinct was the correct one. In Leinster the council's patience with Preston eventually paid dividends because, after Ormond's departure, the general honestly applied himself to the task of confronting Jones, ignoring the idea, which Digby had been advocating, of preserving his troops for French service. This was not the case in Munster. Unfortunately for the clerical moderates, the troops in Munster were immediately targeted by Digby as replacements for the Leinster forces lost at Dungan's Hill.[125] In August Muskery resigned his command to another member of the 'Ormondite' faction, Viscount Taaffe, who with some of his chief officers became willingly involved in Digby's scheme. The outlines of the plan can be seen clearly in the letters of the French agents written at this time.[126] Muskery had apparently engaged himself to supply 2,000 men. Viscounts Taaffe and Dillon, the latter thereby rather confirming the validity of O'Neill's suspicions concerning the fortress of Athlone, were also partners in the enterprise.[127] So also was Alexander MacColla, the celebrated Scots Irish veteran of Montrose's campaigns[128] who in turn hoped to contribute 2,000 men. Thus it seems clear that at least 4,000 men, over half the Munster army, were involved in the scheme.[129] Ultimately, Mazarin showed little enthusiasm for the plan once it became clear that any troops shipped from Ireland in this fashion would lack a safe conduct from the English parliament. This, however, was not known in Ireland until October or November.[130] In the interim the expectation of entering French service dictated the tactics adopted by the Munster army in 1647. In the crudest of terms the Munster officers made sure that they would not lose their valuable men in combat with Inchiquin.[131] On 27 September de la Monerie wrote to Mazarin that in compliance with this advice, 'my lords Muskery and Taafe are conserving their troops for the design of which my lord Digby has informed your Eminence'.[132]

---

[125] Indeed, from the moment of Muskery's mutiny in June, Digby had become interested in involving the Munster army in the scheme: see Digby to Ormond, 17 July 1647 (Carte, *Ormond*, vi. 526).

[126] De la Monerie to Mazarin, 25 Aug. (ns?) 1647 (AMAE, Correspondence Politique (Angleterre) 55, fos. 318ʳ–319ᵛ).

[127] Ibid.

[128] In this regard see David Stevenson, *Scottish Covenanters and Irish Confederates* (Belfast, 1981), 170–82; Ohlmeyer, *Civil War and Restoration*, 187–8.

[129] *Comment. Rinucc.*, ii. 711.

[130] Indeed Digby continued to bombard the cardinal with memorials on this subject during these months: see correspondence between Digby and Mazarin (AMAE, Correspondence Politique (Angleterre) 55, fos. 373ʳ–374ʳ, 379ʳ–380ᵛ, 401ʳ⁻ᵛ).

[131] Before leaving for France, Digby had impressed on Taaffe the absolute necessity of avoiding a battle: see Digby to Taaffe, 31 Aug. 1647 (*Comment. Rinucc.*, ii. 707).

[132] 'Messieurs de Muscrey et Taff conservent leur troupes pour le desseing dont Monsieur d'Igby a informé votre eminence': de la Monerie to Mazarin 7 Oct. (ns) 1647 (AMAE, Correspondence Politique (Angleterre) 55, fo. 358ʳ).

This policy of conserving their troops meant that Inchiquin was allowed to ravage the confederate south without opposition from the main body of the Munster army in August and September.[133] The damage which was wrought to the province and to the morale of its population was incalculable: indeed this summer to some extent marked the collapse of the confederate association in the province. By November, when it was becoming clear that the French scheme had come to nothing, it was already too late to protect most of Munster. The eventual defeat of the Munster army at Knocknanuss thus marked merely the final stage in a catalogue of disasters.[134]

The events in Munster revealed the limits of the policy of moderation and compromise which Ferns and Plunkett had espoused during that year. The appeasement of Muskery in Munster led, not to his reconciliation with the clerically dominated Supreme Council, but to his involvement in a plot to transfer the Munster army to France. The nuncio was arguably unlucky that he lacked finance at this point in time because his instinct concerning when to abandon the policy of conciliation seems to have been keener than that of his allies in the council and access to a substantial sum would probably have allowed him to intervene to consolidate his support in the provincial armies, despite the tactics of 'Ormondite' commissioners of supply. The position of the peace party, in particular after the arrival of parliamentary troops in Dublin in June, was, after all, desperately weak. The very fact that Muskery and his associates were planning to go to France indicates how the collapse of the peace had undermined their party.[135] Nor indeed did their French plans ever come to fruition. It can be noted that the Leinster and Munster armies, destitute of alternatives, both eventually did what Rinuccini wished and took the field against the association's protestant foes. Unfortunately for the nuncio, both did so in unfavourable circumstances and after costly delays which had seen a great deal of confederate territory comprehensively ravaged.

VI

The succession of military disasters in 1647 and the extensive devastation of their territory was taken by many confederates as proof that the association

[133] *Comment. Rinucc.*, ii. 648–50; Bagwell, *Ireland under the Stuarts*, ii. 152.

[134] The battle is described by Bagwell, *Ireland under the Stuarts*, ii. 156–8; see also Stevenson, *Covenanters and Confederates*, 188–9; Ó Siochrú's analysis of this episode, *Confederate Ireland*, 151–2, differs from mine in that he sees the Munster army as more probably preparing themselves for a potential coup d'état. He does not refer, however, to my detailed argument in ' "Far from Terra Firma": The Mission of GianBattista Rinuccini to Ireland', 1645–9' (2 vols., unpub. Ph.D thesis, European University Institute, 1995), 310–14.

[135] In this regard see Sir Robert Talbot to Clanricard, 20 Mar. 1647 (*Clanricard Letter Book 1643–7*, 370): Talbot's belief that the failure to accord with Ormond condemned the Old English either to 'be slaves to the parliament or to the Ultonians' and his conviction that 'begging or banishment' was preferable indicates the desperation of those who embraced the French option: Clanricard to Henrietta Maria, 20 Feb. 1647 (ibid., 356–7); see also Digby's account of peace party despair in his letter to Ormond, 22 July 1647 (Bodl. Carte MS 21, fos. 330ʳ–335ᵛ).

was too weak to pursue the militarily aggressive policy in which Rinuccini believed and this conviction was to set the tone at the second assembly of 1647.[136] It was to be of crucial importance that Rinuccini formed a different interpretation of the events of these months.

Preston's defeat in August had certainly shaken the nuncio's belief in the entire Irish enterprise. Short of money even for his household needs, ignorant of Massari's whereabouts, uncertain of O'Neill's ability to check Jones in Leinster, his confidence in his capacity to oversee the maintenance of the war was clearly low.[137] Yet, unlike many of the confederates, he recovered his spirits surprisingly quickly. An important element in this development was probably the manner in which he came to rationalize the defeat of the catholic army at Dungan's Hill. In the aftermath of the battle the nuncio became increasingly sure that Preston had been involved in some plot with Digby and Ormond's confederate supporters, although he was ignorant of the precise details. Rinuccini thus became willing to believe that Dungan's Hill might have been something of a blessing in disguise which had led to the replacement of Preston by the more reliable O'Neill in Leinster.[138] O'Neill's success in checking Jones may have increased the nuncio's confidence in this analysis and, more importantly, it removed the threat of immediate collapse from the association. News of the heroic conduct of the abandoned confederate infantry during the battle also moved and uplifted him greatly,[139] and seems to have confirmed his belief that the war in Ireland was a great religious struggle in which at least some of the Irish were worthy participants.[140] In September he was greatly relieved to hear that Massari had arrived in France with the papal subsidies and began to hope once again to retrieve the clerical position in Ireland with the money which he had so sorely missed during the previous period.[141]

Taaffe's refusal to confront Inchiquin in Munster in August and September inclined him to conclude that he too was involved in some plot, which he surmised would involve bringing the prince of Wales to Ireland,[142] and which he feared might well precipitate a civil war between the armies of Taaffe and O' Neill.[143] Rinuccini thus may well have decided that the battle

[136] Corish, 'Ormond, Rinuccini, and the Confederates, 1645–9', 324–5.

[137] Rinuccini to dei Bagni, 14 Aug. 1647 (Aiazzi, *Nunziatura*, 237–8).

[138] Rinuccini to Cardinal Capponi, 6 Sept. 1647 (ibid., 248); Rinuccini to Pancirolo, 23 Aug. 1647 (ibid., 242); same to same, 29 Aug. 1647 (ibid., 245); *Comment. Rinucc.*, ii. 680, 772.

[139] Rinuccini to Pancirolo, 30 Aug. 1647 (Aiazzi, *Nunziatura*, 247); see also Rinuccini to the Pope, 29 Aug. 1647 (ibid., 246).

[140] He commented that the Irish 'Hanno pur questo d'insigne, che per qualsivoglia accidente son risoluti di lasciar prima la vita che la Fede': Rinuccini to the nuncio of Spain, 1 Sept. 1647 (Aiazzi, *Nunziatura*, 248).

[141] In addition to everything else, this allowed him to obtain credit more easily: Rinuccini to Pancirolo, 16 Sept. 1647 (Aiazzi, *Nunziatura*, 253–4); see also same to same, 6 Oct. 1647 (ibid., 256).

[142] Rinuccini to Pancirolo, 6 Oct. 1647 (Ibid., 256).

[143] Same to Same, 3 Nov. 1647 (*Comment. Rinucc.*, ii. 773).

of Knocknanuss on 13 November, while a severe blow to the association, actually strengthened his own party within the assembly which had just congregated in Kilkenny to discuss the situation. Certainly, it can be noted that his position hardened following the battle.

Prior to the assembly Rinuccini had informed his superiors that if the delegates adopted a policy of which he could not approve he would neither oppose nor support it but would instead stand aloof.[144] Once the assembly opened, the nuncio found his worst fears confirmed as those whom he termed the malignant party controlled most of the votes.[145] Nevertheless, with the military balance within the association having swung strongly in favour of O'Neill, and finding himself very strongly supported by the large episcopal presence in the assembly,[146] the nuncio soon abandoned the idea of cold neutrality and reconciled himself to the idea of siding actively with one of the alignments in a confederate civil war.

He outlined his own analysis of the situation to the assembly in a Latin address on 20 November:

It is to be pronounced with unsurpassable tears that God in his just judgement has withdrawn from the catholic association, and it is certain from sacred scripture that he is not accustomed to act thus in matters of faith unless our sins demand it. Now therefore is the time, most illustrious lords, to show him penitence and amendment by unifying all, by embracing all, without distinction of region, or blood, or profession. Who does not see the enemy insulting us with a double triumph, namely one through the army and the other through your discords and perhaps more through the second than the first? What external persons will not deem the title of your war a fiction, if a sincere reconciliation should not be made manifest with the men of the church, whom God always wished honoured and whom he has constituted as the defenders and interpreters of his will?[147]

---

[144] Ibid., 774.   [145] Rinuccini to Pancirolo, 8 Dec. 1647 (Aiazzi, *Nunziatura*, 271).
[146] At least 19 were present but there may have been as many as 24. To the fury of Rinuccini's opponents, even unconsecrated bishops were allowed take their seats in the assembly: see Rinuccini to Mazarin, 27 Dec. 1647 (Aiazzi, *Nunziatura*, 279); Rinuccini to Pancirolo, 4 Dec. 1647 (ibid., 270); *Comment. Rinucc.*, ii. 793; Cregan, 'Social and Cultural Background', 87.
[147] 'Pronunciandum est maximis cum lacrimis Deum recessisse iusto eius iudicio a Confaederatione Catholica, certumque est ex Sacra Scriptura non solere illum id agere in causis fidei, nisi peccatis nostris exigentibus. Nunc ergo tempus est, Illustrissimi Domini, paenitentiam et emendationem illi repraesentare, omnes uniendo, omnes amplectendo sine discrimine vel regionum, vel sanguinis, vel professionis. Quis non videt hostes nobis insultantes duplici triumpho, uno nempe de exercitu, altero de discordiis vestris, et magis fortasse de secundo quam primo? Quis iam exterorum non existimabit titulum vestri belli confictum, se reconcilatio sincera non appareat cum personis ecclesiasticis, in quibus semper Deus honorari voluit, et quos voluntatis suae interpretes ac defensores constituit?': *Comment. Rinucc.*, ii. 788; the nuncio expressed himself in similar terms to Pancirolo five days later: 'Si vede che Iddio per le loro dissensioni e peccati si e pur troppo ritirato dall'aiutar la sua causa per qualche tempo' (One sees that God because of their dissensions and sins has unfortunately withdrawn from helping their cause for some time): Rinuccini to Pancirolo, 26 Nov. 1647 (Aiazzi, *Nunziatura*, 267).

The nuncio soon realized that the dominant faction in the assembly failed to appreciate what was to him clear evidence of divine displeasure[148] but he was able to use the unprecedented number of bishops who attended the assembly to counter their voting superiority. Many of the bishops present later opposed the nuncio over the Inchiquin truce and some already had misgivings about his leadership,[149] but in a general convocation of bishops the nuncio was in an excellent position to dominate any critics and force them to subscribe to a united clerical position.[150]

And in 1647 this position proved to be the most radical that had yet been articulated by the leadership of the Irish church. In contrast even with August 1646, when the clergy had been prepared to allow the assembly to decide concerning the acceptance of the Ormond peace, in 1647 Rinuccini and the bishops declared that they would not accept any decree of the assembly which threatened the interests of the church.[151] This declaration was certainly a reaction to the bishops' position as a minority within a rather hostile assembly and it considerably heightened the already tense atmosphere. In fact the nuncio anticipated that a confrontation at this juncture might well precipitate a confederate civil war. Several of his advisors, in particular O'Neill, were evidently eager for such a development and, as events transpired, the nuncio and his party would have enjoyed a stronger position if the breach had come at this point.[152] Rinuccini, however, although he did not shrink from such an eventuality, was not prepared to precipitate it.[153] Some of his opponents also seem to have contemplated forcing a decisive breach in the assembly but like the nuncio they eventually thought better of it.[154] Instead they concentrated their energies on weakening the clerical position.

One important manner in which this was achieved was through the nomination of Plunkett and Ferns for a mission to Rome which had the effect of remov-

---

[148] Rinuccini to Pancirolo, 26 Nov. 1647 (Aiazzi, *Nunziatura*, 266–7).

[149] See Same to Same, 29 Aug. 1647 (*Comment. Rinucc.*, ii. 763).

[150] Although, in 1647, few bishops seem to have questioned the nuncio's leadership: Rinuccini was actually very pleased with the bishops' behaviour in the course of the assembly and wrote warmly of them to Rome: see Rinuccini to Pancirolo, 24 Dec. 1647 (Aiazzi, *Nunziatura*, 276).

[151] In this regard see *Comment. Rinucc.*, ii. 792–3; Patrick Darcy also believed that some of the bishops were eager to reinstate a dictatorship based on O'Neill's forces: see Darcy to Muskery, 6 Nov. 1647 (Bodl. Carte MS 21, fo. 517ʳ).

[152] At this point O'Neill's army was in a position to dominate Kilkenny, the bishops were assembled and ready to support him and his opponents could not count on military support from Inchiquin: Rinuccini to Pancirolo, 24 Dec. 1647 (Aiazzi, *Nunziatura*, 277) details the nuncio's own analysis of the importance of O'Neill's strength at this juncture.

[153] Concerning his reasoning on this point see Rinuccini to Pancirolo. 24 Dec. 1647 (Aiazzi, *Nunziatura*, 277–8).

[154] The decision to escalate the crisis over the refusal of the bishop of Clogher to accept a confederate mission to France is difficult to explain in any other terms than a deliberate attempt by the nuncio's enemies to force a confrontation: see the account of the treatment of the bishop of Clogher (Aiazzi, *Nunziatura*, 272–4); *Comment. Rinucc.*, ii. 794–8; in October also an offer had been made to Ormond through an intermediary that the confederate peace party were prepared to reintroduce the peace by force: Eustace to Ormond, 8 Oct. 1647 (Bodl. Carte MS 21, fo. 488ʳ).

ing the most influential of the confederate moderates from Ireland.[155] Secondly, the nuncio's opponents acquired crucial influence in the new twelve-person Supreme Council. This was nominated by two representatives from the faction which had originally introduced the Ormond peace, Muskery and Geoffrey Browne, and the two most influential members of the existing council, Plunkett and Ferns, in whom the nuncio reposed his trust. Ultimately, after weeks of negotiation, the essentially moderate representatives Plunkett and Ferns flouted Rinuccini's instructions by allowing seats to four candidates whom he had expressly forbidden them to accept.[156] Thus some of the nuncio's most implacable opponents were established in the confederate executive.[157]

The second assembly of 1647 thus represented an important turning point in the nunciature. It marked the end of the domination of the Supreme Council by supporters of the clergy and with the nomination of Plunkett and Ferns as envoys to Rome it removed the principal advocates of the strategy of compromise and conciliation which Rinuccini had been persuaded to countenance since the failure of the Dublin campaign. As was noted previously, the chief policy decision of the deeply divided assembly was ultimately to offer the government of Ireland to the queen of England and the prince of Wales, according to religious conditions acceptable to the pope, and if this proved impossible to seek a protector. To a large extent, the missions to Rome and France which had been made necessary by these decisions of the assembly represented a postponement of open hostilities between now irreconcilable factions in the hope of acquiring tactical advantages through fresh developments. Two of the envoys to France, Muskery and Browne, were bitter opponents of the nuncio who were to use their mission successfully as a means to undermine his position in Ireland. Rinuccini, for his part, hoped to use the confederate mission to Rome to obtain fresh financial resources.

The outlines of the nuncio's analysis of the situation in Ireland following this assembly can be seen in a number of memorials which he composed at this time. The cardinal point of Rinuccini's perception of the situation was the conviction that the entire position in Ireland could still be transformed by the application of a large sum of papal money.[158] Although the ordinary

---

[155] The same trick was tried unsuccessfully with the bishop of Clogher and successfully with the marquis of Antrim: see Rinuccini to Pancirolo, 24 Dec. 1647 (Aiazzi, *Nunziatura*, 274); Jane Ohlmeyer, basing her analysis on Spanish sources, suggests that Antrim was selected merely for his royalist connections and to satisfy the Old Irish interest: *Civil War and Restoration*, 201–2.

[156] The four were the baron of Athenry, Sir Lucas Dillon, Richard Bellings, and Gerrott Fennell: see *Comment. Rinucc.*, iii. 531–4.

[157] Also, at the same time a reserve pool of councillors was established who were to fill any vacancies which might arise if any of the selected 12 were missing. This provision ultimately allowed the peace party to co-opt new councillors in the wake of the Inchiquin truce when the nuncio's supporters withdrew from the council: see Corish, 'Ormond, Rinuccini, and the Confederates, 1645–9', 325; Rinuccini to Pancirolo, 24 Dec. 1647 (Aiazzi, *Nunziatura*, 277); Rinuccini's relation to the pope (ibid., 418).

[158] Rinuccini to Pancirolo, 28 Dec. 1647 (Aiazzi, *Nunziatura*, 284); *Comment. Rinucc.*, iii. 7.

revenue of the Holy See was at this point massively overextended,[159] Rinuccini was aware that the pope could provide such money by drawing on the special treasury created by Sixtus V in Castel St Angelo.[160] Alternatively, he believed the resources of the Italian clergy could be tapped for this purpose as had been done in 1634 on behalf of the emperor.[161] Probably conscious of the pope's parsimony and of his reluctance to support unsuccessful enterprises, Rinuccini carefully coached the confederate envoys on how to convince him to invest in Ireland.[162] Rinuccini was clearly not wholly blind to the weaknesses of the association but he continued to believe that they stemmed principally from internal dissension. He refused therefore to accept that the military situation was critical but insisted that the transfer of units of the Ulster army to the south would be sufficient to ward off Inchiquin while still leaving sufficient forces to protect Leinster from Jones.[163] The arrival of papal aid would then allow the confederates to renew the offensive. To some extent, the nuncio's analysis in this regard was proved correct in February 1648 when the confederates successfully repelled a double thrust against them by Inchiquin and Jones.[164] Yet Rinuccini's evaluation of confederate strengths and weaknesses evidently underestimated the debilitating effect on the association of the widespread hatred and distrust which was felt for O'Neill and the Ulster army, by the common people because of the soldiers' onerous exactions and by many of the gentry because of the general's supposed ambitions.[165]

Rinuccini was certainly conscious of the growing hatred for the Ulster army because increasingly he personally was becoming the butt of the people's anger on this score. In December 1647 another mob of women besieged the nuncio's residence, complaining of the wrongs which they had suffered at the hands of the Ulster army.[166] Some months previously, the French agent de la Monerie informed Mazarin concerning Rinuccini that: 'today he receives from the people as many curses as he once received accla-

---

[159] Pastor, *History of the Popes*, xxx. 366–7.

[160] *Comment. Rinucc.*, iii. 7; even at the end of the eighteenth century, literally millions of scudi remained in this treasury and there was certainly an argument that Ireland satisfied the conditions which Sixtus had laid down before the money could be used: see Wolfgang Reinhard, 'Finanza pontificia e Stato della Chiesa nel xvi e xvii secolo', in Aldo De Maddalena and Hermann Kellenbenz (eds.), *Finanza e ragion di Stato in Italia e Germania nella prima età moderna* (Bologna, 1984), 381.

[161] *Comment. Rinucc.*, iii. 7; Pastor, *History of the Popes*, xxviii. 328.

[162] *Comment. Rinucc.*, iii. 1–8.

[163] Rinuccini to Pancirolo, 28 Dec. 1647 (ibid., 1–2); see also the report of the state of Ireland (Aiazzi, *Nunziatura*, 287–90).

[164] *Comment. Rinucc.*, iii. 61–3.

[165] Which later point was clearly revealed in the violent reaction to the arrival in Ireland of Conor O'Mahoney's *Disputatio Apologetica*, which was seen as a theological text legitimizing the transfer of the Irish kingship to O'Neill: see Corish, 'Ormond, Rinuccini, and the Confederates, 1645–9', 324.

[166] *Comment. Rinucc.*, ii. 807–8.

mations from them.'[167] In June of that year, Thomas Talbot claimed in a memorial to Mazarin that when Rinuccini passed a village on his journeys:

the common people run and cry after him, cursing him and all who sent him to Ireland to create ruin there and to cause so many families to die of hunger; they go and cry in the same way before his house in Kilkenny, throwing stones against the windows and this because he supports O' Neill.[168]

Yet although Rinuccini was aware of the people's anger against O'Neill he found it difficult to accept that this should be allowed to dictate the association's policy. He was now more disposed to trust O'Neill than ever before[169] and was convinced that his own enemies fomented the hatred against the Ulster army and emphasized its connection with the clergy to turn the common people against himself.[170] The anger which the nuncio felt over this point almost defies exaggeration. Indeed, much of his later bitterness towards the Old English community can plausibly be attributed to the nuncio's conviction that he had been the victim of wilful and vindictive slander in this matter. This burning sense of injury probably made it more difficult for the nuncio to accept his enemies' legitimate criticisms of the Ulster army. Nor does it seem far-fetched to suggest that Rinuccini's repressed resentment of the soldiers who actually committed the crimes was projected onto those who calumniated him about them. Thus the increasing antagonism towards O'Neill was made doubly destabilizing to the association because of Rinuccini's refusal to take it into account. Apart from anything else, this refusal was rooted in the religious context in which Rinuccini saw the war in Ireland. Although in 1647 he had been willing to conciliate Leinster hostility towards O' Neill by diverting his army into Connacht, he continued to count the Ulster forces as an integral aspect of the association's strength.

Ultimately, from Rinuccini's perspective, there was little difference between protecting Munster and Leinster with Ulster troops and in doing so with the native armies of the provinces under Old English generals. To a large number of confederates, particularly those of Old English stock, the perspective was different. For many, conquest by parliament was little or no

[167] 'Aujourd'huy il recoit autant de maledictions du peuple qu'autrefois il en a recu d'acclamations': de la Monerie to Mazarin, 7 Oct. (ns) 1647 (AMAE, Correspondence Politique (Angleterre) 55, fo. 357ᵛ).

[168] 'Le petit peuple court et crie apres luy, le maudissons et tous ceux qui l'ont envoyés en Irlande pour y ruyner et faire mourir de faim tant de familles; ils vont crier de la mesme sorte devant sa maison a Kilkenny, jettans des pierres contre les fenêtres; et ce à cause qu'il supporte O Neile': Memorial of Fr. Thomas Talbot for Mazarin, June 1647 (AMAE, Correspondence Politique (Angleterre) 55, fo. 209ʳ).

[169] See for instance his analysis of the outcry concerning the *Disputatio Apologetica*: Rinuccini to Pancirolo, 1 Oct. 1647 (Aiazzi, *Nunziatura*, 256–7) and the extract from his letter to Pancirolo of 28 Dec. 1647 (*Comment. Rinucc.*, ii. 461).

[170] *Comment. Rinucc.*, iii. 2–3.

worse than domination by the Ulster army.[171] As the crisis over the Inchiquin truce was to demonstrate, the majority party of the Munster confederates preferred to accept a truce with Inchiquin rather than to allow O'Neill's forces into the province to protect them against the baron. This was an attitude which Rinuccini could hardly understand, let alone condone. There is a note of incredulity in his account of the reception of one of his suggestions in this regard in 1648:

in the business that I suggested of drawing him [O'Neill] at my expense into Munster against the Baron, the Ormondites . . . confused by the offer, gave me no other answer except that in Munster Ulster men were not wanted. Which by a religious person [probably the Jesuit superior, Malone] was confirmed to me again in much cruder terms, when I suggested to him that it was better in the end to have catholics than heretics in the province, he answered me unashamedly and without wavering that this was not always true.[172]

It is in this context that the second excommunication crisis over the Inchiquin truce of 1648 should be understood. The policy which Plunkett and Ferns had attempted the previous year, investing authority in an elected council, marginalizing the Ulster army in Connacht, and pursuing their objectives in Munster and Leinster with armies under Old English command, had failed, a failure capped by the departure of both men from Ireland in February 1648. The previous year had been full of uninterrupted disaster for the confederates of Leinster and Munster. For the first time previously secure territories had been comprehensively devastated: papal subsidies which they had been so often promised by the nuncio had failed to arrive:[173] the armies in which they most trusted had both been comprehensively routed, and they had been forced to rely for protection on O'Neill whom they bitterly distrusted. Nor, even if the beaten armies could be reconstructed, was there any reason to believe that there was a politically and militarily trustworthy general with the capacity to lead them to victory. In this context, acceptance of the Inchiquin truce and then the second Ormond peace over the next year was a logical development.

Crucially, however, Rinuccini saw things in a different light. Increasingly convinced of the fidelity and military prowess of O'Neill, aware that Massari

---

[171] See for instance Sir Robert Talbot's letter to Clanricard, 20 Mar. 1647 (*Clanricard Letter Book 1643–7*, 369–71); Preston to Clanricard, 14 Oct. 1646 (ibid., 292–3); Apologia of the Munster officers, June 1647 (*Comment. Rinucc.*, ii. 616–19); Rinuccini's instructions to Plunkett and Ferns, 28 Dec. 1647 (Aiazzi, *Nunziatura*, 283); Bodl. Carte MS 21, fo. 511ʳ.

[172] 'Nel negoziato che io feci di tirarlo a mie spese nella Momonia contro il Barone, gli Ormonisti . . . confusi dall'offerte, non mi respondevano mai altro, se non che in Momonia non si volevano Ultoniesi. Il che da persona religiosa, in termini assai piu communi, mi fu ancora affermato, quando supponendoli io esser meglio alla fine avere i Cattolici che gli Eretici nella Provincia, con aperta fronte e senza alcuna titubazione mi rispose, che questo non era sempre vero': Rinuccini's relation to the pope (Aiazzi, *Nunziatura*, 424–5).

[173] In this regard note the extreme bitterness of Patrick Darcy towards Rinuccini's promises of papal gold: Darcy to Muskery, 6 Nov. 1647 (Bodl. Carte MS 21, fo. 517ᵛ).

was in France with papal funds, hopeful that the Plunkett-Ferns mission might persuade the pope to invest even more substantially in Ireland, trusting in God to continue the political turmoil in England, and interpreting the military disasters of 1647, not as evidence that the policy which he advocated was impossible, but as the product of the dissensions of a detestable section of the association, he still believed in the possibility of continuing the war. In order to do so, he had accepted (at least by March 1648) that the Ulster army would have to play a critical role, but the nuncio felt it morally impossible to accept the objections which some confederates made to this. Of course, even the nuncio's confidence about ultimate victory had been somewhat shaken but crucially he believed that those confederates who were most insistent on the need to compromise were actually those who bore most responsibility for the failures of 1647. The deep distrust which he felt for this group, now ensconced in the Supreme Council, meant that the nuncio found it greatly difficult to co-operate with them. Increasingly, he saw his choices in Ireland restricted to two options. One was the optimistic strategy of supporting O'Neill in the hope of recovering the clergy's position through the Ulster army: the more pessimistic option was that of washing his hands of the Irish and deciding that his mission was a failure. It was between these two choices that Rinuccini was to waver during his final year in Ireland.

CHAPTER SIX

The End of the Nunciature

I

Rinuccini's last year in Ireland has attracted more attention from Irish historians than any other year of the nunciature.[1] To some extent this is attributable to the fact that this was the year which saw the emergence of the fragile royalist coalition which ultimately and unsuccessfully confronted Cromwell. Thus it marks the beginning of the end of the often confusing intricacies of confederate politics. Those same intricacies have perhaps appeared less worth unravelling because of the degree to which Cromwellian simplicity later rendered them irrelevant. To some degree the interregnum restored 'normality' to seventeenth-century Irish history by re-establishing the centrality of the relationship between a government under control from Britain and the Irish population which, during the confederate period, had been occluded by the collapse of the English state in most of the island. Furthermore, the Cromwellian conquest marked such a decisive landmark in Irish history that it is doubly difficult for any historian of the period to avoid interpreting the entire confederate period from 1649 backwards, rather than forwards from 1642. Viewed in that post-Cromwellian context, Rinuccini's most notable accomplishment was to impede the formation of a unified party capable of resisting the 1649 invasion. This 'complicity' in the Cromwellian conquest may perhaps explain the rather simplistic and prob-

[1] The credit for this is largely due to Patrick Corish who has published a number of articles on the Inchiquin truce and the second Ormond peace, and on the controversies to which they gave rise. The most important of these are: 'Rinuccini's Censure of 27 May 1648', *Irish Theological Quarterly*, 18 (1951), 322–37; 'The Crisis in Ireland in 1648: The Nuncio and the Supreme Council. Conclusions', ibid., 22 (1955), 231–57; 'Bishop Nicholas French and the Second Ormond Peace, 1648–9', *Irish Historical Studies*, 6 (1948), 83–100; 'Two Contemporary Historians of the Confederation of Kilkenny: John Lynch and Richard O'Ferrall', *Irish Historical Studies*, 8 (1952–3), 217–36. Some of the material in these articles was subsequently reformulated in 'The Origins of Catholic Nationalism' in Corish (ed.), *Irish Catholicism*, iii (Dublin, 1968), 45–55, and again in id., 'Ormond, Rinuccini, and the Confederates, 1645–9', in T. W. Moody, F. X. Martin, and F. J. Byrne (eds.), *A New History of Ireland*, iii. *Early Modern Ireland, 1534–1691* (Oxford, 1976), 316–35. The military engagements of the year are detailed in Jerrold Casway, *Owen Roe O'Neill and the Struggle for Catholic Ireland* (Philadelphia, 1984), 193–262 while details of the protestant forces in Ulster and Munster and their reaction to the confederate civil war are outlined in David Stevenson, *Scottish Covenanters and Irish Confederates*, 254–70 and John A. Murphy, 'The Politics of the Munster Protestants, 1641–9', *Journal of the Cork Historical and Archaeological Society*, 76 (1971), 14–19. A narrative summary of the events of this period is presented by Micheál Ó Siochrú, *Confederate Ireland 1642–1649: A Constitutional and Political Analysis* (Dublin, 1999), 172–204.

ably unjust portrait of the nuncio which has occurred in some of the secondary literature.[2]

The essential outline of events in 1648 has already been well recounted. During 1647 the transformation in English politics which followed parliament's victory in the first Civil War began to make Inchiquin increasingly uneasy. The weakening of his authority in February 1647 by parliament's dispatch of Philip, Lord Lisle, as Lieutenant of the kingdom to Munster threatened his position. Vigorous lobbying in Westminster in the spring of 1647 contributed to the ousting of Lisle and the cooling of Inchiquin's anxieties, but the decisive intervention of the army in English politics in August augured badly for the baron and the interests he represented. By January 1648 an open breach with parliament seemed a distinct possibility.[3] In England, at the same time, Charles, having signed an engagement with the Scots, commissioned Ormond to negotiate again with the confederates concerning a peace. Ormond sailed for France from England in February 1648, where he liaised with his brother-in-law, Muskery, who had been sent by the second assembly of 1647 as one of the confederate envoys to Paris. The marquis also dispatched an emissary to Ireland, Colonel John Barry, who first sounded out Inchiquin about declaring for the royalist party and then proceeded to Kilkenny to discuss matters with the confederates. By the beginning of March both Inchiquin and the Supreme Council were seriously considering a mutual cessation of hostilities and towards the end of that month Inchiquin declared for the king against parliament.[4]

The nuncio, then resident in Waterford, where he had gone following the second assembly of 1647, was deeply suspicious about these events and although he returned to Kilkenny to discuss the matter, he could not be brought to countenance the proposed truce between the now royalist Inchiquin and the confederates. Massari had eventually arrived from France in March bringing with him about £8,000, the remnant of the papal subsidies

---

[2] In general, this particular portrait emerges in the less specialized secondary literature. For example, see Louis McRedmond, *To the Greater Glory: A History of the Irish Jesuits* (Dublin, 1991), 69, 73; Brendan FitzPatrick, *Seventeenth-Century Ireland: The War of Religions* (Dublin, 1988), 198–9; see also Corish, 'The Nuncio and the Supreme Council', 257 and 'Rinuccini's Censure', 337: in contrast Casway's criticism of Rinuccini is on account of his supposed irresolution and failure to stand by O'Neill's party in 1649. See Casway, *Owen Roe O'Neill*, 237.

[3] Robert Armstrong, 'Protestant Ireland and the English Parliament, 1641–1647' (unpub. Ph.D. thesis, Trinity College Dublin, 1995), 258–98; John Adamson, 'Strafford's Ghost: The British Context of Viscount Lisle's Lieutenancy of Ireland', in Jane Ohlmeyer (ed.), *Ireland from Independence to Occupation, 1641–60* (Cambridge, 1995), 128–59.

[4] Murphy, 'Politics of the Munster Protestants', 15–16; Corish, 'Ormond, Rinuccini and the Confederates, 1645–9', 327–8, 337; *Comment. Rinucc.*, iii. 70, 76–80; J. C. Beckett, *The Cavalier Duke* (Belfast, 1990), 46; for developments in England in 1647–8 see Robert Ashton, *The English Civil War: Conservatism and Revolution, 1603–1649*, 2nd edn. (London, 1991), 290–319; David Underdown, *Pride's Purge: Politics in the Puritan Revolution* (London, 1985), 45–172; Mark Kishlansky, 'Ideology and Politics in the Parliamentary Armies, 1645–9', in John Morrill (ed.), *Reactions to the English Civil War, 1642–9* (London, 1982), 163–83.

which had been much diminished by his long and expensive sojourn in France.[5] Rinuccini thus once again had access to a not contemptible supply of money. On 27 April 1648 he persuaded fourteen Irish bishops to sign a protest against the truce. Twelve days later, on 9 May, following the stalemate of negotiations with the council, and nervous about his safety in Kilkenny, the nuncio fled to O'Neill's camp at Maryborough. In his absence, on 20 May, the council concluded the truce. A week afterwards, news was brought to O'Neill and the nuncio that Preston's army was on the march towards Maryborough in greater strength than the Ulster army would be able to counter. This was erroneous information but Rinuccini decided to safeguard his position by excommunicating all those who adhered to the truce, particularly with an eye to halting Preston. The council, remembering 1646, had already foreseen this eventuality and decided to appeal Rinuccini's action to Rome. By doing so, they anticipated that the censure would be suspended for at least several months until the result of their appeal was known. Rinuccini, however, although he recognized the council's right to lodge an appeal, declared that the excommunication would remain in force pending the decision in Rome. The failure on both sides to moderate their positions meant that a confederate civil war, between those who adhered to the nuncio and those who supported the council, flared up inevitably during the summer and autumn.[6]

By the end of November the clerical party was in disarray. Rinuccini was confined to Galway and, despite intelligent generalship in difficult positions, O'Neill, the military backbone of his party, was irrevocably on the defensive. Indeed, he was forced to negotiate with the protestant forces in the island just to preserve his army.[7] Ormond returned to Ireland in September and a new assembly, largely representing the interests of Rinuccini's opponents, had reopened negotiations with him about peace. In November Nicholas French and Nicholas Plunkett returned from Rome where they had been frustrated in their attempts to gain more papal aid, or even a clear statement of the terms on which they might negotiate peace with the king. Appalled by the situation in Ireland, they elected more or less to ignore Rinuccini in Galway. Instead they co-operated with the victorious party in the confederate civil war in an attempt to secure certain minimum terms for the catholic religion in the negotiations which the assembly was pursuing with Ormond. These negotiations still presented enormous problems but the threat to the king's life from the November remonstrance of the army provided the spur to compromise and an agreement was reached on 17 January 1649. Rinuccini

    [5] *Comment. Rinucc.*, iii. 229, 56.
    [6] My summary here is based on Corish, 'Rinuccini's Censure', 322–37; see also Corish, 'Ormond, Rinuccini and the Confederates, 1645–9', 328–30.
    [7] The intricate details of these campaigns are covered in Casway, *Owen Roe O'Neill*, 215–36.

had no interest in remaining in a jurisdiction under the authority of a protestant lord lieutenant and he left the island on 23 February 1649.[8]

II

The actual course of action which Rinuccini adopted in 1648 has thus been traced already in the secondary literature. One issue which has previously been inadequately explained, however, is the context in which Rinuccini made the decision to oppose the Inchiquin truce with such vehemence. This is a point of particular importance when account is taken, first, that at face value the agreement with Inchiquin was merely a temporary truce for military utility and thus devoid of the long-term implications of an actual peace treaty; second, that earlier in the year *before* Inchiquin had broken with parliament the nuncio was prepared to countenance a truce with him,[9] and also with the Scots in Ulster;[10] third, that such fervent opposition to the truce went directly against the nuncio's orders from Rome;[11] and fourth, that in the months before the truce Rinuccini's enthusiasm for the Irish mission had diminished to such an extent that he was seriously contemplating washing his hands of the nunciature and returning to Rome.[12]

Rinuccini's behaviour becomes immediately more comprehensible when it is accepted that his real objections to the Inchiquin truce did not concern the merits of the truce itself but were related to his belief that the agreement with Inchiquin was part of an elaborate plot to bring about the return of Ormond and the Ormond peace.[13] It was for this reason that Inchiquin's declaration

[8] Corish, 'Bishop Nicholas French', 83–100; and id., 'Ormond, Rinuccini and the Confederates, 1645–9', 331–5; Ashton, *English Civil War*, 341–3.

[9] See Corish, 'Rinuccini's Censure', 323–4; Supreme Council to Rinuccini, 11 May 1648 (*Comment. Rinucc.*, iii. 151); Rinuccini to Supreme Council, 6 Apr. 1648 (ibid., 96); same to same, 13 Apr. 1648 (ibid., 100–1); see also *Comment. Rinucc*, iii. 124; the damaging accusation that Rinuccini had only turned against the Inchiquin truce when the baron had broken with parliament later became a staple of the council's invective against the nuncio: see Abstract of the charge against the nuncio, 19 Oct. 1648 (Thomas Carte, *An history of the life of James, first duke of Ormonde* (6 vols., Oxford, 1851), 574).

[10] Stevenson, *Covenanters and Confederates*, 255–6; Corish, 'Ormond, Rinuccini and the Confederates, 1645–9', 328–30.

[11] The nuncio's most recent instructions in this regard informed him: 'cumque D. vestra . . . solita virtute et prudentia diligentiam adhibuerit ut Dei cultus et nostra sancta religio in splendore jam introducto conservetur, causam suae Divinae Majestati commendet, nec amplius induciis aut paci se immisceat, cum sufficiat Suae Sanctitati ut cognoscat mundus se ex parte sua non defuisse officio Patris universalis et capitis Ecclesiae': Pancirolo to Rinuccini, 1 July (ns) 1647 (*Comment. Rinucc.*, iii. 103); see also Corish, 'The Nuncio and the Supreme Council', 245.

[12] As he reported afterwards to the pope, his personal inclination was to go in Mar. 1648 when Massari's return had placed a ship at his disposal, he and his household were together in a convenient port, and the activity of parliamentary ships off the southern coast was still low from fear of spring gales: Rinuccini's relation to the pope, (Aiazzi *Nunziatura*, 423).

[13] See Rinuccini to Pancirolo, 18 Feb. 1648 (ibid., 297–8); same to same, 29 Jan. 1649 (ibid., 294); same to same, 8 Apr. 1648 (ibid., 302–3); Statement of Rinuccini's reasons for the excommunication (ibid., 316).

for the king made him less rather than more willing to agree to the truce. The nuncio was perfectly correct in these suspicions, although this has previously received little attention.[14] Despite the accuracy of his intuition concerning the ultimate objectives of the proponents of the truce,[15] it was a problem for Rinuccini that he was unable to prove his suspicions definitively. The nuncio was thus forced to argue against the truce on its demerits as a military agreement and his inability to build a really convincing case meant that in the course of the debate he was made to appear intransigent and also invasive of the temporal authority.[16]

Yet the point must be stressed that Rinuccini's enemies on the Supreme Council were at least as intransigent as the nuncio, while operating in a considerably more duplicitous fashion.[17] This group pushed forward with the truce, choosing to ignore, first the fact that the Supreme Council itself was deeply split on the issue,[18] second that the majority of the Irish bishops supported the nuncio's stance,[19] and third that the nuncio had made it clear that they risked forfeiting the papal subsidies by accepting the truce. A particular pro-truce cabal was in fact as indifferent to the merits or demerits of the truce as Rinuccini himself. Militarily the arrangement was clearly a dubious bargain if it entailed the loss of the papal subsidies and armed resistance from O'Neill. But if it came to a choice then the pro-truce cabal clearly preferred to fight with Inchiquin against O'Neill than vice versa.

---

[14] It has been touched on: see Corish, 'The Origins of Catholic Nationalism', in id., *Irish Catholicism*, iii. 48; Corish, 'Rinuccini's Censure', 324; Murphy, 'Politics of the Munster Protestants', 16–18; Ó Siochrú, *Confederate Ireland*, 171; Inchiquin's letter to Ormond, 29 May 1648 (Carte, *Ormonde*, vi. 549–53) also clearly indicates that Rinuccini was completely correct that the truce was tied up with Ormond's return to Ireland.

[15] In Apr. his adherents intercepted a letter from Inchiquin to John Plunkett which offered strong evidence of the existence of the plot: see *Comment. Rinucc.*, iii. 84 for a Latin version of this letter; in May letters from France about Ormond's activities offered further corroboration of his suspicions: see ibid., 184; see also Rinuccini's relation to the pope (Aiazzi, *Nunziatura*, 418); Rinuccini to Pancirolo, 3 May 1648 (ibid., 308); reasons of the nuncio for the excommunication, 15 June 1648 (ibid., 317).

[16] The council intelligently demanded of the nuncio that he show how specific articles of the truce offended against the catholic religion: see *Comment. Rinucc.*, iii. 94–5, 112–13; on 27 Apr. Rinuccini and the Irish bishops responded rather lamely to this challenge characterizing the truce 'omnino tendere ad ruinam Catholicae religionis, cultorum ejus in hoc Regno' (ibid., 134); see also the defence of the truce presented by Bellings (J. T. Gilbert (ed.), History of the *Irish Confederation and the War in Ireland* (7 vols., Dublin, 1882–91), vii. 78).

[17] Corish, 'Rinuccini's Censure', 336–7 offers a rather generous interpretation of the council's behaviour during the crisis of the truce.

[18] As late as 29 May Inchiquin was aware that only five of the council were certain to support the truce: see Inchiquin to Ormond, 29 May 1648 (Carte, *Ormond*, 551). The five in question were presumably Bellings, Fennell, Athenry, Sir Lucas Dillon, and Robert Devereux.

[19] Although at least six were unhappy with the nuncio's behaviour: see Diary of the Supreme Council, Apr. 1648 (*Comment. Rinucc.*, iii. 141); Corish, 'Rinuccini's Censure', 325: the identity of all six is unclear but from their subsequent alignments after the split one can be reasonably certain that they included the archbishop of Tuam, John Bourke, the bishop of Killala, Francis Kirwan, the bishop of Kilfenora, Andrew Lynch, and the bishop of Limerick, Edmund O'Dwyer.

The councillors in favour of the truce, however, were not actively seeking civil war with the Ulster army and the nuncio. Having completed the truce with Inchiquin they were prepared to try to conciliate O'Neill,[20] although they refused terms from Rinuccini which were designed to prevent them from using the agreement as a springboard to reintroducing the Ormond peace.[21] The irony was that ultimately the peace party seem to have provoked the very confrontation which they had been hoping to avoid.

One of the ways in which this came about was through the council's insistence that Rinuccini return to Kilkenny from Waterford, where he had been domiciled after the departure of Plunkett and Ferns to Rome. Given the manner in which the truce was later concluded, it seems clear that the peace party's intention in bringing Rinuccini to Kilkenny was less to consult with him than to neutralize him in a city under their direct military control. This decision backfired because in Waterford Rinuccini had been drifting away from the confrontational stance which he had adopted during the second assembly of 1647 towards a position of passivity. He still entertained feelings of loyalty to and solidarity with O'Neill and some Irish bishops, which played their part in influencing his decision to stay in Ireland,[22] but by April Rinuccini had decided that he would follow instructions and offer only detached disapproval if the council ignored his advice.[23] He was now pessimistic about the entire Irish mission and Massari's return from Italy seems to have deepened his gloom because, while it provided him with some financial leverage, it offered little hope for the massive subsidies from Rome with which he believed the Irish situation could still be transformed.[24]

The council's inveigling of him to Kilkenny evidently worked on a number of levels to push the nuncio back to a more confrontational stance. Their evident attempts to mislead him were arguably counterproductive with an individual as combative as the nuncio. Moreover, in Kilkenny Rinuccini was once again at the hub of things and in a better position to analyse the

---

[20] They proposed that Rinuccini should devote the papal money at his disposal to O'Neill's forces which would then be used to attack the parliamentary and Scots forces in Trim, Dundalk, Drogheda, and Ulster. In return for this, they were prepared to guarantee the Ulster army secure winter quarters: see *Comment. Rinucc.*, iii. 176–9.

[21] See Rinuccini's propositions to the council, 13 May 1648 (*Comment. Rinucc.*, iii. 155–7); see also Gilbert, *Irish Confederation*, vii. 74–6; Rinuccini's conditions were arguably impossibly stringent but they do indicate that the nuncio was not bent on civil war if he could prevent the reinstatement of the Ormond peace by other means.

[22] Rinuccini's relation to the pope (Aiazzi, *Nunziatura*, 423); see also ibid., 314, 316–17.

[23] Rinuccini to Pancirolo, 10 Apr. 1648 (ibid., 305–6).

[24] In a private letter to his brother, and therefore presumably sincerely, Rinuccini declared that a substantial papal grant of about £100,000 would result in the catholic conquest of the entire island: see *Comment. Rinucc.*, iii. 234. He was well aware that the pope could supply a sum of this kind but he had evidently begun to realize that his chances of goading the confederates into action that might stimulate such generosity were increasingly slim.

situation,[25] and to consult with members of the Irish hierarchy.[26] He was also personally under far greater pressure. Prior to leaving Ireland, the bishop of Ferns had warned Rinuccini to be careful of his safety, which was evidently one of the reasons why Rinuccini remained in Waterford and within easy access of the impregnable fortress of Duncannon during the first part of the year.[27] He was nervous about his personal security on his return to Kilkenny and, in May, his final flight from Kilkenny to O'Neill's camp was partly prompted by fears that a plot existed to assassinate him.[28] Even if his fears for his life were exaggerated,[29] it was logical to worry that his freedom to leave Kilkenny would be restricted by the council, as indeed subsequently happened to Massari during the nuncio's absence.[30]

As it transpired, the enticing of the nuncio away from Waterford ultimately pushed him into the arms of O'Neill. At Waterford Rinuccini had been able to count on a safe and dignified escape from confrontation with the council simply by taking to ship. In Kilkenny this alternative was closed to him. Rinuccini fled to O'Neill in Maryborough under cover of the procession on Rogation Monday on 9 May partly because this was the only secure location he could hope to reach without being intercepted by his enemies' cavalry.[31] And, of course, the eventual excommunication which precipitated the confederate civil war was prompted by Rinuccini's belief that he and O'Neill were in danger from an attack by Preston. It was thus largely a defensive and, it has been convincingly argued, a panicky reaction.[32]

Yet, while stressing the almost accidental nature of the ultimate conflagration, sight must not be lost of the deep structural reasons which ultimately made conflict extremely likely from the moment that Rinuccini had fled from Kilkenny. In a real sense the war which ignited in May 1648 had been foreshadowed in the second general assembly of 1647, if not earlier.[33] The parties which confronted each other in that assembly were substantially similar to those who did so in the summer of 1648, with the major alteration that Inchiquin now supported Rinuccini's enemies. What the events of April

[25] And, in particular, to assess the probable victimization of his own supporters in Munster as a result of the truce. These included Dermot MacCarthy of Dunhallow, O'Sullivan of Castletownbere, Daniel MacCarthy of Castlemaine and, as it later transpired due to a secret article, Viscount Roche of Fermoy, Muskery's most important catholic rival in the province, who were all assigned to Inchiquin's quarters: see *Comment. Rinucc.*, iii. 242–3, 135–7.

[26] The Irish bishops ultimately backed his own position unanimously although some were clearly unhappy with this decision. Given Rinuccini's belief that the Holy Spirit voiced itself in any convocation of bishops, this event probably strengthened his resolve: see *Comment. Rinucc.*, iii. 134.

[27] See Rinuccini to Pancirolo, 18 Feb. 1648 (Aiazzi, *Nunziatura*, 298).

[28] Corish, 'Rinuccini's Censure', 325.

[29] Corish, 'Ormond, Rinuccini and the Confederates, 1645–9', p. 329.

[30] See the extract from Paul King's letter to Rinuccini (NLI MS 345, 941); Massari was not eventually released from Kilkenny until 23 Jan. 1649: see the extract from Massari's letter to Thomas Rinuccini, 8 Feb. 1649 (*Comment. Rinucc.*, iv. 82).

[31] Bodl. Carte MS 64, fo. 457[r].   [32] See Corish, 'Rinuccini's Censure', 328–9.

[33] In this regard see Bodl. Carte MS 21, fo. 367[v].

and early May had accomplished was to harden the nuncio's attitude to a pitch similar to that which he had displayed during the previous assembly. And the evidence suggests that Rinuccini was expectant of and fairly resigned to conflict considerably before the panicky reaction on 27 May to the news of Preston's troop movements. By 11 May he had already decided to distribute the papal money in his possession to O'Neill.[34] Such a course of action arguably flouted his instructions[35] and in concluding this section it is necessary to consider the reasons why Rinuccini was prepared to do this.

In the past the nuncio's willingness to disregard his instructions has been taken as another measure of his rashness and imprudence.[36] There is some justice in this charge. Yet it is important to bear in mind the context in which those instructions were formulated. Bluntly, the possibility exists that the nuncio's actions reflected his suspicion that his superiors' interest in the Irish mission was dominated by a concern to minimize expenditure and to maximize prestige. In view of Pope Innocent's reaction to the successes and failures of 1646, it was logical to assume that a glorious military success would do more for the Irish mission in Rome than strict obedience to instructions.[37] In this context one can note the interesting accusation levelled against the nuncio in October 1648 that

being expostulated by a reverend prelate and a religious father, that it stood not with his lordship's honour to side with Owen O'Neill and his party against the loyal, interested and considerable persons of the kingdom . . . unto which his lordship [Rinuccini] answered, that the prevalent party would be accounted the best catholics in Rome.[38]

This accusation was, of course, made by the nuncio's fiercest enemies. Nevertheless, it seems possible that in the heat of the moment Rinuccini may have responded to the arguments of some of his clerical opponents in the manner quoted above. If he did so, then this would indicate that the nuncio had very few illusions about the nature of papal interest in Ireland. In that context what he attempted was comprehensible but fraught with extreme risk.

The background to the crisis of the Inchiquin truce is, therefore, somewhat more intricate than has previously been presented. The importance of the

---

[34] That he believed that this was the prelude to conflict is indicated by his declaration to his superior: 'Non si è potuto fuggire questo gran cimento, e se vinciamo una volta, si possano sperare grandissimi progressi per la Fede, ma se verrà il contrario, non ci sarà altro che la mano d'Iddio e le orazioni di Sua Sanctità che la possano sostenere': Rinuccini to Pancirolo, 11 July 1648 (Aiazzi, *Nunziatura*, 315).

[35] Pancirolo to Rinuccini, 1 July (ns) 1647 (*Comment. Rinucc.*, iii. 103).

[36] Most importantly by Patrick Corish in 'Rinuccini's Censure', 331; see also Corish, 'The Nuncio and the Supreme Council', 235.

[37] In the wake of the censure's failure, Rinuccini indeed attempted to defend his decision by arguing that it could be seen as a logical repetition of the action of 1646 which had been retrospectively approved in Rome: see Instructions to Arcamoni, 11 Nov. 1648 (Aiazzi, *Nunziatura*, 348).

[38] Charge against the nuncio, 19 Oct. 1648 (Carte, *Ormond*, 576).

action, however, together with the nuncio's refusal to accept the legitimacy of the council's appeal,[39] is beyond doubt as it brought about first a confederate civil war, and second Rinuccini's own departure.

III

Little attention has previously been focused on Rinuccini in the wake of the excommunication, nor is this particularly surprising. The censure of 27 May was the nuncio's last truly decisive action in Ireland. None the less, the repercussions of this act continued to bedevil the association even after his departure. It was not until 20 October 1649 that Owen Roe O'Neill finally came to an accommodation with Ormond, by which time the Cromwellian invasion had already been launched. Even subsequently, catholic distrust of the lord lieutenant materially contributed to the difficulties which he encountered in slowing the momentum of conquest.[40] Essentially, there are three points concerning Rinuccini's stance after the censure which require investigation: the first refers to the nuncio's refusal to take a meaningful part in any attempt to bring about a reconciliation between the warring confederate factions during the summer: the second concerns his eventual dissociation from O'Neill, which meant that in contrast to March 1648 he decided to leave Ireland against the general's wishes: and the third relates to his reaction to the later attempts of the bishop of Ferns to reconcile the clerical party with the supporters of the truce.

With regard to the first of these points, after the censure Rinuccini saw his hopes as inextricably linked to the triumph of O'Neill's army, the very thing which Ferns and Plunkett had struggled to avoid in 1647.[41] O'Neill's skilful generalship, in the face of most difficult odds and acute lack of money,[42] kept the nuncio's hopes of a military victory alive for several months.[43] Consequently, during this time he rebuffed a number of attempts to arrange some degree of confederate reconciliation.[44] When the tide did begin to turn

[39] See Corish, 'Rinuccini's Censure', 335–6 and 'The Nuncio and the Supreme Council', 241–5; see also *Comment. Rinucc.*, iii. 215–17, 221–2.

[40] Corish, 'Ormond, Rinuccini and the Confederates, 1645–9', 339–48.

[41] He informed Rome in the middle of June that if O'Neill was victorious then there was great hope for the catholic religion in Ireland but if the Ulster general was defeated then 'little or no remedy was in sight' (poco o nessun remedio si vede): Rinuccini to Pancirolo, 16 June 1648 (Aiazzi, *Nunziatura*, 320).

[42] During the entire course of 1648 Rinuccini was apparently unable to supply the Ulster army with more than 33,000 livres tournois (less than £3,000): see *Comment. Rinucc.*, iii. 543.

[43] O'Neill's various activities during this period are traced in Casway, *Owen Roe O'Neill*, 211–36; the extent to which the nuncio still cherished hopes of military triumph even in Sept. 1648 is apparent in Rinuccini's letter to Pancirolo, 15 Sept. 1648 (Aiazzi, *Nunziatura*, 335–6).

[44] In this context see his correspondence in June with the Old English bishops of Dublin, Ossory, Meath, Dromore, and Ardagh (*Comment. Rinucc.*, iii. 384–6); on 16 July, the French agent, de la Monerie, in an attempt at mediation tried to arrange a meeting with the nuncio but Rinuccini merely invited the agent to present his views at the national synod in Aug.: see ibid., 433–4.

against his party, the depth of his anger against what he saw as the deeply irreligious conduct of his opponents over the summer, in particular the frustration of a synod which he had attempted to hold to discuss the crisis, placed a huge obstacle in the face of any confederate reconciliation.[45] The nuncio was also emboldened to stand firm because he continued to hope against hope that Ferns and Plunkett might return from Rome with a large sum of money. Indeed, if he had not believed in this possibility it is distinctly plausible that he would never have pronounced the censure in the first place.[46]

The experience of Plunkett and Ferns in Rome, however, was to carry them in a direction directly contrary to the one that Rinuccini had adopted in Ireland. Pope Innocent proved anything but generous to the confederate envoys. He was clearly suspicious of the contemporaneous confederate mission to France,[47] and wary of the rumours which filtered back to Rome about the Inchiquin truce.[48] Consequently, although Plunkett and Ferns arrived in Rome on 23 April, until August they received no answer to their two principal demands, first for a clear statement of the religious terms on which they could make peace with the king, and second for immediate financial aid.[49] When it did come the response was deeply unsatisfactory. Certainly aware of the diplomatic implications which a statement on Ireland might have on contemporary developments in Westphalia, the confederate envoys were blandly informed:

the Apostolic See, whenever it is treated concerning a peace to be contracted between catholics and heretics, is accustomed to do nothing to approve the same, and it will be led by the good hope that the said envoys and all other Irish catholics in all their actions will aim for the greater advantage and utility of the catholic religion.[50]

---

[45] On 16 Aug., in reply to a letter from the archbishop of Tuam, the nuncio demanded impossible conditions, making it clear that he would not accept a reconciliation which did not involve the end of confederate co-operation with Inchiquin and the disowning of all acts 'against the honour of the church and particularly against the national synod' (contra honorem Ecclesiae et praecipue contra Synodum Nationalem): Rinuccini to Tuam, 16 Aug. 1648 (*Comment. Rinucc.*, iii. 479–80); see also the following section.

[46] Ibid., 544.

[47] Rinuccini had been worried about this possibility from the outset. Details of what was happening in Paris arrived in Rome much more quickly than in Ireland: see for instance Pancirolo to Rinuccini, 8 June (ns) 1648 (ibid., 397) and Plunkett and Ferns to Albizzi, 13 July (ns) 1648 (ibid., 400–1).

[48] As is indicated in Pancirolo's letter to Rinuccini, 20 July (ns) 1648 (ibid., 404–5); see also Corish, 'Ormond, Rinuccini and the Confederates, 1645–9', 332.

[49] Plunkett and Ferns to Pancirolo, 27 July (ns) 1648 (*Comment. Rinucc.*, iii. 405–6).

[50] 'Sedem Apostolicam, quoties de pace inter Catholicos et haereticos contrahenda agitur, solere nullas in ea re partes agere ad eam approbandam, seque bona duci spe futurum ut iidem Oratores aliique omnes Iberniae Catholici in cunctis eorum actionibus collinent in majorem religionis Catholicae profectum et utilitatem.': Pancirolo to Rinuccini 31 Aug. (ns) 1648 (*Comment. Rinucc.*, iii. 409).

Moreover, the only money they received was to defray the expenses of their own journey.[51] The frustration, indeed the sense of reproach and betrayal which the Irish envoys felt, can be sensed in a number of memorials which they presented in Rome at this time.[52] Their subsequent conduct when they returned to Ireland, in ignoring the nuncio and exerting themselves to obtain the best possible settlement from Ormond, can be attributed to a large extent to their prolonged disillusionment in Rome.

By the time of their arrival back in Ireland in November, the nuncio's party was in acute decline. Opposition to the censure from the Society of Jesus and in particular from a number of Old English bishops had crucially weakened its force.[53] Ormond had returned to Ireland on 30 September and Rinuccini believed that the Assembly congregated in Kilkenny since 4 September would be mere putty in the marquis's capable hands.[54] After the summer's campaigns, which had included a frightening siege of the nuncio in Galway, O'Neill had been thrown on the defensive and was forced into various shifts and compromises with protestant parliamentary forces in order to keep his army intact.[55] This had an important bearing on the nuncio's stance. Rinuccini disapproved of these tentative contacts and they seem to have convinced him that the Ulster army was now a broken reed, and somewhat harshly, that he himself was free of any further obligation to O'Neill.[56] Unable to contemplate compromise with those whom he had come to see as a party of apostates, and with his hopes of victory gone, he began therefore to make plans for his own departure. A concern both for his own personal dignity, which was beginning to be threatened by insolvency, and that of his position as the pope's representative, was now becoming the chief determinant of his behaviour. Thus, although eager to leave, he was unwilling to have it appear that he had been expelled from the island.[57] By waiting for the

---

[51] Innocent supplemented this rather pitiful donation with a number of cost-efficient ceremonial gestures. Plunkett was made a knight of the golden spur, Ferns an assistant in the pontifical chapel, and they both received a special papal blessing: see Pancirolo to Rinuccini, 20 Aug. (ns) 1648 (*Comment. Rinucc.*, iii. 408) and same to same, 31 Aug. (ns) 1648 (ibid., 409).

[52] These were couched in very frank language: see for example Plunkett and Ferns to Pancirolo, 27 July (ns) 1648 (ibid., 405) and Plunkett and Ferns to Albizzi, 27 July (ns) 1648 (ibid., 407).

[53] Rinuccini himself stressed the damage which his cause had sustained through the reluctance of many bishops to support him: see his report on the truce, Aug. 1648 (Aiazzi, *Nunziatura*, 332): the importance of the bishops' stance in undermining Rinuccini's support was also emphasized by Richard Bellings: see Gilbert, *Irish Confederation*, vii. 68.

[54] Rinuccini to Pancirolo, 10 Oct. 1648 (Aiazzi, *Nunziatura*, 339–41).

[55] Casway, *Owen Roe O'Neill*, 232–3; there had previously been contact between O'Neill and parliament over the exchange of prisoners: see id., 'George Monck and the Controversial Catholic Truce of 1649', *Studia Hibernica*, 16 (1976), 57.

[56] Rinuccini to Cardinal Roma, 23 Dec. 1648 (Aiazzi, *Nunziatura*, 357); Rinuccini seems to have felt somewhat abused by O'Neill's failure to rescue him from the siege of Galway in Aug.: see the implied criticism of O'Neill in his praise for Roger Maguire in Rinuccini's relation to the pope (ibid., 429); see also Casway, *Owen Roe O'Neill*, 236–7 which is highly critical of the nuncio's attitude at this juncture.

[57] Rinuccini's diary entry for 4 Nov. would suggest that he had already received the order to leave Ireland (*Comment. Rinucc.*, iii. 628).

actual publication of peace he hoped to convey the impression that his departure was the dignified refusal of a papal emissary to remain in a jurisdiction where a catholic executive had voluntarily dissolved itself to accept the government of a protestant.[58]

It was in this frame of mind that Rinuccini heard on 21 November of the return of the Roman envoys to Ireland. As an Italian, it was much easier for Rinuccini to dissociate himself from confederate affairs than it was for the Irish born bishop of Ferns. Ferns returned from Italy convinced that an effort had to be made to resolve the confederate crisis through compromise and negotiation.[59] On his arrival in Ireland, therefore, instead of visiting the nuncio in Galway, the bishop, together with Plunkett, went to the assembly in Kilkenny, where eight episcopal opponents of the nuncio had already gathered. There, making use of the vagueness of the papal response, they informed the delegates in the assembly that the pope did not require specific religious conditions but only that the best arrangement possible for the catholic religion be obtained. In addition, using a letter which they had obtained from Cardinal Roma, the envoys seem to have conveyed the impression that the Roman response to Rinuccini's excommunication had been much colder than it really was and thus materially undermined Rinuccini's remaining influence in Ireland. Seeing the negotiations between the confederate assembly in Kilkenny and Ormond as the best hope of salvaging something for the catholic party in Ireland, they also strove to entice additional catholic bishops to Kilkenny both by a direct appeal to the nuncio for permission and by a variety of pretexts.[60]

This represented a considerable volte-face on the part of both men who had of course left Ireland on good terms with the nuncio. The logic which informed this transformation has not previously been fully explained. In the first place, Ferns had always been an apostle of reconciliation within the clerical party and he returned to Ireland at a time when the nuncio's party had already suffered military defeat. More importantly, the bishop had gone to Rome charged with arguments from Rinuccini to convince the pope that it would be worthwhile and meritorious to support the militant catholic party among the confederates, even if the association were to split. Ferns's stay in Rome had convinced him that such assistance would not be forthcoming.[61]

---

[58] See Rinuccini to Pancirolo, 10 Oct. 1648 (Aiazzi, *Nunziatura*, 340) and same to same, 23 Dec. 1648 (ibid., 355).

[59] The role Ferns played on his return to Ireland has been the subject of an excellent analysis: see Corish, 'Bishop Nicholas French', 86–100.

[60] Ibid.

[61] Indeed this was the substance of Roma's letter which informed Rinuccini that there was no hope for renewed aid from Rome unless the confederates reunited: 'certum sit donec dissensionem cessasse innotuerit, hic non cogitandum de subsidiis, quae Dominatio vestra Illustrissima cum tanta ratione desiderat et expectat': Latin version of Roma to Rinuccini, 24 Aug. (ns) 1648 (*Comment. Rinucc.*, iii. 685).

He was thus aware that the clerical party had nothing to lose and a good deal to gain by patching up their differences with Ormond's supporters. Not only did a united party stand a better chance of resisting any invasion from England, but the hope of persuading the Irish bishops to endorse a peace would give the lord lieutenant the best possible incentive to offer the catholic clergy generous conditions. This was the background to the bishop's frantic search for confederate unity and his willingness to marginalize and indeed deceive the nuncio to achieve it,[62] because Rinuccini, as a result of his experiences during the summer, had reached a point where he was deaf to any talk of compromise. Disillusioned with O'Neill, Rinuccini no longer believed that it was worth Rome's while investing in Ireland and, revolted by the excesses of his opponents, he believed that it was morally impossible to contemplate absolving them of his censure unless they made a complete repudiation of what he had come to see as their sacrilegious behaviour.[63]

Rinuccini's subsequent reaction to Ferns's behaviour, and in particular to Ferns's arguments that the bishops should attend the assembly in Kilkenny, has been described somewhat surprisingly as 'rather petulant'.[64] The substance of the nuncio's reply was a refusal to allow the congregation of bishops in Kilkenny, but a willingness to allow them to assemble, under the chairmanship of the moderate archbishop of Cashel and without the nuncio's own participation, in Limerick.[65] Rinuccini sincerely believed that the chief figures in the Kilkenny assembly did not deserve absolution from his censure because of their behaviour in the period after its promulgation. While unwilling to see the clergy assemble officially in a city under the control of excommunicates, he was prepared to allow them to come together to decide clerical policy for Ireland without his personal input.[66] And indeed he did nothing further to impede those bishops who wished to go to Kilkenny from attending the assembly. This was hardly an extreme position. In fact, without Rinuccini's passive acquiescence in his own marginalization it is difficult to believe that the second Ormond peace could ever have been

---

[62] In particular he failed to inform the nuncio that the pope had left the handling of the censure to Rinuccini's own discretion. Rinuccini was forced to wait until the arrival of a letter from Pancirolo in Dec. for this information and, until it arrived, he was evidently very worried that Rome had disowned his action: see the Latin extract from Pancirolo to Rinuccini, 7 Sept. (ns) 1648 (*Comment. Rinucc.*, iii. 682) and Rinuccini to Ferns and Plunkett, 14 Dec. 1648 (ibid., 675).

[63] See Rinuccini's instructions to Arcamoni, 24 Jan. 1649 (ibid., 686).

[64] Corish, 'Bishop Nicholas French', 93.

[65] If this compromise was unacceptable, Rinuccini was prepared to leave it up to the consciences of the individual bishops whether to attend the assembly, although he could not approve of such a decision: see Rinuccini to Plunkett and Ferns, 18 Dec. 1648 (ibid., 676).

[66] The envoys' objection that this suggestion was impractical, because the negotiations with Ormond could not be broken off to allow the bishops to congregate in a completely different city, was arguably valid, but this does not alter the basic good faith in which Rinuccini made the offer: see Plunkett and Ferns to Rinuccini, 30 Dec. 1648 (*Comment. Rinucc.*, iii. 679–80).

achieved.[67] A further indication of the nuncio's retreat from extremism was the fact that he largely dismantled the post-truce interdict prior to leaving the island.[68] By the time of the nuncio's departure, even Kilkenny, the seat of his opponents' government and of one of the most rebellious bishops, had been released from the interdict as a reward for the loyalty of the city's regular clergy.[69]

By January 1649 the nuncio had definitively passed the baton as principal spokesman for the catholic clergy in Ireland back to the native Irish bishops. The release of Massari from his enforced detention in Kilkenny on 23 January followed hard on the formal agreement of the second Ormond peace on 17 January and the conjunction of these two events meant that there was little to keep Rinuccini in Ireland.[70] In leaving he was in a position to declare scornfully that it was impossible for a nuncio of the pope to remain with confederates who 'from the governors that they had been, voluntarily made themselves the servants of a heretic'.[71] Rinuccini was still not quite certain of the precise articles of peace.[72] When he saw the complete draft of the treaty in May, he was already in France and had the dour satisfaction of seeing his worst suspicions vindicated. With an odd mixture of depression and *schadenfreude* he dispatched a copy of the religious article to Rome 'so that the pope and all the congregation [of cardinals] should have full information of what our good bishops have done; it is not other in substance than that which they had concluded before my arrival'.[73] This was somewhat overstated but it was true that the peace contained only a vague possibility that the catholic church would eventually be accorded legal recognition of its right to jurisdiction and ecclesiastical property in Ireland.[74] This was of course the irreducible minimum for which Rinuccini had struggled throughout his nunciature.

[67] Even without the nuncio's active opposition, the bishops at Kilkenny found it extremely difficult to accept Ormond's terms: see Corish, 'Bishop Nicholas French', 96–100.

[68] At the time of his departure the nuncio himself believed that only a tiny minority of the confederates were still barred from the sacraments: see Rinuccini's letter to Pancirolo, 14 Mar. (ns) 1649 (Aiazzi, *Nunziatura*, 363–6).

[69] Ibid., 364; see also Rinuccini's instructions to Arcamoni, 11 Nov. 1648 (ibid., 345.)

[70] See the extract from Massari's letter to Thomas Rinuccini, 8 Feb. 1649 (*Comment. Rinucc.*, iv. 82).

[71] 'Che di padroni che erano, si facevano spontaneamente servi d'un eretico': Rinuccini to Pancirolo, 14 Mar. (ns) 1649 (Aiazzi, *Nunziatura*, 360).

[72] Indeed, from rumours he had heard, he clearly believed that the treaty contained some positive aspects. Any such aspects were, he claimed somewhat defensively, a credit to his own defence of the rights of the church. Nevertheless, overall he was still deeply pessimistic that a parliamentary victory was imminent and almost inconsolable that the confederates in Kilkenny had accepted a protestant as viceroy (ibid.); see also the nuncio's analysis of the peace, 30 Mar. (ns) 1649 (ibid., 368–70).

[73] 'Acciò N.S. e tutta la congregazione abbiano piena notizia di quello che i nostri buoni Vescovi hanno fatto, non e altro in sostanza che quello che avanti la mia venuta avevano concluso': Rinuccini to Pancirolo, 13 May (ns) 1649 (ibid., 380).

[74] Corish, 'Bishop Nicholas French', 93–100.

IV

Rinuccini's refusal to accept that his authority to pronounce on confederate affairs had been neutralized by the confederate appeal to Rome in 1648 meant that the council were forced to adopt unanticipated strategies to weaken and resist his spiritual authority. In this they were reasonably successful. The nuncio was never able to recreate the clerical consensus which had paved the way to the overthrow of the government established by the Ormond peace in 1646. The price which the council paid for its success was the complete alienation of Rinuccini from their party. The bitterness of the nuncio's strictures against his opponents in Ireland has been noted in the past but has not been the focus of a sustained analysis.[75] Yet the manner in which his comments contradict the prevailing historiography about the progress of the counter-reformation in Ireland suggest that these deserve more attention than they have previously been shown. Moreover, the attitude which the nuncio developed during these months materially affected his behaviour in the wake of the censure and his retrospective analysis of his mission.

In the latter part of 1648 and 1649 Rinuccini commented several times on the irreligious actions and attitudes of his opponents, a failing which he consistently associated with the Old English tradition in Ireland. In November 1648 the nuncio denounced the council and the assembly which they had convened as having 'without respect for the Apostolic See' made 'propositions little short of heretical'. Actions like theirs, he believed 'had never occurred to such a degree in the time of any king who was not a complete heretic'.[76] In this document Rinuccini also drew a distinction between the catholicism of the different communities in Ireland. He declared:

Perhaps it was well that at this time the perverse inclinations of the factionaries and of the Old English are uncovered, so that the Apostolic See may consider for the future if aid given to them would not always lead to a strengthening of heresy and the overthrow of ecclesiastical jurisdiction; and on the contrary how well such aid would be employed for the other party and for the Old Irish, of whom there is no memory that anyone of them ever left the Catholic Religion, or confederated with heretics.[77]

---

[75] The most detailed consideration has been in Aidan Clarke's 'Colonial Identity in Early Seventeenth-century Ireland' in T. W. Moody (ed.), *Nationality and the Pursuit of National Independence* (Belfast, 1978), 68–70; see also Corish, 'The Nuncio and the Supreme Council', 233–4.

[76] 'Senza rispetto della Sede Apostolica', 'proposizioni poco meno che eretiche', 'Cose forse non venute mai a questo segno in tempo di alcun Re, se non eretico affato': Instruzioni al P.D. Guiseppe Arcamoni, 11 Nov. 1648 (Aiazzi, *Nunziatura*, 349); see also his comments in a letter to the nuncio of France, 2 July 1648 (ibid., 322); and his description of one of his principal episcopal opponents, Thomas Dease: Rinuccini to Pancirolo, 4 July 1648 (ibid., 323).

[77] 'E forse è stato bene che si scopra in questo tempo perversa la inclinazione dei fazionari ed Anglo-Iberni del Regno, acciò la Sede Apostolica consideri per l'avenire che i suoi aiuti dati a costoro servirebbon sempre per augumento dell'eresia, e per mettere in terra la giurisdizione ecclesiastica; e

He went on to suggest: 'It could have been therefore by God's will that persons catholic only in name, and irreverent towards the church, should feel [at] this time the thunderbolt of the principal see, and draw upon themselves that anger which customarily touches its despisers.'[78] In other letters the nuncio found a certain sour satisfaction in reflecting that his mission had at least exposed the true nature of those Irish who had 'finagled until then the name of good catholics'.[79] He declared his hope that:

I will have done something to uncover the propensities of these anglicised factionaries who dominate, so that in future people there [in Rome] may not be so easily disposed to praise their purity and honesty to the pope and the court, because in effect they have neither reverence nor regard for the Roman church, and they profess almost the same ideas as Henry VIII and Queen Elizabeth.[80]

On his return to Italy the nuncio elaborated on the distinction between Old Irish and Old English, defining the communities according to criteria not dissimilar to those used by contemporary historians. The Old English (antichi Inglesi) he described as:

blood introduced into Ireland in the time of Henry II, fifth king after William the Norman who conquered England, and thus called to differentiate them from the new English, who then arrived with the heresy . . . they are also called new Irish to distinguish them from the old [Irish] and they maintain continual commerce with the English, not only in matrimonial ties but in every other negotiation . . . enriched with the fruits of the monasteries, and as much inclined as constrained towards the king, they neither want nor desire anything other than royal greatness, they do not respect other laws than those of the kingdom, completely English in their affections, and through continual familiarities with the heretics, [are] less jealous [than the Old Irish] of the difference of religion . . .[81]

per il contrario quanto bene saranno impiegati per l'altra parte, e per gli Ibernesi vecchi, dei quali non ci è memoria che mai alcuno abbia lasciato la Religione Cattolica, o si sia confederato con gli Eretici': (ibid.).

[78] 'Può essere dunque stata permissione di Dio che persone cattoliche solo di nome, ed irreverenti alla Chiesa, sentano una volta il fulmine della prima Sede, e si tirino addosso quell'ira che suol esser compagna dei disprezzatori di esso': (ibid., 350).

[79] 'Gente che ha scroccato fino a qui il titolo di buon cattolico': Rinuccini to Pancirolo, 29 Nov. 1648 (ibid., 355).

[80] 'Avrò fatto qualche cosa a scoprir l'inclinazione de questi fazionari inglesati che dominano, acciò per l'avvenire non siano costì le persone tanto facili a celebrare la purità e candidezza loro a N S ed alla corte, poichè in effetto non hanno nè riverenza, nè conto della Chiesa Romana, e tengono quasi i medesimi concetti de Enrico VIII, e della Regina Elisabeta': Rinuccini to Pancirolo, 14 Mar. (ns) 1649 (ibid., 362).

[81] 'Sangue introdotto in Ibernia ai tempi di Enrico II quinto Re dopo Guglielmo Normando, che conquistò l'Inghilterra, e così detti a differenza dei nuovi Inglesi, che vi sono poi entrati con l'eresia . . . vengono ancora chiamati Ibernesi moderni, per differenziarli dagli antichi, e mantengono continuo commercio con gli Inglesi, tanto nei reciprochi matrimoni, quanto in ogni altra contrattazione . . . arricchiti con i frutti dei Monasteri, e obbligati però non meno che interressati col Re, non vogliono nè desiderano altro che la regia grandezza, non stimano altre leggi che quelle del Regno, tutti Inglesi d'affetto, e per le continue domestichezze con gli Eretici, meno gelosi della diversita di religione': Rinuccini's relation to the Pope (ibid., 391–2).

Rinuccini's blanket criticisms of the Old English did not prevent him from enthusiastically praising the fidelity of the inhabitants of Galway and Waterford.[82] Clearly the entire Old English community was not comprehended in the nuncio's denunciations nor, contrarily, did he enjoy the support of all individuals of Gaelic stock. This does not alter the fact, however, that the nuncio did differentiate specifically between the Old English and the Old Irish in favour of the latter.

The views which Rinuccini had formulated about the nature of Old Irish and Old English catholicism run counter to the prevailing orthodoxy in the contemporary historiographical literature. Exactly why his comments have attracted so little attention is uncertain. Possibly the strongly articulated view that the strength of Irish catholicism in the seventeenth and eighteenth centuries lay in its forced *lack* of conformity to the classical European model,[83] has inclined historians to doubt the relevance of Rinuccini's testimony. Since Rinuccini has been identified as unable to distinguish what was 'really essential'[84] for Irish catholicism and as an advocate of some of the practices which supposedly weakened post-tridentine catholicism on the continent,[85] there has been a temptation perhaps to see his strictures against the Old English as another example of the blindness of Italian orthodoxy to the real vitality of catholicism in Ireland. If such a process has been at work, then it must be noted that an important difference existed between the criticisms which Rinuccini levelled in 1646 against such matters as private mass, informal clerical dress and quotidian contact between the laity and the regular clergy,[86] and the attacks which he made in the extracts quoted above. Two different if linked points were at issue: the first concerned the institutional laxity of the Irish church, which Rinuccini criticized but about which he did not despair: the second concerned the heretical strain that the nuncio distinguished in Old English catholicism, which he regarded as a much more fundamental problem.

Another approach to the problem of Rinuccini's comments has been to suggest that he was an unreliable and biased observer because his:

pronounced ultramontane views, his determination to secure the public exercise of catholicism and his increasing preoccupation with the need for a catholic viceroy

---

[82] See for example his relation to the pope (Aiazzi, *Nunziatura*, 433).

[83] Patrick Corish has strongly endorsed John Bossy's arguments and further adapted them to the Irish situation: see Corish, *The Catholic Community in the Seventeenth and Eighteenth Centuries* (Dublin, 1981), 41–2 and id., 'Women and Religious Practice' in Margeret MacCurtain and Mary O'Dowd, *Women in Early Modern Ireland* (Dublin, 1991), 213–14; see also J. G. Simms, 'The Jacobite Parliament of 1689', in David Hayton and Gerard O'Brien (eds.), *War and Politics in Ireland, 1649–1730* (London, 1986), 80.

[84] Corish, 'Ormond, Rinuccini, and the Confederates, 1645–9', 334–5.

[85] Id., *Catholic Community*, 42; John Bossy, 'The Counter-Reformation and the People of Catholic Ireland', *Historical Studies*, 8 (1971), 169.

[86] Noted by Corish, *Catholic Community*, 41–2.

combined to make his choices fundamentally political, as he acknowledged in his first report of the state of Ireland . . . Moreover the measure by which he judged groups and individuals was the degree to which they shared his priorities, so that even estimates of spiritual worth rested upon political criteria.[87]

This position, which owes a good deal to a particular interpretation of the nuncio's first major report from Ireland in 1646, fails fully to evaluate the basis on which Rinuccini formed his judgements and is somewhat unjust in ascribing to him such narrow perceptions of spiritual worth. On his return to Rome, for instance, despite his anger at the bishop of Ferns and Nicholas Plunkett, who had materially assisted in the formulation of the second Ormond peace, Rinuccini was quite prepared to describe both Plunkett and the bishop as good catholics to the pope.[88] Other evidence also suggests very strongly that Rinuccini did *not* base his evaluations of spiritual worth on political criteria and that his criticisms in the last year of his nunciature were rooted in something deeper than mere pique at encountering an analysis of the situation in Ireland which was different from his own. In this regard, the timing of Rinuccini's criticisms is of importance.

The nuncio began his first strong denunciations of what he saw as proto-heresy in Ireland only in the latter half of 1648. Almost from the moment of his arrival in Ireland he had disagreed profoundly with the political pro-gramme of many members of the association. Nevertheless, Rinuccini did not ascribe such disagreements to his opponents' inclination towards heresy. From the nuncio's perspective, the council and their supporters moved towards religious heterodoxy after his rejection of their appeal against his censure in June 1648. It was at this point, he declared: 'a beginning was given to all those excesses which then followed, approaching to the introduction of heresy, or at least an apostasy from the Apostolic See, as Henry VIII had already begun.'[89] What therefore was the precise nature of these excesses?

On his return to Rome, the nuncio explained that he had refused to lift his excommunication from the principal authors of the truce and the second Ormond peace until they had made 'a repudiation of all the acts against the Holy See and ecclesiastical immunity'.[90] It was evidently their sins in this regard which were responsible for his most severe criticisms. From the nun-cio's perspective, the conclusion of the truce was thus actually the least of

---

[87] Clarke, 'Colonial Identity', 70.

[88] 'Buoni cattolici': Rinuccini's relation to the Pope (Aiazzi, *Nunziatura*, 410).

[89] 'Si diede principio a tutte quelle stravaganze che son poi seguite, fino all'avvicinarsi ad intro-durre l'eresia, o almeno una apostasia delle Sede Apostolica, come già cominciò Enrico VIII': Rinuccini's compendium of the truce, 11 Nov. 1648 (ibid., 352).

[90] 'La condannazione di tutti gli atti contro la Santa Sede, e l'immunità Ecclesiastica': Rinuccini's relation to the Pope (ibid., 432); see also the stress which the nuncio laid on his opponents' crimes against ecclesiastical immunity in the instructions to Arcamoni, 24 Jan. 1649 (*Comment. Rinucc.*, iii. 686).

their offences,[91] something which paled into insignificance when compared with other horrors.[92] In his report to the pope, the nuncio expanded on the offences of his opponents *following* his censure of the truce:

Then, as if released from every restraint, the Ormondites relaxed the bridle totally to their proclivities . . . Ecclesiastical jurisdiction collapsed immediately. Decrees were issued that without any distinction all those who defended the censure were to be imprisoned and this was executed against many people . . . Most iniquitous oaths were proposed according to which all were forced to oblige themselves to pay no attention to the censure passed, nor to any other censure whatsoever in future. And to draw the bishops to their side, it was threatened in an edict that they would be deprived of their sees, to which the council declared that it would designate suitable candidates . . . Then when the councillors saw themselves as without hope of my return [to Kilkenny], they immediately placed in custody the Lord Dean [Massari] who had remained in Kilkenny and a little after they deprived him of all the documents which I had left with him . . . And in the end, having warned me by letters at the beginning of the new Assembly to leave the kingdom as a rebel against the crown of England, they wrote to Galway that obedience should be denied to me and that I should be treated as unworthy of the necessaries of life . . .[93]

This passage offers a revealing insight into the nuncio's anger against his opponents. In this regard the introductory metaphor is itself of interest. It recalls several images in *Della Dignita* concerning the corruptions of the human will. Rinuccini evidently believed his opponents had actively embraced evil, rather than merely making misjudgements in the manner of 'good catholics' like Plunkett and Ferns. He reported to Rome his conviction that all opposition to the censure was 'completely the work of the devil'[94] and that Hell was exerting all its forces against him.[95] It was perfectly in character that Rinuccini should believe that the devil would rejoice at the collapse of 'ecclesiastical jurisdiction'. The nuncio's vision of social and spiritual order was founded on the idea of watchful and effective clerical authority, which ideally would always remain in harmony with temporal

---

[91] Rinuccini to Pancirolo, 14 Mar. 1649 (Aiazzi, *Nunziatura*, 365).

[92] Instructions to Arcamoni, 21 July (ns) 1649 (ibid., 386–7).

[93] 'Allora, come sciolto ogni freno, lasciarono gli Ormonisti la briglia totalmente alle inclinazioni . . . La giurisdizione Ecclesiastica andò immantinente per terra. Uscirono ordini che si carcerassero senza distinzione alcuna tutti quelli che difendevano le censure, e fu eseguito contro di molti . . . Si proposero giuramenti iniquissimi, per i quali doveva ognuno obbligarsi a non fare alcun conto delle censure passate, nè di qualunque altra in futuro. E per tirare i Vescovi dalla loro parte, si minacciò in un editto de levarli le chiese, alle quali diceva il consiglio che avrebbe provveduto dei soggetti a proposito . . . Onde quando i Consiglieri si videro senza speranza del mio ritorno, ritennero subito il Signor Decano che era rimasto a Kilchennia, e poco dopo li levarannon tutte le scritture che avevo depositato in sua mano . . . E alla fine avendomi nel principio della nuova Assemblea avvisato con lettere a partirmi del regno come ribelle della corona d'Inghilterra, scrissero a Galvia che mi si negasse obbedienza, e che io fossi trattato come immeritevole delle comodità necessarie alla vita.': Rinuccini's relation to the pope (ibid., 426).

[94] 'Tutta opera del demonio': Rinuccini's report of the truce, Aug. 1648 (ibid., 331).

[95] 'L'inferno s'aiuta con tutte le sue forze': Rinuccini to Pancirolo, 13 June 1648 (ibid., 315).

government but which would reluctantly take precedence in the event of a clash. It is in this light that Rinuccini's strictures in this extract and elsewhere against the abuse of ecclesiastical immunity are best understood. His anger at those who violated clerical immunity, by threatening imprisonment 'without any distinction' of persons, for instance, was not merely an example of clerical particularism, although this aspect was arguably present. His position in this respect was intimately linked to his sincere belief that the clergy needed certain powers to discharge effectively the most important of all human activities.

Moreover it is clear that the nuncio was absolutely correct in his accusations that his opponents had violated clerical immunity on numerous occasions in the course of the summer of 1648. The arrest of such an important figure as the provincial of the Irish Franciscans, Thomas MacKiernan, in August of that year, provoked a particularly angry exchange between Rinuccini and Clanricard on the clergy's right to immunity.[96] In Kilkenny, other members of MacKiernan's order, which supported the nuncio with particular zeal, were forcibly prevented by soldiers from seeking alms in the city and were thus brought into real danger of starvation.[97] From Rinuccini's point of view, however, the persecutions of the bishops, whom he saw as the keystone of spiritual order, were even worse than the sufferings of the regular clergy. The nuncio received letters from Waterford in which the bishop, Patrick Comerford, openly admitted to being afraid for his life.[98] Comerford's colleague in Leighlin, Edward O'Dempsey, was threatened with the penalties of praemunire if he did not attend the General Assembly in September.[99] In October that assembly issued a decree that all clergy should take an oath rejecting Rinuccini's excommunications and that any prelates who refused this oath were to be imprisoned.[100] The nuncio's reaction to these decisions can be seen in the extract from his relation to the pope quoted above, from which it is clear that the nuncio also believed that threats had been made to deprive bishops of their sees and introduce substitutes, something which not only threatened their immunity but also invaded papal jurisdiction. Perhaps the most important attack against episcopal dignity, none the less, was the decision to use soldiers to prevent the assembly of a national

[96] See Rinuccini to Clanricard, 2 Aug. 1648 and Clanricard's response of 8 Aug. (*Comment. Rinucc.*, iii. 471–3).
[97] See the Franciscan petition to the Supreme Council (ibid., 638).
[98] See Comerford to Rinuccini, 17 July 1648 (ibid., 432–3); see also ibid., 320–2 concerning other attacks on Comerford's immunity.
[99] See Richard Blake to Dempsey, 14 Sept. 1648 (ibid., 604; Dempsey had in any case already been pillaged of his goods by Preston's troops. (Dempsey was of course a Dominican and Comerford an Augustinian but it was as bishops rather than as members of their orders that they clashed with the council in these instances.)
[100] Decree of General Assembly, 19 Oct. 1648 (ibid., 606–8).

synod of the catholic clergy in Galway in August,[101] and it is therefore useful to look at this incident in slightly greater detail.

Within days of issuing the general censure against the truce Rinuccini became aware of widespread disapproval of his decision within the ranks of the Irish clergy which militated against the effectiveness of his action.[102] His decision to convoke a national synod at Galway to discuss the issue was almost certainly influenced by a conviction that the synod would back his own position on the truce and strengthen his authority to deal with rebellious clergy on his own terms. Nevertheless, it is unlikely that the nuncio saw the synod merely as a convenient mode of rubber-stamping his decision to censure the truce. He was clearly distressed as well as angered by division within the clergy's ranks. Moreover, a number of Irish bishops, not all of them hardline supporters of the censure, urged the nuncio to convoke the synod.[103] The previous year, also, a congregation of clergy in Clonmell had supported the policy of the Supreme Council against the nuncio's opposition.

Although Galway was a relatively neutral venue for the synod, the council had no intention of allowing it to meet there. They informed the nuncio that a General Assembly had already been convoked for 4 September in Kilkenny. Since that assembly was the 'Supreme Power of the confederates', they argued that its members should be consulted about the date and venue of the synod.[104] This itself was enough to raise the nuncio's hackles.[105] He angrily informed them that the convocation of a synod of the Roman catholic clergy had nothing to do with any assembly but was a matter 'wholly depending upon his Holiness's pleasure'.[106]

The council forbade the bishops to attend the synod and requested the marquis of Clanricard to deploy cavalry to prevent any clergy making their

[101] This seems to have been the abuse which Rinuccini himself resented most: Rinuccini to Tuam, 16 Aug. 1648 (*Comment. Rinucc.*, iii., 479–80).

[102] See for instance the letter from the bishops of Ossory, Dublin, Dromore, Meath, and Ardagh to Rinuccini, 3 June 1648 (ibid., 284–5) and Rinuccini's angry response, 6 June (ibid., 285–6).

[103] Some, most notably the archbishop of Cashel, who later endorsed the second Ormond peace in Jan. 1649, were evidently motivated chiefly by the desire to promote clerical unity and reconciliation on all sides: see the letter from the archbishop of Cashel and the bishop of Emly to Rinuccini, 2 July 1648 (ibid., 429–30).

[104] See Bellings's narrative, (Gilbert, *Irish Confederation*, vii. 91–2); see also the Latin text of the council's letter of 24 July 1648 to Rinuccini (*Comment. Rinucc.*, iii. 436–7).

[105] It was very close to a position which a national synod of the Irish church had already condemned out of hand in 1646, namely that the clergy did not possess a separate authority outside the General Assembly but merely *shared* in that assembly's authority, in which of course they sat by right as lords spiritual. In 1646 the clergy had dismissed this as a reformulation of Henry VIII's heretical theory of the supremacy of parliamentary jurisdiction: see the clergy's response to Richard Bellings, 22 Aug. 1646 (*Comment. Rinucc.*, ii. 336).

[106] See Bellings's narrative (Gilbert, *Irish Confederation*, vii. 92); precisely the same issue had of course raised the temperature between Rome and Philip II's government in Spain during the sixteenth century: see Henry Kamen, *The Phoenix and the Flame: Catalonia and the Counter-reformation* (London, 1993), 56–63.

way to Galway: prelates were to be treated courteously but were not to be allowed to pass.[107] Rinuccini bitterly recorded the result of this request: 'but they placed in all the roads different troops of cavalry, who violently turning back the bishops, and every other ecclesiastical person, added this barbarous example to the other sacrilegious actions.'[108]

The sacrilege which the nuncio identified in this action arguably consisted not only in the physical coercion of clergy but also in the justifications which the council advanced to defend their actions against the synod. Indeed, it was apparently their willingness to justify their actions by reference to English legal tradition which inclined the nuncio to view them as apostates as well as sinners. Just as early modern authority reacted more harshly to organized rebellion than to mere riot, so in the intellectual sphere the principled legitimization of resistance evoked more bitterness than simple dereliction of duty: in religious terms heresy was more heinous than ignorance.

The sight of a catholic government proscribing a catholic synod, in a manner not dissimilar to that of protestant governments in the pre-confederate era, not only confirmed the nuncio's worst suspicions about the irreligiousness of his opponents but also troubled the consciences of many Irish catholics, even of those who supported the truce. The council had urgent tactical reasons for forbidding the synod[109] but the decision also indicated their essential disinterest in the clergy's viewpoint, all protestations to the contrary notwithstanding. Certainly the nuncio was convinced of his opponents' disregard for any opinions which differed from their own and this formed the background to his denunciations. Nor was Rinuccini's belief in the essential intransigence of those who opposed him without grounds. From the outset, only the slenderest of majorities (7 of 12) on the original council was in favour of the truce. Its supporters, nevertheless, pushed forward determinedly with an issue which they realized was extremely divisive.[110] Within a month Roebuck Lynch of Galway seems to have dissociated himself from the actions of the other six. A religiously zealous man,[111] his breaking point seems to have been the decision to sequester the papers which Rinuccini had left in Massari's possession in Kilkenny. This was of course one of the incidents which Rinuccini mentioned specifically in the extract of his relation quoted above. It was an offence not only against ecclesiastical

---

[107] Supreme Council to Clanricard, 25 July 1648 (Comment. Rinucc., iii. 438–9).

[108] '[M]essero però a tutte le strade diverse truppe di cavalli, i quali violentamente respingendo addietro i Vescovi, e ogni altra persona ecclesiastica, aggiunsero questo barbaro esempio all'altre sacrileghe azioni': Rinuccini's relation to the pope (Aiazzi, Nunziatura, 429).

[109] And were probably also under pressure from Inchiquin who believed them to be criminally lax in their toleration of clergy of the nuncio's party: see Inchiquin to Ormond, 10 Aug. 1648 (Bodl. Carte MS 22, fo. 166ʳ).

[110] Comment. Rinucc., iii. 578–9.

[111] See his letters to his wife in K. W. Nicholls (ed.), 'The Lynch Blosse Papers', Analecta Hibernica, 29 (1980), 117–22.

immunity but also directed against a cleric employed in papal service.[112] The oath of which Rinuccini complained so bitterly in the same passage seems to have been one circulated by the council in the immediate aftermath of the censure.[113] The nuncio interpreted this oath in the widest sense as implying that, even if the pope supported his decision against the truce, the council would still assert its right to disagree.[114]

The potential for friction among catholics concerning the extent of papal authority and jurisdiction in Ireland had existed long before Rinuccini's arrival. During the sixteenth century some catholics had been prepared to challenge the papal bull 'Regnans in Excelcis' which had excommunicated Elizabeth I. In the course of the 1630s a number of ecclesiastical figures had maintained that other pontifical edicts were not valid in Ireland, and in particular that the papal bull 'In Coena Domini', which protected the immunities of the clergy,[115] was inapplicable in the island and that catholic clerics could be called before the secular courts to answer civil or criminal charges. This whole issue was sharpened, however, by the emergence of a catholic government in the 1640s.

In 1644, prior to the nuncio's arrival, a congregation of Irish clergy had been willing in certain circumstances to allow the confederate executive to take clerics into custody in cases of *lèse-majesté*, although they insisted that a trial could only be held in the presence of the legitimately constituted ecclesiastical superior of the accused.[116] Three years later Rinuccini found himself involved in a debate over the rights of nomination to Irish dioceses. Originally it had been some of his episcopal colleagues who had argued with him that it was a royal prerogative to nominate bishops to sees but that while the king was a protestant this should be vested in the Supreme Council and

[112] And there were of course other slights to the Holy See identified by the nuncio in the same passage, such as the threats to depose bishops from their sees and appoint alternatives, the framing of oaths against the censure and the order to the nuncio to leave the kingdom as a rebel against the English crown.

[113] This oath apparently enjoined everyone subject to the council's jurisdiction to deny obedience both to Rinuccini and to his excommunications and to observe the truce 'notwithstanding any excommunication whatsoever promulgated or to be promulgated' (nonostante qualsivoglia scomunica fatta, o da farsi): Compendium of wrongs suffered by the nuncio (Aiazzi, *Nunziatura*, 319); see also Rinuccini's report of the truce (ibid., 332) where he denounced 'un giuramento sacrilego, che ciascuno sia obbligato di accetar la tregua senza timore nemmeno delle scomuniche future' (a sacrilegious oath, that everyone should be obliged to accept the truce without any respect for future excommunications).

[114] In Nov. Rinuccini insisted that his opponents had declared that they would continue to reject the censure even if it was confirmed by the pope (Compendium of the Truce, 11 Nov. 1648 (ibid., 352–3).

[115] In Ireland as elsewhere in Europe, the most controversial aspects of the bull were the manner in which it condemned any appeal from an ecclesiastical to a temporal tribunal and its penalty of automatic excommunication for anyone who used force against a cleric: see Samuel J. Miller, *Portugal and Rome c. 1748–1830* (Rome, 1978), p. 35, n. 6.

[116] See the decrees of the congregation held in Kilkenny, 3, 4, 5, 6, and 7 Nov. 1644 (Bodl. Carte MS 97, fo. 52^r).

the metropolitans.[117] Rinuccini naturally disagreed, believing that the nomination of bishops should be a free choice of the pope.[118] To his surprise, the bishops in question informed him that in this matter 'their doctrines differed from those of Rome',[119] a position which was to offend his superiors even more than the nuncio himself.[120] Rinuccini had even less patience with the secular lawyers who then took this point up with him. They informed him that in English law a prerogative was not lost by heresy but passed instead to those who administered the royal authority during the incompetency of the monarch. They also assured him that in English law adequate lay judges were appointed to decide such matters as the validity and translation of patronage. The nuncio was clearly scandalized at being forced to listen to what he termed 'those ascerbic principles which are nourished in temporal courts'.[121] The idea of English jurisprudence adjudicating on papal powers was of course anathema to him but he was anxious not to provoke conflict. The issue, however, evaded the nuncio's attempts to sidestep it and came back to prominence in 1648 when the council found itself effectively at war with the pope's nuncio and declared illegitimate those bishops whom they had not nominated to their sees.[122]

The nuncio saw this declaration as one aspect of a veritable offensive against papal rights and prerogatives. As part of his opponents' denial of his censure, he reported to Rome their argument that: 'as an external power in the kingdom, I had no jurisdiction to excommunicate and this by virtue of I do not know what English laws';[123] and further that: 'the bishops were implicated in the crime of rebellion for having obeyed the nuncio whom they say

---

[117] One can note that this issue surfaced again in the patriot parliament of 1689 which recognized only those catholic bishops nominated as such by the king: see Simms, 'Jacobite Parliament', 77.

[118] If the king of England had ever enjoyed the power of nomination, it was, he believed, as a privilege from the pope rather than by inherent right. Having relapsed into heresy, the king's privilege had naturally been forfeited. Rinuccini was certainly aware of the somewhat similar position in Portugal where the pope had decided to nominate to Portuguese dioceses *motu proprio*: see Pamfili to Rinuccini, 29 May (ns) 1645, quoted in Ludvig Von Pastor (trans. Ernest Graf), *History of the Popes from the Close of the Middle Ages*, (London, 1938–40), xxx. 74–5 n. 5.

[119] 'Replicavano le lor dottrine eser differenti da quelle di Roma': Rinuccini to Pamfili, 1 Mar. 1647 (Aiazzi, *Nunziatura*, 201).

[120] Pancirolo to Rinuccini, 20 May (ns) 1647 (BAV Nunziatura di Inghilterra 8, fo. 45ʳ).

[121] 'Quelle massime acerbe, che si nutriscono nelle corti temporali': (Aiazzi, *Nunziatura*, 201).

[122] See Rinuccini's instructions to Arcamoni, 11 Nov. 1648 (ibid., 349).

[123] 'Che io non avevo giurisdizione alcuna di scomunicare, comè potestà esterna di questo Regno, e ciò in vigore di non so che legge Anglicane': Statement of the Reasons which induced the nuncio to excommunicate 15 June 1648 (ibid., 318); he reported also that 'qualcun dice, che Io per le legge Anglicane non ho autorità di esercitar giurisdizione' (some say that by English law I do not have authority to exercise jurisdiction): Rinuccini to Pancirolo, 13 June 1648 (ibid., 315); see also his statement that 'avevano cominciato a spargere, che i Delegati del Papa, come potestà esterna, non hanno giurisdizione di censurare e questo in virtù di alcune legge anglicane' (they had begun to spread about that the delegates of the Pope, as an external power, do not have the jurisdiction to censure and this by virtue of certain English laws): Rinuccini's report of the truce (ibid., 332).

is an alien power.'[124] In October, as the General Assembly deliberated, Rinuccini was informed that: 'the assembly has declared me a rebel against the crown of England and that it wishes to drive me from the kingdom.'[125] In their 'more execrable excesses'[126] the nuncio found that the secular members of the assembly were prepared to take advantage of the bishops' absence from the deliberations to introduce a decree that 'the ministers of the pope would not be received in future' into the kingdom of Ireland.[127] The return of the bishops the following day led to the revocation of this act but the mere fact that catholics could have contemplated such an idea helped confirm the nuncio's convictions about his opponents' irreverence.

As a papal minister, Rinuccini's reactions to opinions of this nature was entirely comprehensible. It is difficult to believe that many of his colleagues in any other nunciature would have questioned his belief that the propositions of the peace party verged on the heretical. It is of course vital to bear in mind that the chief confederate denials of papal jurisdiction, together with the offences against ecclesiastical immunity, took place during a time of crisis and civil war.[128] The whole issue then became even more urgent as the assembly of 1648 wrestled with a problem which had consistently defeated the association's best efforts at resolution over the previous five years, namely how could peace be made with the king without betraying the catholic religion. Moreover, attacks on both clerical immunity and papal authority were hardly unprecedented in post-tridentine Europe. Urban VIII's decision to establish a special congregation to oversee the implementation of papal bulls with regard to ecclesiastical jurisdiction reflected not only the determination of the papacy to defend its prerogatives but also the degree to which these were under attack.[129] The medieval erastian tradition was continued and developed in both catholic and protestant Europe during the early modern period.[130] Even in the Italian peninsula, catholic governments almost routinely violated the fiscal and legal immunities of the church and invaded papal prerogatives. Tuscany witnessed bitter conflict between the grand-ducal court and the papal nuncio during the 1630s; in 1640 Lucca was interdicted for interference with ecclesiastical jurisdiction and similar action was mooted against both Savoy and Naples in the pontificate of Urban

---

[124] 'I Vescovi incorsi in delitto di rebellione per aver obbidito al Nuncio, il quale dicono essere potestà forestiera': Instructions to Arcamoni, 11 Nov. 1648 (Aiazzi, *Nunziatura*, 349).

[125] 'L'Assemblea mi ha dichiarato rebelle della corana d'Inghilterra e che voglia cacciarmi dal Regno': Rinuccini to Pancirolo, 10 Oct. 1648 (ibid., 340).

[126] 'Nei più esecrabili eccessi'; Rinuccini to Pancirolo, 14 Mar. (ns) 1649 (ibid., 361).

[127] 'Che non si recevessero più i Ministri del Papa': (ibid.).

[128] One can note for instance that in Limerick, where the council could rely on at least the tacit support of the bishop, greater care seems to have been taken not to offend against ecclesiastical immunity: see *Comment. Rinucc.*, iii. 456.

[129] Pastor, *History of the Popes*, xxix. 172.   [130] Wright, *Counter-Reformation*, 269–70.

VIII.[131] Perhaps the most telling example of the manner in which no catholic state could afford to allow the church the degree of autonomy which it wished to arrogate to itself occurred in the pope's own domain. In the immediate aftermath of the council of Trent Cardinal Paleotti found his attempts at the institution of tridentine reforms in Bologna undermined by the opposition of none other than the papal governor. The reforming prelate was consistently rebuffed at Rome in his efforts to obtain papal support for his episcopal activities.[132]

The example of continental Europe was one which the nuncio's confederate opponents were quick to advance to justify their actions. This appeal to contemporary catholic practice was supplemented by reference to English precedent from before the Henrician schism.[133] Just as it was natural for Rinuccini as a papal minister to maintain the most rigorous interpretation of 'In Coena Domini' and the immunities of the clergy, so it was logical for his opponents to look to justify their actions by reference to the activities of other catholic temporal authorities. Neither continental nor pre-reformation English precedent was lacking for attacks on papal jurisdiction. The confederates took their most extreme positions in this regard in 1648 but the issue had been raised previously with regard to the ecclesiastical tribunal which Rinuccini had instituted in Ireland,[134] creating tensions reminiscent of the difficulties between Rome and the governments of the Iberian peninsula.[135]

[131] See the account of the nunciature of G. Fr. Passionei in Toscana (BAV, Barberini Latini MS 5678, fos. 47–8, 151–3); Pastor, History of the Popes, xxix. 171–5, 188; Massimo Bray, 'L'arcivescovo, il viceré, il fedelissimo popolo', Nuova Rivista Storica, 74 (1990), 313–15.

[132] Prodi, Il sovrano pontefice: un corpo e due anime. La monarchía papale nella prima età moderna (Bologna, 1982), 251–93.

[133] Such references were also linked to rather unconvincing protestations of complete canonical and theological orthodoxy, for example: 'nostrum edictum in omnibus et singulis praedictis capitibus quadret ad Sacrorum Canonum normam, ad magnorum Theologorum et Canonistarum sententiam, et ad nationum summopere Catholicarum, interque alias ad Angliae praxim ante schisma citra Cleri renitentiam': The declaration of twelve prominent supporters of the truce, 3 June 1648 (Comment. Rinucc., iii. 281).

[134] As the nuncio noted, there had been bitter resentment on the part of confederate lawyers to the idea of the independent jurisdiction of a papal tribunal in Ireland during the 1640s. One can surmise with reasonable confidence that those who had opposed him on this issue in 1645–6 were also involved in the attacks on his jurisdiction in Ireland in 1648: see the instructions to Arcamoni, 11 Nov. 1648 (Aiazzi, Nunziatura, 350).

[135] In 1639, to the fury of the pope, recourse to the nuncio's tribunal in Spain was made a punishable offence. Increasingly in the late sixteenth and seventeenth centuries, the Council of State in Spanish Flanders insisted that papal decrees could not be promulgated in the Netherlands. From 1532 in Portugal, with the creation of the Mesa da Consciência e Ordens, steady inroads were made against the authority of all ecclesiastical tribunals, a process which culminated in the mid-eighteenth century with John V's claim that all decrees and bulls issued from Rome were subject to the king's approval: see Pastor, History of the Popes, xxix. 197–8; James D. Tracy, 'With and Without the Counter-Reformation: The Catholic Church in the Spanish Netherlands and the Dutch Republic, 1580–1650', Catholic Historical Review, 71 (1985), 549; Miller, Portugal and Rome, 34–5.

In 1648 the nuncio's opponents were quite prepared to quote Iberian precedent to justify their actions.[136] He reported to Rome of their claim that Cardinal Pallotto had been forced to flee from Portugal and that the cardinal's auditor had been imprisoned. The nuncio seems to have been somewhat puzzled by this contention although he admitted his ignorance about the case.[137] It seems likely, however, that his opponents had in mind the former papal collector (the Portuguese equivalent to a nuncio) GianBattista Palotta who had encountered what he considered to be virtually schismatic conditions in Portugal during his term of office there (1624–7).[138]

It is thus possible to view the nuncio's opponents, as they seem to have seen themselves, within a wider European catholic tradition, reflecting a need to adapt their catholicism to the political exigencies of the conditions in which they lived, and in particular insisting on a delineation between temporal and spiritual authority.[139] In that context Rinuccini can be seen as the Irish parallel of a variety of other contemporary papal ministers in Spain, Portugal, France, the Spanish Netherlands, Austria, and Bavaria, vainly attempting to maintain a strict definition of papal prerogatives.

Yet although elements of the 1648 crisis are certainly amenable to such an analysis, the circumstances which Rinuccini encountered in Ireland were also unique, because the confederates did not represent an independent catholic government but an association dedicated to achieving peace, through its own dissolution, with a protestant king. As a result, the conflict with the nuncio was only secondarily jurisdictional. On the continent catholic erastianism and papal claims were ultimately capable of an uneasy co-existence. The Italian incidents previously mentioned were ultimately solved or at least elided by compromise. Even in France the monarchy's enjoyment of very wide powers over the French church continued to be managed through the medium of the concordat of 1516. In the first half of the seventeenth century, although anxious to conciliate the crown, the papacy

[136] There was a definite logic to this as some of the wide range of powers which had been conceded to France in the concordat of 1516 were not duplicated in Iberia. Consequently, the Iberian monarchies could be forced into justifying their actions by more overt references to royal prerogatives: see Christian Hermann, *L'Eglise d'Espagne sous le patronage royal (1476–1834)* (Madrid, 1988), 72–87; in matters of presentation to sees and monastries, however, the power of the Spanish kings did in fact outstrip those of France: see Kamen, *Phoenix and the Flame*, 47.

[137] See Rinuccini to Pancirolo, 29 Nov. 1648 (Aiazzi, *Nunziatura*, 354): it seems eminently possible that the nuncio wrongly assumed that the name Pallotto referred either to the influential Roman cardinal (who was actually the protector of his own diocese of Fermo during Rinuccini's absence in Ireland), or to the Cardinal Pallotto who had been papal nuncio in Vienna during the 1630s.

[138] Or possibly they in turn confused Palotta with one of his successors, Alessandro Castracani, who in 1639 was ordered by the Habsburg authorities to leave Portugal and was then imprisoned for levying an interdict on Lisbon. He was eventually expelled across the frontier into Spain. In 1646 the sub-collector Girolamo Battaglia was also expelled from Portugal, this time on instructions from the Braganza monarchy as part of John IV's continuing efforts to win the right of nomination to Portuguese bishoprics. See Pastor, *History of the Popes*, xxx. 74–7.

[139] See the charges against the nuncio (Bodl. Carte MS 64, fos. 131^{r-v}, 133^r).

contrived not to renounce officially further aspects of its jurisdiction and was not forced to do so.[140] In Spain (where the leadership of the Inquisition was at the beginning of the seventeenth century wrested away from the monarchy by the papacy[141]), and indeed in seventeenth-century Portugal (where the Inquisition explicitly declared its support for the supremacy of papal juris- diction in matters ecclesiastical[142]), despite the very substantial influence which the crown exerted over the church and its extensive rights of patron- age, a complete denial of papal rights and jurisdiction was similarly avoided, even in the tense days of Urban VIII's pontificate. The nuncio's tribunal in Madrid, operating with delegated papal authority, survived the great onslaught of the late 1630s and continued to function throughout the seven- teenth century, although in a more limited fashion after 1640. Also, in early modern Spain, the crown refrained from attempting to legitimize its taxation of the church by an appeal to royal authority alone. The nuncio in Spain, to whom practically all papal prerogatives were delegated, continued to enjoy wide and very lucrative powers of jurisdiction and appointment throughout the seventeenth century.[143]

Such a mode of compromise was arguably the most important feature which distinguished catholic erastianism from its protestant counterpart in Europe.[144] Papal willingness to recognize a very large measure of temporal influence over *de facto* national churches was the key to the maintenance of a certain degree of unity of doctrine and practice in a remnant of the medieval Latin church. If the Thirty Years War demonstrated the deep frac- tures and conflicts of political interest within catholic Europe, it did not render obsolete the idea of a religious tradition not insignificantly common

---

[140] The *modus vivendi* which emerged was in many ways symbolized by the commission of 1622 for the reform of the regular orders. In that year La Rochefoucauld was chosen for the task as the twin delegate of both king and pope and enjoyed not only a papal commission but letters patent to the same end from the king. Moreover, it seems likely that the papacy accepted La Rochefoucauld as the commissioner because he was both persona grata with the king and noted for his ultramon- tane views. See J. A. Bergin, 'The Crown, the Papacy and the Reform of the Old Orders in Early Seventeenth Century France', *Journal of Ecclesiastical History*, 33 (1982), 234–55; and id., *Cardinal de la Rochefoucauld: Leadership and Reform in the French Church* (London, 1987), 136–60; a pos- sible model for this co-operation was the Spain of Philip II: there visitation of the orders was con- ducted by royal commissioners but after consultation with the nuncio: see Kamen, *Phoenix and the Flame*, 68

[141] E. William Monter, 'The New Social History and the Spanish Inquisition', *Journal of Social History*, 17 (1983–4), 706–8.

[142] Pastor, *History of the Popes*, xxx. 77–8.

[143] In 1632 and more successfully in 1640 the crown and its advisors did attempt to limit Roman power in the Spanish church but they eventually did so, not by denying papal authority, but by accepting the nuncio's gracious engagement not to invoke certain papal prerogatives. These pre- rogatives were not definitively renounced and continued to be seen in Rome as inalienable: see Hermann, *L'Eglise d'Espagne* , 68–93. Indeed, into the eighteenth century Spanish bishops could only operate in papally exempt areas of the peninsula under a direct licence from Rome: see Kamen, *Phoenix and the Flame*, 105.

[144] The common tendency towards temporal control of the church in both catholic and protes- tant Europe has been discussed in Wright, *Counter-Reformation*; see especially 264–74.

to the catholic states of the continent. Over the course of more than a century successive popes showed themselves willing to make extensive jurisdictional compromises to conserve princes in communion with Rome,[145] but by doing so they were able to enlist the support of the princes for appreciable portions of the tridentine programme of which the papacy had made itself the champion in the sixteenth and seventeenth centuries. Crucial to this process of 'confessionalization', from a papal perspective, was the fact that the governments to which it ceded much of its jurisdiction were overtly catholic.[146] As the papal state was increasingly integrated into the temporal politics of the early modern state system, catholic states, for their part, increasingly 'sacralized' taking on together with power and ideology many of the actual functions which had previously been within the ecclesiastical domain.[147] Catholicism thus came to constitute a vital aspect of national political identity in Spain, Portugal, Austria, Italy, and France. These absolutist states were consciously intolerant in religious matters and indeed saw such intolerance as an important source of political strength,[148] in the same manner as the Roman church saw it as a source of religious security. The jurisdictional disputes which occurred between successive popes and catholic princes cannot be divorced from the awareness which existed on both sides of a shared agenda of religious reform and a shared *obstacle* in the form of religious dissent. This awareness of a common purpose, naturally, did not exist between protestant states and the papacy. And by 1648 it did not exist between Rinuccini and the confederate Supreme Council.

Rinuccini's personal formation had been within an environment which stressed, and was to a large degree predicated upon, a belief in the mutual

---

[145] See Prodi, *Il sovrano pontefice*, 318–19; see also the letter of Julius III to Francis II of France, 13 Apr. 1552, which he quotes to illustrate the extent to which the papacy was eager to offer inducements to the French king to remain in communion (ibid., 317); as was noted previously, during the 1630s the Roman curia also attempted to convince Charles I of England that only within the catholic faith would he find truly effective ideological support for monarchical government, see Gordon Albion, *Charles I and the Court of Rome* (London, 1935), 191; in the 1570s the curia also attempted to convince John III of Sweden of the solid political benefits which he would receive from embracing the catholic faith: see Oskar Garstein, *Rome and the Counter-Reformation in Scandinavia* (Oxford, 1963), 68–9; see also the discussion of the reasons why the Spanish crown was so eager to seek a resolution of its quarrels with Rome through compromise rather than rupture in Hermann, *L'Eglise d'Espagne*, 86–8.

[146] See Wolfgang Reinhard, 'Reformation, Counter-Reformation and the Early Modern State: A Reassessment', *Catholic Historical Review*, 75 (1989), 383–404; Robert Bireley, 'Early Modern Germany' in John O'Malley (ed.), *Catholicism in Early Modern Europe: A Guide to Research* (Ann Arbor, Mich., 1988), 12–13; Norman Ravitch, *The Catholic Church and the French Nation, 1589–1989* (London, 1990), 29.

[147] Prodi, *Il sovrano pontefice*, 306; Reinhard, 'Reformation, Counter-Reformation', 400; Christina Larner, *Witchcraft and Religion: The Politics of Popular Belief* (Oxford, 1984), 114–16; Rinuccini was wary of the dangers to the church of too close an identification with the power of the state but this was the political universe in which he had been raised and he saw a close co-operation between church and state as fundamental to the well-being of both.

[148] Reinhard, 'Reformation, Counter-Reformation', 384–98; Ravitch, *The Catholic Church and the French Nation*, 1–27; see also Gregorio Penco, *Storia della chiesa in Italia* (Milan, 1978), 7–9.

compatibility of throne and altar. Although a zealous supporter of what he saw as the legitimate rights of the pope and of the bishop, one can note that he was not unaccustomed nor wholly unsympathetic to an interest on the part of the temporal power in the exercise of ecclesiastical authority. He had after all once been offered nomination to the archiepiscopal see of Florence by the Grand Duke of Tuscany. While in Paris he was openly critical of papal unwillingness to conciliate Mazarin's government in the case of de Beaupuis. The earlier jurisdictional disputes of his nunciature were managed without provoking overt conflict. While establishing a papal tribunal, he made extensive efforts to do so in as conciliatory a fashion as possible and won plaudits in Rome for his decision not to charge its applicants for any decisions.[149] Again, when controversy erupted over the nomination of bishops in 1647, Rinuccini did his best to defuse the situation while upholding the rights of the pope. Indeed, his action in resolutely defending the right of the pope to a free choice of bishops, while assuring those who had broached the subject with him that their wishes in this regard would be favourably treated in Rome, was very much within the spirit of seventeenth-century Roman co-operation with temporal authority.[150]

In 1648, however, Rinuccini believed that his opponents were not only prepared to increase the level of their rejection of 'In Coena Domini' to the point of apostasy, but that their motivation in doing so was even more sinister than a mere desire for the aggrandizement of temporal authority. Confederate behaviour was aimed, he believed, not at control of the mechanisms of catholic confessionalization but their abandonment in order to facilitate the re-establishment of protestant authority in Ireland through the Ormond peace. It was the deployment of anti-papal legalism in conjunction with what he perceived as temporizing lack of religious zeal which hardened the nuncio's convictions of the deficiency of Old English catholicism. Rinuccini came to believe that the royalism deeply ingrained in the Old English tradition blunted both their willingness to defend true religion and their ability to identify and resist heresy. In his final report in Rome, this was indeed the climactic point in his denunciations:

I remain greatly astonished at times that arguments are [even] sought to prove that the objective of this party was never respect for religion. And what clearer proof could be given than the common sentiment of the Ormondites, signified to me on many occasions, that the followers of the King should not be taken for heretics, but only those who rebel against the crown, and that in consequence war against the puritans is legitimate in so far as they are rebels, and illegitimate immediately when

---

[149] See Rinuccini to Pamfili, Dec. 1645 (*Comment. Rinucc.*, ii. 93) and Pamfili's response, 20 May (ns) 1646 (ibid., 95).

[150] Rinuccini to Pamfili, 1 Mar. 1647 (Aiazzi, *Nunziatura*, 201–2): it is true that as his awareness of the intricacies of confederate politics developed, the nuncio rather abandoned the policy of privileging the Supreme Council's nominees.

they return to obedience? As if respect for the king alone could qualify heresies or purge the contagion which falsities inflict on souls.[151]

From Rinuccini's perspective, perhaps the most pernicious aspect of Old English tolerance was the peace settlement which his opponents were prepared to accept in order to reconcile themselves to their protestant monarch. From an early stage in his nunciature he had become convinced that those whom he termed 'Ormondites' believed it to be 'superfluous and unjust' to demand more than the private exercise of their religion from the king and were thus willing to abandon what he saw as critical structures of catholic reform.[152] The nuncio was arguably ungenerous in his description. In 1645 when this issue had become of burning importance, the confederate peace party had attempted unsuccessfully in negotiations to secure a right to jurisdiction for the catholic bishops, as well as possession of the churches.[153] Clanricard, who maintained close contact with them during the summer of that year, acknowledged the tenderness of their consciences with regard to the latter issue and was convinced that, although they would not oppose the repossession of ecclesiastical property, they could not be brought to sign to anything involving its explicit concession.[154] Nevertheless, Rinuccini was correct that his confederate opponents placed a greater store on the achievement of peace than the retention of the churches.

Thus, Rinuccini's belief that the rift between himself and the catholic opposition in Ireland centred on differing conceptions of the role which the church was to play within society supplemented his horror at the extremity of their rejection of papal authority. Rinuccini's instinct in this regard was probably correct. The development of a resident hierarchy in Ireland, committed to the achievement of tridentine reform, did not necessarily correspond to the wishes of many Old English gentry. The extension of this pattern of episcopally directed organization to Gaelic Ireland, despite the pastoral imperatives in its favour, aroused opposition even among some Old English clergy during the 1620s. For Rinuccini, on the other hand, these developments were critical aspects of the evangelical process. In this regard he can be identified clearly with the central impulse of the European counter-reformation, namely the desire to regenerate spiritually the entire commu-

---

[151] 'Io alle volte resto grandemente maravigliato che si vadano cercando argomenti per provare, che il fine di questa parte non sia mai stato il respetto di religione. E qual prova più chiara può darsene che il comune sentimento degli Ormonisti, significato a me tante volte, che i seguaci del Re non devono tenersi per eretici, ma solo quelli che si alienano dalla corona, e che per conseguenza sia lecita la guerra coi Puritani insino che sono ribelli, e illecito subito che retornino all'obbedienza? Come se il solo rispetto del Re qualificasse l'eresie o purgasse il contagio, che portano all'anime le falsità . . .': Rinuccini's relation to the pope (Aiazzi, *Nunziatura*, 432).

[152] 'Superfluo ed ingiusto' (ibid., 105).   [153] See for instance Bodl. Carte MS 15, fo. 287^{r-v}.

[154] Clanricard to Ormond, 4 June 1645 (John Lowe (ed.), *The Letter Book of the Earl of Clanricarde, 1643–7* (Dublin, 1983), 164).

nity, to embrace the many and not merely the jansenist or seigniorial few.[155]
His peace party opponents were not necessarily hostile to that notion but
neither were they prepared to subordinate everything to it. The determination to maintain the English constitution of the kingdom of Ireland, as a protection not only against Gaelic Ireland but also against any attempt by the
church to regain impropriated monastic property, was fundamental to their
position. If the price of that constitution, which was inextricably linked to a
protestant monarchy, was a limitation of the structures on which the catholic
church depended to operate a tridentine programme of reform, then it was a
price which the dominant group on the Supreme Council was prepared to
pay both in 1646 and 1649. Rinuccini's belief that this sacrifice was made
willingly, that the acceptance of the Ormond treaties of those years, neither
of which guaranteed the rights and jurisdiction of the catholic clergy, was the
product of choice rather than necessity, was crucial to his later accusations.
Catholics who were prepared to compromise on the freedom of action of the
catholic episcopacy were, in the nuncio's eyes, in thrall to private religious
commodity at the expense of the wider community.

It seems relatively clear, therefore, that it was not merely political dis-
agreement which prompted Rinuccini's criticisms of the catholicism of his
opponents. Rather those criticisms concerned a significantly different view
of the role of the church within society. And it concerned, also, the degree to
which religious allegiance was to be at the centre of the group identity of the
catholic population in Ireland. On one level, the exchanges between
Rinuccini and his opponents mirrored those which took place between
advocates of royal and papal power all over catholic Europe. But the protestantism of the king whose rights Rinuccini's opponents upheld fundamentally altered the nature of this debate, because it meant that jurisdictional
disputes essentially concerned, not the control, but the limitation of the
structures of catholic reform. Taken in this light, therefore, Rinuccini's
analysis of the differences between Gaelic Irish and Old English was quite
acute. The nuncio realized that catholicism lay more or less unchallenged at
the centre of the group identity of those whom he termed Gaelic Irish but
that this did not apply in the same fashion to many Old English.[156] The
national catholic identity of that community differed from that which
became typical in counter-reformation Europe, and with which Rinuccini
was familiar, because its English component necessitated an entirely different perspective towards the alternative confession of the monarch to whom

---

[155] See Wright, *Counter-Reformation*, 276–7; in this context, one can note John Bossy's argument that it is difficult to speak of a counter-reformation 'outside countries where the Catholic
Church retained, at least in theory, its identity with the whole body of society' in the unpaginated
introduction to Jean Delumeau, *Catholicism between Luther and Voltaire* (London, 1977); see also
Tracy, 'With and Without the Counter-Reformation', 565–6.

[156] In the aftermath of the confederate wars this identical point was made in favour of the Old
English by moderate protestant observers. See for example British Library Egerton MS 917, fo. 81r–v.

they were loyal. This was to be clearly typified in the 1660s by John Lynch, the Old English clerical apologist and archdeacon of Tuam, who advanced a sophisticated analysis of the various brands of heresy, concluding that the 'Protestantismus' of Charles I was close to catholicism and thus far superior to all forms of puritanism.[157]

Rinuccini was profoundly unsympathetic to such delicate perceptions and complexities of allegiance. This reflected the limitations of an Italian background which provided no real experience of religious diversity and consequently little tolerance for creative adaptation. But it was symptomatic also of an orthodoxy which appreciated that it was not to Gaelic custom but to English political structures that the most resistant acculturation of tridentine norms in Ireland had occurred. Rinuccini's rather harsh but logical designation of the Old English as apostates was in a sense the mirror image of James I's rejection of catholics as half subjects. The attempt to marry mutually opposed traditions ultimately resulted in a creative deviation from both: a willingness to accept the private exercise of catholicism satisfied neither the demands of the tridentine church nor the royal supremacy. If John Bossy's challenging hypothesis is correct then Rinuccini's intolerance of the Old English included an active blindness to what ultimately became a critical strand in the subsequent vitality of Irish catholicism, namely the strong focus on the home in religious devotion.[158] In part that may be true, although this feature was not confined to the Old English community in the decades that followed. But the more primitive confessionalism which Rinuccini identified as authentically catholic was ultimately at least as central to the evolution of Irish catholic identity and he was certainly correct that this attribute was more strongly represented among those he termed the Gaelic Irish.

V

Rinuccini's final year in Ireland revealed his limitations to a considerable degree. He continued to demonstrate a keen perceptiveness: throughout this period his judgement of his opponents' motivations and intentions was quite acute. But his behaviour was that of a gambler whose luck had begun to exhaust itself. Ultimately no faction of the confederates benefited from his actions in 1648. Even O'Neill, on whose behalf he partially pronounced the censure against the Inchiquin truce, would have been better off if the nuncio had chosen to attempt a reconciliation with the Supreme Council once the Ulster army's survival had been guaranteed. In 1648 Rinuccini had arrived at the point where religious conviction and practical politics diverged sharply from each other. Previously he had been able to count on broad popular

---

[157] Ó hAnnracháin, 'Political Ideology and Catholicism in Ireland', 168–9.
[158] Bossy, 'Counter-Reformation and Catholic Ireland', 169.

support for his insistence on the attainment of a certain position for the church in any political settlement. The disasters of 1647, however, had thinned the constituency prepared to give attention to the nuncio's demands. His refusal to accept the logic of this situation helped precipitate a confrontation which was to the advantage solely of the confederates' enemies. Rinuccini's opponents, none the less, also contributed to the debacle which ensued. To a large extent, the seeds of the nuncio's behaviour had been laid in 1647 when the refusal of the peace party to accept the outcome of the first assembly of that year materially contributed to the sequence of confederate disasters. Rinuccini's passionate distrust and resentment of this group undoubtedly contributed to his obstinacy concerning the issue of the Inchiquin truce and its aftermath. The bitter harvest of this mutual hostility, however, was ultimately shared by all segments of the association.

CHAPTER SEVEN

The Nuncio, Religious Reform and the Irish Clergy

a primitive and persecuted church . . . and I dare to promise that I am confident, if we have a little peace, to shape them so much to my way that they will take and conserve the Roman style.[1]

I

The legatine synod of August 1646 proved emblematic of the manner in which the ecclesiastical aspect of Rinuccini's mission developed. Originally convened to ratify the full acceptance of tridentine decrees and discipline in Ireland,[2] it was almost entirely taken over by political events and developed into the vehicle for the clerical *putsch* against the government of the Supreme Council. In a similar fashion, throughout his four years in Ireland Rinuccini was to find his role as an ecclesiastical organizer in danger of being swamped by the necessity of involving himself in confederate politics. So prominent did he become in this sphere that it is hardly surprising that the more narrowly ecclesiastical aspect of his mission has been passed over by Irish historians.[3]

Yet both Rinuccini and his superiors had originally viewed his mission as primarily one of church reform and ecclesiastical supervision[4] and this always remained the nuncio's chief objective in Ireland.[5] While in France in

---

[1] 'Una chiesa primitiva e perseguitata . . . ed ardisco di promettere che . . . mi basta l'animo, se averemo un poco di pace, di formarli tanto a mio modo, che pighleranno e conserveranno lo stilo Romano': Rinuccini to Pamfili, 30 Dec. 1646 (Aiazzi, *Nunziatura*, 187).

[2] See Rinuccini to Pamfili, 7 Mar. 1646 (ibid., 102).

[3] Patrick Corish, *The Catholic Community in the Seventeenth and Eighteenth Centuries* (Dublin, 1981), 41–2, drawing on John Bossy, 'The Counter-Reformation and the People of Catholic Ireland', *Historical Studies*, 8 (1971), 153–70 does touch very briefly on this aspect.

[4] For Rinuccini's extensive faculties, which included the right to visit all establishments of regular clergy, to constitute an ecclesiastical tribunal, to convoke national synods, to revoke all existing papal faculties, and to override all ordinary exemptions: see *Comment. Rinucc.*, i. 590–600.

[5] His secret instructions (generally a more reliable indicator of his superiors' view of the mission than the public instructions, although in this matter there is no contradiction between them, informed the nuncio that his mission was to 'ristorare ed istabilire il pubblico esercizio della Cattolica Religione nell'Isola d'Irlanda, ed a soggettare quei populi, se non tributari alla Sede Apostolica, come furono già cinque secoli addietro, a ridurli almeno sotto il soave giogo della podestà pontificia nelle materie spirituali, ed a guadagnare in fine anime innumerabili alla gloria del Paradiso' (to restore and establish the public exercise of the catholic religion in the island of Ireland

1645 he had been eager to see a peace signed which would free him in Ireland for the work which he knew best and which he believed to be the most important in which he could be involved,[6] namely the restructuring of the Irish church in conformity with contemporary Italian practices. And following the collapse of his mission he was still able to take a certain amount of pride in the manner in which he had improved the worship of God during his time in Ireland.[7] From Rinuccini's point of view, the service which he had done to God and the souls of the Irish during his four years in Ireland was valuable in itself, even if the structures and practices which he had instituted did not prove to be permanent. To his regret, nevertheless, the nuncio was never free to concentrate on his pastoral and organizational work in the manner, for instance, in which he had functioned in Fermo. Because the terms on which peace was available to the confederates were utterly unacceptable to him, a vast proportion of his time and energy had to be devoted to questions of a political nature and to discussions and negotiations with the secular executive of the confederates.

Even so, although not as free as he would have wished to pursue the more narrowly ecclesiastical dimensions of his mission, the nuncio did not neglect this aspect entirely. As the effective head of the Irish church, he made strenuous attempts to regularize the rites and practices of Irish catholicism and to introduce Italian devotions and ceremonials.[8] In addition, he acted as advisor to Rome concerning new appointments to the Irish clergy and as supervisor and assessor of the existing clerical personnel.[9] Furthermore, it is probably accurate to say that the nuncio saw the border between his ecclesiastical functions and his more political involvements as somewhat indistinct and fluid. His interest in Irish politics was purely to protect the interests of the Roman church. The attention which he paid to the confederate war reflected his hope that victory would establish the church in Ireland on a secure footing. In addition, his politics were informed by a belief in the providential nature of human existence. Thus, not only did the nuncio believe that the creation of a properly functioning church was dependent on the achievement of certain political conditions, but he also believed that prayer and ceremonies of devotion had vital roles to play in the achievement of a settlement. Many of the religious ceremonies which he promoted were designed

---

and to subject the people, if not tributary to the Apostolic See, as they were already five centuries ago, to reduce them at least to the light yoke of pontifical power in spiritual matters, and to win ultimately innumerable souls for the glory of Heaven): Secret Instructions, Dec.(?) 1644 (Aiazzi, *Nunziatura*, p. xxxv): see also above Ch. 3.

  [6] Rinuccini to Pamfili, 14 July 1645 (ibid., 29–30); same to same, 4 Aug. 1645 (ibid., 38).

  [7] What he himself termed 'qualche poco d'augmento al culto divino': Rinuccini to Pancirolo, 14 Mar. (ns) 1649 (ibid., 362).

  [8] *Comment. Rinucc.*, ii. 164.

  [9] In this context see Rinuccini to Pamfili, 3 Dec. 1645 (Aiazzi, *Nunziatura*, 83); 'Viaggio in Irlanda' (APF, Miscellaneae Varie 9, pp. 281–5).

to bring about victory in the war. On occasion they combined a triple purpose, first to impress the general population and thus strengthen their faith, second to introduce the population to contemporary Italian rites, and third, by being pleasing to God, to strengthen the likelihood of divine assistance in the war.

II

Given the importance which Rinuccini attached to the bishop as the key to the functioning of the church, it is hardly surprising that he devoted a great deal of time and attention to the question of new appointments to the Irish hierarchy, which he was very eager to see strengthened in numbers and quality.[10] He sent several detailed memorials to Rome concerning the suitability of various candidates for sees and in the autumn of 1646 he made use of Massari's return to Rome to press his case for the appointment of several individuals even more strongly.[11] Partly through the persuasiveness of Massari's advocacy, Rinuccini's nominees were enormously successful in gaining positions,[12] something which antagonized influential interests in Ireland.

The archbishop of Armagh, Hugh O'Reilly, had always been very insistent that no appointments be made in his province without his approval. Together with many of the other Gaelic Irish clergy of the province, O'Reilly was particularly eager to prevent the appointment of Old English clergy to areas in Gaelic Ulster, a stance which pre-dated Rinuccini's arrival by several decades.[13] The appointment of Patrick Plunkett to Ardagh (who owed his position very largely to Rinuccini's championship of his cause) and of Oliver Darcy to Dromore thus represented a major rebuff to O'Reilly.[14] Other bishops, supported by secular elements on the Supreme Council, argued that the right to nominate to bishoprics belonged to the confederate Supreme Council as the king's proxies, and attempts were actually made in the second assembly of 1647 to exclude bishops who had not been nominated by the

---

[10] The nuncio was particularly critical of the older Irish bishops of whom he complained that they did not pay attention 'to the splendour and majesty of religion' (non fanno conto dello splendore e grandezza della Religione): Relazione del Regno d'Irlanda, 1 Mar. 1646 (Aiazzi, *Nunziatura*, 110).

[11] See for instance Rinuccini to Pamfili, 31 Dec. 1645 (ibid., 83–5); same to same, 7 Mar. 1646 (ibid., 102–3); same to same, 11 Aug. 1646 (ibid., 152–3); Rinuccini to Pancirolo, 16 Jan. 1648 (ibid., 292); Viaggio in Irlanda di Dionysio Massari (APF, Miscellaneae Varie 9, pp. 281–4): see also APF, Acta 1646–7, fos. 297ʳ–298ᵛ; of course Rinuccini also believed a strengthened hierarchy would have beneficial political effects as well as ecclesiastical ones.

[12] Viaggio in Irlanda di Dionysio Massari (APF, Miscellaneae Varie 9, pp. 281–4); a profile of the bishops of this era including Rinuccini's nominees is provided by Donal Cregan in 'The Social and Cultural Background of a Counter-Reformation Episcopate, 1618–60', in A. Cosgrove and D. MacCartney (eds.), *Studies in Irish History Presented to R. Dudley Edwards* (Dublin, 1979), 86–117.

[13] *Comment. Rinucc.*, ii. 183–5.

[14] Rinuccini to Pamfili, 7 Mar. 1646 (Aiazzi, *Nunziatura*, 102–4).

council to their sees.[15] Rinuccini, who was adamant that the appointment of bishops was the pope's free choice, eventually forced the assembly to accept his nominees.[16] Other confederates, both clerical and lay, were unhappy at the number of regulars who were nominated to sees by both Rinuccini and the council.[17] For his part, the Franciscan, Hugh Bourke, appointed to the see of Kilmacduagh in 1647,[18] was furious that he was not given the richer and more important see of Clonfert.[19] Yet the protests of these various interests were largely in vain. For as long as Rinuccini remained in Ireland, major ecclesiastical appointments were effectively dependent on his approval.

The degree of influence which this conferred in political matters was bitterly regretted by Richard Bellings. In the secretary's view, whereas Scarampi had strengthened the Supreme Council:

by declaring that his master was resolved not to grant any provisions at Rome, for benefices or ecclesiastical dignities, but to such as were nominated by the Supreame Councell; which privilege includes so much of the essence of government, that, speaking morally, and with relation to those places where the clergy enjoy their livings, and have a free influence upon the people, it scarce can be in any foreign hand that may not think himself of power to conserve quiet and introduce trouble at his will and pleasure,[20]

with Rinuccini's arrival 'it was no sooner known that promotions passed at Rome by his recommendation, but all the water ran by his channel, all pulpits spoke his sense, and all the observance formerly paid to the orders of the Councell, was transferred to his direction'.[21] It was presumably not only Rinuccini's political influence which was increased by his position as arbiter of ecclesiastical appointments. Hopes for advancement at his hands also probably increased the willingness of the clergy to accept Rinuccini's direction in ecclesiastical matters, and to respond favourably to his attempts to Italianize the ceremonials of the church in Ireland.

Nevertheless, 1648 was to see a profound decline in Rinuccini's influence among the Irish clergy, principally because a majority of the Old English bishops opposed his position on the Inchiquin truce. To that extent, the crisis of 1648 provides a type of stress radiography of the limits and channels of ecclesiastical authority during the nunciature. It is, therefore, interesting to trace the nature and extent of this rebellion of the clergy in some detail.

Clearly, the politics of the truce itself and the manner in which it was perceived, particularly by the Old English population, were the vital factor in

[15] Micheál Ó Siochrú, *Confederate Ireland, 1642–1649: A Constitutional and Political Analysis* (Dublin, 1999), 160.
[16] Rinuccini to Pamfili, 1 Mar. 1647 (Aiazzi, *Nunziatura*, 199–202); see *Comment. Rinucc.*, ii. 787–8; note also the unsuccessful attempt of a number of Irish bishops to have the bishopric of Derry filled without apparently consulting Rinuccini: see ibid., 486.
[17] Rinuccini to Pamfili, 7 Mar. 1646 (Aiazzi, *Nunziatura*, 102).
[18] Cregan, 'Social and Cultural Background', 87.   [19] *Comment. Rinucc.*, ii. 761–3.
[20] Bellings's narrative (*Irish Confederation*, i. 153).   [21] Ibid., 154.

causing clergy to oppose the nuncio. Only two bishops who could comfort-
ably be identified as Old English, Walter Lynch of Clonfert and Robert Barry
of Cork and Cloyne, really exerted themselves in support of the nuncio during the truce crisis.[22] Two other Old English bishops, Nicholas French of
Ferns and Hugh Bourke of Kilmacduagh, were abroad during the summer of
1648 and thus, although both disapproved of Rinuccini's action, were in no
position to intervene at the beginning of the crisis. Bourke's brother John, the
vigorous archbishop of Tuam, was, however, in Ireland and he rapidly
emerged as the leader of the Old English wing of the hierarchy in their opposition to the nuncio. Tuam certainly had more support among the Old
English bishops than Rinuccini could hope to muster. Francis Kirwan of
Killala and Andrew Lynch of Kilfenora were particularly blunt in their
opposition to the nuncio. The aged bishop of Meath, Thomas Dease, who
had adopted a notably royalist stance since 1641 and who was cordially
detested by the nuncio, not surprisingly took his place among the nuncio's
opponents. The similarly ancient and possibly senile bishop of Ossory,
David Rothe, was also persuaded to lend his name to the council's attempts
to undermine Rinuccini's censure. This was particularly useful to the council as Ossory was of course the resident ordinary in Kilkenny, the seat of their
government. Even more galling for the nuncio was the fact that Patrick
Plunkett of Ardagh and Oliver Darcy of Dromore, two bishops whom he had
originally supported as candidates for sees against the wishes of their metropolitan, Hugh O'Reilly, also lent their support to his opponents, very
openly in the case of Dromore and more covertly in the case of Ardagh.[23]

In contrast, what could be termed the Gaelic Irish wing of the hierarchy
aligned itself solidly behind the nuncio. Only Edmund O'Dwyer, the bishop
of Limerick, clearly favoured the truce and disapproved of Rinuccini's censure although, like Ardagh, O'Dwyer tried to avoid the open appearance of
defiance while covertly supporting the council. Unfortunately for Rinuccini,
O'Dwyer was the bishop of Gaelic stock whose stance was most likely to
carry weight among the Old English population of his see. Of wealthy
antecedents and fluent in English, O'Dwyer stood out from many of the
other Old Irish bishops in his capacity to straddle the two worlds of Gaelic
and Old English Ireland.[24]

[22] The archbishop of Dublin, Thomas Fleming, the bishop of Waterford, Patrick Comerford, and
the archbishop of Cashel, Thomas Walsh, also rather tepidly obeyed Rinuccini during the crisis. My
analysis here differs somewhat from that of Hugh F. Kearney, 'Ecclesiastical Politics and the
Counter-Reformation in Ireland, 1618–48', *Journal of Ecclesiastical History*, 11 (1960), 202–12.

[23] This paragraph is based on the material in *Comment. Rinucc.*, iii. 284–8, 327, 335, 342, 491,
500; see also Cregan, 'Social and Cultural Background' and Kearney, 'Ecclesiastical Politics',
202–12.

[24] In fact if one adopts Hugh Kearney's definition of the Old English as 'as much a political label
as anything else' then O'Dwyer might justifiably be seen as Old English: see Kearney, *Strafford in
Ireland, 1633–41: A Study in Absolutism*, 2nd edn. (Cambridge, 1989), 16.

The disunity among the Old English bishops in 1648 was mirrored also among their diocesan clergy. The truce was such a divisive issue because the instinct of obedience to the pope's representative, which had been very evident in previous official congregations of the Irish clergy, clashed with the conviction that the nuncio had made a terrible error. Because the bishop of a diocese adopted a particular position, moreover, did not mean that all the clergy of his diocese followed suit. Respect for Rinuccini's standing as nuncio could come into conflict with obedience to episcopal example. Moreover, traditional resistance to the intrusion of episcopal authority in certain localities also surfaced during the crisis of the truce.

Another factor at work was the recent nature of many of the provisions to the Irish hierarchy. Rinuccini's most fervent Old English supporters among the bishops, Robert Barry and Walter Lynch, had for instance only been consecrated in the spring of 1648.[25] Barry was actually an exile from his diocese which was under Inchiquin's control while Lynch had to deal with a body of clergy who had largely been appointed during John Bourke's stewardship as bishop and vicar apostolic in Clonfert. Bourke, the newly translated archbishop of Tuam and Rinuccini's most important opponent, thus probably still exerted great influence over the clergy of his former diocese in 1648. The logical corollary of this was of course that Bourke's influence in his new archdiocese of Tuam was also somewhat more limited than one might expect at first glance. As it transpired, a considerable number of the diocesan clergy of Tuam, many of whom had been appointed by Bourke's predecessor, Malachy O'Queely, strenuously opposed the truce which their archbishop supported. Of particular importance in this respect was Patrick Lynch, the *praepositus* of the collegiate church of St Nicholas in Galway.[26]

The church of St Nicholas was one of the most important religious institutions in Connacht, carrying great weight with the population of Galway. Without the firm stance of the collegiate church it is probable that Rinuccini would have encountered far more opposition and hostility during his protracted sojourn in Galway in 1648. Yet the alliance between the nuncio and the collegiate church against the local ordinary was in many ways a strange one. The church of St Nicholas had a long history, before the split of 1648, of attempting to emancipate itself from the episcopal supervision of the archbishop of Tuam.[27] Rinuccini was certainly grateful for the commitment which Patrick Lynch and other clergy in Galway showed to his censures but he may well have felt somewhat ambivalent about allying with rebellious local clergy against the authority of their ordinary, since his personal philosophy of church government was based on the necessity of secure episcopal

---

[25] Cregan, 'Social and Cultural Background', 87.
[26] See *Comment. Rinucc.*, iii. 335–43, 354–5.
[27] The collegiate church made use of the disturbances of 1648 to launch another appeal to Rome to free it from Tuam's jurisdiction: see ibid., 598.

authority within a diocese. In normal circumstances Rinuccini's sympathies would almost certainly have been with the archbishop and against the collegiate church but the events of 1648 meant that the nuncio had to accept allies where he could find them.[28]

Several of the bishops who had been appointed since Rinuccini had arrived in Ireland also lacked influence in their sees because they had little or no roots among the population of their dioceses. For this Rinuccini himself could take some of the blame and he may well have felt somewhat chastened about his own role concerning episcopal appointments in the previous years. Unimpressed by localist arguments, Rinuccini had encouraged his superiors to appoint several bishops to dioceses where they were seen as interlopers. This marked a change in Roman policy which had recognized during the 1630s that only bishops with sound local support networks could hope to survive as prelates in an extra-legal church. In 1648 the most embarrassing result for the nuncio of this change of policy was the case of Patrick Plunkett, the Cistercian bishop of Ardagh. Rinuccini had been insistent that Plunkett should be appointed despite local opposition and the misgivings of the archbishop of Armagh. In 1648, however, those whom the nuncio had previously rebuffed in favour of Plunkett supported his censures while Plunkett aligned with the pro-truce party. The nuncio thus found it necessary to appoint a local Dominican to promulgate the censures in the diocese of Ardagh.[29]

The key to the initial opposition in Ardagh to Plunkett's appointment, and to the subsequent gulf between the bishop and most of his clergy, was the fact that the catholic population of the diocese evidently resented the imposition of the scion of an influential Pale family as bishop in their locality. Other Old English bishops who were similarly out of touch with their (largely Gaelic Irish) sees were Francis Kirwan of Killala and Oliver Darcy of Dromore. Kirwan was particularly unpopular in his diocese and his public opposition to Rinuccini provided his diocesan clergy with the opportunity of complaining about him to the nuncio.[30] Again, Rinuccini may have had somewhat mixed feelings about entertaining this complaint. While applauding the clergy of Killala for their support of the censure, he may have suspected (with reason) that much of the resentment against Killala was particularist in nature and had been aroused by Killala's previous attempts to reorganize and reform the see.[31] Possibly for this reason, Rinuccini took no action on the complaint but referred the matter to the national synod which he hoped

---

[28] Martin Coen, *The Wardenship of Galway* (Galway, 1984), 18 suggests that, for their part, the clergy of Galway probably supported Rinuccini because of 'historic anti-Tuam attitudes' rather than 'the merits of the nuncio's case'. Given the length of time that Rinuccini spent in Galway, and the warmth with which he wrote of it, this supposition seems to me unlikely.

[29] *Comment. Rinucc.*, iii. 289–90.

[30] See the complaint of Richard Sayers on behalf of the clergy and people of Killala, ibid., 362–3.

[31] With regard to Killala's reforming zeal see John Lynch, *Pii antistitis icon sive de vita et morte D. Francisci Kirovani Rmi. Alladensis Episcopi . . .* ed. C. P. Meehan (Dublin, 1884).

to hold in August.[32] Old divisions and rifts within the Irish church seem, therefore, to have surfaced again during the controversies of 1648 which was possibly another factor in the developing depression which afflicted the nuncio during the crisis. While convinced of the rectitude of his own actions, the nuncio could hardly ignore the degree to which church discipline and coherence were being affected by the split within the clergy, something which almost certainly caused him greater pain than any rift between secular and clerical interests.

The evidence of Wexford in 1648 indicates the importance of the stance of senior local clergy, such as Nicholas Redmond and Walter Enos, with regard to the application of ecclesiastical authority. Redmond was the vicar general of the diocese and thus the chief ecclesiastical authority in the see in the absence of the bishop of Ferns: Enos was a prominent theologian and canonist. The influence of this duo was evidently of great importance in creating support for the nuncio in the town of Wexford, although military pressure from the Leinster army forced the city to be somewhat circumspect.[33] In the crisis of 1648, wherever, as in Wexford, the major clerical figures in an area promoted the nuncio's censure, the council was fighting an uphill battle to secure the acceptance of the truce. Unfortunately for the nuncio, in 1648 too many key members of the clergy, particularly those of Old English stock, either supported the truce or failed to make a determined stand in favour of the censure.

Rinuccini's relationship with the regular orders in Ireland was complex. Aside from the Jesuits (whom he favoured in other ways),[34] he was careful, despite some local opposition, to conciliate the three most important religious orders in Ireland by recommending the appointment of two of their members as bishops.[35] As was pointed out previously, the great bulk of the regular clergy in Ireland stayed loyal to the nuncio during the split over the Inchiquin truce. However, Rinuccini's criticisms of the standards of the regular clergy in Ireland were among the harshest he made. In the nuncio's view, so accustomed had the regulars become to 'living outside their convents'[36] and 'free from the discipline of the monasteries',[37] that he believed they were

---

[32] Comment. Rinucc., iii. 363.   [33] Ibid., 329–35.

[34] He secured the former Augustinian church of St John in Kilkenny for the Society: see Rinuccini to Pamfili, 3 May 1646 (Aiazzi, Nunziatura, 127); he may also have taken some of the credit for the decree in the General Assembly of 30 Mar. 1647 which raised the status of the Jesuits and Capuchins (both of course post-reformation orders) to the level of the other regular orders in Ireland: see Comment. Rinucc., ii. 562.

[35] Viaggio in Irlanda di Dionysio Massari (APF, Miscellaneae Varie 9, p. 283); Patrick Plunkett (Ardagh) and Arthur Magennis (Down & Connor) were Cistercians: Oliver Darcy (Dromore) and Terrence O'Brien (Emly) were Dominicans: Hugh Bourke (Kilmacduagh) and Boethius MacEgan (Ross) were Franciscans: see also Cregan, 'Social and Cultural Background', 87.

[36] 'Avvezzi di star fuori dei Conventi': Relazione del Regno d'Irlanda, 1 Mar. 1646 (Aiazzi, Nunziatura, 111).

[37] 'Astretti alla disciplina dei Monasteri' (ibid.)

now reluctant to accept a genuinely regular life through the achievement of a peace that would 'involve the restoration of ecclesiastical discipline'.[38] Scarampi was evidently also as unhappy as the nuncio about the standards of the Irish orders. On one occasion Rinuccini went so far as to inform his superiors that 'the Regulars (as Your Eminence will hear also from Father Scarampi) play a great part in the ruin of this kingdom'.[39]

The difficulties of the war meant that it was difficult to get to grips with the problem which the regulars posed. For instance, the exceedingly numerous Franciscan order would, the nuncio believed, benefit from a proposal which was made by some of the friars to split the Irish province into two parts. Quite apart from the difficulty of organizing this in a climate of war, however, it was somewhat uncomfortable for the nuncio that the division was chiefly supported by those friars who were most inclined to peace with Ormond. Consequently, despite the real organizational difficulties which the order faced, he decided that any move to divide the province was best left until the overall political situation in Ireland was stabilized.[40]

The various orders of the regular clergy also split on the issue of the truce and the censure in 1648. Those who supported the truce tended to be of Old English origin while the Gaelic Irish regulars overwhelmingly supported the nuncio. Nevertheless, the nuncio's support even among the Old English regulars seems to have been strong. The Dominican order traditionally attracted a strong proportion of Old English recruits but in October 1648 Gregory O'Ferrall, the Irish provincial of the order, claimed not to know of a single Irish Dominican who supported the truce, although the order had more than 300 members in Ireland.[41] O'Ferrall's testimony is weakened by the obvious fact that the Dominican bishop of Dromore, Oliver Darcy, supported the truce wholeheartedly, yet it does seem clear that he was in a small minority within his order.[42]

The Franciscan order was particularly popular throughout Gaelic Ireland which helps to explain the solid support which they offered the nuncio. A minority, again chiefly of Old English friars, did adhere to the pro-truce party (indeed the chief clerical apologist of the truce was the Franciscan Peter Walsh),[43] but the provincial of the order, Thomas MacKiernan, suggested that the number was as low as twenty from a Franciscan population which

---

[38] 'Che porti la restaurazione del rigore Ecclesiastico' (Aiazzi, *Nunziatura*, 111).

[39] 'Regulares (sicut Eminentia Vestra etiam a Patre Scarampo intelliget) magnam habent partem in huius Regni ruina': Latin version of Rinuccini to Pamfili, 29 Dec. 1646 (*Comment. Rinucc.*, ii. 453).

[40] Ibid., ii. 689–93.   [41] See O'Ferrall to Rinuccini, 19 Oct. 1648 (ibid., ii. 558–9).

[42] Rinuccini also emphasized the degree of support he received from the Dominican order (Aiazzi, *Nunziatura*, 345).

[43] Corish, 'The Crisis in Ireland in 1648: The Nuncio and the Supreme Council Conclusions', *Irish Theological Quarterly*, 22 (1955), 231–57.

may have numbered almost 1,000.[44] Many Old English friars were evidently fiercely opposed to the truce. Even in Kilkenny itself the Franciscan convent provided very stubborn and uncomfortable opposition to the council and the truce.[45]

Of particular interest in this regard are the Irish Capuchins. Originally established in Ireland despite considerable hostility from the observant Franciscans, they had from an early date been identified with Old English Ireland.[46] At the time of the Inchiquin truce membership of the order was still heavily weighted towards the Old English population, and the commissary-general, Barnaby Barnewall, was well connected with the Pale gentry and nobility. Yet the order seems, without a single exception, to have supported the nuncio against the truce.[47] Obedience to Barnewall who gave strict orders on this matter played its part in this rather surprising development but the very austere nature of the order was probably the most important factor.[48] The Capuchins were probably more likely than any other group to put purely religious considerations above temporal ones.

The other religious body in Ireland with a distinctively Old English character was the Society of Jesus. In the course of 1648 the nuncio became extremely bitter about the Irish Jesuits, whom he identified, together with the rebellious bishops, as the chief architects of the failure of his censure.[49] Until 1648 Rinuccini had enjoyed good relations with the Irish Jesuits. He was a warm admirer of the Society, by whom he had been educated, and exerted himself to obtain a number of concessions on their behalf.[50] His relations with the Jesuit superior, Robert Nugent, were initially excellent and Nugent assisted the nuncio with both money and advice in the attack on Dublin in 1646, although this project was unpopular with most of the politically important Old English gentry into whose ranks Nugent had himself been born.[51]

It was Nugent's replacement as superior on the Irish mission by William Malone which marked the beginning of the deterioration of relations between Rinuccini and the Society. The new incumbent spoke no Irish, seems

[44] See MacKiernan to Rinuccini, 19 Dec. 1648 (*Comment. Rinucc.*, iii. 560–1): Corish, 'The Nuncio and the Supreme Council', 45–8.

[45] *Comment. Rinucc.*, iii. 638–9.

[46] The early driving influence behind the order in Ireland, Francis Nugent, had antagonized many Gaelic Irish clergy in the 1620s by his attempts to prevent the archiepiscopal see of Armagh going to a cleric from Gaelic Ulster: see F. X. Martin, *Friar Nugent: A Study of Francis Lavalin Nugent, 1569–1635, Agent of the Counter-Reformation* (Rome and London, 1962), 249–60.

[47] Michelle O'Riordan, *The Gaelic Mind and the Collapse of the Gaelic World* (Cork, 1990), 248 n. 99 suggests otherwise but is, I believe, mistaken.

[48] See *Comment. Rinucc.*, iii. 574–5.

[49] See Rinuccini to Pancirolo, 4 July 1648 (Aiazzi, *Nunziatura*, 323–4) and same to same, 19 May (ns) 1649 (ibid., 380–1).

[50] See ibid., 381–2.

[51] McRedmond, *Greater Glory*, 47–84; Nugent to Rinuccini, 25 Nov. 1648 (*Comment. Rinucc.*, iv. pp. 65–6).

to have veered more towards the wing of the society which opposed Gaelic Irish admissions, and seems to have favoured a much more compromising position *vis-à-vis* protestants, notably Inchiquin.[52] When the crisis of the Inchiquin truce broke, Malone, attempting to find a relatively neutral position, ordered all Jesuit houses to follow the example of the local bishop in terms of observing the interdict. Because Kilkenny and Galway were the sites of the most important residences, most of the Jesuit fathers thus took their example from pro-truce bishops. (There was also a residence in Limerick but this defied the bishop and supported the nuncio.) Rinuccini seems to have decided that Malone's policy was merely a diplomatic way of effectively siding with the council. He was angered further when six Jesuits, including the superior of the Society's house in Kilkenny, Henry Plunkett, publicly expressed their approval of the council's position in August 1648.[53]

It is possible to overestimate the extent to which the Society actively exerted itself against the nuncio. The council for instance were far less convinced than Rinuccini that the Jesuits were doing everything in their power to further the truce. Yet it seems clear that individual Jesuit fathers did play a vital role in maintaining the agreement with Inchiquin by soothing the consciences of those who stood by it. Again, it was not the numbers of the Jesuits which made them significant. Even including novices, there were fewer than seventy members of the Society in the entire country.[54] But within that small group there was a disproportionate number of the sons of the Old English gentry. Of the six Jesuits who publicly endorsed Peter Walsh's answers to the 'queries' about Rinuccini's censures, for instance, five bore distinguished Old English surnames: Plunkett, Dillon, Usher, Bathe, and FitzMaurice, while St Leger was also clearly of gentle birth.[55] Respect for the Jesuits was inspired not only by the aristocratic Old English lineage of many of the Society's members but also by their learning and their commitment to their mission. Their stance in the controversies of 1648 was therefore of an importance out of all proportion with their numbers.

Thus, while it seems clear that a considerable majority of the Irish clergy, and possibly even a majority of what could be identified as the Old English clergy, supported the nuncio in 1648, sufficient important religious figures, particularly bishops and Jesuits, stood out against him to armour the con-

[52] Louis McRedmond, *To the Greater Glory: A History of the Irish Jesuits* (Dublin, 1991), 68–75; it was probably Malone who so incensed the nuncio with the observation that it was not always better to have catholic troops than protestant (see above, Ch. 6).

[53] McRedmond, *To the Greater Glory*, 70–5; *Comment. Rinucc.*, iii. 489.

[54] McRedmond, *To the Greater Glory*, 57–74.

[55] See Corish, 'The Nuncio and the Supreme Council', 45–55; *Comment. Rinucc.*, iii. 489; Plunkett and St Leger had already played not inconsiderable roles in confederate politics, Plunkett as a confederate agent in Brussels and St Leger as a clerical advisor to Bellings and Preston. Robert Bathe was also a prominent figure, a noted scholar who had continued a dangerous ministry in Drogheda after the outbreak of the rebellion: see McRedmond, *To the Greater Glory*, 67–74.

sciences of his secular opponents against his censures. The efficacy of this ecclesiastical minority in blunting the edge of the nuncio's authority was undoubtedly augmented by the fact that many clerics who did oppose the nuncio were precisely those whose opinions would carry most weight among the politically influential Old English families.

Rinuccini seems to have resented the disobedience of the clergy to his censure more than any action committed by his secular opponents. Clerical discipline was at the heart of the programme of religious reform to which he had devoted much of his life. Again, his strictures against the Old English community cannot be divorced from the sense of anger which filled him at the disobedience of many Old English clergy. As was noted previously, Rinuccini believed in two overriding sources of ecclesiastical authority. The first and most important of these was that of the pope, the second was the opinion delivered by a group of bishops who had deliberated together. Rinuccini felt that those clergy who opposed his censure had disregarded both these fonts of authority, namely the papal power which he exercised as nuncio and also the clerical declaration of 27 April which had finally received unanimous backing from all the bishops present at the meeting (although some had been initially unwilling to sign).[56] The temerity of individual bishops in going against both these sources of authority filled the nuncio with anger. The example of the Capuchins, a largely Old English order, which loyally obeyed the censure, may have emphasized to the nuncio the failings of his clerical opponents and indeed sharpened his anger against the rest of the Old English community. Thus, while the issues of 1648 went far beyond a simple question of clerical discipline, it is apparent that the nuncio saw it partly in this light, nor should the importance which Rinuccini attached to the idea of clerical discipline in the abstract, as a necessity for the achievement of the reform of society, be underestimated.

This can be seen in the concern which he showed about reasserting ecclesiastical obedience in the Irish church after his departure from the island. Personal anger and pique almost certainly contributed to Rinuccini's desire in 1649 to see the archbishop of Tuam, the bishops of Killala and Kilfenora, the prior of the discalced Carmelites in Galway, and the Jesuit provincial, Malone, summoned to Rome to answer charges.[57] These men had been the backbone of the ecclesiastical opposition who had eventually contributed to the nuncio's humiliating departure from Ireland. Yet personal anger was, from the nuncio's perspective, completely compatible with a passion for the revival of church discipline. He evidently honestly believed that the measures which he outlined were necessary to force the Irish church to return 'to some sort of obedience to the Apostolic See', an obedience which at that time he

---

[56] See for example Rinuccini's letter to the bishops of Ardagh, Meath, Ossory, Dromore, and the archbishop of Dublin, 6 June 1648 (*Comment. Rinucc.*, iii. 285–6).

[57] See Rinuccini to Arcamoni, 20 Apr. (ns) 1649 (Aiazzi, *Nunziatura*, 376–7).

believed to be 'almost completely lost'.[58] Some months later, made more circumspect by the degree of his opponents' military triumph in Ireland, the
nuncio continued to search for some formula which would hearten and
reward those who had obeyed his authority, without provoking retaliation
from the former Supreme Council.[59] Once again he saw the vindication of
both his own honour and that of the Holy See and the future well-being of
the Irish church as a seamless garment.

Ultimately, the extent of the influence which Rinuccini exerted over the
Irish clergy during the nunciature as a whole was very considerable. For most
of his sojourn in the island there is little evidence of significant clerical opposition to Rinuccini's leadership. When sustained opposition did emerge, it
reflected extraordinary political and ethnic tensions within the confederate
association, in which Rinuccini had vehemently involved himself, rather than
a distaste for the nuncio's ecclesiastical authority. Significantly, in 1648 the
attacks on papal jurisdiction and ecclesiastical immunity to which the nuncio most objected were not publicly defended to any great degree by senior
clerical supporters of the truce. Clerical opposition to Rinuccini in that year
centred around the issue of the truce and only secondarily related to the nuncio's authority, which, he himself noted, had been accepted without question
in previous years.[60] That it took as extraordinary a crisis as the truce to
shake the nuncio's dominance of the Irish clergy suggests the strength of the
ecclesiastical network of authority which Rome had maintained and developed in seventeenth-century Ireland.

III

On his arrival Rinuccini was clearly able to tap into previously developed
ecclesiastical structures but to what extent were his criticisms and analysis of
the Irish church those of an outsider and to what extent did he share a genuinely common religious culture with the Irish? Certainly, the Rinuccini who,
when chased by a protestant privateer in 1645, threw holy water and a picture
of St Nicholas into the water to invoke spiritual protection,[61] would appear
to have been well equipped to understand many of the devotions which he
encountered in Ireland.[62] That same episode, however, pointed up a difference between the Italian group and the Irish with whom they shared the ship.
The nuncio actively disapproved of the intention of the Irish passengers to die

---

[58] 'In qualche obbedienza verso la Sede Apostolica, che adesso e perduto quasi affato' (Aiazzi,
Nunziatura, 377).

[59] Ibid., 385–6.   [60] See ibid., 353.

[61] Letterre di Alessandro Neroni sul viaggio in Irlanda del Nuncio Apostolico (ASF, Mis.
Medicea, 436 ins 19).

[62] Patrick Corish remains the chief authority on the social practice of religion in the first half of the
seventeenth century: see Corish, *Irish Catholic Experience* (Dublin, 1985), 96–116; see also Raymond
Gillespie *Devoted People. Belief and Religion in Early Modern Ireland* (Manchester, 1997).

rather than to surrender to any boarders. For their part, the nuncio and his household were prepared to surrender quietly, confident that 'Ecclesia Dei non est custodienda more castrorum'.[63] This situation was of course rather more exotic for the Italians than for the Irish: to Rinuccini and his party the dangers posed by the existence of an alternate and hostile religious grouping were essentially abnormal. As a psychological strategy for dealing with persecution, such a passive response was possibly more suited to those for whom religious persecution was an anomaly rather than a credible aspect of normal existence. Rinuccini's passivity in this instance probably owed something also to his belief in the essential difference between the clerical and the secular state: very much in the mould of the counter-reformation cleric Rinuccini wished to emphasize the abstraction of the priest from the profane world. In Ireland of course, the extra-legal status of the church meant that the strict separation of the spiritual and the profane was much more difficult to achieve and this aspect of the European counter-reformation was slower to penetrate the island.[64] In this context it is interesting to note how strongly Scarampi (himself a former soldier) disapproved of an Irish priest who so far forgot his sacred status as actually to involve himself in combat,[65] and it is difficult to believe that Rinuccini was content with the bishop of Clogher's later assumption of the command of the Ulster army after the death of Owen Roe O'Neill.[66] The blurring of the border between the sacred and the profane which disturbed the nuncio most, however, was apparently the Irish habit of celebrating Mass in private homes: 'most often on the same table, where, when the altar cloths are taken off, they bring immediately the playing cards, or the jugs of beer with the food for the meal'.[67]

Rinuccini's concern to maintain a distinction between the secular and the ecclesiastical spheres can be glimpsed as well in his expressed reluctance to invoke the excommunications of the church in what he regarded as the purely

[63] Rinuccini to Pamfili, 25 Oct. 1645 (Aiazzi, Nunziatura, 65).

[64] See Bossy, 'Counter-Reformation', 168–70; Corish, Catholic Community, 41–2 discusses Rinuccini's horror at the intermingling of sacred and profane in Ireland and the disgust which it evoked in him; see also Corish, 'Women and Religious Practice', in Margaret MacCurtain and Mary O'Dowd (eds.), Women in Early Modern Ireland (Dublin, 1991), 211–13.

[65] The priest in question was Oliver Walsh: see Comment. Rinucc., ii. 731; one can, however, contrast Walsh with the Franciscan Brian MacEgan who seems to have almost sought martyrdom, deliberately putting himself in a defenceless position of prayer while the Franciscan chapter was under imminent danger of attack (ibid., 689–90).

[66] In the great Neapolitan revolt, one can note that Cardinal Filomarino refused permission to the clergy of the city to take up arms: see Massimo Bray, 'L'arcivescovo, il viceré, il fedelissimo popolo', Nuova Rivista Storica, 74 (1990), 311–32.

[67] 'Il più delle volte in quella medesima tavola, dove sparecchiate che siano le tovaglie dell'Altare, si porteranno subito le carte del guioco, o i vasi di birra con le vivande del pranzo': Relazione del Regno d'Irlanda, 1 Mar. 1646 (Aiazzi, Nunziatura, iii. 2); the nuncio not only found this intermingling of the sacred and the profane repugnant but he also regretted the useful opportunities of impressing the population with formal ceremonies which were being lost through the habit of private mass; this same passage is also discussed in Corish, Catholic Community, 41–2.

secular matter of the command of the garrison at Athlone.[68] Political calcu-
lation probably had something to do with Rinuccini's stance on this issue,
yet this was possibly not the only factor. The nuncio's belief in the importance of maintaining a distinction between secular and spiritual authority
was very genuine. Convinced that the goals of the church were different and
higher than those of the state, he was deeply worried that the general population might see too close an identification between secular and ecclesiastical authority. He was delighted, for example, at the manual work undertaken
by the clergy and in particular the Jesuits in the preparation of the defences
of Kilkenny in 1647: this he believed was 'to the great edification of the
people'. The tension created by the high status of the Jesuits (many of whom
were of noble stock) within society and the low status of manual labour
served to confer the moral authority of voluntary humility on the clergy and
to emphasize the greatness of the God they served.[69]

The nuncio's fierce determination to protect ecclesiastical immunity operated within the context of this desire to protect the independent identity of
the church. In this he seems to have been more unyielding than the Irish
clergy who, in November 1644, had legitimized the apprehension of clerics
accused of *lèse-majesté* by officials of the Supreme Council.[70] Rinuccini was
of course very bitter about breaches of ecclesiastical immunity following the
split over the Inchiquin truce[71] but, even before matters came to this, he was
forced to remind the council that they had no authority to imprison a priest,
and indeed to warn them reluctantly that they had probably incurred excommunication for having done so. Interestingly, the council's representative in
this debate was the bishop of Limerick, Edmund O'Dwyer, which again indicates that the Irish clergy may have been less zealous about this question than
Rinuccini.[72] In addition, few if any of the Irish bishops seem to have been as
concerned as the nuncio about the threat to the bishop of Clogher's ecclesiastical immunity in the second assembly of 1647.[73] (After the experience of
protestant government, the Irish clergy may well have felt that subjection to
the jurisdiction of a catholic executive was a relatively light burden.)

Not only was the ecclesiastical sphere to be defined by its difference and
separation from the secular domain, but the nuncio was also keen to see the

---

[68] See *Comment. Rinucc.*, ii. 536–8; as was noted in Ch. 1 the Irish clergy had thrown the power
of excommunication behind the Supreme Council at the beginning of the war.

[69] (In maximam populi aedificationem): see ibid., 613.

[70] See the decrees of the clerical convocation of 3, 4, 5, 6, 7, Nov. 1644 (ibid., i. 498–9).

[71] See above, Ch. 6.

[72] See Rinuccini to O'Dwyer, 12 Mar. 1648 (*Comment. Rinucc.*, iii. 65–6).

[73] Rinuccini became almost apoplectic at the suggestion that the assembly was competent to punish the bishop: 'that which was then said by the upholders of the English laws concerning the punishment of a bishop, it is hardly possible to relate. There was no insolence which was not voiced'
(quello che fosse poi detto dai Professori delle leggi anglicane circa le punizioni d'un Vescovo e
difficile a poterlo raccontare. Non fù temerità che non si sentisse): Rinuccini to Pancirolo, 8 Dec.
1647 (Aiazzi, *Nunziatura*, 273).

Irish church generate a sense of corporate identity from within its own ranks. As a pastor in Fermo, he had seen synods chiefly as a means of promoting solidarity among the clergy and during the General Assembly of 1647 (and probably on other occasions) he convened the bishops every second day to reinforce mutual solidarity and to protect in a united fashion the rights and immunities of the clergy.[74] This was of course a recent development in Ireland: not only had it been highly dangerous for the catholic clergy to assemble as a corporate and jurisdictional entity prior to 1641,[75] but the deep cultural divisions in the island also disrupted the unity of the clergy as a body. The fruits of that disunion were to be seen in the split of 1648 when the hierarchy divided into rival wings along substantially ethnic lines, something which deeply depressed the nuncio. Even prior to this, however, Rinuccini had been disgusted by the passivity of the Irish bishops with regard to the captivity in Ulster since 1643 of John O'Cullenan, the bishop of Raphoe.[76] In the nuncio's view, the clergy should have been willing to pay almost any price to free a bishop: as it was, the bishop was finally ransomed by the Ulster army following its victory at Benburb, perhaps a revealing indication of the difference between provincial and episcopal solidarity.

Again, the historical experience of the Irish church as an extra-legal institution was almost certainly the key to two further areas in which the nuncio found the Irish deficient: namely in the degree of tolerance which both clergy and laity were prepared to accord protestants; and in the clergy's reluctance to spend time and money on ecclesiastical ceremonial and 'splendore'. Rinuccini, for instance, found the city of Limerick's willingness to tolerate protestant preaching utterly repugnant and finally managed to put an end to it in 1646.[77] Nor in any truce arrangement with Ormond in 1647 was he prepared to grant protestants in confederate quarters the right to listen to public preaching by their own clergy.[78] And the nuncio was positively incensed, first by the idea in 1647 that protestant royalists should be allowed to join the confederate armies, and second by the bishop of Ferns's temerity in arguing the point with him.[79] As the product of a religious tradition which stressed the value of carefully constructed and beautiful ceremonies and buildings, Rinuccini found the idea of allowing protestants the freedom to create rival public displays abhorrent. In this way, his conviction of the usefulness and importance of catholic 'splendore' as a stimulus to worship and belief was

---

[74] See the bishop of Ferns' memorial to the pope, June(?) 1648 (*Comment. Rinucc.*, iii. 42); the practice of the clergy sitting in convocation during the assembly pre-dated Rinuccini but he seems to have amplified and regularized the process.

[75] See above, Ch. 2.   [76] See *Comment. Rinucc.*, ii. 760.   [77] See Ch. 3.

[78] See his arguments against the truce arrangements, Mar. 1647 (*Comment. Rinucc.*, ii. 526).

[79] Ibid., 695–9.

linked to his desire to prevent protestants from enjoying similar opportunities of impressing the general population.[80]

The nuncio found the Irish bishops, particularly the older members of the hierarchy, depressingly blind to the merits of 'splendore':

the old bishops, accustomed to perform their limited functions in secret and without inconveniences and instigations, they make little of the splendour and grandeur of Religion, foreseeing that this could put them to great expense, and doubting always that they will be unable to maintain it either because of new dissolutions in the kingdom or because of the necessary diversion of revenues to the war. Whence one rather sees in them revulsion than anything else from subjecting themselves to the vestments and ceremonies, nearly all being used to celebrate [Mass] like ordinary priests, and to minister, for example, the sacrament of confirmation, not only without mitre and vestments, but in little less than secular garb; and these also would not be averse to contenting themselves if the king and the marquis [of Ormond] would concede free exercise, even if secret, to preserve as they believe, the substance of the Faith, and to not draw upon themselves any difficulty.[81]

This distinction between the style and substance of religion was one which Rinuccini resisted strenuously, not only by mobilizing his vast influence against any peace which promised mere toleration of secret catholic worship, but also by personal example and the instigation of Italian ceremonies. His time in Ireland was to be full of elaborately planned and staged set-pieces of ritual and commemoration. The suppression of protestant worship in Limerick in 1646 was, for instance, followed by extensive ceremonies of celebration which drew large crowds because of the 'novelty of the spectacle'.[82] The previous month Limerick had been treated to an equally elaborate procession, in the organization of which the nuncio had evidently played a key role and in which music which he had brought from Italy was played, to mark the victory at Benburb.[83] In Kilkenny, Massari was to play an important part

---

[80] He insisted to Ferns that if protestants were allowed freedom of worship in the confederate army there was a real danger of what he saw as perversion, on the grounds that 'it is impossible that other soldiers will see these rites without danger because heresy comes easily to the nature and facility of uneducated people' (impossible est ut illi ritus a militum caeteris videantur absque communi illo periculo, quod haereseos naturam et idiotarum sequitur facilitatem) Rinuccini to Ferns, Sept. 1647 (ibid., 699).

[81] 'Avvezzi a far le loro poche funzioni in segreto e senza incomodi e suggezioni, non fanno gran conto dello splendore e grandezza della Religione, prevedendo che questa gli può mettere in grandi spese, e sempre dubitando di no lo poter mantenere, o per nuove risoluzioni del Regno, o per la diversione necessaria dell'entrate ai bisogni della guerra. Onde si vede in loro più presto aborrimento che altro a soggetarsi agli abiti ed alle cerimonie, usando quasi tutti da celebrare come sacerdoti ordinari, e da ministrar per esempio il Sacramento della Confermazione non solo senza mitra e paramenti, ma poco manco che in abito secolare; e però questi ancora non sarebbono alieni a contentarsi che il Re ed il marchese concedessero esercizio libero, ancorchè occulto, per salvare com'essi credono, la sostanza della Fede, e non tirarsi addosso alcuna difficoltà': Relazione del Regno d'Irlanda, 1 Mar. 1646 (Aiazzi, Nunziatura, 110–11).

[82] 'Ob spectaculi novitatem': Comment. Rinucc., ii. 273.

[83] See ibid., 247; it seems eminently possible that the institutional poverty of the Irish church since the reformation had hampered the development of religious music in Ireland. The nuncio's use of

in the staging of an equally elaborate pageant of rejoicing for O'Neill's victory.[84] In the same city, also, in January 1648, the adoption of the Virgin Mary as the protectress of Ireland[85] was marked by an intricate procession which bore the signs of much Italian organization.[86] In 1646 Kilkenny had previously acted as the site of Rinuccini's ceremonial and public acceptance of Viscount Costello's conversion to catholicism.[87] The nuncio also baptized a number of Muslims publicly in Waterford in 1648.[88]

Not surprisingly the nuncio concentrated much of his evangelical energy in the period around Easter, particularly in 1646 and 1647, when he introduced a number of new rites to Ireland.[89] In the latter year, indeed, he went on something of an ecclesiastical tour in several confederate cities to supervise the performance of Italian ceremonies. Of the new practices he introduced, the one in which he took most pride was the washing of the feet of thirteen paupers on Holy Thursday.[90] He performed this ceremony in Kilkenny in 1646 and in Wexford in 1647.[91] On the first occasion he was assisted by members of the Supreme Council and by aldermen of the city. In the presence of a large throng of people, these exalted personages provided the paupers with white tunics, publicly washed their feet, and then personally waited on them at table during a repast in the castle.[92] It is not surprising that this ceremony appealed to the nuncio so strongly. Through this controlled violation of temporal and ecclesiastical status codes he was able to transmit a powerful message concerning the relationship between the secular and profane spheres and the authority of the clergy as the arbiters and organizers of humanity's relationship with God. Indeed he cheerfully informed his superiors: 'the people have remained so conscience-stricken, that I have heard it said by some that one sight of this spectacle is a sufficient stimulus to retain the Catholic Religion in the kingdom and to defend it for always.'[93] The impact of such ceremonies

music therefore in his ceremonies may well have made an even greater impact for this reason: see also ibid., 165, 496, and 568 for the nuncio's recitation of the litany with music and Aiazzi, *Nunziatura*, 117 concerning the musical accompaniment to his Lenten preaching in 1646. The nuncio's experience as Secretary of the Congregation of Rites in the 1620s may well have sharpened his interest in the incorporation of music in the liturgy: concerning seventeenth-century developments in Italian church music, see Alec Harman and Anthony Milner (eds.), *Man and his Music* ii, *Late Renaissance and Baroque Music*, rev. edn. (London, 1988), 498–530.

[84] Viaggio in Irlanda di Dionysio Massari (APF, Miscellaneae Varie 9, pp. 117–19).

[85] Itself evidently an idea inspired by Rinuccini: see *Comment. Rinucc.*, ii. 496–7.

[86] Ibid., 568–9.   [87] See ibid., 467–8; again music was incorporated into the ceremony.

[88] Ibid., iii. 54.   [89] See ibid., ii. 164–5, 653–4.

[90] This practice was evidently popularized north of the Alps by the Pénitents Blanc de l'Annonciation in the France of Henri III. See Frances A. Yates, *Astraea: The Imperial Theme in the Sixteenth Century* (London, 1993), 180: the ceremony was apparently unknown in Ireland prior to Rinuccini.

[91] *Comment. Rinucc.*, ii. 165, 653.   [92] Ibid., 165.

[93] 'Sono restati il popolo cosi compunti, che ho sentito pronunziare ad alcuni esser bastante stimolo il vedere una sol volta questo spettacolo a far ritenere nel Regno la Religione Cattolica e difenderla per sempre': Relazione del Regno d'Irlanda, 1 Mar. 1646 (Aiazzi, *Nunziatura*, 113).

confirmed Rinuccini in his belief that the Irish clergy who played down the importance of achieving public exercise of their religion were appallingly and dangerously wrong. Not only did he find their arguments repugnant but he was very worried about the effect which they might have on the general public. As he reported to Rome, some clergy:

have dared to preach almost seditiously in the pulpits, where some of them have dared to advance an argument that Churches are not necessary for the substance of the faith, that already in the Old Testament the Jewish people existed for centuries without having a Temple; and in the new that the Saviour instituted the Eucharist in a private house. And if those who believe otherwise had not written to contradict them, and managed to remedy the matter through reason, the common people would have easily been influenced by this opinion.[94]

In his fight to infuse Irish catholicism with some of the baroque confidence and style of contemporary Italy, the nuncio undoubtedly became impatient with a general lack of ardour and optimism. As he reported

this nation perhaps more than any other in Europe is most negligent by nature towards any industry or vivacity to improve or perfect things, but contents itself with great quiet of mind in that alone which nature itself suggests to each by means of the first apprehensions, whence, neither in matters ecclesiastical nor in secular affairs, one never sees a special solicitude or diligence, nor an ardour to promote their success, and in the same way neither does one see much indignation when a design does not succeed . . . in the worship in the churches, in the ecclesiastical ceremonies and ornaments, and in whatever other matter, even profane, which requires the stimulus of application, one does not discern even a thought or an effect which surpasses ordinary conditions.[95]

They were a people who had 'become accustomed to a mass in hovels'[96] and had 'accommodated themselves without bother to the conditions of the time'.[97] Rinuccini, almost like a nineteenth-century European in the South

---

[94] 'Si sono arditi a predicarlo quasi sediziosamente nei pulpiti, dove alcuno di loro si e avanzato temerariamente a provare non esser necessario per la sostanza della fede aver le Chiese, giacchè nel vecchio Testamento il popolo Ebreo stette tante centinaia d'anni senza aver Tempio; e nel nuovo il Salvatore institui l'Eucarista in una casa privata. E se di quelli che sentano altrimente non si fosse scritto in contrario, e procurato di remediare con le ragioni, il popolo basso facilmente si sarebbe impressionato di questo parere': Aiazzi, *Nunziatura*, 111.

[95] 'Questa nazione forse più d'ogn'altra d'Europa è negligentissima per natura a qualsivoglia industria o vivacità per migliorare e perfezionare le cose, ma si contenta con gran quieto d'anima in quel solo che l'istessa natura va dettando a ciascuno per mezze delle prime apprensioni, onde non si vede mai tanto nelle cose Ecclesiastiche, quanto nelle profane una sollecitudine o diligenza straordinaria; nemmeno un ardore a promuovere il bene di esse, siccome nè molto sdegno, quando non riesca l'intento . . . nel culto delle Chiese, nelle cerimonie ed ornamenti ecclesiastici, ed in qualunque altra cosa anco profana che richieda stimoli d'applicazione, non si scorge pure un pensiero, or un effetto che trapassi le condizioni ordinarie': ibid., 112.

[96] 'Una messa per le capanne' (ibid.).

[97] 'Accomodati senza fastidio alle condizioni del tempo': ibid. In his quotation from this report Patrick Corish rather untypically follows the Hutton translation which renders the phrase as '*quietly* accommodate themselves to the *misery* of the times', (my emphasis); this translation of 'senza

Sea islands, was inclined to put some of the blame for the 'cold spirits' of the Irish on the fact that they managed to 'feed themselves from that alone which the earth produces, without toil or sweat'.[98]

But the national character was not, he believed, a cause for despair. Even in March 1646 he admitted that, if strictly supervised, the Irish were well capable of living life with all the ecclesiastical rigour that anyone could wish. This, he suggested, was proved by the discipline of the nuns in the country and the nuncio was hopeful that all the rest of the clergy would attain the same standard when they were properly disciplined and supervised.[99]

Nine months later he was even more optimistic about the prospects for a thorough reformation of the Irish church and urged his superiors not to adopt too pessimistic a view of the criticisms which he had already made. There was, he explained, in Ireland 'a primitive and persecuted church' but the Irish offered 'docility and respect' when 'one shows them authority and example'. And he declared in ringing terms: 'I dare to promise that I am confident, if we have a little peace, to shape them so much to my way that they will take and conserve the Roman style.'[100] His experiences in Galway in 1647 and 1648 confirmed him in this opinion. Galway indeed became the site of Rinuccini's most intense ecclesiastical activity. Although *in toto* he actually spent more time in Kilkenny, the nuncio was freer to concentrate on ecclesiastical matters in Galway, whereas in the confederate capital a great deal of his time was occupied by his negotiations with the Supreme Council. From the moment of his arrival there in June 1647, he was greatly impressed not only by the 'very exemplary' clergy of Galway,[101] but also by the public devotions imploring divine assistance in the war which he declared 'were frequented with no less assembly and assiduity than is customary in the most secure kingdoms in the christian world'.[102] As he prepared to leave the city in November he wrote to Rome that there was still cause for optimism in Ireland because: 'the Catholic Religion is exercised in this city as in Italy, and I in Galway have performed my offices and the processions as I would have done in Fermo.'[103] On his

---

fastidio' and 'condizioni' seems to underemphasize the nuncio's note of criticism of the Irish: see Corish, *Catholic Community*, 42.

[98] 'Spiriti freddi'; 'pascersi di quel solo che la terra produce senza fatica e sudore': Relazione del Regno d'Irlanda, 1 Mar. 1646 (Aiazzi, *Nunziatura*, 112).

[99] Ibid., 113.

[100] 'Docilita e timore . . . quando si mostra loro l'autorità l'esempio'; 'una chiesa primitiva e perseguitata . . . ed ardisco di promettere che . . . mi basta l'animo, se averemo un poco di pace, di formarli tanto a mio modo, che pigheranno e conserveranno lo stilo Romano': Rinuccini to Pamfili, 30 Dec. 1646 (ibid., 187).

[101] 'Valde exemplarem': Extract from Rinuccini's diary, 3 July 1647 (*Comment. Rinucc.*, ii. 765).

[102] 'Fuisse frequentata non minori concursu et sedulitate, quam in orbis Christiani Regnis maxime securis fieri solet': Extract from Rinuccini's diary, 10 July 1647 (ibid.).

[103] 'La Religione Cattolica si esercita in questa città come in Italia, ed Io qui a Galvia ho fatto le mie funzioni quest'estate e le processioni, come avrei fatto a Fermo': Rinuccini to Pancirolo, 5 Nov. 1647 (Aiazzi, *Nunziatura*, 262).

return to Galway in 1648 the piety of the population once again made a deep impression on him. Indeed, the 'singular loyalty'[104] of the Galway people to his person when he had been stripped of political influence moved him to suggest Ireland could actually serve as a model for the rest of the catholic world:

Perhaps the most distant country of Christendom in reverence of the Supreme Pontiff, and in the defence of his ministers will serve as a standard for its nearer adherents; and to understand the subjection of the faithful to its head, it will be necessary that the peoples nourished in the light of truth should go to discover a climate where one never sees the sun.[105]

Thus, even though towards the end of his mission the nuncio was forced to inform his superiors that certain Italian practices were impossible to institute in Ireland,[106] the dominant impression which abides is of mutual intelligibility between Rinuccini and the Irish in terms of religious culture and practice. Variations on the basic theme of European post-tridentine catholic culture had undoubtedly occurred in Ireland, reflecting the extra-legal position of the catholic church in the island for most of the period between 1534 and 1641. Nevertheless, the ease with which the nuncio and the city of Galway established a mutually harmonious relationship indicates the degree to which the basic pattern of post-tridentine catholicism was already present in the island prior to his arrival.

[104] 'Lealtà singolare': Rinuccini's relation to the pope (Aiazzi, *Nunziatura*, 433).

[105] 'Forse il più lontano paese della Cristianità nell adorazione del Sommo Pontificato, e nella difesa dei suoi ministri servirà di norma alle comittele dei più vicini; e per intendere la soggezione dei dedeli al suo capo, bisognerà che i popoli nutriti nella luce del vero vadano a trovare un clima dove non si vede mai sole': ibid.

[106] In particular, the Italian mode of appointing parish priests through synodal examinations and other competitions was, the nuncio judged, impractical in Ireland: see Rinuccini to Pancirolo, 4 May 1648 (ibid., 310).

CHAPTER EIGHT

Conclusion

I

Barely eight months after Rinuccini's departure from Ireland the Cromwellian conquest began. In some respects, it is ironic that neither the nuncio, nor Owen Roe O'Neill, the two figures of this time easiest to portray as catholic crusaders, directly engaged in the struggle against God's Englishman. That conflict between the catholic population of Ireland and the saints of the English revolution was certainly harsh enough to qualify as another outcrop of the ferocity of the European religious wars, and it distinguished the Irish experience of the interregnum from anywhere else in the archipelago. In that context it might seem suited to personalities of their stamp. Yet any irony is perhaps more apparent than real. Owen Roe O'Neill did not confront Cromwell because the peace party of the confederates had chosen to align not with him but with Inchiquin, who had impeccable credentials as a protestant priest-killing demon in the eyes of catholic militants, and Rinuccini was not present in the island because the confederates had forced him to leave its shores. These occurrences were emblematic of other contemporary developments in European catholicism.

Rinuccini was not the only papal nuncio retreating to Italy in the late 1640s following the collapse of his mission. Fabio Chigi, the papal delegate at Münster, had endured a similar fate following the Treaty of Westphalia. Both the Chigi and the Rinuccini nunciatures were creations of the period covered in this book and their frames of reference were remarkably similar. Perhaps the most striking parallel between Chigi's German mission and that of Rinuccini in Ireland was the depth of their dissatisfaction with the peace ultimately accepted by the catholics to whom they were accredited. Although Rinuccini went further in his opposition to the Irish treaty, Chigi not only refused to sign the peace, but also argued strongly in favour of a papal bull to dissociate the pope from the peace, declaring that he saw such a bull as

most necessary and that it should be printed and distributed in upper Germany, in the Swiss [cantons], in Poland and other kingdoms also, as well as in those parts . . . because in seeing the hand of secular princes put in the sanctuary of God and this thrown one could say to the ground if it is not protected and if such great sacrileges are not condemned, by this omission only, catholics will be perverted. Now because the heretics give themselves the churches, the bishoprics and the ecclesiastical goods, all will pervert and will accuse the Holy See of somnolence if not of connivance when his Beatitude does not do that which in his piety and prudence he has already thought to do so.[1]

Such an attitude is clearly consistent with that which Rinuccini expressed in the wake of the Second Ormond peace of 1649.[2] Moreover, although Chigi objected to Westphalia because of its concessions to heretics, he clearly identified the peace as the product of catholic pressure. The nuncio very pointedly refused to accept a French gift as he left Münster. In this regard, Chigi's indignation mirrored that of Rinuccini against those he termed the Old English on his departure from Ireland. The religious wars of Europe polarized the continent not only between protestant and catholic forces but between militants and *politiques* as well.

There was a certain logic to the collapse of the Rinuccini mission so shortly after the peace of Westphalia. The reorganization and the expansion of the institutions of the Irish catholic church in the second quarter of the seventeenth century was not an isolated phenomenon but rather the product of a more generalized mood of confessional confidence. That not only Ireland but also Britain could be reintegrated into the European catholic fold seemed possible to the Roman curia during this period. In the late 1630s hopes were entertained in Rome that Charles I's struggle with English and Scottish puritanism might encourage his conversion, hopes bolstered by the king's willingness to acknowledge parallels between his position and that of his brother-in-law *vis-à-vis* the Huguenots of France.[3] These expectations were further raised by the manner in which the papal agent, George Conn, was able to develop a personal relationship with the king which he could exploit to intercede on behalf of the king's catholic subjects.[4]

The Rinuccini mission of the 1640s represented the high point of Roman hopes for a radical revision of the confessional map in the North Atlantic. Both the confederates and the nuncio himself saw Ireland as a potential

---

[1] 'La vedo necessarissima et che si stampi et che si sparga per la Germania alta, per gli Svizzeri, per la Polonia e per gli altri Regni ancora, nonchè per queste parti . . . Poichè nel vedersi messa la mano dei Principi secolari nel santuario di Dio, e questo gettato può dirsi a terra, se non si rimostra e se non si condannano tanti sacrilegi, da questa sola omissione si perverteranno i Catholici. Ora poi che egli Heretici si danno le Chiese, i Vescovadi ed i beni Ecclesiastici, tutti si perverteranno, et accuseranno la S. Sede di sonnelanza, se non di connivenza, quando non facesse S. Beatitudini quel che per sua pietà e prudenza ha già pensato di fare': quoted in Laura Schiavi, *La Mediazione di Roma e di Venezia nel congresso di Münster* (Bologna, 1923), 141.

[2] Rinuccini to Pancirolo, 13 May (ns) 1649 (Aiazzi, *Nunziatura*, 380).

[3] Geoffrey Parker, *The Thirty Years' War* (London, 1984), 7, 84; Gordon Albion, *Charles I and the Court of Rome* (London, 1935), 191; the papal agent George Conn did all in his power to foster these attitudes in the king: see Caroline Hibbard, *Charles I and the Popish Plot* (Chapel Hill, NC, 1981), 94–5.

[4] Hibbard, *Popish Plot*, 48–9; among those who wished to avail themselves of Conn's good offices was the bishop of Kildare, Ross MacGeoghegan: see APF, Scritture Originali Referite nelle Congregazioni Generali, 140 (1640), 308.

springboard for further catholic advances into the protestant fastnesses of northern Europe. But Westphalia ushered in a new era of stability in the confessional frontiers of the continent. In that context, and in the context of the Cromwellian triumph in Ireland, the Rinuccini mission rapidly took on the appearance of a product of another era. There would be no repeat: Rome did not turn its back completely on the innovations of the period covered by this book, the episcopal model of the 1620s and the 1630s was reintroduced when the easing of persecution permitted, but the notion of re-establishing the public exercise of the catholic religion was now untenable. Nor during the rest of the early modern era did the catholic episcopate regain the political position which it had enjoyed in the 1640s. Even in the Patriot parliament under a catholic king, the bishops who sat in the House of Lords were of the established not the catholic church.[5]

Rinuccini's mission was thus the culmination of a particular phase of the Irish counter-reformation, a period during which the institutional strength of the catholic church in Ireland had steadily increased. The peak in that process was arguably the legatine synod of 1646 when the clergy, under the nuncio's leadership, not only insisted that their demands for property and jurisdiction be placed at the centre of the Irish political agenda but actually deposed a government established by an unsatisfactory peace. The subsequent collapse of Rinuccini's influence and his departure in 1649, however, ushered in the greatest period of devastation of the institutional structure of the catholic church in Ireland during the entire early modern period. Consequently, it is impossible to judge the nunciature a success, whether the point of view taken is that of the papal curia, or of the confederates or of the nuncio himself.

This is most obvious from the perspective of Rome. The avowed purpose of the mission had been the full and public restoration of the exercise of the catholic religion in Ireland.[6] This was also Rinuccini's own principal interest concerning his nunciature.[7] Even as he left Ireland, although taking some comfort from the religious changes which he had instituted,[8] the nuncio was extremely pessimistic that a military victory for the English parliament in Ireland would sweep away his work.[9] His fears in this regard were entirely justified: the Cromwellian conquest shattered the catholic church in Ireland, reducing its organization to a level far below that of 1641, let alone during

[5] See J. G. Simms, 'The Jacobite Parliament of 1689' in David Hayton and Gerard O'Brien (eds.), *War and Politics in Ireland, 1649–1730* (London, 1986), 65–88.

[6] Rinuccini's instructions, Dec.(?) 1644 (Aiazzi, *Nunziatura*, p. xxxv).

[7] *Comment. Rinucc.*, ii. 278; see also ibid., i. 632.

[8] His rather disparaging comment that he had 'somewhat strengthened divine worship' ('dar qualche augmento al culto divino') reflected the nuncio's consciously humble tone at a time when he was feeling particularly jaundiced: see Rinuccini to Pancirolo, 14 Mar. (ns) 1649 (Aiazzi, *Nunziatura*, 362).

[9] Ibid., see also p. 360.

the confederate era.[10] By the latter part of 1650 Rinuccini was making no attempt to disguise the magnitude of the failure of the Irish mission.[11]

Roman interest in the Rinuccini mission had never been wholly confined to the reorganization of the Irish church. A sizeable element of the mission had been diplomatic, both as a demonstration of the pope's paternal solicitude towards his flock, and, more narrowly, as a mechanism through which diplomatic contact with the hostile French court could be reopened. In neither of these respects could the mission be deemed a success. However much care Rinuccini took to make it appear that he had left Ireland at his own volition, it was quite clear that the confederates had rebuffed Rome's interest in their affairs.[12] Nor in the course of his four years in Ireland did the presence of the nuncio and the papal investment of funds produce the reward of spectacular advances for the catholic religion.[13] With regard to the French dimension of his mission, the nuncio failed to mollify the anger of the French court towards the new pope in 1645. He eventually departed from France in that year without having been able to confer the papal rose on the Queen Regent, Anne of Austria.[14] In Ireland, the policy he pursued antagonized Mazarin's agents, particularly in 1646 when he overthrew a peace they had helped bring to fruition. In his actions, Rinuccini was not motivated by any hostility towards France but French observers proved unable to appreciate this and believed him to be an active partisan of Spain in Ireland. This was communicated to him openly and with malice in 1649 on his return to France and was one of the reasons why he was not able to remain within Bourbon territory to observe the unfolding of events in 1649.[15] The hostility between Paris and Rome during this period sprang from deeper sources than Rinuccini's conduct in Ireland, but his mission, which was originally designed to help dissipate tension between Mazarin and the Holy See, in the long run served to increase it.

For the confederate peace party the arrival of Rinuccini in Ireland was an unmitigated disaster. Rinuccini's successful opposition to the first Ormond treaty in August 1646 meant that they were forced to wait until January 1649 before concluding peace with the lord lieutenant. The second agreement with Ormond provided greater concessions than had been obtained in 1646

[10] Toby Barnard, *Cromwellian Ireland, English Government and Reform in Ireland* (Oxford, 1975), 172–3; Patrick Corish, *The Catholic Community in the Seventeenth and Eighteenth Centuries* (Dublin, 1981), 47–50.

[11] See for example his letter to Innocent, 23 Sept. (ns) 1650 (ASV, Lettere di Vescovi e Prelati 22, fo. 405).

[12] Rinuccini to Pancirolo, 14 Mar. (ns) 1649 (Aiazzi, *Nunziatura*, 359, 360).

[13] The major exception to this was the battle of Benburb, news of which was received with great enthusiasm in Rome, while the standards captured at the battle were hung in St Peter's basilica in Rome: see *Comment. Rinucc.*, ii. 249–51.

[14] Ibid., 644–6, 652.

[15] See Rinuccini to Pancirolo, 28 Apr. (ns) 1649 (Aiazzi, *Nunziatura*, 377–8 and same to same, 9 May (ns) 1649 (ibid., 379); Pancirolo to Rinuccini, 31 May (ns) 1649 (*Comment. Rinucc.*, iv. 119).

but from their perspective had certainly not been worth the wait.[16] The delay of more than two years which this involved was also highly significant in terms of the politics of the three kingdoms, because in 1649 the new royalist coalition in Ireland was left with scant months to prepare to resist the retribution of the English parliament. Moreover, the preparations which they did make were gravely hampered by the open military opposition of Owen Roe O'Neill who continued to resist the peace even after Rinuccini's departure in February 1649.[17] When finally the various ex-confederate factions did manage to patch together their differences, the lingering distrust of Ormond by the clerical party and its supporters continued to weaken the unity of the royalist coalition.[18]

Rinuccini was not, of course, solely responsible for these difficulties. Even prior to his arrival the confederate peace party had been encountering increasing difficulties with the clericalist wing of the association. Nevertheless, without Rinuccini's leadership in convoking and leading the legatine synod of 1646, it seems unlikely that the French-brokered peace of 1646 would have been overturned. Furthermore, it seems probable that without Rinuccini's arrival Owen Roe O'Neill and the Ulster army would have remained but minor players in the confederate drama.

Yet if the peace party had bitter cause to regret Rinuccini's arrival, the nuncio did not bring any long-term success to the hardline confederate clericalists or to Owen Roe O'Neill and the Ulster army. In 1646 he prevented a peace which would have left the clergy without effective guarantees concerning the lands in their possession and concerning the exercise of papal jurisdiction in Ireland, but as it transpired he had only staved off this agreement because the 1649 peace certainly did not ensure the attainment of these conditions.[19] Worse was to follow after Rinuccini's departure for no sector of the population was to suffer more from the Cromwellian conquest than the catholic clergy.[20] Similarly, although Rinuccini's money and support allowed Owen Roe O'Neill to come to the fore in a new way in the years 1646–8, in particular through the victory at Benburb and the subsequent increase in the size of the Ulster army, the gains proved transitory. By 1649 O'Neill was a

[16] To Rinuccini the peace was not 'other in substance than which they had concluded before my arrival' (altro in sostanza che quello che avanti la mia venuta avevano concluso'): Rinuccini to Pancirolo, 13 May (ns) 1648 (Aiazzi, *Nunziatura*, 380) but Micheál Ó Siochrú, *Confederate Ireland 1642–1649: A Constitutional and Political Analysis* (Dublin, 1999), 198–201 has pointed out a number of fairly significant further concessions; see also Patrick Corish, 'Bishop Nicholas French and the Second Ormond Peace, 1648–9', *Irish Historical Studies*, 6 (1948), 99–100.

[17] Jerrold Casway, *Owen Roe O'Neill and the Struggle for Catholic Ireland* (Philadelphia, 1984), 237–62.

[18] Patrick Corish, 'The Cromwellian Conquest, 1641–53', in T. W. Moody, F. X. Martin, and F. J. Byrne (eds.), *A New History of Ireland*, iii, *Early Modern Ireland, 1534–1691* (Oxford, 1976), 336–52.

[19] Ó Siochrú, *Confederate Ireland*, 198–201.

[20] Benignus Millett, 'Survival and Reorganization 1650–1695', in Corish (ed.), *History of Irish Catholicism*, iii (Dublin, 1968), 1–12.

marginalized figure, whose army represented a bargaining counter rather than a tool to reshape the political and military situation in Ireland.[21]

For Rinuccini personally, rather than opening the door to new and greater responsibilities, the end of the Irish nunciature foreshadowed the close of his varied ecclesiastical career. Having reached Florence in October 1649 he was eager to return to his archiepiscopal duties in Fermo. As it transpired, he was never really to settle back fully into his pastoral role in the see. Once returned to Italy, he could not escape going to Rome where he presented the pope with a long report on his nunciature.[22] His sojourn in Rome was quite extended, but by August 1650, having refused the newly vacant post of secretary to the congregation of *Propaganda Fide*,[23] he had returned to Fermo.[24] His distance from Rome, the fact that the situation in Ireland was changing at such speed, and the fact that Massari as secretary of *Propaganda Fide* was better placed to monitor and report on developments there, meant that Rinuccini was no longer of great value to the curia as an advisor on Ireland. Even in Fermo, the archbishop found himself increasingly bypassed by events. The city itself was still under military government at this time because the hunt for those who had been involved in the 1648 rebellion was still being conducted with some vigour, something which probably had the effect of limiting Rinuccini's influence.[25] In any case, the archbishop's health was not good and it seems to have broken down almost completely towards the end of 1651.[26] He spent much of 1652 completely absent from Fermo for reasons of ill health although he did return to his see prior to his death in 1653.[27]

II

If the mission was clearly not a success, then to what extent may its various failures be ascribed to the nuncio's personal decisions and actions? Rinuccini

---

[21] Casway, *Owen Roe O'Neill*, 237–62.

[22] Rinuccini to Pancirolo, 19 Oct. (ns) 1649 (ASV, Lettere di Vescovi e Prelati 31, fo. 410); Rinuccini's report to the pope (Aiazzi, *Nunziatura*, 391–433); *Comment. Rinucc.*, v. 433–4.

[23] *Comment. Rinucc.*, iv. 189; the post instead was given to Massari. The fact that Rinuccini was offered the post was proof that he was not judged to have been derelict in his duties in Ireland; in this regard see also Albizzi to Rinuccini, 26 Apr. (ns) 1649 (ibid., 114) and Pancirolo to Rinuccini, 3 May (ns) 1649 (ibid., 114–15). Nevertheless, the nuncio did not receive any extraordinary promotion such as elevation to the college of cardinals, although this may also have reflected his own disinclination to receive such a post: in this regard see Viaggio in Irlanda di Dionysio Massari (APF, Miscellaneae Varie 9, p. 296).

[24] Rinuccini to Pancirolo, 1 Sept. (ns) 1650 (ASV, Lettere di Vescovi e Prelati 32, fo. 333).

[25] See Francesco Caetano to Pancirolo, 24 Mar. (ns) 1651 (ASV, Lettere di Vescovi e Prelati 32, fo. 574ʳ) and same to same, 13 May (ns) 1650 (ibid., fo. 42ʳ⁻ᵛ).

[26] In that year, nevertheless, he had the gratification of seeing the belated publication of what he considered his principal work, the *Della Dignita*.

[27] Rinuccini to Innocent, 27 Jan. (ns) 1652 (ASV, Lettere di Vescovi e Prelati 33, fo. 19; Rinuccini to Cardinal Pamfili, 28 Feb. (ns) 1652 (ibid., 30); Rinuccini to Innocent, 3 Nov. (ns) 1652 (ibid., fo. 258).

evidently deserved few reproaches from his superiors. In terms of the primary ecclesiastical objective of his mission, namely the supervision of reform in the Irish church, he did all that could reasonably have been asked of him. It is true that political activity absorbed an enormous amount of his time and attention. Nevertheless, he did not neglect the ecclesiastical dimensions of his mission and was very active, particularly in 1647, in investigating religious procedures and in visiting areas which were militarily secure. Moreover, it is clear that Rinuccini engaged in intensive political activity almost exclusively because he saw this as the key to the consolidation of the ecclesiastical settlement which he had been sent to attain. As soon as a confederate executive in which the nuncio had trust was installed after the first assembly of 1647, he turned his attention with alacrity to more purely ecclesiastical affairs. That most of his energies were once again diverted to political matters towards the end of that year reflected, not his personal interests, but a conviction that such involvement was necessary to protect the interests of the church.

Rinuccini's perception that ecclesiastical reform was inseparable from a particular political settlement accorded with that of his superiors in Italy. It was for this reason that the nuncio had been equipped with 50,000 scudi as well as a wide-ranging ecclesiastical mandate on his departure from Italy, and had been given permission to make extensive donations from Irish church revenues to the confederate cause.[28] Rome had thus intended from the beginning that its nuncio would use the resources with which he had been supplied to acquire political leverage in Ireland, and they could have few complaints concerning the efficiency with which Rinuccini set about this task. Indeed, considering the total level of papal investment during this period, which did not amount to more than 150,000 scudi (less than £40,000),[29] Rome actually acquired more political influence in Ireland in the course of the confederate period than it had any real right to expect, a development due in large measure to Rinuccini's own efforts. Moreover, the policy which Rinuccini pursued in Ireland in opposing the Ormond peace, which his superiors found as unsatisfactory as the nuncio himself, was faithfully in accordance with his instructions.[30]

The one area where a significant difference between the nuncio and his superiors can be detected was in the scale of his personal involvement in the great confederate crisis of 1648. That his superiors would have wished him to avoid taking such a definite stance seems highly probable. The principal

---

[28] See *Comment. Rinucc.*, i. 590–600.

[29] One can note that the dowry of the pope's great grand-niece in 1653, assembled largely thanks to papal generosity, amounted to 70,000 scudi, a sum greater than any individual donation made to the confederates in the course of Innocent's pontificate (Ignazio Ciampi, *Innocenzo X Pamfili e la sua corte* (Rome, 1878), 20–1).

[30] Instruzione (Aiazzi, *Nunziatura*, p. xlv).

reason for this was the Roman disinclination to provide the level of finance which Rinuccini's interventionist policy required if it was to enjoy realistic chances of success. Naturally cautious, particularly about the expenditure of money,[31] the pope was ultimately more concerned with cutting expenditure on the Irish mission than with providing the nuncio with extra funds to consolidate the position of dominance which he had acquired by September 1646. However, although the pope would evidently have preferred if the nuncio had accepted the effective failure of his mission somewhat earlier, from a papal perspective relatively little was lost by Rinuccini's actions in 1648. Roman interest in Ireland was not particularly pronounced, as successive confederate envoys had discovered to their cost, and the fact that the Irish had finally managed to antagonize a prelate as religiously zealous as the nuncio merely strengthened Roman suspicions that the island was not really worth the trouble and attention it had received. The failure of the nunciature certainly left Irish catholicism in an undesirable state from a papal perspective, but Rome had found the situation in the island unsatisfactory prior to Rinuccini's arrival as well. A highly Italocentric church 're-Latinized at the Council of Trent',[32] had forged an identity based on the eradication of protestantism in the heartland of catholic Europe. Catholic reform and missionary work was, to no small extent, seen in Rome as the degree to which conformity with Italian practice could be achieved outside the peninsula, a process symbolized by the insistence on the liturgical use of Latin even in the most un-European conditions.[33] The Rinuccini nunciature had not just been a mission from the centre of the Roman church to its periphery: it was also the mission of an Italian to the 'ultramontani'.[34] That the interlude of the nunciature was followed by the Cromwellian conquest of Ireland was certainly regretted in Rome. It is obvious that a settlement under the Ormond peace would have been more acceptable to the Roman authorities than this, but that should not disguise the degree to which the Ormond peace itself was seen as inadequate by Rinuccini's superiors. From Rome's perspective, its policy had failed first in 1649, not in 1653.

Ultimately, therefore, Rinuccini's personal responsibility for the failure of papal policy in Ireland during this period would appear to be relatively slight. Rome failed to achieve its objectives in the island not because of his personal deficiencies but because those objectives were extremely difficult to secure, indeed effectively unattainable without a far greater investment of money than Innocent was prepared to make.

[31] When cardinal of the datary, Innocent had apparently been nicknamed 'Monsignor non si può' ('Monsignor it's not possible'): see Ciampi, *Innocenzo X*, 319–27.

[32] A. D. Wright, *The Counter-Reformation: Catholic Europe and the Non-Christian World* (London, 1982), 32–5.

[33] Ibid., 138–46; Henry Kamen, *The Phoenix and the Flame: Catalonia and the Counter-reformation* (London, 1993), 53.

[34] See Albizzi's instructions to Rinuccini, Dec.(?) 1644 (Aiazzi, *Nunziatura*, p. li).

In terms of the confederate association, it is difficult to determine the extent to which Rinuccini's actions were of genuine long-term significance. The Cromwellian conquest was the shockwave which entirely altered the political landscape of 1650s Ireland. Whether this could have been prevented or its nature altered by any action of the confederates or of the nuncio is open to question. Certainly, it was of military significance that Cromwell was able to land his forces in parliamentary held Dublin in 1649.[35] Recently some of the military deficiencies of the 'invincible' New Model Army in Ireland have been highlighted.[36] Nevertheless, it seems probable that the resources available to the English parliament would have been adequate for the reconquest of Ireland unless a most unusual concatenation of circumstances had prevailed. Thus only if Irish intervention in Britain had come much earlier in the decade does it seem possible that the dynamic of events might have been altered. To follow that particular counter-factual is, however, beyond the scope of this study.

Counter-factuals aside, it is none the less evident that during the 1640s Rinuccini was an actor of quite extraordinary significance in the affairs of the confederates. He was the prime mover in the rejection of the first Ormond peace in 1646; it was he who brought the association to the brink of civil war with the attack on Dublin of that year and it was his ecclesiastical censure against the Inchiquin truce which effectively ignited the confederate civil war of 1648. A common thread links these three events, namely the nuncio's willingness to initiate positive action which carried with it the great probability of escalating the level of conflict, in Ireland as a whole, and within the confederate association itself. Rinuccini's gambler's instinct brought success in the first instance, a severe but potentially recuperable setback in the second, and ultimate defeat in the third. Yet, although the wisdom of Rinuccini's actions in all these cases is open to some question, it is vital to bear in mind the context within which he took them.

His opposition to the Ormond peace in 1646 was intimately related to his growing suspicions of the good faith and motivations of the confederate Supreme Council who introduced the treaty. Rinuccini was arguably correct to believe that a relatively unrepresentative clique dominated the council at this juncture. This is indicated both by the behaviour of the confederate General Assembly in February 1646 and in the manner in which the peace was rejected, first by the populations of the towns and the soldiers of the confederate armies, and then at the first assembly of 1647. That this clique also had no real desire to accommodate the demands of the catholic clergy had been suggested in the debates of May 1645 and was demonstrated again in their response to the legatine synod of 1646. When account is taken, first of

[35] Simms, 'The Jacobite Parliament of 1689', 1–10.
[36] James Burke, 'The New Model Army and the Problems of Siege Warfare, 1648–51', *Irish Historical Studies*, 27 (1990), 1–29.

the nature of Rinuccini's convictions concerning the necessity of the public exercise of catholicism, second of the confederate military victories of the summer of 1646, third of the inadequacy of the religious conditions of the Ormond peace following the complete undermining of Glamorgan's authority, and fourth of the firm support which the legatine synod gave to the nuncio, then his developing conviction that the council were prepared to ignore the interests of the church for their private commodity was enough to make his opposition to the peace close to inevitable. The ease with which the nuncio masterminded victory at this juncture was a further proof of the strength of his case, although in hindsight it is clear that Rinuccini gave insufficient weight to the French involvement in the Ormond peace.

Thus one can suggest that the nuncio emerged with more credit from the crisis of the first Ormond peace than did the peace party in the council. Like Rinuccini, this party represented an essentially sectional interest, in their case a largely Old English group who saw their position in Ireland threatened by returned military exiles, by the religious orders of the catholic church, and, most of all, by the English parliament. From the perspective of this group, union with the (unfortunately practically moribund) royalist cause represented the best mode of protecting their interests. Their willingness to use their position of influence on the council to direct the association as a whole in the direction of peace with the king was certainly understandable, but ultimately they had little justification for complaint when the nuncio, in defence of the interests of the clerical wing of the association, simply outmanœuvred them.

Having assumed effective control of the association in September 1646, Rinuccini made his most significant blunder by launching an attack against Ormond. Given that the lord lieutenant had respected his side of the peace, the morality of this action was intensely dubious, while the political consequences were disastrous. The campaign against Dublin alienated many moderate confederates, and its failure diminished the pope's interest in subsidizing the Irish mission. The nuncio appears to have been influenced in deciding on this aggressive strategy by a mixture of motives, including determination to end Ormond's baleful influence within the association, intoxication with a sense of divine favour as a result of the summer's successes, and hope that the capture of Dublin would stimulate further papal generosity.

The dismal failure of the Dublin campaign inaugurated a new period in the nuncio's policy during which time the leadership of the still dominant clerical faction within the association passed largely into the hands of the bishop of Ferns and Nicholas Plunkett. Rinuccini's half-reluctant acquiescence in this development arguably made sound sense. Without an independent source of finance, his own powers of initiative were limited, and, as had been suggested in late 1646 and was to be demonstrated again in 1648, the support of the Ulster army alone was inadequate to allow him to dominate the association. Moreover, and hardly to the nuncio's discredit, he evidently found the Ulster army's treatment of the civilian population of Leinster distasteful and he remained doubtful about O'Neill's motives. Yet, the nuncio covered his options to a certain extent by securing service for the Ulster army in Connacht, thereby contributing to its survival during the summer of 1647.

Unfortunately for the nuncio, three factors, none of which was under his control, combined to undermine the policy of the clerical party in 1647. The first of these was the non-arrival of any money from Rome. This was something which Rinuccini had not anticipated and it severely weakened the amount of influence he was able to exert within the politics of the association and within the confederate military. The failure of these subsidies to arrive was itself due to a combination of factors: to some extent the fiasco at Dublin contributed, as did the reluctance of Mazarin to allow the export of coin from France to Ireland, but a prime reason was Pope Innocent's basic parsimony. The second factor at work in weakening the nuncio's position was the refusal of the peace party to reconcile themselves with the clerical faction's control of the council. As a result, both the Leinster and Munster armies became riven by faction and involvement in plots to desert to French service which compromised their military efficiency. The third factor concerned Preston's military inability to fulfil the hopes of the clerical party, who had entrusted him with the crucial campaign against Dublin. The military disasters which afflicted the association in 1647, therefore, did not spring primarily from independent decisions made by Rinuccini. To a large extent, he followed a reasoned policy during this period which was ultimately undermined by events outside his control.

Rinuccini's reactions to the disasters of 1647, however, certainly set the stage for his behaviour in 1648. The factionalism in the confederate armies during 1647 further confirmed his suspicions of the untrustworthiness of the confederate peace party. Thus he continued to adopt a hardline policy in the second assembly of 1647. The fact that this assembly resulted in the peace party regaining effective control of the Supreme Council narrowed the nuncio's options considerably in 1648. Convinced, and with justification, that they were plotting to bring about Ormond's return, Rinuccini had little choice but to oppose them or to make preparations to leave Ireland. Ultimately, partly because of the council's own actions, the nuncio decided on overt opposition. His wisdom in doing so was certainly questionable. The hope he still entertained in 1648 that the Roman envoys might return with additional papal subsidies was arguably unrealistic. Furthermore, the issue on which he chose to confront the council, namely the Inchiquin truce, was relatively weak and he failed to assemble the coalition of support which he had enjoyed in 1646. Consequently, he found himself outmanœuvred by essentially the same group whom he had humbled in the crisis of the first Ormond peace. The manner of his subsequent departure was inglorious and he left the confederates bitterly divided. Yet this was to a certain extent inevitable. The nuncio's enemies had antagonized him to such an extent by what he saw as sacrilegious behaviour that he could not contemplate reconciliation with them. Indeed, the fact that he left so few under sentence of excommunication was perhaps surprising. Moreover, in leaving Ireland, he expected to be in a position to supervise the development of events from either Flanders or France, not anticipating the attitude of the French court which forced him back to Italy in the summer of 1649.

Any attempt to understand Rinuccini's political career in Ireland must take into account his relationship with the confederate peace party. It is they who have remained the most shadowy figures in the existing literature on the 1640s, while the nuncio's role has been highlighted to a greater degree. There has been a general failure even in those analyses which have acquitted the nuncio of some of the most serious accusations against him[37] to confront the self-interested and often duplicitous nature of the confederate opposition to his policies, particularly in 1647 and 1648. This group, Bellings, Browne, Muskery, and Fennell in particular, was arguably at least as intransigent as the nuncio: their protection of what they saw as their interests within the association was in many ways natural, but certainly in 1647 the plotting in which they engaged contravened the oath of association and undermined the genuine attempts of Nicholas Plunkett and the bishop of Ferns to reunite the confederate catholics.

Rinuccini's personality, and above all the nature of his religious convictions, must also be considered in any evaluation of his nunciature. Money, and the respect which accrued to him from his office, only partly explain the nuncio's influence during this period. His own intelligence and capacity for work were also essential ingredients in this regard. In addition, the intensity of his religious belief was significant. Rinuccini's conviction in the necessity of achieving a position for the catholic church in Ireland roughly equivalent to that which it enjoyed in Italy was fervent and firm. It accorded with his conscience as well as his instructions to oppose any political settlement which did not offer a secure probability of this. The need for faith in providence also influenced his political stance. The nuncio believed in the necessity of willing sacrifices from catholics in order to safeguard the honour of God, a conviction strengthened by the trust that eventually, and perhaps even in the short term, such sacrifices would be rewarded by heavenly assistance and intervention. Certainly the nuncio saw God's hand in the victories of 1646 and his belief that the confederates had incurred divine displeasure through their sins in 1647 seems to have influenced his later position concerning the Inchiquin truce.

[37] In this context, see in particular Patrick Corish, 'Ormond, Rinuccini, and the Confederates, 1645–9', in T. W. Moody, F. X. Martin, and F. J. Byrnes (eds.), *A New History of Ireland*, iii, *Early Modern Island, 1534–1691* (Oxford, 1976), 334–5; the exception to this general rule is Ó Siochrú, *Confederate Ireland*: see for example 105–6, 171–5.

To many Old English confederates, particularly Richard Bellings, an insistence on the necessity for renewed faith in the aftermath of military disaster bordered on irrationality.[38] Yet Rinuccini's religious convictions also seem to have separated him somewhat from his superiors. Where Rinuccini saw the Irish mission in terms close to that of a crusade, more disinterested attitudes were adopted in Rome. Innocent X's commitment to the mission on religious grounds certainly did not match that of the nuncio and this contributed to his unwillingness to invest money in Ireland. The nunciature therefore was to become filled with frustration for Rinuccini, who believed passionately in the worth of the cause in Ireland, and who considered that with additional money he could make great gains for the catholic party, but who was unable to persuade his superiors to commit the necessary resources. And in trying to force the confederates into performing actions likely to stimulate papal generosity, it is arguable that he overreached himself.

III

So devastating was the Cromwellian conquest of the 1650s that it is difficult to speak with any confidence of the long-term effects of Rinuccini's mission. That mission was in a real sense the culmination of the episcopal strategy which Rome had been employing in Ireland since 1618. The episcopate, however, which reached its peak under Rinuccini in 1648 was to have no immediate successors.[39] When Rome gradually began to rebuild the structures of the Irish church in the late 1650s, the essential starting point was the damage of the Cromwellian settlement, not the foundations which Rinuccini had laid.[40] In the history of the Irish church, Rinuccini's legacy was thus largely subsumed by that of Cromwell. Ormond's return as lord lieutenant in the 1660s and the survival and renewed prominence of a number of Rinuccini's confederate opponents did help to keep some of the controversies of his nunciature alive.[41] A number of these former confederates were prominent in producing the 'Loyal formulary' or 'Remonstrance' of 1661 which, one historian has suggested, can be characterized to some extent as an attempt by Rinuccini's opponents 'to rationalize the position adopted for political reasons in 1648'.[42] None of the Irish bishops, even those who had opposed Rinuccini, was prepared to endorse the formulary. Whether this represented

[38] Bellings's narrative (Gilbert, *Irish Confederation*, vii. 5).
[39] D. F. Cregan, 'The Social and Cultural Background of a Counter-Reformation Episcopate, 1618–60', in A. Cosgrove and D. MacCartney (eds.), *Studies in Irish History Presented to R. Dudley Edwards* (Dublin, 1979), 85.
[40] Millett, 'Survival and Reorganization', 13–20.
[41] James Brennan, 'A Gallican Interlude in Ireland', *Irish Theological Quarterly*, 24 (1957), 219–37, 283–309.
[42] Patrick Corish, 'The Origins of Catholic Nationalism', in id. (ed.), *History of Irish Catholicism*, iii. 60–1.

'the first public vindication of the nuncio' and an indication that his career in Ireland had put certain points, such as the refusal of Irish catholics to compromise their declarations of allegiance to Rome, 'outside the scope of discussion in the future', remains, however, debatable.[43] The failure of Irish catholics to find an oath of allegiance acceptable both to their religion and their monarch long pre-dated Rinuccini. The Remonstrance arguably sprang more from the desire to conciliate Ormond, who had been left rather jaundiced about the nature of catholic allegiance, and the intervention of the catholic clergy into politics, by his experiences in the 1640s.[44]

The Rinuccini excommunication also fizzled out rather than anything else: the nuncio believed that only a tiny handful of confederates remained to be absolved on his departure.[45] He had left faculties in the hands of various Irish prelates to absolve those who feared they were affected and after his death Rome dealt quietly with the matter by granting the bishops of Raphoe, Leighlin, Clonfert, and Cork (all supporters of the nuncio) the right to grant absolution from the censure to all individual applicants.[46]

Yet if the trail of Rinuccini's legacy runs cold surprisingly quickly after this departure from Ireland, that does not undermine his importance as an actor in the confederate association and in particular, from the perspective of a modern historian, as an observer of the confederates. The ecclesiastical activity of this byproduct of the Italian counter-reformation, and his analysis of Irish catholicism offer a different picture of the nature of religious change in mid-seventeenth-century Ireland. For Rinuccini, the Old English catholic tradition, particularly outside the towns, was more anomalous than that of the Gaelic Irish. His own quest to secure a position for the church closer to that which it enjoyed in Italy ultimately foundered. But the ease with which Rinuccini came to grips with his task of ecclesiastical reform, and his optimism that a satisfactory political settlement would lead to the complete remodelling of Irish catholicism on Italian lines, is evidence of the deep penetration of tridentine attitudes and organization into all parts of Ireland, even prior to his arrival. That Rinuccini did not manage to complete the process of integrating Ireland into the European norm contributed, it has been suggested, to the subsequent strength of Irish catholicism.[47] But perhaps one element of the nuncio's vision did survive in a significant fashion. In Chapter 3, a certain paradox was noted between the nuncio's belief in the establishment of firm and authoritative ecclesiastical structures to maintain

---

[43] Corish, 'The Origins of Catholic Nationalism', 60–1.

[44] J. C. Beckett, *The Cavalier Duke* (Belfast, 1990), 95.

[45] See Rinuccini to Pancirolo, 14 Mar. (ns) 1649 (Aiazzi, *Nunziatura*, 363–6).

[46] Ibid., v. 244–7; the various stages of the controversy, and the attempts of the various Irish factions to convince Rome to adopt a position favourable to them, are detailed in *Comment. Rinucc.*, iv. 185–90, 369–83, 400–1, v. 207–8.

[47] John Bossy, 'The Counter-Reformation and the People of Catholic Ireland', *Historical Studies*, 8 (1971), 169–70.

religious orthodoxy on the one hand and, on the other, his conviction that nothing strengthened the church more than persecution and martyrdom. In Ireland his attempts to achieve his organizational goals were swept away by the repression of the catholic church and clergy during the 1650s. Yet, if this was truly the decade that the 'tradition of the 'Mass-rock' stamped itself on the Irish experience',[48] then according to his own beliefs the nuncio ironically may have succeeded more than he had imagined.

---

[48] Corish, *Catholic Community*, 49.

Appendix A. The Irish Episcopacy during the Nunciature

Name	Diocese and Year of Consecration	The Nuncio's Evaluation pre-1648	Stance in 1648
1. David Rothe	1. Ossory (1620)	1. Pious but old.	1. Anti-nuncio.
2. Richard Arthur	2. Limerick (1623)	2. Little contact.	2. Already dead (1646).
3. Maurice O'Hurley	3. Emly (1623)	3. Little contact.	3. Already dead (1646).
4. Thomas Dease	4. Meath (1622)	4. Old, troublesome.	4. Strongly anti-nuncio.
5. William Tirry	5 Cork and Cloyne (1623)	5. Old but accommodating.	5. Already dead (1646).
6. Thomas Fleming	6. Dublin (1623)	6. Fat but well meaning.	6. Moderate pro-nuncio.
7. Hugh O'Reilly	7. Armagh (1626)[2]	7. Reliable but defensive.	7. Pro-nuncio.
8. John O'Cullenan	8. Raphoe (1626)	8. Old but reliable.	8. Strongly pro-nuncio.
9. Boethius MacEgan	9. Elphin (1626)	9. Old but reliable.	9. Pro-nuncio.
10. Thomas Walsh	10. Cashel (1626)	10. Mild but well meaning.	10. Very moderate anti-nuncio.
11. Eugene MacSweeny	11. Kilmore (1630)	11. Little if any contact.	11. Pro-nuncio.
12. Patrick Comerford	12. Waterford and Lismore (1629)	12. Old but reliable.	12. Very moderate pro-nuncio.[4]
13. Malachy O'Queely	13. Tuam (1630)	13. Lamented his death.	13. Already dead (1645).
14. John O'Moloney	14. Killaloe (1630)	14. Little apparent contact.	14. Pro-nuncio.
15. Richard O'Connell	15. Ardfert (1643)	15. Old but committed.	15. Pro-nuncio.
16. John Bourke	16. Clonfert (1642)[3]	16. Mediocre, troublesome.	16. Strongly anti-nuncio.
17. Edward O'Dempsey	17. Leighlin (1643?)	17. Reliable, unimpressive.	17. Pro-nuncio.
18. Heber MacMahon	18. Clogher (1643)	18. Reliable, too political.	18. Strongly pro-nuncio.
19. Nicholas French	19. Ferns (1645)	19. Best Irish bishop.	19. Anti-nuncio.
20. Edmund O'Dwyer	20. Limerick (1645)	20. Reliable and able.	20. Anti-nuncio.
21. Francis Kirwan	21. Killala (1645)	21. Little apparent contact.	21. Strongly anti-nuncio.

22. Patrick Plunkett	Ardagh (1648)	Politically useful.	22. Anti-nuncio.
23. Anthony MacGeoghegan	Clonmacnoise (1648)	Reliable.	23. Strongly pro-nuncio.
24. Arthur Magennis	Down/Connor (1648?)	Reliable.	24. Strongly pro-nuncio.
25. Oliver Darcy	Dromore (1648)	Influential with Preston.	25. Strongly anti-nuncio.
26. Terrence O'Brien	Emly (1648)	Reliable, zealous.	26. Strongly pro-nuncio.
27. Boethius MacEgan	Ross (1648)	Reliable, close to O'Neill.	27. Strongly pro-nuncio.
28. Andrew Lynch	Kilfenora (1647)	Weak, unimpressive.	28. Strongly anti-nuncio.
29. Walter Lynch	Clonfert (1648)	Reliable, zealous.	29. Strongly pro-nuncio.
30. Robert Barry	Cork/Cloyne (1648)	Reliable, zealous.	30. Strongly pro-nuncio.
31. Hugh Bourke	Kilmacduagh (1648?)	Able.	31. Anti-nuncio

[1] Much of the information in this and the following column is based on D. F. Cregan, 'The Social and Cultural Backgrund of a Counter-Reformation Episcopate 1618–60', in A. Cosgrove and D. MacCartney (eds.), *Studies in Irish History Presented to R. Dudley Edwards* (Dublin, 1979), 87.

[2] He was consecrated as bishop of Kilmore and transferred to Arnagh in 1628.

[3] Subsequently transferred to Tuam in 1647.

[4] However, he ultimately participated in the negotiation of the second Ormond peace.

Appendix B. Supplementary Biographical Details

Albizzi, Francesco: Secretary of the Congregation of Irish affairs in Rome; framer of Rinuccini's instructions and important adviser on Irish affairs to Pope Innocent X; also a regular correspondent with Fabio Chigi in Münster.

Alexander VII: see Chigi, Fabio.

Barberini, Antonio: cardinal protector of Ireland up to 1645; also cardinal protector of France and of the Dominican order; nephew of pope Urban VIII; suspected of complicity in the murder of one of cardinal Pamfili's retainers; together with his brothers contributed 20,000 scudi to confederate cause, 1642–3.

Barberini, Francesco: cardinal, nephew of Pope VIII, brother of the above; personal enemy of cardinal Pancirolo; Pope Innocent's most important adviser in the college of cardinals.

Barberini, Maffeo: Pope Urban VIII; acceded to papal throne in 1623, died in 1644; notorious for nepotism, considered to be pro-French in politics but provided financial assistance to the Austrian Habsburgs at intervals during the 1620s and 1630s; involved by his nephews in the expansionist War of Castro, 1642–4; appointed Scarampi to Ireland in 1643.

Baron, Geoffrey: lawyer, nephew of Luke Wadding; played an important role in bringing Waterford into the original rebellion against the wishes of the mayor; did duty as a confederate agent in France, 1645–8; nuncioist in the split of 1648.

Barry, Colonel John: emissary of Ormond to Inchiquin and to the confederate peace party in 1648.

Bellings, Richard: arguably the single most important confederate; a trained lawyer, he possessed substantial allotments of former monastic property and was married to Margaret Butler, the daughter of Viscount Mountgarrett; member of most confederate Supreme Councils where he discharged the office of secretary; was appointed extraordinary confederate ambassador to Italy in 1644; returned with Rinuccini to Ireland in 1645; ardent advocate of the first Ormond peace; imprisoned after nuncio's coup of 1646; returned to office in the Supreme Council against the nuncio's furious opposition in December 1647; intimately involved in the negotiation of the Inchiquin truce and Ormond's return in 1648; went into exile with Ormond in 1650; composed his history of the confederate period in the 1670s.

Blake, Sir Richard: native of Galway; president of confederate assembly of 1648; member of the confederate peace party and ardent anti-nuncioist in 1648.

Borlase, Sir John: English-born master of the Ordinance in the 1630s; appointed lord justice with William Parsons in 1641 and was joint head of the Irish government at outbreak of 1641 rebellion.

Bourke, Hugh, OFM: confederate agent in Flanders during the 1640s; appointed bishop of Kilmacduagh on Rinuccini's advice in 1647; had hoped for appointment to Clonfert to succeed his brother John and resented that his brother Oliver, the vicar apostolic, had not been given Kilmacduagh; absent from Ireland at the time of the truce crisis in 1648 but opposed the nuncio.

Bourke, John: brother of the above; vicar apostolic of Clonfert in the 1630s; appointed bishop of the see in 1641; succeeded to archdiocese of Tuam with Rinuccini's somewhat grudging consent in 1647; emerged during that year as Rinuccini's most important episcopal opponent; finally broke with the nuncio over Rinuccini's censure of May 1648; thereafter headed clerical resistance to the nuncio.

Browne, Geoffrey: prominent member of the confederate peace party; confederate envoy to France in 1648 where he played an active part in the plot to bring Ormond back to Ireland.

Burke, Ulick: catholic earl (later marquis) of Clanricard; also earl of St Albans in the English peerage; English raised and educated; domiciled in county Galway of which he was the royalist commander for most of the 1640s; threatened with excommunication by catholic bishops for his refusal to take the confederate oath but consistently refused to do so; supported both Ormond peaces; in late 1646 almost detached Preston from the nuncio's camp during the campaign against Dublin; in December 1650 was appointed Ormond's deputy when the lord lieutenant left Ireland.

Butler, James: earl (later marquis, later Duke) of Ormond; appointed lieutenant-general of king's army in Ireland in Nov. 1641; in Nov. 1643 appointed lord lieutenant; oversaw the transport of most of the crown army back to England after the truce of Sept. 1643; thereafter held Dublin with a small force through a series of truces with the confederates; chief royalist negotiator with the confederates 1643–6; exerted great influence on the confederate peace party, many of whom were related to him; concluded first Ormond peace with the confederates in March 1646; consented to its publication on Digby's advice in July; visited Kilkenny in late August but driven back to Dublin by the clerical coup; saved Dublin from Rinuccini through an appeal to parliament and Clanricard's manipulation of Preston; negotiated the transfer of Dublin to parliament in 1647; left Ireland for England; involved in a new series of royalist plots; liaised with confederate envoys to France in Paris in 1648; returned to Ireland in September of that year; negotiated the second Ormond peace which was signed in January 1649; defeated by Jones in August of that year; failed to halt Cromwell's campaign of conquest; went into exile in 1650; an important member of Charles II's court in exile in the 1650s; appointed lord lieutenant after the Restoration in 1662; oversaw the restoration settlement of Irish land; returned as lord lieutenant in 1677; left office in 1685; died in 1688.

Butler, Richard: Viscount Mountgarrett; president of the confederate catholic association until the first Ormond peace; possibly semi-senile by 1647 when he attempted to imprison the Supreme Council; anti-nuncio in 1648 but did not play a particularly active role in the latter part of the decade.

Castlehaven, earl of: see Touchet, James.

Chigi, Fabio: papal nuncio in Cologne 1629–51; represented the papacy at the peace negotiations at Münster until the peace of Westphalia in 1648; urged an official papal condemnation of the peace which was finally issued in 1651; elected pope as Alexander VII in 1655.

Darcy, Patrick: a lawyer and important confederate closely linked to Clanricard; opposed Wentworth's attempts to find for the king's title in Connacht in the 1630s; emerged as the outstanding constitutionalist in the Irish parliament with his *Argument* of 1641 which asserted the legislative independence of the Irish parliament; the *Argument* was published by the confederates in 1643; Darcy served on several Supreme Councils; was closely linked to the peace party but was respected also by the clerical party; together with Nicholas Plunkett, played an important role in moderating the clergy's position in May 1645; failed to persuade the legatine synod of the worth of the Ormond peace in August 1646 but escaped imprisonment; worked unsuccessfully to bring Clanricard into the association in 1647; anti-nuncioist in 1648.

Dease, Thomas: bishop of Meath; most important cleric to oppose original rebellion; consistently denied the rights of catholics to take up arms against their lawful monarch; greatly disliked by Rinuccini whom he opposed with vehemence in 1648; his great age, however, limited his degree of influence.

de Bellièvre, Pompone: French ambassador to England in 1646; acted according to instructions to integrate the Irish confederates into plans for the restoration of Charles' authority and to protect their existing religious liberties.

de la Torre, Don Diego: Spanish agent to the confederates; supported Rinuccini and O'Neill in the coup against the council in 1646; in 1648, however, allowed the council to make use of him to harass the nuncio concerning a ship which Massari had captured on his return to Ireland; eventually recalled to Spain and replaced by O'Sullivan Beare in 1648.

Digby, George: son of the earl of Bristol and the king's chief secretary during the first Civil War; arrived in Ireland towards the end of 1645; responsible for the imprisonment of Glamorgan in Dublin; led an expedition to the Scilly isles and then on to France in the spring of 1646; returned to Ireland in July equipped with money and instructions from France and from the queen of England to facilitate the Ormond peace. Played an important role in persuading Ormond to publish the peace; after the deposition of the council worked hard with Clanricard to detach Preston from the nuncio; in March 1647 managed to interest the French agents in bringing confederate soldiers to France; intrigued with the Leinster and Munster armies to that purpose and in this way contributed to their costly military inactivity during that year.

Digby, Sir Kenelm: cousin of the above; emissary of queen of England to Pope Innocent in 1645; signed the 'papal peace' with Innocent in November but this treaty came ultimately to nothing.

du Moulin, Claude: French agent to Ireland in 1646–7; under instructions to support the Ormond peace which he did ardently; communicated intelligence to Digby during Rinuccini's campaign against Dublin in 1646; opposed the nuncio publicly in the first confederate assembly of 1647; involved in the plot to transport confederate soldiers to France later that year.

Fennell, Gerrott: important member of the confederate peace party; a physician by profession, he served on several Supreme Councils where he was identified as a particular supporter of his patron, Ormond; imprisoned after the clerical coup of 1646; eventually brought back into the council against Rinuccini's wishes in December 1647; involved in the preparation of the Inchiquin truce and in the plot for Ormond's return in 1648; strongly anti-nuncioist and in favour of both treaties with Ormond.

FitzGerald, Pierce: Old English confederate generally known as 'MacThomas'; an important military commander whose support was important in the nuncio's victory over the council in 1646; in 1648, however, he supported the Inchiquin truce and opposed O'Neill.

French, Nicholas: appointed bishop of Ferns in 1645; made a deep impression on the nuncio who considered him the best of the Irish bishops; secretary to the synod of 1646 which opposed the first Ormond peace; selected for the Supreme Council which oversaw the campaign against Dublin; one of the architects of clerical strategy in 1647; worked closely with Preston during that year in supplying and equipping the Leinster army; played a part in convincing Preston to confront Jones at Dungan's Hill; one of the nominators of the Supreme Council in December 1647 where he flouted the nuncio's instructions and consented to the elevation of several prominent members of the peace faction; confederate envoy to Rome in 1648; returned much chastened in November and played a prominent role in the negotiation of the second Ormond peace which was concluded in 1649; subsequently disavowed responsibility for the second Ormond peace; published a bitter attack on Ormond during the restoration.

Jones, Michael: chief parliamentary commander in Ireland from July 1647 until Cromwell's arrival in August 1649; inflicted a heavy defeat on Preston in August 1647 but was prevented from following the victory up by O'Neill; his forces suffered heavily from O'Neill's scorched earth policy during the winter of 1647–8; in August 1649 routed Ormond's forces at Rathmines thus preserving a safe bridgehead for the arrival of the Cromwellian army of conquest.

La Monerie, le sieur de: French agent to Ireland on several occasions during the 1640s; supported Digby in the plot to suborn the Munster army in 1647; was convinced that Rinuccini was pro-Hispanic and advised the French court not to trust him.

Lynch, Walter: appointed bishop of Clonfert on Rinuccini's recommendation in 1647; his appointment aroused great hostility because he was not the Supreme Council's nominee for the see; one of the Old English bishops who stood firmly by the nuncio during the crisis of 1648.

MacCarthy, Donough: Viscount Muskery; most influential confederate in Munster and one of the leaders of the confederate peace party; married to Helena Butler, Ormond's sister; personal rival of the viscount of Fermoy; important figure in the negotiations of the first Ormond peace; made commander of the Munster army in 1646; voluntarily joined other members of the peace party in prison after the clerical coup; returned to the Supreme Council after the first assembly of 1647 with the assistance of Nicholas Plunkett; helped paralyse the Munster army in the first half of 1647 before reassuming command in a mutiny in June; plotted with Digby to bring confederate soldiers to France later that year; helped select the Supreme Council of 1648; went to France in 1648 as a confederate envoy; plotted with Ormond concerning the marquis's return; a major figure in the anti-nuncioist camp following the Inchiquin truce.

MacDonnell, Randal: earl (later marquis) of Antrim; husband of Duchess of Buckingham; involved in various schemes in late 1630s and 1640s to raise his Scottish and Irish kin for the royalist cause; in 1644 sent 2,000 troops to Scotland to fight with Montrose; became president of the nuncioist Supreme Council of 1647; went as confederate envoy to France where he was marginalized from the plans of Browne and Muskery; declared an innocent papist by the court of claims and restored to his estates in 1665.

MacMahon, Heber: appointed bishop of Down and Connor in 1642; transferred to the see of Clogher where he had previously been vicar apostolic in 1643; played a prominent role in the synod of the province of Armagh in March 1642; worked closely with Owen Roe O'Neill throughout the decade; one of the two bishops whom Rinuccini was instructed to liaise with closely on his arrival in Ireland; considered by the nuncio to be motivated almost purely by political considerations; came close to provoking a decisive rupture in the association during the second assembly of 1647 when he refused the embassy to France; opposed the Inchiquin truce in 1648; appointed commander of Ulster army after Owen Roe's death in 1650 but was defeated and killed at Scarrifhollis in June of that year.

Massari, Dionysio: dean of Fermo and in 1649 made secretary of the Congregation of *Propaganda Fide* in Rome; accompanied Rinuccini to Ireland in 1645; auditor-general and datary of the nuncio's tribunal in Ireland; liaised with Preston and O'Neill on the nuncio's behalf on several occasions; returned to Rome in November 1646 on a mission from the Irish clergy; successfully convinced Pope Innocent to make a further contribution to the Irish mission in December; was delayed in Rome until May 1647 by the pope's disappointment with the failure of the Dublin campaign; subsequently delayed in France until March 1648 when he returned to Ireland; en route captured a vessel and money which was subsequently claimed as Spanish by Don Diego de la Torre who brought a court case against Massari; promulgated the nuncio's censure of May 1648 in Kilkenny and was imprisoned; returned to France with Rinuccini; met Mazarin in Paris in April and discovered his hostility to Rinuccini; preceded the nuncio back to Rome; as secretary to *Propaganda Fide* hampered the attempts of the confederate peace party to have Rinuccini's censure overturned.

O'Connell, Richard: appointed bishop of Ardfert in 1641 having previously been vicar apostolic in the see; supported the 1641 rebellion as a war in defence of religion from an early stage, but offered protestants in his diocese protection if they would convert; met Rinuccini on his arrival in Kerry in 1645; a consistent and firm supporter of the nuncio but came infrequently to Kilkenny during the 1640s.

O'Connell, Robert: capuchin friar and co-author of the *Commentarius Rinuccinianus* in the 1660s in Florence.

O'Ferrall, Richard: capuchin friar, and principal author of the *Commentarius*; superior of capuchin friary in Galway in 1648; sent by Rinuccini to Rome in that year to explain the nuncio's censure; nominated by Rinuccini in 1650 to aid the nuncio in preparing a detailed history of his mission; in 1659 began the compilation of the *Commentarius* (work completed in 1666).

O'Ferrall, Richard: important officer in the Ulster army, greatly liked by Rinuccini; after some indecision supported the nuncio openly in the great crisis of 1648; resisted the Cromwellian invasion but survived to go with an Irish regiment to Spain in 1653.

O'Neill, Owen Roe: nephew of the great earl of Tyrone and colonel in the Spanish service until 1642; returned to Ireland in that year and became general of the Ulster army; defeated at Clones in June 1643 but recovered to threaten the royalist position in Dublin by September; blamed Castlehaven for the failure of the confederate offensive in Ulster in 1644; supplied to a limited extent with money and arms by Rinuccini in 1646 and won a major victory over the Scots at Benburb; supported the nuncio in the crisis of the 1646 peace and took part in the offensive against Dublin; alienated the nuncio through the looting of his soldiers in the first months of 1647; was sent to Connacht but inadequately supplied at the beginning of the summer; recalled to Leinster after Dungan's Hill and successfully defended Kilkenny from Jones; helped persuade the nuncio not to leave Ireland in March 1648 and offered him refuge in Maryborough in May of that year; encouraged the censure against the Inchiquin truce; carried the nuncio's hopes in the civil war of 1648 but lacked the resources for victory; opposed the nuncio's departure in 1649; co-operated briefly with pro-parliamentary forces from April to August, 1649; negotiated an agreement with Ormond in October; died in November 1649.

O'Neill, Sir Phelim: original leader of the 1641 rebellion in Ulster; largely displaced as a figure of importance in Ulster by Owen Roe's arrival in 1642; maintained a covert rivalry with the Ulster general until 1648 when he sided against the nuncio's party; executed in Dublin by parliamentarians in 1653.

O'Queely, Malachy: appointed archbishop of Tuam in 1630; prominent ecclesiastical reformer during the following decade; acted as a controlling influence when the rebellion spread into Connacht in 1641–2; emerged as most important confederate figure in Connacht; Rinuccini was instructed to liaise closely with him on his arrival but O'Queely was killed in a skirmish with Scottish troops in October 1645.

O'Reilly, Hugh: appointed archbishop of Armagh in 1628, having previously been bishop of Kilmore; became involved early in the rebellion and presided over the synod of the clergy of the province of Armagh which legitimized the rebellion as a war for the defence of religion in March 1642; also played an important role in the national synod of May 1642; was disappointed with several of Rinuccini's nominees to Ulster sees but remained firmly in the nuncio's camp throughout the nunciature; bitterly hostile to Ormond, he may have encouraged Rinuccini in the offensive against Dublin in 1646.

Pamfili, cardinal Camillo: nephew of Innocent X and elevated to the purple following his uncle's coronation in November 1645; proved an indolent failure as cardinal-nephew, where his duties included supervision of the Rinuccini mission; in January 1647 he renounced his cardinalate for a glittering marriage with Olimpia Aldobrandini.

Pamfili, cardinal GianBattista: elected Pope Innocent X in September 1644; seen as pro-Spanish, having been nuncio in Madrid but disappointed Spanish hopes to a considerable degree; nevertheless was regarded with furious hostility by Mazarin; renowned for his parsimony and considered to be under the influence of his sister-in-law, Olimpia Maldachini; created the Irish mission in March 1645; disappointed with its progress until November 1646 when he decided to invest further money upon news of the rejection of the first Ormond peace; delayed sending the money until May 1647; thereafter showed little inclination to devote more funds to Ireland.

Pancirolo, cardinal Giovanni: son of a Roman tailor; a protégé of GianBattista Pamfili to whom he owed his early advancement; appointed nuncio first in Milan and then in Spain by Urban VIII; made cardinal in 1643; eventually gave strong support to Pamfili in the conclave of 1644; was rewarded with the post of secretary of state; following Camillo Pamfili's resignation from the Sacred College, Pancirolo took over supervision of the Irish mission; helped persuade the pope to send Massari to Ireland with further funds in 1647.

Parsons, Sir William: representative of the planter interest who became joint lord justice following the collapse of Wentworth's government in 1641; greatly suspected by the catholic population of Ireland; was accused of welcoming the rebellion as a means to introduce the repression of all Irish catholics; suspected of pro-parliamentary inclinations and displaced from the leadership of the Dublin government by Ormond's elevation to the lord lieutenancy in 1643.

Plunkett, Sir Nicholas: deeply religious lawyer and son of the baron of Killeen; one of the most influential of the Leinster confederates; a member of various Supreme Councils; played a role in the negotiation of the first Ormond peace despite the tenderness of his conscience; together with Patrick Darcy quieted the fears of the clerical party in May 1645; impressed the nuncio greatly from an early stage of the nunciature; was shocked and disturbed by Rinuccini's condemnation of the peace and the council's proceedings in June 1646; attempted to conciliate the legatine synod in August of that year but eventually threw in his lot with the clergy; nominated to the council by the clergy in September 1646; took part in the offensive against Dublin; combined with Ferns to moderate Rinuccini's approach at the beginning of 1647; secured Muskery's election to the new council as a gesture of reconciliation to the peace party; worked closely with Ferns throughout 1647; helped select the Supreme Council of 1648 when he allowed the elevation of various individuals against Rinuccini's wishes; departed for Rome with Ferns as an envoy in February; immensely proud to have been created a knight of the Golden Spur in Rome; on his return to Ireland in November 1648 co-operated with Ferns in securing the second Ormond peace.

Plunkett, Patrick: brother of the above; appointed bishop of Ardagh in 1647 against the wishes of the archbishop of Armagh and the local clergy; owed his elevation to the support of the council and Rinuccini's desire to reward his brother Nicholas for fidelity to the clerical party; to the nuncio's great chagrin he supported the Inchiquin truce in May 1648 and covertly worked against the nuncio for the remainder of the nunciature.

Preston, Nicholas: sixth Viscount Gormanston; a major influence in bringing the Old English of the Pale into rebellion in 1641–2; possbly the most important secular figure in the creation of the confederate association; died in 1643 thereby altering the internal balance of the Old English party among the confederates.

Preston, Thomas: uncle of the above; a colonel in Spanish service until his return to Ireland in 1642; largely responsible for the creation of a functioning Leinster army but lost several encounters in the open field; passed over for Castlehaven in the expedition into Ulster in 1644; captured Duncannon in March 1645; took part in the failed confederate offensive in Munster in the summer of that year; was given the bulk of Rinuccini's money and arms in the Spring of 1646; took Roscommon and won several skirmishes against the Scots of Sligo before the eruption of the crisis of the peace in August 1646; eventually sided with the clergy in September 1646; participated unwillingly in the campaign against Dublin during which he almost defected to Ormond; delayed mounting any offensive against Dublin in 1647 until Ormond had departed; was defeated by Jones at Dungan's Hill in August 1647; openly fought against O'Neill and the nuncio in the civil war of 1648; accepted the second Ormond peace in 1649.

Roche, Maurice: viscount of Fermoy; Muskery's major rival in Munster; provided a focus for opposition to Muskery's domination of the Munster army in 1647; opposed the Inchiquin truce, partly because of fear that his own lands would be assigned to Inchiquin's quarters.

Scarampi, PierFrancesco: Oratorian priest appointed to the Irish mission in 1643; opposed the confederate policy of truce with Ormond but without success; supplied Preston with the funds to finish the siege of Duncannon in 1645; opposed the Glamorgan treaty unsuccessfully in August and September of that year; hoped to leave Ireland on Rinuccini's arrival and was disgruntled at being detained in the island; helped persuade the nuncio to favour Preston from the papal subsidies; warned Rinuccini that the first Ormond peace had been signed prior to June 1646 but failed to convince him; one of the delegates appointed by the legatine synod of 1646 to oversee the negotiations with the Supreme Council; favoured the attack on Dublin and Preston's inclusion in the campaign; on his return to Rome in 1647 apparently voiced some criticism of the nuncio; subsequently became *praeposito* of the Oratory in Rome.

Somerset, Edward: Lord Herbert, earl of Glamorgan and later marquis of Worcester; fervent catholic royalist sent by Charles I to Ireland in 1645; used a private mandate from the king to negotiate a subsidiary treaty with the confederates covering religious concessions in August and September 1645;

denounced for this by Digby in December and briefly imprisoned in Dublin; released on bail, he went to Kilkenny where he arranged a bargain with the nuncio which allowed him to transport an advance force of Irish troops to Britain; the fall of Chester undermined this expedition; thereafter was disowned by the king; was appointed commander of the Munster army by clergy following the coup of 1646; proved unable to muster forces in the face of the hostility of his commissioners of supply; eventually lost command of the army to a Muskery-inspired mutiny in June 1647.

Talon, Jean; French agent who arrived in Ireland in March 1647; favoured the plan of transporting Ormond and confederate soldiers to France and attempted to convince the French court of the worth of the idea.

Touchet, James: earl of Castlehaven; related by marriage to Ormond and prominent member of the confederate peace party; commander of the confederate expedition into Ulster in the summer of 1644 where O'Neill accused him of incompetence; commanded the expedition into Munster in 1645 where it was rumoured he deliberately undermined the attack on Youghal for fear that its fall would strengthen the intransigence of the confederate war party; left the association in disgust when an agreement was not reached with Ormond and Glamorgan in 1645; played a military role against the nuncio's party in 1648.

Wadding, Luke, OFM: Irish franciscan, an important voice concerning the appointment of bishops to Ireland in the 1620s and 1630s; also played a part in the selection of Scarampi for the Irish mission in 1643; worked hard in Rome to increase the level of papal funding for Ireland; evidently believed that Rinuccini's censure of 1648 was an error but did not publicly oppose the nuncio. Following the Cromwellian conquest was accused by many Old Irish of Old English and anti-nuncioist sympathies.

Walsh, Thomas: appointed archbishop of Cashel in 1626; of merchant stock, he complained of considerable poverty throughout the 1630s; relatively moderate in politics he was reluctant to oppose the nuncio openly even in 1648 when he evidently believed that Rinuccini's censure was an error; attempted to convince the nuncio to summon a synod in the summer of 1648; when this failed he was willing to accept the second Ormond peace in January 1649.

Appendix C. Chronology

1536–7 (Ireland) 'Reformation Parliament' (Dublin). Act 28 Hen. VIII, c. 5 recognizing king as Supreme Head of Church in Ireland. Act 28 Hen. VII, c. 6 forbidding appeals to Rome. Act 28 Hen. VIII, c. 13 against the authority of the bishop of Rome.

1541 (Ireland) Act 33 Hen. VIII, c. 1 declaring Henry of England to be king of Ireland.

1545 (Europe) General Council of catholic church opens at Trent.

1553 (Britain) Accession of Mary to throne.

1555 (Europe) Peace of Augsburg in Germany. Bull of Paul IV making Ireland a kingdom.

1557 (Ireland) Parliament in Dublin. Repeal of statutes against see of Rome.

1558 (Britain) Accession of Elizabeth.

1560 (Ireland) Parliament in Dublin. Act of Supremacy (2. Eliz., c. 1), Act of Uniformity (2 Eliz., c. 2).

1560 (Europe) David Wolfe, SJ appointed nuncio to Ireland.

1570 (Europe) Papal bull, 'Regnans in excelsis' excommunicates Elizabeth.

1573 (Ireland) David Wolfe leaves Ireland.

1577 (Europe) Pope Gregory XIII provides James FitzMaurice with a brief in support of his expedition to Ireland.

1579 (Ireland) FitzMaurice and papal legate, Nicholas Sanders, land on Dingle peninsula.

1580 (Ireland) Papal force lands at Smerwick but are defeated and killed.

1580 (Europe) Pope grants city of Limerick to Sir John of Desmond.

1582 (Europe) Gregorian reformation of the calendar.

1584 (Ireland) Easter celebrated according to Gregorian calendar by O'Neill, O'Donnell, and Maguire.

1588 (Britain) Defeat of the Spanish Armada.

1592 (Ireland) Charter of Trinity College Dublin.

1592 (Europe) Philip II approves the Irish college of St Patrick at Salamanca. Birth of Rinuccini in Rome.

1594 (Europe) College of St Patrick at Douai founded.

1595 (Europe) Kingship of Ireland offered to Archduke Albert, Spanish governor of the Netherlands, by Ulster lords.

1598 (Ireland) Tyrone's victory over queen's forces at the battle of the Yellow Ford.

1598 (Europe) Treaty of Vervins between France and Spain. Death of Philip II.

1600 (Europe) Plenary indulgence granted to supporters of Tyrone's rebellion by Clement VIII but those who support the queen are not excommunicated.

1601 (Ireland) Arrival of Spanish fleet in Kinsale. Ulster confederates defeated in subsequent battle.

1601 (Europe) Ludovico Mansoni, SJ appointed nuncio in Ireland by Clement VIII.

1603 (Ireland) Treaty of Mellifont ends Nine Years' War.

1603 (Britain) Death of Elizabeth and accession of James VI and I.

1607 (Ireland) Flight of the Earls.

1608 (Ireland) Suppression of Cahir O'Doherty rebellion in Ireland. Survey of six counties in Ulster opens the way to the Ulster plantation.

1611 (Europe) *An teagasg criodaidhe*, the first catholic devotional work to be printed in Irish, is produced in Antwerp.

1618 (Europe) Defenestration of Prague ignites Thirty Years War. David Rothe, first of the new residential bishops, appointed to the see of Ossory.

1622 (Europe) Recatholicization begins in Habsburg Bohemia. Foundation of *Propaganda Fide* in Rome.

1623 (Europe) Maffeo Barberini elected Pope Urban VIII.

1625 (Britain) Accession of Charles I. Anglo-Spanish war begins.

1625 (Europe) Rinuccini appointed archbishop of Fermo.

1626 (Ireland) King offers 'graces' to his subjects in Ireland in return for subsidies.

1628 (Ireland) (May) Charles issues 51 'graces' in return for the promise of a subsidy of £40,000 per annum for three years. (Oct.) Parliament to confirm 'graces' aborted.

1628 (Europe) Rinuccini holds his first provincial synod in Fermo.

1629 (Europe) Edict of Restitution in Germany.

1629 (Britain) Anglo-French treaty of peace.

1630 (Britain) English peace with Spain.

1630 (Ireland) John O'Moloney, the last episcopal appointment for 11 years, nominated for see of Killaloe.

1633 (Ireland) Wentworth arrives as Lord Deputy.

1634 (Ireland) Beginning of Charles's first Irish parliament which fails to confirm the 'graces'.

1636 (Ireland) Wentworth successfully intimidates a jury in Galway which ultimately finds in favour of the king's title to land in Galway.

1638 (Britain) National Covenant in Scotland.

1639 (Ireland) 'Black oath' required of Scots in Ulster.

1639 (Britain) First 'Bishops' War'.

1640 (Ireland) (Mar.) First session of Charles's second Irish parliament.

1640 (Britain) 'Short Parliament' in England. (Aug.) second 'Bishops' War' begins. (Nov.) 'Long Parliament' meets in England.

1640 (Europe) Rebellion of Catalonia and secession of Portugal from Castile.

1641 (Ireland) (Oct.) Outbreak of rebellion in Ulster. (Nov.) Irish parliament assembles but is prorogued after one day. (Dec.) At Knockcrofty Old English of Pale join Ulster rebels.

1641 (Britain) (Jan.) Strafford (Wentworth) impeached by English Parliament (executed in May).

1641 (Europe) Resumption of episcopal appointments to Ireland.

1642 (Ireland) Clergy of province of Armagh meet at Kells. (Apr.) Arrival of Scottish army in Ulster. (May) Synod of catholic clergy at Kilkenny where they are joined by influential catholic laity. (July) Owen Roe O'Neill arrives back in Ireland. (Sept.) Return of Preston to Ireland. (Oct.) Beginning of first confederate assembly at Kilkenny.

1642 (Britain) (Mar.) 'Adventurers' Act' of English parliament offering forfeited Irish land in return for monetary contributions. (Aug.) Outbreak of first English Civil War.

1642 (Europe) Beginning of War of Castro consumes nearly all available papal finance for next two years.

1643 (Ireland) (Mar.) Preston defeated at New Ross. (Apr.) Ormond receives royal commission to parley with confederates. (May) Second confederate assembly begins. (June) O'Neill defeated at Clones. (July) Scarampi reaches Kilkenny. (Sept.) Against Scarampi's advice confederates purchase a one-year truce with royalist forces. (Oct.) Confederates request that Scarampi be appointed nuncio. (Nov.) Third confederate assembly meets and nominates delegates to go to England to treat with Charles. Ormond appointed lord lieutenant.

1643 (Britain) (Sept.) Parliamentary alliance with Scots.

1643 (Europe) (Apr.) Scarampi appointed as papal minister to Ireland. (Nov.) Swedish victory at Breitenfeld. (Dec.) Death of Richelieu. Succeeded by Mazarin as chief minister of French crown.

1644 (Ireland) (June) Charles remits negotiations with confederates to Ormond in Ireland. An Irish force raised by Antrim with confederate assistance sails for Scotland. (July) Inchiquin defects to parliament in Munster. Fourth confederate assembly begins. (July-Sept.) Indecisive confederate campaign in Ulster. (Dec.) Richard Bellings sent to the continent to seek aid.

1644 (Britain) (July) Royalist defeat at Marston Moor in England.

1644 (Europe) Olivares dismissed in Spain. French victory over Spanish at Rocroi. Opening of peace negotiations in Germany. Death of Urban. Coronation of Pamfili as Innocent X. Publication of *Il Cappuccino Scozzese*. Decision made to send Rinuccini to Ireland.

1645 (Ireland) (Mar.) Preston, with money from Scarampi, takes Duncannon. (May) Fifth confederate assembly begins. (June) Glamorgan arrives in Ireland. (Aug.-Sept.) Confederate offensive in Munster peters out. Secret treaty prepared between Glamorgan and confederates. (Oct.) Rinuccini arrives in Kenmare. (Nov.) He reaches Kilkenny. (Dec.) Glamorgan imprisoned in Dublin.

1645 (Britain) (June) Royalist defeat at Naseby in England.

1645 (Europe) Outbreak of Turko-Venetian war. Republic appeals to pope for financial assistance. (Mar.) Emperor's forces routed at Jankov. Rinuccini leaves Rome. (May) Rinuccini arrives in Paris. (July) Rinuccini ordered to delay in Paris to negotiate with the French court. (Sept.) The nuncio reaches La Rochelle. Antonio Barberini flees to France. (Nov.) Draft of 'Papal Peace' signed between Kenelm Digby and Pope Innocent in Rome. (Dec.) Fabio Chigi at Münster prepares a draft protest against any prejudice to the catholic religion in any proposed treaty, taking as a model Cardinal Augusta's declaration concerning the Peace of Augsburg (1555).

1646 (Ireland) (Jan.) Glamorgan released. (Feb.) Sixth General Assembly convenes. Bargain reached between Rinuccini and confederate peace party. (Mar.) Peace party secretly violate the bargain by concluding peace. (Apr.) Peace party borrow money from Rinuccini which is sent to Ormond. (June) O'Neill wins major victory at Benburb. (July) Confederate success in Connacht. Rinuccini supervises the successful siege of Bunratty. Digby arrives in Ireland and convinces Ormond to allow the publication of peace. (Aug.) Supreme council proclaims peace. Legatine synod repudiates it. Massari leaves for Rome to solicit aid from pope. (Sept.) Clergy overthrow government. Rinuccini becomes president of new council. Decision made to attack Dublin. (Sept.–Dec.) Failure of Dublin campaign.

1646 (Britain) (May) Charles surrenders himself to the Scots. Forbids peace in Ireland.

1646 (Europe) (Jan.) Taddeo and Francesco Barberini also flee to France. Collapse of papal peace. Letter informing Rinuccini of this lost in transit. (June) French plans for Britain and Ireland co-ordinated. Digby given 10,000 pistols to support the peace. (Oct.) French take Dunkirk. (Nov.) Massari arrives in Rome. (Dec.) Decision made to send more aid to Ireland.

1647 (Ireland) (Jan.) Seventh confederate assembly. Rinuccini resigns presidency. (Feb.) Peace rejected. Ormond opens negotiations with parliament. (Mar.) New French agents arrive. Plot with Digby to lead confederate troops to France developed. (Apr.) Confederates offer Ormond renewed truce. (May) Inchiquin takes Dungarvan and Cappoquin. Decision taken to divert O'Neill to Connacht. (June) Mutiny of Munster army. (June–July) Transfer of Dublin to parliament. (Aug.) Leinster confederate army routed at Dungan's Hill. Regiments of Munster army commit themselves to the plot to desert to France. (Sept.) Inchiquin takes Cashel. (Nov.) Eighth General Assembly convenes. Decision taken to send envoys to France and Rome. Inchiquin routs Munster army. (Dec.) New Supreme Council nominated which includes several bitter enemies of the nuncio.

1647 (Britain) (Jan.) King handed over to parliament. (June) Rapid politicization of the army. King is seized and parliament confronted successfully concerning the eleven members. (Dec.) Charles signs 'Engagement' with the Scots.

1647 (Europe) (Jan.–Apr.) Additional papal subsidies delayed in Rome. (May) Massari leaves Rome. Is delayed for almost a year in France. (June) Rinuccini's criticisms of O' Neill dampen papal enthusiasm for Ireland still further. (July) Rinuccini ordered not to involve himself too deeply in opposition to peace. Neapolitan revolt. (Oct.) Spanish bankruptcy.

1648 (Ireland) (Feb.) Confederate envoys set out for Rome and Paris. Colonel Barry, Ormond's emissary, arrives in Ireland. (Mar.) Massari returns to Ireland. (Apr.) Rinuccini reluctantly leaves Waterford for Kilkenny. (May) Rinuccini flees Kilkenny. Inchiquin truce concluded. Rinuccini excommunicates those who support it. (June) Rinuccini decides to convoke a national synod in August. Council prevents it assembling. (Aug.) Rinuccini refuses attempt of archbishop of Tuam to organize a reconciliation. Is besieged in Galway. (Sept.) Last confederate assembly meets in Kilkenny. Ormond lands in Cork. (Nov.) Plunkett and Ferns return to Ireland. Promote peace with Ormond.

1648 (Britain) (May–Aug.) Second Civil War in England. (Dec.) Pride's purge in England.

1648 (Europe) Turkish siege of Candia begun which increases the urgency of Venetian appeals to the pope for aid. (Mar.) Ormond arrives in Paris and begins to plot with confederate envoys. (Apr.) Plunkett and Ferns arrive in

Rome. (July–Nov.) Rebellion in Fermo which is savagely repressed by papal forces. Fronde begins in France. (Aug.) Non-committal papal response to envoys. No subsidies are given. Envoys leave Rome. (Oct.) Peace of Westphalia.

1649 (Ireland) (Jan.) Second Ormond peace concluded. Rinuccini hears of the rebellion in Fermo. (Feb.) Rinuccini leaves Ireland. (Aug.) Ormond defeated at battle of Rathmines. Cromwell lands in Ireland. (Sept.) Cromwell takes Drogheda with great slaughter. (Oct.) Cromwell takes Wexford. Owen Roe O'Neill comes to an agreement with Ormond. (Nov.) Death of O'Neill. (Dec.) Synod of catholic bishops issue declaration for religion and king against Cromwell.

1649 (Britain) (Jan.) Trial and execution of the king. (Mar.) Cromwell accepts command for Ireland.

1649 (Europe) (Apr.) Massari meets Mazarin who makes insinuations concerning Rinuccini's pro-Spanish affiliation. (May) Rinuccini ordered to leave France and return to Italy. He is also informed that absolution from his excommunication will be left in his hands. (Aug.) Rinuccini reaches Turin. (Dec.) He reports on the nunciature.

1650 (Ireland) (Mar.) Kilkenny surrenders to Cromwell. (May) Cromwell leaves Ireland, Ireton assumes command of English forces. (June) Ulster army routed. (Aug.) Waterford surrenders to Ireton. Catholic bishops repudiate Ormond. (Sept.) Catholic bishops excommunicate supporters of Ormond. (Dec.) Ormond appoints Clanricard as his deputy and leaves Ireland.

1650 (Britain) (June) Charles II takes Covenants. Beginning of Third Civil War in Britain. (Aug.) Charles II repudiates the 'bloody Irish rebels'.

1650 (Europe) (Aug.) Rinuccini re-installed in Fermo.

1651 (Ireland) (June) Limerick besieged. (Oct.) Surrender of Limerick. (Nov.) Death of Ireton.

1651 (Britain) (Jan.) Charles II's coronation in Scotland. First exile of Mazarin. (Sept.) Cromwell defeats Charles II.

1651 (Europe) (Jan.) Papal protest against the Peace of Westphalia. Publication of the *Della Dignita* in Rome. First exile of Mazarin.

1652 (Ireland) (Apr.) Surrender of Galway. (May) Leinster army surrenders. (July) Fleetwood appointed commander-in-chief in Ireland. (Aug.) Act for the settling of Ireland.

1653 (Ireland) (Jan.) Edict expelling all catholic priests from Ireland. (Mar.) Parliament votes that Ireland will be represented with 30 seats in the new British assembly of 460 seats.

1653 (Europe) Death of Rinuccini in Fermo.

Bibliographical Note

THE MATERIAL relevant to the analysis of Rinuccini's mission and its wider contexts is scattered in a dozen cities situated in six separate countries and written in an equal number of different languages. This variety undoubtedly contributes to the difficulty of the subject. The very partisan nature of the sources is also a factor of some importance. Most original English-language material is hostile to the nuncio. The vast deposits of the Carte papers in Oxford are of fundamental importance to any understanding of the 1640s in Ireland but few of the multitude of correspondents with the lord lieutenant showed any notable understanding of Rinuccini or of his mission. Analysis of his motivations was largely lacking or at the level of caricature. He was never mentioned by name, appearing as the 'Italian bishop' or as the pope's nuncio. Thus, although the Carte papers are integral to an understanding of the context in which Rinuccini operated, they offer only an external perspective on his behaviour and that of the catholic clergy in general.

The most notable exception to the rule of bias in the original English-language material is the narrative text generally called the 'Aphorismical Discovery', which contains material of great importance, but its blanket and ludicrous accusations against Ormond and his sympathizers among the confederates do more to convince a historian of its unreliability than of its value. The 'Aphorismical Discovery' appears even more incredible when contrasted with the highly plausible and meditative narrative of Richard Bellings. Bellings's measured tone and the manner in which he eschews simplistic judgements of the nuncio's supporters render his exposition of events doubly convincing. A note of fatalistic humility also pervades the text, strengthening the impression of balance:

where God is pleased to exercise the mercy of his chastisements (for mercies they are, when, by a willing and entire submission to them and a sincere acknowledgement of our sins, the cause of them, we endeavour to appease his wrath) that he gives us the reins and permits us to feel the effects of original prevarication in the blindness of our judgments . . .[1]

Nevertheless, an alert critical judgement is even more necessary with Bellings than with the anonymous author of the 'Aphorismical Discovery', precisely because of the plausibility with which Bellings presented his case. The former secretary of the confederate catholics was a highly partisan author who, as an actor in the 1640s, was a personal as well as a political enemy of Rinuccini. The passage quoted above, in fact, modulated into a scathing attack on the nuncio, made all the more effective because of the manner in which Bellings confessed his own human weakness.

Caution is needed for entirely different reasons concerning the extremely rich and important Latin and Italian sources. The single most important of these is the *Commentarius Rinuccinianus* which was a posthumous apologia of the nunciature. The narrative tone of its authors, O'Ferrall and O'Connell, was not as smooth as

---

[1] Bellings's narrative (Gilbert, *Irish Confederation*, vii. 84).

that of Richard Bellings but the great strength of the work lies in the degree to which the seventeenth-century Capuchin compilers were content to let the original documents present their case for them.[2] The force of their argument, sustained over five massive Latin volumes totalling over 3,300 pages, is undeniable. Rinuccini's own intelligent and elegantly expressed Italian correspondence from Ireland, conveniently collected in one volume by an excellent editor,[3] strengthens their case even further. Rinuccini's chief subordinate, Dionysio Massari, during his tenure as secretary of *Propaganda Fide*, also compiled a retrospective narrative of the Irish mission which echoed the position of the nuncio on all major matters. This is currently extant in the archives of the Congregation whose considerable Irish holdings represent the other great Italian lode which was mined in the course of this research.

Taken together the thrust of the Italian material is the mirror image of the English-language sources. Its authors and compilers demonstrated little sympathy with the nuncio's opponents: Ormond indeed is as externalized a figure in the *Commentarius* as Rinuccini in the Carte papers. As such the two principal deposits of material act as a balance and a complement to each other, although charting the correct course away from the Charybdis of Italian apologia without being lured into the Scylla of English dismissiveness remains a formidable task. There is currently no absolutely reliable modern translation of any of these key Italian sources. However, they are not entirely inaccessible to an English-language audience. A translation of much of the rather chaotic original of Massari's text was published between 1916 and 1919 in volumes 6, 7, 8, and 9 of the *Catholic Bulletin*. Aiazzi's volume of the correspondence of Rinuccini's nunciature was also translated, at times somewhat eccentrically, in 1873 by Annie Hutton.[4] Plans are currently afoot to publish an English translation of the *Commentarius* itself. Until this formidable task is completed those for whom the original Latin presents grave difficulties have recourse to two principal aids: the first is Michael Hynes's *The Mission of Rinuccini* (Louvain, 1932) which is effectively a skilful compression rather than a critical analysis of the material and arguments of Rinuccini and his Capuchin partisans. The second is volume 6 of the original work itself which provides a summary of the contents of the previous five volumes as well as a series of detailed indexes.

[2] Donal Cregan's description of the *Commentarius* as a collection of documents held together by a narrative thread is both accurate and elegant: see his review of the work in *Irish Historical Studies*, 2 (1944–5), 274.

[3] Aiazzi, *Nunziatura*.

[4] Id., *The Embassy in Ireland of Monsignor G. B. Rinuccini, archbishop of Fermo in the years 1645–49* (Dublin, 1873).

Bibliography

Manuscript Sources

ITALY

Fermo

Archivio Arcivescovile di Fermo

iii C/10, Letters of Rinuccini to Alessandro Celli (?).
iii C/11, Miscellaneous letters of Rinuccini.
iii C/13, 'Instruttione pratica per la cura episcopale di Monsignor Gio. Battista Rinuccini, Arcivescove di Fermo'.
Synodus Civitatis et Dioecesis Firmane, Decrees of synod of 1628.

Florence

Archivio di Stato di Firenze

Miscellanea Medicea, 436 ins 19, Lettere di Alessandro Neroni sul viaggio in Irlanda del Nuncio Apostolico, 1654.
Deputazione sopra la nobilità, Filza 7, Details concerning the Rinuccini family.

Milan

Archivio Storico Comunale di Milano

Biblioteca Trivulziana, cod. n. 1958, Rinuccini's Compendio di Geografia.
Biblioteca Trivulziana, cod. n. 1963, Rinuccini's Quaestiones in octo libros Aristotelis de phisica.
Biblioteca Trivulziana, cod. n. 1964, Rinuccini's Libellus de recta argumentandi ratione ad quaestiones logicas intelligendas.

Rome

Archivio Segreto Vaticano

Acta Miscellanea 97, Details concerning the archbishopric of Fermo.
Acta Vicecancellarii, 17, Details concerning Rinuccini's elevation to the see of Fermo.
Epistulae ad Principi, 53, Letters concerning the appointment of Scarampi in 1643.
Lettere di Cardinali, vols. 12–14, 17, Letters of bishop of Clogher, Rinuccini, Rossetti, and the Grand Duke of Tuscany to Pamfili and Pancirolo, 1647–53.
Lettere di Vescovi e Prelati, vols., 16, 23, 24, 25, 27, 29, 30, 31, 32, 33, 35, Letters from Rinuccini, Visconti, Imperiali, Caetano, the council of Fermo, San Felice, cardinal Montalto, the bishops of Clonfert, Raphoe, and Ossory, and the archbishop of Cashel to Pancirolo and Pamfili, 1645–53.

Lettere di Vescovi e Principi, vols., 29, 31, Letters from Rinuccini and military governors of Fermo to Pancirolo, 1646–9.

Particolari, vols. 17, 24, Miscellaneous letters concerning Bellings's embassy to Rome in 1644, the Catalonian request for a nuncio in 1644, and details concerning Massari.

Pontificio, Miscellanea, ii, Details concerning the influence of Cardinal Bandini in Rome.

Processus Episcoporum Sacrae Consistorialis, 21, Details concerning Rinuccini and Fermo in 1625.

Secretarius Brevium Apostolicorum, 657, Details of Rinuccini's privileges as a referendary in 1622.

Archivio della Sacra Congregazione di Propaganda Fide

Acta Sacrae Congregationis, 1644–5, Details concerning ecclesiastical faculties in the province of Tuam following Rinuccini's appointment and the finance of the Rinuccini and Scarampi missions in Ireland.

——1646–7, Details concerning the appointment of bishops in Ireland during Rinuccini's nunciature.

Lettere Latine, vol. 9, Letters from the Roman curia to the earl of Westmeath, the conde de Tirconnel, the four archbishops, the bishops of Elphin, Kildare, Killaloe, Ferns, Waterford, and others concerning church affairs in Ireland.

Lettere Volgari, vols. 7, 22, Letters to archbishop of Dublin and Scarampi concerning catholicism in Scotland.

Miscellaneae Varie, vol. 9, Massari's account of the Rinuccini nunciature.

Scritture Originali Referite nelle Congregazioni Generali, vols. 14 (1635), 89 (1644), 140 (1640), 141 (1642), 142 (1643), 143 (1645), 145 (1647), 294 (general up to 1636), 295 (general up to 1648), Material relating to Irish dioceses.

Scritture riferite nei Congressi", 1, Irlanda, Material relating to Irish dioceses, 1618–53.

Fondo di Vienna, vols. 14, 39, Miscellaneous material relating to Ireland.

Archivio della congregazione per le cause dei Santi

Decreta Liturgica, 1622–6.

Biblioteca Apostolica Vaticana

Barberini Latini MSS 3631, 4994, 5253, 5653, 6485, 6827, 8223, 8238, 8649, 8651, 8653, 8655, Letters to Barberini concerning Irish and British affairs.

——4729, Account of Scarampi in Ireland.

——4886, Account of the life of Scarampi.

——5678, Account of nunciature of Passionei in Toscana.

Nunziatura di Fiandra, vols. 32, 33, 45, Letters relating to Britain and Ireland 1645–9.

Nunziatura d'Inghilterra, vol. 8, Letters to Rinuccini and Scarampi in Ireland.

IRELAND

Dublin

Dublin City Pearse Street Library

MS 254, Memoirs of George Leyburn.

Franciscan Archive in Killiney

D II, D III, D IV, Correspondence of Luke Wadding relating to affairs in Ireland.

National Library of Ireland

MSS 7–12, Collectanea de rebus Hibernicis.
MS 345 (Plunkett-Dunne MS), 'The war and rebellion in Ireland begun in 1641'.
MS 476, 'A light to the blind'.

National Archives

Carte Transcripts, vols. 15–23.

Trinity College

MS 846, Aphorismical discovery of treasonable faction.
MS 1071, Cín Lae Ó Mealláin.

GREAT BRITAIN

London

British Library

Egerton MS 917, Miscellaneous papers, 1623 –1728.
Egerton MS 2533, Miscellaneous papers, 1640s.
Egerton MSS 2541–2, Papers of secretary Nicholas, 1598–1659.
Harleian MS 4551, Diplomatic papers of Brienne.
Harleian MS 6807, Miscellaneous papers, chiefly 1649–1650.
Sloane MS 1008, Papers of Edmund Borlase.

Oxford

Bodleian Library

Carte MSS 14–24, 27, 63–5, 67, 97, 99, 118, 156, Ormond corresponence and miscellaneous papers.
Clarendon MSS 22–5, 98, Papers of the earl of Clarendon.
Rawlinson MS A 110, Parliamentary orders 1642–1643.

FRANCE

Paris

Archives du Ministère des Affaires Étrangères

Correspondence Politique (Angleterre), vols. 48, 49, 51, 52, 54, 55, 57, 60, Letters of Mazarin, Brienne, Rinuccini, Talbot, Digby, du Moulin, Talon, de la Monerie, and others relating to affairs in Ireland.
Correspondence Politique (Rome), vols. 90, 91, 92, Letters of Mazarin, Pamfili, and others.

Archives de la Guerre (Vincennes)

AI Côtes 79, 86, 100, 110, 116, 118, 119, 128, 133, 134, 137, 158, Letters of Digby, Muskery, du Moulin, and others concerning the recruitment of Irish soldiers for French service.

Bibliothèque Nationale

Fonds Français, 4168, 4169, 4170, Letters from the King and Queen Regent to the Supreme council and to de la Monerie 1644–5.
4173, du Moulin's instructions of January 1646 and letters of Queen Regent to Ormond and others.
4175, Instructions to Talon and de la Monerie in February and March 1647 with miscellaneous letters to Ireland.
15996–8, Correspondence between Brienne, le Tellier, and a variety of French agents (consulted on microfilm in National Library of Ireland).

SPAIN

Simancas

Archivio General (consulted on microfilm in National Library of Ireland)

Segretaría de Estado, Negociaciones de Inglaterra 1628–48, 1644–50.
Negoc. de Roma, 1613–99.

Pamphlets

Lough Fea Collection (consulted on microfiche in National Library of Ireland)

No. 225, *Exceeding good newes from Ireland* (London, 1647).
No. 227, *A true and brief relation of Lord Lisles departure from his command in Ireland* (London, 1647).
No. 234, *The declaration and the protestation of the Lord Inchiquin and all the officers under his command* (London, 1648).
No. 278, *A relation of the particulars of the reduction of the greatest part of the province of Munster in Ireland* (London, 1648).

British Library Thomason Tracts (consulted on microfilm in University College Dublin)

E 60 (19), *Orders established in the popish general assembly held (under the specious pretence of supreme authority, and being his majesty's good subjects) at the city of Kilkenny* (London, 1642).

E 110 (9), *A remonstrance of the beginnings and proceedings of the rebellion including the acts of the Kilkenny congregation 10–12 May 1642* (London, 1642).

E 113 (4), *The popes brief or bull of dispensation* (London, 1642).

E 131 (23), *The rebels letter to the pope, 20 January 1642* (London, 1642).

E 155 (22), *The copy of a letter written from the lord viscount Gormanston unto Sir Phelim O'Neal* (London, 1642).

E 294 (24), *A sad relation of the miseries of the province of Munster in the realm of Ireland* (London, 1645).

E 346 (5), *Very sad and bloody newes from Ireland on the loss of Bunratty in Munster and Roscommon in Connaught* (London, 1646).

E 386 (16), *The bloody diurnall from Ireland being the papers and propositions, orders, an oath and several bloody acts and the proceedings of the confederate catholics assembled at Kilkenny* (London, 1647).

E 407 (5), *A great and glorious victory obtained by the Lord Inchiquin, lord president of Munster over the Irish rebels, not far from the castle of Conmell* (London, 1647).

E 416 (22), *Newes from Dublin in Ireland* (London, 1647).

E 418 (10), *A perfect narrative of the battle of Knocknones within the county of Cork and province of Munster* (London, 1647).

E 419 (8), *Two letters of the Lord Digby to the Lord Taaffe, the rebels general in Munster* (London, 1647).

E 608 (15), *A history or a brief chronicle of the chief matters of the Irish wars* (London, 1649).

Printed Sources

Aiazzi, G., *Nunziatura in Irlanda di Monsignor Gio. Baptista Rinuccini Arcivescovo di Fermo negli anni 1645 à 1649* (Florence, 1844).
——(Annie Hutton, trans.), *The Embassy in Ireland of Monsignor G. B. Rinuccini, archbishop of Fermo, in the years 1645–1649* (Dublin, 1873).
Balázs, Mihály, Ádám Fricsy, László Lukács, and István Monok (eds.), *Erdélyi és Hódoltsági Jezsuita Missziók*, I/2, *1617–1625* (Szeged, 1990).
Bibliothèque de L'Institut Historique Belge de Rome, Fascicule ix, *D'après les Lettere dei Particolari Conservée aux Archives Vaticanes, 1525–1796.*
Bindon, S. H. (ed.), *The historical works of the right reverend Nicholas French, bishop of Ferns* (Dublin, 1846).
Calendar of State Papers and Manuscripts Relating to English Affairs, Existing in the Archives and Collections of Venice, 1643–7 (London, 1926), *1647–52* (London, 1927).
Calendar of State Papers, Domestic Series.
   1640 (London, 1880).
   1641–3 (London, 1887).
   1644–5 (London, 1890).

1645–7 (London, 1891).

1648–9 (London, 1893).

Calendar of State Papers Relating to Ireland.

1615–25 (London, 1880).

1625–32 (London, 1900).

1633–47 (London, 1901).

Adventurers Act 1642–59 (London, 1903).

Callaghan, John, *Vinciciarum Catholicorum Hiberniae Authore Philopatio Irenaeo ad Alilophilum Libri duo* (Paris, 1651).

Casway, Jerrold, 'The Clandestine Correspondence of Father Patrick Crelly, 1648–9', *Collectanea Hibernica*, 20 (1978), 7–20.

——'Unpublished Letters and Papers of Owen Roe O'Neill', *Analecta Hibernica*, 29 (1980), 222–48.

Clarendon Historical Society, 'The memoirs of George Leyburn' in *Five Scarce Books in English Literature* (London, 1886).

Clarke, Aidan (ed.), 'A Discourse between Two Councillors of State, the One of England, the Other of Ireland', *Analecta Hibernica*, 26 (1970), 159–76.

Corish, P. (ed.), 'Two Reports on the Catholic Church in Ireland in the Early Seventeenth Century', *Archivium Hibernicum*, 22 (1959), 140–62.

de Boccard, E., *Recueil des instructions donnés aux ambassadeurs et ministres de France depuis les traités de Westphalie jusqu'a la révolution française, xxiv (Angleterre)*, i, *1648–1650* (Paris, 1929).

de Burgh, Ulick, *The memoirs and letters of Ulick, marquiss of Clanricarde* (London, 1757).

de Burgo, T., *Hibernia dominicana sive historia provinciae Hiberniae ordinis praedictorum* (n.p., 1762).

Decreta Synodi Secundae Dioecesis Firmanae (Fermo, 1650).

De Ecclesia Firmana eiusque Episcopis et Archepiscopis Commentarius (Fermo, 1783).

Gilbert, J. T. (ed.), *History of the Irish Confederation and the War in Ireland* (7 vols., Dublin, 1882–91).

——(ed.), *A Contemporary History of Affairs in Ireland (1641–1652)* (3 vols., Dublin, 1879).

Glynn, Marcellus and F. X. Martin, (eds.), 'The *Brevis Relatio* of the Irish Discalced Carmelites, 1625–1670', *Archivium Hibernicum*, 25 (1962), 136–63.

Historical Manuscripts Commission, *Calendar of the Manuscripts of the Marquess of Ormonde KP*, NS (8 vols., London, 1902–20).

——*Report on Franciscan Manuscript* (Dublin, 1906).

Hogan, J. (ed.), *Letters and Papers Relating to the Irish Rebellion between 1642–46* (Dublin, 1935).

Jennings, Brendan, 'Brussels MS 3947: Donatus Moneyus Provincia Hiberniae S. Francisci', *Analecta Hibernica*, 6 (1934), 1–249.

——'Miscellaneous documents II, 1625–40', *Archivium Hibernicum*, 14 (1949), 1–49.

——'Documents of the Irish Colleges at Douai', *Archivium Hibernicum*, 10 (1943), 179–92.

——*Wild Geese in Spanish Flanders, 1582–1700. Documents Relating Chiefly to Irish Regiments from the Archives Générales du Royaume, Brussels, and other Sources* (Dublin, 1964).

Jennings, Brendan, (ed.), *Louvain Papers 1606–1827* (Dublin, 1968).

Jones, F. M. (ed.), 'Papal Briefs to Father Mansoni, Papal Nuncio to Ireland', *Archivium Hibernicum*, 17 (1953), 51–68.

Journal of the House of Commons of the Kingdom of Ireland, i, *1613–1666* (Dublin, 1796).

Kavanagh, Stanislaus (ed.), *Commentarius Rinuccianus, de sedis apostolicae legatione ad foederatos Hiberniae catholicos per annos 1645–9* (6 vols., Dublin, 1932–49).

Kybal, V., and G. Incisa Della Rochetta (eds.), *La Nunziatura di Fabio Chigi, 1640–1651* (Rome, 1946).

Lowe, John (ed.), *The Letter Book of the Earl of Clanricarde, 1643–7* (Dublin, 1983).

Lynch, John, *Alithinologia, sive Vendica reponsion ad invectivam mendaciis, falaciis calumniis et importunis foetam in plurimos antistites proceres et omnis ordinis Hibernos à R.P.P.F.C.* (St Malo, 1664).

——*Supplementum Alithinologiae quod partis invectivae in Hibernos cusae in Alithinolgia non oppugnatas evertit* (St Malo, 1667).

——*Cambrensis eversus, seu potius historiae fides in rebus Hibernicis Giraldo Cambrensi abrogata . . .* ed. Matthew Kelly (3 vols., Dublin, 1848–52).

——*Pii antistitis icon sive de vita et morte D. Francisci Kirovani Rmi. Alladensis Episcopi . . .* ed. C. P. Meehan (Dublin, 1884).

——*De Praesulibus Hiberniae potissimis Catholicae religionis in Hibernia serendae propagandae, et conservandae Authoribus . . .*, ed. John. F. O'Doherty (2 vols., Dublin, 1944).

MacLysaght, Edward, 'Report on Documents Relating to the Wardenship of Galway', *Analecta Hibernica*, 14 (1944).

Moran, Patrick Francis (ed.), *Spicilegium Ossoriense: Being a Collection of Original Letters and Papers Illustrative of the History of the Irish Church* (3 vols., Dublin, 1874–84).

Nicholls, K. W. (ed.), 'The Lynch Blosse Papers', *Analecta Hibernica*, 29 (1980), 113–218.

O'Donnell, T. J. (ed.), *Selections of the Zoilomastix of Philip O'Sullivan Beare* (Dublin, 1960).

Olden, Michael (ed.), 'Episcopal Comments on the *Decreta pro recta regime ecclesiarum Hiberniae*', *Archivium Hibernicum*, 27 (1964), 1–12.

O'Mahoney, Connor, *Disputatio Apologetica de Iure Regni Hiberniae pro Catholicis Hibernis, adversus haereticos Anglos* (Lisbon, 1645).

O'Sullivan Beare, Philip, *Historiae Catholicae Iberniae Compendium . . .*, ed. M. Kelly (Dublin, 1850).

Rinuccini, G. B., *Considerazioni sopra la Storia Romana e Greca di Dionigi d'Alicarnasso, Tito Livio, Polibio, Plutarco, Tacito ecc.* (Rome, 1634?).

——*Il Cappuccino Scozzese* (Rome, 1645; repr. 1863).

——*Della Dignita et Offitio dei Vescovi: Discorsi Quaranta di Monsignor Gio. Battista Rinuccini, Arcivescovo e Prencipe di Fermo* (Rome, 1651).

Talbot, Peter, *A treatise of the Nature of the Catholick Faith, and Heresie, with reflexion upon the nullitie of the English Protestant Church, and Clergy* (Rouen, 1657).

——*The Politicians Cathechisme, for his Instruction in Divine Faith and Morall Honesty* (Antwerp, 1658).

Touchet, James, earl of Castlehaven, *The earl of Castlehaven's review: or his memoirs* (London, 1684).

Walsh, Peter, *The history and vindication of the loyal formulary or Irish remonstrance* (1674).

Secondary Material

Acquaviva, S. S., *The Decline of the Sacred in Industrial Society* (Oxford, 1979).

Alberigo, G., 'Studi e problemi relativi all'applicazione del Concilio di Trento', *Rivista Storica Italiana*, 70 (1958), 239–98.

——'The Council of Trent', in John O'Malley (ed.), *Catholicism in Early Modern Europe: A Guide to Research* (Ann Arbor, Mich., 1988) 213–21.

Albion, Gordon, *Charles I and the Court of Rome* (London, 1935).

Armstrong, Robert, 'Protestant Ireland and the English Parliament, 1641–1647' (unpub. Ph.D. thesis, Trinity College Dublin, 1995).

Ashton, Robert, *The English Civil War: Conservatism and Revolution, 1603–1649*, 2nd edn. (London, 1991).

Aringhi, Paolo, *Memorie istoriche della vita del venerabile servo di Dio Pier Francesco Scarampi* (Rome, 1744).

Aylmer, G. E., *Rebellion or Revolution: England from Civil War to Restoration* (Oxford, 1986).

——'Presidential Address: Collective Mentalities in Mid-seventeenth-Century England, 2, Royalist attitudes', *Transactions of the Royal Historical Society*, 37 (1987), 1–30.

Bagwell, Richard, *Ireland under the Stuarts and during the Interregnum* (3 vols., London, 1909–16).

Baker, J. H., 'The Common Lawyers and the Chancery: 1616', *Irish Jurist*, 4 (1969), 368–92.

Barnard, Toby, *Cromwellian Ireland, English Government and Reform in Ireland* (Oxford, 1975).

——'Crises of Identity among Irish Protestants, 1641–1685', *Past and Present*, 127 (1990), 39–83.

——'1641: A Bibliographical Essay', in Brian Mac Cuarta (ed.), *Ulster 1641: Aspects of the Rising* (Belfast, 1993), 173–86.

Beckett, J. C., *The Making of Modern Ireland, 1603–1923* (New York, 1977).

——*The Cavalier Duke* (Belfast, 1990).

——'The Confederation of Kilkenny Reviewed', *Historical Studies*, 2 (1959), 29–41.

Bennett, Martyn, *The Civil Wars in Britain and Ireland, 1638–1651* (Oxford, 1997).

Bercé, Yves-Marie (trans. J. Bergin), *Revolt and Revolution in Early Modern Europe: An Essay on the History of Political Violence* (Manchester, 1987).

Bergin, J. A., 'The Crown, the Papacy and the Reform of the Old Orders in Early Seventeenth Century France', *Journal of Ecclesiastical History*, 33 (1982), 234–55.

——*Cardinal de la Rochefoucauld: Leadership and Reform in the French Church* (London, 1987).

——'Cardinal Mazarin and his Benefices', *French History*, 1 (1987), 1–22.

Bireley, Robert, *Religion and Politics in the Age of the Counter-Reformation. Emperor Ferdinand II, William Lamormaini, S.J., and the Formation of Imperial Policy* (Chapel Hill, NC, 1981).

——'Early Modern Germany', in John O'Malley (ed.), *Catholicism in Early Modern Europe: A Guide to Research* (Ann Arbor, Mich., 1988).

——'The Thirty Years' War as Germany's Religious War', in K. Repgen (ed.), *Krieg und Politik, 1618–1648* (Munich, 1988), 85–106.

Black, Christopher, 'Perugia and Post-Tridentine Church Reform', *Journal of Ecclesiastical History*, 35 (1984), 429–51.

Bluche, François, *Louis XIV* (Paris, 1986).

Bolster, Evelyn, *A History of the Diocese of Cork: From the Reformation to the Penal Era* (Cork, 1982).

Bonney, Richard, *The European Dynastic States* (Oxford, 1991).

Bossy, John, 'The Counter-Reformation and the People of Catholic Europe', *Past and Present*, 47 (1970), 51–70.

——'The Counter-Reformation and the People of Catholic Ireland', *Historical Studies*, 8 (1971), 153–70.

——*The English Catholic Community, 1570–1850* (London, 1976).

——'The Mass as a Social Institution, 1200–1700', *Past and Present*, 100 (1983), 29–61.

——*Christianity in the West, 1400–1700* (Oxford, 1985).

Bottigheimer, K. S., *English Money and Irish Land* (Oxford, 1971).

Boyd, Andrew, 'Rinuccini and Civil War in Ireland, 1644–9', *History Today*, 41 (1991), 42–8.

Bradshaw, Brendan, *The Dissolution of the Religious Orders under Henry VIII* (Cambridge, 1974).

——'The Bardic Response to Conquest and Colonisation', *Bullán: An Irish Studies Journal*, 1 (1994), 119–22.

——and P. Roberts (eds.), *British Consciousness and Identity* (Cambridge, 1998).

Brady, Ciarán, *The Chief Governors: The Rise and Fall of Reform Government in Tudor Ireland, 1536–1588* (Cambridge, 1994).

——and Raymond Gillespie (eds.), *Natives and Newcomers: Essays on the Making of Irish Colonial Society, 1534–1641* (Dublin, 1986).

Bray, Massimo, 'L'arcivescovo, il viceré, il fedelissimo popolo', *Nuova Rivista Storica*, 74 (1990), 311–32.

Breatnach, Caoimhín, *Patronage, Politics and Prose* (Maynooth, 1996).

Bremond, H., *Histoire littéraire du sentiment religieux en France. Depuis la fin des guerres de religion jusqu'à nos jours* (Paris, 1924–33).

Brennan, James, 'A Gallican Interlude in Ireland', *Irish Theological Quarterly*, 24 (1957), 219–37, 283–309.

Briggs, Robin, *Communities of Belief: Cultural and Social Tensions in Early Modern France* (Oxford, 1989).

Burke, James, 'The New Model Army and the Problems of Siege Warfare, 1648–51', *Irish Historical Studies*, 27 (1990), 1–29.

Butlin, R. A., 'Irish Towns in the Sixteenth and Seventeenth Centuries', in R. A. Butlin (ed.)., *The Development of the Irish Town* (London, 1977), 61–100.

Caball, Marc, 'Faith, Culture and Sovereignty: Irish Nationality and its

Development, 1558–1625', in Brendan Bradshaw and P. Roberts (eds.), *British Consciousness and Identity* (Cambridge, 1998).

Canny, Nicholas, 'The Treaty of Mellifont and the Re-organization of Ulster, 1603', *Irish Sword*, 9 (1969), 249–62.

——*The Formation of the Old English Elite in Ireland* (Dublin, 1975).

——'Dominant Minorities: English Settlers in Ireland and Virginia, 1550–1650', in A. C. Hepburn (ed.), *Minorities in History*, Historical Studies, 12 (Belfast, 1978), 17–44.

——'The Formation of the Irish Mind: Religion, Politics and Gaelic Irish Literature, 1580–1750', *Past and Present*, 95 (1982), 91–116.

——*The Upstart Earl. A Study of the Social and Mental World of Richard Boyle, first Earl of Cork, 1566–1643* (Cambridge, 1982).

——'Migration and Opportunity: Britain, Ireland and the New World', *Irish Economic and Social History*, 12 (1985), 7–32.

——*From Reformation to Restoration: Ireland, 1534–1660* (Dublin, 1987).

——*Kingdom and Colony: Ireland in the Atlantic World, 1560–1800* (Baltimore, 1988).

——'In Defence of the Constitution? The Nature of Irish Revolt in the Seventeenth Century', in Louis Bergeron and Louis Cullen (eds.), *Cultures et pratiques politiques en France et en Irelande XVIe–XVIIIe siècles* (Paris, 1991), 23–40.

——'The Attempted Anglicisation of Ireland in the Seventeenth Century: An Exemplar of "British History"', in J. F. Merritt (ed.), *The Political World of Thomas Wentworth, Earl of Strafford, 1621–1641* (Cambridge, 1995).

——'What Really Happened in 1641', in Jane Ohlmeyer (ed.), *Ireland: From Independence to Occupation* (Cambridge, 1995).

——'Religion, Politics and the Irish Rising of 1641', in Judith Devlin and Ronan Fanning (eds.), *Historical Studies*, 20, *Religion and Rebellion* (Dublin, 1997), 40–70.

——and Anthony Pagden (eds.), *Colonial Identity in the Atlantic World, 1500–1800* (Princeton, NJ, 1987).

Capucci, Martino, 'Caratteri e Fortune di un cappucino scozzese', *Studi Secenteschi*, 20 (1979), 43–88.

Cardinale, Igino, *Le Saint-siège et la diplomatie* (Paris, 1962).

Carlton, Charles, *Charles I: The Personal Monarch* (London, 1983).

Carte, Thomas, *An history of the life of James, first duke of Ormond* (6 vols., Oxford, 1851).

Carter C. H. (ed.), *From the Renaissance to the Counter-Reformation: Essays in Honour of Garrett Mattingly* (London, 1966).

——*The Western European Powers, 1500–1700* (New York, 1971).

Casway, Jerrold, 'Owen Roe O'Neill's Return to Ireland in 1642: The Diplomatic Background', *Studia Hibernica*, 9 (1969), 48–64.

——'George Monck and the Controversial Catholic Truce of 1649', *Studia Hibernica*, 16 (1976), 54–72.

——*Owen Roe O'Neill and the Struggle for Catholic Ireland* (Philadelphia, 1984).

——'Two Phelim O'Neills', *Seanchas Ardmhacha*, 11 (1985), 331–41.

——'The Belturbet Council and Election of March 1650', *Clogher Record*, 22 (1986), 159–70.

Catalano, Gaetano and Federico Martino (eds.), *Potestà civile e autorità spirituale in Italia nei secoli della riforma e controriforma* (Milan, 1984).

Chaunu, P., 'Jansénisme et frontière de catholicité. A propos du Jansénisme lorrain', *Revue historique* (1962), 115–38.

Ciampi, Ignazio, *Innocenzo X Pamfili e la sua corte* (Rome, 1878).

Clarke, Aidan, 'The Earl of Antrim and the First Bishops' War', *Irish Sword*, 6 (1963–4), 108–15.

—— 'The Army and Politics in Ireland, 1625–30', *Studia Hibernica* 4 (1964), 28–53.

—— *The Old English in Ireland, 1625–42* (London, 1966).

—— *The Graces, 1625–41*, Irish Historical Series, 8 (Dundalk, 1968).

—— 'Pacification, Plantation and the Catholic Question', 'Selling Royal Favours', 'The Government of Wentworth', and 'The Breakdown of Authority', in T. W. Moody, F. X. Martin, and F. J. Byrne (eds.), *A New History of Ireland*, iii, *Early Modern Ireland, 1534–1691* (Oxford, 1976), 187–288.

—— 'Colonial Identity in Early Seventeenth-century Ireland', in T. W. Moody (ed.), *Nationality and the Pursuit of National Independence* (Belfast, 1978), 57–72.

—— 'The Colonization of Ulster and the Rebellion of 1641, 1603–1660', in T. W. Moody and F. X. Martin (eds.), *The Course of Irish History* (Cork, 1978), 189–203.

—— 'The Genesis of the Ulster Rising of 1641', in Peter Roebuck (ed.), *Plantation to Partition. Essays in Ulster History in Honour of J. L. McCrocken* (Belfast, 1981), 29–45.

—— 'The 1641 Depositions', in P. Fox (ed.), *Treasures of the Library, Trinity College Dublin* (Dublin, 1986).

—— 'Sir Piers Crosby, 1590–1646: Wentworth's "Tawney Ribbon"', *Irish Historical Studies*, 26 (1988), 142–60.

—— 'The 1641 Rebellion and Anti-popery in Ireland', in Brian Mac Cuarta (ed.), *Ulster 1641: Aspects of the Rising* (Belfast, 1993), 139–58.

—— 'Patrick Darcy and the Constitutional Relationship between Britain and Ireland', in Jane Ohlmeyer (ed.), *Political Thought in Seventeenth-Century Ireland: Kingdom or Colony* (Cambridge, 2000), 35–55.

Clifton, Robin, 'The Popular Fear of Catholics During the English Revolution', *Past and Present*, 52 (1971), 23–56.

Coen, Martin, *The Wardenship of Galway* (Galway, 1984).

Conlan, Patrick, *Franciscan Ireland* (Mullingar, 1988).

Connors, Thomas Gilroy, 'The Impact of English Colonial Expansion on Irish Culture' (unpub. Ph.D. thesis, University of Illinois at Urbana-Champaign, 1997).

Coonan, T.L., *The Irish Catholic Confederacy and the Puritan Revolution* (Dublin, 1954).

Corish, Patrick, 'Bishop Nicholas French and the Second Ormond Peace, 1648–9', *Irish Historical Studies*, 6 (1948), 83–100.

—— 'Rinuccini's Censure of 27 May 1648', *Irish Theological Quarterly*, 18 (1951), 322–37.

—— 'Two Contemporary Historians of the Confederation of Kilkenny: John Lynch and Richard O'Ferrall', *Irish Historical Studies*, 8 (1952–3), 217–36.

—— 'John Callaghan and the Controversy among the Irish in Paris', *Irish Theological Quarterly*, 21 (1954), 32–50.

——'The Crisis in Ireland in 1648: The Nuncio and the Supreme Council. Conclusions', *Irish Theological Quarterly*, 22 (1955), 231–57.

——'The Origins of Catholic Nationalism', in P. Corish (ed.), *History of Irish Catholicism*, iii (Dublin, 1968), 1–64.

——'The Rising of 1641 and the Catholic Confederacy, 1641–45', 'Ormond, Rinuccini, and the Confederates, 1645–9', 'The Cromwellian Conquest, 1649–53', and 'The Cromwellian Regime, 1650–1660', in T. W. Moody, F. X. Martin, and F. J. Byrne (eds.), *A New History of Ireland*, iii, *Early Modern Ireland, 1534–1691* (Oxford, 1976), 289–386.

——*The Catholic Community in the Seventeenth and Eighteenth Centuries* (Dublin, 1981).

——*The Irish Catholic Experience* (Dublin, 1985).

——(ed.), *Radicals, Rebels and Establishments*, Historical Studies, 15 (Belfast, 1985).

——'Women and Religious Practice', in Margaret MacCurtain and Mary O'Dowd (eds.), *Women in Early Modern Ireland* (Dublin, 1991), 212–22.

Coville, Henry, *Études sur Mazarin et ses séméles avec le pape Innocent X, 1644–8* (Paris, 1914).

Coward, Barry, *The Stuart Age: A History of England, 1603–1714* (London, 1980).

Crawford, W. H., 'Landlord–Tenant Relations in Ulster, 1609–1802', *Irish Economic and Social History*, 2 (1975), 5–21.

Cregan, D. F., 'Daniel O'Neill. A Royalist Agent in Ireland, 1644–50', *Irish Historical Studies*, 2 (1941), 398–414.

——'Some Members of the Confederation of Kilkenny', in S. O'Brien (ed.), *Measra i gCuimhne Mhichíl Uí Chleirigh* (Dublin, 1944), 34–44.

——'The Confederation of Kilkenny: Its Organisation, Personnel and History' (unpub. Ph.D. thesis, National University of Ireland, 1947).

——'An Irish Cavalier: Daniel O'Neill', *Studia Hibernica*, 3 (1963), 60–100.

——'An Irish Cavalier: Daniel O'Neill', *Studia Hibernica*, 4 (1964), 104–33.

——'An Irish Cavalier: Daniel O'Neill in Exile and Restoration, 1651–1664', *Studia Hibernica*, 5 (1965), 42–76.

——'Irish Recusant Lawyers in Politics in the Reign of James I', *Irish Jurist*, 5 (1970), 306–20.

——'The Confederation of Kilkenny', in Brian Farrell (ed.), *The Irish Parliamentary Tradition* (Dublin, 1973), 102–15.

——'The Social and Cultural Background of a Counter-Reformation Episcopate, 1618–60', in A. Cosgrove and D. MacCartney (eds.), *Studies in Irish History Presented to R. Dudley Edwards* (Dublin, 1979), 85–117.

Cunningham, Bernadette, 'Political and Social Change in the Lordships of Clanricard and Thomond, 1569–1641' (unpub. MA thesis, University College, Galway, 1979).

——'Native Culture and Political Change', in Ciarán Brady and Raymond Gillespie (eds.), *Natives and Newcomers: Essays on the Making of Irish Colonial Society, 1534–1641* (Dublin, 1986), 148–70.

——'Seventeenth-century Interpretations of the Past: The Case of Geoffrey Keating', *Irish Historical Studies*, 25 (1986), 116–28.

——*The World of Geoffrey Keating: History, Myth and Religion in Seventeenth-Century Ireland* (Dublin, 2000).

De Maddalena, Aldo, and Hermann Kellenbenz (eds.), *Finanza e ragion di Stato in Italia e Germania nella prima età moderna* (Bologna, 1984).

De Martino, E., 'Mito Scienze, religiosità e civiltà moderna', *Nuovi Argomenti*, 37 (1959), 1–23.

Degert, A., 'S. Charles Borromée et le clergé français', *Bulletin de littérature ecclésiastique*, 4 (1912), 145–59, 193–213.

del Re, Niccolò, *La Curia Romana: Lineamenti Storico-Giuridici* (Rome, 1970).

Delumeau, Jean, *Catholicism between Luther and Voltaire* (London, 1977).

Deutscher, Thomas, 'Seminaries and the Education of Novarese Priests, 1593–1627', *Journal of Ecclesiastical History*, 32 (1981), 303–19.

——'The Growth of the Secular Clergy and the Development of Educational Institutions in the Diocese of Novara (1563–1772)', *Journal of Ecclesiastical History*, 40 (1989), 381–97.

Dickens, A. G., *The Counter-Reformation* (London, 1979).

DiDomizio, Daniel G., 'Spirituality and Politics: Seventeenth Century France', in M. Fox (ed.), *Historical Spirituality* (Chicago, 1982), 296–313.

Ditchfield, Simon, *Liturgy, Sanctity and History in Tridentine Italy* (Cambridge, 1995).

Duffy, Eamon, 'The English Secular Clergy and the Counter-Reformation', *Journal of Ecclesiastical History*, 34 (1983), 214–30.

Dunlop, Robert, 'The Forged Commission of 1641', *English Historical Review*, 2 (1887), 527–33.

Dunne, T. J., 'The Gaelic Response to Conquest and Colonization: The Evidence of the Poetry', *Studia Hibernica*, 20 (1980), 7–30.

Dupront, A., 'Le Concile de Trente et la réforme tridentin', in Actes du Convegno de Trente, 1963, *Le Concile de Trente et la réforme tridentin* (Rome, 1965) ii. 525–38

——'Réflexions sur l'hérésie moderne', in A. Dupront *Hérésies et sociétés dans l'Europe préindustrielle* (Paris, 1968).

Elliott, J. H., 'Revolts in the Spanish Monarchy', in Robert Forster and Jack P. Greene (eds.), *Preconditions of Revolution in Early Modern Europe* (London, 1970), 109–30.

——*Richelieu and Olivares* (Cambridge, 1984).

——'Foreign Policy and Domestic Crisis: Spain, 1598–1659', in K. Repgen (ed.), *Krieg und Politik, 1618–1648*, (Munich, 1988), pp. 185–202.

——'The Spanish Monarchy and the Kingdom of Portugal, 1580–1640', in Mark Greengrass (ed.), *Conquest and Coalescence: The Shaping of the State in Early Modern Europe* (London, 1991), 48–67.

Ellis, S. G., *Tudor Ireland* (London, 1985).

——'Economic Problems of the Church: Why the Reformation Failed in Ireland', *Journal of Ecclesiastical History*, 41 (1990), 239–65.

Ferri Antonio e Roversi, Giancarlo, *Storia di Bologna* (Bologna, 1978).

Fincham, Kenneth and Peter Lake, 'The Ecclesiastical Policies of James I and Charles I', in Kenneth Fincham (ed.), *The Early Stuart Church, 1603–1642* (London, 1993), 28–48.

FitzPatrick, Brendan, *Seventeenth-Century Ireland: The War of Religions* (Dublin, 1988).

Flynn, Thomas S., *The Irish Dominicans, 1536–1641* (Dublin, 1993).

Ford, Alan, *The Protestant Reformation in Ireland, 1590–1641* (Frankfurt, 1985).

——'The Reformation in Kilmore before 1641', in Ray Gillespie (ed.), *Cavan: Essays on the History of an Irish County* (Dublin, 1995).

Forrestal, Alison, *Catholic Synods in Ireland, 1600–1690* (Dublin, 1998).

Forster, Robert (ed.), *Ritual, Religion and the Sacred* (London, 1982).

Foster, R. F., *Modern Ireland, 1600–1972* (London, 1988).

Franciscan Fathers, *Father Luke Wadding: Commemorative Volume* (Dublin, 1957).

Gabrieli, Vittorio, 'La Missione di Sir Kenelm Digby alla Corte di Innocenzo X (1645–1648)', *English Miscellany*, 5 (Rome, 1954), 247–88.

García García, Antonio, 'The Faculties of Law', in Hilda de Ridder-Symoens, *A History of the University in Europe* (Cambridge, 1992), 388–408.

Garstein, Oskar, *Rome and the Counter-Reformation in Scandinavia* (Oxford, 1963).

Gaudemet, Jean, 'Patristique et Pastorale: La Contribution de Grégorie le Grand au "Miroir de l'Evêque" dans le décret de Gratian', in Centre National de la Recherche Scientifique, *Études d'histoire du droit canonique dédiées à Gabriel Le Bras* (Paris, 1965), i. 129–40.

Geertz, Clifford, *The Interpretation of Cultures* (London, 1973).

Giblin, Cathaldus, 'Vatican Library: MSS Barberini Latini. A Guide to the Material of Irish Interest on Microfilm in the National Library, Dublin', *Archivium Hibernicum*, 18 (1955), 67–144.

——'The *Processus Datariae* and the Appointment of Irish Bishops in the Seventeenth Century', in Franciscan Fathers, *Father Luke Wadding: Commemorative Volume* (Dublin, 1957), 508–616.

——'Catalogue of Material of Irish Interest in the Collection *Nunziatura di Fiandra*, Vatican Archives', *Collectanea Hibernica*, 1 (1958), 7–125.

Gillespie, Raymond, 'Harvest Crises in Early Seventeenth-century Ireland', *Irish Economic and Social History*, 2 (1984), 5–18.

——*Colonial Ulster: The Settlement of East Ulster 1600–41* (Cork, 1985).

——'Mayo and the 1641 Rising', *Cathair na Mart*, 5 (1985), 38–44.

——'The End of an Era: Ulster and the Outbreak of the 1641 Rising', in Ciarán Brady and Raymond Gillespie (eds.), *Natives and Newcomers: Essays on the Making of Irish Colonial Society, 1534–1641* (Dublin, 1986).

——*Conspiracy. Ulster Plots and Plotters in 1615* (Belfast, 1987).

——'Destabilising Ulster, 1641–2', in Brian Mac Cuarta (ed.) *Ulster 1641: Aspects of the Rising* (Belfast, 1993), 107–22.

——*Devoted People: Belief and Religion in Early Modern Ireland* (Manchester, 1997).

Ginzburg, Carlo, 'Folklore, Magia e Religione nelle Campagne Italiane', in Carla Russo (ed.), *Società Chiesa e vita religiosa nell'Ancien Regime* (Naples, 1976), 434–8.

Golden, Richard M., *The Godly Rebellion: Parisian Curés and the Religious Fronde, 1652–62* (Chapel Hill, NC, 1981).

Gouhier, Pierre, 'Mercenaires irlandais au service de la France (1635–1664)', *Irish Sword*, 7 (1965–6), 58–75.

Greengrass, Mark (ed.), *Conquest and Coalescence: The Shaping of the State in Early Modern Europe* (London, 1991).

Grisar, J., 'Päpistliche Finanzen, Nepotismus und Kirchenrecht unter Urban VIII', *Xenia Piana: Miscellanea historiae pontificae*, vii (Rome, 1943), 205–366.

Gurr, T. R., *Why Men Rebel* (Princeton, NJ, 1971).

Haigh, Christopher, 'From Monopoly to Minority: Catholicism in Early Modern England', *Transactions of the Royal Historical Society*, 5th ser., 31 (1981), 129–47.

——'Revisionism, the Reformation and the History of English Catholicism', *Journal of Ecclesiastical History*, 36 (1985), 394–405.

Harold, F., *Vita Fratris Lucae Waddingi*, 3rd edn. (Karachi, 1931).

Hale, J. R., *War and Society in Renaissance Europe, 1450–1620* (Glasgow, 1985).

Hallman, B. M., *Italian Cardinals, Reform and the Church as Property, 1492–1563* (London, 1985).

Harman, Alec, and Anthony Milner (eds.), *Man and his Music II: Late Renaissance and Baroque Music*, rev. edn. (London, 1988).

Harris, F. W., 'The Rebellion of Sir Cahir O'Doherty and its Legal Aftermath', *Irish Jurist*, 15 (1980), 298–325.

Haskell, F., *Patrons and Painter: A Study in the Relations between Italian Art and Society in the Age of the Baroque* (New Haven, Conn., 1980).

Hazlett, Hugh, 'The Financing of the British Armies in Ireland, 1641–9' *Irish Historical Society*, 1 (1938), 21–41.

——'A History of the military forces operating in Ireland' (unpub. Ph.D. thesis, Queen's University, Belfast, 1938).

Henry, Grainne, *The Irish Military Community in Spanish Flanders, 1586–1621* (Dublin, 1992).

——'Ulster Exiles in Europe, 1605–41', in Brian Mac Cuarta (ed.) *Ulster 1641: Aspects of the Rising* (Belfast, 1993).

Hermann, Christian, *L'Eglise d'Espagne sous le patronage royal (1476–1834)* (Madrid, 1988).

Hibbard, Caroline, *Charles I and the Popish Plot* (Chapel Hill, NC, 1981).

Hoffmann, P., *Church and Community in the Diocese of Lyons, 1500–1789* (New Haven, Conn., and London, 1984).

Hook, Judith A., 'Urban VIII: The Paradox of a Spiritual Monarchy', in A. G. Dickens (ed.), *The Courts of Europe: Politics, Patronage and Royalty, 1400–1800* (London, 1977), 213–31.

Hutton, Ronald, 'The Royalist War Effort', in John Morill (ed.), *Reactions to the English Civil War, 1642–9* (London, 1982), 51–66.

Hynes, Michael, *The Mission of Rinuccini, Nuncio Extraordinary to Ireland, 1645–49* (Louvain, 1932).

——'The Irish Republic in the Seventeenth Century', *Catholic Historical Review*, 23 (1937), 293–311.

Irwin, Liam, 'Politics, Religion and Economy: Cork in the Seventeenth Century', *Journal of the Cork Historical and Archaeological Society*, 85 (1980), 7–25.

Jennings, B., 'The Career of Hugh, Son of Rory O'Donnell, Earl of Tyrconnel in the Low Countries 1607–42', *Studies*, 30 (1941), 219–34.

——'Ecclesiastical Appointments in Ireland, Aug. 1643–Dec. 1649', *Collectanea Hibernica*, 2 (1959), 18–64.

Kamen, Henry, 'Clerical Violence in a Catholic Society: The Hispanic World, 1450–1720', in W. J. Sheils *The Church and War*, Studies in Church History, 20 (London, 1983), 201–16.
——*European Society, 1500–1700* (London, 1984).
——*The Phoenix and the Flame: Catalonia and the Counter-reformation* (London, 1993).
Kearney, Hugh F., 'Ecclesiastical Politics and the Counter-Reformation in Ireland, 1618–48', *Journal of Ecclesiastical History*, 11 (1960), 202–12.
——*Strafford in Ireland, 1633–41: A Study in Absolutism*, 2nd edn. (Cambridge, 1989).
Kennedy, Mary Catherine, 'Eagla an Ghallsmacht: The Religion and Politics of Irish Catholics, 1620s–1670s' (unpub. MA thesis, University College, Galway).
Kenyon, John, *The Civil Wars of England* (London, 1989).
Kerney Walsh, Micheline, 'O'Neills in Exile', *Seanchas Ardmhacha*, 8 (1976–7), 55–68.
——*Destruction by Peace: Hugh O'Neill after Kinsale* (Monaghan, 1986).
Kierkegaard, Soren, *Fear and Trembling*, trans. Alastair Hannay (London, 1985).
Kiernan, V. G., *State and Society in Europe, 1550–1650* (Oxford, 1980).
Kishlansky, Mark, 'Ideology and Politics in the Parliamentary Armies, 1645–9', in John Morill (ed.), *Reactions to the English Civil War, 1642–9* (London, 1982).
Knox, R. Buick, *James Ussher, Archbishop of Armagh* (Cardiff, 1967).
Krogh Rasmussen, Niels, 'Liturgy and Liturgical Arts', in John O'Malley (ed.), *Catholicism in Early Modern Europe: A Guide to Research* (Ann Arbor, Mich., 1988), 273–92.
Larner, Christina, *Witchcraft and Religion: The Politics of Popular Belief* (Oxford, 1984).
Le Bras, Gabriel, 'La Pratica Religiosa nelle Campagne Francesi', in Carla Russo (ed.),, *Società Chiesa e vita religiosa nell' Ancien Regime* (Naples, 1976), 185–201.
Lee Malcolm, Joyce, 'A King in Search of Soldiers, Charles I in 1642', *Historical Journal*, 21 (1978), 251–73.
——'All the King's Men: The Impact of the Crown's Irish Forces on the English Civil War', *Irish Historical Society*, 22 (1979), 239–64.
Leerssen, J. T., 'Archbishop Ussher and Gaelic Culture', *Studia Hibernica*, 22–3 (1982–3), 50–8.
Legendre, Pierre, 'Le Droit romain, modèle et langage. De la signification de l'*Utrumque Ius*', in Centre National de la Recherche Scientifique, *Études d'histoire du droit canonique dédiées à Gabriel Le Bras* (Paris, 1965), 913–30.
Lenihan, Pádraig, 'The Leinster Army and the Battle of Dungan's Hill, 1647', *Irish Sword*, 71 (1991), 139–53.
——*Confederate Catholics at War, 1641–49* (Cork, 2001).
Lennon, Colm, *Sixteenth-Century Ireland: The Incomplete Conquest* (Dublin, 1994).
Lindley, Keith, 'The Impact of the 1641 Rebellion upon England and Wales', *Irish Historical Society*, 18 (1972).
Loades, D. M., *Politics and the Nation, 1450–1660* (London, 1974).
Lowe, John, 'Charles I and the Confederation of Kilkenny', *Irish Historical Society*, 14 (1954), 1–19.

Lowe, John, 'Some Aspects of the Wars in Ireland, 1641–49', *Irish Sword*, 4 (1959), 81–7.

——'The Glamorgan Mission to Ireland', *Studia Hibernica*, 4 (1964), 155–96.

MacCarthy-Morrogh, Michael, *The Munster Plantation* (Oxford, 1986).

Mac Cuarta, Brian (ed.) *Ulster 1641: Aspects of the Rising* (Belfast, 1993).

MacCurtain, Margaret, and Mary O'Dowd (eds.), *Women in Early Modern Ireland* (Dublin, 1991).

MacInnes, Allan I, 'Scottish Gaeldom, 1638–51': The Vernacular Response to the Convenanting Dynamic', in John Dwyer, Roger A. Mason, and Alexander Murdoch (eds.), *New Perspectives on the Politics and Culture of Early Modern Scotland* (Edinburgh, 1982), 59–94.

——'The Impact of the Civil Wars and Interregnum: Political Disruption and Social Changes within Scottish Gaeldom', in Rosalind Mitchison and Peter Roebuck (eds.), *Economy and Society in Scotland and Ireland, 1500–1939* (Edinburgh, 1988).

McRedmond, Louis, *To the Greater Glory: A History of the Irish Jesuits* (Dublin, 1991).

MaGrath, Patrick, 'English Catholicism: A Reconsideration', *Journal of Ecclesiastical History*, 35 (1984), 414–28.

Maltby, W., 'Spain', in John O'Malley (ed.), *Catholicism in Early Modern Europe: A Guide to Research* (Ann Arbor, Mich., 1988), 31–48.

Mancini, A. N., 'Il Romanzo nel Seicento. saggio di bibliografia', *Studi Secenteschi*, 12 (1971).

Marocchi, Massimo, 'Spirituality in the Sixteenth and Seventeenth Centuries', in John O'Malley (ed.), *Catholicism in Early Modern Europe: A Guide to Research* (Ann Arbor, Mich., 1988), 162–87.

Marshall, R., *Henrietta Maria* (London, 1990).

Marston, Jerrilyn Greene, 'Gentry Honour and Royalism in Early Stuart England', *Journal of British Studies*, 13 (1973), 21–43.

Martin, F. X., *Friar Nugent: A Study of Francis Lavalin Nugent, 1569–1635, Agent of the Counter-Reformation* (Rome and London, 1962).

Mathias, Peter (ed.), *Science and Society, 1600–1900* (Cambridge, 1973).

Meehan, C. P., *The Rise and Fall of the Irish Franciscan Monasteries and Memoirs of the Irish Hierarchy in the Seventeenth Century* (Dublin, 1877).

Merritt, J. F. (ed.), *The Political World of Thomas Wentworth, Earl of Strafford, 1621–1641* (Cambridge, 1995).

Miller, Samuel J., *Portugal and Rome c. 1748–1830* (Rome, 1978).

Millett, Benignus, 'Irish Literature in Latin', in T. W. Moody, F. X. Martin, and F. J. Byrne (eds.), *A New History of Ireland*, iii, *Early Modern Ireland, 1534–1691* (Oxford, 1976), 566–82.

——'Catalogue of Irish Material in 14 Volumes of Scritture originali riferite nell congregazioni generali in Propaganda Archives', *Collectanea Hibernica*, 10–12 (1967–9).

Mitzman, A., 'The Civilizing Offensive: Mentalities, High Culture and Individual Psyches', *Journal of Social History*, 20 (1987), 662–78.

Monter, E. William, 'The New Social History and the Spanish Inquisition', *Journal of Social History*, 17 (1983–4).

——*Ritual, Myth and Magic in Early Modern Europe* (Brighton, 1983).

Moody, T. W., *The Londonderry Plantation, 1609–1641. The City of London and the Plantation in Ulster* (Belfast, 1939).

——F. X. Martin, and F. J. Byrne (eds.), *A New History of Ireland*, III, *Early Modern Ireland, 1534–1691* (Oxford, 1976).

Morgan, Hiram, 'The End of Gaelic Ulster: A Thematic Interpretation of Events between 1534 and 1610', *Irish Historical Studies*, 26 (1988), 8–32.

——*Tyrone's Rebellion: The Outbreak of the Nine Years' War in Tudor Ireland* (Dublin, 1993).

Morill, John, *The Revolt of the Provinces: Conservatives and Radicals in the English Civil War, 1630–1650* (London, 1976).

——(ed.), *Reactions to the English Civil War, 1642–9* (London, 1982).

——*The Scottish National Covenant in its British Context, 1638–51* (Edinburgh, 1990).

——*The Impact of the English Civil War* (London, 1991).

——*The Nature of the English Revolution* (London, 1993).

Morrissey, Thomas, 'Archdevil and Jesuit: The Background, Life and Times of James Archer from 1550 to 1604' (unpub. MA thesis, University College Dublin, 1968).

——'The Strange Letters of Matthew O'Hartigan SJ', *Irish Theological Quarterly*, 37 (1970), 159–72.

——*James Archer of Kilkenny* (Dublin, 1979).

Mousnier, Roland, 'Les Crises intérieures françaises de 1610 à 1659 et leur influence sur la politique extérieure française, surtout de 1618 à 1648', in K. Repgen (ed.), *Krieg und Politik 1618–1648*, (Munich, 1988), 169–84.

Munck, Thomas, *Seventeenth Century Europe: State, Conflict and the Social Order in Europe, 1598–1700* (London, 1990).

Murphy, Elaine, 'God's Providence: Inchiquin and the Survival of Protestant Munster' (unpub. M.Litt. thesis, National University of Ireland, 1999).

Murphy, John A., 'The Politics of the Munster Protestants, 1641–9', *Journal of the Cork Historical and Archaeological Society*, 76 (1971), 1–20.

Newman, P. R., 'Catholic Royalist Activists in the North, 1642–6', *Recusant History*, 15 (1977), 26–38.

——'Catholic Royalists of Northern England, 1642–5', *Northern History*, 15 (1979), 88–95.

Nicholls, Kenneth, *Gaelic and Gaelicised Ireland in the Middle Ages* (Dublin, 1972).

Nolan, William, and Kevin Whelan (eds.), *Kilkenny: History and Society. Interdisciplinary Essays on the History of an Irish County* (Dublin, 1990).

Nussdorfer, Laurie, 'The Vacant See: Ritual and Protest in Early Modern Rome', *Sixteenth Century Journal*, 18 (1987), 173–89.

Ó Bric, Breandán, 'Galway Townsmen as Owners of Land in Connacht, 1585–1641' (unpub. MA thesis, University College, Galway, 1974).

Ó Buachalla, Breandán, '*Annála Ríoghachta Éireann* is *Foras Feasa ar Éirinn*: An Comhthéacs Comhaimseartha', *Studia Hibernica*, 22–3 (1982–3), 59–105.

——'Na Stíobhartaigh agus an t-aos léinn: Cing Seamas', *Proceedings of the Royal Irish Academy*, 83 (1983), sect. c, 81–134.

——*Aisling Ghéar: Na Stíobhartaigh agus an t-aos léinn* (Dublin, 1997).

O'Cahan, T. S., *Owen Roe O'Neill* (London, 1968).

Ó Cearbhaill, Diarmaid (ed.), *Galway Town and Gown* (Dublin, 1984), 90–109.

Ó Danachair, Caoimhín, 'Montrose's Irish Regiments', *Irish Sword*, 4 (1959), 61–7.

O'Dowd, Mary, 'Land Inheritance in Early Modern County Sligo', *Irish Economic and Social History*, 10 (1983), 5–18.

——*Power, Politics and Land: Early Modern Sligo, 1568–1688* (Belfast, 1991).

——'Women and War in Ireland in the 1640s', in Margaret MacCurtain and Mary O'Dowd (eds.), *Women in Early Modern Ireland* (Dublin, 1991), 91–111.

Ó Dúshláine, Tadhg, *An Eoraip agus Litríocht na Gaeilge, 1600–1650, Gnéithe den Bharócachas Eorpach i Litríocht na Gaeilge* (Dublin, 1987).

Ó Fiaich, Tomás, 'Republicanism and Separatism in the Seventeenth Century', *Léachtaí Cholm Cille*, 2 (1971), 74–87.

O'Gorman, Thomas, 'Occurrences from Ireland: Contemporary Pamphlet Reactions to the Confederate Wars, 1641–49 (unpub. M.Litt. thesis, National University of Ireland, 2000).

Ó Gráda, Cormac, *Ireland Before and After the Famine: Explorations in Economic History, 1800–1925* (Manchester, 1988).

Ó hAnnracháin, Tadhg, 'Vatican Diplomacy and the Mission of Rinuccini to Ireland', *Archivium Hibernicum*, 47 (1993), 78–88.

——'Far from Terra Firma: The Mission of GianBattista Rinuccini to Ireland, 1645–9' (2 vols., unpub. Ph.D. thesis, European University Institute, 1995).

——'Rebels and Confederates: The Stance of the Irish Clergy in the 1640s', in John Young (ed.), *Celtic Dimensions of the British Civil Wars* (Edinburgh, 1997).

——'"Though Hereticks and Politicians Should Misinterpret their Good Zeale": Political Ideology and Catholicism in Early Modern Ireland', in Jane Ohlmeyer (ed.), *Political Thought in Seventeenth-Century Ireland: Kingdom or Colony* (Cambridge, 2000), 155–75.

Ohlmeyer, Jane, 'The "Antrim plot" of 1641—A Myth', *Historical Journal*, 35 (1992), 905–19.

——*Civil War and Restoration in the Three Stuart Kingdoms: The Career of Randal MacDonnell, Marquis of Antrim, 1609–1683* (Cambridge, 1993).

——(ed.), *Ireland from Independence to Occupation, 1641–60* (Cambridge, 1995).

——(ed.), *Political Thought in Seventeenth-Century Ireland: Kingdom or Colony* (Cambridge, 2000).

O'Malley, John (ed.), *Catholicism in Early Modern Europe: A Guide to Research* (Ann Arbor, Mich., 1988).

O'Malley, Liam, 'Patrick Darcy, Galway Lawyer and Politician', in Diarmaid Ó Cearbhaill (ed.), *Galway Town and Gown* (Dublin, 1984), 90–109.

Ó Mórdha, P. B., 'The Battle of Clones, 1643', *Clogher Record*, 4 (1962), 148–54.

Ó Mórdha, Séamus, 'Hugh O'Reilly (1581?–1653), A Reforming Primate', *Breifne*, 4 (1970), 345–69.

——'Heber MacMahon, Soldier Bishop of the Confederation of Kilkenny', in Joseph Duffy (ed.), *Clogher Record Album. A Diocesan History* (Monaghan, 1975).

Ó Murchadha, Ciarán, 'Land and Society in Seventeenth Century Clare' (unpub. Ph.D. thesis, University College, Galway, 1982).

O'Riordan, Michelle, *The Gaelic Mind and the Collapse of the Gaelic World* (Cork, 1990).

——'The Native Ulster *Mentalité* as Revealed in Gaelic Sources, 1600–50', in Brian Mac Cuarta (ed.), *Ulster 1641: Aspects of the Rising* (Belfast, 1993), 61–92.

O'Riordan, S., 'Rinuccini in Galway, 1647–49', *Journal of the Galway Archaeological and Historical Society*, 23 (1948), 19–51.

Ó Siochrú, Micheál, *Confederate Ireland, 1642–1649: A Constitutional and Political Analysis* (Dublin, 1999).

O'Sullivan, Harold, 'The Franciscans in Dundalk', *Seanchas Ardmhacha, The Journal of the Armagh Diocesan Historical Society*, 4 (1960–1), 33–72.

Parker, Geoffrey, *The Thirty Years' War* (London, 1984).

——*The Military Revolution: Military Innovation and the Rise of the West* (Cambridge, 1988).

Partner, Peter, 'The Papal State: 1417–1600', in Mark Greengrass (ed.), *Conquest and Coalescence: The Shaping of the State in Early Modern Europe* (London, 1991).

Pasquini, A., *Eresia e riforma cattolica al confine orientale d'Italia* (Rome, 1951).

Pastor, Ludvig Von (trans. Ernest Graf), *History of the Popes from the Close of the Middle Ages*, xxviii–xxx (London, 1938–40).

Patterson, Nerys, 'Gaelic Law and the Tudor Conquest of Ireland: The Social Background of the Sixteenth-century Recensions of the Pseudo-historical Prologue to the *Senchas már*', *Irish Historical Society*, 27 (1991), 193–215.

Pawlisch, Hans S., *Sir John Davies and the Conquest of Ireland: A Study in Legal Imperialism* (Cambridge, 1985).

Penco, Gregorio, *Storia della chiesa in Italia* (Milan, 1978).

Perceval-Maxwell, Michael, 'Strafford, the Ulster Scots and the Covenanters', *Irish Historical Studies*, 18 (1973), 524–51.

——'The Ulster Rising of 1641 and the Depositions', *Irish Historical Society*, 21 (1978–9), 144–67.

——'Ireland and the Monarchy in the Early Stuart Multiple Kingdom', *Historical Journal*, 34 (1991), 279–95.

——'Ulster 1641 in the Context of Political Developments in the Three Kingdoms', in Brian Mac Cuarta (ed.), *Ulster 1641: Aspects of the Rising* (Belfast, 1993), 93–106.

——*The Outbreak of the Irish Rebellion of 1641* (Dublin, 1994).

Po-Chia Hsia, R., *The World of Catholic Renewal, 1540–1770* (Cambridge, 1998).

Prendergast, J. P., 'Records of the Kilkenny Confederate Assembly, AD 1642–1650', *Journal of the Royal Society of Antiquaries of Ireland*, 1 (1849–51), 420–7.

Prodi, Paolo, 'S. Carlo Borromeo e il cardinale Gabriele Paleotti: due vescovi della riforma cattolica', *Critica Storica*, 3 (1964), 135–51.

——*Il Cardinale Gabriele Paleotti* (2 vols., Rome, 1959–67).

——*Il sovrano pontefice: un corpo e due anime. La monarchia papale nella prima età moderna* (Bologna, 1982).

Pullan, Brian, 'Catholics and the Poor in Early Modern Europe', *Transactions of the Royal Historical Society*, 5th ser., 26 (1976), 15–34.

Ranger, Terrence, 'Richard Boyle and the Making of an Irish Fortune, 1588–1614', *Irish Historical Studies*, 10 (1957), 257–97.

——'Strafford: A Revaluation', in T. Aston (ed.), *Crisis in Europe, 1560–1660. Essays from 'Past and Present'* (London, 1965), 271–93.

Ravitch, Norman, *The Catholic Church and the French Nation, 1589–1989* (London, 1990).

Reay, Barry (ed.), *Popular Culture in Seventeenth-century England* (London, 1988).

Reinhard, Wolfgang, 'Finanza pontificia e Stato della Chiesa nel xvi e xvii secolo', in Aldo De Maddalena and Hermann Kellenbenz (eds.), *Finanza e ragion di Stato in Italia e in Germania nella prima età moderna* (Bologna, 1984).

——'Reformation, Counter-Reformation and the Early Modern State: A Reassessment', *Catholic Historical Review*, 75 (1989), 383–404.

Repgen, K., *Die römische Kurie und der westfälische Friede. Papst, Kaiser und Reich 1521–1644* (Tübingen, 1962).

——(ed.), *Krieg und Politik, 1618–1648* (Munich, 1988).

Rice, G., 'Thomas Dease, Bishop of Meath, and Some Questions Concerned with the Rights to Ecclesiastical Property Alienated at the Reformation', *Ríocht na Midhe*, 6/1 (1975), 69–89.

Richet, Denis, 'Sociocultural Aspects of Religious Conflict in Paris during the Second Half of the Sixteenth Century', in Robert Forster (ed.), *Ritual, Religion and the Sacred* (London, 1982).

Roebuck, Peter, 'The Making of an Ulster Great Estate: The Chichesters, Barons of Belfast and Viscounts of Carrickfergus, 1599–1648', *Proceedings of the Royal Irish Academy*, sect. c, 72 (1979), 1–25.

Romeo, Giovanni, *Inquisitori, esorcisti e streghe nell'Italia della Controriforma* (Florence, 1990).

Roots, Ivan, *The Great Rebellion, 1642–1660* (London, 1983).

Rothkrug, Lionel, 'Icon and Ideology in Religion and Rebellion, 1300–1600: Bauernfreiheit and Religion Royale', in J. M. Bak and G. Benecke (eds.), *Religion and Rural Revolt* (Manchester, 1984), 31–61.

Rowen, Herbert, 'Kingship and Republicanism in the Seventeenth Century: Some Reconsiderations', in C. H. Carter (ed.), *From the Renaissance to the Counter-Reformation: Essays in Honour of Garrett Mattingly* (London, 1966), 420–31.

Rüegg, Walter, 'The Rise of Humanism', in Hilda de Ridder-Symoens, *A History of the University in Europe* (Cambridge, 1992), 442–68.

Russell, Conrad, 'The British Background to the Irish Rebellion of 1641', *Historical Research*, 61 (1988), 165–82.

——*The Causes of the English Civil War* (Oxford, 1990).

——*The Fall of the British Monarchies* (Oxford, 1991).

Russo, Carla (ed.), *Società Chiesa e vita religiosa nell'Ancien Regime* (Naples, 1976).

Ryan, Conor, 'Religion and State in Seventeenth-century Ireland', *Archivium Hibernicum*, 33 (1975), 122–32.

Sauzet, Robert, *Contre réforme et réforme catholique en Bas-Languedoc* (Paris, Brussels, and Louvain, 1979).

Schiavi, Laura, *La Mediazione di Roma e di Venezia nel congresso di Münster* (Bologna, 1923).

Sharpe, James, 'The People and the Law', in Barry Reay (ed.), *Popular Culture in Seventeenth-century England* (London, 1988), 244–70.

Sheehan, A. J., 'The Recusancy Revolt of 1603: A Reinterpretation', *Archivium Hibernicum*, 38 (1983), 3–13.

——'Irish Towns in a Period of Change, 1558–1625', in Ciarán Brady and Raymond Gillespie (eds.), Natives and Newcomers: Essays on the Making of Irish Colonial Society, 1534–1641 (Dublin, 1986), 93–119.

Silke, J. J., 'Primate Lombard and James I', Irish Theological Quarterly, 22 (1955), 124–50.

——'Primate Peter Lombard and Hugh O'Neill', Irish Theological Quarterly, 26 (1959), 15–30.

Simms, Hilary, 'Violence in County Armagh, 1641', in Brian Mac Cuarta (ed.) Ulster 1641: Aspects of the Rising (Belfast, 1993), 123–38.

Simms, J. G., 'The Jacobite Parliament of 1689', in David Hayton and Gerard O'Brien (eds.), War and Politics in Ireland, 1649–1730 (London, 1986).

Simms, Katherine, From Kings to Warlords: The Changing Political Structure of Gaelic Ireland in the Later Middle Ages (Woodbridge, 1987).

Snyder, G., La Pédagogie en France au xvii et xviii siècles (Paris, 1965).

Sparks, May, 'Archbishop Rinuccini, papal nuncio', Old Kilkenny Review, Journal of the Kilkenny Archaeological Society, 7 (1954), 35–9.

Springhetti, A., 'Urbanus VIII PM Poeta Latinus et Hymnarum et Breviarium Emendator', Archivium Historiae Pontificiae, 6 (1968), 163–90.

Stevenson, David, 'The Desertion of the Irish by Coll Keitach's Sons, 1642', Irish Historical Studies, 21 (1978), 75–84.

——'The Irish Franciscan Mission to Scotland and the Irish Rebellion of 1641', Innes Review, 30 (1979), 54–61.

——Scottish Covenanters and Irish Confederates (Belfast, 1981).

Stradling, R. A., The Spanish Monarchy and Irish Mercenaries: The Wild Geese in Spain, 1618–68 (Dublin, 1994).

Tapié, Victor, 'Iconografia Barocca e Sensibilità Cattolica' in Carla Russo (ed.), Società, Chiesa e vita religiosa nell' Ancien Regime (Naples, 1976), 309–26.

Torre, Angelo, 'Politics Clothed in Worship: State, Church and Local Power in Piedmont, 1570–1770', Past and Present, 134 (1992), 42–92.

Tracy, James D., 'With and Without the Counter-Reformation: The Catholic Church in the Spanish Netherlands and the Dutch Republic, 1580–1650', Catholic Historical Review, 71 (1985), 547–75.

Treadwell, Victor, Buckingham and Ireland, 1616–1628: A Study in Anglo-Irish Politics (Dublin, 1998).

Trevor-Roper, Hugh, Archbishop Laud, 1573–1645 (London, 1940).

——Catholics, Anglicans and Puritans. Seventeenth-century Essays (Chicago, 1988).

Turner, Bryan S., The Body and Society: Explorations in Social Theory (Oxford, 1984).

Underdown, David, Pride's Purge: Politics in the Puritan Revolution (London, 1985).

——Revel, Riot and Rebellion: Popular Politics and Culture in England, 1603–1660 (Oxford, 1987).

Vaccari, Pietro, 'La storia del diritto nell'Italia settentrionale: Diritto romano e diritto canonio', in Centre National de la Recherche Scientifique, Études d'histoire du droit canonique dédiées à Gabriel Le Bras (Paris, 1965), i. 997–1006.

Vecchi, Alberto, Correnti Religiose nel sei-settecento Veneto (Venice and Rome, 1962).

Wall, Thomas, 'Irish Enterprise in the University of Paris (1651–1653)', *Irish Ecclesiastical Record*, 5/64 (1944), 94–106, 159–72.

Whelan, Kevin (ed.), *Wexford: History and Society. Interdisciplinary Essays on the History of an Irish County* (Dublin, 1987).

Wiener, Carol, 'The Beleaguered Isle, A Study of Elizabethan and Early Jacobean Anti-Catholicism', *Past and Present*, 51 (1971), 27–62.

Wilson Yeates, F., 'The Coinage of Ireland during the Rebellion, 1641–52', *British Numismatic Journal*, 15 (1919–20), 185–223.

——'Further Notes on the Irish Coinage, 1641–1652', *British Numismatic Journal*, 16 (1921–2), 189–93.

Wright, A. D., *The Counter-Reformation: Catholic Europe and the Non-Christian World* (London, 1982).

Yates, Frances A., *The Rosicrucian Enlightenment* (London, 1972).

——*Astraea: The Imperial Theme in the Sixteenth Century* (London, 1993).

Zagorin, Perez, *Rebels and Rulers, 1500–1660, i, Society, States and Early Modern Revolution. Agrarian and Urban Rebellions, ii, Provincial Rebellion. Revolutionary Civil Wars, 1560–1660* (Cambridge, 1982).

Zemon Davis, Natalie, *Society and Culture in Early Modern France* (Stanford, Calif., 1975).

——*Women on the Margins: Three Seventeenth-century Lives* (Cambridge and London, 1995).

Glossary of Key Ecclesiastical Terms

Dean	See vicar forane
Diocese	Area under the ecclesiastical jurisdiction of a bishop
Nuncio	Papal diplomatic representative to a catholic power
Praeposito/praepositus	Chief dignitary of a chapter or other ecclesiastical foundation
Provincial Synod	An ecclesiastical council of an archiepiscopal province
Suffragans	Bishops other than the archbishop of a metropolitan province, each governing individual dioceses
Vicar apostolic	A prelate nominated by the pope discharging ordinary jurisdiction in a diocese where a bishop has not been appointed
Vicar forane	Or dean; clerical representative of a bishop appointed as the head of an aggregation of parishes within a diocese
Vicar general	A prelate appointed by a bishop to assist in the administration of a diocese by exercising ordinary jurisdiction in his name
Visitation	Formal visit for the purpose of examination of parishes, religious houses and their inhabitants by a bishop

Index

Act of Appeals 73
Act of Marriages 73
Act of Supremacy 42, 73
Adventurers' Act 20, 24 n. 43, 144
Agostini, Gerolamo, Venetian secretary 30
   n. 72
Albizzi, Francesco 272
Alexander VII, Pope *see* Chigi, Fabio
Allerheim, battle of 123
Anglo-Spanish war 17
Annesley, Arthur 168 n. 11
Antrim, earl of *see* MacDonnell, Randal
Aphorismical Discovery 34, 36
Aran islands 60
Archer, James 76 n. 220
Ardagh, diocese of 171 n. 30, 234, 238
   bishop of *see* Plunkett, Patrick
Ardfert, diocese of 63, 64
   bishop of *see* O'Connell, Richard
Armagh, archdiocese of 42, 47, 49, 65, 241
   n. 46
   archbishop of, *see* O'Reilly, Hugh
   provincial synod of 68, 75
Athenry, baron of *see* Bermingham, Francis
Athlone 181, 182, 188, 246
Avignon 70

Bandini, Cardinal Ottavio 83, 85
Bandini, Virginia 83
Barberini, Cardinal Antonio 69, 70, 75, 76, 79
   n. 240, 112, 272
Barberini, Cardinal Francesco 69, 76, 86, 112,
   272
Barnewall, Barnaby 241
Barnewall, Sir Patrick 32 n. 81,
Baron, Geoffrey 72, 159 n. 196, 272
Barry, Colonel John 131, 199, 272
Barry, Robert, vicar apostolic of Ross and
   bishop of Cork and Cloyne 72, 151,
   236-7, 266
Battaglia, Girolamo 224 n. 138
Bellarmine, Robert 84
Bellings, Richard 23, 73 n. 200, 272
   advice to nuncio on travel to Ireland 116
   n. 188
   as member of peace party 34, 80, 128, 153,
   156 n. 179, 264
   attitude to Rinuccini 67, 131, 146, 149, 235,
   265
   hatred of Preston for 161

letter to clergy of 151
narrative of 29 n. 70, 36, 67, 135 n. 69, 202
   n. 16, 208 n. 53
owner of former monastic land 74 n. 210, 80
return to Supreme Council of 193 n. 156
Benburb, battle of 50 n. 69, 155, 160, 247-8,
   256 n. 13
   effects of 125, 137, 138, 164, 170, 257
Benignius, Julius 83 n. 13
Bermingham, Francis, baron of Athenry 193
   n. 156, 202 n. 18
Bernini, GianLorenzo 132
Bethlen, Gábor 39
Biblioteca Trivulziana 84
Bishops' wars 18
Blake, Sir Richard 74 n. 210, 131, 173 n. 40,
   217 n. 99, 272
Bollini, Domenico, bishop of Brescia 88
Bologna 83, 88, 223
Book of Common Prayer 79 n. 239
Borlase, Sir John 18, 23, 272
Borromeo, Cardinal Carlo, archbishop of
   Milan 82, 87, 88, 92, 98, 102 n. 114, 111
Bourke, Hugh, bishop of Kilmacduagh 152,
   239 n. 35, 273, 235-6
Bourke, John, vicar apostolic and bishop of
   Clonfert and archbishop of Tuam 44, 70,
   173, 202 n. 19, 236-7, 273
   links to secular Old English 48, 152
   many of clergy in Tuam appointed by his
   predecessor 243
   on committee representing clergy 151
   slow to receive promotion to bishopric 47
Bray, Thomas 54 n. 95
Brescia, bishop of *see* Bollini, Domenico
Briver correspondence 24 n. 40
Browne, Geoffrey 169, 193, 273
   as holder of monastic lands 74 n. 210
   as member of the peace party 34, 81, 128,
   153, 174
Bruno, Giordano 108 n. 150
Buckingham, Duchess of *see* Manners,
   Katherine
Bunratty, castle of 96 n. 86, 125, 138, 139
Burke, Ulick, earl and marquis of Clanricard
   32, 34, 67, 125, 273
   as Ormond's intermediary 160 n. 198, 228
   attitude to rebellion of 24 n. 40, 129 n. 33
   clergy's objection to 156 n. 176
   Ormond Peace deposited with 145

Burke, Ulick (*cont.*):
  Plunkett's overtures to 186 n. 113
  proposed military position 157 n. 186
  relations with Preston 155 n. 173, 158
    n. 187, 161 n. 202, 162
  Rinuccini's anger with 217
  role in prevention of synod of 1648 218
Butler, Edmund 180 n. 78
Butler, Edward, viscount of Galmoy 74 n. 210
Butler, James, earl and marquis of Ormond
    76, 81, 177, 201, 248, 265–6, 273
  anger at repudiation of peace 176
  Archbishop O'Reilly's dislike of 50 n. 69
  attacked in Dublin 158–164
  attitude to Glamorgan articles 79, 149
    n. 137
  catholic distrust of 206, 257
  confederate concealment of treaty with 135–7
  confederate supporters of 166, 171, 185,
    190, 210, 240, 256
  decision to publish the peace 144–7
  departure to France of 199
  influence with confederates 22–3, 174
  negotiations with confederates 27–31, 33–5,
    42, 80, 111, 124–7, 128 n. 28, 175, 187,
    208–9, 247
  negotiations with French agents 177–80
  opposition to the demands of the clerical
    party 72–4, 78, 129
  reaction to attacks on peace 150, 152, 153,
    156, 157, 165
  return to Ireland of 200, 202 n. 14, 263
  Rinuccini's distrust of 130, 133–4, 262
  transfer of garrisons to parliament 167, 184,
    188
Butler, Richard, viscount of Mountgarrett 23,
    46, 117, 135, 273
  as member of peace party 34, 80, 128, 153
  as owner of former monastic lands 74 n. 210
  embarrassment of nuncio by 182 n. 90

Cahill, Patrick 43, 44
Camus, Jean-Pierre 111
Candia 115, 170
Capponi, Cardinal 190 n. 138
Cappoquin 168, 186
Carlingford 35
Carlow 154
Casey, Donal 43
Cashel, archbishop of, *see* Walsh, Thomas
  archdiocese of 46, 51, 168
  prelates of province of 57 n. 111
Castlehaven, earl of *see* Touchet, James
Castracani, Alessandro 224 n. 138
Castro, war of 70
catholic clergy 125, 130 n. 39, 137 n. 80, 214,
    255, 266–7

acceptance of tridentine reform by Gaelic
    wing of 60–6
  and Confederate erastianism 217–30
  attempts to address concerns of 124, 134,
    136, 261
  clergy's military campaign against Ormond
    158–63
  development of hierarchy of 40–59
  limits of power of 175 n. 53
  Massari as agent of 146 n. 125
  nature of clerical faction 173–4
  Plunkett and Darcy's arguments to 144
    n. 110, 148
  political objectives of 103
  reaction to military success 138
  relationship with Preston 177
  relationship with Rinuccini 232–52, 257
  rejection of Ormond Peace by 147–58
  repressive activity of 39 n. 1
  respect for 67–8
  response to rebellion of 68–9
  Rinuccini's relinquishing of leadership
    210–1
  role within association before nuncio's
    arrival 70–81
  stance within second assembly of 1647
    192–3
  support for Glamorgan in Munster 185
  zenith and nadir of influence 255
catholic reformation 106, 107 n. 145, 148, 229,
    255, 260
  and Gaelic Ireland 60–66
  evangelical techniques of 102 n. 116, 104
    n. 123, 228
  historiography of in Ireland 212
  power of in Rinuccini's hands 68
  Rinuccini as exemplar of 82, 84, 93, 99,
    103, 110, 118, 245, 266
  spread of 41, 57, 66–7, 255
  structures of in Ireland 40
Celli, Alesio 117 n. 193
cessation *see* truce
Charles I 57, 124, 248, 262
  and negotiations with the Confederates
    27–35, 45, 71–2, 76
  and the Engagement 199
  and the Graces 17
  attempted conversion of 226 n. 145,
    254
  capture by army 168
  clemency of 49
  Confederate attitudes towards 20, 81, 159,
    228–30
  declining position of 74, 123
  defence of his prerogatives 68, 220–1, 234
  disowning of Ormond by 125
  doubts concerning good faith of 79 n. 235

effect of November remonstrance 200
French attitudes towards 139–45, 177
Glamorgan's mandate from 78, 124,
    129–30, 134 n. 63, 135 n. 69
impact of his Scottish negotiations 19
protection of reputation by Digby 124
Rinuccini's attitude towards 128, 133, 185
Chester 134 n. 63
Chigi, Fabio, papal nuncio at Münster, later
    Pope Alexander VII 112 n. 171, 113, 115,
    253–4, 274
Church of England 129 n. 31
    bishops of 31 n. 76
Church of Ireland 30, 32, 71, 81
Clanmalier, Viscount see O'Dempsey, Terence
Clanricard, earl and marquis of see Burke,
    Ulick
Clogher, bishop of see MacMahon, Heber
Clonfert, vicar apostolic of, see Bourke, John
    bishop of see Bourke, John and Lynch,
    Walter
    diocese of 235
Clonmacnoise, vicar apostolic of, see Coghlan,
    Terence
Clonmell 153, 180, 218
Cloyne, diocese of 74 n. 210
    bishop of see Tirry, William and Barry,
    Robert
Coghlan, Terence, vicar apostolic of
    Clonmacnoise 44
Comerford, Edward 150 n. 139
Comerford, Patrick, bishop of Waterford and
    Lismore 44, 79 n. 237, 217, 236 n. 22
    reforming activity 51–3
    residence with his brother 46
confederate armies 178–9, 184–5, 189, 261,
    263
    and attack on Dublin 161
    and intervention in England 141 n. 99
    and rejection of the peace 154
    nuncio's opposition to the recruitment of
        protestants 247, 248 n. 80
    see also Connacht army, Leinster army,
        Munster army, Ulster army
confederate catholic association:
    and appointment of bishops 235
    and negotiations with Ormond 42, 159,
        124–39
    and the city of Limerick 96 n. 86
    and the rebellion of 1641 19
    appointment of nuncio to 85, 111–5
    Bellings's history of 67
    conclusion of peace with Ormond in 1646
        145–7, 256
    crisis of 1648 206–11
    ethnic tension within 244
    evolution of 27–37

French attitudes towards 141–3
Genoa as model for its relations with Rome
    118
influence and policy of Plunkett and Ferns
    166–76, 184–89, 192–3, 196
pursuit of unpopular policies 162–3
Rinuccini as nuncio to 86, 119, 206–7,
    261–5
Rinuccini's evaluation (1646) 132–4
Rinuccini's evaluation (1647) 194–7, 231
Rinuccini's evaluation (1648) 212–30
role and demands of the clergy 41, 45, 50,
    56, 68–82, 103
sources of political legitimization 25–6, 153
confederate catholics see confederate catholic
    association
confederate civil war 200, 204, 206, 233, 261
confederate government 111, 130, 134 n. 63,
    149
Congregation of Rites 83, 84
Conn, George papal agent 56 n. 108, 254
Connaght army 149
Conway, Richard 67 n. 165
Coote, Sir Charles 22
Cork, bishop of see Tirry, William and Barry,
    Robert
    diocese of 51, 186
counter-reformation see catholic reformation
Court of Wards 29 n. 69
Cregan, Donal 40
Cromwell, Oliver 198, 253, 261, 265
Cromwellian conquest 143, 198, 206, 253,
    255, 257, 260–1, 265

Darcy, Oliver, bishop of Dromore 234, 236,
    238, 239 n. 35, 240, 243 n. 56
Darcy, Patrick 192 n. 151, 196 n. 173, 274
    as representative to the clergy in Waterford
        148, 150, 152, 156 n. 174
    breach of trust with the nuncio 135
    suspicions of 34
    tender conscience of 144 n. 110
Dease, Thomas, Bishop of Meath 65, 212
    n. 76, 243 n. 56, 274
    campaign against regular clergy 53–4
    in favour of Glamorgan peace 79 n. 237
    not insisting on the retention of the churches
        35 n. 98, 50 n. 70
    opposition to the nuncio 236
    refusal to assist the archbishop of Dublin 44
    relationship with the baron of Delvin 47–48
de Bellièvre, Pompone 140, 142–4, 178 n. 65,
    274
de la Torre, Don Diego 157, 174, 177 n. 62,
    274
de la Tour d'Auvergne, Henri, vicomte de
    Turenne 123

Derby House Committee 179
Derry 46
de Sales, François 91 n. 59, 93 n. 69
Descartes 100
Devereux, Robert 202 n. 18
Digby, Lord George 159 n. 193, 161 n. 202,
    179 n. 72, 184 n. 105, 185 n. 110, 274
  and conclusion of peace in 1646 143–7
  and imprisonment of Glamorgan 124, 129
  and transport of soldiers to France 178, 180,
    188, 190
Digby, Sir Kenelm 124 n. 6, 131, 274
Dillon, John 167 n. 7, 181, 188
Dillon, Sir Lucas 128, 153, 193 n. 156, 202 n. 18
Dini, Petro 89 n. 43
Doge, of Venice 30 n. 72, 141 n. 98
Douai, college of 55
Dowling, Moriarty, vicar apostolic of Leighlin
    44
Down and Connor, bishop of see O'Devaney,
    Conor, Dungan, Edmund and Magennis,
    Hugh
  diocese of 58 n. 121
Drogheda 57 n. 112, 203 n. 20
Dromana 168
Dromore, bishop of see Darcy, Oliver
  diocese of 234
Dublin 130 n. 38, 133, 144, 146, 149, 263
  archdiocese of 44
  archbishop of , see Fleming, Thomas
  actions of catholic population 67
  clergy of 43
  1646 campaign against 123, 125, 145 n. 115,
    147, 155, 158–63, 165, 166, 169–73, 181,
    193, 241, 261–2
  devastation of area around 167
  establishment of parliamentary forces in
    176, 180, 183–4
  imprisonment of Glamorgan in 124, 134
  officers in garrison of 136
  Ormond's slow departure from 153
  Plunkett's departure for 137
  printing of peace in 150
  Rinuccini's desire to renew attack against
    175, 177, 182, 185
  Talon's negotiations in 179
Dublin government 76, 81, 103
du Moulin, Claude 132 n. 52, 144, 145, 156
    n. 174, 177, 178 n. 64, 274
Duncannon, siege of 34–5, 155, 157
  fortress of 204
Dundalk 203 n. 20
Dungan, Edmund, bishop of Down and
    Connor 42, 43, 46
Dungan's Hill, battle of 167, 178, 184, 188,
    190
Dungarvan 168, 186

Elizabeth I 24, 29 n. 67, 67, 213, 220
Elphin, bishop of see MacEgan, Boethius
  diocese of 58
Emly, bishop of see O'Brien, Terrence
Enos, Walter 36
English Civil War 1642–46 25, 27, 30, 123,
    162
  confederate fear of parliamentary victory in
    20, 128
  Irish rebellion as cause of 19
Everard, Sir Richard 167 n. 7

Fennell, Gerrott 34, 81, 128, 193 n. 156, 202
    n. 18, 264, 275
Ferdinand I, Holy Roman Emperor 95, 113,
    115
Fermo, archbishop of see Rinuccini,
    GianBattista
  archdiocese of 85, 98, 113, 224 n. 137, 251
  rebellion in 258
  Rinuccini's pastoral experience in 87, 89,
    101, 107, 233, 247
Fermoy, viscount of see Roche, Maurice
Ferns, bishop of see Roche, John and French,
    Nicholas
  diocese of 51
Field, Owen 52 n. 86, 53 n. 91
FitzWilliam, Oliver 149 n. 137, 161 n. 206
Fleming, Thomas, archbishop of Dublin 43,
    44, 46, 151, 236 n. 22
Fleming, William, baron of Slane 46
Flight of the Earls 20 n. 23
Florence 63, 82, 84, 86, 113, 227, 258
French government 139–42, 144, 145, 177–9
French, Nicholas, bishop of Ferns 166, 239,
    275
  account of synod of 1646 148
  advice concerning Rinuccini's safety 204
  and inclusion of Preston in attack on Dublin
    161
  and mission to Rome 192, 196, 203,
    207–8
  attempts to reconcile confederate factions in
    1648 206, 209–10
  disapproves of Rinuccini's actions 236
  involvement in attempt to impeach Preston
    177
  moderate policies of 172–5, 184–5, 189,
    196, 262, 264
  return to Ireland in 1648 200
  Rinuccini's argument with concerning
    recruitment of protestants 247, 248
    n. 80
  Rinuccini's attitude towards 171–2, 215,
    216
  selects Supreme Council 193
  shocked by conduct of Ulster troops 181

Gaelic rebels in Ulster 32
Galmoy, Viscount of *see* Butler, Edward
Galway 131, 200, 208–9, 216, 243
  and collegiate church of St. Nicholas 45,
    237–8
  as site of Jesuit residence 242
  Malachy O'Queely's problems 46
  prevention of synod in 1648 149, 218–9
  respect for the nuncio 67
  Rinuccini's praise of 214, 251–2
  site of retraining of inadequate priests 58
    n. 121
General Assembly 130, 148, 149, 156, 180
  composition and nature of 25, 31, 70–1, 151
    n. 148
  decrees of 26, 75, 78, 239 n. 34
  relationship with Supreme Council 135
    n. 67, 164
  Assembly of 1642 25, 26, 75
  of 1645 35, 77, 116, 148
  of 1646 134, 36, 138, 152, 164, 261
  of 1647 (first) 31, 125, 162, 166–7, 172,
    174–7, 181, 185, 231, 239 n. 34, 259, 261
  of 1647 (second) 168, 172, 174, 190–3, 199,
    203–5, 234–5, 246–7, 263
  of 1648 200, 208, 210, 212, 216–8, 222
Genoa 70, 116, 118
Glamorgan, earl of *see* Somerset, Edward
Gormanston, Viscount *see* Preston, Nicholas
Graces, the 17, 18
Graham, James, marquis of Montrose 123,
  188
Gregory the Great, Pope 88, 89 n. 48
Grimaldi, Cardinal 69 n. 176, 70 n. 180, 72
  n. 196

Habsburg, dynasty of 140
Harmon, Thomas 154 n. 165
Harris, Paul 43, 44
Henrietta Maria, Queen of England 116, 193
  and papal peace 124 n. 6, 134 n. 63, 147
    n. 127
  to be offered the government of Ireland 168
  influence on French policy and conclusion of
    peace in 1646 143–5
  Leyburn as emissary of 180
  plot with Muskery and Browne 169
  probable disapproval of Ormond's
    settlement with parliament 177
Henry VIII 16, 213, 215, 218 n. 105
High Commission, Court of 56
Holy Roman Emperor *see* Ferdinand I

Inchiquin, Baron of *see* O'Brien, Murrough
Inchiquin truce 141, 192, 196, 246, 261, 263–4
  importance of clerical leadership during 239
  Jesuit reaction to 242

literature concerning 198 n. 1
new councillors co-opted after 193 n. 157
nuncio's failure to unify clergy against 41
opposition from Old English friars 241
revealing limits of ecclesiastical authority
  235–7
Rinuccini and the crisis 200–7, 230–1
shakes Rinuccini's dominance of clergy 244
Independent party 141 n. 99
Ingoli, Francesco 55 n. 103
Innocent X, GianBattista Pamfili 278
  aid other than financial 208 n. 51
  and creation of the Irish mission 111
  and Massari's mission 170
  and papal peace 134 n. 63
  and rights of jurisdiction in Ireland 219–222,
    235
  and Rinuccini's report to 215, 216, 217, 258
  and the Plunkett-Ferns mission 207–9
  and threats to his dignity 127, 136, 208
  capacity to provide finance 194
  decision on crisis of 1648 not communicated
    to Rinuccini by Ferns 210 n. 62
  diplomatic advantage from Rinuccini's
    mission 112, 116, 256
  dissociation from Peace of Westphalia 253
  election of 112
  his views to be canvassed 149, 168, 193
  innovative idea concerning former monastic
    land 76, 77 n. 227
  parsimony of 263
  reverence of province of Ulster for 154
  Rinuccini as representative of 131, 132, 208,
    211, 237
  Rinuccini's hopes for further aid 197, 205
  Supreme Council's wish to avoid
    antagonizing 126, 137
  suspect enthusiasm for the Irish mission
    182, 260, 262, 265
  Ulster forces as army of 155 n. 170, 181
Invernizzi, Carlo 57, 72, 112

James I 16, 29 n. 67, 230
Jankov, battle of 123, 140 n. 93
Jones, Michael 188, 190, 194, 275
  and establishment in Dublin 167, 176, 180,
    184
Jones, Oliver 181 n. 85

Kells, abbey of 74 n. 210
Kenmare 63, 82, 117, 132
Kildare, bishop of *see* MacGeoghegan, Ross
Kilfenora, bishop of *see* Lynch, Andrew
Kilkenny 132, 149, 162, 192 n. 152, 251
  Antrim's opposition to Ormond's influence
    in 174
  arrival of Glamorgan in 78

Kilkenny (*cont.*):
  arrival of Rinuccini in 117–8, 123
  Barry's mission to 199
  confederate assemblies in 75, 191, 218
  demonstrations in 181, 195
  ecclesiastical congregation of 220 n. 116
  Franciscan friars in 217, 241
  gentry of 154
  Jesuit presence in 239 n. 34, 242, 246
  Massari's imprisonment in 216
  number of priests in 58
  O'Neill's securing of 159 n. 197
  Ormond's presence in 125, 152–3, 156, 158
  Ossory as ordinary of 236
  Plunkett and Ferns's arrival in 209
  Preston's invitation to 157
  processions and ceremonials in 248–9
  ratification of peace in 146
  relaxation of interdict in 211
  Rinuccini forbids congregation of bishops in
    210
  Rinuccini's flight from 200, 204
  Rinuccini's return in 1648 199, 203
  Scottish thrust against 155 n. 171
  sequestering of nuncio's papers in 219
  synod of 69, 75
  post peace vacuum of authority in 150
Killala, bishop of *see* Kirwan, Francis
Killaloe, diocese of 46, 59, 60
  vicar apostolic of *see* O'Queely, Malachy
Killashee 74 n. 210
Kilmacduagh, bishop of *see* Bourke, Hugh
  diocese of 235
Kilmore, bishop of *see* MacSweeney, Eugene
  and O'Reilly, Hugh
Kilrush, battle of 25 n. 44
King, Paul 204 n. 30
Kirkby, William 150 n. 144
Kirwan, Francis, bishop of Killala 58 n. 121,
    151, 202 n. 19, 236, 238, 243
Knocknanuss, battle of 168, 189, 191

La Monerie, le sieur de 140 n. 92, 179, 188,
    194, 206 n. 44 , 275
Lamormaini, William 138 n. 86
Lane, George 153 n. 158, 176 n. 57
La Rochelle 116 n. 188
Leicester, earl of *see* Sidney, Robert
Leighlin, vicars apostolic of *see* Roche,
    Matthew and Dowling, Moriarty
  bishop of *see* O'Dempsey, Edward
Leinster army 149, 155, 177–8, 180, 189,
    263
  and Dublin campaign 161–3
  and Preston's decision to support Rinuccini
    in crisis of 1646 158
  capture of Roscommon by 139

committee of makes little attempt to supply
    O'Neill 181
  defeat of at Dungan's Hill 167, 184
  pressures Wexford in 1648 239
  Rinuccini's subsidies to 154
Leyburn, George 180, 184 n. 102
Limerick 210, 222 n. 128
  bishop of *see* O'Dwyer, Edmund
  defiance of bishop by Jesuit residence of 242
  resistance to publication of peace in 153
  Rinuccini's journey to 117
  site of Council's meeting with Rinuccini 146
  suppression of protestant ceremonies in 96,
    247–8
Lisbon 224 n. 138
Lismore, bishop of *see* Comerford, Patrick
Loftus, Dudley 178 n. 69, 179 n. 71
London 168, 176 n. 56, 178 n. 65
Lord Chief Justice 43
Lough Derg 182
Louis XIII of France 95
Louis XIV of France 132 n. 52, 140, 145, 151
    n. 148
Loyala, Ignatius 111
Lucca 222
Lynch, Andrew, bishop of Kilfenora 202 n. 19,
    236, 243
Lynch, John, archdeacon of Tuam 230
Lynch, Patrick 237
Lynch, Roebuck 219
Lynch, Walter, bishop of Clonfert 236–7, 266,
    275

MacCarthy, Daniel 204 n. 25
MacCarthy, Dermot, 204 n. 25
MacCarthy, Donough, Viscount Muskery 23,
    149, 204 n. 25, 275
  and embassy to France 169, 199
  and the Munster army in 1647 185–9
  and the Supreme Council of 1647 167 n. 7
  as member of the peace party 34, 80, 128,
    153, 174, 264
  deception of the nuncio 135
  one of four who selects the Supreme Council
    174, 193
MacColla, Alexander 188
MacDonnell, Francis 46, 47
MacDonnell, Randal, 1st earl of Antrim 46,
    47
MacDonnell, Randal, 2nd earl and 1st
    marquis of Antrim 173 n. 40, 180 n. 80,
    193 n. 155, 276
  and confederate politics in 1647 172 n. 34,
    174, 177 n. 63
  and forces to Scotland 28
  and Spanish pension 177 n. 63
MacEgan, Brian 245 n. 65

MacEgan, Boethius, bishop of Elphin 46,
    50–1, 63, 239 n. 35
MacGeoghegan, Ross, bishop of Kildare 44,
    47, 50, 254 n. 4
MacKiernan, Thomas 217, 240
MacMahon, Heber, bishop of Clogher 173,
    177 n. 63, 246, 276
    and the embassy to France in 1647 172
        n. 34, 192 n. 154, 193 n. 155
    as general of the Ulster army 50 n. 69, 245
    delegate of the synod of 1646 151
    long pastoral experience 50
    of an eminent but impoverished family 47
MacSweeny, Eugene, bishop of Kilmore 42,
    46, 65
Madrid 115, 225
Magennis, Arthur, bishop of Down and
    Connor 239 n. 35
Magennis, Hugh (Bonaventure), bishop of
    Down and Connor 49, 65
Magennis, John 49 n. 64
Maguire, Roger 208 n. 56
Malone, William 241–3
Manners, Katherine, duchess of Buckingham
    31 n. 75, 73 n. 207
Martin, Richard 34, 75 n. 217
Mary I 16, 75
Maryborough 200, 204
massacres of 1641 30
Massari, Dionysio, dean of Fermo 190, 196,
    276
    and mission to Rome 160, 170, 234
    and pageant to celebrate victory at Benburb
        248
    as liaison with confederate generals 145
        n. 115, 155 n. 172
    as secretary of Propaganda Fide 258
    description of Hugh O'Reilly by 50 n. 69
    enjoyed the food of Gaelic Ulster 117 n. 193
    freedom to leave Kilkenny restricted 204,
        211, 216
    helps mislead Supreme Council 146
    his account of confederate duplicity 136
    impressed by the state of religious
        instruction in Gaelic Ireland 63, 64–5
    return to Ireland in March 1648 199, 201
        n. 12, 203
    sequestering of papers in his possession 216,
        219
Matthews, Francis 54 n. 96, 55 n. 100
Maximilian of Bavaria 115
Mazarin, Cardinal Jules 140, 141, 194–5, 256,
    263
    and antagonism towards Innocent X 112,
        116, 227
    and donation of subsidies to Rinuccini 79
        n. 240

Digby's and Ormond's gratitude towards 146
levies of troops supercede other aspects of
    his Irish policy 178
loses enthusiasm for Digby's recruitment
    scheme 188
priorities of his agents clash with Rinuccini's
    143
Talon the trusted emissary of 132 n. 52
Meath, bishop of see Dease, Thomas
    vicar general of see Plunkett, James
    diocese of 74 n. 210
Messingham, Thomas 55 n. 103
Milan, archbishop of see Borromeo, Carlo
Montereul, Jean de 140 n. 92
Montrose, marquis of see Graham, James
Mooney, Donncha 57, 67
Moore, Bartholomew 44
Moore, Roger 32
Mountgarrett, Viscount see Butler, Richard
Munster army 149, 168, 185–9, 263
Münster, 113, 115, 253–4
Muskery, Viscount see MacCarthy, Donough

Nani, Giovanni (GianBattista), Venetian
    ambassador 116 n. 185, 141 n. 98
Naples 222
Naseby, battle of 123, 140
Neri, Filippo 111
Neroni, Alessandro 136
Newcastle 143
New Model Army 261
Nine Years' War 20 n. 23, 67
Nördlingen, battle of 138 n. 86
Nugent, Francis 241 n. 46
Nugent, Richard, earl of Westmeath 74 n. 210,
    75
Nugent, Robert 151, 241
Nugent, Sir Thomas 153 n. 158, 176 n. 57
nuncio, of Ireland see Rinuccini, GianBattista

oath of association 26, 69, 129, 148–9, 264
O'Brien, Barnaby, earl of Thomond 24 n. 40,
    139 n. 88
O'Brien, Murrough, Baron of Inchiquin 237,
    242, 253
    and truce of 1648 199, 201–4
    as commander of protestant enclave in
        Munster 28
    clerical coup of 1646 prevents offensive
        against 162, 185
    military advances of 167–8, 186, 189
    Munster army avoids engagement with 188,
        190
    nuncio demands an end to co-operation with
        207 n. 45
    Ormond's outrage concerning confederate
        policy towards 176

O'Brien, Murrough (*cont.*):
  pressures peace party to restrict clergy 219
    n. 109
  Rinuccini favours use of Ulster army against
    194
  1645 offensive against 33
O'Brien, Terrence, bishop of Emly 239 n. 35
O'Connell, Richard, bishop of Ardfert 63, 64,
  276
O'Cullenan, John, bishop of Raphoe 65, 266
  imprisonment of 42, 43
  poverty of 46, 48
  ransomed by the Ulster army 247
O'Dempsey, Edward, bishop of Leighlin 47,
  50, 217, 266
O'Dempsey, Terence, Viscount Clanmalier 47
O'Devaney, Conor, bishop of Down and
  Connor 67
O'Donnell, Hugh, earl of Tyrconnel 61
O'Dwyer, Edmund, bishop of Limerick 132
  n. 52, 151, 173, 202 n.19, 236, 246
  as secret papal agent 69, 75
O'Ferrall, Gregory 240
O'Hartigan, Matthew 34 n. 87, 111 n. 166,
  132 n. 52
O'Mahoney, Conor 33, 194 n. 165
Oneilland 157 n. 181
O'Neill, Daniel 157 n. 181, 159 n. 194, 168
  n. 16
O'Neill, John, earl of Tyrone 61
O'Neill, Owen Roe 158, 172, 184–5, 190–1,
  253, 263, 277
  accommodation with Ormond in 1649 206
  and Connacht campaign 167, 182–83
  and monetary support from Scarampi 73
  and relationship with the bishop of Clogher
    173
  and relationship with Rinuccini 154, 155,
    180–3, 195–7, 203, 206, 210, 257, 263
  and the civil war of 1648 200, 204–6, 208,
    230
  and the Dublin campaign 161, 163
  and the fortress of Athlone, 181–2, 188
  and the victory of Benburb 137, 164, 249
  and truces with protestant forces 208
  clerical interests regret his exclusion from
    command of 1644 campaign 33
  continued resistance to second Ormond
    Peace 257
  his soldiers ravage Leinster 179–80
  nuncio's flight to his camp 204
  offers to attack Dublin 144, 145 n. 115
  pact of co-operation with Preston 162 n. 211
  peace party prefers to align with Inchiquin
    202–3
  proposed by clergy for military command
    156 n. 176

return to Ireland in 1642 25
role in Leinster changes in 1647 177
succeeded as Ulster general by Heber
  MacMahon 50 n. 69, 245
supports the clergy in 1646 125, 157
suspicion and hatred of 32, 194–5
unwillingness of Munster confederates to
  accept his protection 195–6
O'Neill, Sir Phelim 32, 277
O'Queely, Malachy, vicar apostolic of Killaloe
  and archbishop of Tuam 46, 62–4, 237,
  277
  and pastoral impact 59–60
  forced into hiding 44
O'Reilly, Hugh, bishop of Kilmore and
  archbishop of Armagh 236, 238, 277
  eager to prevent the appointment of Old
    English clergy to Ulster 234
  imprisonment of 42, 43
  militant perspective of 50 n. 69
  of an eminent but impoverished family 47
  pastoral impact of 59, 65
Ormond earl of *see* Butler, James
Ormond peace 1st 183, 185, 228–9
  and deceptions of the nuncio concerning
    134–9
  and French involvement 143–7, 157, 164,
    177–8, 256, 257
  and Preston 155, 157–8, 161, 182
  and the contemporary negotiations in
    Germany 113
  attack on Dublin follows its rejection
    158–60
  evolution of Rinuccini's attitudes towards
    125–31, 163–5, 261–2
  inevitable friction between nuncio and
    Supreme Council concerning 81
  Inchiquin a beneficiary of rejection 162
  lack of catholic control of university a
    deficiency 99
  most important issue confronted by first
    assembly of 1647 166
  opposition in towns 67
  originally accepted by Nicholas Plunkett
    172
  Ormond's attitude in wake of rejection 176,
    180
  outline of its negotiation 1645–46 123–5
  peace party commitment to negotiation of
    30
  peace party undermined by collapse of
    189
  ratification 145–6, 162
  rejection by first assembly of 1647 166, 167,
    174, 176
  rejection by synod of Waterford 41, 147–54,
    156, 163, 192, 212, 256–7

Rinuccini expects further papal aid after
rejection 169
Roman attitudes towards 259–60
two supporters of among four who select
Supreme Council 193
Ulster army introduced into Leinster after
rejection 181
Ormond peace 2nd 141, 196, 198 n. 1, 200–3,
210–1, 215, 227–9
and peace of Westphalia 254
does not provide guarantees to clergy 257
endorsed by archbishop of Cashel 218 n.
103
offers greater concessions than first peace
256–7
Ormondite party see peace party
Ossory, bishop of see Rothe, David
diocese of 51, 58, 100 n. 103
Oxford 30, 72, 123

Pale, Lords of 23, 32 n. 81
Paleotti, Cardinal Gabriele 87, 88, 107 n. 146,
108 n. 150, 109 n. 154, 223
Pallotto, Cardinal 224
Palotta, GianBattista 224
Pamfili, Cardinal Camillo 126, 130, 138, 144,
278
Pamfili, GianBattista see Pope Innocent X
Pancirolo, Cardinal Giovanni 170, 210 n. 62,
278
Papal Bulls
In Coena Domini 220, 223, 227
Regnans in Excelsis 220
papal excommunication 29 n. 67, 149
Paris 140 n. 97, 141, 256
anonymous letter from 111 n. 164
clergy dismiss Digby's machinations in 147
collapse of papal peace in 135 n. 65
fresh policy adopted in 178
fruitless papal mission to of 1632 115
news from arrives more quickly in Rome
207 n. 47
O'Hartigan the confederate agent in 132
n. 52
Ormond and Muskery liaise in 199
Rinuccini's sojourn in 1645 116, 131, 227
worries in concerning du Moulin's
demeanour 144 n. 112
parliament (English) 164, 201, 255, 257, 261–2
and French levies of troops 178–9, 188
and Ormond 162, 167, 176–7
confederates committed to war with 127
n. 21
confederates see truce as means to
strengthen king against 28
conquest by considered no worse than
domination by Ulster army 195–6

differing attitudes concerning prospect of its
victory 128
Digby's declaration a protection for
Ormond from 145 n. 118
expects intervention from Ireland after
settlement 30
Inchiquin's declaration for 28
Inchiquin's defection from 199, 201
parliament (Irish) to be convened after peace
159
parliamentary armies 119, 203 n. 20, 208
at Bunratty 139
in Dublin 162, 167, 176, 179, 189
parliamentary fleet 170
Parsons, Sir William 18, 22, 168 n. 11, 278
Pascal, Blaise 91 n. 59, 93 n. 69
peace party 157, 172 n. 35, 173–4, 253
and co-option of new councillors in 1648
193 n. 157
and failed arguments to clergy in 1645 35
and negotiations with clergy in
August/September 1646 152, 156, 158
and Rinuccini's opposition to 66, 124, 134,
256–7, 262
alienation after rejection of peace 31, 192
n. 154, 231, 263
attempt to neutralize Rinuccini in Kilkenny
203
concern to conclude peace before elapse of
Ormond's mandate 135
covets Rinuccini's subsidies 79
deceits of 78, 135
desperate to prevent a parliamentary victory
in England 128
imperfect communications with Ormond in
August 1646 150
reaction to constraints on Ormond 129, 145
n. 116
Rinuccini's criticisms of their catholicism
222, 228–9
suspicions concerning 34, 74
tender consciences of 228
their position threatened by military success
34, 36
weak position in 1647 189
Pécs 57 n. 112
penal laws 30
Perugia 83
Philiphaugh, battle of 123
Pisa 83
Plunkett, Henry 242
Plunkett, James, vicar general of Meath 57
Plunkett, John 202 n.15
Plunkett, Sir Nicholas 166, 203, 278
and mission to Rome 192–3, 196–7, 207–8,
263
approved by Rinuccini 149 n. 135, 215–6

Plunkett, Sir Nicholas (*cont.*):
  as representative to the clergy in Waterford
    148, 150, 152, 156 n. 174
  charged with persuading Ormond to
    countenance Rinuccini 137
  moderate policies of 171–5, 184–6, 189,
    206, 262, 264
  particularly eager to conciliate Muskery
    186
  return to Ireland from Rome 200, 208–9
  tender conscience of 144 n. 110
  selects Supreme Council 193
Plunkett, Patrick, bishop of Ardagh 234, 236,
    238, 239 n. 35, 243 n. 56, 279
  elevation to bishopric urged by Rinuccini as
    reward for his brother 171 n. 30
Pole, Cardinal Reginald 74, 75, 76
pope, deposing power of 29 n. 67
post-tridentine reform 16
Pozsony 39
Preston, James 157 n. 185
Preston, Nicholas, Viscount Gormanston, 32,
    279
Preston, Robert 180 n. 78, 181 n. 87
Preston, Thomas 137, 188, 217 n. 99, 263, 279
  and Dublin campaign 161–3, 165, 172
  and levies of soldiers for France 178
  attempted impeachment of 173, 177, 181
  captures Roscommon 139
  confirmed as confederate general in Leinster
    175, 177, 184
  defeated at Dungan's Hill 167, 183, 184–5,
    190
  fiasco at Youghal ascribed to his rivalry with
    Castlehaven 36 n. 105
  offers Rinuccini to attack Dublin 144, 145
    n. 115
  proposed for military command by clergy
    156 n. 176
  movement of his army precipitates the
    censure of 1648 200, 204–5
  receipt of aid from Rinuccini and Scarampi
    154–5
  return to Ireland in 1642 25
  supports clergy against the Ormond peace
    125, 157–9, 164
  uncertainty about his position concerning
    the Ormond peace 154, 155
Prince of Wales 168, 169, 177, 190, 193
Propaganda Fide, congregation of 48, 49, 54,
    63, 64, 258
Purcell, Patrick 187

Raphoe, bishop of *see* O'Cullenan, John
  diocese of 43
rebellion of 1641 49, 57, 66, 68, 80
Redmond, Nicholas 239

Richelieu, Cardinal 69
Rinuccini, GianBattista 19, 23, 27, 33, 39, 50,
    79–81
  and crisis in Munster army 185–9
  and former monastic land 76–7
  and French involvement in Ormond peace
    144–5, 147
  and legacy of Trent 88, 89, 98
  and national character of the Irish 250–52
  and opposition to peace party 30, 31, 66,
    124, 134, 256–7, 262
  and relationship with Irish clergy 25 n. 49,
    41, 56–7, 67–8, 71, 210–1, 232–52, 257
  and relationship with Owen Roe O'Neill
    154, 155, 180–3, 195–7, 203, 206, 210,
    257, 263
  and subsidies from France 79 n. 240
  and suppression of protestant worship 96,
    247–8
  and synod of 1646 125, 147–52, 164–5, 232,
    255, 257, 261–2
  and the Chigi nunciature 113–5, 253–4
  and the Dublin campaign 158–63
  and the need for a catholic university in
    Ireland 99
  and the recruitment of protestants to
    confederate armies 247, 248 n. 80
  and town of Galway 67, 214, 251–2
  and town of Limerick 96, 117, 146, 153,
    247–8
  and Ulster army 154–5, 171, 180, 181–2,
    196–7, 206 n. 42, 208, 257, 262–3
  anger at Clanricard 217
  appointment as nuncio 85, 111–5
  appointment to see of Fermo 85–6
  approval of Gaelic Irish as catholics 60–2,
    65, 66
  approval of Nicholas Plunkett 149 n. 135,
    171 n. 30, 215–6
  arrival in Ireland 82, 116–7
  arrival in Kilkenny 117–8, 123
  as exemplar of catholic reformation 82, 84,
    93, 99, 103, 110, 118, 245, 266
  attitude towards bishop of Ferns 171–2,
    215, 216
  attitude towards Charles I 128, 133, 185
  attitude towards Glamorgan peace 124,
    125–30, 164, 262
  attitude towards John Bourke 47
  attitude towards reform of clergy 58–9,
    103–109
  authoritarian nature of his vision 110–1
  Bellings's attitude to 67, 131, 146, 149, 235,
    265
  conversion of Viscount Dillon 181
  criticisms of Old English catholicism 61,
    212–30

curial experience 83–4
deceptions by confederates of 134–7
demonstrations against 181–2, 194–5
departure from Ireland 197, 201, 211
dissatisfactions with confederate
    government 132–4, 138–9, 152,
    163–4, 261–2
distrust of Ormond 130, 133–4, 159, 262
education in Italy 83
evaluations of confederate association
    132–4, 194–7, 212–31
evolution of attitude to first Ormond peace
    125–31, 163–5, 261–2
family background 82–3
flight from Kilkenny in 1648 200, 204
formal difficulties with Supreme Council
    131–2
ignorance of protestantism 89–91
influence concerning Irish appointments
    147, 233–5, 238
instructions 40, 53, 80, 81
introduction of ecclesiastical ceremonial
    248–9
journey to Ireland 36, 115–7, 244
legacy of nunciature 265–7
literary career 82–3
opposition to Inchiquin truce 199–206
papers sequestered by confederates 219
personality 91–3, 102–3, 119, 264
presidency of Supreme Council 160, 161,
    174
protection of ecclesiastical immunity 217,
    246
reception into Kilkenny 117–8
restricted by lack of finance in 1647 169–71,
    177, 180
return to Kilkenny in 1648 199, 203
significance of Irish career 261–5
sojourn in Paris in 1645 116, 131, 227
subsidies to Leinster army 154
system of ecclesiastical reform 98–111
view of relationship between temporal and
    spiritual authority 93–6
writings on episcopal duties 86–111
Rinuccini's works: Considerazioni sopra la
    Storia Romana e Greca di Dionigi
    d'Alicarnasso, Tito Livio, Polibio,
    Plutarco, Tacito ecc. 84 n. 19;
    "Compendio di Geografia" 84; Della
    Dignita et Offitio dei Vescovi 86–92, 94
    n. 74, 95–8, 105, 106, 110, 216, 258 n. 26;
    Il Cappuccino Scozzese 85, 90, 92;
    "Instruttione pratica per la cura
    episcopale" 86, 88, 98, 101, 105;
    "Libellus de recta argumentandi ratione
    ad quaestiones logicas intelligendas 84 n.
    21; "Quaestiones in octo libros Aristotelis

de phisica" 85 n. 22; "Varie consider-
    azioni sulla Storia Ecclesiastica" 84 n. 19
Rinuccini, Tomasso 82, 204 n. 30, 211 n. 70
Roberts, William 150
Roche, Maurice, viscount of Fermoy 204 n. 25,
    279
Roche, John, bishop of Ferns 48, 53, 151
Roche, Matthew, vicar apostolic of Leighlin
    44, 53
Rochford, Luke 43, 173 n. 40
Roma, Cardinal 208 n. 56, 209
Roman Treaty 130, 147 n. 127, 163, 164
    attempt to postpone peace until arrival of its
        articles 134
    details of suppressed by Rinuccini 135
    knowledge of increases nuncio's distrust of
        Ormond 159
    terms of 129 n. 37
Rome 149, 205, 213, 227, 254–6, 265–6
    and creation of Irish mission 111–2, 127
    and failure of its Irish policy 260
    and former monastic property 74–7
    and jurisdiction derived from 42, 72
    and Massari's mission to 146, 160, 170–1
    and Plunkett-Ferns mission to 172, 192–3,
        207–9
    and representatives of 71
    and tensions with governments of Spain and
        Portugal 223–6
    and the rebellion of 1641 69–70
    appeals to 46, 61–2, 112, 169, 200, 212, 237
        n. 27
    complaints to 45, 55
    doctrines in Ireland declared different from
        221
    finance from 67, 138, 160–1, 169, 203, 210,
        259, 263
    grants no further missionary faculties 58
    importance of proximity to 88
    instructions from 44, 115, 116, 201
    Irish church organized from 39, 47, 50, 56
    Irish ecclesiastical disputes transmitted to 40
    its religious splendour not a suitable
        comparison to Ireland 132, 144
    papal peace negotiated in 124 n. 6, 135 n. 65
    reports to 49, 63, 182, 206 n. 41, 211, 216,
        250–1
    requests to 79–81, 111
Rinuccini's birth, education and
    employment in 82–4, 96, 131
Rinuccini's influence in concerning Irish
    appointments 147, 233–5
Rinuccini's resignation of presidency
    welcomed in 174
Rinuccini's return to 215, 258
Rinuccini wishes his opponents be
    summoned to 243–4

Rome (*cont.*):
  synod of Tuam approved in 59
  undercutting episcopal authority 51–2
Roncati, Hilario 112 n. 171
Roscommon 138, 139
Rothe, David, bishop of Ossory 243 n. 56
  and campaign against regular clergy
    53–4
  diocesan organization of 58–9, 60
  less militant than other bishops 35 n. 98, 48,
    50 n. 70, 79 n. 237
  opposition to censure of 1648 236
  residence of 46
Royalist party in England 36

St Ambrose 88, 95 100 n. 1 n. 02
St Augustine 84, 88
St Leger, Sir William 24 n. 40
St Nicholas, collegiate church of Galway
  237–8
St Patrick's Purgatory 182, 183
St Peter of Alcantara 111
St Wolstans, Allens of 74 n. 210
Savoy 222
Scarampi, PierFrancesco, papal agent 73,
  78–80, 112, 279
  and former monastic lands 75–6
  and Preston 155, 157, 161
  and reverence of Irish population 117 n. 194
  as delegate of the synod of 1646 151
  attempts to awaken Rinuccini's suspicions
    137
  boosts authority of Supreme Council 70,
    111, 235
  critical of regular clergy 240
  disapproval of clergy taking arms 245
  foreshadows Rinuccini's stance 124, 127
  hostility towards policy of truce 28, 72
  opposes Glamorgan peace 78
  radicalism of clergy not solely attributable to
    his influence 27
  spoke neither English nor Irish 131
  supplies funds to Preston 35
  Supreme Council untroubled by 73, 80
Segnatura di Giudizio 84
Segnatura di Grazie 84
Seville, Irish college of 55
Sidney, Robert, earl of Leicester 18 n. 10, 19
Slane, baron of *see* Fleming, William
Sligo 167, 182
Solsona, diocese of 49 n. 62
Somerset, Edward: Lord Herbert, earl of
    Glamorgan, marquis of Worcester 144,
    149, 279
  as commander of Munster army 185–6
  confederate acceptance of his proposals
    78–9

imprisonment in Dublin 129, 134, 135 n. 69,
    138 n. 83, 159
  Rinuccini's attitude to his proposed treaty
    124, 125–30, 164, 262
Spenser, Edmund 103 n. 122
Spinola, Domenico 127
Strafford, earl of *see* Wentworth, Thomas
Strange, Thomas 54 n. 96, 55 n. 100
Stuart dynasty 69, 70, 113, 140
Stuart kingdoms 139, 141, 143, 178
Stuart monarchy 128, 124 n. 6, 162 n. 209
Supreme Council 199–200, 244, 251
  and Athlone 181 n. 85
  and deception of the nuncio 134–7
  and difficulty of asserting authority over
    towns 24, 67
  and diplomacy with Rome 72, 75, 111, 118
  and former monastic property 75, 77
  and Inchiquin truce 199–200, 201 n. 9,
    241–2
  and Munster 187–9
  and Muskery's reinstatement 186 n. 113
  and negotiations with nuncio concerning
    Glamorgan peace 123–6, 129–30
  and nomination of bishops 234–5
  and removal of O'Neill from Leinster 183
  and the confederate oath 26
  and the declaration of the Ormond peace
    145–7, 149
  as tribunal for ecclesiastical cases 71, 246
  changes wrought by Rinuccini's arrival
    79–81
  clerical dissatisfaction with 33–5, 74
  clerical representation on 70–1
  creation of a new body after clerical coup
    147, 158, 163, 165, 232
  disjunction from main body of association
    162
  does not control Rinuccini's use of papal
    subsidies 154
  dominated by clerical sympathizers after first
    assembly of 1647 167, 172–5, 186, 262–3
  formal difficulties with Rinuccini 131–2
  lapse of its authority after Ormond peace
    149–50
  legitimization of 25, 69
  members' assistance at Holy Thursday
    foot-washing 249
  peace party regains dominance 193, 197,
    263
  policy of peace councillors towards
    Rinuccini in 1648 202–6, 212, 236,
    239
  relief in Rome at Rinuccini's resignation of
    presidency 160
  resumption of negotiations with Ormond in
    1647 180

Rinuccini's anger at its sacrilegious actions
215–30
Rinuccini's dissatisfactions with government
of 132–4, 138–9, 152, 163–4, 261–2
Rinuccini's presidency 160, 161
selected by four individuals after second
assembly of 1647 168–9, 174, 193
synod's condemnation of 149, 151
Szini, István 59 n. 126

Taaffe, Theobold, viscount of Taaffe 139
n. 90, 176, 188, 190
Taaffe, viscount of see Taaffe, Theobold
Talbot, Sir Robert 32 n. 81, 34, 157 n. 183,
167 n. 7, 196 n. 171
Talbot, Thomas 195
Talon, Jean 132 n. 52, 178–9, 280
Theodosius I 95
Thirty Years' War 94, 225
Thomond, earl of see O'Brien, Barnaby
Tirry, William, bishop of Cork and Cloyne 35
n. 98, 48, 50 n. 70, 51 n. 75, 53, 79 n. 237
Touchet, James, earl of Castlehaven 280
accusations of sabotage concerning Munster
campaign of 1645 35, 36
and rivalry with Preston 157 n. 186
as member of peace party 34, 36, 81
cattle stolen in 1642 23
clergy prefer Preston and O'Neill for
military command after peace 156 n. 176
informs Ormond concerning power of clergy
150 n. 141, 153
Trent, Council of 110, 111, 223, 260
acceptance of its decrees by synod of Tuam
59
and establishment of dioscesan seminaries
55
and the revival of preaching 101
importance of pastoral bishop in its
aftermath 39
nature of episcopal institution debated at 87
pastoral reforms of not only component of
post-tridentine catholicism 65
Rinuccini and its legacy 88, 89, 98
Rinuccini instructed to secure full
acceptance of its decrees 40
Trim 203 n. 20
truce of 1643 27, 28, 30
Tuam, archbishop of, see O'Queely, Malachy
and Bourke, John
archdeacon of see Lynch, John
archdiocese of 57, 58 n. 121, 60, 100 n. 103,
152, 237
synod of 44, 52
Turenne, vicomte de see de la Tour
d'Auvergne, Henri
Tuscany 222, 227

Tyrconnel, earl of see O'Donnell, Hugh
Tyrone, earl of see O'Neill, John

Ulster army 119, 157, 200, 203, 230, 262–3
after 1646 Rinuccini unable to supply major
assistance 155, 180, 206 n. 42
and its diversion to Connacht 175, 181–4
and the bishop of Clogher 173, 245
and the Dublin campaign 161
anger and anxiety concerning 177, 187
n. 123, 195–6
its reputation for rapine and pillage 154
limits to what Rinuccini could achieve
through 171, 262
nuncio loses faith in 208
receives support from Rinuccini 154,
257
Rinuccini's anger at 181–2, 263
Rinuccini's refusal to accept objections made
about 196–7
Urban VIII 76, 222, 225
distaste created by his nepotism 112
offers Rinuccini archbishopric of Florence
86
promotes Rinuccini to archbishopric of
Fermo 85

Venice, Senate of 30 n. 72, 116 n. 185, 141
n. 98, 170 n. 24
town of 70, 170
Vienna 115, 224 n. 137
Vitelleschi, Muzio 59 n. 126

Wadding, Luke 44, 48, 118, 280
and former monastic property 75
importance influence in appointment of
Rinuccini and Scarampi 111–2
Walsh, John 150 n. 139
Walsh, Nicholas 159 n. 193
Walsh, Oliver 245 n. 65
Walsh, Peter 240, 242
Walsh, Thomas, archbishop of Cashel 280
and campaign against regular clergy 53–5
and imprisonment 44
and obedience to Rinuccini 236 n. 22
bitterness concerning poverty 45
moderate political views 79 n. 237, 210
resentment at lack of attention to episcopal
recommendations by seminary authorities
55
residence with his brother 46
war party 33, 126 n. 18
Ward, Maurice 43
Waterford, bishop of see Comerford, Patrick
Waterford, city of 67, 148, 151–3, 156 n. 174,
178, 217
clerical declaration published in 159

Waterford, city of (*cont.*):
  nuncio's residence in early 1648 199, 203–4
  poor choice for first proclamation of peace
    150
  Rinuccini praises fidelity of inhabitants
    214
  Rinuccini's baptism of muslims 249
Waterford, diocese of 46, 51

Waterford, Legatine synod of 125, 147–52,
  165, 232, 255, 257, 261–2
Wentworth, Thomas, earl of Strafford 17, 21,
  32 n. 84, 53, 56
Westmeath, earl of *see* Nugent, Richard
Westminster 199
Westphalia, treaty of 3, 115, 207, 253–5
Wexford, city of 239, 249